COLLECTED WORKS OF ERASMUS

VOLUME 69

Marriage of the Virgin (B.82.M.194) from the series
The Life of the Virgin (probably 1504–5), by Albrecht Dürer.

COLLECTED WORKS OF
ERASMUS

SPIRITUALIA and PASTORALIA

PRECATIO AD VIRGINIS FILIUM IESUM
PAEAN VIRGINI MATRI
OBSECRATIO AD VIRGINEM MARIAM
PRECATIO DOMINICA
LITURGIA VIRGINIS MATRIS
PRECATIO PRO PACE ECCLESIAE
PRECATIONES ALIQUOT NOVAE
VIRGINIS ET MARTYRIS COMPARATIO
EPISTOLA CONSOLATORIA
INSTITUTIO CHRISTIANI MATRIMONII

edited by
John W. O'Malley and Louis A. Perraud

University of Toronto Press

Toronto / Buffalo / London

The research and publication costs of the
Collected Works of Erasmus are supported by
University of Toronto Press.

© University of Toronto Press 1999
Toronto / Buffalo / London
Printed in Canada

ISBN 0-8020-4382-8

Printed on acid-free paper

Canadian Cataloguing in Publication Data

Erasmus, Desiderius, d. 1536
[Works]
Collected works of Erasmus

Partial contents: v. 69. Spiritualia and Pastoralia /
edited by John W. O'Malley and Louis A. Perraud.
Includes bibliographical references and index.
ISBN 0-8020-4382-8 (v. 69)

1. Erasmus, Desiderius, d. 1536. I. Title.

PA8500 1974   876'.04   C74–006326-x rev

University of Toronto Press acknowledges the financial assistance
to its publishing programme of the Canada Council and the Ontario Arts Council.

Collected Works of Erasmus

The aim of the Collected Works of Erasmus
is to make available an accurate, readable English text
of Erasmus' correspondence and his
other principal writings. The edition is planned
and directed by an Editorial Board, an Executive Committee,
and an Advisory Committee.

Contents

Introduction

The ten works of Erasmus contained in this volume are among the twenty that the editors of CWE have selected for inclusion in the series of spiritual and pastoral works, *spiritualia* and *pastoralia*. The basis for this category is Erasmus' famous enclosure with his letter to Hector Boece of 15 March 1530, in which he listed his writings and divided them into nine categories or *ordines*.[1] The fifth *ordo* consists of writings pertaining to *pietas*, the starting-point for our designation. For further discussion of the issues raised by this category, I refer the reader to the pertinent pages of my general introduction to this series, CWE 66 ix–xii.

That introduction is presupposed as background for what I have to say here, and I urge the reader to consult it. By editorial decision it was meant to serve for all five of the volumes in the series and to deal in a comprehensive way with the wide variety of issues connected with these twenty works and with Erasmian *pietas*. It would be redundant to repeat its arguments for the present volume. Towards the end of that introduction, I dealt briefly but in somewhat more detail with the three works contained in volume 66. I indicated that similar treatments would introduce the works in the subsequent volumes of the series, and such a treatment is what I will undertake for the ten in this volume.

This volume is obviously special in that it contains such a large number of the works in the series – half of the twenty are here, with the remaining half distributed over the other four volumes. Except for 'The Institution of Christian Matrimony,' all the pieces in this volume are relatively short, and they are gathered here primarily for reasons of editorial convenience. None the less, in two regards the volume has a certain coherence. First, seven of the pieces, if we include the 'Liturgy of Loreto,' are prayers of

* * * * *

1 Allen Ep 2283. See also CWE 24 694–702.

various types. The volume thus provides ample material for examining a genre important to Erasmus that until quite recently scholars have ignored. Moreover, these seven pieces range chronologically from some of his very first published works, 1503, to the prayers he published in 1535, the year before his death. Accordingly they provide a small but handy specimen that upon investigation might betray changes in Erasmus' religious sensibilities over the years.

Second, many of the pieces deal to a greater or lesser degree with issues of gender or even sexuality, if we take those terms in their broadest senses. These issues find their focus here especially in discussions of virginity and marriage. Virginity and marriage are professed subjects in the last three works in the volume, but virginity of course is at least an implicit subject in the three Marian works that appear earlier. The volume is thus special also in that so many of the pieces it contains are about women, prompted by women, addressed to women, or, as with 'The Institution of Christian Matrimony,' dedicated to women. The 'Institution,' by far the most substantial work in the volume and second in length in the whole series of spiritual and pastoral works only to the *Ecclesiastes*, is of great interest for any number of reasons, but surely among them is Erasmus' delineation of women's role in the relationship between spouses.

In that delineation in the 'Institution' as well as in his other works in this volume and elsewhere, Erasmus is not easy to interpret. As Erika Rummel has pointed out, 'Erasmus' comments on women range from ad hoc remarks in his letters to lengthy treatises on marriage and widowhood, from lively dialogues with a mixed cast of virgins and mothers, housewives and harlots, to a funeral oration for a matriarch.'[2] Erasmus 'appropriates a variety of voices'; what he says and how he says it are often governed by well-established conventions of the various literary traditions in which he writes. On some questions the heat and glare of the religious situation after 1517 made him more cautious than he would have been otherwise, made him even elusive. The interpreter faces further problems. Erasmus' sense of irony, his sense of the complexity of human motivation, and sometimes the technical sophistication of opinions seemingly simply expressed add to the difficulty.

Even with these problems, at least two things are clear about what Erasmus has to say about women. First and most obvious, Erasmus was a person of his times, and we will not find in him the sensibilities of the

* * * * *

2 *Erasmus on Women* ed Erika Rummel (Toronto and London 1996) 3

late twentieth century. Jennifer Tolbert Roberts pointed out a decade ago how in his treatise 'On the Christian Widow' the 'usual clichés about the natural inferiority of women to men abound.'[3] Women were naturally given to vanity, idleness, and frivolity; wives were to be subject to their husbands; and so on.

The second is that, none the less, Erasmus at certain points transcends the clichés to pay more attention to women and to assign them greater dignity in a variety of roles than did practically any other major sixteenth-century author. True, by the 1520s the *querelle des femmes* was well under way, especially in vernacular literatures, with women having ardent detractors and just as ardent champions, among whom Henricus Cornelius Agrippa would be outstanding.[4] None the less, one would be hard pressed to find many significant figures in the western cultural tradition – at least until quite recently – who could best Erasmus here.

On this issue interpreters must move between these two poles. In any case, as with so many of the other works in the series of *spiritualia* and *pastoralia*, those in this volume represent an 'Erasmus nobody knows.' Scholarship on these writings has been virtually non-existent until quite recently, and the bibliography is still sparse. Except for 'Some New Prayers,' none of them has appeared before in a modern English translation. The result is that the Erasmus that dominates our imagination is still either the genial humanist, or the caustic critic of superstitious rites, or the supposedly dilettante theologian unequal to the debate with Luther. That is to say, the Erasmus of these volumes has received little consideration by scholars outside a narrow group of Erasmus specialists, and has not figured at all in textbooks and the popular media. Yet the works in these volumes, taken as a whole, are as characteristic of Erasmus as anything he wrote, and some of them – like 'The Institution of Christian Matrimony' in this volume and the *Ecclesiastes* – are of towering importance in the history of their subjects.[5]

* * * * *

3 CWE 66 181
4 See Henricus Cornelius Agrippa *Declamation on the Nobility and Preeminence of the Female Sex* trans and ed Albert Rabil, Jr (Chicago and London 1996); and C. Fantazzi and C. Matheeussen 'Introduction' to J.L. Vives *De institutione feminae christianae: liber primus* (Leiden 1996) xxiii–xxvii.
5 See eg John W. O'Malley 'Erasmus and the History of Sacred Rhetoric: The *Ecclesiastes* of 1535' ERSY 5 (1985) 1–29. Despite the importance of 'The Institution of Christian Matrimony,' however, it is hardly mentioned in the most recent study of marriage in the sixteenth century, John Witte, Jr *From Sacrament to Contract: Marriage, Religion, and Law in the Western Tradition* (Louisville 1997).

More shocking is how the posthumous vilification of Erasmus by his religious enemies, especially Catholics, meant that the very memory of his works 'pertaining to *pietas*' was obliterated.[6] In the sixteenth century Erasmus' 'Lord's Prayer,' for instance, ran through perhaps as many as a dozen editions or printings in Latin within two years of publication, and it was translated into German in 1523, English in 1524, Czech in 1526, Spanish in 1528, Polish in 1533, and Dutch in 1593. The English translation, which reappeared in three subsequent editions, was done by Margaret Roper, Thomas More's daughter.[7] Yet in the authoritative *Dictionnaire de spiritualité* the article on that prayer fails to mention Erasmus' work, though it lists those by other authors that surely had a much smaller diffusion and influence.[8] The *Dictionnaire* also ignores 'On Praying to God' (*Modus orandi Deum* CWE 70), another highly influential and widely circulated work by Erasmus on a related topic.[9]

The silence of the *Dictionnaire* is symptomatic of the collective amnesia about Erasmus in the mainstream of scholarship dealing with Christian spirituality. Once excluded from the canon, Erasmus has never after been able to break into it, for everybody has forgotten he might even be a candidate. His is a sobering tale about the lasting impact of censorship and social disciplining.

I

Although the 'Liturgy of Loreto' is a special case because of its highly formalized structure, the seven works appearing first in CWE 69 belong, as I have said, to the genre of prayers. Moreover, they are all relatively short, and three of them are addressed to the Virgin Mary. I will discuss them, therefore, as a unit.

* * * * *

6 See eg Bruce Mansfield *The Phoenix of His Age: Interpretations of Erasmus, c 1550–1750* (Toronto 1979) especially 7–64; and Silvana Seidel Menchi *Erasmo in Italia, 1520–1580* (Turin 1987).
7 See E.J. Devereux *Renaissance English Translations of Erasmus: A Bibliography to 1700* (Toronto 1983) 176–8. See also Germain Marc'hadour 'Erasmus' Paraphrase of the "Pater Noster" (1523) with Its English Translation by Margaret Roper (1524)' *Moreana* VII (August 1965) 9–64; and Rita M. Verbrugge 'Margaret More Roper's Personal Expression in the *Devout Treatise upon the Pater Noster*' in *Silent but for the Word: Tudor Women as Patrons, Translators, and Writers of Religious Works* ed Margaret Patterson Hannay (Kent 1985) 30–42.
8 'Pater noster' DS XII-1 especially 389–95
9 'Prière' DS XII-2 especially 2295–317

Perhaps the first thing that needs to be emphasized is how important prayer and prayers were to Erasmus, as Hilmar M. Pabel's recent and welcome study of the subject makes clear.[10] Among Erasmus' first published works was the triad consisting of the 'Prayer to Jesus, Son of the Virgin,' the 'Paean in Honour of the Virgin Mother,' and the 'Prayer of Supplication to Mary.' Although, as Stephen Ryle and John N. Grant point out below, Erasmus afterwards somewhat dismissed these efforts by saying he had composed the prayers to the taste of the lady of Veere, Anna van Borssele, and of her young son, Adolph of Burgundy, he none the less allowed them to be published again and again and included them in the catalogue of his works. He continued to compose and publish prayers until the very end of his days. Moreover, he inserted prayers into other works, such as the *Colloquies*, and a number of these he singled out for separate publication in his collection of 1535, 'Some New Prayers.'

Despite differences among his many prayers, composed as they were over the course of a lifetime, certain similarities stand out. Among them the Latin style is perhaps the most obvious. Even though in that early triad one catches strong hints of medieval piety, Erasmus articulates his ideas and sentiments in a classicizing or humanistic Latin. Indeed, in the 'Paean' he likens Mary to Diana and Lucina, and he designates Christ 'ruler of Olympus' – a practice he would later criticize.[11] But the very style of the prayers would have given them a freshness and attractiveness to educated ears, and that style is characteristic of them all. The new style of language must have suggested to contemporaries that a new style of piety was in the offing.

The prayers also evince strong continuity with one another in their content. They are characterized by a piety based solidly on traditional Trinitarian and Christological doctrines. Moreover, in all of them we recognize as typical of Erasmus the unmistakably biblical undergirding and especially the themes of membership in the body of Christ and of the transforming power of grace.

None the less, the first three prayers stand apart from the rest. Their style, while classicizing, is more effusive and lyrical than that of the later prayers, and they have a tenderness reminiscent of the imaginings of late-medieval devotion, as when in the 'Prayer of Supplication' Erasmus speaks of the kisses exchanged between Mary and the child Jesus (49).[12] The content, especially regarding Mary, is thus even more distinctive than the style.

* * * * *

10 Pabel *Conversing*
11 See ASD I-2 640 / CWE 28 388.
12 See also Trapman 771–2.

Had Erasmus not yet found his true voice, or was he, as he averred, trying to accommodate his patrons? It was probably a mixture of the two. Certainly, over the course of the years his *pietas* evolved and, for one thing, moved its centre ever closer to the paschal mystery of the death and resurrection of Christ as interpreted in the Pauline Epistles. These early prayers, somewhat diffuse in their sentiments, lack that centre in a clearly articulated way.

Another important difference from his later works is his view of Mary's role in the economy of salvation. When in the 'Paean in Honour of the Virgin Mother' he says to her that her Son willed she 'should share with him the sovereignty of the universe' (21), we are reminded of the great medieval paintings and mosaics of Mary's coronation in heaven by the Trinity or by Jesus, but not of Erasmus' later insistence on the unique sovereignty of God, shared with no saint. When a few pages later he tells Mary, 'You alone ... possess the power to appease the anger of the judge' (23),[13] and when in the 'Prayer of Supplication' he calls Mary 'my saviour, my salvation, my sole and certain refuge' (45), he moves far, far beyond what he would later deem appropriate. It is worth noting that in his collection 'Some New Prayers,' 1535, he included the 'Prayer to Jesus' from this triad but not the two prayers directed to Mary.

None the less, Erasmus' thinking was far too traditional not to have a place in it for the Virgin. His prayer to her in 'Some New Prayers' reflects his mature ideas and sentiments on the matter. He praises the Virgin highly but clearly distinguishes her role from her Son's, as when he says that at the mention of the name of Jesus 'every knee bends' in adoration, whereas at the mention of her name all souls simply rejoice (127). The difference is clear, with none of the blurring found in the 'Paean' and the 'Supplication.'

Somewhat surprising is Erasmus' adherence to the doctrine of the Immaculate Conception of Mary, since its first forceful articulation had been by medieval Franciscans and its validity had been challenged by the Dominicans of Erasmus' own day. It might have seemed another 'recent' doctrine over which the friars waged their theological wars with one another, and therefore an issue of no concern to Erasmus. The fact is, however, that he takes his stand in favour of the doctrine in the 'Prayer of Supplication' in 1503, and never wavers thereafter.[14]

Erasmus wrote no treatise on Mary, and his statements about her are scattered in many works composed across the years. The stuff for recon-

* * * * *

13 See also 20, 23.
14 See Halkin 'Mariologie' especially 39–43; and O'Donnell 'Women Saints' especially 106–8. On this doctrine see G.M. Lechner 'Unbefleckte Empfängnis' in *Marienlexikon* VI 519–32.

structing his Mariology is less ample than for reconstructing his Christology and perhaps in some regards less consistent. None the less, when the relevant material is viewed in the large, Léon-E. Halkin's summary judgment about it twenty years ago remains sound: Erasmus' Mariology was founded essentially on the Bible, the Fathers, and the tradition of the church[15] rather than on, say, speculative theology or vernacular piety.

In this regard his recourse to the liturgical tradition of the church perhaps needs to be underscored, for he often silently quotes or paraphrases from it prayers and antiphons used on feasts of the Virgin.[16] In his monastic days Erasmus had acquired a profound knowledge of liturgical texts, which he was able to recall as sharply as he recalled the Bible. They were second nature to him.[17]

What is therefore surprising is not that Erasmus wrote a liturgy or wrote a liturgy honouring the Virgin Mary, but that he wrote a liturgy for Our Lady of Loreto, that is, in connection with the miraculous translation by angels of Mary's house in Nazareth to the Italian town of Loreto in the late thirteenth century. It was a tale Erasmus surely considered outlandish, though he makes no comment on it. It is clear that he undertook the composition of the liturgy in 1523 because a friend requested that he do so. He complied perhaps gladly, we may surmise, because the task provided him with an opportunity to show how in such a situation one could still adhere to appropriate traditions of veneration of Mary and even act silently to correct popular credulity.[18] The next year he came close to suggesting such a course while discussing superstitious practices relating to the saints in his 'On Praying to God.'[19] That is what he does, in any case, without mentioning either in the assembled liturgical texts or in his sermon anything about the curious way in which Loreto became a place of special veneration of the Virgin. In other words, he composed a liturgy honouring Mary – who happened to be venerated in a particularly intense way at Loreto.

Erasmus added the sermon for the second printing by Froben, 1525, with the explanation that he did so 'to make the liturgy complete' (85).

* * * * *

15 Halkin 'Mariologie' 54. See also O'Donnell 'Women Saints' 105–15.
16 See, besides the notes for these prayers, Clarence H. Miller 'The Liturgical Context of Erasmus' Hymns' in *Acta Torontonensis* 481–90.
17 See Léon-E. Halkin 'Erasme contre la liturgie?' in *Miscellanea Moreana: Essays for Germain Marc'hadour* ed Clare M. Murphy, Henri Gibaud, and Mario A. di Cesare (Binghamton 1989) 421–5.
18 See Halkin 'Mariologie' 50.
19 CWE 70 145–230

The explanation indicates his correct theological understanding of the intimate relationship between word and sacrament in Eucharistic celebrations. He wrote during an era, however, when the almost inevitable practice was to separate the two, with most masses being celebrated without a sermon or homily, which in some instances was provided on its own in the afternoon, or in perhaps most instances was not provided at all. Only in the mid-twentieth century have Catholic theologians insisted on the homily as integral to the full and proper celebration of the mass. With the explanation 'ne non esset integra liturgia,' Erasmus again showed how much more in touch with the tradition of the church he was than were many of his contemporaries.

But by 1532, the year he composed his 'Prayer to the Lord Jesus for Peace in the Church,' Erasmus was being subjected to vituperation from and condemnation by the theological establishment precisely for his interpretation of that tradition.[20] He suffered accordingly, not only because he himself had become an object of suspicion and vilification but because he saw what was happening to him as a symptom of what was happening on a much broader scale, as the church was torn apart by controversy and division – and now, with the formation in 1530 of the Schmalkaldic League, by the threat of war in the cause of religious truth. This is the situation in which he composed this prayer, one of his most obviously heartfelt cries. The 'Prayer for Peace' is filled with typically Erasmian themes – the overriding importance of concord and harmony in Christian life, for instance, and peace as a sign of God's presence and pleasure. The next year Erasmus published 'On Mending the Peace of the Church,' a long commentary on Psalm 83 (Vulg 84), and he attached to it the 'Prayer for Peace,' which in many of its sentiments anticipates the commentary.[21]

Less anguished but similarly heartfelt is Erasmus' 'Lord's Prayer,' 1523.[22] It falls into the tradition of sermons or commentaries on the Our Father that began with Tertullian, Origen, and Cyprian, a tradition that Erasmus knew better than did any of his contemporaries and that influenced this work. Special about Erasmus, however, is the literary form he adopts,

* * * * *

20 See Rummel *Catholic Critics*.
21 See Pabel *Conversing* 182–8, and his 'The Peaceful People of Christ: The Irenic Ecclesiology of Erasmus of Rotterdam' in Pabel *Erasmus' Vision* 57–93, especially 84–9.
22 By far the best commentary is Pabel *Conversing* 109–54. See also his 'Erasmus' Esteem for Cyprian: Parallels in Their Expositions of the Lord's Prayer' ERSY 17 (1997) 55–69.

which he described in the second edition of the catalogue of his publications, 1524, as a 'paraphrase.'[23] His descriptive term indicates that instead
of producing a series of comments on the Lord's Prayer he has turned what
he has to say into a prayer itself – or rather into a series of seven prayers,
addressed to God the Father. In the *editio princeps* by Froben, the heading
of each of the seven sections indicates the day of the week when that section might be recited.[24] The result was a prayer-book – a slender, easily
portable volume containing seven prayers, all based on the Lord's Prayer,
that would accompany the devout Christian through the seven days of the
week.[25]

Here, then, is Erasmus publishing in what was for him the new genre
of the prayer-book. Here, also, is Erasmus showing in actual practice and in
a fully fleshed-out model how one might pray the Lord's Prayer in a more
sustained way than by simply reciting the formula. He puts the appropriate
sentiments into appropriate words – almost a definition of the humanist's
métier. Pabel, who has written the most thorough examination to date of
what Erasmus has to say about prayer, sees Erasmus' publication of prayers
as a form of ministry exercised through the printing press.[26] In Erasmus'
'Lord's Prayer,' with its unusual but pastorally effective restructuring of a
tradition of commentary, Pabel's judgment is particularly verified.

Erasmus was not, however, the first to use the form. Earlier, Luther,
for one, had paraphrased the same prayer in his 'Personal Prayer-Book' or
Betbüchlein, 1522.[27] Even earlier than that, he had appended to his 'Exposition of the Lord's Prayer for Simple Laymen,' 1519, a short colloquy between the soul and God according to the sevenfold division of the Lord's
Prayer.[28] Erasmus' use of the prayer form is best understood as an aspect
of his larger project of paraphrasing books of the New Testament, already
well under way by this date, rather than as directly influenced by Luther. In
1535 Vives published his 'commentary' on the Lord's Prayer; like Erasmus,
he paraphrased it in the form of a prayer.[29]

* * * * *

23 Ep 1341A:1586
24 See Pabel *Conversing* 113.
25 See Pabel *Conversing* 113.
26 See Pabel *Conversing* 6–7 and passim.
27 See Pabel *Conversing* 113. Cf Luther's 'Personal Prayer Book' in LW 43 5–45,
   especially 29–38.
28 Cf 'An Exposition of the Lord's Prayer for Simple Laymen' in LW 42 15–81,
   especially 78–81.
29 Juan Luis Vives 'In ipsam precationem dominicam commentarius' in *Opera
   omnia* ed G. Majansius 8 vols (Valencia 1782–90; repr London 1964) I 136–62

Luther's *Betbüchlein* was one of his most immediately well received works, running through nine editions the year it was published. Luther composed it as an antidote to the *Hortulus animae* and other late-medieval prayer-books. The *Hortulus*, first published in a Latin and German edition in Strasbourg in 1496, had widespread diffusion thereafter, as did some similar works, modelled for the most part on the traditional and widely diffused *Book of Hours*, of which the *Hortulus* was not much more than an expanded version.[30]

The starting-point for the *Book of Hours* was the so-called Little Office of the Blessed Virgin Mary, which consisted in modified form of some or all of the eight liturgical hours of Matins, Lauds, Vespers, and so on, daily recited or chanted by the clergy. The Psalms thus constituted much of the content of the *Book of Hours*, but until some standardization occurred with the invention of printing, that content in any given *Hours* would vary considerably and, besides the Little Office, consist of various hymns, prayers, litanies, the seven penitential psalms, and similar pieces. This was the book known in England as the Primer, on which Stephen Ryle comments below (118–19). The *Book of Hours* and variations on it would remain popular in Catholic territories well after the Reformation.

Luther's *Betbüchlein* or 'Personal Prayer-Book' broke radically with this tradition, but in a peculiar way. It contained brief explanations of the Decalogue and the Apostles' Creed, a paraphrase on the Lord's Prayer, an explanation of the Hail Mary, some psalms, and the Epistle to Titus. Thus the substance of it was the invariable centre of late-medieval catechisms and catechesis – Decalogue, Creed, Our Father, and Hail Mary. What Luther in fact provided under the name of a prayer-book, therefore, was a 'small catechism,' anticipating the famous work by that name published by him in 1529. By calling his earlier work a prayer-book, by professedly offering it to the public as a substitute for the *Hortulus* and similar works, and by making a connection between prayer and catechesis, Luther influenced the content of future prayer-books, both Protestant and Catholic.[31]

It should now be clear how much the prayer-book of Erasmus published by Froben in 1523 in easily portable format under the title of the Lord's Prayer, *Precatio dominica*, differed from Luther's *Betbüchlein* of the previous year and from other, more traditional prayer-books already in

* * * * *

30 On the *Book of Hours* see eg *Time Sanctified: The Book of Hours in Medieval Art and Life* ed Roger S. Wieck (New York 1988).
31 See Kenneth F. Korby 'Prayer: Pre-Reformation to the Present' in *Christians at Prayer* ed John Gallen (Notre Dame 1977) 113–36, especially 121–4.

wide circulation. The book that Froben published a dozen years later, in
1535, entitled 'Some New Prayers,' *Precationes aliquot novae*, carried this new
form of the genre even further. It was a substantial little collection, consisting of twenty-seven properly called 'new prayers' and of thirty-five shorter
prayers, the so-called *eiaculationes*, described by Ryle in his introductory
note; to these were added three prayers published earlier – the 'Prayer to
Jesus, Son of the Virgin' (1503), the 'Prayer to the Lord Jesus for Peace in
the Church' (1532), and the 'Lord's Prayer' (1523).

Some Protestant prayer-books made up of prayers taken directly from
the Bible or adapted from it had meanwhile begun to appear, the most notable of which was *Precationes biblicae* by Otto Brunfels, published in Strasbourg in 1528.[32] Wittingly or unwittingly the authors of such books followed
Erasmus' recommendation in his 'On Praying to God' that prayers consist
for the most part in the words of Scripture.[33] In twenty-two of his *eiaculationes* of 1535 Erasmus follows his own recommendation precisely, weaving
together especially verses from the Psalms. The other prayers in the book
are, with a few exceptions, Erasmus' own words, in some instances professedly lifted from his other works, but they abound in allusions to Scripture
and paraphrases on it. The first in the volume, 'Prayer to the Father,' for instance, is another extended paraphrase on the Lord's Prayer, though considerably shorter than the one published in 1523 and then republished as part
of this collection of 1535.

Erasmus dedicated the book to David Paumgartner, then fourteen
years old, the son of one of his patrons. The dedication to such a young man
reminds us of Erasmus' abiding concern for the education of the young in
letters and *pietas* and of his conviction that if foundations in the devout life
were not laid in youth they would be forever shaky. Erasmus did not, however, design a book especially for adolescents, for with a few exceptions the
prayers are appropriate for young and old alike. They embody sentiments
redolent of the 'philosophy of Christ,' described in detail by Pabel in his commentary on them.[34] Individual prayers are sometimes succinct summaries
of Erasmus' thoughts and sentiments on a given subject; Peter G. Bietenholz
pointed out some years ago, for instance, that the prayer 'In Grave Illness'
was 'nothing less than the essence' of Erasmus' 'Preparing for Death.'[35]

* * * * *

32 See Pabel *Conversing* 158.
33 ASD V-1 161–2 / CWE 70 209–10
34 Pabel *Conversing* 155–90
35 See Peter G. Bietenholz 'Ludwig Baer, Erasmus, and the Tradition of the "Ars
   bene moriendi"' *Revue de littérature comparée* 52 (1978) 164.

As both Ryle and Pabel have noted, we have evidence that this little volume had considerable impact on private devotional literature, even though its *Nachleben* has not been examined by scholars in a comprehensive way.[36] Erasmus once again took an established genre and refashioned it. His prayer-book and those influenced by it look considerably different in style, structure, and content from their earlier counterparts. In 1535, the year of the publication of 'Some New Prayers,' Juan Luis Vives published his *Exercitationes animi in Deum*, which contained prayers and points for meditation that made it a prayer-book similar in many ways to Erasmus' though with some notable differences. It too was influential.[37] Erasmus' was thus but one voice among many in a century that experienced significant changes in this genre expressive of piety. None the less, his importance can hardly be overestimated.

II

In 1524 Erasmus published his 'Comparison of the Virgin and the Martyr,' *Virginis et martyris comparatio*, an expanded version of a piece he had written the previous year as an expression of gratitude to a convent of Benedictine nuns in Cologne for a small gift the nuns had sent him. Louis A. Perraud in his introductory note describes in detail the further circumstances of its composition and provides an analysis of its content and style. It was a popular work in Erasmus' day, as Perraud says, and was eventually translated into at least six vernacular languages.

Yet one searches almost in vain for any notice of it by modern scholars; it is one of the more neglected works in the already neglected category of Erasmus' writings 'pertaining to piety.' There are surely special reasons for this lack of interest, including the shortness of the piece. Moreover, the merits of virginity have hardly been in the forefront of scholars' concerns since the great revival of interest in Erasmus began about thirty years ago. Perhaps most important, Erasmus praising virginity is not an Erasmus that conforms to our image of him. Is it not true that he praised marriage and disparaged celibacy and virginity? Is it not true that he praised holiness in the world and found corruption and ungodliness in the cloister, which is where virginity traditionally was best guarded and fostered?

* * * * *

36 See 118–19 below, and Pabel *Conversing* 158–9, 198–202. See also Alice Tobriner 'The "Private Prayers" of Erasmus and Vives: A View of Lay Piety in the Northern Renaissance' ERSY 11 (1991) 27–52, especially 35–9.

37 Juan Luis Vives *Opera omnia* (see n29 above) I 49–131

Questions like these keep recurring about Erasmus, and their persistence indicates, once again, that he is not always easy to interpret, especially when he is dealing with matters controversial in his day or in our own. At such times he used and professed using *dissimulatio*, that is, the saying of something less than the whole truth in the interest of peace.[38] Nor do the encomiastic genre and style of the present work lessen the problems for the interpreter. But to dismiss the 'Comparison of the Virgin and the Martyr' as essentially duplicitous is to go too far.[39]

This is not the place to settle the still vexing questions about where Erasmus stood on the many issues revolving around virginity, celibacy, and marriage. A good case can be made for the opinion, however, that the rhetorical mode of his thought inclined him away from what was in principle 'best' towards what his experience of real men and women showed him actually worked in practice. In this regard his approach was not unlike that of the casuists he sometimes decried.[40] There is at any rate no doubt that his experience of most 'monks,' especially friars of the mendicant orders, gave him an unfavourable view of them. The real issue was not what was better in some speculative sense but what was better in the concrete for a given individual – and de facto the vast majority of individuals were called to the married state, where by God's design they could live holy and devout lives.

The same rhetorical approach, however, also inclined him to emphasize how God accommodates to the individual, so that a call to virginity or celibate chastity, though rare, was still viable and holy and, indeed, a manifestation of the marvellous *varietas* of styles of life possible in the following of Christ. Just as God accommodates himself to us in his Word, so does he accommodate himself to us in his call.[41]

In trying to sort out what Erasmus really believed on these matters certain further considerations and distinctions must be kept clearly in mind. First, for him there was all the difference in the world between celibacy freely chosen and celibacy institutionally imposed. Second, he needs to be taken seriously when he distinguishes between what may have been appropriate in earlier times and what was appropriate in his own day. Third, in his praise of matrimony he was trying to correct what he saw as a bad imbalance in pastoral practice and in devout literature that praised virginity and celibate chastity to the detriment of marriage.

* * * * *

38 See Tracy *Erasmus* 117–21, 175–82.
39 See Telle 255.
40 See Tracy *Erasmus* 118 and John W. O'Malley *The First Jesuits* (Cambridge, Mass 1993) 144–5.
41 See Ep 1202:73–119; *Paraclesis* LB V 140A.

Finally, it is crucial to distinguish between what Erasmus says about monks (and nuns) properly so-called on the one hand, and about friars (members of the mendicant orders such as the Franciscans and Dominicans) on the other. For several reasons he had a special animus against the latter. It was from the ranks of the 'mendicant tyrants,' for instance, that came some of the most rabid enemies of the 'new' style of theology he advocated, and it was their pastoral practices that for him most reeked of superstition and quackery. He gave voice to these and other complaints in different tones and with different emphases in different periods of his life, but in the main he was consistent in his disdain.[42]

In any case, he had none of these complaints against the nuns at the convent of the Maccabees. Might this piece, however, still be interpreted as a political ploy, meant to deflect the criticism and antagonism that his *Encomium matrimonii*, first published in 1518, had aroused and that he probably anticipated for 'The Institution of Christian Matrimony,' which he had already promised to write? Possibly, of course, but the origins of the 'Comparison of the Virgin and the Martyr' and the identity of the persons to whom it is addressed seem to preclude that as his uppermost motive for writing it. Relatively short though the 'Comparison' is, it would represent a rather long-winded attempt on Erasmus' part to dissemble his true convictions.

If his praise here for virginity is genuine, then almost *a fortiori* we must take in earnest his commendation of the ideal of Christian martyrdom, an ideal that, like virginity, was deeply imbedded in the tradition of the church and celebrated in the liturgy. Here too, *lex orandi, lex credendi*. In the Sequence for his own Liturgy of Our Lady of Loreto, below, Erasmus similarly joins virgins and martyrs as deserving of praise.[43]

* * * * *

42 On these issues see Joseph C. Linck 'Erasmus' Use of Scripture in *De vidua christiana*' ERSY 11 (1991) 67–87, especially 85–7; Alan W. Reese 'Learning Virginity: Erasmus' Ideal of Christian Marriage' BHR 57 (1995) 551–67; Tracy *Erasmus* 79–81, 90–4, 136–48, 206–8; Joseph Coppens 'Erasme et le célibat' in *Sacerdos et célibat* ed Joseph Coppens (Gembloux 1971) 443–58; Léon-E. Halkin 'Erasme et le célibat sacerdotal' *Revue d'histoire et de philosophie religieuses* 57 (1977) 497–511; Jacques Chomarat 'Erasme et le monachisme' in *Acta Conventus neo-Latini Hafniensis: Proceedings of the Eighth International Congress of Neo-Latin Studies, 1991* ed Rhoda Schnur (Binghamton 1994) 5–19; Erika Rummel ' "Monachatus non est pietas": Interpretations and Misinterpretations of a Dictum' in Pabel *Erasmus' Vision* 41–55. On a related topic, see Germain Marc'hadour 'Erasmus as Priest: Holy Orders in His Vision and Practice' in Pabel *Erasmus' Vision* 115–49.
43 89 below

In his 'Letter of Comfort in Adversity,' written some years later, Erasmus again addresses a convent of nuns and repeats, sometimes using the same mystical language from the Song of Solomon that he employed so extensively in the 'Comparison,' his sentiments of admiration for the life they lead. The subject of the 'Letter' is, however, altogether different from the subject of the 'Comparison.' The 'Comparison' is an encomium of virginity and martyrdom, but the 'Letter' is a message of comfort in tribulation.

Comfort in tribulation was a theme beloved by humanists beginning with Petrarch, whose writings on the topic culminated in his *De remediis utriusque fortunae*. As George W. McClure has observed, 'The psychological domain of grief and consolation – as it applied both to moral theorists and to rhetorical practitioners – was an urgent part of this realm of humane letters both in antiquity and in the Renaissance.'[44] It is first and foremost in this tradition that the *Epistola consolatoria* must be placed. But comfort and consolation were frequent and insistent subjects also in a wide variety of religious literature in the late Middle Ages and Renaissance beyond the domain of the humanists.[45] For instance, the third book of *The Imitation of Christ*, the flagship of the Devotio Moderna, was entitled 'On Inner Consolation.' True, comfort was often coupled with fear and dread in an ongoing struggle for possession of the Christian soul,[46] but comfort's resources in both argument and style were not small.

Curious about the 'Letter of Comfort' is what seems to be a discrepancy between the subject it discusses and the audience it addresses. The tribulation causing the distress Erasmus describes is the vicious disagreement over doctrine unleashed during the previous decade. What he says in the early pages is probably true of the nuns – there cannot be anyone not occasionally overcome with grief and mental anguish in the midst of such disturbances. But we have no evidence that these nuns were touched by the situation in any special way, and we might well wonder how apprised they were, in their English convent in 1528, of the doctrinal goings-on, or how interested they would have been. Later in the 'Letter' Erasmus seems to concede as much: 'These storms raging in the world do

* * * * *

44 George W. McClure *Sorrow and Consolation in Italian Humanism* (Princeton 1991) ix. See also Anne M. O'Donnell 'Cicero, Gregory the Great, and Thomas More: Three Dialogues of Comfort' in *Miscellanea Moreana* (see n17 above) 169–97.
45 See eg John W. O'Malley *The First Jesuits* (Cambridge, Mass 1993) 19–20, 41–3, 82–4, 139–41, 176–7, 315.
46 See eg Jean Delumeau *Sin and Fear: The Emergence of a Western Guilt Culture, 13th–18th Centuries* trans Eric Nicholson (New York 1990).

not disturb you so much, dear sisters' (197). Concerned they should have been, of course, because within eleven years their convent would be confiscated by the Crown and the nuns dispersed, but that eventuality could hardly have crossed their minds in 1528. Henry VIII's problems with the Holy See over his marriage to Catherine of Aragon were just beginning to surface.

Whom, then, was Erasmus really trying to comfort with this piece? Perhaps himself, first and foremost. By this date controversies were raging everywhere in northern Europe, he had already had his fateful confrontation with Luther in the debate over free will, he was being attacked by his Catholic critics, and he had suffered his first condemnation by the faculty of theology of the University of Paris. The anguish he experienced at his personal setbacks was augmented by his witnessing the crumbling of his ideal of concord and harmony in the church as a whole. The 'Letter,' that is to say, is something of a prelude to his 'Prayer to the Lord Jesus for Peace in the Church' of 1532, discussed earlier, and a harbinger of worse tribulations to come.

III

The present translation of 'The Institution of Christian Matrimony' is the first into modern English of this long and especially important work. Erasmus wrote a great deal concerning marriage – beginning with the *Encomium matrimonii* and including several of the colloquies – but this is his considered and major statement on a subject that was for him, as Jean-Claude Margolin said some years ago, 'd'une importance capitale.'[47] It has been relatively little studied, and interpreters, as we have come to expect, have not always agreed on what Erasmus really thought about all aspects of a subject that aroused such bitter controversy in his day.[48]

* * * * *

47 Introduction to *Encomium matrimonii* ASD I-5 339
48 The major study is still Telle, 1954. See also his 'Erasme et les mariages dynastiques' BHR 12 (1950) 7–13; *Declamation des louenges de mariage* (Geneva 1976); 'Marriage and Divorce on the Isle of Utopia' ERSY 8 (1988) 98–117; 'La Digamie de Thomas More, Erasme, et Catarino Politi' BHR 52 (1990) 323–32; 'Le Chartreux du colloque *Militis et Carthusiani* et Erasme' BHR 55 (1993) 231–43. See also Jean-Claude Margolin's introduction to the *Encomium matrimonii* ASD I-5 335–82; Olsen 2–42; *Erasmus on Women* ed Erika Rummel (Toronto and London 1996) 3–14; Alan W. Reese 'Learning Virginity: Erasmus' Ideal of Christian Marriage' (see n42 above); Joseph C. Linck 'Erasmus' Use of Scripture in *De vidua christiana*' (see n42 above); Michael J. Heath

Erasmus placed the work squarely in the category 'pertaining to piety,' for the central message of the piece is that matrimony is a holy state and, when properly entered into and then fostered by the spouses, conducive to a devout life. This message in and of itself was not controversial in the early sixteenth century, but the circumstances surrounding Erasmus' publication of it in 1526 provided ample ammunition for his enemies to use against him – and they did.

Michael J. Heath in his introductory note ably presents 'The Institution of Christian Matrimony' and indicates the issues it raised in the sixteenth century and still raises for the historian and interpreter today. In those regards little more needs to be added here. To appreciate Erasmus' achievement, however, it will be helpful to sketch briefly the history of the genre into which his treatise falls. But before doing so we need to have some idea of the topics he treats and the order in which he treats them.

In one of the opening paragraphs he says he will discuss only 'the following subjects: how to ensure the best possible start to matrimony, how to develop and bring it to a successful conclusion, and, finally, how to bring up offspring, who are the most precious fruit of marriage' (217). He fulfils that promise, but the description is too sketchy to guide the reader through Erasmus' sometimes complex argument and gives no indication of the large number of issues about which he speaks.

The outline that follows provides more details. But it too gives only a faint indication of how deeply Erasmus probes into every corner of the institution, and it is deceptive in so far as it suggests a straight developmental line. Erasmus tends to take up a topic, develop it, and then many pages later return to it. The outline also perforce omits mention of many topics treated in passing by Erasmus, such as syphilis, slavery, and lascivious painting, and it conveys nothing of its author's moralizing war against cosmetics, idleness, drunkenness, and similar human vanities and frailties.

Dedicatory letter to Catherine of Aragon
  I.   Some general considerations on the nature, dignity, and importance of marriage, especially among Christians
 II.   Theological foundations for the holiness of the married state
III.   The choice of a partner, a matter of great importance

* * * * *

'Erasmus and the Laws of Marriage' in *Acta Conventus neo-Latini Hafniensis* (see n42 above) 477–84; Payne especially 109–25; Albert Hyma 'Erasmus and the Sacrament of Matrimony' *Archiv für Reformationsgeschichte* 48 (1957) 145–64.

    A. Problems arising from the ease with which marriage can be contracted

    B. Problems arising from canon law: the eighteen impediments to marriage

    C. Measures the church might take to deal with the aforementioned problems

    D. Some suggestions for making a good choice of spouse, with examples from Scripture and history

IV. Ways to ensure that harmony and good will are established between the partners once they are married – the importance of mutual respect, mutual tolerance, conversation, and prayer, and similar matters

    A. Advice about observing Christian propriety in the wedding ceremony and celebration itself

    B. The secret of a successful marriage is contained in charity (or love), faith (or fidelity), and hope, the most important of which is the first.

       (Mutual deference; some principles of household management; simplicity of dress and furniture; restraint in sexual relations; the authority of the husband; similar matters)

V. The rearing of children

    A. Pregnancy, breast-feeding, the care and training of infants

    B. The education of children in learning and piety – where, when, how, and by whom it is to be undertaken

The textual tradition into which Erasmus' treatise must be fitted begins with the Fathers of the church. Erasmus was not too wide of the mark when he indicated that the Fathers wrote more extensively and enthusiastically about virginity than about marriage. True, with a few exceptions the Fathers spoke of the dignity and even sanctity of marriage, and their sometimes special enthusiasm for virginity has to be understood in the context of the contemporary polemics against it, which came even from Christians. None the less, most of what they wrote about marriage was said in passing – in sermons or in treatises devoted to other subjects. Augustine, for instance, dealt with aspects of marriage in Sermons 51, 288, and 292.

But Augustine was also one of the few to write on the subject professedly. His *De bono coniugali* ('The Good of Marriage') has been called 'the most complete patristic consideration of the duties of married persons,' and it was highly influential in the subsequent tradition.[49] It is, however, slight

* * * * *

49 Charles Wilcox 'Introduction' to 'The Good of Marriage' in *The Fathers of the Church* vol 27 ed Roy J. Deferrari (New York 1955) 3; PL 40 373–96

in length and scope compared with Erasmus' work. Augustine's *De coniugiis adulterinis* ('Adulterous Marriages')[50] and *De nuptiis et concupiscentia* ('Marriage and Concupiscence')[51] are longer but specific in the topics they deal with.[52]

In Augustine's day his works were known and read not only by clerics but also by lay persons, for whom they were often intended. With the radical decline in literacy in the early Middle Ages, however, very few books continued to be read by or written for a lay audience, and with the advent of scholasticism in the late twelfth century the highly technical and academic nature of the enterprises of theology and canon law further precluded discussion of their subject-matter by non-professionals. Serious reflection on marriage retreated almost exclusively into the courtrooms of the canonists and the lecture halls of the theologians, and it was recorded solely in the books they produced, which were intended for their peers and intelligible only to them. The canonists and theologians generated an immense body of literature on the subject, which eventually brought about consensus on many points earlier debated – for example, on various aspects of the sacramental character of matrimony – and resulted in what Gabriel Le Bras has called 'la doctrine classique.' But it also gave rise to a tangle of legal and theological opinion sometimes almost impossible to unravel, which made writings on matrimony even more inaccessible to non-professionals – that is, to large numbers of the clergy as well as to the laity.[53]

With the humanists in fifteenth-century Italy the situation began to change. The humanists by definition wrote for a broad audience and used an elegant but non-technical style of discourse. They were interested in moral questions related to everyday life. As early as 1416 Francesco Barbaro composed his treatise *De re uxoria* ('On Wifely Duties'), a sign of things to come. The work was widely read and circulated in many manuscript copies before its appearance in print in the early sixteenth century. Two decades later Leon Battista Alberti wrote his *Della famiglia* ('On the Household'), a treatise on a related topic. Marsilio Ficino published a short *Matrimonii laus* in 1497 as part of the collection of his *Epistolae*.[54] Bishop Giovanni Antonio Campano's treatise on the excellence of matrimony, *De dignitate matrimonii*,

* * * * *

50 PL 40 451–86
51 PL 44 413–74
52 See the article by L. Godefroy under 'Mariage' in DTC IX-2 2077–123.
53 See the article by Gabriel Le Bras under 'Mariage' in DTC IX-2 2123–317. For a much briefer treatment that also touches on other matters related to marriage, see Lawrence Stone *Road to Divorce: England, 1530–1987* (Oxford 1990) 51–71.
54 Marsilio Ficino *Opera omnia* 2 vols (Basel 1576; repr 1962) I 778–9

an expanded version of an oration he had delivered on the subject, appeared in a Roman edition in 1495 and a Venetian edition in 1502. Erasmus knew the earlier edition of Campano's works by 1497, when he was in Paris.[55] In 1524 Juan Luis Vives published his *De institutione feminae christianae*, in which the second of the three books dealt with wifely conduct.

Meanwhile, delivering encomiastic orations on the subject at weddings had become almost an avocation for humanists, as indicated by the many such speeches that survive from them, a good number of which were printed in the late fifteenth or the early sixteenth century. Among them, for instance, are seven by Francesco Filelfo published in 1496,[56] and six Latin and thirteen Italian by Agostino Dati published in 1503.[57] The practice spread north of the Alps, and in 1518, to take another instance, Cuthbert Tunstall, who had studied in Padua for six years, published his *In sponsalibus Delphini et Mariae filiae regis*, an oration given at the betrothal of the future Queen Mary (then three years old) to the still younger dauphin of France; the oration was reprinted the next year in Basel.[58] Thus not only had the subject moved into broader forums, but through the panegyrical form it had been given a notably positive interpretation. Marriage was praised in these orations as an institution of surpassing excellence, with arguments drawn from history, from philosophers, and often enough from the Bible and the Christian tradition – it was a sacrament and therefore holy. In some of the orations were the explicit comparisons of marriage with other states of life that got Erasmus into such trouble, beginning with the publication of his *Encomium matrimonii* in 1518.

By the late fifteenth century works of different inspiration or focus began to appear, such as *Les Quinze Joyes de mariage*, an anonymous and virulent satire against marriage written probably much earlier. That same year the famous expert in jurisprudence André Tiraqueau published the second edition of his book on marriage legislation, *De legibus connubialibus*, which had first appeared in 1513.

Especially important of course were the works by Luther, beginning with his *Babylonian Captivity* of 1520, in which he attacked 'la doctrine

* * * * *

55 Epp 61:153, 101:37. See Telle 182 n67.
56 Francesco Filelfo 'Nuptialium orationum annotatio' in *Orationes cum aliis eiusdem operibus* (Basel c 1496). I am indebted to Mr Anthony D'Elia of Harvard University for calling these and other humanist orations on matrimony to my attention.
57 Agostino Dati *Opera* (Siena 1503) fols 101v–113v
58 See CEBR III 351.

classique' in a number of ways, by denying, for instance, that marriage was a sacrament. The next year he published his *Judgment on Monastic Vows*, in which he condemned the vows as unchristian, and in 1522 he published his sermon/treatise *The Estate of Marriage*, in which he dealt with divorce and similar matters and, like Erasmus but much more briefly, addressed the problem of the eighteen canonical impediments to a valid marriage. These three works set off an explosion of controversy that was still raging when Erasmus published his 'Institution of Christian Matrimony' just a few years later.

The acrid and turbulent situation after 1517 is principally responsible for the success in many quarters of the attacks on Erasmus' treatise. But even aside from the situation, Erasmus' penchant for comparing marriage favourably to celibacy and virginity provided just the excuse his enemies from the scholastic establishment needed to rail against him as a heretic. High praise for the dignity and holiness of the married state was not new in the early sixteenth century, especially not in Italy, but by 1518, when Erasmus published his *Encomium matrimonii*, and even more so by 1526, when he published 'The Institution of Christian Matrimony,' the stage was set for onslaughts against what Erasmus had to say and how he said it.

That is the context and longer tradition in which Erasmus' treatise appeared, and the review above makes two things clear about the work. First, the 'Institution' did not appear in a void, nor can it be understood simply as a reply to Luther or as a clarification, justification, or even retractation of the *Encomium matrimonii*. It must be seen as part and parcel of a new way of speaking and writing on the topic that had been in the making for several generations, a new approach to the subject that was mightily propelled forward by the invention of printing and that reached a climax in the second decade of the sixteenth century. This new approach owed much, moreover, to the humanist movement, which gave the tradition the new form of panegyric, never before applied to the subject in a Christian context. This form influenced treatment of the subject in a positive direction. Form and content – *verba et res* – were reciprocally influential here, as the great teachers of rhetoric maintained they always were. Moreover, the form – a speech – by definition moved the subject out of the classroom and courts to a more general public.

Second, the review reveals the originality of Erasmus' treatise. As Heath says below, Erasmus produced a work 'profoundly serious and deeply researched . . . a detailed and painstaking examination of the institution from every conceivable angle' (204). Nothing like it had existed earlier – not in the patristic, medieval, humanist, or Reformation tradition. That is to say, nobody had undertaken to write a lengthy work that for all its complexity would be intelligible to non-specialists; that would deal with all aspects of the subject; that at least in a few instances would deal with them in a novel way; and that would try to give firm theological foundation to an ideal of a godly life lived as husband or wife.

Thus, as John B. Payne said some years ago, 'Marriage for Erasmus, the Christian pedagogue, is then a school for Christian living, in which husband and wife maintain with each other a chaste and holy relationship determined not by perverse pleasure but by a desire for progeny to be educated in the principles of the *philosophia Christi*.'[59] For that reason the treatise depicting marriage deserves to be included in the list of Erasmus' works 'pertaining to piety.'

In 'The Institution of Christian Matrimony' Erasmus ranges from a subtle theology of the Incarnation, which is a basis for his recurring reflections on the devout sentiments necessary for the spouses if their match is to endure, to the most down-to-earth issues, such as the advantages of breast-feeding by the mother. His lucidity in negotiating the labyrinth of canon law concerning marriage and the persuasiveness of his solutions, many of which were repudiated by the Catholic church in the sixteenth century only to be accepted by it in the twentieth, are remarkable for a 'mere' humanist. Erasmus drew from a wide variety of sources. Like any great artist, he was of course dependent on those who had preceded him, but he put the pieces together in a way that created something new.

Scholars often fail to recognize this aspect of Erasmus' achievement, for they are generally more intent on examining his ideas than the genre in which he expressed them, another instance of the priority routinely granted to *res* over *verba*, to content over form. One of the most striking aspects of many of the works in CWE 69 and CWE 70, however, is how Erasmus reshaped various literary forms or genres, sometimes to the point of creating a new tradition even as he moved within established frames of reference. This certainly applies to 'The Institution of Christian Matrimony,' and it constitutes one of the treatise's chief claims to our attention and respect.

JWO'M

* * * * *

59 Payne 111

ACKNOWLEDGMENTS

The individuals and institutions who assisted in the preparation of the various pieces in this volume are acknowledged in the introductions to those items. Once again we are indebted to Mary Baldwin, Lynn Burdon, Penny Cole, Theresa Griffin, and Philippa Matheson for their indispensable contribution of preparing the text for publication and bringing it into print.

PRAYER TO JESUS, SON OF THE VIRGIN

Precatio ad Virginis filium Iesum

translated and annotated by
STEPHEN RYLE

The *Precatio ad Virginis filium Iesum*, together with the *Paean Virgini Matri* (20–38) and the *Obsecratio ad Virginem Mariam* (41–54), owed its origin to the patronage Erasmus received from Anna van Borssele, the lady of Veere,[1] during the final years of the fifteenth century. While Erasmus was studying in Paris with a view to gaining a doctorate in theology, his friend Jacob Batt[2] obtained employment as tutor to Anna van Borssele's young son, Adolph of Burgundy.[3] During the autumn of 1498 Batt persuaded Anna van Borssele to invite Erasmus to the castle of Tournehem, between Calais and Saint-Omer, which was her family's principal residence. After some initial doubts Erasmus accepted the invitation,[4] and having arrived at the castle he apparently spent the first five weeks of 1499 there.[5] During that time he composed the *Paean*, the *Obsecratio*, and the *Precatio ad Virginis filium Iesum*. Subsequently he presented the three prayers to Adolph of Burgundy, together with the *Oratio de virtute amplectenda*.[6] In the closing lines of *De virtute amplectenda* he stated that the prayers had been composed at the request of Anna van Borssele and with Batt's encouragement; they were intended, however, for Adolph of Burgundy, and their style had been adapted to his tender age (he was about ten years old in 1499).[7] Some twenty years after they had first appeared in print Erasmus drew a distinction between the *Precatio* and the prayers to the Virgin, maintaining that the latter had been written in order to win the favour of Anna van Borssele, but that the *Precatio* was 'more after my own heart' ('magis ex animo meo').[8]

The *Precatio* occupied second place in the collection of Erasmus' works published by Dirk Martens at Antwerp in February 1503 under the title *Lucubratiunculae aliquot*. It immediately followed *De virtute amplectenda* and preceded the *Paean* and *Obsecratio*. The *Lucubratiunculae* were reprinted by Martens in November 1509 and again in 1514, using the same formes but with a few errors corrected. In September 1515 a new edition, retitled *Lucubrationes*, was published by Matthias Schürer in Strasbourg, having been seen through the press by Nikolaus Gerbel. After the appearance of this edition the most important work in the collection, the *Enchiridion*, began to

* * * * *

1 See CEBR I 173–4.
2 See CEBR I 100–1.
3 See CEBR I 223–4.
4 See Ep 80.
5 For the chronology see Epp 87–8, with Allen's notes I 223–4. Erasmus left Tournehem after 4 February 1499.
6 LB V 66D–72D / CWE 29 1–13; extracts printed as Ep 93
7 *De virtute amplectenda* LB V 72D / CWE 29 13 (=Ep 93:113–14)
8 Allen I 20:18–21 / CWE Ep 1341A:740–5

enjoy great popularity,[9] and the *Lucubrationes* were reprinted by Schürer in 1516 and 1517 and by Johann Froben at Basel in 1518. Ten years later the *Precatio* was again reprinted, together with its original companions the *Paean* and *Obsecratio*, at Cracow, on the initiative of Anselmus Ephorinus, who prefaced them with a dedicatory epistle.[10] From 1535 onwards the *Precatio* was included among the collection of Erasmus' prayers published under the title *Precationes aliquot novae* (120–51).

In 1872 Charles S. Coldwell published an English version of the *Precatio ad Virginis filium Iesum* among his selection of Erasmian prayers.[11]

For the present translation the text of LB has been collated with the 1503 and 1509 Martens editions, the Schürer edition of 1515, and the Basel *Omnia opera* of 1540. Significant variants have been registered in the notes.

SR

* * * * *

9 Cf Epp 412:26–8, 1341A:736–40.
10 See Allen Ep 2539 introduction; CEBR I 436–7.
11 *The Prayers of Erasmus* trans and ed Charles Simeon Coldwell (London 1872) 21–42

PRAYER OF ERASMUS OF ROTTERDAM
TO JESUS, SON OF THE VIRGIN,[1]
REDEEMER OF THE HUMAN RACE

With prostrate, suppliant soul I adore you, saviour of the human race, Jesus Christ, at once Son of God and of the Virgin. You are the true undying light,[2] utterly unbounded by time, flowing forth in an indescribable manner from the Father, the source of all light.[3] Together with the bond of the Holy Spirit, which is beyond our comprehension, you are joined in such a way that neither the simplicity of the Monad confuses the differences of the Persons, nor does the particularity of the Triad divide the unity of the substance.[4] For you are the new Sun of Righteousness:[5] ever rising from the Father who is ever giving life,[6] you have risen once and for all before the eyes of a world condemned to eternal night, and have driven out the infernal darkness of our sins;[7] and shining forth with fresh lustre you have brought back that bright and truly life-giving day, most eagerly awaited by humanity, the day that the Lord has uniquely

* * * * *

1 This is the form of the title as printed in editions of the *Lucubrationes* from Matthias Schürer's edition of 1515 onwards, and in LB. In the *editio princeps* of the *Lucubratiunculae* (Antwerp: Dirk Martens, February 1503) and its 1509 reprint the full title of the work is *Precatio qum erudita tum pietatis plena ad Iesum Dei Virginisque filium* (A Prayer, both learned and full of devotion, to Jesus, Son of God and of the Virgin).
2 Cf John 1:4–5, 9; 8:12.
3 Cf Gen 1:3–5; 1 Tim 6:16; James 1:17; 1 John 1:5.
4 For 'substance' Erasmus employs the Greek term *usia* (οὐσία); see G.W.H. Lampe *A Patristic Greek Lexicon* (Oxford 1965) 983–4. In 1527 Erasmus quoted this passage, beginning with the words 'from the Father,' as evidence of his consistent orthodoxy concerning the doctrine of the Trinity: Allen Ep 1877:85–9 and *Apologia adversus monachos* LB IX 1027C.
5 Cf Mal 3:20 (Vulg 4:2).
6 Cf *Precationes* 127 below.
7 Cf Isa 9:2, 60:1–3; *In Prudentium* LB V 1339E–1340A / CWE 29 175–6.

made,[8] scattering the loathsome blackness of the night (which we ourselves had caused). Nor do you ever cease to rise unseen in the hearts of the faithful, continually new, but the same, refusing no one the rays of your life-giving grace, unless that person himself refuses them and shuts them out.

Perpetually at rest, you turn and revolve all things; always remaining within yourself, you encompass the universe in its eternal revolution; you illuminate all things, and there is nothing that escapes your regard or your active involvement. Manifest, but also unseen; small in scope, and yet immeasurable; embracing all things, and at the same time incomprehensible; pervading all things, yet of absolute simplicity. Unfettered by time, you are the author of time; in tranquil order you govern all things.

You penetrate human souls imperceptibly[9] with your innate fire and steal them away to your Father: you purge them of the filth of their earthly desires, as far as is possible, and ravish them to the heights of your own nature; ravished, you lighten them; lightened, you transform them, so that just as you are one with God the Father by nature, so we may be one with you by adoption.[10] With your health-giving rays you cause all things to flourish and gain new life: you give them birth and nourishment, you are the origin and goal of all things that come into existence. To be influenced by your star is to revive, to be protected by your light is to advance, to be kindled by your flames is to be made perfect, to be abandoned by you is to perish. O thrice happy, those for whom your rising is gentle and dew-laden; eternal woe to those with whom you are angry at your setting. To gaze upon your face is absolute joy; to be deprived of your sight is chaos and everlasting horror. Where you shine, there is final immortality; where you do not shine, there is the pit of hell. I pray you, be favourable and gracious to me in your rising, O light that my eyes long for, and dispel the clouds of my mind, which my earthly nature wraps in darkness; spread your radiance serenely upon the eyes that are accustomed to see you, and shine with the face with which you make both heaven and earth joyful. You illuminate all things on earth with your flames;[11] do not ignore, I pray you, this poor soul that you yourself have fashioned. Do not be ashamed, kind Jesus, to remake what in your goodness you have

* * * * *

8 Cf Ps 118 (Vulg 117):24. In liturgical texts this verse recurs as applied to Easter Day; cf *Missale Romanum*.
9 Reading *insensibiliter* with the early editions (*sensibiliter* 1540 and LB)
10 Cf Rom 8:14–17, 23; Gal 4:5–6; Eph 1:5–6.
11 Virgil *Aeneid* 4.607

made; restore what you have established. Do not refuse to renew your own image. Let your mercy repair by its operation what has been squandered through my wrongdoing. Put right in your handiwork what has been perverted through my fault. Acknowledge and bring to perfection what you in your supreme goodness had supremely well created. Vindicate what is yours, so that we attribute all our ills to no one but ourselves; let us, however, accept all the benefits of your mercy, since in your unrivalled generosity you also habitually, by some divine art, turn our sinfulness into your good.

It was your power, Jesus, kindest of parents, that miraculously brought me into being when I was nothing. To this slight body, equipped with organs perfectly adapted to every kind of use and joined together in a wonderful harmony of all its parts, and, furthermore, endowed with an incredible acuteness of the senses, your wisdom imparted a living soul,[12] catching fire from your sacred breath, immortal, engendered from on high,[13] fashioned in your own image, so that it could partake of your nature, who are the highest good. In addition, from your light you showered upon it some sparks as it were of understanding, so that, placed at the centre of the universe as if in some supremely beautiful theatre of your creation, it might, through the knowledge of things seen (none of which you have fashioned less than supremely well), search for you, their unseen maker. Again, after I had fallen back into nothingness, owing not only to the sore[14] of our inherited guilt but also to my own sinfulness, your mercy set me back on the path to life through the remedy of your healing death, and you, O most innocent one, paid from your resources the debt that I had incurred through my fault.

Your goodness knows no bounds, most merciful Creator. Yet again, having thus freely ransomed me, your all-embracing generosity fortified me with so many wonderful gifts, lest having once been given back my freedom I should revert to the wretched condition of a slave. You strengthened me with so many life-giving sacraments, continually welling up from the spring of your most sacred death:[15] with water you gave me life and washed me clean, with holy oil you gave me strength; you fed me with the

* * * * *

12 Cf Gen 2:7; Wisd of Sol 15:11; 1 Cor 15:45.
13 Cf Virgil *Aeneid* 7.281; Silius Italicus *Punica* 15.77.
14 The Latin word used by Erasmus, *serpigo*, appears to be taken from the *Regimen sanitatis Salernitanum*; see C. DuCange *Glossarium ad scriptores mediae et infimae Latinitatis* 7 vols (Paris 1840–50) VI 205.
15 Erasmus here describes the sacraments of baptism, Eucharist, and confirmation.

riches of your own body and blood, and hardened your soldier with a powerful ointment in the face of spiritual combat; you enriched me with a variety of graces and secret gifts, drawing me to you with the soul's silent promptings when I went astray and rousing me when I had fallen asleep. And as if all these things were not enough, in our times of peril your loving-kindness comes to our aid with the saving remedies of your mystical Scripture. You instruct those who err, strengthen waverers, confirm with your promises those in difficulties, arouse the willing with your encouragement; you set us on fire by your example, and inspire us with fear by your dire warnings; now you attract us by your generosity, now you punish us with the scourge of merited disaster. Finally, in addition to all these mercies, so many and so great, though I have so often rejected you, so often mortally offended you, still again and again, most merciful Redeemer, you call me back, ungrateful and stubborn as I am. When I am already on the way to perdition you throw open the refuge of life-giving repentance, and open it as often as I turn away from myself and flee back to you: for you are yourself the highest beauty, and you do not desire the destruction of anything that you had so beautifully fashioned, or that you, no inexperienced or foolish merchant, had bought so eagerly and at so high a price.[16]

Trusting in your goodness, which is beyond all calculation, here I am, a runaway slave, daring to return to you, my master and master of all creation, after wandering aimlessly for so long.[17] Claim what is yours by right of recovery, Lord Jesus, and restore me at the same time to you and to myself, since I am lost to both. Wretch that I am, to how many masters, how domineering, how shameful, have I become a slave, while in my utter insanity I took excessive delight in my wanderings in Egypt[18] and my captivity in Babylon,[19] and, crazed as I was, cast from my shoulders your truly sweet yoke.[20] To serve you is the highest, the only, freedom;[21] to be claimed by you is to be rescued; to be possessed by you is to be blessed; to flee from you is to be lost.

* * * * *

16 Cf Matt 13:45–6.
17 Cf Luke 15:18–21.
18 Cf Gen 42–50.
19 An allusion to the deportation of the Jews to Babylon and their period of exile there, c 597–538 BC
20 Cf Matt 11:30.
21 Cf *Missale Romanum*, Collect for Peace ('cui servire regnare est'); *Book of Common Prayer*, Morning Prayer, 2nd Collect, for Peace ('whose service is perfect freedom'). For the various editions of the *Book of Common Prayer* see F.E. Brightman *The English Rite* 2 vols (London 1915).

Yet the sheep, once more gone astray,[22] dares to return to its all-forgiving shepherd. Earlier you had sought me long and often through the thickets of sin,[23] joyfully brought me back on your shoulders,[24] and returned me, clothed anew in the snow-white fleece of innocence, to the communal folds of your church, within which I should no longer have to fear the prowling of wolves.[25] The spendthrift son dares to return to his all-loving father.[26] I have wickedly wasted both the best years of my physical strength and my gifts of character, in other words the whole of my father's boundless substance, with the worst sort of wastrels and with foreign prostitutes, that is, in the lusts of the flesh. From a distant and unknown region of sin (the only thing unknown to you, who are eternal knowledge) I return, naked, needy, famished, bringing with me nothing from the great bounty bestowed on me by a generous parent, except an unhappy conscience, overwhelmed by wickedness and shame. But your essential goodness proves greater than this accumulated burden, vast though it is, of my sinfulness, and you summon this most wicked servant not to a criminal's death, not to chains, which I had otherwise deserved to wear eternally, but to forgiveness; you do not deliver me up to punishment, but take me back, purged of guilt, into your household. This scabbed, lost sheep you judge worthy of healing rather than punishment. You do not disinherit or disown your son, so disobedient to your word, so ignobly departing from his father's ways, but overcome by a father's love you run spontaneously to embrace him when he comes to his senses. You do not bar him from your home on his return, you do not cast the suppliant away from your knees, but immediately at the first expression of sorrow you take him in your arms and bestow a kiss on him; after enduring his sinful ways for so long you gladly welcome him when he repents, and you order a new robe to be brought out for your son clothed in rags. He deserves death, but you prepare a banquet for him, now by all means at your own expense; you forgive all his old crimes. And in the overwhelming joy of regaining your child there is not time to recall former offences: no savage tongue-lashing gives vent to a father's anger; not even Micio's gentle rebuke is

* * * * *

22 Cf Ps 119 (Vulg 118):176; Isa 53:6; 1 Pet 2:25. With this image and that of the prodigal son which immediately follows, compare *Precationes* 135 below ('A Penitent's Prayer').
23 Cf Ezek 34:16; Matt 18:12–13; Luke 15:4–6.
24 Cf Isa 40:11.
25 Cf John 10:12.
26 Cf Luke 15:11–32.

heard.[27] Has any skilful portrayer of human nature ever produced a similar example of an indulgent father?

Alas for the winter within our nature, most merciful Saviour, if in response to your unheard-of love for us we do not grow warm so as to love you in return, who have so loved us first.[28] Alas for the sluggishness of our souls, if they are not awakened when roused by such great favours. Alas for the more than adamantine hardness of the human heart,[29] if it cannot be softened by such great forgiveness on your part. But who will pluck out this impenetrable heart of stone, and restore our simple heart of flesh,[30] except you alone, our only hope, who yourself became flesh in order thus to overcome the hardness of our nature? Rather, who will refashion this entire human creature from head to toe, except you, the absolutely spotless lamb,[31] who renew the whole of creation,[32] not by incantations or magic herbs but by the sprinkling of your most holy blood? You do away with the old world, and you alone create a new heaven and a new earth.[33] Who will restore this putrid corpse to newness of life, except you, who alone with your life-giving breath revive dry, forsaken bones,[34] and who by a simple word summoned Lazarus, even after he had been dead for four days, back to the light?[35] I pray you, awaken my dead soul as well, since you are the life of every creature; heal my sick condition, since you are our souls' true medicine. May your freely offered mercy take hold of this pitiable victim of dropsy,[36] who thirsts after nothing but what is transitory and of no value, and feeds his sickness to no effect with wretched excess; and instead of his insatiable desire for water that is not sweet, instil in him a thirst for you. Whoever drinks from your spring will never be thirsty again.[37] Rouse up in him a hunger for you: you are the bread of life,[38] and once anyone has eaten of you he will

* * * * *

27 Cf Terence *Adelphi* 679–96. The character Micio is represented as an indulgent stepfather, in contrast to his brother Demea, the strict father of two sons, one of whom has been adopted by Micio.
28 Cf 1 John 4:19.
29 Cf Zech 7:12.
30 Cf Ezek 11:19, 36:26.
31 Cf Exod 12:5; 1 Pet 1:19; Rev 5:6.
32 Cf 2 Cor 5:17; Gal 6:15.
33 Cf Isa 65:17; Rev 21:1, 5.
34 Cf Ezek 37:1–10.
35 John 11:39, 43
36 Cf Luke 14:2–4.
37 Cf John 4:14, 6:35, 7:37–8.
38 Cf John 6:48, 51.

surely be sickened by the fleshpots of the Egyptians.[39] By your all-powerful will release this paralysed soul, tied to bodily appetites as if to a slothful bed,[40] and restore it to life and the practice of virtue. Pour on to the mortal wounds of this injured man both the wine of life-giving penitence and the oil of your consolation.[41] Open the inner eyes of this blind man so that they may see you, the light that never dies,[42] and so that all the illusions of this world may vanish in an instant. Finally, since you alone have fashioned the new creature, take away completely this old Adam, such as he is, who has no knowledge of anything other than the earth from which he was made, and let the new one, formed by you, created on your pattern, emerge.[43]

You, most sweet Jesus, are the kindly enchanter and magician: you refashion not only the body but also the soul, not by means of magical charms from Thessaly or Colchis but through your all-powerful mercy, and you do not merely restore its youth in place of old age[44] but also banish death and give it life and immortality. Come quickly, then, and transform me totally through the hidden enchantments of your Spirit and the elixirs of your grace. Take away this rotten, irremediably corrupt flesh, continually warring against the spirit,[45] and give me instead a new flesh modelled on your own, pure, undefiled, responsive to the spirit. Let this flesh, which is grass, and will have no sight of you, wither away;[46] let the flesh that will see the salvation of God take its place.[47] Remove this dull, earthbound, proud, ungovernable spirit that conspires with the flesh and is frequently unfaithful to you; give me a share of yours, sweet, gentle, tasting of heaven, despising things that are seen because they are transitory, flying to things that are unseen but are everlasting; so that, no longer alive, as it were, for myself, I may breathe through you, and live in you and for you alone, dead to myself and to the world.[48] Indeed, those who live by their own spirit are truly dead; but those who are led by your spirit are neither in the flesh nor subject to the Law;[49] they lead the life that lasts for

* * * * *

39 Cf Exod 16:3.
40 Cf Matt 9:2–7; Mark 2:3–12; Luke 5:17–25.
41 Cf Luke 10:30, 34.
42 Cf John 1:4–5, 9; 8:12; 9:5.
43 Cf 1 Cor 15:45–9.
44 Cf Ps 103 (Vulg 102):5.
45 Cf Gal 5:17.
46 Cf Isa 40:6–8; James 1:10–11; 1 Pet 1:24.
47 Cf Job 19:26.
48 Cf eg *Enchiridion* LB V 31B / CWE 66 71; *Colloquia* ASD I-3 383:297, 688:82 / CWE 39 457:8, 40 1003:1; *Epistola consolatoria* 197 below.
49 Cf Rom 8:1–4.

ever, having become immortal members of the head who will never die. So therefore take me away from myself, or rather restore me to myself, Jesus Christ, only bringer of salvation; cut me out of myself, so that I may be grafted on to you; let me be lost to myself, so that I may find safety in you; let me die to myself, so that I may live in you; let me wither to myself, so that I may flower in you; let me be empty in myself, so that I may overflow in you; let me begin to be nothing in myself, so that I may be all things in you.

It is a great thing that this wretched worm[50] asks of you (the fact does not escape me), something greater not only than human beings can deserve but also than they can desire or even comprehend: that is, to be one with you, and for a mere human creature to be transformed into a god.[51] But what is it that is so wonderful, if a mere human creature is transformed into a god? It is more wonderful that God has been transformed into a man. Both are inconceivable, both incomprehensible; but this is truly worthy of your incomprehensible mercy, to bestow upon us gifts that are beyond our comprehension.

Therefore I beseech you, not through my merits,[52] which are either of no worth or weigh against me, but through your own self, best and greatest Creator, and through all the ways by which we assuage and entreat your godhead: through the power you share with the Father, by which you created me from nothing as a great and wonderful good; through the identity of goodness you share with the Holy Spirit, by which you have bestowed such riches upon me with so many gratuitous gifts; through your wonderful wisdom, by which, as you span the universe from one limit to the other in your power and sweetly order all things,[53] you have in your indescribable purpose condescended to redeem us. And above all through the adorable source of our renewal, your incomparable love, which brought you, crazed as it were and drunk with new wine, down from the bosom of God the Father to a virgin's womb,[54] from the height of heaven to this vale of tears, the place of our exile,[55] and compelled you (totally willing as you were) to clothe

* * * * *

50 Cf Ps 22:6 (Vulg 21:7).

51 Cf Augustine *Sermones* 371 PL 39 1660–1.

52 The 1503 *editio princeps* highlights the beginning of this litany, in which 'through' (*per*) is repeated forty-two times, with the marginal lemma *Obsecrationes* ('Supplications').

53 Cf Wisd of Sol 8:1.

54 Cf *Paean Virgini Matri* 33 below; *Carmina* 110:286–8 ASD I-7 371 / CWE 85 292–3.

55 Cf the eleventh-century Marian antiphon *Salve, regina*: 'in hac lacrimarum valle . . . post hoc exilium' ('in this vale of tears . . . after this our exile').

yourself with this mud. And through all the hurts of the human condition, and the thousand troubles of this life, which you, the Lord of all, voluntarily endured through thirty-three years for the sake of a worthless slave.

Through hunger and thirst, by which you paid for our gluttony; through weariness, labours, sleepless nights, heat and cold,[56] by which you atoned for our fatal extravagance. Through your extreme poverty, in which you willed to be born, to live, and to die, so that you might enrich our impoverished condition. Through malice, contempt, abuse, through the complete humility of your whole life, by which you shattered our pride. Through those most holy tears that you shed so often for our crimes.[57] Through the extreme mental anguish that in your total innocence you endured, and which in the shadow of the cross you willingly undertook, not by any means because of any fear of death, which you so longed for, but out of an incredible love of your members;[58] you transferred our helpless condition to yourself, so that your weakness might strengthen us,[59] and your distress absolve us from everlasting grief. Through the drops of blood that you sweated from your whole body,[60] when you were about to take upon your shoulders the heavy weight of our sins.[61] Through your bonds,[62] which freed us from the fetters of eternal imprisonment. Through your condemnation, by which we were absolved from our real crime. Through the insults and wicked taunts heaped upon you, when you, the wholly innocent one, took on the shame incurred by our sins. Through the spittle that smeared your face, through the blows rained on you, which our faults had merited.[63] Through the enormous shame of your noble and absolutely pure mind, which your immeasurable love willingly and eagerly took upon itself, when, exactly like some criminal at the hands of most brutal executioners, you were publicly dragged from one seat of judgment to another, from one judge to another; and when, after being savagely scourged by the lictors' rods you were brought out to

* * * * *

56 Cf 2 Cor 11:27.
57 Cf Luke 19:41; John 11:35; Heb 5:7.
58 Cf Matt 26:36–44; Mark 14:32–40; Luke 22:39–44. In *De taedio Iesu* Erasmus argues that in his human nature Christ feared death, but that in his divine nature he ardently desired it in order to bring about the redemption of the human race. See eg LB V 1289A–D / CWE 70 63–4; Ep 109:78–96.
59 Cf 2 Cor 12:9.
60 Cf Luke 22:44.
61 Cf Isa 53:4, 6.
62 Cf Matt 27:2; Mark 15:1; John 18:12, 24.
63 Cf Isa 50:6; Matt 26:68; 27:27–31, 39–44; Mark 14:65; 15:16–20, 29–32; Luke 22:63–5; 23:11, 35–9; John 19:2.

be displayed to a crazed populace,[64] transferring our disgrace onto yourself, so that you might claim us for your glory. Through your stripes, by which we have been healed of our injuries.[65] Through your wounds, our remedy. Through your lashes, by which you paid the penalty of this wretched slave's offences. Through your most holy blood, which you have so often shed without stinting, in order to wash away our uncleanness. Through the cross, thrice worthy of adoration, your shame, our glory.[66] Through your most precious death, the undeserved penalty you paid for the life of us all, by which you restored the human race to the birthright of undying life, so that whereas our life had been our entry to death, your death might be for us the beginning of life.

Through the inestimable merits of your fidelity to God the Father and of your love for us, by which you most handsomely discharged the bad debts of our sins. Through the praiseworthy power of your most pure sacrifice, by which, as both priest and victim, you reconciled us to God the Father and to yourself.[67] Through that adorable mystery revealed when your side was pierced, and even in death you opened your secret source of blood and water,[68] so that by the one we might be brought back to life when we were dead, and by the other might be washed clean from our filthy state. Through your magnificent triumph, which you celebrated to the applause of heaven after returning to life from the underworld with the tyranny of death abolished. Through your undying glory, to which you have adopted us as joint heirs.[69] Through the faithfulness and merits of your spouse the church, the spotless virgin, joined to you by an indissoluble bond,[70] which receives the warmth of life from your blood and is animated by your Spirit. Through my hardships, the reason for your generosity. Through my evil deeds, from which only your mercy will deliver me. Through your good deeds, for which, to be sure, I have nothing to recompense you except myself, who have been yours now for a long time; but I cannot give you even this, such as it is, unless you yourself take possession of it and liberate also by love what is yours by right.

* * * * *

64 Cf Matt 26:57–68, 27:11–14; Mark 14:57–65, 15:1–5; Luke 22:66–71, 23:1–11; John 18:12–14, 19–24, 28–38; 19:1–16.
65 Cf Isa 53:5; 1 Pet 2:24.
66 Cf Gal 6:14.
67 Cf Heb 7:27, 10:10–12.
68 Cf John 19:34; 1 John 5:6–8.
69 Cf Rom 8:17.
70 Cf 2 Cor 11:2; Eph 5:24–7.

Therefore, not for the sake of my merits but for the sake of your abundant mercy,[71] claim for yourself what is yours. Lay your hand upon your slave, reforge the work that you, the artificer, have fashioned, and create a gift worthy of you. Drive far from my heart, a temple sacred to you, the unspeakable abominations of the Egyptians, with which I have so wickedly profaned it; cleanse it with the gift of true faith; when it is cleansed let it be enlightened by your sacred hope, which deceives no one;[72] when it is illuminated bring it to perfection by the fire of charity; and link my spirit, now transfigured, with yours in such a way, or rather, let your spirit so absorb mine, that our happy unanimity cannot be divided, whether by worldly prosperity or adversity, by life or death;[73] so that I may in future love nothing apart from you alone, nothing unless it is both in you and on account of you. Raise up this flesh, still creeping upon the ground, to the victorious height of your cross, and there fix it to yourself with your blessed nails, so that my love, as it looks down in freedom from the lofty tree upon all earthly things, may pant only after you.

May you alone become sweet for me, you alone have savour for me, you alone give me delight, you alone be the sole object of my wonder and longing. O true happiness, may this deceiving world, with its tricks and enchantments, with its fatal allurements which seduce me from you, become more and more sordid in my sight. Cleanse my palate, which once, alas, was saturated with sweet poisons, so that after I have tasted your sweetness,[74] the pleasures of the flesh, which before were sweet to the point of my destruction, may immediately become bitter to me. After this may I be sickened by the tainted delights of the world which I once, wretch that I was, devoured so avidly. May nothing captivate my eyes, however outwardly beautiful it may be, that is not pleasing in your sight. In fact nothing is pleasing that is not holy, since you are holiness itself; nothing that is not pure, since you are purity itself. You hate what is false, since you are truth itself; you reject anything that savours of the flesh, since you are spirit pure and simple. You detest the wisdom of this world,[75] since you are the wisdom of the Father. You abhor what the world admires, since for so long the world has hated

* * * * *

71 Cf Pss 51:1 (Vulg 50:3), 69:16 (Vulg 68:17).
72 Cf Rom 5:5; Phil 1:20.
73 Cf Rom 8:35–9.
74 Cf Ps 34:8 (Vulg 33:9); 1 Pet 2:3.
75 Cf 1 Cor 2:14, 15:44–6.

you[76] and you in turn have hated the world, from which you withdraw all those whom you wish to be called your own.[77] Thus, as you draw me little by little to you, let my soul die in your love, so that it may feel utter amazement at the idea of either good or evil fortune. For without you can any kind of good at all happen to me, or with you any kind of harm? Or rather, what is not sweet if you are there? Or what is so evil that you do not turn it to good for those you love? And so let everything else be thrown into confusion, let everything become topsy-turvy, as long as you do not remove yourself from me. May you alone be the object of my love and passion, since you are the undying form of beauty itself, and in communion with you whatever gives pleasure by its outward form is beautiful; to perish with desire for you is to be saved; to be mad with love for you is the only sanity.

May you be my pleasure, since to enjoy you is the height of happiness. May you be my wealth, the highest good, since for anyone who possesses you there is nothing else to be desired.[78] May you be my pride, who are the glory of the Father and the worship of all the saints. May you be my stronghold, who can by the simple exercise of will save anything you wish; but you wish to save all things. May you be my sure hope, at the same time guarantor and pledge and prize. May you be my trust, in no sense a broken reed, pricking and piercing the hand of anyone who leans on you,[79] but the reliable rock, on which anyone who lays his foundations need fear no fall.[80] May you be a parent to me, to whom I owe my life many times over. May you be my consolation, the joy of my heart, my peace, my tranquillity. Finally, for you alone let me hold all things in contempt, so that you alone may in turn be everything for me: compared to you all things are as nothing, and in you everything that is exists. For nothing exists that is not like you, whose essence is goodness and beauty. What is it to grow apart from you, other than to tend towards nothingness? The closer one approaches your likeness, so one grows more and more perfect. Therefore, most gentle Jesus, so that you may in your mercy make this poor creature,

* * * * *

76 Cf Matt 10:22, 24:9–10; Mark 9:13; Luke 21:18; John 7:7, 15:18, 17:14; 1 John 3:13.
77 Cf John 15:19, 17:14–16.
78 The text between 'my pleasure' and 'for anyone who possesses you' is omitted in LB.
79 Cf 2 Kings 18:21; Isa 36:6; Ezek 29:6–7.
80 Cf Matt 7:24–5; Luke 6:47–8.

such as he is, perfect, I give myself and place myself in your hands, so that you may restore me with you and you with me to myself, you who are the highest of all goods,[81] ever to be adored with the Father and the Holy Spirit. Amen.

* * * * *

81 Reading *bonorum* with the early editions (*honorum* LB)

PAEAN IN HONOUR OF THE VIRGIN MOTHER

Paean Virgini Matri dicendus

translated and annotated by
STEPHEN RYLE

Erasmus composed the *Paean Virgini Matri* during the early weeks of 1499, at the same time as the *Obsecratio ad Virginem Mariam* and the *Precatio ad Virginis filium Iesum*, while staying at the castle of Tournehem as the guest of Anna van Borssele, the lady of Veere. The three prayers were later dedicated, together with the *Oratio de virtute amplectenda*, to Anna van Borssele's young son, Adolph of Burgundy.[1]

The imagery upon which Erasmus drew for the *Paean Virgini Matri*, derived in the first instance from Scripture, but also from patristic sources and from the traditions of Latin homiletic literature and hymnography, seems to have borne further fruit later in 1499 with the composition of his longest poem, a hymn in Sapphic stanzas entitled *Paean divae Mariae atque de incarnatione Verbi*.[2] The numerous motifs common to the two paeans add weight to the hypothesis, argued convincingly by Harry Vredeveld, that the hymn was composed during the spring of 1499.[3]

Within two years of the initial publication of the *Paean* Erasmus had begun to adopt a somewhat defensive attitude with regard to its content and that of the *Obsecratio*. When presenting John Colet with a copy of the *Lucubratiunculae* in 1504 he stated that apart from the *Enchiridion* the contents of the volume had been written 'almost against the grain' ('reliqua omnia pene alieno scripsi stomacho'); and in revising his letter to Colet for publication in 1521 he added that this was particularly true of the *Paean* and *Obsecratio*: they had been composed 'in deference to the wishes of my friend Batt and the sentiments of Anna, princess of Veere.'[4] He used similar language when he referred to the *Paean* and *Obsecratio* in the *Catalogus lucubrationum*: the two works had been written, he said, 'to please [Adolph of Burgundy's] mother Anna, lady of Veere, in a childish style designed to suit her feelings rather than my judgment.'[5]

However, despite these reservations about the style and tone that he had adopted in composing the *Paean* and *Obsecratio*, it is clear that the two

* * * * *

1 For the background to the composition of the *Paean Virgini Matri* and for its early publication history see the introductory note to *Precatio ad Virginis filium Iesum* 2–3 above.
2 *Carmina* ed Harry Vredeveld 110 ASD I-7 355–77 / CWE 85 276–99
3 See Harry Vredeveld 'Some "Lost" Poems of Erasmus from the Year 1499' in *Fide et amore: A Festschrift for Hugo Bekker on His Sixty-Fifth Birthday* ed William C. McDonald and Winder McConnell, Göppinger Arbeiten zur Germanistik 526 (Göppingen 1990) 329–39; also the introductions to his commentaries on *Carmina* 110 ASD I-7 355 / CWE 86 646–8.
4 CWE Ep 181:60–2; Allen Ep 181:53–4n
5 Ep 1341A:743–4

works represent a genuine expression of Erasmus' devotion to the Blessed
Virgin. In later life he was able to cite the *Paean* in answer to conservative
critics who accused him of paying insufficient honour to the Mother of God.[6]

The *Paean Virgini Matri* was translated into English, probably between
1533 and 1544, by Henry Parker, Lord Morley (1476–1556), who presented
his translation to Henry VIII's daughter Mary Tudor, the future queen Mary
I of England.[7]

For the present translation the text of LB has been collated with the
Martens edition of 1514 and the Schürer edition of 1516.

SR

* * * * *

6 See n46 to the text. On the question of Erasmus' ideas about the role of Mary
within the context of Christian theology see especially Halkin 'Mariologie';
also O'Donnell 'Women Saints'; and John W. O'Malley's introductions to CWE
66 and this volume.

7 On Henry Parker, Lord Morley see *Dictionary of National Biography* 63 vols (London 1885–1900) 43 238–9; also the 'Introduction' to his *Forty-Six Lives Translated
from Boccaccio's 'De claris mulieribus'* ed Herbert G. Wright, Early English Text
Society o s 214 (London 1943); and E.J. Devereux *Renaissance English Translations of Erasmus: A Bibliography to 1700* (Toronto 1983) 140–1. Parker's translation of the *Paean Virgini Matri* is preserved in BL MS Royal 17A xlvi, and its
preface is printed in Wright's edition of the *Forty-Six Lives* 171–2.

PAEAN IN HONOUR OF THE VIRGIN MOTHER COMPOSED IN GRATITUDE TO THE LADY OF VEERE BY DESIDERIUS ERASMUS OF ROTTERDAM

Singular glory of heaven, earth's surest safeguard, virgin mother Mary. See, this poor soul of mine longs to propitiate your godlike majesty as if with the burning incense of its praise. Not relying on its own merits, but strengthened by your graciousness, it dares to encompass the vast ocean of your praises with the limitations of human language. Only he can comprehend its breadth who is immeasurable and beyond understanding, whom you were privileged to bear enclosed in the narrow confines of your most pure womb.[1] He did not sprinkle your virginal soul with a few drops of grace but transferred the very source of all graces into your person, so that those four famous rivers might flow forth from you as if from a most abundant paradise,[2] able to irrigate with their life-giving streams the parched and unproductive gravel of our hearts and to adorn them with smiling verdure and the spangled flowers of different virtues. So it is, O queen beyond compare, that a huge gulf stretches between your exalted state and my lowliness, between your more than angelic purity and my uncleanness, between your splendour and my darkness. You gaze upon the spirits of heaven placed far beneath your feet, we murmur from the depths of a valley. And yet the less we are able to achieve your praise, the more zealously we should strive to do so.

You[3] are the mightily powerful mistress of the world,[4] who alone among mortal creatures have deserved to be called upon by that most

* * * * *

1 Cf *Missale Romanum*, Common of feasts of the Blessed Virgin, Gradual: 'quem totus non capit orbis, in tua se clausit viscera factus homo'; Jerome Ep 77.7 CSEL 55 44:16.
2 Cf Gen 2:8–14; *Carmina* 110:117–20; 112:348 ASD I-7 364, 404 / CWE 85 282–3, 330–1; Salzer 7, 388–91; *Marienlexikon* II 87–8.
3 On the repetition of 'You' (*Tu*) as a feature of prayers and hymns in the ancient world see Eduard Norden *Agnostos Theos* (Leipzig 1913; repr 1929) 149–63, 220–3; A.D. Nock 'A Traditional Form in Religious Language' *Classical Quarterly* 18 (1924) 185–8.
4 Cf Salzer 450–5; *Marienlexikon* III 161–2.

auspicious title, Virgin Mother of God,[5] since your fecund virginity brought forth for us one and the same man from human stock (but without sin), who is God from God the Father, born from the beginning, who is to come to birth eternally. You are the exalted queen of heaven and earth:[6] your all-powerful Son willed that you should share with him the sovereignty of the universe bequeathed to him by the Father; before your holy power even the depths of hell tremble; this entire world, placed at the centre, worships you with dedicated altars in every region,[7] and at your revered name pope and emperor bare their heads and bow them in worship. Before your feet the purity of virgins, the martyrs' crown of laurel,[8] the prophets' authority, the dignity of the apostles, the blessed state of the angels, and all the exalted host of heaven kneel in submission; and the Godhead itself in its entirety holds you worthy of particular honour. The Father joyfully acknowledges you as the mother of your common offspring, and enfolds you in love. The Son, in accordance with his own filial devotion and the reverence due to his mother, loves and honours the woman who gave him birth. The Holy Spirit, proceeding from them both, permeates you entirely;[9] he willingly acknowledges his own spotless workshop, in which, to the amazement of nature, he accomplished that previously unheard-of act of creation, when with divine skill he formed within your virginal breast[10] the threefold giant:[11] he joined together in an indescribable mixture the word of God with

* * * * *

5 Erasmus uses the Greek term *Theotokos*, which had been employed as an epithet for Mary at least as early as the time of Origen (c 185–c 254), and which was accepted by the councils of Ephesus (431 AD) and Chalcedon (451 AD) as the authentic expression of her relationship to Jesus Christ. See *Marienlexikon* VI 390–1.

6 Cf Salzer 461–7; *Marienlexikon* III 589–96.

7 Cf 38 below; *Liturgia Virginis Matris* 90 and 108 below, with nn28 and 144.

8 Cf *Liturgia Virginis Matris* Sequence 89 below (= ASD I-7 444:5 / CWE 85 360): 'the laurel-crowned band' (*laureata turma*).

9 Cf *Precationes* 126 below.

10 Cf *Liturgia Virginis Matris* 91 and 101 below.

11 Cf 25 and 28 below; *Institutio christiani matrimonii* 231 below; *Liturgia Virginis Matris* 101 below. This image of the nature of Christ seems to have no exact precedent in patristic literature. Giants were normally represented both in the Hebrew scriptures and in Greek mythology as forces of anarchy, threatening to destroy the established order that governed the world. The Septuagint and Old Latin versions of the Psalms, however, used *gigas* in a favourable sense at Ps 19:5 (Vulg 18:6), within a double simile portraying the sun in its course. The simile was applied to Christ, the 'sun of righteousness' (Mal 3:20 [Vulg 4:2]). Ambrose, in his Christmas hymn *Veni, redemptor gentium*, employed the expression *geminae gigans substantiae*, 'twin-substanced giant,' to convey the idea of the two natures in the person of Christ. This phrase

the human spirit, the soul of man with mortal flesh, and cemented three things absolutely contrary to one another in such a way that the simplicity of the hypostasis should by no means confuse the differences of their natures. Therefore each of them holds you in special honour, and all of them in common award you the place second in rank, so that after the Godhead the panoply of heaven should have no more wondrous sight to gaze upon than you alone.

If, then, the highest ranks of the heavenly court look up to her as raised so far above them, with what confidence can I, poor worm that I am, turn my face upwards? What sound can I utter in my stammering attempts to express your praises, to which not even the voices of angels are able to prove themselves equal? But I am taught boldness, O Mary, not by arrogance but by the necessity of my wretched state; insupportable poverty overcomes my reticence, devotion prompts this alacrity within me, your singular favour fills me with confidence. If you were merely a source of wonder, O Virgin Mother of God, and not also a source of mercy, if you revealed less compassion than surpassing greatness, our mortal nature would have no one to turn to. But now as much as your sublime state makes our mean nature discouraged, so your graciousness raises it up; as much as your excellence separates us from you, so your kindness draws us to you; as much as the splendour of your virtues dazzles our eyes, so the shade of your mercy gives us relief. Nor are you so distant from us through the pre-eminence of your merits as you are close to us through your readiness to come to our aid. You gave birth to God – heaven is amazed; but you undoubtedly gave birth for us – humanity revives. You brought forth God – nature stands stupefied; but you brought forth not a thunderer, not a wielder of the thunderbolt,[12] but a

* * * * *

was taken up by Augustine during the Christological controversies of the early fifth century, and was frequently quoted by later writers. For Erasmus' emphasis on the triple aspect of Christ's nature, embracing the elements of word, soul/spirit, and flesh, compare Augustine *Contra sermonem Arianorum* 7.6–9.7 PL 42 687–90, and see further Brian E. Daley 'The Giant's Twin Substances: Ambrose and the Christology of Augustine's *Contra sermonem Arianorum*' in *Augustine: Presbyter factus sum* ed Joseph T. Lienhard, Earl C. Muller, and Roland J. Teske, Collectanea Augustiniana (New York 1994) 477–95.

12 Zeus (Jupiter), the supreme deity of the Greco-Roman pantheon, was principally the god of the sky, and the thunderbolt was the weapon with which he punished those who offended him. For the epithet 'the Thunderer' (*Tonans*) cf eg Ovid *Metamorphoses* 1.170, 2.466. Cf also *Carmina* 110:310–12 ASD I-7 373 / CWE 85 294–5.

crying baby;[13] not one who punishes, but one who atones; who brings about redemption, not revenge. You gave birth to God, but so that we might be reborn. You gave birth as a virgin, not so that our unclean nature should lose hope, but so that it should be expunged. You are the Mother of God, but you are also called the mother of mercy,[14] and you could not be the mother of mercy if you had not deserved to be the Mother of God. You were filled to superfluity with spiritual gifts, so that your surplus might overflow into our emptiness. You are placed next to the Godhead so that we should not lack an advocate in that quarter. You have the greatest influence with God so that there might be one to whose prayers and authority he might entrust his righteous anger against us. Therefore, O Mary, all the qualities you possess are intended for our help: the greater your excellence, the surer is our confidence, since as you are most great you are also most good.

Do not reject the paean of praise, however unpolished, that rises from those whose nature your Son did not despise. Look favourably, Mother, on our hymns, however feeble, since your son valued more highly the poor widow's mite than the riches of the rest.[15] Do not allow yourself to ignore the prayers of those whom your son prized so highly that he devoted himself to their salvation. If you rejoice to be called mother of the Creator, look kindly upon your son's flesh and blood. Look kindly upon what your son has gained, mother of the Redeemer. Look kindly also upon those who are the cause of your title and the subject of your praise, mother of clemency:[16] for to what fate do you consign wretched mortals, mother of mercy, if you exclude them from your embrace? Indeed, who else is there for suffering humanity to call upon with hymns and prayers than you, Mary, who alone among the heavenly host, by virtue of your merits, favour, and dignity, possess the power to appease the anger of the judge?

In the same way you are so ready to listen and so kindly disposed that there is no one whose prayers you turn away. You are so patient that you are never wearied by the importunate requests of those in need; so forgiving and ready to be placated that no crimes on our part, however heinous, will deter you from coming to our aid; so generous that you allow

* * * * *

13 Cf *Carmina* 110:325–6 ASD I-7 374 / CWE 85 294–5.
14 The title 'mother of mercy' (*mater misericordiae*) occurs immediately after the invocation *Salve, regina* in the eleventh-century Marian anthem of that name sung in many places daily at the conclusion of the Divine Office. Cf also Salzer 554–6, 582–6; *Marienlexikon* I 364–70, IV 552.
15 Mark 12:41–4; Luke 21:1–4
16 Cf Salzer 569–70.

no one to part from you unrewarded; so rich that your wealth can never be exhausted by your giving; with the result that you seem to have been granted to mortals by the true Jupiter, who is not only your foster-child but also your son, as if you were some golden horn, from which they will not fail to receive anything that they request.[17] Finally your nature is such, most blessed Virgin, that no earth-born creature has not experienced your goodness, and not even the heavenly spirits can comprehend your greatness.

You are assuredly the Woman of renown:[18] both heaven and earth and the succession of all the ages uniquely join to celebrate your praise in a musical concord. Already before the earth was formed you were living at the very source of creation, delighting in the world.[19] When the angels were created in the beginning, you, shining out from the mirror of the mind of God,[20] conferred an additional measure of joy. The Creator himself, at the very outset when the world was still newly fashioned, uttered his first prophecy about you, saying that a woman would come who would crush the head of the deadly serpent with her heel.[21] During the centuries of the previous age the oracles of the gentiles spoke of you in obscure riddles. Egyptian prophecies, Apollo's tripod, the Sibylline books, gave hints of you.[22]

* * * * *

17 An allusion to the *cornucopia*, or horn of Amaltheia, which was said to belong to the she-goat which suckled Zeus (Jupiter); alternatively Amaltheia was the name of the nymph who owned the she-goat. The horn was regarded as providing its possessor with everything he desired. See *Ausführliches Lexikon der griechischen und römischen Mythologie* ed W.H. Roscher 6 vols in 9 (Leipzig 1884–1937) I 262–6; A.B. Cook *Zeus* 3 vols in 4 (Cambridge 1914–40) I 500–2; J.G. Frazer on Apollodorus *Bibliotheca* 2.7.5, Loeb Classical Library (Cambridge, Mass and London 1921); *Reallexikon für Antike und Christentum* ed Theodor Klauser (Stuttgart 1950–   ) 16 524–74 under 'Horn I' especially 539–40, 560–1. See also *Carmina* 87:6 ASD I-7 252 / CWE 85 166–7, 86 556; *Adagia* I vi 2: *Copiae cornu*, 'A horn of plenty' CWE 32 4–5.
18 The Latin word for 'Woman' used here by Erasmus – *Virago* – is taken from Gen 2:23, the only instance of its use in the Vulgate Bible. Erasmus uses it again at *Enchiridion* LB V 17D / CWE 66 48. For the epithet – *nobilis* – cf *Liturgia Virginis Matris* Sequence ASD V-1 98:44 / 89 below (= ASD I-7 445:16 / CWE 85 360–1). Erasmus no doubt also has in mind a play on *Virgo/Virago*.
19 Cf Prov 8:22–31. Erasmus equates Mary with the figure of Wisdom, as was done in liturgical texts honouring her. See eg DS X 448, 450.
20 Cf Salzer 76–7, 337–9; *Marienlexikon* VI 237–9.
21 Gen 3:15; cf Rev 12:1–6, 17; *Carmina* 110:57–60 ASD I-7 360 / CWE 85 278–9.
22 In late antiquity pagan oracles were interpreted by Christians as evidence for the coming of the Messiah in the person of Jesus, born of Mary. The so-called Sibylline Oracles, originally collected in fifteen books of Greek hexameters, incorporate Jewish and early Christian Messianic prophecies, and were known

The mouths of learned poets predicted your coming in oracles they did not understand.[23]

You are the virgin who has restored the golden age.[24] You are the true Diana, both origin and model of perpetual virginity.[25] You are the deity of triple form[26] who gave birth to the threefold giant,[27] thrice-powerful, whom the rulers of the underworld dread, the heavenly powers revere, and this middle earth adores. The epithet Lucina[28] is uniquely appropriate to you, since you both brought forth the true light and opened for us the portals of everlasting light so that we might be reborn.

Both the Old and the New Testament, like two cherubim with wings joined[29] and unanimous voices, repeatedly sing your praise. The mystic synagogue foreshadowed you in symbolic images; the trumpet of the Gospel proclaims with piercing clarity its paean in your honour. Hebrew literature represented you by adumbration, in the most appropriate colours;[30]

* * * * *

to Lactantius and Augustine. See *The Oxford Dictionary of the Christian Church* ed F.L. Cross and E.A. Livingstone 3rd ed (Oxford 1997) 1496–7; *Marienlexikon* VI 153.

23 Cf *Carmina* 110:69–80 ASD I-7 360–2 / CWE 85 280–1.

24 A reference to Astraea, the virgin goddess of justice, the last of the deities to depart from the earth at the end of the primordial golden age; see Virgil *Georgics* 2.473–4; Ovid *Metamorphoses* 1.149–50. Her return would be the harbinger of its restoration; see Virgil *Eclogues* 4.5 ('Iam redit et Virgo'). Cf *Carmina* 110:315–16 (of Christ): 'saecla … daturus aurea' (ASD I-7 373 / CWE 85 294–5).

25 Cf *Obsecratio ad Virginem Mariam* 45 below. The Italian goddess Diana, identified at an early stage of Rome's history with the Greek Artemis, was traditionally regarded as a virgin-goddess, particularly associated with woods and hills, and worshipped as the patron deity of huntsmen. Cf Catullus *Carmina* 34.9–12; Horace *Odes* 3.22.1, *Carmen saeculare* 1. See also *Marienlexikon* I 248–9, II 185–6, and the following note.

26 Like Artemis, Diana came to be associated with other female deities, particularly Lucina (the Greek Eileithyia, goddess of childbirth) and Hecate, a goddess of the underworld. In art she was represented as a triple figure, with three faces in different directions. Cf Horace *Odes* 3.22.4 ('diva triformis'); Virgil *Aeneid* 4.511 ('tria virginis ora Dianae').

27 See n11 above.

28 See n26 above.

29 Cf Exod 25:18–20, 37:7–9; 1 Kings (Vulg 3 Kings) 6:23–8; 2 Chron 3:10–13; Heb 9:5.

30 This may simply allude to the Old Testament passages which Christian writers interpreted as referring to Mary; but Jewish commentators and cabbalistic authors attributed special significance to the letters of the Hebrew alphabet, which were described as 'woven from all the colours of the light,' and in view

Christian books adorned you in your virtues. Thus indeed have writers religiously vied to proclaim you, on the one hand inspired prophets, on the other eloquent Doctors of the church, both filled with the same spirit, as the former foretold your coming in joyful oracles before your birth and the latter heaped prayerful praise on you when you appeared. The first group make no empty promises, but rouse a mourning world to hope, while the second raise devout souls to contemplation of your wonder. The heralds are certainly distinguished, but both groups are overshadowed by the scale of your virtues. The insight of the prophets, foretelling the future, yields to your godlike merits, as does the superabundant eloquence of the Doctors; and the copious flood of their words acknowledges that it is unequal to expressing your glory.

You are the fertile shoot sprung from the stock of Jesse[31] (yet you carry with you no taint of the impurity of childbirth):[32] a humble offshoot which has produced no deadly fruit but the incomparably fragrant flower that with its most charming appearance has filled both earth and heaven with joy, and whose scent attracts us to the love of heavenly life.[33] You are the woman of prophecy who by means of a new and unheard-of miracle conceived a child within the girdle of your unblemished body without the working of a man. You are the rich sun-filled paradise, not broken by the plough or disturbed by the hoe, that brings forth every kind of delight and relief for souls.[34] You are the tree of life whose fruit, life-giving and unfailing, has taken away the poison of the tree that to our misfortune was tasted of old.[35]

You are the celebrated house that the Son of God himself, the wisdom of the eternal Father, the wonderful architect, built for his own use, basing it on seven tall, solid pillars,[36] so that he, who lives only in the highest heavens,[37] might dwell in its recesses, far removed from earthly concerns. You

* * * * *

of later references in his letters it is possible that Erasmus had some knowledge of the Cabbala. See Epp 798, 967, 1033, 1160, and, further, *Encyclopaedia Judaica* 16 vols (Jerusalem 1971–2) II 747–9 under 'Alphabet, Hebrew, in Midrash, Talmud and Kabbalah.'

31 Cf Isa 11:1; *Marienlexikon* VI 768–70.
32 Cf *Obsecratio ad Virginem Mariam* LB V 1236E (47 below): 'per sacratum partum tuum ab omni cruciatu, ab omni pudore, nostrique puerperii sordibus … immunem'; *In Prudentium* LB V 1340E–F / CWE 29 178. See also Halkin 'Mariologie' 37.
33 Cf Song of Sol 1:4 (Vulg 1:3).
34 See n2 above.
35 Cf Gen 2:9, 3:22; Salzer 7, 113 n6, 301–2; *Marienlexikon* I 328–34.
36 Prov 9:1; Salzer 116 n3, 321.
37 Cf Ecclus 24:4 (Vulg 24:7).

are the ivory throne of Solomon, adorned with gold,[38] from which the king of kings,[39] clad in the robe of the flesh,[40] gives judgment to mortals. You are the palanquin of that fastidious lover, constructed from wood of Lebanon, which he wondrously decked out for himself in gold, silver, and radiant purple,[41] a worthy resting-place, to be sure, in which he might be carried for ten months. Your snow-white breast[42] was symbolized by his verdant bed,[43] which the Son of God, lover of purity, so protected with squadrons of the heavenly host and the entire chaplet of virtues that no approach ever lay open even for a thought that was less than holy, and where alone nothing was ever found that might offend the Bridegroom as he took his delight, or disturb his slumber. You are the most sacred temple[44] of the king who brings peace, into which he has transmitted all his art and all his treasure: so sanctified that the absolute Holy of Holies was entrusted to its recesses;[45] so splendid that the ruler of Olympus took his seat there; so sacred that it could never be defiled by any stain of sin.[46]

Your pregnant virginity was prefigured by the mystic bush that falsely seemed to Moses to be on fire:[47] you alone among mortal women deserved

* * * * *

38 Cf 1 Kings (Vulg 3 Kings) 10:18, 20; Salzer 39; *Marienlexikon* VI 113–18.
39 Cf Deut 10:17; 1 Tim 6:15; Rev 17:14, 19:16.
40 Cf *Carmina* 110:323 ASD I-7 373 / CWE 85 294–5; *Liturgia Virginis Matris* 101 below; Salzer 88:3–4.
41 Cf Song of Sol 3:9–10.
42 Cf *Carmina* 110:358 ASD I-7 375 / CWE 85 296–7; *Liturgia Virginis Matris* Sequence 89 below (= ASD I-7 445:22 / CWE 85 362–3).
43 Cf Song of Sol 1:16 (Vulg 1:15).
44 Cf Salzer 36–7, 119 n2; *Marienlexikon* VI 367–9.
45 Cf Exod 26–34; 1 Kings (Vulg 3 Kings) 6:16; Heb 9:1–5.
46 A reference to the doctrine of the Immaculate Conception of the Blessed Virgin. Erasmus here uses language that is more specific than the words contained in the *Obsecratio ad Virginem Mariam*, written at about the same time as the *Paean*: there he describes Mary as 'ab omni libidine aliena' LB V 1236E (47 below). In 1527 Erasmus asserted that he had always believed in the Immaculate Conception, and recalled the expressions of his adherence to the doctrine 'nearly thirty years ago' ('ante annos ferme triginta'); *Supputatio* LB IX 569F–570A. This must refer to the *Paean* and the *Obsecratio*; and in the *Apologia adversus rhapsodias Alberti Pii* of 1531 he specifically cited the two early works in again declaring that he had always held that belief: 'quam magnifice sentiam de sacratissima Virgine declarant *Paean* meus et *Obsecratio*, iam toties excusa [sic], praeterea *Liturgia* cum concione, quam edidi adversus obtrectatores Virginis, semperque favi sententiae quae liberat eam ab omni peccato, etiam originali' (LB IX 1163E). See further Halkin 'Mariologie' 39–43.
47 Cf Exod 3:2–3; *Breviarium Romanum*, third Psalm-antiphon at Vespers, 1 January: 'Rubum quem viderat Moyses incombustum, conservatam agnovimus

the title of mother although you never held that of wife. Your virginal fertility was wonderfully foreshadowed by the priestly rod,[48] neither sown by human agency nor watered by earthly moisture: you flowered by means of your heavenly conception and, giving birth without pain,[49] brought forth your life-giving fruit.[50] The snow-white fleece of Gideon presented an image of you:[51] far removed from fleshly taint, but sprinkled three times with heavenly dew, by the working of the Trinity you conceived your threefold child[52] in purity, gave birth in purity, and remained pure after your child was born.[53]

You were signified by the tower of David: you alone were equipped by the illustrious man of war with ramparts, a thousand bucklers, and the armour of every kind of virtue[54] against all the weapons of the most wicked enemy, so that neither your body nor your spirit has ever been attacked, not to say captured, by any assault of carnal desire.[55] The divine prophet was speaking of you when he described the outstanding gate,[56] not facing the north, whence every kind of evil breaks forth,[57] but the east, whence the new sun arises, renewing everything: the prince of peace[58] in entering and in going out has not tampered with the bonds of your integrity, but made them inviolate.

* * * * *

tuam laudabilem virginitatem'; *Carmina* 110:81–4 ASD I-7 362 / CWE 85 280–1; Salzer 13–14, 114 n6, 413:1–3.

48 Cf Num 17:16–24 (Vulg 17:1–9); Salzer 34–5; *Marienlexikon* I 8–9.

49 See n32 above.

50 Cf Salzer 66:18–21.

51 Cf Judg 6:36–40; Ps 72 (Vulg 71):6; *Breviarium Romanum*, second Psalm-antiphon at Vespers, 1 January: 'Quando natus es ineffabiliter ex Virgine, tunc impletae sunt Scripturae: sicut pluvia in vellus descendisti, ut salvum faceres genus humanum: te laudamus Deus noster'; *Carmina* 110:91–2, 120:20–2 ASD I-7 362, 422 / CWE 85 280–1, 342–3; Salzer 41–2, 120 n2; *Marienlexikon* II 636–7.

52 See n11 above.

53 Cf *Missale Romanum*, Mass for feasts of the Blessed Virgin, Alleluia-verse and Tract: 'Post partum Virgo inviolata permansisti.'

54 Cf Song of Sol 4:4; Salzer 12, 286–91; *Marienlexikon* II 153–4.

55 Cf *Obsecratio ad Virginem Mariam* LB V 1236E (47 below): 'tu fueras ab omni libidine aliena.'

56 Cf Ezek 43:1–4, 44:1–3; *Carmina* 110:97–100 ASD I-7 362–3 / CWE 85 280–1; *Explanatio symboli* ASD V-1 245:198–246:213 / CWE 70 291; *In Prudentium* LB V 1339F / CWE 29 176; Salzer 28, 117 n7, 283:37–9; *Marienlexikon* V 191–3. Erasmus chose Ezek 44: 1–3 as one of the two alternative Old Testament readings for the *Liturgia Virginis Matris* (87 below).

57 Cf Jer 1:14, 4:6, 6:1.

58 Isa 9:6

You are the new Eve[59] of the new Adam,[60] not a stepmother like the one of old who destroyed her offspring even before she could give birth,[61] but a mother, and not a mother of mortal creatures as the other was, but of beings restored to life.[62] Through a mystery impossible to comprehend you have given birth from your own flesh to the very one from whose bone you came to birth;[63] and you became pregnant by none other than the one whom you bore, so that by a paradox impossible to resolve you have become daughter, wife, and mother of the same being. You have turned back the poison of that supreme liar, the serpent, on its own head.[64]

You are the courageous woman who dared to carry out a most splendid deed and transfixed the heathen commander, the common enemy of the human race, with a tent-peg.[65] You are Judith, worthy of celebration through all ages: alone you slaughtered the hellish tyrant who rampaged far and wide,[66] and in place of certain despair brought your people sudden deliverance and triumph.[67] You are beautiful Esther, delight of the heavenly king:[68] you warded off the grim sentence of death and turned the swords that were poised at your people's throats onto the very man who had plotted their massacre.[69]

You are the mountain, hard as adamant, from which was hewn, without the work of human hands,[70] the cornerstone that makes two into

* * * * *

59 Cf *Carmina* 110:54–6, 205–8 ASD I-7 360, 367 / CWE 85 278–9, 286–7; *Enchiridion* LB V 17D / CWE 66 48; *Explanatio symboli* ASD V-1 245:186–8 / CWE 70 290; *Marienlexikon* II 418–21.
60 Cf 1 Cor 15:45.
61 An allusion to the goddess Hera (Juno), who attempted to destroy the offspring of several of the extramarital liaisons of her husband Zeus (Jupiter), especially Hercules and Dionysus. In Latin literature Juno was frequently referred to as 'stepmother' (*noverca*), eg Virgil *Aeneid* 8.288; Ovid *Metamorphoses* 6.336, 9.15, 135, 181. Cf Otto 1239–41; *Adagia* II ii 95: *Odium novercale*, 'Stepmotherly hatred'; and see further Patricia A. Watson *Ancient Stepmothers* Mnemosyne Supplement 143 (Leiden 1995).
62 Cf Salzer 581–6, especially 584:27–35.
63 Cf Gen 2:22–3.
64 Cf Gen 3:15.
65 This refers to the slaying of Sisera by Jael, Judg 4:21–2, 5:24–7. Cf Salzer 492; *Marienlexikon* III 344–5.
66 Holofernes: cf Jth 2:19–3:8 (Vulg 2:11–3:12).
67 Jth 13:8–16:20 (Vulg 13:10–16:24); cf *Carmina* 110:95–6 ASD I-7 362 / CWE 85 280–1; Salzer 492–4; *Marienlexikon* III 451–3.
68 Cf Esther 2:16–17; Rest of Esther 5:2 (Vulg 15:16–17).
69 Esther 7:10; cf *Carmina* 110:93–5 ASD I-7 362 / CWE 85 280–1; Salzer 261:22–6, 473–6; *Marienlexikon* II 403–4.
70 Cf Dan 2:34–5, 45; Salzer 7–8, 113 n7.

one,[71] on which every structure is aligned,[72] which will not yield to the storms of this world:[73] anyone who falls on it will be dashed to pieces.[74]

You, a rose-bush of Jericho,[75] have given birth to the flower of the field:[76] you were nourished not by the crags of pride but by unassuming simplicity and lowly modesty; God's love has suffused you with the purple of high dignity; though you were born from earth you absorbed nothing of earth's uncleanness. You, mother of the lily of the valleys, and yourself a lily among brambles,[77] springing up without thorns, have joined supreme modesty to your milk-white virgin purity. You are the sealed fountain[78] whose supremely clear waters have never been troubled by any sensual appetite, and in which no earthly desire has disturbed the resplendent image of your Bridegroom: you divert your healing waters into the heads of every channel, and to drink them gives us not eloquence, like the waters of the Castalian spring, but immortality.[79] You are the divinely protected garden,[80] enclosed by a fence in such a way that not even a wanton thought can penetrate it; in which the supreme gardener has with wonderful skill marked out beds of spices,[81] where he himself pastures his flock among the lilies[82] and gives it rest at noon.[83]

* * * * *

71 Cf Ps 118 (Vulg 117):22; Isa 28:16; Matt 21:42; Mark 12:10; Luke 20:17; Acts 4:11; 1 Pet 2:6; *Virginis et martyris comparatio* 160 below; *Epistola consolatoria* 199 below.

72 Cf Eph 2:20–1.

73 Cf Matt 7:24–5; Luke 6:48.

74 Cf Luke 20:18; *Epistola consolatoria* 200 below.

75 Cf Ecclus 24:14 (Vulg 24:18); Salzer 183–92; *Marienlexikon* v 548–9.

76 Cf Song of Sol 2:1; *Virginis et martyris comparatio* 161–2 below; Salzer 14–15, 145–50; *Marienlexikon* I 510–13.

77 Song of Sol 2:1–2; cf *Virginis et martyris comparatio* 161–2 below; Salzer 14–15, 68, 115 n1, 121 n7, 162–70; *Marienlexikon* IV 121–2.

78 Song of Sol 4:12; Salzer 9–10, 114 n4; *Marienlexikon* v 383–5.

79 The spring of Castalia, rising on Mount Parnassus in the region of Delphi, was regarded as sacred to Apollo and the Muses. Roman poets made the spring a metaphor for poetic inspiration and eloquence. Here Erasmus is recalling Statius *Silvae* 5.5.2: 'Castaliae vocalibus undis.' He neatly inverts the context of Statius' poem, which is a lament on the death of a child.

80 Song of Sol 4:12; cf Salzer 15–16, 115 n2, 281–4; *Marienlexikon* III 247–50; and see further Brian E. Daley 'The "Closed Garden" and the "Sealed Fountain": Song of Songs 4:12 in the Late Medieval Iconography of Mary' in *Medieval Gardens* ed Elisabeth B. MacDougall, Dumbarton Oaks Colloquium on the History of Landscape Architecture 9 (Washington, DC 1986) 255–78.

81 Cf Song of Sol 5:13, 6:2 (Vulg 6:1); Salzer 283:7–14.

82 Cf Song of Sol 2:16, 6:3 (Vulg 6:2).

83 Cf Song of Sol 1:7 (Vulg 1:6).

You are the holy city of Sion,[84] whose walls have never been breached by any battering-ram of the Babylonian enemy:[85] the one who was born in that city, the all-highest who established it, has protected it with impregnable defences, since he himself is its wall and rampart.[86] You are Jerusalem, the one city in which the peacemaker has chosen to dwell, where he has built his palace and temple.[87]

You are the mirror of life, so polished and pure that the image of the Godhead could receive no clearer reflection.[88] You are the column of smoke, breathing myrrh and frankincense and every perfume the merchant knows:[89] burning so intensely with heavenly charity, so deeply moved by love of fallen nature, you continually sought divine mercy with prayers of such purity as to evoke the wonder even of the inhabitants of heaven.

You are the new earth, so often promised by God:[90] implanted with divine seed, you have brought forth not thorns and thistles like the accursed earth of old,[91] but the food of life.[92] You are the noble vine from whose branch the famed cluster has sprung:[93] uniquely, it is supported on the shoulders of the two covenants, of such weight that when placed in the scales it has counterbalanced the immense burden of all our sins; its wine is so potent and distinctive that after tasting it many thousands of men and women have suddenly become soberly drunk, to the point of abandoning the world.[94]

You are the tall cedar of Lebanon,[95] spreading the fragrance of your virtues far and wide: you alone among mortals have not experienced the decay of sin, but in your concern for our souls you ward it off, while so many young men and women everywhere, inspired by your example, pursue the path of blameless purity of life.

* * * * *

84 Cf Salzer 121 n3, 377.
85 Cf 2 Kings (Vulg 4 Kings) 24:10, 25:4.
86 Isa 26:1
87 Cf 2 Sam 5:9; 1 Kings (Vulg 3 Kings) 7:1–10; Pss 78 (Vulg 77):68–9, 132 (Vulg 131):13–14; Ecclus 24:10 (Vulg 24:15); Salzer 36–8; *Marienlexikon* III 367–9.
88 Cf Wisd of Sol 7:26; Salzer 74, 76–7, 337–9; *Marienlexikon* VI 237–9.
89 Song of Sol 3:6
90 Isa 65:17, 66:22; 2 Pet 3:13; Rev 21:1; Salzer 494–5
91 Gen 3:17–18
92 Cf John 6:35, 48, 56; Salzer 495–6.
93 Cf Song of Sol 1:13; Ecclus 24:17 (Vulg 24:23); Salzer 39–40, 196–7, 309.
94 Cf Acts 2:13, 15; *Liturgia Virginis Matris* 91 and 105 (= *Precationes* 149) below. See also Phillips 35, 39; and DS VIII-2 2312–37 under 'Ivresse spirituelle.'
95 Cf Ecclus 24:13 (Vulg 24:17); Ezek 31:3–9; *Liturgia Virginis Matris* Sequence 89 below (= ASD I-7 445:15 / CWE 85 360–1); Salzer 151–3; *Marienlexikon* VI 780–1.

You are the olive tree in the plain,[96] beautiful and ready to be pruned: from your spotless body the destined evergreen shoot was plucked for us by the one whose characteristic sign is to appear to mortals in the form of a dove; he placed it in the ark of the church as an absolutely certain pledge of the end of the flood of sins and a symbol of the renewal of the world.[97] The healthy bitterness of its berries has brought an instantaneous remedy for the poison, too sweet, alas, of the deadly fruit; human souls, wiped clean of their former filthy condition and the mud of the earthly Adam[98] by means of its oil, shine once again as if with their youth restored;[99] and through its constant nourishment the lamp of faith is fed so that it can never be put out.

You are the brightly glowing dawn:[100] emerging in a gentle glow of dewy crimson, to the wonder even of those who watch over the heavenly citadel, you have banished all the dread of night and, appearing beforehand, have revealed to mortal eyes the sun that they especially longed for.

You are the evergreen palm:[101] prosperity cannot make even the slightest alteration in you, nor can adversity depress you. You are the plane-tree, spreading wide your most welcome shade for weary mortals.[102] You are the terebinth, stretching out to the utmost extent the branches of your bounty to every class and race of humankind.[103]

You are as it were a second mother of all the living,[104] the sister of the church. The mysteries are so closely parallel that whatever mystic language is used of the church in the sacred books can be seen to apply in a wonderful way to you as well. Thus the church, guided by the heavenly Spirit, gives us new life in Christ: you, filled to overflowing by the power of the Godhead, have given us the one in whom we are all reborn. You, in mystic guise, are the village which the world's redeemer entered, to be greeted by the two sisters with most welcome cheer.[105]

* * * * *

96 Cf Ecclus 24:14 (Vulg 24:19); Salzer 177–80; *Marienlexikon* IV 673–5.
97 Cf Gen 8:8–11, 9:9–17; Salzer 5–6, 279–80, 472.
98 Cf 1 Cor 15:45–9.
99 Cf Ps 103 (Vulg 102):5; Isa 40:31.
100 Cf 2 Sam 23:4; Song of Sol 6:10 (Vulg 6:9); Salzer 24, 122 n4, 384–8.
101 Cf Ecclus 24:14 (Vulg 24:18); Salzer 180–3.
102 Ibidem (Vulg 24:19); Salzer 140–1.
103 Cf Ecclus 24:16 (Vulg 24:22); Salzer 193.
104 Cf Salzer 102–10, 581–6.
105 Cf Luke 10:38–41; Salzer 122 n3, 289–91; *Marienlexikon* IV 27.

You are the matchless woman[106] seen by the eagle eyes[107] of the one who had taken the place of your son.[108] Your snow-white brow is adorned by a crown of starry lights woven from the orb of all the virtues:[109] you are entirely clothed in the brightness of God's sun, and you have set beneath your feet the moon, never shining with the same face since it is the mistress of what is transient, and made it for ever subject to you.

You are bride,[110] concubine,[111] beloved,[112] unique dove.[113] You are love, you are fire, you are the special delight of the one who is the fairest of the sons of men.[114] You are the precious lover uniquely desired by the Son of God. So passionate that you fainted with love for the one you desired,[115] so beautiful that the lustre of your eyes[116] caused the Word of God to fly from the bosom of his Father into your own womb.[117] Worthy of such great respect that you merited an angel as your marriage-promoter.[118] So spotless that without a man you conceived a man.[119] So free from blemish that you gave birth as a virgin. So blessed that you enclosed within your chaste body the secret word, the tetragrammaton,[120] that it was sacrilege for others to express with their mouths. So highly favoured that you brought forth the saviour of all.

* * * * *

106 Cf Rev 12:1; Salzer 373–7; *Marienlexikon* VI 201–4.
107 A reference to the eagle as the symbol of St John the Evangelist, considered by Erasmus to be the author of the book of Revelation; cf Ezek 1:10; Rev 4:7; *Carmina* 110:65–8 ASD I-7 360 / CWE 85 280–1.
108 John 19:26–7
109 Cf 27 above; *Liturgia Virginis Matris* Sequence 89 below; Salzer 331–2.
110 Cf Song of Sol 4:8–12, 5:1; Salzer 98–100; *Marienlexikon* I 561–71.
111 Cf Song of Sol 6:8–9 (Vulg 6:7–8).
112 Cf Song of Sol 1:8, 14; 2:2, 10, 13; 4:1, 7; 5:2; 6:4 (Vulg 6:3); Salzer 97–8, 562–3.
113 Cf Song of Sol 6:9 (Vulg 6:8); Salzer 134–40.
114 Cf Ps 45:2 (Vulg 44:3); *Carmina* 110:369 ASD I-7 375 / CWE 85 298–9.
115 Cf Song of Sol 2:5, 5:8.
116 Cf Song of Sol 1:14, 4:1.
117 Cf *Precatio ad Virginis filium Iesum* 11 above; *Carmina* 110:286–8 ASD I-7 371 / CWE 85 292–3.
118 Cf Luke 1:26–38. Erasmus here uses the term *pronubus* as he does at *Liturgia Virginis Matris* ASD V-1 102:184 (96 below). See also *Carmina* 110:238 ASD I-7 369 / CWE 85 290–1; and *Institutio christiani matrimonii* LB V 622D (230 below), where the angel is described as *paranymphus*.
119 Cf Luke 1:35; John 1:13.
120 A reference to the Hebrew name of God, expressed in the four letters YHWH or JHVH. See further *The Oxford Dictionary of the Christian Church* ed F.L. Cross and E.A. Livingstone 3rd ed (Oxford 1997) 1593.

Hail, noble descendant of kings, splendour of priests, glory of patri-archs,[121] triumph of the heavenly host, terror of the powers below, hope and consolation of Christians![122] You are more brilliant than the morning sun.[123] You are gentler than the silver moon,[124] more beautiful than the golden day-star,[125] purer than a fresh lily,[126] whiter than driven snow,[127] more comely than a spring rose,[128] more precious than a single pearl,[129] no-bler than gold,[130] more graceful than agate,[131] lovelier than the lodestone,[132] more fragrant than balsam,[133] more pungent than marjoram,[134] sweeter than honey,[135] more delightful than life, more fertile than a watered garden,[136] more abundant than paradise,[137] more exalted than heaven,[138] more chaste than the angels.[139] Hail, sanctuary of the eternal Deity,[140] resting-place of the Godhead,[141] storehouse of the Holy Spirit![142]

But why do we even attempt, in our lack of eloquence, to stammer out your inexpressible praises? Whatever the human mind may be able to conceive or the tongue to utter, even though it may be well beyond our talent, will fall far short of what you deserve. Yet although your greatness, O Mary, is such that every highest authority in heaven and on earth bows to

* * * * *

121 Cf Salzer 375:26.
122 Cf 36 below; *Liturgia Virginis Matris* 107 below; Litany of Loreto (see NCE VIII 790–1): 'consolatrix afflictorum'; Salzer 592–4; *Marienlexikon* IV 33–44.
123 Cf Salzer 394–9; *Marienlexikon* VI 201–4; *Carmina* 110:61–4 ASD I-7 360 / CWE 85 278–81.
124 Cf Salzer 380–4; *Marienlexikon* IV 188–9.
125 Cf Salzer 24:23–25, 394:25.
126 Cf n77 above.
127 Cf Salzer 335–6.
128 Ibidem 186–92; *Marienlexikon* V 548–52
129 Cf Salzer 243–8.
130 Ibidem 227–9
131 Ibidem 200–2
132 Ibidem 315–16
133 Cf Ecclus 24:15 (Vulg 24:20–1); Salzer 143–5.
134 Cf Catullus *Carmina* 61.7; Virgil *Aeneid* 1.693; Columella *Res rustica* 10.296.
135 Cf Ecclus 24:20 (Vulg 24:27); Salzer 489–92.
136 Cf Song of Sol 4:12; Salzer 282–4.
137 Cf Salzer 388–91.
138 Ibidem 427–30
139 Ibidem 419–23
140 Ibidem 20:33–6; 330:8; 340:22, 27–8
141 Ibidem 18:24–5, 228:23, 534:23
142 Ibidem 320:27–32, 513:12–13

you and venerates you as mistress,[143] queen,[144] empress,[145] you still do not consider it unworthy to be called mother of the lowly and wretched,[146] nor, after assuming the queenship of heaven, have you abandoned your concern for us. Should I call this quality of yours more admirable than mere human feelings, or more lovable? Even now your supremely gentle heart is troubled by the suffering of mortals, touched by their prayers, moved by their sighs, and overcome by their tears. So it is that on all sides the mass of suffering humanity besieges your most willing ears with their requests. Every age, every rank, every condition implores the help of Mary alone. Boys and girls, old men and women, the greatest and the least, without distinction call on Mary. *To whom*

Who else but Mary does the rash sailor pray to with hands uplifted, when roaring gales have split his mast and sails, when a wave has torn away a plank of his hull, when menacing squalls buffet the sides of his ship, when everything threatens imminent death? When he is clinging naked to a shattered spar and being tossed among the tops of the waves, whom does he call upon in prayer except Mary? Surrounded by robbers, whom does the unfortunate traveller invoke other than Mary? Those held tight in the grip of incurable disease, prisoners in chains, pitiable women in the pangs of a difficult childbirth turn to Mary in their prayers. Whether the hiss of lightning-flashes brings terror to a guilt-stricken world, or earthquakes tear the land apart, or the collapse of buildings or raging fire brings death in its wake – in a word, whatever disaster overcomes suffering mortals, whatever fear of impending evil causes them to be terrified, they turn to you alone for help in their desperation, and you at once come to their aid.

To you the anxious merchant entrusts his hope for profit; to you the voyager by sea commits his life; to you the farmer bent over the plough[147] pledges his hopes for the year in his prayers. To you the soldier facing the hazard of battle makes his vows. The bearer of a conscience oppressed by wrongdoing adopts you as advocate.[148] Our poverty even sets down as items debited to you things from the store of evils to which it is subject by the thousand.

* * * * *

143 Cf n4 above.
144 Cf n6 above.
145 Cf Salzer 457–8; *Marienlexikon* III 496–7.
146 Cf Salzer 583–6.
147 Cf Virgil *Eclogues* 3.42.
148 Cf Salzer 594–6.

Orphans call upon you as mother,[149] children as guardian,[150] the accused as patron,[151] prisoners as liberator,[152] wanderers as guide,[153] the afflicted as comforter.[154] You are both invoked and experienced as nurse by the sick,[155] port of safety by the shipwrecked,[156] protection by the destitute,[157] consolation by mourners,[158] relief by the oppressed, salvation by the lost,[159] hope by the desperate.[160] For the human race, prone to calamity, you are the source of trust: they depend solely on you, look solely to you, since they are thoroughly convinced – and their faith is not in vain – that there is nothing that you would refuse to grant if you were asked or that you could not grant if you wished.[161]

We see wandering birds, fierce lions, and savage panthers flee to humans for aid in times of want; no doubt hardship shows them where they should look for help. Similarly we in our necessity are taught by our very misfortunes where we should seek protection. We know that you are the most secure sanctuary, intended by the supremely tolerant king to be ever open to the guilty, as the last refuge in extreme disaster.[162] We know that you are the golden watercourse[163] to be approached by those who wish to draw water from the fountain of mercy;[164] the inexhaustible storehouse of divine generosity, from which he has commanded to be unlocked whatever he wishes to grant us; the door of the celestial granary at which those who lack their three loaves may knock.[165]

* * * * *

149 Ibidem 583:16, 20, 23; 584:1, 12–13
150 Ibidem 548:35, 571:17, 572:16, 573:6.
151 Ibidem 548:31; 571:15; 572:35, 39; 595:29; 596:25
152 Ibidem 572:22, 25, 31
153 Ibidem 380:16, 530:1–2, 572:28, 579:2–20
154 Ibidem 572:32
155 Ibidem 513–15
156 Ibidem 528–31
157 Ibidem 548:29–34, 549:12, 573:17–20
158 See n122 above.
159 Cf Salzer 571–3.
160 Ibidem 575–7; *Marienlexikon* III 227–8
161 Cf the prayer known as the Memorare, probably dating from the late fifteenth century: 'It is a thing unheard of that anyone ever had recourse to your protection, implored your help, or sought your intercession, and was left forsaken.' See NCE IX 639.
162 Cf Salzer 598–9.
163 Cf Ecclus 24:30–1 (Vulg 24:40–1); Salzer 533–4.
164 Cf Salzer 521–3, 554–6; *Marienlexikon* V 383–5.
165 Cf Luke 11:5–10.

Where then, Mary, shall we flee for refuge with greater confidence than to the one whom God has willed to be our complete safeguard?[166] To whom shall we turn in our human poverty other than to the one whom God has made the keeper and distributor[167] of his inexhaustible bounty, so that he may grant us everything through the one by whose agency he had earlier given himself to us? To you we owe the beginning of our redemption; from what other source can we more suitably hope for its completion? Who is more recognized as the source of help in life than the one who gave life? And to whom can the wretched flee more securely than to the one who is most merciful? To whom can criminals turn, other than to the one who is most forgiving?[168] Fugitives, other than to their sanctuary?[169] Those threatened with judgment, other than to the mother of the judge? Those found guilty, other than to their advocate,[170] who is at the same time most gentle, since she is the mother of mercy,[171] and most powerful, since she is the mother of the judge?

Because you are the mother of the king we are confident that there is nothing that is beyond your power, and because you are the mother of mercy we are confident that there is nothing that you will not wish to do for the sake of those who call upon you. And the confidence of wretched souls is not in vain. For who has ever requested your aid with prayers that were unrewarded? Who has ever worshipped your godlike majesty with devotion that proved fruitless? Who has ever returned from your altars with prayers unanswered?[172] So far are you from rejecting hard-heartedly those who fly to your knees for protection that of your own accord you invite the hesitant, go forth to meet those who hold back, spontaneously stretch out your hand to those who are laid low, so that there is now no human being who cannot testify, from some great experience, to your goodness towards him. It would be like counting the sand[173] for anyone to try to enumerate how many people you have brought back to the light from the depths of the underworld; how many you have snatched from imminent danger; to how many who had already abandoned all hope you have brought undreamt-of

* * * * *

166 See n157 above.
167 Cf Plautus *Pseudolus* 608.
168 Cf Salzer 569–70.
169 See n162 above.
170 See n148 above.
171 See n14 above.
172 See n161 above.
173 Otto 786

salvation; how many you have restored from the furthest depths of sin[174] to a more disciplined life.

As a result Christians have not been ungrateful and have dedicated churches to you everywhere; from innumerable altars throughout city and countryside candles are burned in your honour;[175] all over the world choirs devoted to sacred music sing your praises unceasingly; around your altars thank-offerings are hung, tablets are fixed, and memorials of your kindness are dedicated to you. Indeed you are so deeply implanted in the hearts of all that no one fails to be refreshed even by your very name.

Among this multitude, brightest of virgins, I too have now sung my paean to you: may you be pleased with it and, I pray you, reconcile me with your son, whose most righteous anger I have aroused by my most grievous faults. For only you will be able to appease the anger of the judge, because only you were able to give him birth. You are both able and willing: since you are the mother of mercy[176] you have borne a most merciful son, most like yourself; so that strengthened by your help and guidance I may conduct my voyage through this sea of life in such a way as to reach the homeland of everlasting light, where with your son you live in glory for ever and ever. Amen.

* * * * *

174 Cf *Carmina* 110:398 ASD I-7 377 / CWE 85 298–9.
175 Cf 21 above, with n7.
176 See n14 above.

PRAYER OF SUPPLICATION TO MARY, THE VIRGIN MOTHER, IN TIME OF TROUBLE

Obsecratio ad Virginem Matrem Mariam in rebus adversis

translated and annotated by
JOHN N. GRANT

The *Obsecratio sive oratio ad Virginem Mariam in rebus adversis* (the usual modern title of the work) was composed by Erasmus for the young Adolph of Burgundy, heer van Veere, at the request of his mother, the widowed Anna van Borssele. Erasmus tell us this in a letter written to Adolph in 1499 (Ep 93:112–15). The work was first published in 1503 in a volume entitled *Lucubrationes aliquot*, printed by Dirk Martens in Antwerp. Erasmus sent a copy of this volume to John Colet in 1504, and in the accompanying letter there is a note of defensiveness about the prayers included in the edition. 'I wrote them,' he says, 'almost against the grain [*pene alieno . . . stomacho*], especially the *Paean* and *Obsecratio*' (Ep 181:60–1). Similar sentiments are found in the *Catalogus*, written to Johann von Botzheim: Erasmus says that the prayers were 'written to please the boy's mother Anna, lady of Veere, in a childish style [*stilo iuvenili*] designed to suit her[1] feelings rather than my judgment' (Ep 1341A:742–4).

Since the *Obsecratio* is so short, it is not surprising that few textual discrepancies are found among the printed editions. The translation follows the text of the Leiden edition of 1703–6 (LB V 1233–40) except where that edition is clearly in error – for example, *falsas* for *salsas* at 1235C and *futilis* for *sutilis* (see n4 to the translation). Other editions that have been consulted are the *editio princeps* of 1503; the 1515 edition printed by Matthias Schürer in Strasbourg, entitled *Lucubrationes*; the 1516 edition by the same printer, which, at least as far as the *Obsecratio* is concerned, is virtually a reprint of the 1515 edition, with the same page breaks (but see n3 to the translation); and the 1518 edition of the *Enchiridion militis christiani* of Johann Froben (Basel), in which the *Obsecratio* and other short works are included.

In the *editio princeps* the title of the work is *Obsecratio ad Virginem Mariam semper gloriosam*. This becomes *Oratio ad deiparam Virginem* in a later edition of Dirk Martens (*Lucubratiunculae*, Louvain 1514), and *Obsecratio ad Virginem Matrem Mariam in rebus adversis* in the 1515 and 1518 editions of Schürer and Froben respectively.[2]

I am indebted to Dr Hans Trapman for information about the readings in the *editio princeps* as well as for valuable suggestions relating to the translation and the notes.

JNG

* * * * *

1 Her feelings (*illius affectum*): more probably '*his* disposition,' since Erasmus says in his letter to Adolph that he has adapted the language to suit the boy's age (Ep 93:115)
2 The running heads in Schürer's edition read *Oratio ad Mariam* (verso) and *In adversis* (recto).

A PRAYER OF SUPPLICATION TO MARY, THE VIRGIN MOTHER, IN TIME OF TROUBLE[1]

Mary, Virgin and Mother, sole hope to us in our afflictions, you see, yes, you see the frightening storms by which we are tossed on this mortal voyage. In our wretchedness we strive in every way to return to our homeland, thoroughly weary of the miserable exile into which we were cast by the shamelessness of Eve, who was not a mother to us, but a stepmother.[2] As we are carried this way and that in the blackest darkness by the currents of this life, you alone shine forth like a propitious star, and at the same time you ever breathe on us the breezes of your favour. For we would have no hope at all of reaching our haven on this long and very dangerous journey if amid such dangers your divine majesty did not beam for us continuously and with all its power and benevolence. O holy Mary, you who have always pitied the hard toils of the human race, surely[3] you do not abandon us on our journey? For you know well that this body of ours, the tiny vessel in which we travel, has a weak frame, has no more protection than that of skins stitched together,[4] and is by no means watertight; yet it is buffeted by the waves of many evils and surrounded by many dangers. Destructive evil

* * * * *

1 In his discussion of the interpretation of the name *Maria* as meaning *maris stella*, 'star of the sea,' St Bernard urges praying to Mary when one is 'in dangers, in straits, and in difficulties' (*Homilia* 2 of *De laudibus Virginis Matris* PL 183 70D). In the same context he uses the common image of the sea of life that Erasmus employs at the beginning (and end) of this work.

2 Eve and Mary are often contrasted by the church Fathers and medieval writers, as in hymns such as *Ave, maris stella*, where play is made on the same letters in *Ave* and *Eva* (Raby no 71:5–8; see also nos 59:25–32 and 151:25–32). On Mary as the 'Second Eve,' see Warner 50–67. For the image of human exile and its connection with Eve cf 'exules filii Evae' ('exiled sons of Eve') in the hymn *Salve, regina misericordiae* Raby no 141:3.

3 LB reads *num*, as do Froben's edition of 1518 and Schürer's edition of 1516. The *editio princeps* and Schürer's edition of 1515 offer *non*.

4 LB reads *futilis*, 'worthless.' The translation reflects the reading *sutilis*, 'stitched together,' found in the *editio princeps* as well as in Schürer's editions of 1515

spirits envelop it with their frightening, roaring blasts and strive with all their might sometimes to smash it on the sharp rocks of ambition, sometimes to run it aground on the shallow Syrtes[5] of seething passions, sometimes to offer it to be sucked up by the monstrous mouths of Charybdis.[6] To be sure, those evil spirits are like the winds unleashed from the Tartarean cave that 'from egress given, rush out and with their blasts assail the world':[7] the wanton Auster, the roaring Boreas, the violent Africus, the rain-bearing Notus.[8] In common cause they batter us daily with mighty storms. They shipwreck many: some are carried headlong into every crime 'on the vainglorious chariot of renown,'[9] others cannot struggle free from the mire of foul desires, still others in their efforts to keep and increase their material goods unhappily are themselves lost. Though freed by the precious blood of your son, we are pursued on one side by a cruel pirate intent on dragging us back again into the foulest servitude. On the other a Siren, the most seductive of wantons,[10] assails our ears and our minds with her sweet but deadly songs; we forget our homeland, we forget who we are, we rush unswervingly to certain death.

How dangerous is fortune in its vicissitudes. Like the changing tide sometimes it is favourable and heaps upon us gifts, corrupting though they may be,[11] lifting our humble vessel to the heights; sometimes fortune is

* * * * *

and 1516 and Froben's edition of 1518. Erasmus here evokes the description of Charon's bark at Virgil *Aeneid* 6.413–14 as a 'cumba sutilis et . . . rimosa.'

5 Two gulfs on the north coast of Africa. The Greater Syrtis, the one referred to here (note *vadosas*, 'shallow'), was dangerous for its sandbanks and quicksands, the Lesser for treacherous rocks.

6 A whirlpool on the northern edge of the Straits of Messina, often conceived of as a monstrous being that sucked up and disgorged the sea three times a day

7 Virgil *Aeneid* 1.83

8 Auster and Notus are both names for the south wind. Boreas is the north wind, while Africus is the south-west wind, though often thought of as western rather than southern. The epithets used by Erasmus are conventional, with the exception of *procax*, 'wanton' or 'shameless.' In using this adjective with *Austri* Erasmus here is probably echoing Virgil *Aeneid* 1.536: 'procacibus Austris.' The epithet for Boreas (*sonorus*) may be a learned pun on a supposed etymology of its name from the Greek word βοή, 'shout'; see Aulus Gellius *Noctes Atticae* 2.22.9.

9 Horace *Epistles* 2.1.177

10 The Sirens, which vary in number in the sources, caused the death of sailors by luring them with song to their island, where the sailors wasted away. The most familiar description of the Sirens in classical literature is at Homer *Odyssey* 12.158–200.

11 The editions consulted (see the introductory note) offer *venenatis muneribus*, literally, 'poisoned gifts'; cf Cicero *Philippicae* 13.35. In the context of the

hostile and rages furiously, hurling our vessel down from the top of a wave[12] to strike the sand at the bottom of the sea.[13] Are we not sometimes so engulfed by the tumult and whirlwind of our daily business that our ship no longer obeys the rudder and cannot hold a fixed course? Are we not sometimes deceived by the gentleness of a tranquil sea, which even then can be more treacherous than any storm? Often we are trusting and too confident when the sky is clear and the sea is calm, and we are taken by surprise by a sudden change of weather. We who were a moment ago joyfully calling out the stroke to the rowers, as if already in port, are suddenly swimming in the open sea.

But why should I list all the monstrous beasts that are nourished by the sea, with jaws ever agape for us as prey? Land too has its own poisons, which breathe fatal venom upon us from all sides. Some persons deceive us by flattery, some distract us from the path of honour by their deadly advice, some urge us on to destruction. One person openly wants to do us wrong, another is a secret enemy; both do us harm. Some abuse us to our face and disturb our peace of mind; others play the part of friends, but their shining teeth inject a viper's venom. One person, steeped in the black ink of a cuttlefish, tries to stain our reputation; another, like the ray fish, stuns us with chilling poison and strives to extinguish the ardour of our concern for others. But it is especially when the pitch-black 'clouds' of ignorance 'snatch away the heavens and the light of day from our eyes'[14] that our 'bodies are benumbed by cold'[15] that chills. Then we wander rudderless over dark seas, our sails in tatters, the sailyards lost. Then great 'fear everywhere abounds, and we see many an image of death.'[16] The course of this life of ours, which we began in chains and wailing, is ever a sea of tears, ever fraught with disaster. Not even in times of calm are we free of danger.

O queen of heaven,[17] you see all this, and in your compassion you hasten to aid those in danger. You cannot fail to see the misfortunes of mortals. This very title of yours shows that you are the lofty Helice,[18] you are the

* * * * *

enjoyment of *good* fortune, *veneratis muneribus*, 'revered gifts' or 'gifts we have prayed for,' would make better sense.

12 Cf Virgil *Aeneid* 1.106.
13 Cf Virgil *Aeneid* 1.111.
14 A close echo of Virgil *Aeneid* 1.88
15 Virgil *Aeneid* 1.92
16 Virgil *Aeneid* 2.369
17 A common appellation of Mary, as shown by the antiphons *Regina caeli* and *Ave, regina caelorum* sung at the conclusion of the Divine Office
18 The constellation Ursa Major (the Great Bear)

brightly shining Cynosura,[19] at the very top of heaven's vault. You alone
have never touched the salty waves of the western sea, you have not felt the
moisture of even its finest spray. It is right that nothing at all of what happens on earth escapes your eyes, for you are the beautiful moon,[20] sister and
mother of the eternal sun, and look down on our toils from near at hand;
you are the star that is nearest and most familiar to our world and much the
most powerful in influence. You make our night glimmer with your gentle
light; ever fixed, you never grow old; ever constant, you never wane, never
set.[21] Unfailingly you shine with full orb, ever facing the sun, from which
you draw your light and power, shedding them on us; you nourish and
make all things grow with your health-giving power. Since you are both the
star of our sea[22] and moon of our earth, you cannot fail to see our human
misfortunes. Since this world of ours has long called you not only mother
but also mother of mercy,[23] and since you willingly acknowledge that title,
you cannot fail to be moved by them.

You cannot but look on the troubles of us mortals as an anxious mother
since the son you bore so loved us that he shared our exile, sacrificed himself
to redeem our race, and exposed himself so willingly to all our misfortunes.
Accordingly, you do not fail to see our troubles and pity them when you
do; you cannot but put them right when you pity them, for the son you bore
listens readily to your entreaties, and, what is more, so reveres you (since
he is a most loving and dutiful son) that he never denies anything you ask.

* * * * *

19 The constellation Ursa Minor (the Little Bear) or the North Star itself, with
which Mary is often associated; cf 'O Maria, stella maris ... in supremo sita
poli' ('O Mary, star of the sea ... placed at the very top of the sky') in the
Victorine Sequence (Raby no 163:63, 67). See Marjorie O'Rourke Boyle *Erasmus
on Language and Method in Theology* (Toronto 1977) 81.

20 In the later Middle Ages Mary was frequently associated with the moon; see
Warner 258–64, who sees this as developing in part from the images of Christ
as the sun and of the church, his bride, as the moon. See also Raby no 163:49–52.

21 Erasmus seems here to move from the image of Mary as the moon to the
image of her as the polestar, before reverting to the former image in the next
sentence.

22 An echo of a common designation of Mary as *stella maris*, as in medieval hymns
such as *Alma redemptoris* and *Ave, maris stella* (see nn1, 17 above); see F.J.E.
Raby *A History of Christian-Latin Poetry from the Beginnings to the Close of the
Middle Ages* (Oxford 1953) 226. Here the image is paraphrased by Erasmus as
stella huius nostri pelagi.

23 Another common designation of Mary, as in a version of the hymn *Quem terra,
pontus, aethera colunt* sung in the Divine Office on some Marian feasts. Cf also
the hymn *Salve, regina misericordiae* (see n2 above).

In the same way the Son never asks anything of his Father in vain, such is the limitless love which they share. As the Father is omnipotent, so is the Son, since omnipotence is begotten of omnipotence. You too, therefore, are omnipotent, for your son sets all store by your godliness and honour. By these thoughts we mortals, who are not born with sense but acquire it from the needy circumstances in which we live, reason that you are the only one, O Virgin Mother of God, from whom we must ask for and hope for help in our afflictions. You are the one who can do everything, and whatever you can do you do on our behalf. With unwavering faith, therefore – see how I throw myself prostrate at your feet, those feet before which even the angels and saints abase themselves – I stretch out my hands in supplication to your ever present divine power. But I do so not without a flood of bitter tears that spring from deep within me, in part because of the labours of this our exile, in part because of the remorse I feel for the sins I have committed against your son.

Help me, I beg you, my saviour, my salvation, my sole and certain refuge; shine forth, Mary, as star of salvation to me in darkness, guide me when I err, assist me in my suffering, strengthen me in my weakness, support me when I waver, help me in danger, lest perchance the proverbial tenth wave[24] engulf this shattered vessel, already defenceless, already breaking apart. Nay more, restore it to safety, even though it is stuck fast on rocks, already wrecked, already close to destruction. Sweet glory of mine,[25] save my soul; insignificant though it be, it dedicates itself to you. If you grant this prayer, even that which is on the point of death is immediately yours. I beg you, do not allow to be lost what your son, the wise architect, so carefully fashioned, so diligently equipped, and redeemed at the immeasurable cost of his own blood. Return to the Creator his creation, return to the Redeemer what he redeemed.

But since you are our Diana, powerful in triple majesty,[26] and even rejoice in being importuned by humans in their prayers, why have I been

* * * * *

24 A reference to the belief in antiquity that the tenth wave was the largest; cf Ovid *Metamorphoses* 11.530; Lucan 5.672.

25 Sweet glory of mine: Erasmus here closely echoes Horace *Odes* 1.1.2: 'o . . . dulce decus meum.'

26 Diana is referred to in Roman literature as 'the goddess of three shapes' (*diva triformis*), being Luna in her heavenly aspect, Diana in her earthly aspect, and Hecate in her underworldly aspect. See Horace *Odes* 3.22.4 and Ovid *Metamorphoses* 7.94; Virgil *Aeneid* 4.511; Catullus *Carmina* 34.13–16. The association of Mary and Diana is not unexpected because of the connection of both with the moon and virginity (cf *Ciceronianus* LB I 995C / CWE 28 388). Here Erasmus

soliciting you for so long now with holy supplications, as if with prayers of sorcery? Surely holiness carries weight with you, a true goddess, when superstition swayed a false one? Surely pure worship wins your favour, when sacrilegious rites won hers? Surely the tears of Christians move you, when evil incantations stirred her? Surely holy prayers touch you, when she heard unholy curses? I pray to you, therefore, O queen of all,[27] invoking both your heart that can be moved by our entreaties and whatever can appease your heavenly majesty and your son's; your holy conception,[28] which was kept free of all taint by him whom you later conceived in similar purity; and your birth, worthy of adoration, whereby, like the morning star[29] rising with its gentle light, you gave mortals certain hope of the sun that was to come. I invoke your childhood, devoted to studies most pleasing to God.

I invoke the consummate purity of your mind, your humility, your godliness. It was by the fragrance of these virtues[30] that you allured the only-begotten Son of God to come to earth, like a suitor drunk with love,[31] but undoubtedly in such a way that you, a virgin, were betrothed to a virgin groom; that you, most pure, conceived an equally pure child; that you, unsullied, gave birth to an unsullied son. I invoke that creation thrice worthy of adoration and the thrice-blessed happiness in your heart. For it was with your awareness and consent that the Holy Spirit, that unique worker,

* * * * *

develops the association in terms of the nature of Jesus, who is described as an *opus triforme*, 'a creation, threefold in nature,' in the next paragraph.

27 Cf the list of titles of Mary in the Litany of Loreto (see NCE VIII 790–1): 'Queen of Angels,' 'Queen of Patriarchs,' 'Queen of Prophets,' etc.

28 Here Erasmus seems to subscribe to the teaching of Franciscan theologians of the Middle Ages such as Duns Scotus that Mary was immaculately conceived, a teaching generally disputed by Dominican theologians. See also *Paean Virgini Matri* 27 n46.

29 The morning star (*stella matutina*) is a designation of Mary found in the Litany of Loreto (see n27 above), here paraphrased as *luciferi sidus*. For the image of Mary as the morning star prefiguring the sun cf 'luciferi mater pueri' ('mother of the light-bearing child') in a prayer of Marbod of Rennes (Raby no 150:17).

30 The fragrance of virtues is often associated with Mary; cf the Victorine Sequence (Raby no 163:22–4, 35–6): 'myrtus temperantiae, rosa patientiae, nardus odorifera ... tu dulcoris et odoris habes plenitudinem' ('the myrtle of temperance, the rose of patience, fragrant nard ... you have the fullness of sweetness and fragrance'). See also Raby no 150:5–6; Warner 99–100.

31 Erasmus applies erotic imagery to Christ's desire for Mary, thus reversing the allegorical interpretation of the imagery in the Song of Solomon as describing the soul's love for God; see St Bernard *Sermones* 7.3 PL 183 807 on the Song of Solomon: 'anima ... ita proprio ebriatur amore'; and E. Gilson *The Mystical Theology of Saint Bernard* (Kalamazoo 1990) 112–13, 238 nn164–6.

brought to completion in the workshop of your womb a creation, threefold in nature, in a sacred triad. The Holy Spirit in an instant fashioned the perfectly pure body of your son from a tiny drop of your virgin blood; at the same time he created from nothing that blessed soul and infused it in a body that, though mortal, was completely free of impurity; with the clearest part of the soul he added divinity. Thus he brought together clay, the principle of life, and God in such harmonious diversity and diversified harmony that though the elements kept their own separate nature, they nevertheless came together to form one person.

I invoke the holy services that you, a young girl, heavy with child and pregnant with the Redeemer, carefully performed for your relative, an old woman, when she had just given birth, having been pregnant with the herald of Christ;[32] the indescribable joy in your heart when you, a mere girl who had not known union with a man, were carrying in your womb and nourishing with your blood that golden child, the hope of the whole world, experiencing the sweet but heavy weight of carrying a child, but not fretting at the long term of pregnancy as most women do; your most auspicious feelings of anticipation when, anxiously counting off the regular stages of pregnancy, you promised yourself the name of parent, untroubled by thoughts of your virginity.[33] I invoke the holy birth itself, which was as free from all pain, all shame, and the uncleanness of our birth as you were free from all carnal desire; how your mind leapt with holy joy when, with the angels

* * * * *

32 See Luke 1:39–56, the account of how Mary, herself pregnant, attended Elizabeth, pregnant with John the Baptist, during the last three months of her cousin's pregnancy. Luke's account makes sense if Mary stayed with Elizabeth until she gave birth, since she went to her in her sixth month and stayed there for about three months (see verses 36 and 56). But the account implies, rather strangely, that Mary left Elizabeth just before the time of John the Baptist's birth (see verses 56 and 57). Erasmus describes Elizabeth as *feta*, which can mean 'pregnant' or 'having given birth.' The twofold contrast between Mary as *virgo* and *gravida* and Elizabeth as *anicula* and *feta* suggests that here the meaning of *feta* is the latter.

33 Untroubled by thoughts of your virginity: there may be an allusion to Mary's initial reaction to the prophecy of Gabriel that she would conceive Jesus: 'How shall this be, seeing I know not a man?' (Luke 1:34). Erasmus draws a contrast between Mary's anxious worrying (*sollicite numerans*) about how her pregnancy is developing and her lack of concern about her virginity (*secura integritatis*). On the passage in Luke St Augustine contrasts the reactions of Zacharias and Mary to Gabriel's prophecies in *Sermones* 291 PL 38 1318; see also St Bernard PL 183 80. The meaning 'secure in your virginity' in the sense of 'your virginity still intact' would suit the context but is difficult to extract from the Latin.

as midwives, that sweet infant came from the wedding chamber of your body.[34] To you he brought the name of mother, to us his birth revealed the hope of being born again.[35]

I invoke the indescribable merit of your poverty, O Mary, for in the cruel weather of December it was not at home but abroad, not in a palace but in a lowly hut, that you took into your arms your newborn child, the source of life for all.[36] He was wrapped not in purple swaddling clothes but in rags. You laid him down to rest in a hard manger, not in a cradle with fancy flounces.[37] I invoke the devout pleasures of your mind when you saw that the coming of your child was announced by angels, that he was sought out by shepherds, that he was honoured with mystical gifts by wise men whom the star had informed and summoned.

I invoke the pure love of a mother that you felt much more passionately for your sweet child Jesus than other mothers do for theirs; the indescribable holiness of your love for each other, of you as mother for your divine son, of him as son for his virgin mother; those feelings – by far the happiest of all – that stirred your maternal heart whenever you kissed your son's beautiful and gentle eyes (eyes that resembled and reflected the pleasing sweetness of yours), whenever, as you gazed upon him, you recognized how his brow was like your brow, his mouth like your mouth, his face like your face, his little hands like your hands. I invoke the mother's care you bestowed so dutifully on Jesus in his cradle, immediately after childbirth, or when you cherished your shivering child in your warm embrace, or when you put your arms around him and pressed him to your virginal bosom, or when you brought sleep to your crying child with soothing lullaby; or when you put him to the breast he knew, and he who balances the mighty universe on his finger hung on a virgin's nipple; or when he cried, and your lips, caressing him with loving kisses, drew in the teardrops that streamed from his eyes. I invoke the nectar of a mother's milk that flowed plentifully from the fount of your virginal breast when you nourished with snow-white liquid the nourisher of the universe.

I invoke that dutiful anxiety you showed when you fled the wickedness of the mad Herod and carried the hope of us all into Egypt so that

* * * * *

34 St Augustine describes the womb of Mary as the wedding chamber of the union of the Word and the flesh (*Sermones* 291 PL 38 1319).
35 See John 3:3.
36 For this paragraph see Luke 2:7–29; Matt 2:9–11.
37 Cradle with fancy flounces: Erasmus uses a phrase found at Juvenal *Satires* 6.89: 'segmentatis . . . cunis.'

he would not perish before the day that was to save us all;[38] that humility of yours, by far the most pleasing of all to God, whereby you did not deem it unworthy for your son to go through the rites of circumcision, or for you yourself those of purification – as if there were anything impure that needed to be cut out in him who alone was pure enough to abolish the stains of all; or as if you needed any expiation, when compared to you at the time you gave birth, any virgin would be most foul.[39] I invoke the pleasant, lisping strains of your little child's voice, his friendly smiles, his love then expressed by gesture instead of by word, the kisses you exchanged, the way you carried about your dear child, no heavy burden to you; the blessed loving devotion of your son, when, learning to speak our language, he often called you 'Mother' in his sweet, lisping voice; the gentle words, full of love, which you said to each other; the conversations about ordinary things, and the very holy nature of your discussions; the troubled longings of a mother's heart when you searched everywhere for your son, now almost grown up, thinking him lost;[40] the anxious worries and the pure prayers with which you accompanied your only son as he matured through the stages of mortal life. I invoke the cold, the heat, the thirst, the hunger, the sleeplessness, the poverty, and all the hardships of human existence, none of which, with you as witness, he refused to endure; your hard work and the most holy labours of your hands, with which you, a poor woman, reared a poor son; the hidden joy you silently felt in your heart when you saw your son, a mortal whom you, a mortal, had borne, giving proof of his divinity when he turned water into wine, cured diseases with a simple word, raised the dead, commanded the waves, forgave sins, and drove out demons.

I invoke the torments of your son (you shared and endured them with him through a mother's bond, so that we might owe our renewed salvation to your son, but also to you, his mother); the bitter tears that he often shed for our sins, the shameful abuse that he so often received on our behalf from the Jews, the natural aversion your son felt when the thought of how we were to destroy him caused him anguish in that place,[41] the bloody sweat

* * * * *

38 Matt 2:13–14. Erasmus here departs from the chronological order of events that he usually follows in this section by referring to the flight to Egypt (not mentioned in Luke 2) before the circumcision of Christ and the purification of Mary (referred to at Luke 2:21–2, but not in Matthew).

39 See Luke 2:21–4.

40 The occasion is the teaching of Jesus in the temple at the age of twelve; see Luke 2:41–50.

41 The Latin here (*cum illic nostro exitio angeretur*) is ambiguous. It could also mean 'when he suffered anguish at the thought of how we were perishing / would

with which our crimes drenched him from head to toe,[42] the bitter shame of you and your only son when that snow-white lamb was seized before a great rabble, led away like a wicked parricide by sacrilegious ministers of God,[43] taken from judge to judge,[44] taunted by the people; the even greater sense of shame when he heard the calumny of suborned witnesses and yet said nothing. I invoke the screaming catcalls of that throng, the curses heaped upon him, and the smashing blows he suffered; the foul spit that bespattered the holy countenance of your only son,[45] the shameful ropes that bound him who freed the world from sin, all his limbs unmercifully furrowed by the lictors' whips;[46] the thousand rivulets of red blood that spurted forth over all his body, the most shameful derision to which he was subjected, the robe given him in jest,[47] his holy head struck by a stick,[48] the nails driven into his bleeding hands, the mockery of a crown of wounding thorns that pierced your heart when it pierced the sacred temples of your son, the sentence of death unjustly pronounced on the most innocent of defendants.

I invoke the sad steps you are said to have taken as he carried that shameful tree on his shoulders, you, a mother accompanying your only son to see his shameful punishment; the wound in your maternal breast[49] when you saw your only son being raised between two thieves; those most holy arms so violently stretched out; those hands of a creator and those guiltless feet, pierced by hateful iron; the raging thirst and the sponge soaked in

* * * * *

perish.' But since Erasmus often refers to specific details in the Gospels, he probably has in mind here the appeal of Jesus to his Father to relieve him of the cup of suffering (Matt 26:36–9; Mark 14:36; Luke 22:42). That is supported by the presence of *illic* (translated as 'in that place', ie the garden of Gethsemane, although it could have a temporal significance, 'at that time'), which suggests a well-known incident. The interpretation of Jesus' words in the garden is the subject of *De taedio Iesu* CWE 70 13–67.

42 See Luke 22:44. This verse (with 43) does not appear in some early manuscripts and is regarded as an interpolation by many modern critics. Erasmus accepts both verses as genuine in his edition of the New Testament. He thinks that they were erased 'by those who were afraid to attribute to Christ such clear proof of human weakness' (*Annotationes in Novum Testamentum* LB VI 322 n22).

43 Translated as a reference to the chief priests and elders referred to at Luke 22:52. But the Latin (*sacrilegi ministri*) may refer simply to lowly servants.

44 Caiaphas, Pilate, Herod, and then Pilate again (Luke 22:54, 23:1, 23:7, 23:11)

45 See Matt 27:30.

46 See Matt 27:26; Mark 15:15.

47 See Matt 27:28.

48 See Matt 27:30.

49 An allusion to the prophecy reported at Luke 2:35 (see n54 below)

vinegar and gall that was offered to him in his thirst.[50] I invoke the emotions you felt in your heart as a mother, known to you alone, when, addressing you as 'Woman' from the cross, he entrusted you to his disciple and his disciple to you,[51] a virgin to a virgin; the feelings in your heart at the moment when your son freely accepted death and with a great cry entrusted his precious soul into his Father's hands;[52] the holy mystery that you saw with your own eyes when that fount thrice worthy of adoration flowed from his side as he slept in death,[53] the water a pledge to cleanse us and the blood a pledge to give us life; the cruel sword of sorrow (which the old seer had prophesied to you soon after you gave birth)[54] that pierced a mother's body with the most terrible wounds as your only son suffered each torment.

I invoke how you longed most passionately for the redemption of the human race. Although you experienced all the pains of your son with almost the same intensity of his suffering, nevertheless you felt incredible joy along with the pain because it was our salvation that was being won by your sacrifice and your son's. I invoke what your faith accomplished at a time when the disciples were stunned and wavering. As you alone meditated in silence on the mystery of our redemption, and held fast to the sure and everlasting hope of resurrection, your joy at the thought of our life surpassed your grief over your son's death. I invoke the joy in your heart, joy that no words can express, when your beloved Jesus, now victorious, now risen, now immortal, showed himself first to your eyes,[55] luminous to behold,[56] adorned with eternal trophies and the spoils of the greatest victory. I invoke the devout pleasures of your mind when you saw that the thrice-holy name of your only-begotten son was becoming celebrated throughout the whole world,

* * * * *

50 See John 19:28–9.
51 See John 19:26–7.
52 See Luke 23:46.
53 See John 19:34.
54 The prophecy of Simeon (see Luke 2:35: 'and a sword will pierce through your own soul also')
55 Like many theologians and writers of devout literature in the Middle Ages, Erasmus here departs from the evidence of the New Testament to postulate that after his resurrection from the dead Christ appeared to his mother before showing himself to anyone else. See eg Ignatius Loyola *The Spiritual Exercises* trans Louis J. Puhl (Chicago 1951) no 299.
56 Literally, 'clearly seen in much light.' Luminosity is often linked with the glory of the resurrected body. Cf Matt 13:43: 'Then the righteous will shine like the sun in the kingdom of their Father.' Aquinas in *Summa theologiae* III q 54 art 1–2 speaks of the *claritas* and *gloria* of the resurrected body of Christ.

and when you rejoiced that he who had been made flesh from your flesh and whom you alone had conceived alone in the flesh and had begotten in the flesh was now being conceived in spirit by so many thousands.

I invoke the sighs of motherly love, the holiest feelings of longing, the purest of prayers, the blessed tears that you, a mother who had survived her son, shed copiously on earth whenever you remembered how sweet it had been to live with him, whenever you conversed with his friends and disciples about his plan of human redemption and about his mystical words and deeds, or whenever devotion guided your steps and you visited again the holy places where something would remind you of your only son. 'This was the cradle in which he first cried as a baby. This was the temple where I found him with those who were learned in the Law.[57] This was the dining-room in which he brought joy to the banquet when water was changed into wine.[58] On this river bank he was baptized. In this desert he fasted. In this lonely place he satisfied the appetite of such a large crowd with the little food at his disposal.[59] This was the place where he told such and such a parable. This was the mountain where he sat and presented his teachings on different things.[60] This portico holds the traces of his feet as he walked.[61] Here he ate with his companions. This was the ground that was soaked by his tears. This was what he looked like when he drove the moneylenders from the temple precinct.[62] How pale he was, how he moaned, how he wept when he restored his friend Lazarus alive to his sisters.[63] He stood here when he gave the blind man sight.[64] It was at this well that he rested when he was tired from travelling.[65] Here he said various things to me alone. Here they led him, here he hung. This was the tomb in which he was laid.[66] This was the spot where he appeared. From here he said his final farewell to us when he was about to return to his Father.[67] It was in this upper room that he sent us his and his Father's Spirit.'[68]

* * * * *

57 See Luke 2:41–51.
58 See John 2:1–10.
59 See Matt 14:16–21; Mark 6:37–44; Luke 9:13–15.
60 See Matt 5:1.
61 See John 5:1–9.
62 See John 2:15.
63 See John 11:1–44.
64 See eg John 9:1–8.
65 See John 4:6.
66 See Matt 27:60.
67 See Mark 16:19; Luke 24:50–1; Acts 1:1–11.
68 See John 20:19–23.

I invoke the blessed memory of these and similar things that brought your absent son back to you and gave you even more happiness than before, when he had been present in the flesh; the frequent travels of the angels, who, often visiting you as their friend, carried a mother's prayers to her son, and a son's gifts to his mother; your holy weariness with this mortal life, when you yearned to be removed from earthly things and to be joined with your son, immortal with immortal; the joyful applause of all heaven when your son carried you beyond where the angels sit and placed you next to him and gave you sway over all things; your ineffable devotion to the human race; and your heart, by far the most compassionate of all. I invoke your happiness and our toils, your joys and our pains.

I invoke this devotion of mine with which, such as it is, I venerate your divine power as best I can. Through the power of the prayers of all who have fixed their hopes on you I beg and entreat you, Virgin undefiled, take up the cause of this sinner with your son the judge, ask him to cast aside his wrath, the wrath I have stirred up by my sins. Reconcile this sinful man to him whom you nourished with your breasts, so that illuminated by his light I may distinguish what is harmful from what is beneficial, and strengthened by his anointing I may with constant love pursue whatever I know to be pleasing to him and in turn shun completely and avoid what he finds offensive. Win for me, my pleader, I beg you, the greatest boon from your son, that with all my heart and soul I may hate my evil actions; that I may not love or have regard for anything but your only son; that I may deserve to be transfigured into his image, so that it may become sweet even for me to lift up the cross with him and, through hope and endurance, to continue to do so steadfastly[69] and auspiciously till the very end of my life; that everything may be completely changed, and what in my spiritual folly used to give me pleasure may begin to seem bitter in my soul; and that those things that I once used to think of as the worst of evils may give me pleasure, lest the allurements of the flesh snatch me off[70] the narrow path of your only-begotten son, or a storm of evils assail and overwhelm me. And since I sail a dangerous

* * * * *

69 The translation 'to continue to do so steadfastly' (*in ea ... perseverare*) takes *in ea* to refer to the cross (= *in ea tollenda*) rather than to the image of Christ (*illius imaginem*). With the latter interpretation Erasmus would be saying, 'that I may deserve to be transfigured into his image so that it may become sweet ... to persevere in it.' This seems weak and lacks point.

70 The *editio princeps* reads *me ab arcta ... via*. The preposition is omitted in the other editions consulted.

sea in a fragile little boat into which he too deigned to descend, I pray, O Mary, that with him as ruler of the winds and the sea, and with you ever shining brightly, it may befall me to reach the haven of the heavenly Jerusalem, where you will enjoy the blessed company of your son for ever. Amen.

THE LORD'S PRAYER

Precatio dominica

translated and annotated by
JOHN N. GRANT

Since praying is an essential part of the Christian life, and the Lord's Prayer is the pre-eminent example of prayer, it is in no way surprising that, from the early Fathers down to modern times, churchmen and theologians have devoted much attention to interpreting and discussing the prayer that Jesus instructed his disciples to use.[1] For Tertullian the Lord's Prayer represented 'an epitome of the whole Gospel,'[2] a sentiment that is often repeated in later commentaries and treatises. In his essay on prayer, the *Modus orandi Deum* (CWE 70), a small section of which is devoted to the Lord's Prayer, Erasmus states that 'we should ask God for nothing that is not in harmony with one of the seven parts of the Lord's Prayer.'[3]

The pre-eminence of the Lord's Prayer meant that it was an invariable component of Christian catechisms, including the one Erasmus composed and published in 1533 (*Explanatio symboli* CWE 70). Unlike Luther, however, and most others who wrote large catechisms in the sixteenth century, Erasmus devotes only a few lines there to the Lord's Prayer, referring readers to commentaries on it and mentioning explicitly the present work, the *Precatio dominica*. Erasmus describes this as a 'paraphrase' (Ep 1341A:780–1), by which term he meant an interpretative expansion of the bare text. Significant in other respects, the *Precatio dominica* therefore must also be interpreted as part of Erasmus' catechetical enterprise.[4]

As the prefatory letter reveals, Erasmus wrote the *Precatio dominica* at the request of Justus Ludovicus Decius, and did so quickly. The work was printed as a separate work by the Froben press in Basel, probably in late 1523, since the date of the dedicatory letter is 28 October of that year, and in Ep 1408, written to Willibald Pirckheimer on 8 January 1524, Erasmus says that Decius had not received the copy of the work that Erasmus had sent him.

The translation is based on the text in the Leiden edition (LB). The abbreviated headings of each section of the essay in that edition have been expanded in this translation.

JNG

* * * * *

1 See Matt 6:9–13 and (in shorter form) Luke 11:2–4. For a list of writings on the Lord's Prayer see DS XII 389–95.
2 Tertullian *De oratione* 1.6 CCSL 1 258
3 CWE 70 205
4 For a valuable assessment of the content of the *Precatio dominica* and of its relationship to Erasmus' other writings on prayer, see Pabel *Conversing* especially 109–54. See also Hilmar M. Pabel 'Erasmus' Esteem for Cyprian: Parallels in Their Expositions of the Lord's Prayer' ERSY 17 (1997) 55–69.

DESIDERIUS ERASMUS OF ROTTERDAM TO JODOCUS OR JUSTUS
LUDOVICUS OF WISSEMBURG, SECRETARY AND ENVOY OF HIS MOST
SERENE MAJESTY THE KING OF POLAND, GREETINGS.

For good reason, honoured sir,[1] many generations have approved the mime-
writer's adage 'When a man of power says "please," he means "you must"';[2]
but I am inclined to think that this applies more to you than to anyone, for
along with your learned letter you have sent me an elegant gift, one indeed
coming from such a distance that if I refused it I would have to throw it
away![3] Your letter is such that it would extract anything from the most stubborn of men, to say nothing of me, who am too easily won over. It is well
equipped with many stratagems to break down resolve: forceful persuasiveness, pressing arguments, sparkling erudition, and overpowering eloquence. Nothing, however, gives it more power than its exceptional and admirable modesty. I am so influenced by this that I could agree to undertake
not only the task you request, which is both congenial and pious, but also
one more difficult and much less to my liking. Accordingly, as soon as I received your letter – and it took a long time to reach me, until the very end
of August – I snatched up my pen and did as you wished. Modest though
the work may be, it will provide a happy token of our friendship and of my
good will towards the Polish or, if the ancient name is more to your liking,
the Sarmatian people.

I congratulate that people. In the past they were thought of as bar-
barians. Nowadays, literature, law, Christianity, culture, and all else that
can protect them from the charge of barbarism so flourish there that they
can match the most eminent and highly regarded nations. And yet even
in antiquity, when the Sarmatians were reckoned among savage and barbarous peoples, that stern moral critic Juvenal placed them above the highly
cultured Athenians for their integrity: 'Neither Sarmatian nor Thracian he /

* * * * *

1 The addressee is Justus Ludovicus Decius (Jost Ludwig Dietz), who became
   secretary to Sigismund I of Poland in 1520. He visited Erasmus in Basel in
   1522 and arranged the reprinting of *De conscribendis epistolis* in Cracow in 1523;
   see CEBR I 380–2. This prefatory letter is Ep 1393; the translation here is heavily
   indebted to the translation of that letter in CWE 10 103–4.
2 One of the *sententiae* in collections of aphorisms ascribed to the mime-writer
   Publilius Syrus of the first century BC. The transmitted corpus includes material whose authorship is uncertain, as is true for the *sententia* quoted here (*ro-
   gando cogit qui rogat potentior*). See *Publilii Syri mimi Sententiae* ed O. Friedrich
   (Berlin 1880) 97 (no 54).
3 Probably the gilded cup which was still in Erasmus' possession at his death;
   see Ep 1393 n3.

Who put on wings, but one in the midst of Athens born.'[4] I say nothing of
their realm, which embraces White Russians and Lithuanians and stretches
from the Vistula to the Tauric Chersonese and from the Baltic Sea to the
Carpathians. This broad expanse is ruled by King Sigismund,[5] who not only
excels in all the qualities worthy of a great prince but also is renowned for
his many great victories over his Tartar and Muscovite enemies, victories
needed more than any others to protect the boundaries of Christendom.

Perhaps, however, it will be more appropriate to speak of such matters
on another occasion. For the moment I offer you the Lord's Prayer, which I
have divided into seven parts as you asked me to do and as I see others have
done.[6] Yet I think it is as wrong to separate the last two clauses, 'And lead
us not into temptation, but deliver us from evil,' as it would be to divide
'And forgive us our trespasses, as we forgive those who trespass against
us.'[7] If your devotion is not satisfied by taking seven days to go through the
whole work, you can divide each day into seven times for prayer, as I see
our predecessors have also done.[8] Farewell.

Basel, 24 October 1523

* * * * *

4 Juvenal *Satires* 3.79–80. In the context of the satire, a tirade against the Greeks,
the comparison of the Sarmatians with the Athenians is much less flattering
to the former than Erasmus suggests.

5 Sigismund I (1467–1548); see CEBR III 249–51.

6 Augustine talks explicitly of the seven petitions in the Lord's Prayer as corre-
sponding to the seven (by his count) Beatitudes of the Sermon on the Mount
in Matt 5 (*De sermone Domini in monte* 2.38 CCSL 35 128–30).

7 Augustine sometimes advocates the division of the prayer into six parts since
the last two petitions form one concept; see *Enchiridion* 116 CCSL 46 111. Other
Christian Fathers do the same; see J. Carmignac *Recherches sur le Notre Père*
(Paris 1969) 312–13; Pabel *Conversing* 148–9.

8 Erasmus' words do not seem to fit a reference to the canonical hours of prayer
(see *Modus orandi Deum* CWE 70 168 n167). He may be referring to Ps 119 (Vulg
118):164: 'Seven times a day I praise thee'; cf Clement of Alexandria *Stromateis*
7.305 PG 9 450.

THE LORD'S PRAYER
DIVIDED INTO SEVEN PARTS FOR THE SEVEN DAYS OF THE WEEK
BY DESIDERIUS ERASMUS

Our Father who art in heaven, hallowed be thy name

O Father, dwelling in heaven, hear the petitions of your children who are still held fast on earth in their mortal bodies but who in their souls pant for their heavenly homeland and their Father's house. They realize that there a treasure of everlasting joy has been laid away for them,[1] the inheritance of eternal life.[2] O creator, preserver, and ruler of all that is in heaven and on earth, we acknowledge your majesty, we acknowledge our lowly state. Unworthy of being called your servants, we would not dare to address you as 'Father' or to claim for us that most honourable title of 'children,' of which you did not deem even your angels worthy, if you had not in your freely given goodness adopted us and given us the honour of that name.[3] We were 'slaves of sin,'[4] unhappily begotten from Adam; we were the children of Satan, whose spirit drove us to every kind of sin.[5] You, however, pitied us and through your only-begotten Son Jesus removed us from our servitude to sin, freed us from having Satan as our father,[6] and saved us from the inheritance of eternal fire.[7] You deigned to adopt us, engrafted through faith and baptism onto the body of your Son, so as to share in his name and inheritance.[8] So that we might not lack faith in your devotion to us you sent from heaven into our souls the Spirit of your Son as

* * * * *

1 For the comparison of the kingdom of God with a hidden treasure cf Matt 13:44.
2 Cf Titus 3:7.
3 Cf Gal 4:4–5; John 1:12.
4 John 8:34
5 Cf John 8:44.
6 Cf Gal 4:4–7; John 1:12.
7 Cf Mark 9:43.
8 Cf Gal 3:24–7.

a pledge of your love for us.[9] The Spirit repulses the fear of servitude and is not afraid to call out again and again within our hearts, 'Abba, Father.'[10] Born again by your Spirit,[11] through baptism we renounced Satan as our father and ceased to have an earthly father.[12] Then your Son, through whom you bestow everything upon us, also taught us to acknowledge only our heavenly Father, by whose power we were created when we were nothing, by whose goodness we were restored when we had perished, by whose wisdom we are guided and prevented from slipping back into perdition.

Your Son also gave us the confidence to address you; he laid out a formula of prayer.[13] Acknowledge your Son's prayer, acknowledge the Spirit of your Son, which importunes you for us through us.[14] You will not deem it unworthy to be called 'Father' by those whom your Son, so like you, deigned to call his brothers.[15] We have no cause to take pride in ourselves; rather, we have cause to glorify your kindness and that of your Son, since our merits can win nothing in this life and all that we have comes from your freely given generosity. Words of love and devotion have pleased you more than words showing fear. You would rather hear 'Father' than 'Master.' Your wish is for us to return your love as your children rather than to fear you as your servants. You showed your love for us first, and our love for you in turn is itself part of your gift. Father of spirits,[16] hear your spiritual children, worshipping you in spirit.[17] Your Son, who was sent by you into this world so that you might teach us all truth,[18] taught us that you take pleasure in such worshippers.

Hear our prayers for harmony. For it is not right that brothers, whom you in your goodness have made equal in your freely given gift, should contend with each other through ambition, rivalry, hatred, and jealousy. We all spring from the same Father, we all ask for the same things. We do not ask for anything peculiar to ourselves. Instead, like members of one body,

* * * * *

9 Cf Gal 4:6.
10 Cf Rom 8:15.
11 Cf John 3:5.
12 Cf Matt 10:37, 19:29; Mark 10:29.
13 The Lord's Prayer; Matt 6:9–13; Luke 11:2–4. Erasmus uses the fuller form of the prayer, found in Matthew.
14 Cf Rom 8:26.
15 Cf Matt 12:49; Mark 3:35; Luke 8:21.
16 Cf Heb 12:9.
17 Cf John 4:23; Eph 6:18.
18 Cf John 16:13.

enlivened by the same spirit, we ask for what will benefit all of us together.[19] We would not dare to ask you for anything other than what your Son bade us or ask in any way other than the way he prescribed. Your Son promised that if we petitioned in this way we would receive whatever we asked for in his name.[20]

When our Lord Jesus, your Son, lived on earth, his most ardent prayer was that your holy name should shine not only in Judaea but among all nations of the world.[21] By his urging and example we too pray with burning longing that the glory of worshipping your name should fill heaven and earth and that every creature should tremble before your inescapable power, worship your eternal wisdom, and love your ineffable goodness. Your glory is immeasurable; it had no beginning and will have no end,[22] ever flourishing in itself; it cannot increase or diminish. It is of great concern to the human race, however, that your glory be revealed to all. For to us 'it is eternal life to know you who are alone true God and Jesus Christ whom you sent.'[23] Let the splendour of your name obscure and extinguish all human glory within us. Let there be no one who will dare to claim even the smallest part of glory for himself. For any glory of which you have no part is nothing but ignominy.

Children born of physical union have a natural devotion to their parents and deeply desire that they win honourable fame. We see how joyful and exultant and proud of themselves children are if an outstanding honour befalls their parents: a triumph, for example, or a statue placed in the forum with an honorific inscription, or the highest office of state. For children regard a parent's glory as their own. Similarly, how sad and dejected they are if their father's name is smeared by disgrace. It is so deeply ingrained in human hearts for parents and children to take pride in each other. But since our love of God is so much stronger than our feelings for our fellow humans, we thirst all the more eagerly for the glory of your name and we suffer especial anguish if your name – you to whom alone all glory is owed – is besmirched. This is not because the splendour of your glory can

* * * * *

19 Cf 1 Cor 12:12–26.
20 Cf John 14:13, 15:16.
21 Cf Matt 24:14, 28:19. In this paragraph Erasmus is explaining the significance of 'Hallowed be thy name'; cf Augustine *De sermone Domini in monte* 2.19 CCSL 35 109.
22 Cf the Collect spoken in a mass celebrated at the beginning of the civic year in the *Missale Romanum*.
23 John 17:3 (a close but not exact rendering)

be defiled by disgrace. Rather, from our viewpoint, your name is insulted in some way when pagans, who do not know or who despise the creator of all things, worship and adore – through stone or wooden or colourfully painted representations, for example – even the most contemptible of creations: cattle, rams, apes, leeks, onions, and the evil spirits contained within all of these.[24] For these they sing hymns, sacrifice victims, and burn incense as if they are gods. When we, your children, see such things, we feel anguish on two accounts: you are being cheated of the glory owed to you, and these poor wretches are perishing through their own madness. The Jews too never cease from vilifying your only Son in their synagogues. Abuse heaped on Jesus, your only Son, who is the splendour of your glory,[25] is also heaped on you. They fasten on us the glorious name of your Son to insult us, thinking that it is more shameful to be called a Christian than a thief or a murderer; they cast up in reproach the cross of your Son, which is our glory.[26] We owe it to your mercy that we acknowledge you as the source of all salvation, that we worship your Son as equal to you, that we have been filled with the Spirit proceeding from both of you. May you in your clemency, heavenly Father, have pity on those others also, so that the pagans will give up the cult of images and worship you alone, and so that the Jews, who acknowledge God, from whom all things come, will be taught by your Spirit to abandon their superstitious adherence to their Law and also will acknowledge the Son of God, through whom all things come, and the Holy Spirit, who shares in the divine nature, and will worship in three Persons the same majesty, recognizing in a single essence the triple character of these Persons.[27] May every nation, every tongue, every man and woman, every generation everywhere agree in glorifying and praising your most holy name.

May we too, who are called your children, not disgrace your glory in the eyes of those who do not know you. For just as a wise son is a source of glory to his father, so wicked sons bring shame to their parents. And indeed, he who does not strive with all his might to emulate the good character and

* * * * *

24 Erasmus seems to have in mind the first part of Juvenal *Satires* 15, where the Latin poet lists animal and other objects of worship among the Egyptians. Note the presence of leeks and onions at line 9 of Juvenal's poem, though this is an echo of Horace *Epistles* 1.12.21. Erasmus also refers to the objects of cult among the Egyptians in *Adagia* III vii 1: 'The beetle searches for the eagle.'
25 Cf Heb 1:3.
26 Cf Gal 6:14.
27 Cf the Preface for the feast of the Blessed Trinity in the *Missale Romanum*.

behaviour of his parents is not a true son. Your Son Jesus is the purest son because he is the perfect image of his Father,[28] whom he recalls and represents in totality. We who are not your natural children but your children by adoption[29] model ourselves according to the example of your Son and try to become as like you as our strength allows. As you are perfectly glorified through your Son, so may you be glorified also through us to the extent that our weakness permits. You are glorified if the world sees us living in accordance with your Son's teaching, loving you above all, loving our neighbour as we love ourselves,[30] wishing well of those who wish us evil and doing good to those who do us harm.[31] For this was your Son's teaching. He called upon us to imitate the heavenly Father, who orders 'his sun to rise upon the righteous and the unrighteous.'[32] What great dishonour is brought to your glory by those who are called Christians, but who also steal, fornicate, quarrel, wage wars, seek political power, exact vengeance, cheat, swear false oaths in your holy name, and sometimes even utter blasphemous abuse! Their god is their belly.[33] They despise you and serve mammon.[34]

I say this because most people appraise God on the basis of his worshippers. Certainly, when they see those who profess your name living wicked lives, they say, 'Away with that God who has such worshippers, away with that Lord who has such servants, away with that Father who has such children, away with that king who has such subjects.' This is why your Son taught us to shine light on the glory of your name as best we can by pure and blameless behaviour, just as he glorified your name both in his life and in his death.[35] He said, 'Let your light shine before mortals, so that they may see your good deeds and that they may glorify your Father who is in heaven.'[36]

O heavenly Father, there is no light in us that has not proceeded from you, who are the everlasting source of all light.[37] No good deed of ours can proceed from us. May your goodness work in us and may your light

* * * * *

28 Cf 2 Cor 4:4; Col 1:15.
29 Cf Gal 4:5; Eph 1:5.
30 Cf Matt 19:19; Lev 19:18.
31 Cf Matt 5:44; Luke 6:27–8.
32 Matt 5:45
33 Cf Phil 3:19.
34 Cf Matt 6:24; Luke 6:27–8.
35 Cf John 17:1–5.
36 Matt 5:16
37 Cf Isa 60:19.

shine in us, just as there shines in your whole creation your eternal power, your inscrutable wisdom, and your inestimable kindness, which you wished to reveal especially to the human race. Accordingly, wherever we turn our eyes everything sings of the glory of your name. Day and night the heavenly spirits honour their king with praise. The wonderful creation of the heaven to which we raise our eyes, the harmonious union of discordant elements,[38] the fixed tides of the sea, the gushing forth of springs,[39] the neverending flow of rivers, the many different types of objects, trees, plants, and living things, each with its own innate particular power, as a magnet attracts iron and plants provide a powerful remedy against disease – what else, I say, do all these things express to us but the glory of your name? They tell us that you alone are true God, you alone are eternal, immortal, powerful, wise, good, merciful, just, truthful, wonderful, you alone are worthy of love and worship. Anyone who appropriates to himself anything of these qualities wrongs your glorious name. For whatever part of these is within us proceeds in its totality from your generosity. Grant, therefore, Father, that your name be glorified everywhere. Let the glory of your name shine forth in our actions as much as in the angels and in all your other creations. Just as those who contemplate this world can infer the greatness of the Creator from his wonderful work, so may those who do not know you be stirred by our example and not only recognize their evil ways but also wonder at your generosity. Changed in this way, may they glorify along with us your most holy name and the name of your Son Jesus and of the Holy Spirit that proceeds from both. To these equally is owed all glory, for ever and ever. Amen.

Thy kingdom come

Heavenly Father, source, creator, preserver, renewer, and ruler of all things in heaven and on earth, from you alone flows all authority, power, kingship, rule over things hidden and not hidden, over things 'visible and invisible.'[40] Your throne is heaven, your footstool is earth,[41] your sceptre is your eternal and immovable will. No power can withstand you. In times past through prophets inspired by your Spirit you promised your people a

* * * * *

38 The oxymoron (*discors concordia*) is found in Horace *Epistles* 1.12.19 ('rerum concordia discors'). Cf also Seneca *Naturales quaestiones* 7.27.4.
39 Cf Pliny *Naturalis historia* 5.1.1.6.
40 Col 1:16
41 Cf Matt 5:34–5; Isa 66:1.

spiritual kingdom for the salvation of the human race.[42] This would liberate those born again in you, freeing them from the tyranny of the devil, who had reigned a long time in this world, which is so addicted to sin. To claim this kingdom you deigned to send from heaven to earth your only-begotten Son to redeem us by his death[43] and transform us from servants of the devil into children of God.[44] For while he was on earth he often called his gospel teaching the 'kingdom of heaven' and 'kingdom of God.'[45] He taught that this was concealed and hidden among us.[46] Your children desire and ask with urgent prayer that this kingdom, which our Lord Jesus began to claim for you, should grow greater day by day and be extended daily on earth until your Son hands it over to you full and complete,[47] after subduing all whom your eternal purpose had marked out for this kingdom.

They also pray that, with the quelling of all the rebellious evil spirits and desires that even now fight against your sovereignty and destroy the tranquillity of your state, there be peace and calm throughout all your kingdom. For this world still assails your children with all its arsenal, burdened as they are with a mortal body. Human desires and the remnants of ancient sin still try to rebel against the spirit; wicked spirits, whom you cast down from your heavenly realm, still attack with fiery weapons from the upper air those whom you in your freely given goodness chose from the kingdom of this world and appointed to your heavenly kingdom as 'fellow heirs with your Son.'[48] Grant, omnipotent Father, that those whom you in your devoted love wished to be freed once and for all from the tyranny of sin and to be received as citizens in your kingdom may stand firm in their freedom through the kind offices of that same love of yours. Grant that none may defect from you and your Son and return to the tyranny of the devil. In this way we shall reign happily in you through your Son, and you will reign in us for the glory of your name. Your glory will be our happiness; our happiness will be your generous gift.

Your Son Jesus taught us how to despise the kingdom of this world; it rests on wealth, bodyguards, armies, and weapons; it is administered with

* * * * *

42 Cf Ex 19:5–6; Deut 7:6.
43 Cf John 3:16.
44 Cf Gal 4:4–7; John 1:12.
45 Cf Luke 4:43: 'I must preach the good news of the kingdom of God'; Matt 4:23.
46 Cf Matt 13:44: 'like a treasure hidden in a field'; Matt 13:33; Luke 13:18–20.
47 Cf 1 Cor 15:24.
48 Rom 8:17

arrogance and violence; it is procured and defended by cruelty. With the heavenly Spirit he conquered the evil spirit that is 'the prince of this world.'[49] By his purity he overcame sin, by his mildness he prevailed over cruelty. Through the greatest shame he regained eternal glory, through death he restored life, through the cross he triumphed over evil spirits. In this wondrous way, Father, you waged a victorious war, and now triumph and rule in your Son Jesus, through whom you chose us to share in your kingdom. In this way you reign and triumph in your holy martyrs, in your chaste virgins, in your blameless confessors.[50] For it was not by their own strength and force that those persons prevailed over the cruelty of tyrants or the desires of the flesh or the dangers of their time of service in this world. It was your Spirit, which you deigned to bestow on them, that undertook, developed, and completed all their achievements for the glory of your name and the salvation of the human race.

We pray that your kingdom may ever flourish in us too. We do not perform miracles (for time and circumstances do not demand them), we are not incarcerated, tortured, cut to pieces, burned, nailed to a cross, plunged into the sea, or beheaded. Nevertheless, the power and splendour of your kingdom will shine in us as well if the world sees that through the strength of your Spirit we are indomitable when confronted by all Satan's onslaughts, by the flesh that lures us to actions that are in no way in harmony with the Spirit, by the world that incites us with every kind of weapon to give up the confidence that we have fixed once and for all in you. Whenever because of love of you we spurn the kingdom of this world and follow the promises of the heavenly kingdom, whenever we reject mammon and grasp that unique pearl of the gospel,[51] whenever we repudiate all the apparent pleasures of the flesh that temporarily allure us and endure bravely all cruelty in the hope of eternal happiness, whenever we ignore through love of you the strongest of human emotions and what is dearest to us (parents, children, wives, relatives),[52] whenever we control the passion of anger and, through respect for you, return abuse with friendly words or injury with kindness[53]

* * * * *

49 Cf John 12:31, 14:30, 16:11.
50 In the early church the term 'confessor' was applied to martyrs, but from the third century on it denoted those who witnessed to their faith through their holiness and suffered for it, without, however, losing their lives. See NCE IV 141–2.
51 Perhaps an allusion to Christ's admonition to his disciples not to cast pearls before swine (Matt 7:6)
52 Cf Matt 19:29; Mark 10:29–30; Luke 18:29–30.
53 Cf Rom 12:17–21.

– on all those occasions you conquer through us the kingdom of Satan and reveal the power of your kingdom. You decided in your wisdom, Father, to exercise and strengthen the virtue of your children by such a constant and difficult struggle. Increase their strength so that they may always be more powerful when they leave the battlefield and so that, with the gradual weakening of our enemy's forces, you may rule more and more in us as each day passes.

Not yet, however, good Father, has the whole world submitted its neck to your yoke; the tyrant Satan still controls many nations. Not yet is there 'one fold and one shepherd,'[54] as we expect will come to pass, when the Jews too join the kingdom of the gospel. Many still do not know the great freedom, honour, and happiness of being a subject in your heavenly kingdom. For that reason they prefer to be slaves of the devil rather than to be your children, 'fellow heirs with Jesus,'[55] sharing in your heavenly kingdom. Even among those who now live within the walls of your church and display the insignia of your kingdom there are far too many, alas, who conspire with the enemy and, to the extent that they can, disgrace the glory of your kingdom and weaken its strength. We pray especially, therefore, for that time, which you wanted to be known to you alone,[56] when in accordance with your Son's promise the angels will be sent to cleanse the threshing-floor of your church; they will remove the weeds and gather the pure wheat and put it into a barn;[57] they will remove all causes of evil from your kingdom.[58] There will be no hunger or poverty or nakedness or disease or death or persecution. There will be no evil at all, or the fear of evil. The whole body of your only Son will be joined together with its head and will enjoy a happy share of the heavenly kingdom. Those, however, who have in the meantime preferred to be the slaves of the tyrant devil will be bound over with their master to eternal punishment.[59] This, of course, is the kingdom of Israel that the disciples asked to be restored soon when your Son Jesus Christ was about to leave earth and return to you.[60] As you made heaven peaceful and free of all revolt when you cast out Lucifer and his follow-

* * * * *

54 John 10:16
55 Rom 8:17
56 Cf Matt 24:36; Mark 13:32.
57 An interpretation of the parable of the wheat and the tares, relating to the kingdom of heaven, as told in Matt 13:24–30, 37–41
58 Cf Matt 13:41.
59 Cf Matt 25:46.
60 Cf Acts 1:6.

ers,[61] so, when human bodies have been restored to life, will you separate the sheep from the goats.[62] Those who have embraced with all their heart the kingdom of the gospel in this world will be invited to join the eternal kingdom that you in your goodness had marked out for them before the creation of the world.[63]

O Father, dwelling and reigning in heaven, this is the day, promised by your Son Jesus, that we pray for, we, your children on earth, in exile, as it were, weighed down by living in an earthly body and groaning because in the meantime we are exposed to many troubles and are separated from a share of your abode. We shall experience perfect happiness only when we see our king and Father with uncovered face in the beauty of his glory.[64] Our merits, which we know are worthless, do not provide us with this confidence. It comes from you. In your generosity you gave your Son in entirety to us, you imparted to us the heavenly Spirit as a pledge of this inheritance. If you grant that we constantly stand firm in your Son Jesus, you will not be able to exclude us from sharing in your kingdom. To you, your Son, and the Holy Spirit is owed all honour, splendour, and glory, for ever and ever. Amen.

Thy will be done, on earth as it is in heaven

Father, nourisher and guide of all those acknowledged by your Son as his brothers (for he acknowledges whoever have in true faith professed his name in baptism), your children call from earth to you who are in heaven and are far removed from all the transience of the world. They pray that they may come to join your heavenly kingdom, which will not be defiled by any contamination of evil, but they understand that only those who try with devout zeal to be in this world what they will be in your realm can be received into that tranquil existence. For the heavenly and earthly kingdoms and cities are the same, except that in this existence we have a great struggle with the flesh, with the world, and with Satan. Although there is nothing there that disfigures or contaminates the happiness of the blessed spirits, one thing is needed to make their happiness complete, the gathering together of all members of your Son and the joining of the whole body, pure and chaste, with the head. Christ thereby will have all of his members,

* * * * *

61 Cf Rev 12:7–9; Luke 10:18.
62 Cf Matt 25:32.
63 Cf Matt 25:34.
64 Cf Rev 22:4.

and the souls of the devout will be rejoined to their bodies, which long to share in the pleasures in heaven, just as they partook of earthly afflictions.

Those who, like good and obedient children, strive to do in their mortal body what your will dictates and not what their desires tempt them to do are practising here on earth the harmony of the heavenly kingdom. They do not consider why you wished this or that; satisfied that it is your will, they firmly believe that you wish only what is best. We have learned your will from your only-begotten Son. This he 'obeyed even unto death,'[65] and he uttered these words for us: 'Father, if it is possible, remove this cup from me; nevertheless, not my will, but yours, be done.'[66] Accordingly, it is shameful now for any one of us to prefer our will to yours. The flesh has its own will, which humans love to cling to,[67] as does the world, and Satan has his will, very different from yours. 'For the flesh has desires against the Spirit'[68] that you imparted to us, and the world tries to allure us to the love of transient things. Satan's will is for that which drags us into eternal death. It is not sufficient for us to profess at baptism that we will obey your commands and that we have renounced Satan as our ruler unless we constantly do all our lives what we have professed. We cannot do so, however, without your giving strength to our efforts, so that it is not our will, but your will, Father, that does in us what you in your wisdom have judged best. Those who live for the flesh are dead to you and are no longer your children.[69] In fact, as long as we carry round our earthly bodies, the will of the flesh frequently causes trouble for your children, itching as it does to have precedence over your will. Grant that your will may always prevail, whether you wish us to die or live, whether you wish us to be afflicted so that we may be set right or be lifted up so that we may thank you for your kindness. The will of Satan is followed by those who sacrifice to idols, who hurl abuse at your most holy Son Jesus Christ, who do not trust his promises, who prepare to rebel against the gospel, who through envy plan the murder of their neighbour, who hasten to become rich in this world by fair means or foul, who are defiled by base pleasures. Your will, however, is for us to keep body and soul pure and free from all the contaminants of this world, to honour you and your Son above all else, never to envy or be angry with or inflict vengeance on anyone, but rather to repay harmful acts with kindness;

* * * * *

65 Phil 2:8
66 A close paraphrase on Matt 26:39 and Mark 14:36; cf Luke 22:42.
67 Cf Rom 8:5–8.
68 Gal 5:17
69 Cf Rom 8:6–8.

finally, to suffer hunger, exile, imprisonment, torture, death more readily than to deviate from your holy will. Heavenly Father, help to give us the strength to do this more and more each day, so that, as each day passes, the flesh may struggle less against our spirit and our spirit may be more and more at one with yours.

At the present time there are many lands where those who obey your Son's gospel follow your will; may the same happen throughout the whole world so that all may understand that you alone are the monarch of all things and so that all may obey your divine laws willingly and gladly, just as in heaven there is no one who resists your will. We cannot wish effectively what you wish unless your divine will has drawn us to you. You bid us comply with your will; for we will not deserve the name of children unless we obey our Father's commands in every matter. In your holy love you have deigned to adopt us, though we have in no way deserved such an honour; in the same love you will deign to bestow on us a ready and constant desire not to stray from the prescriptions of your divine will but to mortify the flesh and be impelled by your Spirit towards all that is holy and pleasing in your eyes. You, Father, will thereby acknowledge that your children are not wicked, and your Son acknowledge us as his true brothers.[70] In other words, both Father and Son will recognize their own kindness in us. With them the Holy Spirit shares the glory, for ever and ever. Amen.

Give us this day our daily bread

Our heavenly Father, who in your ineffable kindness generously nourish all that 'you wonderfully created,'[71] provide spiritual and heavenly food for us your children, chosen to be members of the heavenly family and dependent on you, so that, serving your will, we may grow in strength and perform more virtuous acts as each day passes, until, to the extent that our nature allows, we may attain the complete fullness that is in Jesus Christ.[72] As long as the children of this world have kind parents and are not disinherited they are not concerned about food, since they are provided for by the generosity of their father. We whom your Son Jesus has taught to have no thought of the morrow[73] should be much less worried. We have been chosen to be God's

* * * * *

70 Cf Luke 8:21.
71 From the Collect 'Deus qui humanae substantiae' of the mass *in die* on Christmas Day
72 Cf Eph 4:13.
73 Cf Matt 6:34.

children, and Jesus assures us that his rich, generous, and loving Father, who cares deeply for us, will not allow us to lack food or clothing. For he provides food even for the sparrows that have no fixed abode,[74] and clothes the lilies of the field in much splendour.[75] Ignoring all else, we should strive after what pertains to your kingdom and your Son's righteousness.[76] For you take no pleasure in the righteousness of the Pharisees, for that is of the flesh.[77] The spiritual righteousness of your kingdom lies in pure faith and unfeigned love.[78] It is no great act for you in your bounty to provide our weak bodies with bread made of wheat. Even if they do not perish through starvation, they will soon perish through illness, old age, or something else. We, however, your spiritual children, entreat the Father of spirits[79] for the spiritual and heavenly bread that allows all of us who are truly called your children to live true lives.

That bread is your Word,[80] an omnipotent bestower and nourisher of life, which you deigned to send to us from heaven when we were dying of hunger. For the bread of the philosophers or of the Pharisees did not satisfy our souls, but that bread of yours, which you sent us, has given life to those who were dead. Whoever partakes of it will never die.[81] Through it we have lived again, through it we are nourished and filled, through it we grow into the full strength of the Spirit. We must absorb this deep within our soul every day; and it does not nourish us, Father, unless you give it every day. The body of your only-begotten Son is the bread, and all who live in your great home that is the church partake of it. There is one bread, shared by all, just as we are one body, consisting of members that are different but strengthened by the same Spirit.[82] Yet, although it is taken by all,

* * * * *

74 Erasmus may be confusing Luke 12:24, where Christ refers to God's feeding of ravens, with Matt 10:29 and Luke 12:6–7, where God's general concern for sparrows is enunciated. Cf also Matt 6:26 (God's feeding of 'the birds of the air').
75 Cf Matt 6:28–9; Luke 12:27.
76 Cf Matt 6:33; Luke 12:31.
77 See Matt 23 for Christ's indictment of the Pharisees.
78 Cf 2 Cor 6:6.
79 See n16 above.
80 Word: a translation of *sermo*; see James K. McConica *Erasmus* (Oxford 1991) 64–5. For the different ways in which the 'bread' in this petition has been interpreted, see J. Carmignac *Recherches sur le Notre Père* (Paris 1969) 144–66; Pabel *Conversing* 138–9.
81 Cf John 6:58.
82 Cf 1 Cor 12:20.

it brings death to many.[83] For it does not bring life unless you give it every day with the spice of your heavenly grace so that it may be wholesome to those who take it. Your Son is the truth,[84] and the truth of the gospel is the bread that he left us for spiritual nourishment. Yet this bread is bitter to many whose spiritual palate is infected by the fever of evil desires. If you, however, offer it, Father, it will be sweet tasting, it will refresh the afflicted, it will raise up the fallen, it will strengthen the weak, it will encourage the timid, and, finally, it will confer eternal life. But since we always slip backwards through the weakness of human nature, and our souls are assailed each day by many battering-rams, each day you should strengthen your children with your bread. For otherwise we will be unequal to so many strong enemies, so many assaults, so many objects of terror. If we are not continually strengthened by your holy bread, who among us can endure to be the laughing-stock of the world, to be exiled, thrown into prison, chained, condemned, tortured, stripped of our property, deprived of our dear wife and sweet children, and, finally, to perish by a cruel death? Those who teach the words of the Gospel offer us this bread, but they offer it in vain unless you too give it. Many persons receive the body of your Son, many hear the words of the Gospel, but they do not depart any stronger than they came because they do not merit their Father's invisible offering of the bread.

Most generous Father, impart this bread to your children each day until it befalls them to partake of it at your heavenly table. This happily will fill the children of your kingdom with a never-ending supply of eternal truth. To enjoy this truth is supreme joy, which knows no longing for anything else, whether in heaven or on earth. All things are in you alone, and nothing that is not in you is worthy of being sought. With your Son Jesus and with the Holy Spirit you live and reign, for ever and ever. Amen.

And forgive us our trespasses, as we forgive those that trespass against us

Heavenly Father, source of peace and lover of harmony, in your goodness you have joined together your children with many bonds of unanimity; you infuse them with the same Spirit and cleanse them with the same rite of baptism; you bring them together in the same house that is the church;

* * * * *

83 Cf 1 Cor 11:27–30.
84 Cf John 14:6.

you sustain them with the sacraments of the church, which are common to all; you have called them equally to inherit the kingdom of heaven. It is assuredly your will that they be strengthened by living together in your family at one with each other, by being joined together in mutual love with no dissent among the members of the same body. Since, however, they still carry round their mortal bodies, it is scarcely possible, because of their weak nature, for them not to commit some offences that, though not destroying the serenity of their brotherly harmony, will impair it and finally destroy it if you in your clemency do not every day forgive their daily sins. Whenever we offend against our brothers and sisters, we offend against you too, Father, who told us to love our neighbour as ourselves.[85] Your Son, however, knew well the weakness of his members and pointed out a remedy for this evil. He gave us the certain hope that you in your mercy would forgive us our sins if we for our part had truly forgiven the sins our neighbour committed against us.

This condition for being granted forgiveness, prescribed by your Son Jesus, is a most just one. How shamelessly do those who are preparing to avenge a brother's trifling offence pray that their Father may not punish them! How brazenly do some say to you, 'Give up your anger,' when they themselves persist in their anger against their brother. Your Son was free of all sin, but he prayed to you on the cross to forgive his murderers.[86] How arrogant then are those who boast of being members of your Son when, though naturally prone to sin themselves, they do not forgive a brother when he sins against them, and immediately sin against him! Here, instead of forgiveness there is an exchange of sins.[87] Those who worship without forgetting their anger or with no thought of reconciliation with their neighbour

* * * * *

85 Cf Lev 19:18; Matt 19:19.
86 Cf Luke 23:34.
87 The text at this point reads *ut hic sit potius mutua veniae permutatio quam ignoscentia*, 'so that here there is an exchange of *venia* [pardon/forgiveness] rather than forgiveness [*ignoscentia*].' The clause must refer to what immediately precedes: the example of those who not only are unwilling to forgive a brother's sin against them, but also commit a sin against that brother in retaliation. Erasmus may have made a slip, writing *veniae* instead of *peccati*, 'of sin,' through mental anticipation of *ignoscentia* – unless *veniae* can mean 'occasion for / cause of forgiveness,' that is, 'sin.' In her 1525 translation Margaret Roper translates 'so that amongst us it maye be called rather as mutuall chaunge of pardone than very forgyvenesse,' taking *hic* to mean 'amongst us.' More naturally *hic* refers specifically to the circumstances that have just been described.

are unpleasing to your eyes. Your Son taught us that we should hurry to achieve harmony with our brethren even if we have to abandon our sacred duties at the altar.[88]

Noblest Father, we follow what your Son taught, we imitate what he did. If you recognize the terms prescribed by your Son (and there is no doubt that you do), we ask you to bestow what he gave us certain hope of receiving. He told us to pray in this way, and he asserted more than once that we would receive whatever we asked for from you in his name.[89] He gave us the confidence to ask; Father, grant through him forgiveness to those who seek it. We acknowledge our weakness, and because of it we realize to what depths of evil we would fall if you did not watch over us and protect us from more serious sins. In your devotion to us you left this very weakness in us as a cure against the danger of arrogance. Every day we lapse so that every day we may glorify your mercy. Father, grant us the ability sincerely to forgive our brethren, so that you will always look kindly upon us because we are in harmony with each other. If we offend in any way, and we often offend in many ways, may you as our Father correct and cleanse us. Only do not renounce us, do not disinherit us, do not cast us into hell. In baptism you forgave our sins once and for all.[90] That was not enough for you in your holy love for us. You also revealed an unfailing and readily available remedy for the daily sins of your children. For this we give thanks to you in your generosity. By such kindnesses and through your Son and the Holy Spirit you deem us worthy of the everlasting glory of your most holy name. Amen.

And lead us not into temptation

Our Father, dwelling in heaven, there is nothing that we fear terribly if you are well disposed to us; our mutual love makes us, your children, stronger to face every onslaught of evil. Nevertheless, we cannot be free of worry when we think of the weakness of human nature and are uncertain about whom you in your goodness deem worthy of strengthening in love of you to the very end of this life. As long as we live here, we are tempted in a thousand ways to ruin. This whole life is filled with the devil's snares.[91] That tempter, who was not afraid to assail even your Son Jesus with his

* * * * *

88 Cf Matt 5:23–4.
89 Cf John 14:13.
90 Cf John 3:5–8.
91 Cf 2 Tim 2:26.

tricks,[92] is never idle. We reflect upon the many weapons with which Satan attacked your servant Job.[93] We call to mind Saul, first chosen, then cast out from your sight.[94] We remember how David, who was called 'a man of your heart,'[95] was dragged down to such baseness that he added adultery to murder.[96] We think of how Solomon, to whom at the beginning of his reign you had given wisdom beyond all other humans, was led to such madness that he sacrificed to foreign gods.[97] We recall what happened to the leading apostle; he professed loyalty to Christ even if he had to die with him, but then denied his Lord three times.[98]

When we consider these and many other such happenings, we cannot help fearing the danger of temptation. You in your fatherly love wanted us always to have this fear. Having it, we would not become lazy or negligent and trust in our own resources; we would continually fortify ourselves against the tempter's attacks through sobriety, wakefulness, and prayer;[99] we would remember our weakness and not challenge the enemy; despite that weakness we would stand fast with unbreakable resolution against the storm of temptation when it assails us, by relying on your help, without which we can do nothing.[100] Admittedly, you allow temptations to fall upon us sometimes, either to test and then prove the endurance of your people, just as Job and Abraham[101] were tested, or to censure and correct our sins by such scourgings. Whenever you allow this to happen, we ask you, however, also to provide a happy outcome of the temptation and grant us strength that will match the weight of the evils rushing upon us. There is great danger when we are threatened with the seizure of our possessions, with exile, disgrace, imprisonment, or chains, with terrible torture and a dreadful death. There is no less danger, however, from delusory prosperity than from terrifying adversity. Countless persons succumb, right and left. Some, terrified by the fear of punishment, sacrifice to evil spirits; others are crushed by their misfortunes and blaspheme against your holy name. Similarly, others become

* * * * *

92 Cf Matt 4:1–11; Luke 4:1–13.
93 Cf Job 1:12–22, 2:1–9.
94 Cf 1 Sam 9:15–17, 15:10–26.
95 1 Sam 13:14 (with a slight change in wording)
96 David arranged the murder of Uriah the Hittite, then committed adultery with Uriah's wife; see 2 Sam 11:14–17, 26–7.
97 Cf 1 Kings 11:4–9.
98 Cf Matt 26:33–5, 69–75; Mark 14:29–31, 66–72; Luke 22:33, 56–62.
99 Cf Matt 26:41; Mark 14:38.
100 Cf John 15:5.
101 Cf Gen 22:1–19.

drunk with the poisonous draughts of worldly happiness; they spurn your gifts and slip back to wallow in their former filth. Take, for example, that son in the Gospel who dissipated all his father's money on whores; he came to such misery that he grudged giving even husks to pigs.[102]

We know that our adversary has no power over us unless you allow it. Accordingly, we do not refuse to be exposed to any kind of danger provided that in your mercy you control our adversary's attack and our own strength. For even if we come off worse in the battle, your wisdom will turn this to our good. When your Son, ever worthy of reverence, prevailed over Satan, over the flesh, over the world, he won the greatest triumph at the moment when he seemed to be totally crushed. It was for us he fought, for us he prevailed, for us he triumphed. Let us too prevail through his example, through your help, and through the Holy Spirit proceeding from both, for ever and ever. Amen.

But deliver us from evil

Omnipotent Father, by your freely given kindness you have purified us once and for all of our sins, through your Son Jesus Christ you have freed us from having the devil as our foul father, and have adopted us to share in the honour of your name and inheritance. The terms, however, are that as long as we are on this earth we have a perpetual struggle with our enemy, who grudges us your kindness and tries everything to drag us back under his sway. We shudder whenever we think of the evil father we had when we were 'slaves of sin,'[103] of the unhappy inheritance for which we were marked, of the pitiless master we served. We are well aware of his persistently evil ways, and of how well equipped he is for our destruction, not only with strength but also with countless tricks and stratagems. He never sleeps, never is idle, but ever is prowling about us like a lion roaring with hunger that searches out, stalks, hunts for someone to devour.[104] To be sure, he is completely unlike you, Father. For you are good and kindly by nature: you carry back the lost sheep to the fold,[105] you cure the sick, you call back the dead to life. You overcome by your love even your enemies who blaspheme against your name, and invite them to eternal life.

* * * * *

102 The prodigal son of the parable told in Luke 15:11–32. For the pigs see Luke 15:15–16.
103 John 8:34 and Rom 6:16–17
104 An expanded paraphrase of the simile in 1 Pet 5:8, also describing the devil
105 Cf Matt 18:12; Luke 15:3–7.

The devil is filled with insatiable hatred of us, who have never done him harm; all his endeavours are directed at dragging as many as possible to perdition. It is the mark of consummate evil for someone to wish to destroy, gratuitously and with no advantage to himself, those who have never assailed him unjustly. Yet the devil strives to harm, even at great cost to himself, those whom you have called into your guardianship. He was not like this when you created him, but fell to such depths of evil when, through pride, he did not wish to be subject to your majesty.[106] Accordingly, he was goaded on by envy and after tricking the first parents of our race lured them to spiritual death;[107] he grudged them the pleasures of paradise since he had deprived himself of the joys of heaven. Now he burns with fiercer brands of envy because you raise into heaven those who were driven out of paradise, because you invite those who had been marked out for death to partake of blessed immortality through faith in your Son Jesus Christ, because you use even his evil to enhance your glory, our salvation. Although he is deservedly feared by many, your goodness gives us comfort. For it has more power to save us than all his evil has to destroy us. We acknowledge our weakness, but we are not terrified by the enemy's assaults, whether we live or die, as long as we deserve to have you as our protector. We do not fear destruction at the hands of that evil as long as we can cling fast to what is good.

Eternal Father, if these petitions are proper ones and expressed according to the form prescribed by your Son Jesus Christ, we have the certain faith that in your goodness you will grant what we ask for.

* * * * *

106 At Job 1:6–12 Satan is still in heaven, though clearly subservient to God. Here Erasmus is following the version in which Satan left or was expelled from heaven prior to the creation of the human race.

107 Cf Gen 3:1–7.

LITURGY OF THE VIRGIN MOTHER VENERATED AT LORETO

Virginis Matris apud Lauretum cultae liturgia

translated and annotated by
JAMES J. SHERIDAN†

with additional annotation by
ERIKA RUMMEL and STEPHEN RYLE

Erasmus composed the *Liturgia Virginis Matris* at the request of Thiébaut Biétry,[1] parish priest of Porrentruy, a small town in the Jura mountains. Biétry had probably become acquainted with Erasmus as a result of a mutual connection with the prince-bishop of Basel, Christoph von Utenheim, whose patronage had been one of the key factors in persuading Erasmus to settle in that city.[2] The castle of Porrentruy was Christoph von Utenheim's favoured residence, especially after 1519, when his advanced age and the disaffection of the citizens of Basel towards his authority prompted him to withdraw from active participation in affairs. Biétry, whose family had been established in Porrentruy since the fourteenth century, was also a prominent member of the Confrérie Saint-Michel, an association of clergy from the surrounding region devoted to religious and cultural activities, perhaps with a particular interest in liturgy and church music.[3] The *editio princeps* of the *Liturgia Virginis Matris*, consisting of five pages of text, the shortest of Erasmus' works ever to be printed separately, was issued by Johann Froben in November 1523.

The legend of the Holy House of Loreto, said to have been miraculously transported from Nazareth to the Adriatic coast of Italy during the last decade of the thirteenth century, had by the end of the fifteenth gained wide circulation.[4] The cult had received papal recognition from Paul II in 1470 and Julius II in 1507. Presumably Biétry had visited the shrine, and he may even have met Erasmus in Italy, though neither man mentions such an encounter in their surviving correspondence.

When he composed the liturgy Erasmus made no reference to the reputed miraculous origin of the Holy House, but gave emphasis to the miracles of Christ and to his relationship with his mother by choosing as the gospel passage St John's account of Christ's first miracle at the marriage feast of Cana. For the second printing of the liturgy in May 1525 he added a homily, in which he dwells on the virtues of the Blessed Virgin, in particular her purity, humility, prudence, and fortitude.

* * * * *

1 See CEBR I 146–7.
2 See CEBR III 361–2; Epp 598, 756:47–8.
3 For the background to Erasmus' connections with Porrentruy see André Chêvre 'Erasme le prince des humanistes et ses amis de Porrentruy' *Actes de la Société jurassienne d'émulation* 77 (1974) 369–92.
4 See Ulysse Chevalier *Notre-Dame de Lorette: étude sur l'authenticité de la santa casa* (Paris 1906); NCE VIII 994.

The second edition was further amplified by a commendation from Antoine de Vergy,[5] the archbishop of Besançon, within whose diocese Porrentruy lay. De Vergy's commendation, to which was added an indulgence of forty days for anyone taking part in the celebration of the liturgy, was dated 20 April 1524, and must have been drawn up in the course of the journey that Erasmus undertook to Porrentruy and Besançon in the company of Biétry during that month.[6]

The *Liturgia* enjoyed a generally favourable reception, at least among those of a traditionalist outlook. Udalricus Zasius, however, while expressing admiration for the homily, made some light-hearted comments at the expense of the legend concerning the Holy House in a letter to Bonifacius Amerbach.[7] Erasmus himself was able in *Manifesta mendacia* to use the evidence of his authorship of the *Liturgia* to rebut the charge of failing to honour the Blessed Virgin levelled against him by 'Taxander' (Vincentius Theoderici).[8]

After the second Froben edition the *Liturgia* was printed at Venice in 1526. It was later included among the works appended to the *editio princeps* of *De pueris instituendis* published by the Froben firm in September 1529. In 1733 P.V. Martorelli printed the Latin text of the *Liturgia* in the course of a study of the legend of the Holy House.

Erasmus' admirer Giovanni Angelo Odoni[9] reported in 1535 that he had translated the *Liturgia* into Italian, but no copy of the translation has survived.[10] An English version of the homily was printed by Robert Wyer in about 1533.[11] The *Liturgia* was also one of the Erasmian works translated into Spanish by Lorenzo Riber in 1956.[12]

This first complete English version of the *Liturgia* is a translation by the late Reverend James J. Sheridan. Additions to his notes have been made by

* * * * *

5 See CEBR III 388–9.
6 For Erasmus' account of the journey see Ep 1610. He left Basel on or after 14 April and had returned by 8 May (Epp 1440, 1445).
7 *Die Amerbachkorrespondenz* ed Alfred Hartmann and B.R. Jenny (Basel 1942–   ) III Ep 1030:30–44
8 See *Manifesta mendacia* CWE 71 126, 169 n81; also Allen Epp 1679:104–6, 1956:35–7.
9 See CEBR III 23–4.
10 Allen Ep 3002:618–19
11 See E.J. Devereux *Renaissance English Translations of Erasmus: A Bibliography to 1700* (Toronto 1983) 74–5.
12 *Erasmo. Obras escogidas* trans Lorenzo Riber (Madrid 1956; repr 1964) 546–59.

Erika Rummel and Stephen Ryle, and the translation has been amended in a few places. The annotations also incorporate Harry Vredeveld's notes on the Introit and Sequence, which appeared in his editions of Erasmus' *Carmina*.[13] The translation has been checked against the Latin text edited by Léon-E. Halkin in ASD V-1 95–109.

SR

* * * * *

13 ASD I-7 443–4 / CWE 86 719–21

ERASMUS OF ROTTERDAM TO THIÉBAUT BIÉTRY, PARISH PRIEST
OF PORRENTRUY, GREETING.[1]

Look at this! In future you can expect to see Erasmus dancing in the market-
place if you tell him to.[2] Only remember that the fewer the people who agree
with your judgment, the larger the debt you owe me for my compliance. I
foresee one danger, that our Lady of Loreto may not listen when you are
singing this at Porrentruy.[3] Paul condemns neither hymns nor psalms, provided that he who sings psalms with the spirit sings also with the understanding.[4] But you have been summoned to fill the office of a prophet, which
means to be a shepherd. If shepherds thought their flocks would grow fat
on singing, they would sing to them and do nothing more. As it is, they take
them out to pasture, as you see, every day, and do not leave them at home
to starve. A shepherd of sheep ought not to know his job better than a shepherd of souls. You too must lead your flock out and back again, and you
will find pastures, for the Gospel provides food both privately and in public. You must not say, I am no doctor of divinity. Set before the people with
a good courage precisely what Jesus provided, and you will see that today
as of old a few loaves and still fewer small fishes can feed many thousands
of men.[5] Farewell.

* * * * *

1 This letter is Ep 1391, trans R.A.B. Mynors and Alexander Dalzell.
2 Cf Ep 1573:3–5, the prefatory letter of 1525 below, and Ep 404:22.
3 Biétry seems to have taken a special interest in church music; see Ep 1573:5–19.
4 1 Cor 14:15; Eph 5:19
5 Matt 14:13–21, 15:32–8; Mark 6:31–44, 8:1–9; Luke 9:10–17; John 6:1–13

DESIDERIUS ERASMUS OF ROTTERDAM TO THIÉBAUT BIÉTRY,
PARISH PRIEST OF PORRENTRUY, GREETING.[1]

I have played the fool so often to please you, dear Biétry, that I think I would even do the rope dance[2] in the centre of the town square or the Cyclops' jig[3] if you told me to. I am not asking you in return to transform yourself from an old musician into a new preacher. From every quarter of the world music of every style rises from every kind of instrument to assault the ears of the Blessed Virgin, who hears every day the song of the angelic choirs – unless I am mistaken, a far sweeter song than ours. It is only because men listen often to the din of voices and the noise of instruments and never or rarely to the message of the Gospel that in our villages and even in some of our towns there is such naïvety and such ignorance of the Christian faith. Yet it is the music of the Gospel which casts its spell upon us and frees us gently from the spirit of this world and implants within us the spirit of Christ. If Amphion[4] could work such wonders with the sound of his lyre and if Orpheus' lute had such power that it could move rocks and oaks,[5] how much more powerful must be David's lyre, whose music drove the evil spirit from Saul![6] And how much more effective must be the music of the Gospel!

To be sure, a priest has fulfilled a good part of his duty if, by living a pure and sober life, he provides a light for the guidance of his flock. But although I have no fault to find with you on this score, remember, my dear Thiébaut, that when we make allowance for priests who compensate for their lack of eloquence by the special saintliness of their lives, it is because they are unable to be competent in both, and the conduct of one's life has, so to speak, an eloquence of its own. Thus allowance was made for Valerian, the bishop of Hippo,[7] who delegated half his duties to Augustine because he

* * * * *

1 This letter is Ep 1573, trans Alexander Dalzell.
2 Cf Terence *Adelphi* 752. This reference is to a figure dance in which the dancers were joined together by a rope.
3 Horace *Satires* 1.5.63 refers to dancing the role of the Cyclops in the mime; cf Horace *Epistles* 2.2.125.
4 Amphion drew the stones together by the magic of his music to build the walls of Thebes. Apollodorus *Bibliotheca* 3.5.5 is one of several classical sources.
5 Cf Aeschylus *Agamemnon* 1629–30; Ovid *Metamorphoses* 10.86–105, 11.1–2.
6 Cf 1 Sam 16:14–17, 23.
7 Valerian (in other texts, the name appears as Valerius) was an elderly Greek bishop who spoke Latin but not the local Punic vernacular. See Augustine Ep 31.4 CSEL 34 part 2 4 and cf Peter Brown *Augustine of Hippo* (Berkeley 1967) 139. Because he saw the need to uphold the Catholic faith in the presence of a

spoke a language which the people did not understand. But I shall not allow you to be half a priest, since you can perform both functions well; and the Virgin Mother will think that her cherished Loreto is crowned with success[8] only if you use your persuasive powers to draw as many people as you can to the love of her son. But perhaps all along you have been doing what I am now urging you to do.

I have added a short homily[9] to make the liturgy complete. Farewell.
Basel, 4 May 1525

* * * * *

Donatist majority and an active Manichean minority, he relied on Augustine as a preacher. The reference is especially suitable because one of the revisions made in this second edition was the addition of a *concio* or sermon.

8 There is a play on words here. As well as referring to the city of Loreto with its cult of the Blessed Virgin, Erasmus alludes to the Lauretum, a site on the Aventine Hill in Rome. Cf Varro *De lingua Latina* 5.152; Pliny *Naturalis historia* 15.138. He also has in mind the laurel as a symbol of victory.

9 Cf n7 above.

LITURGY OF THE VIRGIN MOTHER
VENERATED AT LORETO

Introit[1]

The laurel gives delight with its aroma; it is beautiful with its perennial verdure. So too, Virgin Mother, will your praise bloom throughout all the ages.[2]

Verse

Draw us after you, Virgin Mary descended from Jesse. We will follow in the fragrance of your perfumes.[3] Glory be to the Father, etc.

Collect

O God, creator, renewer, and ruler of all things, who are glorified, indeed, in all your saints but in a special manner in Mary, the mother of your Son, and who rejoice in the glory brought to you by the innumerable miracles wrought through her both in the world at large and especially at the shrine of Loreto: grant, we pray you, that those who with piety worship you in the Son and the Son in you, and venerate the

* * * * *

1 Erasmus has composed the text of the Introit in the form of a couplet of dactylic hexameters.
2 The laurel held a prominent place in Rome. Its branches were used to decorate poets, priests, ancestral images, victorious generals. See Pliny *Naturalis historia* 15.127, 133–7. In Italian, *laurea* was used for 'victory' or 'triumph.'
3 Cf Song of Sol 1:3. The Vulgate does not have the phrase *Virgo Jesse Maria*, which is a play on words recalling Isa 11:1. It is not known to whom the Song of Solomon was directed, but it certainly was not to the Virgin Mary. Erasmus is using the words in an accommodated sense.

Son in the Mother and the Mother because of the Son, may by heavenly protection be freed from all evils. Through the same Jesus Christ, our Lord.

Lesson from Ezekiel chapter 44

Then he brought me back to the outer gate of the sanctuary which was facing east, and it was closed. And the Lord said to me: 'This gate shall be shut, and it shall not be opened and no man shall enter by it, because the Lord, the God of Israel, has entered by it, and it shall be closed to the prince. The prince himself shall sit in it to eat bread before the Lord. He shall enter by way of the vestibule of the gate and go out by the same way.'[4]

OR: ISAIAH 11
'There shall come forth a shoot from the stock of Jesse' to 'and on that day the Lord will extend.'[5]

Gradual

There came forth a shoot from the stock of Jesse, and a branch grew from his roots, and the spirit of the Lord came to rest upon him.[6]

Alleluia

The rod of Aaron alone sprouted without being planted;[7] the Virgin Mary alone, without the embrace of man, brought forth an unfading flower,[8] Jesus, who restrained the complaints of the people of Israel.[9]

* * * * *

4 Ezek 44:1–3. In *Explanatio symboli* Erasmus uses this passage as a prophecy of Mary's perpetual virginity (ASD V-1 245:189–246:213 / CWE 70 291). Cf also *Paean Virgini Matri* 28 above; *Carmina* 110:97–100 ASD I-7 362–3 / CWE 85 280–1; *In Prudentium* CWE 29 176; Salzer 26–8, 117 n7, 283:37–9; *Marienlexikon* V 191–3.
5 Isa 11:1–11
6 For the Gradual Erasmus uses the opening two verses of Isa 11. However, he changes the verbs from the future to the past tense. What was a prophecy for Isaiah has become a reality.
7 Cf Num 17:8.
8 Cf Tertullian *De Corona* 15.2 CCSL 2 1065: 'Habes florem ex virga Iesse ... incorruptum, immarcescibilem, sempiternum.'
9 Cf Num 17:1–10.

Sequence[10]

Fair choir of virgins, take up the zither, take up the lyre.[11] The Virgin Mother must be celebrated in song, in a virginal ode.[12] The angels, joining in the song, will re-echo your voice. For they love virgins, being virgins themselves.[13]

* * * * *

10 The liturgical sequence evolved during the ninth century when words began to be set to the very long melodies (*melismata*) which were sung to the final syllable of the word *Alleluia* at the end of the processional chant immediately preceding the Gospel at solemn masses. The practice was to set one syllable to each note. Since the musical phrases were of unequal length the texts at first had no coherent pattern, with the result that they were regarded as prose; hence the term *prosa* for a sequence text. The first stage in imposing the characteristics of verse on the sequence occurred when the various melodic units began to be repeated, a practice encouraged by the tradition of antiphonal singing in churches, especially in monastic communities. This produced a pattern of couplets displaying syllabic response-sion, but since the melodic units were unequal in length the different verse-couplets did not exhibit any regular structure. Sequences continued to be composed in this form until the mid-eleventh century, when a tendency towards greater regularity and the use of rhyme began to become evident. From the twelfth century onwards metrical consistency (but not uniformity) and rhyme came to be employed as universal features of the liturgical sequence.

In this sequence Erasmus has ignored rhyme altogether (apart from two internal rhymes); and has modified the principle of syllabic response to produce couplets based on classical metres, in which the metrical units form patterns of long and short syllables. This method of composition was alien to the medieval sequence. Erasmus has also introduced a further classical feature by combining his couplets into sense-units consisting of a quatrain. In doing so he has made the poem conform as closely to the normal structure of a Horatian ode as he could achieve within the constraints of the sequence form. The final quatrain has a coda of an additional couplet.

On the sequence in general see eg *Dictionary of the Middle Ages* ed Joseph R. Strayer 13 vols (New York 1982–9) XI 162–7. On this poem see Clarence H. Miller 'The Liturgical Context of Erasmus's Hymns' in *Acta Torontonensis* 481–90. For the metrical scheme see Harry Vredeveld's notes in ASD I-7 443–4 / CWE 86 719–20.

11 These instruments are among the ones played for the procession in which David brought the ark of the covenant into Jerusalem; see 1 Chron 15:28. The ark was considered a prefiguration of Mary. See *Carmina* 110:85–8, with note, ASD I-7 362 / CWE 85 280, 86 653.

12 Cf *Virginis et martyris comparatio* LB V 591D (163 below), where Erasmus says that the virgin spouse Christ delights in the songs of virgins: 'Virgineis cantilenis delectatur virgo Sponsus.'

13 On the affinity of virgins and angels see *Virginis et martyris comparatio* 175–6 below.

The laurel-crowned band, who once spared not their life and their blood,[14] will add their odes. The martyr conquers the executioner; the virgin subdues the flesh.[15] Both the one and the other deserve the laurel.

The melodious throng of heavenly beings will show their applause, all heaven will sing of the holy Virgin;[16] no song is more pleasing to the Virgin's only son.

As the cedar stands out among the trees that Lebanon bears,[17] so shines the noble[18] Virgin among all the heavenly beings. As the morning star is prominent among the stars, so does the lady of light shine among all virgins.[19]

Amid the starry brightness of all the flowers,[20] lilies excel in whiteness, roses in redness,[21] nor is any other crown more pleasing to the snow-white mother of Jesus.[22]

* * * * *

14 Cf *Paean Virgini Matri* LB V 1228E (27 above): 'martyrum laurea.'
15 Cf *Analecta hymnica medii aevi* ed Guido M. Dreves, Clemens Blume, and Henry M. Bannister 55 vols (Leipzig 1886–1922; repr New York 1961) 48 230.1: 'Virgo carnem, / martyr hostem superat' ('A virgin overcomes the flesh, a martyr the enemy'); *Virginis et martyris comparatio* 175–6 below.
16 Cf *Carmina* 110:13–28 ASD I-7 357–8 / CWE 85 276–9.
17 For the image see Ecclus 24:13 (Vulg 24:17), traditionally interpreted to refer to Mary; Salzer 151–3; *Marienlexikon* VI 780–1; *Paean Virgini Matri* 31 above.
18 A favourite adjective; see eg Prudentius *Cathemerinon* 11.53; *Analecta hymnica* (n15 above) 53 103.12, 54 224.1, 54 267.1; *Paean Virgini Matri* 24 above.
19 Mary is traditionally praised as the morning star, *stella matutina* or *lucifer*, who heralds the sun and the new day of salvation. See Salzer 23–4, 408:7–26; *Marienlexikon* IV 517.
20 Venantius Fortunatus *Carmina* 3.9.13; cf *Carmina* 2:207 ASD I-7 94 / CWE 85 22–3.
21 Cf Venantius Fortunatus *Carmina spuria* 1.233, of Mary: 'rubore rosas, candore ... lilia vincens'; *Analecta hymnica* (n15 above) 30 58 *Ad tertiam* 9: 'O rosa cum lilio, / Tibi candor cum rubore, / Tibi decus cum decore'; *Paean Virgini Matri* 30 above. The lily and the rose, as the two most beautiful and fragrant of flowers, are traditional symbols of the Virgin; See Salzer 162–70 and 183–92; *Marienlexikon* IV 121–2, V 548–9. In *Virginis et martyris comparatio* 161–3, 169 below the lily is associated with virgins and the rose with martyrs. This is relevant here because Mary was sometimes considered both a virgin and a martyr. See Honorius Augustodunensis *Sigillum b. Mariae* PL 172 517D: 'Per rosas martyres, per lilia intelligimus virgines ... Beata autem Dei Genitrix virgo et martyr fuit'; Salzer 191–2. The idea is based on Luke 2:35, where Simeon prophesies that a sword will pierce through Mary's soul also (at the crucifixion).
22 Mary's purity was commonly likened to snow; see Salzer 335–6; *Carmina* 110:358 ASD I-7 375 / CWE 85 296–7; *Paean Virgini Matri* 27 and 33 above. Cf Otto 1231.

Among the fragrant trees[23] there is none more pleasing than the laurel; it brings peace,[24] puts an end to savage wars, wards off the lightning that causes fire,[25] has health-giving berries,[26] shines a perennial green.

Be favourable, O Virgin, to those who celebrate your praise in pious melodies. Turn aside the anger of God that he may not strike the guilty with the lightning that burns. Be a laurel and rejoice always in being called the Virgin of Loreto,

Even though far and wide in the confines of the vast world,[27] many an altar has the smoke of sacrifice.[28] Amen.

Gospel[29]

A marriage was taking place at Cana in Galilee, and the mother of Jesus was there. Jesus also and his disciples were invited to the marriage. And when the wine had run out, the mother of Jesus said to him, 'They have no wine.' Jesus said to her: 'Woman, what part have you with me in this?[30] My

* * * * *

23 Cf the first line of the Introit above; *Carmina* 110:236 ASD I-7 368 / CWE 85 290–1; *Paean Virgini Matri* 31 above; Salzer 157–61 and 282:1–2.

24 Cf Pliny *Naturalis historia* 15.133. Mary is traditionally both peace itself and the bringer of peace; see Salzer 563.

25 The laurel was believed to be immune from lightning. People who were afraid of being hit by lightning wore a laurel wreath to protect themselves. See Pliny *Naturalis historia* 2.146 and 15.134–5. Mary, as mother of the Prince of Peace, can ward off God's avenging lightning bolts; cf *Carmina* 110:310–12 ASD I-7 373 / CWE 85 294–5, and 'the lightning that burns' below.

26 The berries of the laurel tree yield a fragrant oil believed to have medicinal value; see Pliny *Naturalis historia* 23.86.

27 Cf Ps 19:4 (Vulg 18:5); Rom 10:18.

28 Cf the conclusion of Antoine de Vergy's letter granting permission for the use of Erasmus' liturgy within the archdiocese of Besançon, 108 below. Erasmus here also refers to the incense burned at mass. Cf also *Paean Virgini Matri* 21 and 38 above.

29 John 2:1–11. Erasmus quotes his own translation (cf LB VI 348D–350A), not the Vulgate.

30 The Vulgate has 'Quid mihi et tibi est?' Its meaning has been much discussed. The same idiom is found a dozen times in the Bible: Judg 11:12; 2 Sam 16:10, 19:22; 1 Kings 17:18; 2 Kings 3:13; 2 Chron 35:21; Matt 8:29; Mark 1:24, 5:7; Luke 4:34, 8:28; John 2:4. These instances refer to uncalled-for interference, unprovoked, allegedly unprovoked, or imaginary attacks. Erasmus' explanation is that Christ knew that he would perform his first miracle at the wedding

hour has not yet come.' His mother said to the attendants, 'Whatever he shall say to you, do it.' Now there were six stone jars arranged according to the Jewish rite of purification, each holding two or three measures.[31] Jesus said to them, 'Fill the jars with water.' And they filled them to the brim. And he said to them, 'Pour it now and bring it to the master of the feast.' And they brought it. When the master of the feast tasted the water turned to wine and did not know where it had come from (but the attendants, who had drawn the water, knew), he called the bridegroom and said to him, 'Everyone sets forth good wine at first and, when the guests have drunk deep, that which is inferior; you have kept the good wine until now.'

Homily

Dearly beloved brothers and sisters in Christ:

I am scarcely able to do justice in words to the extent of the joy that flows over me when I see you come together in such crowds and with so much enthusiasm for a solemn commemoration of the Virgin Mother. This love for the Mother is an act of piety towards the Son. There is, indeed, a custom handed down from days of old that some more elaborate fare be served on a feast day. Would that I, who am your father and pastor, could draw forth from the exceedingly rich storehouse of sacred writings food for you, my children and sheep in the Lord, food which does not pass away but nourishes and invigorates souls unto eternal life.[32] Would that I could draw the wine of the Spirit, which would gladden your hearts with sober intoxication,[33] so that amid the evils of this world you would sing and chant in spiritual hymns to the Lord,[34] who, while glorious in all the saints, yet manifested in a special way the riches of his glory in his mother.

Thus in prayer said in common let us implore the Spirit, who, overshadowing Mary, consecrated her virgin breast as a temple for the Divine

* * * * *

feast and did not wish any mortal to have any part in it. It was to come from the will of his Father alone; cf Paraphrase on John CWE 46 40. He states that the correct Latin translation of the Greek is 'Quid mihi tecum?' (LB VI 349 n2). The Vulgate version, he says, is grecizing ('Graece reddidit').
31 The Attic measure (metreta) was about eight and a half gallons. The total then would be between 102 and 153 gallons.
32 Cf John 6:27, 55–8.
33 Cf Acts 2:13, 15; 103 and 105 below; *Paean Virgini Matri* 31 above; see also Phillips 35, 39; and DS VII-2 2312–37 under 'Ivresse spirituelle.'
34 Eph 5:19

Triad[35] and made her immaculate womb a workshop for a wondrous birth,[36] which brought forth for all of us Jesus Christ, the saviour of the whole world, whose coming had been awaited by all the ages.

First of all, your love is not unaware of this, that the cult of the most holy Virgin consists principally in four things – praise, honour, invocation, and imitation. The final one is so superior that the others without it would be unfruitful, and this one also embraces the others in itself. For the one who, to the best of his power, imitates Mary's continence, Mary's chastity, Mary's modesty, has praised her satisfactorily. However, those who with perverted judgment endlessly sing Mary's praises and exaggerate them, who honour her with candles, votive offerings, sanctuaries, and shrines, who solicit her aid with long and ostentatious prayers, not giving even a thought to imitating her whom they extol,[37] run the risk of hearing from the Mother what the Jewish worshipper heard from the Father in the prophet's words: 'This people honours me with their lips, but their hearts are far from me.'[38] Again, there is what is heard from the Son in the Gospel: 'Not everyone who says to me, "Lord, Lord," will enter the kingdom of heaven, but the one who does the will of my Father in heaven.'[39]

And so let it be your first concern, my very dear friends, to imitate as far as possible in your life and practices the virtues of Mary, lest she too say of us: 'This people honours me with songs, pipes, and flutes, but their hearts are in these things which I, with Jesus, my son, ever hate, in riches, pleasures, impious games, filthy stories, arrogance and pride. They give me first place in shrines and on altars, but they grant me no place in their heart. They sing in my honour, "Queen of heaven," "Mistress of the angels," "Our life, our sweetness, and our hope."[40] On

* * * * *

35 See Salzer 36–8; *Marienlexikon* VI 367–9.

36 Cf 101 below; *Paean Virgini Matri* 21 above.

37 Cf *Moria* ASD IV-3 134:170–3 / CWE 27 120: 'Think of the many who set up a candle to the Virgin ... and of the few who care about emulating her chastity of life, her modesty, and her love of heavenly things.'

38 Isa 29:13; Matt 15:8; Mark 7:6

39 Matt 7:21; cf Luke 6:46.

40 These phrases are taken from three of the four Marian anthems sung at the conclusion of the daily office at different seasons of the year. 'Queen of heaven' (*Regina coeli*) is the opening of the anthem sung during Paschaltide, 'Mistress of the angels' (*domina angelorum*) is taken from the anthem *Ave, regina coelorum* sung from 2 February to Wednesday of Holy Week, and 'Our life, our sweetness, and our hope' (*vita, dulcedo, et spes nostra*) from the *Salve, regina* sung from Pentecost to Advent.

every side I am saluted with the most honorific titles, but not everyone who says to me, "Lady, Lady," will enter the kingdom of my son, but those who, following his example, obey the commands of God and, striving zealously to copy my example, seek the grace of the Son by imitating the Mother, in whom whatever is worthy of imitation is the gift of the Son.' Let us not, then, believe that the most holy Virgin takes delight in these fasts with which some honour her on certain days, fasting for one purpose only – that the next day they may drink more abundantly; nor that she is won over by songs chanted by certain people, who are completely corrupted by lust and luxury; nor that she is captivated by the votive offerings of those who are polluted on every side by prostitutes and adulteries. It is not that the most clement Virgin would turn away sinners, but those who are already ashamed of and repent this depravity cease to be sinners. Whatever is displeasing to the Son cannot please the Mother.

I know that in some places there is on view a shrine of Mary[41] filled with silks, silver, gold, and gems, so that those who adore the Virgin there seem to be adoring mammon. How much more pleasing would it be to Mary if these riches were disbursed and expended in the relief of the members of Christ,[42] in whom the Mother is in a certain manner either cast down or revived together with the Son. If a statue of the Virgin is decided on, let it be fashioned as of one who has herself pleased God and whom it is an act of piety for us to imitate; let chastity, modesty, and restraint be reflected in her countenance, in the posture of her entire body, even in her dress.

I shall now explain in a few words what it is particularly fitting to imitate in Mary, when I have first reminded you, my beloved ones, that the form and rule of holiness cannot be sought more perfectly or more securely from anyone other than her son,[43] even though it is certain that there is nothing in the Mother that is at variance with the teaching of the Son. Pay strict attention here, boys and girls, wives and widows, grown men, older

* * * * *

41 Cf Mary's mock complaint that before Luther spread his ideas she 'was clothed in gold and jewels . . . I had golden and jewelled offerings made to me,' in the colloquy *Peregrinatio religionis ergo* ('A Pilgrimage for Religion's Sake') ASD I-3 473:111–13 / CWE 40 625:37–9. See also *Exomologesis* LB V 159E.

42 For this idea see also *Peregrinatio religionis ergo* CWE 40 641:1–642:8. It is one of Erasmus' most characteristic themes.

43 On the Christocentric nature of Erasmus' faith see the introduction to Halkin's edition of the *LiturgiaVirginis Matris* ASD V-1 89–91; also Halkin 'Mariologie' especially 49–54, and his *Erasmus: A Critical Biography* trans John Tonkin (Oxford 1993) 221–30.

men and women, for there will be something for all of you to imitate in Mary. These are the targets: the simplicity of a virgin united with the highest wisdom, the greatest bliss united with the greatest modesty, the highest degree of chastity in wedlock, a mother's diligence in her duty, invincible strength of mind in a member of the weaker sex. What virginal purity was in that heart is clear even from this: she was disturbed at the entrance of an angel, as Luke reports.[44] Without doubt she understood what an enormous treasure chastity was, but, as opposed to this, because it is subject to covert attacks, how many have lost it before they could realize how great a good they possessed! How far removed from Mary's example are the virgins who, of their own accord, rush forth to games and conversations with young men who are very unlike the angel, who by nods, pleasantries, blandishments, little presents, and love letters provoke the circumstances that lead to the ruin of virginity.

Mary had a spouse with whom she lived under the same roof, and yet she is disturbed at the entry of an unknown figure, fearing all things, even what was safe. By marrying a spouse, she yielded to the custom of the Jewish race, she yielded to the authority of her parents, and yet virginity was her wish. She shows this when she says, 'I know not man.'[45] Here the verb in the present tense indicates the intention of her mind. Fear of disgrace prevents many women from lewdness. While Mary in her love for virginity ignored the disgrace of sterility, she merited both, namely, that she should as a virgin beget God. Those women who have taken an actual vow of virginity and yet lead lives of shameless depravity, those women who are already elderly and worn out but still itch with an untimely lust, by what effrontery do they proclaim that they are worshippers of this Virgin? Now what is disgraceful in the female sex is much more disgraceful in the male. Let those women who wish to be regarded as virgins be complete virgins after Mary's example. For some of them have undefiled bodies, but their appearance, not free from the use of cosmetics, is far from chaste: the eyes are wanton, the speech is lascivious, the gait is mincing. If the mind is really chaste, let its integrity shine forth even in outward appearances. Someone will say, 'What disgrace is it if a virgin seek to gain a spouse?' If she chases after any spouse, she is not a virgin. If she is seeking a good man, no enticement is more effective with good men than modesty, silence, simple cleanliness in

* * * * *

44 Luke 1:29; for Erasmus' interpretation of 'disturbed' and the ensuing debate cf LB VI 224B–F n37, LB IX 1084E.
45 Luke 1:34

appearance.[46] There is harlotry in marriage, too, to the extent that chastity is most pleasing to God. Let married people imitate the marriage of Joseph and Mary, at least in so far as the weakness of the flesh allows.[47] Those who shamelessly vie with their wives in lust, who play with them and converse with them with more lewdness than they are wont to do with prostitutes, are not husbands, nor do they treat their wives as wives. In a chaste marriage even the act of lovemaking should be modest. At present the perversity of man has discovered how adultery may also be committed with his wife. This was the proof of Mary's innocence, that since she loved perpetual virginity in a singular fashion, the maiden was still living in innocence of heart with her young spouse.

Now listen to an account of the prudence of this young virgin. (For the bridegroom rejects foolish virgins.)[48] Mary does not immediately return the angel's salute, she does not leap up, she remains calm and considers what sort of greeting this might be.[49] Again, on the promise of a birth so distinguished, she does not distrust the one who promises or exult with immoderate joy, but modestly asks the angel how that which was being promised to her, with her unimpaired treasure of virginity, could come to pass.[50] She saw the gathering of the shepherds[51] and the veneration of the Magi,[52] she heard the prophecies of Anna and Simeon,[53] and yet she gossips about none of these things with the levity characteristic of women but in silence gathers them together and preserves them in her heart.[54] It is a most definite proof of prudence, even in men, to be able to maintain silence about a happiness so great. What is the source of so much prudence in a young virgin, in a tender maid with no experience of the world? Late and pitiable is the prudence that is acquired from long experience of misfortunes.[55] The Holy Spirit fills

* * * * *

46 Erasmus here recalls a famous phrase from Horace *Odes* 1.5.5: 'simplex munditiis.'

47 For Erasmus' views on chastity within marriage see especially *Institutio christiani matrimonii* 386–94 below, and on marriage in general, J.-C. Margolin in ASD I-5 367–81.

48 Cf Matt 25:12.

49 Luke 1:29

50 Luke 1:34

51 Luke 2:8–18

52 Matt 2:1–11

53 Luke 2:25–38

54 Luke 2:19

55 Cf *Adagia* I i 31: *Malo accepto stultus sapit*, 'Trouble experienced makes a fool wise.'

the heart even of girls and boys with the prudence of an old man.[56] Let each one purge his heart of vices so that this Spirit, the bestower of wisdom, may deign to enter there.

Really what need is there to speak of the happiness of Mary? Who was ever saluted in more honourable terms by an angel? To whom were more splendid promises made? He who is the creator of heaven and earth sends an embassy to the Virgin; Gabriel acts the part of marriage-promoter,[57] offspring is promised such as was promised to no other: 'He will be great, and will be called the Son of the Most High, and the Lord will give him the throne of his Father; and he will reign over the house of Jacob for ever, and of his kingdom there will be no end.'[58] What could be more sublime than these promises? When a guarantee of these things had now been given by the angel, surely a happiness so great lessened the young virgin's modesty? By no means; it rather increased it: 'Behold,' she says, 'the handmaiden of the Lord.'[59] From something so great, she claims no glory for herself; she simply proclaims herself a handmaiden, obedient and ready to follow wherever the will of the Lord may call. Already pregnant with her heavenly offspring, she does not refuse to visit, for courtesy's sake, her kinswoman, an aged woman and also pregnant.[60] She hears Elizabeth say, 'Why is this granted to me, that the mother of my Lord should come to me?'[61] She, however, in keeping with her character, sings, 'He has shown regard for the humility of his handmaiden.'[62] She proclaims her happiness, not her dignity; she does not say, 'because I deserved it,' but 'because he who is powerful has done great things for me.'[63] Nor does she say, 'and holy is my name,' but 'holy is his name.'[64]

Although she realized that she had such a progeny in her womb, she did not disdain her husband. Whatever service a compliant wife performs

* * * * *

56 Cf Ernst Robert Curtius *European Literature and the Latin Middle Ages* trans Willard R. Trask (London and Henley 1953; repr 1979) 98–105.
57 Erasmus here uses the term *pronubus*. Cf *Paean Virgini Matri* LB V 1232C (33 above). At *Carmina* 110:238 ASD I-7 369 / CWE 85 290, 86 657, and *Institutio christiani matrimonii* LB V 622D (230 below) he describes Gabriel as *paranymphus*.
58 Luke 1:32–3. Erasmus omits 'David' after 'Father.'
59 Luke 1:38
60 Cf Luke 1:36, 39.
61 Luke 1:43
62 Luke 1:48
63 Luke 1:49. On the debate regarding Mary's merits and God's grace cf LB VI 225F–227B n53 and LB IX 498D, 597E–600F, 913B–914E.
64 Ibidem

for her spouse, this she performed in much richer abundance for Joseph. She sets out with him to the census which Caesar had decreed.[65] With him she circumcises the child,[66] with him she goes through the entire rite of purification,[67] she follows him to Egypt.[68] The angel had appeared to Joseph not Mary, so that authority might rest with the man; she clings to him on her return journey from Egypt;[69] she does not disdain to be commonly spoken of as a carpenter's wife; she is not ashamed of lowly brothers and sisters;[70] she does not resent her son being regarded as the son of Joseph, whom she herself also used to call the father of Jesus.[71] There never was another wife who obeyed her husband with greater reverence than the Mother of God. Give heed, women who worship the Virgin. What here will be the comments of newly wed wives, who, somewhat emboldened by their beauty and youth, spurn their spouses? What will married women say who continually cast their dowry in their husbands' teeth, sometimes even drive them out of the house, just as if they were women of superior status, and not wives? What will those say who upset the whole house with quarrels and contentions? Mary does her Joseph's will most scrupulously and respects him, and she never resists her husband or leads the way for him. Are you ashamed to obey your husbands, without whom you are sterile and lacking in honour, and to whom the authority of the Lord and of the apostle Paul has made you subject?[72]

There is no doubt but that she will have cared for her son with as much assiduity as she showed obedience to her husband. She brings him to the temple each year to show him from his tender years that piety must be absorbed. With what solicitude does she seek him when he is missing? She does not rest until she finds him.[73] Why did Mary fear for her son? Was it because she had seen some sign of levity in him? By no means. She was warning you, mothers, that no care that can be shown is too great for one of tender years. That stage of life is frail and eager to pursue every vice. Those who take no care of their children worship Mary in an impious fashion,

* * * * *

65 Luke 2:1–2
66 Luke 2:21. It is not definitely stated that Mary was present at the circumcision of Jesus.
67 Luke 2:22–39
68 Matt 2:13–14
69 Cf Matt 2:21.
70 Cf Matt 13:54–5; Mark 6:3; Luke 4:23.
71 Luke 2:48
72 Cf Eph 5:22–4; Col 3:18.
73 Luke 2:41–8

acting as though it is enough to have given them birth. Indeed, some by impious devices get rid of the irksomeness of child-bearing and the labour of
nursing. And the actions of those who by bad example corrupt one weak in
years, who teach a lisping infant bad moral qualities, are no less sinful. Mary
was solicitous about her son, Jesus, and do you expose and betray your son
and daughter to every type of lewd behaviour? Without doubt this is why
many women regret their fertility, because they bring up well-born children to be ill-breds, while the proper function of parents is rather the training than the begetting of children. Who, however, can give a good training
if they spend their time away from home or live disgracefully at home, so
that by association with their parents children become acquainted with foul
language, wantonness, drunkenness, brawls, gambling, vanity, detraction?[74]
Indeed, a vast field is laid open to us, should we wish to compare the extraordinary virtues of the most holy Virgin with our life. We shall, however,
gain the greatest benefit if we give diligent attention to amending, with her
as our exemplar, our morals that have grown thoroughly corrupt.

It remains for us to touch to some extent on the fortitude of the Virgin. Not to grow haughty in prosperity and not to break down in adversity are both signs of greatness of soul. Nowhere do we read that, when the
adorable name of Jesus was becoming famous by so many miracles, the most
holy Virgin laid claim to any part of the praise; rather we read that she was
hardly present at any miracle except when at the marriage feast he turned
water into wine.[75] She heard all his words and silently stored them in her
heart,[76] ever manifesting the character of a handmaiden to which she had
laid claim.[77] She bore it with like constancy when her one and only beloved
son was frequently in danger from the secret plots of the Pharisees,[78] and
finally when he was captured, bound, scourged, condemned, led away. The
other women wept and were reproved by the Lord.[79] What did a mother's
heart feel here? She was not without feeling. She suffered through the sufferings of her son, but she restrained her human feeling by the strength of
her spirit, she repressed her sobs, she held back the tears that were bursting
forth, and when the other disciples had melted away in fear,[80] she alone to-

* * * * *

74 For similar sentiments cf *De pueris instituendis* CWE 26 308–9.
75 John 2:3–9
76 Cf Luke 2:19, 51.
77 Cf Luke 1:38.
78 Cf Luke 22:2; John 11:47–52.
79 Luke 23:27–31
80 Matt 26:56; Mark 14:50–2

gether with John kept her place beside the cross of her son.[81] The pictures are insulting which represent her in a state of collapse, benumbed by a faint and rendered senseless by grief.[82] She did not wail, she did not tear her hair, she did not beat her breast, she did not proclaim aloud her unhappiness. Her consolation from the redemption of the human race was greater than her sorrow at the death of her son. Here too she offered herself as a handmaiden to him who decided to restore the race of mortals in this way. She thought that she had been fortunate in giving birth since she had borne the author of salvation for the world; she set the happiness of the many above her private grief. Where now are the women who, on account of the loss of money or even a lesser misfortune, miscarry through grief? Where are the men who because of the death of a little daughter throw everything into confusion by their senseless complaints and wailings? It is on record that Mary beheld the most bitter death of her son;[83] there is no record that she wept or complained. Other women kept weeping, and in their longing for the Lord who had been taken away and whom they did not yet love in a spiritual manner, they were practically deranged;[84] Mary alone with unshaken heart is silent, awaiting the will of the Most High. Perhaps you suppose that it is a lowly and feeble thing to be the servant or handmaiden of the Lord: nothing is more invincible. Those who have once and for all handed themselves over to the direction of the Lord direct their praise nowhere else if some good fortune comes their way, hope for protection from no other source if misfortunes burden them, and cannot be shaken by any tricks or terrors of Satan.

Perhaps an opportunity will be given us at another time to discuss these things at greater length; but now today's feast demands that we extract from the Gospel which was read to you something bearing on the glory of the Son and Mother and on our own salvation. Those who have already reached the married state and those who are eager to attain it rejoice to hear that this honour was shown to wedlock: that Christ, when invited

* * * * *

81 John 19:25: 'There stood by the cross of Jesus his mother and his mother's sister, Mary of Cleophas, and Mary Magdalene.'
82 On representations of the grief of the Virgin during the crucifixion see Gertrud Schiller *Iconography of Christian Art* trans Janet Seligman 2 vols (London 1971–2) II 174–81; ASD V-1 105:242–56n.
83 John 19:25–7
84 Cf Luke 23:27. Luke states that 'a great multitude of the people and of women' followed Jesus on his way to Calvary. He says that the women 'plangebant et lamentabantur eum' ('beat their breasts and wept for him'). Erasmus certainly adds details and assigns reasons for which there is no warrant in Scripture.

to a marriage feast with his disciples and his mother, did not refuse to go and did not disdain to honour it with an extraordinary miracle.[85] Thus the Lord, a virgin and the son of a virgin, once and for all honoured marriage to prevent us from dishonouring it by our foul conduct. Indeed, even today, wherever husband and wife cling together in chaste and faithful wedlock, with minds in harmony and with a like zeal for piety, the Lord Jesus does not disdain to be present with his mother.[86] She does not regard it as a burden to speak to the Son on behalf of such people if there should be anything lacking that has a bearing on the happiness of the marriage, even if the resources of the household are slender and the family large. The wine that Jesus lavishly bestows sweetens all things, however disagreeable and bitter they may otherwise be. This, too, should be noticed, that just as it shows respect for sons to obey a mother's wish, so too it befits the authority of parents to cede to the fulfilment of the gospel: here, indeed, nothing is to be kept in view other than what contributes to the glory of God and the salvation of the people. The fact that the mother says, 'They have no wine,'[87] is a mark of a certain benign solicitude; the fact that she yields to the authority of the Son when he answers in words that seem somewhat stern – 'Woman, what part have you with me in this?'[88] – is a sign of wise restraint. On the other hand, the fact that she secretly says to the attendants, 'Do whatever he tells you,'[89] is a sign of marvellous reliance on the Son.

Today parents abuse their authority over their children when they force them to become involved in marriage against their will, or to enter an institution for priests or monks,[90] or when they withdraw them from the teaching of the law of the gospel, or when a ruler urges his son to undertake a war that is destructive to the state. The ruler's son, since he acts in a public capacity, will, with dutifulness unimpaired, answer his father: 'In this instance you will not be my father. Concern for the welfare of the state, which I have undertaken, will carry more weight with me than the private authority of a father.' Someone has a wife and children at home, and his mother orders him to set out for Compostella[91] because she has herself made such

* * * * *

85 The marriage feast at Cana, John 2:1–11
86 Here and in what follows, Erasmus has the marriage feast at Cana in mind.
87 John 2:3
88 John 2:4
89 John 2:5
90 This accusation was brought by Erasmus against his own guardians: cf Ep 447:82–5; *Compendium vitae* CWE 4 405:56–7.
91 For other references to the famous pilgrimage-centre in north-western Spain, traditionally believed to be the burial-place of St James the apostle, and for

a vow. Let him say to the mother, 'You will be a mother in other matters;[92] here we must listen to God, who orders that I take care of those who are my own, for whose sake it is an act of piety to leave even a parent.'[93]

Moreover, these statements were made on a lower level of meaning. But now that the Lord has changed the taste[94] of the insipid Law into choice wine,[95] it is reasonable that we too elicit from them some more profound meaning. There was nothing outstanding in the fact that a maiden was being united in marriage with a man. It is the greatest mystery and something to be adored even by the angelic spirits themselves that the Spirit, that is, the Son of God, is joined with human flesh, the divine nature with the human. The Son of God embraced our flesh, and by a marvellous bond it came to pass that the same being was God and man. There were present in the same Lord Jesus bridegroom and bride; there was present at the feast that blessed womb in which that ineffable union had been celebrated, in which that threefold giant, destined to vanquish the entire tyranny of Satan, had been formed in the workshop, so to speak, of the Holy Spirit.[96]

Marriage bespeaks yet another marvel. The Son of God loved the church, which he purified with his own blood so that he might have a spouse worthy of himself, without spot or wrinkle.[97] Through love of her a wonderful suitor descended from heaven, came into a virgin's womb, and, clad in the robe of our flesh,[98] came forth from there, like a bridegroom

* * * * *

Erasmus' misgivings about pilgrimages, see *Moria* ASD IV-3 136:229–138:231 / CWE 27 122; the colloquies *De votis temere susceptis* ('Rash Vows') ASD I-3 148:761–149:776 / CWE 39 38:24–39; *Naufragium* ('The Shipwreck') ASD I-3 328:92–4 / CWE 39 355:35–7; *Exorcismus, sive Spectrum* ('Exorcism, *or* The Spectre') ASD I-3 422:194 / CWE 39 540:3; and *Peregrinatio religionis ergo* ASD I-3 470:14 / CWE 40 623:9; also *De utilitate Colloquiorum* ('The Usefulness of the Colloquies') ASD I-3 747:215–16 / CWE 40 1104:4–5. Cf also *Supputatio* LB IX 647A: 'Do they not act impiously who, neglecting parents, wife, and children dependent on the father for sustenance, hurry to Compostella?'

92 Echoing Paraphrase on John 2 CWE 46 39; cf *Supputatio* LB IX 625E–629E, especially 626C.

93 Cf Luke 18:29.

94 In the original edition of the homily (1525), Erasmus used the word *sensum*; in the 1529 reprint he changed the text to *aquam*, making the metaphor more straightforward.

95 Cf 103 below; Paraphrase on John 2 CWE 46 40; Phillips 35.

96 Cf 92 above; *Paean Virgini Matri* 21, 25 and 28 above; *Institutio christiani matrimonii* 231 below.

97 Cf Eph 5:25–7.

98 Cf *Paean Virgini Matri* 27 above; *Carmina* 110:323 ASD I-7 373 / CWE 85 294–5.

from his chamber.[99] This without doubt was that gate which Ezekiel saw facing towards the east[100] from which the light, Jesus Christ, arose for those sitting in darkness and the shadow of death.[101] The gate remained closed awaiting the entrance of the prince, the Son of God, and, without damage to the seal of chastity, it brought him forth for us in a human body, as if clothed in a nuptial robe. When he came forth from this chamber, then, he took as his betrothed the new church. He took it without a dowry, he took it when it was a captive, he took it when it was contaminated, but he cleansed it from its stains by the washing of his most precious blood;[102] he ransomed it from captivity by his precious death; when it was destitute, he enriched it with an abundance of gifts.

Dearly beloved, the soul of each one of us is the spouse of Christ. We have been ransomed at a very great price;[103] let us not of our own accord return to the bondage of Satan. We have been cleansed gratuitously; let us not like pigs return to the mire of vice.[104] We have once drunk the teaching of the gospel and imbibed the most sweet spirit of Jesus; let us not, ungrateful for such great generosity, turn back to the deceitful devil, but persevering in the faith of our baptism, by which we have renounced Satan and all his pomps, let us always remember that we are pledged to one man, so that we may present a chaste virgin to Christ, the spouse, and not allow our inclinations to be misled by the cunning of the serpent away from the simplicity which is in Christ Jesus.[105] Rightly is Christ the jealous lover,[106] who has at so high a price joined his spouse to himself. Let us take care that we always share in spiritual nuptials of this kind: through a faith that is not feigned and charity that is sincere[107] let us remain in the embrace of our spouse. Let us continue to be the branches in the vine,[108] let us continue to be the members in the body,[109] so that through the Spirit that joins all things together[110] we may be one with him just as he is one with the Father.[111]

* * * * *

99 Ps 19:5 (Vulg 18:6)
100 Ezek 44:1; cf n4 above.
101 Ps 107 (Vulg 106):10, 14; Isa 9:1, 42:7; Luke 1:79
102 Cf Heb 9:13–14; 1 Pet 1:19.
103 Cf 1 Cor 6:20, 7:23.
104 Cf 2 Pet 2:22.
105 Cf 2 Cor 11:2–3.
106 Cf *Virginis et martyris comparatio* 179 below.
107 Cf 1 Tim 1:5.
108 John 15:5
109 1 Cor 6:15, 12:27; Eph 5:30; Rom 12:5
110 Cf 1 Cor 12:11.
111 John 10:30, 17:11, 21, 22

Let the synagogue, which has lost its spouse, drink its cold and taste-less water.[112] Everyone drinks water who relies for salvation on ceremonies, externals, human powers.[113] Let us, reclining at the table of our spouse, be intoxicated with the spiritual wine of instruction which the spouse pours forth for us in abundance. Let us be nourished by his most sacred body; by drinking his most sacred blood let us ever regain our youthful vigour ac-cording to the interior man, even if this exterior man is collapsing.[114] Those who are not yet capable of taking solid food must be nourished by milk, until they have progressed so far that they are capable of taking this drink and this food.[115] Paul says, 'It is not the spiritual that is first, but the phys-ical.'[116] The Jews had a physical law to which that unfortunate people still hold fast; for us, who have imbibed the Spirit of Christ and have become spiritual, it would be disgraceful to suck milk forever like infants,[117] but more disgraceful to return to the water of the Jews after tasting the wine of heavenly doctrine. It is characteristic of others to slip down from the higher to the lower. Christ changed the order: he set forth the best wine in the last place;[118] in this order we ever progress from the weaker to the stronger.[119]

Let us, then, pray to the Lord that he grant the richest fertility to his spouse, that is, that the seed of the gospel be spread as widely as possi-ble and that there be born daily living offspring to fill the house of God. We see that because of our vices the church becomes ever smaller, and that even among those who profess the name of the church there are so few that the spouse would acknowledge. Some of us blame one party, others blame another; the common man blames the rulers, the people blame the priests. Why do we not work in harmony for this result: that each per-son set his own life right rather than inveigh against the life of someone else?[120] Thus the spouse of Christ will flourish, thus the marriage feast will

* * * * *

112 Cf 101 above, with n95.
113 Echoing Paraphrase on Matt 1 LB VII 1E, which was cited as objectionable by the syndic of the Paris faculty of theology, Noël Béda (cf Erasmus' defence at LB IX 565E–568E). Erasmus' opposition to the superstitious observance of ceremonies was frequently criticized by conservative theologians, but Béda's investigation was very much on his mind at this time (cf Ep 1571 to Béda, which was written a few days before the dedicatory letter for the *Liturgia Virginis Matris*).
114 Cf 2 Cor 4:16; Eph 3:16.
115 Cf 1 Cor 3:1–2; Heb 5:12–13; 1 Pet 2:2; *Precationes* 122 below.
116 1 Cor 15:46
117 1 Cor 3:2; 1 Pet 2:2
118 John 2:10
119 Cf Heb 5:12–14.
120 Cf *Epistola consolatoria* 196 below.

grow cheerful. Paul cries out, 'Husbands, love your wives, just as Christ loved the Church.'[121] Let no man hate his own flesh, but let him nourish it and cherish it,[122] paying honour to the weaker vessel,[123] just as Christ supported his spouse and sustains her, forgiving her sins, ever drawing her to better things. Let wives, in turn, in keeping with the teaching of the Apostle, be subject to their husbands, as is fitting in the Lord,[124] and let there be between husband and wife such proportion of authority and obedience that the unbelieving husband is made holy by the believing wife and the unbelieving wife is made holy by the believing husband.[125] Thus I would wish that all would frequently come together to praise the Virgin, in the hope that, by the gift of the Son and the example of the Mother, each one may return to his home a better person, get rid of some vices, and add something to his virtues. In such devotion Mary takes delight, in such the Son rejoices. To him with the Father and the Spirit be eternal glory. Amen.

Offertory

Who is this that comes forth like the dawn, fair as the moon, bright as the sun, terrible as an army with banners?[126]

Secret[127]

Jesus, source of every good: at the prompting of the Virgin Mother you brought gladness to the guests by changing water into wine;[128] grant to your servants that, aided by the prayers of the same person,[129] we may be

* * * * *

121 Eph 5:25
122 Cf Eph 5:29.
123 Cf 1 Pet 3:7.
124 Cf Eph 5:22; Col 3:18.
125 Cf 1 Cor 7:14. However, in that passage Paul is dealing with a marriage where one party is a Christian and the other a pagan.
126 Song of Sol 6:10 (Vulg 6:9)
127 The term 'Secret' (*Secreta*) is an abbreviation for *Oratio super secreta*, 'Prayer over the offerings (ie bread and wine) set aside for consecration.' Erasmus included this prayer among the *Eiaculationes* in the collection of prayers that he published in 1535, the *Precationes aliquot novae* (149 below).
128 Cf John 2:3–10.
129 This phrase (*eiusdem suffragiis adiuti*) was omitted when the prayer was reprinted among the *Precationes aliquot novae*; see n127 above.

made healthfully drunk by the new wine of your Spirit.[130] Who live and reign for endless ages.

Communion

Blessed be the womb of the Virgin Mary, which bore you, Jesus, according to the flesh, and blessed be the breasts that suckled you,[131] and, indeed, blessed be all those who receive in a spiritual manner the heavenly seed of divine teaching and hold fast to it until it begets eternal life in them.

Collect (Postcommunion)

God, whose glory fills heaven and earth,[132] as you manifest it where you will and when you will for the salvation of mankind, we humbly beseech you that those who return thanks to your bounty for the favours bestowed on them through your Son's mother, who is piously worshipped at the church of Loreto, may, after spending a blameless life here, deserve to enjoy eternal happiness. Through the same Jesus Christ, our Lord.

Antoine de Vergy, by the favour of God and of the apostolic see, Archbishop of Besançon:[133] To all of Christ's faithful, greetings in the Lord. Both the love of piety, which should be in all who profess in common the religion of Christ, and especially the pastoral office which we hold, warn us that, just as we are tortured in soul whenever we notice that the zeal for piety is growing cold in the flock entrusted to us, so we should rejoice exceedingly whenever we perceive that the love of sincere piety is increasing and spreading in the souls of men. Moreover, we are more favourably disposed towards those who devote their attention to stirring up and increasing piety from the fact that we hear that at the present time certain people have come to the fore

* * * * *

130 See n33 above.
131 Cf Luke 11:27–8; see also *Modus orandi Deum* ASD V-1 172:785–6 / CWE 70 224; *Apologia adversus monachos* LB IX 1086E; Ep 1642:73–9; Allen Epp 1679:94–106, 1956:24–40.
132 Cf Isa 6:3; also the Sanctus, the hymn introducing the Eucharistic Prayer in the Roman rite of mass. See Joseph A. Jungmann *The Mass of the Roman Rite* 2 vols Eng trans (New York 1955) II 132–5; NCE XII 1047.
133 For Antoine de Vergy (1488–1541) see the introductory note, with n5. His permission would be necessary for the celebration of a mass that contained new sections.

who, led by what spirit I know not, are endeavouring to dim the glory of canonized men and women, maintaining that saints who have passed out of this life should not be invoked in the prayers of the faithful since they have no influence with God, denying that any worship is due to them since their merits are of no account.[134] We, however, following the example of Christian people handed down to us over a span of so many centuries as though from hand to hand,[135] willingly embracing, moreover, the judgment of orthodox believers approved by the long-standing consent of the ages, and above all resting on the authority of Sacred Scripture, consider it devout and pious and in keeping with the exhortation of the psalmist to praise the Lord in his saints,[136] and with the teaching of Ecclesiasticus, who says, 'Let the peoples declare the wisdom of the saints, and the assembly proclaim their praise';[137] and with our whole heart we promote the glory of the saints and especially of the Virgin Mother, from whose most holy body Jesus, the first of all saints and their exemplar, chose to come forth into the world. If it is an act of piety to give glory to the goodness, power, and wisdom of God in all created things, even indeed in gnats and spiders, how much more righteous is it to do likewise in regard to the saints, in whom he has set forth in a special manner the proofs of his glory. If we rightly venerate living people in whom the grace of God shines forth, although they still could turn aside to evil,[138] how much more reasonable is it to venerate their memory when they are already reigning with Christ their prince; and if God grants many favours here on earth when he is importuned by the prayers of people of piety, who themselves at times need someone to pray for them, how much more likely is it that the saints who have been taken away from this world have not laid aside their concern for their brothers and sisters, and that God grants many things to us on the intervention of those whom he has already deemed worthy of fellowship in his kingdom.[139] For instance, kings, if they wish to recommend anyone to the good will of the people, often prefer to grant, through the prayers of this or that friend, what they had

* * * * *

134 A reference to Luther; cf *Peregrinatio religionis ergo* ASD I-3 473:80–1 / CWE 40 624:41–625:1 '... a follower of Luther ... busily persuading people that the invocation of saints is useless.' Erasmus himself was accused of taking this stand, cf LB IX 914F–915A, 1090D. See also Allen Ep 2443:196–228.
135 Cf Livy 5.51: 'tradere per manus religiones.'
136 Ps 150:1
137 Ecclus 44:15. The scriptural text reads *ipsorum* where Erasmus has *sanctorum*. However, *ipsorum* refers to good people who have died.
138 Cf Ezek 3:20, 18:24, 33:12–13.
139 See also *Modus orandi Deum* ASD V-1 148:939–46 / CWE 70 190.

intended to grant of their own accord. God has performed so many miracles through the intercession of his saints while they were still burdened with a mortal body: is it to seem incredible if he performs miracles through the intercession of the same ones when they are already crowned with heavenly glory and honour?[140] Anyone who venerates the saints venerates Christ in the saints; anyone who praises the saints praises Christ in the saints; anyone who imitates the saints imitates Christ in the saints; anyone who invokes the saints invokes the help of Christ through the saints; anyone who adores the saints adores the gifts of God in the saints. He is in all things and above all things to be worshipped, adored, glorified, invoked, and imitated. God's own glory, which can be shared with no one, abides in himself. Yet just as we do not deny that all glory redounds to the Father and the Son and the Holy Spirit, as to its principal and inexhaustible fount, so, too, we do not approve the efforts of those who cry out against the faithful when, with feelings of piety, they worship and adore those whom God deems worthy of such great honour. Nor is the cult of the saints to be abolished if some worship them in a superstitious manner. In relation to this, just as we say that the principal veneration of the saints is from the love of God, when one imitates the virtues by which they pleased God, so too we have no doubt but that God is pleased with the feeling of piety on the part of those who venerate, even with religious honours, the same saints whom they are trying with all their strength to emulate.

Again, as we say that examples of holiness are most appropriately sought in Christ, in whom all things are most perfect, it is, then, not in keeping with fraternal charity to attack the devout sentiments of those who admire and imitate Christ in his saints,[141] just as we admire the sun reflected in a stream and fashion the image produced by a mirror. If the case were otherwise, Paul, the Apostle, would have fallen short in piety when he wrote, 'Be imitators of me as I am of Jesus Christ.'[142]

Nor can there be any doubt that, among all the ranks of saints, the principal honour is owed to the Virgin Mother. At the mere mention of her name pious souls feel consolation.[143] It is not for us to discuss how God manifests his power and glory in this place or that through his saints. It is

* * * * *

140 Cf Ps 21:5 (Vulg 20:6).
141 The Latin text should read *admirantis et imitantis* as in the 1525 and 1529 editions and LB.
142 1 Cor 11:1. The Vulgate does not have 'Jesus.'
143 Cf *Paean Virgini Matri* 34 and 36 above; Salzer 592–4; *Marienlexikon* IV 33–44, especially 38–9.

the role of our piety to adore the majesty of God in all things and to return thanks for favours, howsoever granted. Influenced by these and other reasons, we have willingly approved the mass, or liturgy, in praise of the same Virgin, honoured at Loreto and renowned for great prodigies and miracles. Desiderius Erasmus of Rotterdam, a man who has deserved well from his learning and piety, has recently composed this liturgy. Accordingly, as we have been importuned by the pious sentiments of certain people, we willingly agree that on those days on which it is customary to celebrate the memory of the most holy Virgin, this same mass or liturgy may be read or sung in honour of the forenamed Virgin in the churches of our diocese. Not that she who is worshipped at Loreto is different from the one who is honoured and invoked in the pious devotions of all people throughout the whole world,[144] wherever the name of Christ is held sacred, but because God in his goodness shows forth in different places his generosity and mercy towards us through his mother, so that he may render her memory sacred. To elicit further devotion to the cult of the most holy Virgin by spiritual rewards, and relying confidently on the mercy of the omnipotent God and on the intercession of his most holy mother and of St John, the apostle, and St Stephen, the first martyr, we mercifully remit to all who with pious intent shall on the said days celebrate this mass, forty days of the temporal punishment imposed on them.[145]

Given at our town of Gy, under the small seal of our exchequer, on the twentieth day of April in the year of the Lord one thousand five hundred and twenty four.

Antoine de Vergy

* * * * *

144 Cf the final couplet of the Sequence, 90 above; *Paean Virgini Matri* 21 and 38 above.
145 Erasmus himself frequently expressed reservations about the doctrine of indulgences. Cf the exchange in *Peregrinatio religionis ergo* CWE 40 635:29–31: 'How much do they grant?' 'Forty days.' 'Are there days even in the underworld?' Cf also *Apologia adversus monachos* LB IX 1090C: 'What significance indulgences have in the underworld is questioned even by the pope himself, I think.' See also Ep 1341A:381–5 (*Catalogus lucubrationum*); Epp 786:26, 916:132–5, 1188:42–4, 1299:63–6, 1301:140–5; Allen Epp 2205:76–84, 2285:86–114, 2853:15–17.

PRAYER TO THE LORD JESUS FOR PEACE IN THE CHURCH

Precatio ad Dominum Iesum pro pace ecclesiae

translated and annotated by
CHRISTOPHER J. McDONOUGH

As Erasmus' prefatory letter to Johann Rinck explains, the *Precatio pro pace ecclesiae* was written as a response to a letter from Rinck deploring the calamities he foresaw for Germany as a result of the religious controversies there.[1] Rinck came from a distinguished family of Cologne, where his father had been burgomaster.[2] Rinck himself had studied at the University of Cologne, then received a doctorate in both canon and civil law at Bologna in 1517. The next year he received the same degree from Cologne and joined the law faculty there, where he remained until his death in 1566. He and Erasmus became friends sometime before 1530, the year in which Erasmus addressed to him his *De bello Turcico*.

Rinck's letter evoking this prayer from Erasmus is no longer extant, so we do not know what in particular prompted it. It would not be unreasonable to surmise, however, that what especially alarmed Rinck at this moment was the breakdown of negotiations between Catholics and Lutherans at the Diet of Augsburg, 1530, and the subsequent creation of the Schmalkaldic League, a military alliance of Lutheran princes that by its very existence raised to a much heightened level the spectre of religious war in Germany. The impassioned rhetoric of Erasmus' prayer reveals how deeply Erasmus also feared the outcome of the controversies. He wrote the piece at a particularly difficult time in his own life, the very month in which he was to publish his response to the censures against him of the theological faculty of the University of Paris, which in his mind were surely another instance of the aggressive dogmatizing that was tearing the church apart.

The *Precatio pro pace ecclesiae* was first printed in 1532 in Freiburg by Johannes Faber Emmeus to accompany the *Duae homiliae divi Basilii de laudibus ieiunii*, and then reprinted the next year by Froben at the end of the first edition of the *Liber de sarcienda ecclesiae concordia*. In 1535 Froben included it in the collection *Precationes aliquot novae*, where it was retained in volume v of the Leiden edition, from which this translation was made.[3]

CJMCD

* * * * *

1 Allen Ep 2618
2 See CEBR III 161–2.
3 LB V 1215–18. The work also appears in LB IV 653–6.

DESIDERIUS ERASMUS OF ROTTERDAM TO THE ILLUSTRIOUS
DOCTOR OF LAWS JOHANN RINCK, GREETINGS.

Your letter, most honoured sir, in which in keeping with your good judgment you wisely and devoutly deplored the heaven-sent calamities threatening Germany, stirred my soul to write a prayer with which we might all
together call upon Christ, the almighty peacemaker and, as Paul calls him,
mediator,[1] who is angered, it seems, yet ever ready to be moved by our
entreaties.

You with fondness and constancy, but too late, warn about not moving Camarina.[2] The vile wickedness of some of them is worthy of such
behaviour, nor were friends lacking who by their writing encouraged it.

Freiburg. 5 March 1532

* * * * *

1 1 Tim 2:5
2 *Adagia* i i 64 CWE 31: *Movere Camarinam*, which Erasmus interprets to mean
   inviting trouble for oneself. When the citizens of Camarina in Sicily asked the
   Delphic oracle about the advisability of draining a lake north of the city, the
   oracle advised against it. Allen suggests that this is an allusion to the Paris
   theologians, with Rinck possibly urging Erasmus not to respond to them, Ep
   2618.

A PRAYER TO THE LORD JESUS
FOR PEACE IN THE CHURCH

Lord Jesus Christ, who in your omnipotence did form all creation, visible and invisible alike, in your divine wisdom you govern and arrange the universe in the most glorious order, in your ineffable goodness you preserve, protect, and animate all things, in your boundless compassion you restore what has fallen apart, shape anew what has fallen in ruins, and give new life to the dead. Now be pleased, we beseech you, at length to turn your face towards the special object of your love, your bride, the church, that serene and gracious face with which you illuminate all that is in the heavens and on the earth, and all that is above the heavens and below the earth.

Deign to turn upon her those gentle and merciful eyes with which you gazed upon Peter, the supreme shepherd of your church, who repented at once after denying you;[1] with which you looked upon the wandering throng and were moved to pity, because, like sheep scattered and driven apart, they strayed about for want of a shepherd.[2] You, good shepherd, see how many different kinds of wolves have burst into your sheepfolds. Each one of them shouts, 'Christ is here, Christ is here,' to lead astray and into error even the perfect, if possible.[3] You observe the winds, waves, and squalls that toss about your little bark,[4] outside of which it is your will that none shall find salvation.[5] If that should sink beneath the waves, what awaits us all except that we perish?

We acknowledge and confess that our sins have summoned this storm. We acknowledge your righteousness and lament that we are unrighteous,

* * * * *

1 Cf Luke 22:61.
2 Cf Matt 9:36.
3 Cf Matt 24:23–4.
4 Cf Matt 14:24.
5 Erasmus paraphrases the classic expression of St Cyprian, 'extra ecclesiam nulla salus' (Ep 73.21 PG 3 1163).

but we call upon your mercy, which surpasses all your works, according to the prophetic psalm.[6] We have already paid a heavy penalty, worn down by so many wars, drained by so many taxes, brought to our knees by so many types of diseases and plagues, shaken by so many floods, and terrified by so many menacing portents from heaven. Yet as we grow weary amid these continually recurring disasters, no haven appears anywhere, but we see more dreadful calamities threatening. Most gentle Saviour, we do not complain of your harshness, but we recognize in this affliction also your compassion, since we have deserved a far more severe punishment.

But, most merciful Jesus, do not consider what our just deserts have earned but what befits your mercy, without which not even angels could subsist, much less we clay vessels.[7] Have mercy on us, Redeemer who hear our prayers, not because we are worthy in ourselves, but grant this glory to your holy name.[8] Do not suffer the Jews, the Turks, and the others who are ignorant of you or begrudge your glory to triumph eternally over us and say, 'Where is the God, Redeemer, Saviour, and Bridegroom of whom they boast?'[9] Their insults fall back on you when your goodness is judged on the basis of our afflictions. They do not understand that we are being chastised, and they believe that we have been abandoned. Once when you were asleep in a boat and a tempest had arisen to threaten destruction to everyone, you awoke at the cries of a few disciples, and then before your all-powerful voice the waves subsided, the winds were hushed, and suddenly the turmoil was turned to deep calm.[10] The silent elements acknowledged the power of the Creator. Now in this far more serious tempest, which imperils not the bodies of a few people but innumerable souls, we beseech you to awake at the cries of your entire church in peril. Countless thousands cry, 'Lord, save us, we perish.'[11] The tempest is too much for human endeavour; indeed, we see the efforts of those who want to help go completely awry. We need your voice, Lord Jesus; only speak the words 'Storm, be still' and immediately there will dawn the calm we have prayed for.

If ten just men had been found in Sodom, you were going to spare countless thousands of utterly sinful men.[12] Now so many thousands of

* * * * *

6 Cf Ps 145:9 (Vulg 144:9).
7 Cf Jer 18:4–6; 2 Cor 4:7.
8 Cf Ps 115:1 (Vulg 113:1bis).
9 Cf eg Ps 79:10 (Vulg 78:10).
10 Cf Matt 8:24–6.
11 Matt 8:25
12 Cf Gen 18:16–33.

people love the glory of your name and long for the beauty of your house.[13] Will you not abate your anger before their prayers, and will you not remember your former mercies?[14] With your divine skill will you not transform our folly into a source of glory for you? Will you not turn the evil of the wicked to the good of your church? For your mercy is usually at hand most of all when men lack the strength and wisdom to be able to help a situation that is utterly desperate. Unaided, you return affairs, however disordered, to harmony; you are the sole creator and guardian of peace. It was you who set in order that chaos of old, wherein the discordant elements of the universe lay in confusion, without order and beauty; and you joined in an eternal covenant elements that are naturally at war, and created an order at which we marvel.[15] But how much uglier is the chaos wherein there is no love, no faith, no covenants, no respect for laws and those in authority, no agreement on basic doctrines, but, as in a cacophonous choir, everyone sings his own song? Among the heavenly spheres discord does not exist, each element keeps its own place, each part discharges its own function. Will you allow your bride, for whose sake you have created everything, to perish because of never-ending dissension? Will you suffer unholy spirits who promote disharmony to exercise their tyranny in your kingdom with impunity? Will you permit the Power of Evil you once subdued and ejected to seize your camp again?

When you lived as a mortal man among men, demons used to flee before your voice.[16] We beseech you, Lord, to send forth your Spirit,[17] which will drive out from the hearts of all people who profess and adore your name the evil spirits who teach excess, greed, ambition, lust, vengeance, and discord. To use the words of the prophet, 'Our God and King, create in us a clean heart and within our hearts renew your holy Spirit, take not your holy Spirit from us.'[18] Return to us the joy of your salvation, and strengthen your bride and the shepherds of your bride with your ruling Spirit.[19] Through this Spirit you have reconciled heaven with earth, through it you have united so many languages, so many nations, and so many different kinds of people

* * * * *

13 Cf Ps 26:8 (Vulg 25:8).
14 Cf Ps 89:50 (Vulg 88:50).
15 Cf Gen 1:1–19.
16 Cf eg Matt 8:16.
17 Cf Ps 104:30 (Vulg 103:30).
18 Cf Ps 51:12–13 (Vulg 50:12–13).
19 Cf Ps 51:14 (Vulg 50:14).

into the one body of the church, which through the same Spirit is joined to you, its head. If you deign to renew this Spirit in everyone's heart, even those external disasters will abate, or if they do not, at least for those who love you they will result in an increase of their piety. Set this chaos in order, Lord Jesus, let your Spirit spread out over these waters of doctrine that rage about to our detriment.[20] And since your Spirit, which according to the word of the prophet is all-embracing, knows also what is said,[21] bring it about that just as for all who dwell in your house there is one law, one baptism, one God, one hope, and one Spirit,[22] so there also should be a single voice of the people who profess the Catholic truth.

In your ascent into heaven, like those celebrating a triumph, you scattered from on high your precious largesse, you showered gifts upon the human race and lavished the various gifts of your Spirit. Once again from on high renew your former bountifulness, grant to your church as it totters what you gave it at its birth. Instil into princes fear of yourself that they may so govern the state as if they will shortly make account to you, the king of kings, concerning every single item. Bestow on them the prudence that always attends your throne, that they may see in their hearts the best course of action and carry it into effect. To your shepherds, whom you have deigned to designate as your vicars, grant the gift of prophecy, that they may interpret the mysteries of the Scriptures not according to human understanding but in accord with your inspiration. Grant the love thrice demanded from Peter as you were about to entrust the sheep to his care.[23] To your priests grant that they may love sobriety and chastity. To your people grant a will prompt to obey your commandments, and a readiness to comply with those through whom you have willed human affairs to be carried out according to your plan. Thus it will transpire that, if princes give orders worthy of you and of your gift, if shepherds teach truths worthy of you, the people will obey good rulers and holy teachers, and, along with order, the church's pristine dignity and tranquillity will return to her, to the glory of your name.

As soon as the people of Nineveh turned to repentance, you spared them, even though you had marked them out for destruction.[24] Will you

* * * * *

20 Cf Gen 1:2.
21 Wisd of Sol 1:7.
22 Cf Eph 4:5.
23 Cf John 21:15–17.
24 Cf Jon 3:1–10.

reject your bride, prostrate at your feet? Instead of being covered in sack-cloth she is full of sighs, instead of ashes, tears. You promised pardon to those who turned to you. But to be able to turn to you with all one's heart is itself your gift, so that all our righteousness redounds to your glory.

You are the Creator; renew your creation. You are the Redeemer; save what is yours. You are the Saviour; do not allow those who utterly depend on you to perish. You are the Lord; claim your possessions. You are the head; come to the aid of your members. You are the king; bestow respect for your laws. You are the Prince of Peace; inspire in us love for one another. You are God; have mercy on those who implore your protection. Be, as Paul said, 'all in all,'[25] that the universal choir of your church, with hearts in harmony and voices as one, may give thanks to the Father and the Son and the Holy Spirit for the mercy that we have obtained. As the supreme paradigm of harmony, you are distinct in your persons but one in nature; to you be praise and glory for ever. Amen.

* * * * *

25 Cf 1 Cor 15:28.

SOME NEW PRAYERS

Precationes aliquot novae

translated and annotated by
STEPHEN RYLE

The collection of Erasmus' prayers issued under the Froben imprint with the title *Precationes aliquot novae* in August 1535 was divided into three parts. The first consisted of twenty-seven previously unpublished prayers. It was prefaced by a short letter of dedication[1] addressed to David, the youngest son of Johann Paumgartner, one of the leading citizens of Augsburg.[2] The second section of the work was made up of twenty-two brief prayers (some no more than a single line in length) drawn from Scripture, mostly from the Psalms, followed by thirteen prayers taken from Erasmus' own works; all of the latter, with one exception, had originally appeared in the *Colloquia*.[3] This second section was entitled *Eiaculationes*, and was introduced by another short letter addressed to David Paumgartner.[4] The remainder of the volume was taken up by three longer prayers which had appeared in print before: the *Precatio ad Virginis filium Iesum*,[5] the *Precatio pro pace ecclesiae*,[6] and the *Precatio dominica*.[7]

The publication of the *Precationes* had an immediate and far-reaching effect on private devotional literature, especially in those regions of Europe where the ideas of the Reformers had taken hold.[8] In England the first edition of the Primer, the traditional manual of private prayer, to be printed in the vernacular had appeared in 1529.[9] From 1537 onwards Erasmian prayers began to be included in versions of the Primer, whether Latin, English, or bilingual.[10] Thomas Cromwell, according to John Foxe's account, recited the prayer 'In Grave Sickness' (appropriate for someone facing imminent death) as he knelt on the scaffold before his execution on 28 July 1540.[11] That prayer

* * * * *

1 Ep 2994. The letter is dated 13 February 1535.
2 See the entries for David Paumgartner and Johann (II) Paumgartner, CEBR III 58–9 and 60–1.
3 See Trapman.
4 Ep 2995, undated
5 LB V 1210E–1216B (4–16 above)
6 LB V 1215E–1218D (111–16 above)
7 LB V 1219A–1228C (57–77 above)
8 On Erasmus' prayers and their reception in German-speaking countries see W.P. Eckert *Erasmus von Rotterdam, Werk und Wirkung* 2 vols (Cologne 1967) II 463–4, 476–9.
9 See Charles C. Butterworth *The English Primers (1529–1545)* (Philadelphia 1953) 11–17.
10 See Edgar Hoskins *Horae beatae Mariae virginis, or, Sarum and York Primers* (London 1901; repr Farnborough 1969). Hoskins failed to recognize the Erasmian authorship of several prayers listed in his volume.
11 John Foxe *Acts and Monuments* ed G. Townsend and S.R. Cattley 8 vols (London 1837–41) V 403

and several others from the *Precationes* were included in the first officially
sanctioned Primer to be printed in English, the so-called 'King's Primer' of
May 1545, which became the standard for successive editions of the Primer
published during the reign of Edward vi (1547–53).[12] After the accession
of the Catholic queen Mary i (1553–8) these prayers were retained when a
bilingual edition of the Primer was issued with the authority of Cardinal
Pole in June 1555.[13] Finally, under Elizabeth i (1558–1603) more than thirty
of Erasmus' *Precationes* and *Eiaculationes* featured in a Latin Primer entitled
Preces privatae published with royal authority in 1564.[14]

In 1872 Charles Coldwell brought out a translation of eight of the *Precationes*, together with the two longer prayers to Jesus and the *Precatio dominica*.[15] Margaret Mann Phillips' versions of the *Precationes* and *Precatio pro pace ecclesiae* were published after her death in 1987,[16] and were later
supplemented by Alice Tobriner's translation of the *Eiaculationes*.[17]

For the present translation the text of LB has been collated with the
Freiburg edition of 1537.

SR

* * * * *

12 See Hoskins (n10 above) 235–44; Butterworth (n9 above) 269–72; Eamon Duffy
The Stripping of the Altars (New Haven and London 1992) 446–7; Diarmaid
MacCulloch *Thomas Cranmer: A Life* (New Haven and London 1996) 334–6.
13 See Hoskins (n10 above) 186–90; Duffy (n12 above) 537–43.
14 See Hoskins (n10 above) 257–67.
15 *The Prayers of Erasmus* trans and ed Charles Simeon Coldwell (London 1872)
16 ERSY 8 (1988) 12–34
17 Alice Tobriner 'The "Private Prayers" of Erasmus and Vives: A View of Lay
Piety in the Northern Renaissance' ERSY 11 (1991) 27–52. The translation of the
Eiaculationes is contained in an appendix, 45–52.

TO DAVID, A YOUNG MAN OF THE HIGHEST PROMISE, SON OF
THE DISTINGUISHED JOHANN PAUMGARTNER OF PAUMGARTEN,
GREETING.[1]

One should learn first what is best;[2] yet nothing in human life is better than
piety. For that reason your father, a man of singular good sense, considers nothing more important than to educate his children from their earliest
years in piety, so that he may reveal himself to you as a true and blameless parent. He understands, no doubt, that he has been far more fortunate
in the possession of piety than in the great wealth that he has honourably
acquired, and has gained far greater eminence than through the distinction
of his noble pedigree, the friendship of kings, popular acclaim, outward authority, and the other great marks of esteem that he has obtained, having
deserved greater still. For these things make him worthy of honour and love
among his fellow men; piety alone makes him worthy in the sight of God. I
for my part, in accordance with my good will towards him, and in order to
satisfy to some extent both his wishes and your endeavours, send you some
prayers, by means of which you may from this time onwards become accustomed to conversing with God,[3] who will graciously reward your youthful
devotion with his favour. Farewell.

From Freiburg im Breisgau, 13 February 1535.

* * * * *

1 This dedicatory letter is Ep 2994. For David and Johann (II) Paumgartner see
n2 to the introductory note.
2 Cf *De ratione studii* ASD I-2 113:11–12, 148:9–10 / CWE 24 666:14–15; *De pueris
instituendis* ASD I-2 47:22–3 / CWE 26 318; Quintilian *Institutiones oratoriae* 2.3.2.
3 Cf *Modus orandi Deum* ASD V-1 134:483 / CWE 70 169.

SOME NEW PRAYERS,
SUPPLEMENTED BY FURTHER ADDITIONS,
BY MEANS OF WHICH YOUNG PEOPLE
MAY BECOME ACCUSTOMED TO
CONVERSING WITH GOD,
BY DESIDERIUS ERASMUS OF ROTTERDAM

Prayer to the Father

Most gracious Father, supreme ruler of the highest heavens, hear the prayers of your servants still in exile on earth. In accordance with your inexpressible generosity you have honoured them with the name of children, and by granting them the most precious pledge of your Spirit have bestowed on them the privilege of daring to call upon you, in humble confidence, with the cry, 'Abba, Father.'[1] We pray that the glory of your name, supremely worthy of praise, may so increase throughout the entire world that just as in the heavenly city you alone are the glory of all, so on earth no one may boast about himself, but that all, acknowledging their own unworthiness and your liberality, may make their boast in you,[2] the only true glory. And since we have a constantly changing and difficult struggle against the world, against Satan and his accomplices, and against the flesh we carry about with us, we ask, sighing, May your kingdom come:[3] so that just as in heaven all things submit with trembling to your supreme power, so your Spirit may reign in our hearts as they acknowledge that you are king of all kings, and that nothing can be either greater or better than you. And just as in your holy palace no voice of sedition is heard, so may all mortal creatures, setting aside all their human passions, observe wholeheartedly your royal commands, in both prosperity and adversity, in life as in death; understanding, to be sure, that you alone can will nothing other than what is best, and that it is best by the very fact that it is pleasing to you.

You have desired, most loving Father, that your will should be made known to us and set forth in the Sacred Scriptures; but no human beings can do justice to your commandments unless you have given us the ability

* * * * *

1 Cf Rom 8:14–16; 2 Cor 1:22, 5:5; Gal 4:6; Eph 1:13–14.
2 Cf 1 Cor 1:31; 2 Cor 10:17–18.
3 Matt 6:10; Luke 11:2

and, in accordance with your indescribable mercy, have excused our frailty. And because, as your Son taught us, we take no thought for the future[4] but depend totally on the loving care of our most bounteous Father, grant us each day through your will what the needs of this life require.[5] But before everything, since (as your most beloved apostle Paul teaches) you are especially the Father of spirits,[6] feed our souls with spiritual nourishment, whether we need milk in our weak condition or solid food as we grow in maturity.[7] The food that truly bestows life[8] is knowledge of you through the Sacred Scriptures,[9] and the grace of your Spirit, through which we grow in you according to our inner self[10] by means of daily advances in virtue, until we develop into the mature man and into the measure of the fullness of your only-begotten Son Jesus Christ.[11] Through your word you brought us into existence when we were nothing; through the same word you regenerated us after our unhappy birth from Adam;[12] and by the same word you feed and enliven those you have regenerated. For this is the bread of heaven, this is the new wine,[13] which gives continuous and fruitful nourishment to all the blessed spirits who dwell in your house and praise you world without end; and if you grant your children some share of it each day, hunger and thirst for the things of this world will daily diminish in us.

However, although you have forgiven all our sins once and for all in the sacred font of baptism through faith, yet because we are still burdened with this mortal flesh and carry the treasure of your grace in earthenware jars,[14] we daily commit sin through human weakness and daily have need of your mercy. Pardon our failings, so that we may not fall from your favour, but may persevere in the peace by which we have been reconciled to you through the blood of your only-begotten Son.[15] Grant also that just as you in your mercy have forgiven us all our sins, so may we each day forgive

* * * * *

4 Cf Matt 6:34.
5 Cf Matt 6:11; Luke 11:3.
6 Cf Heb 12:9.
7 Cf 1 Cor 3:1–2; Heb 5:12–14; 1 Pet 2:2; *Liturgia Virginis Matris* 103 above.
8 Cf John 6:51, 56.
9 Cf John 17:3.
10 Cf Eph 3:16.
11 Cf Eph 4:13.
12 Cf John 3:3–8. See also the prayer 'To the Son' below, with n20.
13 Cf Matt 26:29; Mark 14:25; Luke 22:18; John 6:51.
14 2 Cor 4:7
15 Cf Col 1:20.

one another's petty offences and foster among ourselves mutual peace, harmony, and love. God of peace, no one who hates his neighbour can enjoy your good will.[16] But while we for the present pursue the battle in these tents,[17] the wicked tempter, from whose tyranny you have freed us through Jesus your Son, does not cease to employ every stratagem to draw us back into slavery. Therefore we pray that you will not leave us destitute of your protection and deliver us into the hands of the one who thirsts after the destruction of our souls, but that persevering through faith and love in communion with your most gracious Son we may reach the life where there is no sin and no danger from Satan. Amen.

To the Son

Creator and redeemer of the human race, Jesus Christ. You have said, 'I am the Way, the Truth, and the Life':[18] the way, through your teaching, precept, and example; the truth, in your promises; the life, in your reward. I pray you, through your indescribable love, by which you have sacrificed yourself entirely for our salvation, not to allow me ever to depart from you,[19] who are the way, or ever to lose faith in your promises, who are the truth, fulfilling whatever you promise, or to be satisfied with any other thing, since you are eternal life, and apart from you there is nothing in heaven or on earth to be desired. Through you we have learned the sure and direct path to true salvation, so that we may not wander in the twisting ways of this world any longer. You have taught us openly what we should believe, do, hope for, and in what we should find contentment. Through you we have learned how unhappily we have been born from the first Adam.[20] Through you we have learned that there is no hope of salvation except through faith in you.[21]

You are the one light that shines for all who set out from the darkness of the Egyptians[22] through the desert of this world[23] and the night of our souls towards the blessed land that you have promised to the meek[24]

* * * * *

16 Cf Matt 5:22; 1 John 3:14–15.
17 Cf 2 Cor 5:4.
18 John 14:6
19 Cf the prayer before Communion 'Domine Jesu Christe, Fili Dei vivi' in *Missale Romanum*: '. . . et a te numquam separari permittas.' Cf also the popular medieval prayer 'Anima Christi'; see DS 1 670–2.
20 Cf Gen 3:17–19; Rom 5:12. See also the prayer 'To the Father' above, with n12.
21 Cf Rom 5:1–2.
22 Cf Exod 10:21–3; Wisd of Sol 17:1–18:19.
23 Cf Exod 15:22–16:3; John 6:31.
24 Cf Matt 5:3–4.

and to those who imitate your gentleness;[25] since in us there was nothing but a profound darkness,[26] and we could neither recognize our disastrous condition nor see where we should look for relief from our misfortune. In your generosity you descended to the earth and assumed our nature, so that by your teaching you might dispel the darkness of our ignorance and by your commandments direct our feet into the way of peace.[27] By the example of your life you have laid down for us the path to immortality, and what had been rough and stony you have made, once it had been trodden by your footsteps, easy and smooth for us. So you have become for us a path that cannot lead us astray; and to prevent us from growing weary you have given us in your goodness the support of great and sure promises. Who could grow weary, considering that the inheritance of heavenly life is prepared for anyone who treads in your footsteps? Thus while we are on this road you have willed that we should have a sure hope to support us like a staff. And in your goodness you were not content with these gifts, but taking into account the weakness of our flesh you meanwhile through the consolation of your Spirit restore our strength continually, so that we run eagerly towards you.

Having become the way for us you remove the possibility of wandering; similarly, having become our truth you dispel all doubts. Finally, having become our life you grant to those here who are dead through sin life[28] through your Spirit that enlivens all things, until in the resurrection, when all death is completely done away with, we shall live for ever with you and in you, when Christ will be for us all in all.[29] Eternal life is to know that the Father and the Son and the Holy Spirit are the one true God.[30] We now see you only through faith, a dim reflection in a mirror;[31] but then we shall look upon the glory of the Lord face to face and be transformed into the same image.[32]

Therefore I beseech you, most merciful Saviour, to increase the faith of your servant, so that my belief in your heavenly teaching may never waver; to increase my obedience, so that I may never turn aside from your

* * * * *

25 Cf Matt 11:29; Eph 4:1–2.
26 Cf Isa 5:30, 8:22, 60:2; Luke 1:79.
27 Luke 1:79
28 Cf Rom 6:2, 11.
29 Cf Col 3:11.
30 Cf John 17:3.
31 1 Cor 13:12
32 2 Cor 3:18

commandments; to increase my constancy, so that treading in your footsteps I may neither be seduced by Satan's wiles nor cast down by his terrors, but may persevere until death in you, who alone are true life. Increase my trust, so that relying on your promises I may never grow weary in the pursuit of holiness, but forgetting what I have left behind me may always strive for greater perfection.[33] Increase your grace within me, so that as I daily become more and more dead to myself I may live and be moved by your Spirit:[34] fearing nothing other than you, since nothing is greater or more powerful; loving nothing other than you, since nothing is more worthy of love; glorying in nothing other than you, the true glory of all the saints; seeking after nothing other than you, since nothing is better; desiring nothing other than you, who are full and perfect happiness, with the Father and the Spirit through all ages. Amen.

To the Holy Spirit

Spirit worthy of adoration, proceeding from the Father and the Son[35] and completing the all-powerful Trinity, equal to both in all things, differing only in the particularity of your person: in your goodness you pardon the sins of those who repent; with your holy breath you purify our souls, console them in distress,[36] gladden with holy joy those who mourn, give your serene light to those whose souls are darkened,[37] guide into all truth those who err, kindle with the fire of love those whose hearts have grown cold,[38] reconcile with the bond of peace those who are at variance,[39] and in various ways build up and enrich those who through your inspiration profess the name of the Lord Jesus. Through your action all things live that truly have life: your delight is to dwell in the hearts of the innocent,[40] and you yourself

* * * * *

33 Cf Phil 3:13.
34 Cf Acts 17:28.
35 Cf the Latin version of the Nicene Creed: 'Credo ... in Spiritum Sanctum ... qui ex Patre Filioque procedit.'
36 Cf the Sequence for the feast of Pentecost, *Veni, sancte Spiritus* Raby no 249:7: 'Consolator optime.' Cf also the invocation to the Blessed Virgin from the Litany of Loreto (see NCE VIII 790–1): 'Consolatrix afflictorum.'
37 Cf Pliny *Naturalis historia* 2:13, a passage describing the properties of the sun.
38 Cf the Alleluia-verse *Veni, sancte Spiritus* for the feast of Pentecost and at votive masses of the Holy Spirit in the *Missale Romanum*: 'Veni, sancte Spiritus, reple tuorum corda fidelium, et tui amoris in eis ignem accende.' Cf also the Sequence *Veni, sancte Spiritus* Raby no 249:23: 'fove quod est frigidum.'
39 Cf Eph 4:3.
40 Cf Prov 8:31; Phil 2:15; 'For the Preservation of Chastity' 137 below.

have graciously consecrated them as your own temples.[41] I pray you, protect in me the gifts of your kindness and increase day by day what you have so generously bestowed upon me, so that under your guidance the desires of the flesh may more and more be done to death within me, and the desire for the life of heaven may grow; led by your light may I pass through the gloomy wasteland of this world in such a way that I am neither tainted by the impurities of Satan nor entangled in any errors that dissent from the unassailable truth handed down to us by the Catholic church through the prompting of your divine power: with the Father and the Son you live and reign eternally. Amen.

To the Virgin Mother

Hail Mary,[42] queen of wise virgins:[43] you have turned the curse of the foolish virgin Eve into a blessing for us.[44] Hail, splendour of chaste mothers: you have borne the saviour of us all. Rejoice, glory of angels and men: you have given birth, without loss of your virginity, to the source of heavenly joys. Your perfectly modest chastity was so pleasing to the supreme Deity that from so many thousands of virgins he gave his complete love uniquely to you, and judged you alone to be the woman from whose perfectly chaste womb it was fitting that the Son of God should be born for the redemption of the world. It is a mark of outstanding favour that, while God is present to all who revere him, he united himself with no one more closely or more wonderfully than with you. The Father chose you as his bride; the heavenly Spirit filled you completely.[45] The Son graciously consented to assume the body of a man from the substance of your virginal body, to be carried within the confines of your womb for ten months, to be fed by your milk, to be sheltered in your bosom; and, though he was God and the Son of God, yet he is content both to be and to be called the son of a virgin.

But just as the Lord was with you[46] in a unique way, so through you he has begun to be with us as well in a special sense. First, he was seen on

* * * * *

41 Cf 1 Cor 3:16–17, 6:19; 2 Cor 6:16.
42 The opening words of the best-known prayer to the Blessed Virgin in the western church, based on Luke 1:28–30. See further *The Oxford Dictionary of the Christian Church* ed F.L. Cross and E.A. Livingstone 3rd ed (Oxford 1997) 729–30; NCE VI 898.
43 Cf Matt 25:2–9; Litany of Loreto (see n36 above), 'Regina virginum.'
44 Cf Gen 3:15, where in the Vulgate the enemy of the serpent and its descendants is characterized as a woman; Rev 12:1–17; also Matt 25:1–12.
45 Cf *Paean Virgini Matri* 21 above.
46 Cf Luke 1:28.

earth for more than thirty years, living as a human being among human beings; now, through his Holy Spirit, he dwells in the hearts of the faithful,
refreshing us with food and drink through his own living flesh and sacred
blood in the Eucharist.[47] The entire universe recognizes both how great an
honour God has bestowed upon you and how much good it has itself received through you, and therefore venerates two names above all others:
Jesus, your Son, at whose name every knee bends, in heaven, on earth, and
under the earth;[48] and the Virgin Mary, mention of whom gives joy and
fresh heart to the souls of all who love the name of Jesus. He like the sun
overshadows with his brightness the glory of all the saints; you shine among
all women who have merited praise in just the same way as the moon with
her full orb among the lesser stars.[49] Yet to such a degree is the splendour of
your name linked to the glory of your son, that whenever the adored name
of Jesus is heard, the memory of Mary his most blessed mother is simultaneously called to mind. Once you shared in the sorrows of your son as he
suffered for us; now you are seated with him as he reigns, sharing in his
dignity and his joys. Amen.

Prayer to Christ at Daybreak

Lord Jesus Christ, true Sun of the universe, ever rising, never setting,[50] who
by your redeeming gaze bring to birth, preserve, nourish, and give joy to
all things both in heaven and on earth;[51] graciously shine, I pray you, in my
heart, so that, shaking off the night of sin and the fog of error, I may go
forward without stumbling through my whole life, with you as my inner
light; and may I walk decently as in the day, untainted by the works of
darkness:[52] who live and reign with the Father and the Spirit for all ages.
Amen.

Night Prayer

Lord Jesus Christ, to whose inexhaustible goodness we owe everything, you
have granted the most brilliant light of day equally to all, good and bad

* * * * *

47 In this sentence Erasmus' language recalls the well-known hymn *Pange, lingua,
gloriosi corporis mysterium* composed by St Thomas Aquinas for the feast of
Corpus Christi; see Raby no 263 especially lines 9, 19–21.
48 Cf Phil 2:10.
49 Cf *Obsecratio ad Virginem Mariam* 44 above; Salzer 380–4.
50 Cf *Precatio ad Virginis filium Iesum* 4 above; *Carmina* 111:76 ASD I-7 382 / CWE
85 304, 86 666–7; *In Prudentium* LB V 1339D–1340A / CWE 29 175–6.
51 Cf 'In Summer' 129 below, with n62.
52 Cf Rom 13:12–13.

alike,[53] so that we may fulfil our tasks and duties, and in your mercy have given the friendly quietness of the night to restore the strength of our bodies with rest, relieve our minds' anxious cares, and mitigate our sorrows. You yourself inwardly manifest all these things much more happily for those who love you: in response to every religious action you shine upon them by the grace of faith far more brightly than the sun shines upon the world, and your promises never permit them to grow weary; the consolation of your Spirit eases all the burdens of their minds far more effectively than bodily sleep, and the human person as a whole gains no more secure or sweeter rest in anything other than your mercy, most gracious Redeemer.

I pray that if I have this day done anything through human negligence that has offended your eyes you may in your accustomed goodness forgive me, and at the same time grant that under your prospering hand this night may be happy for me, that you will keep me pure and protect me from the assaults of demons during the night,[54] so that both my body and my mind may through this night's sleep be made more eager to serve you. Furthermore, since there is no certainty in this life about the hour when its evening will come and the body will be oppressed by the sleep from which we shall not awake until the dead are roused to answer the trumpet-call of your angel,[55] I beg you to shine then upon the eyes of my soul, so that I may not fall asleep for ever with my faith extinguished but may take my rest in you, for whom the dead are also alive:[56] you who live and reign with God the Father and the Holy Spirit for ever. Amen.

In Springtime
Lord Jesus, all-powerful, making all things new,[57] you have created this supremely beautiful world for our delight, and have adorned the heavens with so many lights, for our use by day and our comfort by night.[58] By means of the changing seasons you regulate the earth, which you have desired to be a kindly nurse for all living things, and among them also for human beings.

Now with your rising again all things revive, and confirm for us the hope of resurrection that you have promised for us. The fields, formerly

* * * * *

53 Cf Matt 5:45.
54 Cf Ps 91 (Vulg 90):5–6.
55 Cf 1 Cor 15:52.
56 Cf Rom 6:10–11.
57 Cf Rev 21:5.
58 Cf Gen 1:14–18; 1 Cor 15:40–1.

bare, grow green again with new verdure, the grass is adorned with varied flower-buds, crops put out green shoots, buried seeds spring up from the furrows, trees, formerly lifeless, grow young again with new foliage and with the colours of their fresh blossoms fill us with the hope of fruit. The sun itself increases the bounty of its light, and wherever we cast our eyes, the face of universal nature, as if coming to new birth, speaks of your goodness towards the human race, by which you mitigate with so many consolations the exile we have merited, expelled from paradise on account of our fault. Grant that we who have once been reborn[59] in you through baptism and put aside our former selves,[60] becoming a new creation,[61] may never fall back into our old ways, but through the gentle inspiration of your Spirit may flourish in constantly blameless lives and may daily more and more be adorned with the flowers of the virtues as we progress towards the fruit that is worthy of the gospel: you who reign with the Father and the Holy Spirit for all ages. Amen.

In Summer

Jesus Christ, who with supreme wisdom govern and guide the universe: in obedience to your commands the year grows very warm through the heat of your sun, as it prepares to produce its harvests for your servants' profit. We humbly pray you, who are our true Sun, without whom there is no light in our souls, nor does anything come to birth or bear fruit,[62] pour down the radiance of your grace upon the earth of our souls, so that it may daily more and more be warmed by the fire of your love, and bring forth varied fruits of good works. For it was food and drink of this kind that you declared in the Gospel to be your chief delight.[63] This is the wine for which your love towards us caused you to thirst;[64] this is the food for which the Apostle hungered though he did not yet understand.[65] You came upon earth to bring fire to it, and you desired nothing more than that it should be set ablaze;[66] but it is not set ablaze unless our heart is touched by the radiance of your grace. Increase, Lord Jesus, what you have bestowed; bring to perfection

* * * * *

59 Cf John 3:3; 1 Pet 1:23.
60 Cf Rom 6:6; Eph 4:22; Col 3:9.
61 Cf 2 Cor 5:17; Gal 6:15.
62 Cf 'Prayer to Christ at Daybreak' 127 above, with nn50, 51.
63 Cf John 4:32–4.
64 Cf John 19:28.
65 Possibly an allusion to 1 Cor 4:11
66 Cf Luke 12:49.

what you have begun, until we grow into the perfect man, to the measure of your fullness.[67] You have laid aside our mortal nature; you have not, however, laid aside your love for us, but now in addition act on our behalf as a powerful and friendly advocate with your Father, with whom, together with the Holy Spirit, you reign as an equal. Amen.

In Autumn

We thank you, most generous Father, creator of heaven and earth, that through your merciful providence the year has reached its harvest-time and poured out for us on every side an outstandingly rich abundance of produce. Grant, we pray, that just as your goodness provides a rich and varied surplus of crops for the nourishment of our bodies, so through the grace of your Spirit, without which nothing good comes into being, lives, or grows, feelings of love may grow to maturity and perfection in our hearts, so that persevering in the faith of your only-begotten Son we may bear fruit throughout our lives in good works, and achieve a rich harvest in the resurrection of the just: through the same Jesus Christ our Lord, who lives and reigns with you together with the same Holy Spirit for endless ages. Amen.

In Winter

O God, you have created the world and you sustain it with supreme wisdom: in obedience to your command the yearly cycle changes in a constant pattern and accordingly returns upon itself. Now in winter we witness as it were the old age and death of the year; its harshness and discomforts are alleviated by the sweetness of spring that will shortly follow. Indeed, in a similar way to the year, our outward appearance has a springlike freshness in childhood, grows warm in youth, matures with manhood, and declines and dies in old age. But the dread of death is mitigated by the hope of rising to new life, which we regard as absolutely certain especially for this reason, that it was promised by your Son, who is eternal truth, and who cannot deceive or be deceived[68] any more than he cannot be your Son. Through him our inner being[69] does not feel old age or death, but by his unchanging gift it flourishes in innocence, is fervent with desire for virtue, bears fruit, and pours out on others what it receives from him; and the more its bodily strength diminishes the more the spirit overflows with vigour. We pray that

* * * * *

67 Cf Eph 4:13.
68 Cf *Epistola consolatoria* 190 below; Augustine *Enarratio in Psalmum 123* 2.10 CCSL 40 1826; *Speculum virginum* 2.58–60 CCCM 5 43.
69 Cf Rom 7:22; 2 Cor 4:16; Eph 3:16.

you will in your gracious mercy preserve and increase what you have bestowed upon us through your only-begotten Son, who lives and reigns with you for ever. Amen.

A Pupil's Prayer

Hear my prayers, Lord Jesus, eternal wisdom of the Father. You have blessed the years of youth with the added gift of aptitude for learning: grant, I pray you, as well as natural inclination the help of your grace, so that I may more quickly gain a mastery of literature and the liberal arts, those, that is, that will serve your glory; with their support may my intellect come to a more complete knowledge of you, since to know you is the summit of human happiness; and on the pattern of your perfect childhood may I advance day by day in age, wisdom, and favour with God and with those I meet.[70] Who live and reign in union with the Father and the Holy Spirit for endless ages. Amen.

Against Temptation

Lord Jesus Christ, only safeguard of our mortal condition, our only hope, our salvation, our victory, glory, and triumph. You took flesh for our sake, and in the flesh you allowed yourself to be tempted by Satan.[71] You alone conquered sin, death, the world, Satan, and the entire kingdom of the underworld, and whatever you conquered you conquered specifically for our sake. You did not wish your people to engage in battle with those forces except in order to crown them with greater glory. In your own person you vanquished the enemy, and you wished also to overthrow him in your members. I pray you, invincible lion of the tribe of Judah,[72] grant your soldier increased strength against the roaring lion who is always on the prowl, looking for someone to devour.[73] You are the serpent that brings salvation, raised high upon a standard:[74] grant me in my weakness increased astuteness against the snares of the supremely cunning serpent.[75] You are the lamb white as snow,[76] who have vanquished the tyranny of Satan: give your little sheep the strength of your Spirit, so that, frail in itself but strong in you,

* * * * *

70 Cf Luke 2:52.
71 Matt 4:1–11; Mark 1:12–13; Luke 4:1–13
72 Cf Gen 49:9; Rev 5:5.
73 1 Pet 5:8
74 Cf Num 21:6–9; Wisd of Sol 16:5–7; John 3:14.
75 Cf Gen 3:1.
76 Cf Rev 5:6, 12–13; 7:9–10; 22:1, 3.

it may overcome all the assaults of the devil; let my enemy not boast about me, but may I, victorious through you, give thanks to your mercy, which never leaves bereft those who trust in you:[77] who live and reign with the Father and the Holy Spirit for ever. Amen.

Prayer of Thanksgiving for Victory

I give thanks to you, Lord Jesus: at the breath of your grace the storm ceases and is followed by calm;[78] for you is sung the song of triumph, yours is the victory; by your name, not by your arms, the pride of Goliath has been laid low;[79] everything that has been achieved is of your gift. As for me, as far as it concerns my strength, the disgrace of my fall and the disaster into which I had plunged were dreadful; but for that reason I stood firm, since I had rooted my hope not in myself but in you alone, constantly repeating in my mind what was said by your outstanding soldier, 'If God is for us, who can be against us?'[80] and 'I can do all things in him who gives me strength.'[81] He also taught us that when we have fulfilled all the duties of an active soldier we should not give ourselves over to idleness and unconcern, but, for as long as we carry out our service in this world, we should stand, equipped with spiritual armour, ready to face the onslaughts of our enemies, who never sleep. Therefore I ask you, saviour of all who believe in you, to increase my trust in you, so that as the gift of faith grows day by day within me the strength of my enemies may more and more be weakened, until you choose to call me away to that place where there is no contention, no toil, no danger, but everlasting safety and triumph in you; under your protection the victory will be won, when you hand over the kingdom to God the Father,[82] with whom you live and reign in union with the Holy Spirit for ever. Amen.

In Affliction

Most gentle Redeemer, you are always merciful, always our Saviour, whether you send us sadness or joy. It is a mark of great mercy that through external afflictions you bring healing to our inner nature[83] as if by means of bitter medicine, and through temporary troubles prepare us for eternal bliss,

* * * * *

77 Cf Ps 35 (Vulg 34):9.
78 Cf Matt 8:23–7; Mark 4:35–41; Luke 8:22–5.
79 Cf 1 Sam 17:4, 46–51.
80 Rom 8:31
81 Phil 4:13. Erasmus substitutes *corroborat* for the *confortat* of the Vulgate.
82 Cf 1 Cor 15:24.
83 Cf Eph 3:16.

seeing that you have yourself marked out for us with your footsteps this path to true happiness. Grant that I may drink to the full, patiently and obediently, this cup that you have as it were held out to me.[84] These things are certainly very troublesome to frail human nature, but not only have you suffered worse things[85] for my sake, but I have deserved far worse, I who have so often deserved hell-fire.[86] You, however, know the frailty of the human condition, and therefore like the good Samaritan you pour into our wounds the wine that dissipates our faults, but add the oil of your consolation,[87] so that we can bear what is insupportable for us. If it is your will to increase my sufferings, increase also your gift of patience, and make bodily afflictions yield as their result the forgiveness of my sins. Or if your fatherly love is content with this mild punishment, let this storm be greeted with serenity, so that I may give you thanks for two reasons: that you have gently corrected your unprofitable servant,[88] and that you have taken away the bitterness of my affliction with the sweetness of your consolation; on the one hand taking account of what is needed, on the other keeping in mind my weakness. To you be praise and thanksgiving for ever. Amen.

In Grave Sickness[89]

Lord Jesus, only health of the living, eternal life of the dying, I submit and entrust myself entirely to your most holy will, whether you decide that this soul of mine should remain longer in the shelter of this feeble body in order to serve you, or whether you wish that it should pass from this world. Certain that what has been entrusted to your mercy cannot perish, I shall willingly lay down this frail and wretched flesh, seeing that I do so in the hope of the resurrection, which will restore it to me in a much happier condition. I pray that you will strengthen my soul with your grace against all temptations; protect me against all the assaults of Satan with the shield of your mercy,[90] with which in former times you made your martyrs invincible in the face of horrific tortures and most cruel deaths. I see that there is no help in me at all; my trust is entirely in your indescribable goodness. I have no merits or good works to plead in your presence; alas, I see too many

* * * * *

84 Cf Matt 20:22–3, 26:39; Mark 10:38–9, 14:36; Luke 22:42.
85 Cf Virgil *Aeneid* 1.199; Horace *Odes* 1.7.30.
86 Cf Matt 5:22, 29–30.
87 Cf Luke 10:33–4; *Institutio christiani matrimonii* 394 below.
88 Cf Matt 25:30.
89 See the introductory note.
90 Cf Wisd of Sol 5:17–19; Eph 6:14–17.

evil actions, but through your justice I am confident that I shall be counted among the righteous. For me you were born, for me you thirsted, for me you hungered, for me you taught, for me you prayed, for me you fasted, for me you carried out so many good works in this life, for me you suffered so bitter a passion, for me you gave up your precious soul to death on the cross. Let me now profit from these things that you have freely given, who have given yourself totally for me. May your blood wash away the stains of my offences,[91] and may your righteousness make up for my sinfulness.[92] May your merits commend me to the supreme judge. As my suffering grows worse increase your grace, so that my faith may not fail, my hope waver, my love grow cold, and my human weakness be overcome by the fear of death; but once death has taken possession of the eyes of my body, may those of my soul not turn their gaze from you, and when I have lost the use of my tongue, may my heart yet insistently cry to you, 'Into your hands, O Lord, I commit my spirit.'[93] To you be honour and glory for ever. Amen.

A Penitent's Prayer

Supreme creator of all things, when I reflect on the sublime goodness that I have offended by my sins, I shudder at my temerity; when I consider how kind and generous a father I have abandoned, I curse my ingratitude; when I call to mind the rich freedom of the spirit from which I have cast myself down into such wretched slavery, I condemn my madness. I find nothing good in myself, and I see nothing before my eyes but hell and despair, since my conscience is overcome with terror at the prospect of your inescapable judgment. But on the contrary when I contemplate your boundless mercy, which according to the prophet's witness 'surpasses all your works,'[94] and by means of which you are in some sense greater than yourself, seeing that you are in all respects greatest of all, a more cheerful light soon shines upon me and gives me fresh hope. Why indeed should I despair of pardon for my sins from the one who in the prophetic writings so often freely invites sinners to repentance, exclaiming that he does not desire the death of the sinner, but rather that he should be converted and live?[95] Again, how ready your pardon is for those who repent has been impressed on us by your only-begotten Son in many parables, such as that of the drachma lost and

* * * * *

91 Cf Matt 26:28; Heb 9:12–14; Rev 1:5, 7:14.
92 Rom 3:25–6, 5:6–9; 2 Cor 5:21
93 Ps 31:5 (Vulg 30:6); Luke 23:46; cf Acts 7:59.
94 Cf Ps 145 (Vulg 144):9.
95 Cf Ezek 18:23, 32; 33:11.

found,[96] or of the wandering sheep brought back on its master's shoulders,[97] but more clearly in that of the prodigal son,[98] whose portrait I thoroughly recognize in myself. I have ungratefully abandoned a most loving parent, I have squandered in shameful ways all the property that I have received from you, and while I indulged in the desires of the flesh, forgetting your commandments, I have steeped myself in the foulest slavery to sin and have been reduced to utter destitution; and I cannot see where I should turn to, except to the one from whom I have fled. In your mercy take back the suppliant whose errant ways you have so far suffered with patience. I am not worthy to raise my eyes to you or to address you by the name of Father; but, I pray you, do not refuse to turn your eyes towards me. It is your gaze that makes the mortal sinner come to life again, the lost soul return to his true self. Indeed, the fact that I am now unhappy within myself I owe to your regard for me. In your goodness you gazed upon me as I wandered far from you,[99] and you restored the sight of my eyes,[100] so that I could see how deeply I was sunk in sin. You ran to meet me, breathing the recollection and desire of my lost innocence. A slave deserving every form of punishment, I do not ask for your embrace or kiss. I do not demand the robe and ring, marks of my former rank that I have thrown away. I do not ask you to restore me to the honoured status of your children: it will be more than I deserve if you admit me to the most degraded ranks of your slaves, those marked with the branding-iron and the recaptured fugitives, so that I may at least have some share among those who belong to you, since in your household there are many dwellings.[101] I will not be ashamed to be considered among the outcasts in this life, to have harsh punishments inflicted on me, to be begrimed by mourning, as long as I am not separated from you for ever.[102] I pray you, Father, and implore you through the death of your only-begotten Son, the beloved,[103] grant me your Spirit, to purify my heart and strengthen me with his grace, so that I may not sink back through my thoughtlessness to the place from which your mercy has rescued me. Amen.

* * * * *

96 Luke 15:8–10
97 Matt 18:12–13; Luke 15:4–6; cf Ezek 34:16. For the remainder of this prayer compare *Precatio ad Virginis filium Iesum* 8 above.
98 Luke 15:11–32
99 Cf Luke 22:61–2.
100 Cf Matt 9:27–30, 20:30–4; Mark 8:22–5, 10:46–52; Luke 18:35–43; John 9:1–41.
101 John 14:2
102 Cf the prayer before Communion 'Domine Jesu Christe, Fili Dei vivi' in *Missale Romanum* (see n19 above).
103 Cf Matt 3:17, 17:5; Mark 1:11, 9:7; Luke 3:22, 9:35.

A Communicant's Prayer

What tongue or heart could give you the thanks you deserve, Lord Jesus, in return for your indescribable love for us?[104] To redeem the lost human race you condescended to take on human nature and to accept in your person all the harm that attaches to our human condition; and ultimately, as a lamb free from any blemish,[105] you endured the fate of becoming a victim for our sake on the altar of the cross, cancelling out the punishment due for our sins[106] in order to reconcile us to the Father: indeed in life and death you spent, gave, and dedicated yourself totally for us. Nor did your great goodness consider this sufficient, but so that we should never be overtaken by forgetfulness of such great love or begin to lose faith in you, even now as you reign in heaven you continually refresh our souls with the food of your body and gladden our hearts with the sacred cup of your blood. I pray you, let your Spirit purify my heart, so that I do not approach unworthily the heavenly banquet and the table that inspires the angels themselves with awe; but, when I have received you into the recesses of my soul, may I grow strong in you and become more vigorous with an increase of spiritual gifts, so that I may persevere in the blessed company of your mystical body, which you have desired to be as closely united with you as you are with the Father,[107] and bound together by the Holy Spirit, to whom be praise and thanksgiving for ever. Amen.

A Traveller's Prayer

Most faithful guardian of the human race, Jesus Christ, who did not reject the name of Samaritan, turning the slander of the wicked to our salvation:[108] under your protection no danger exists, without your protection no safety exists in any place. By means of your angel you have crowned with success the journey of your servant Abraham,[109] and of the son of Tobit,[110] and of all those who believe in you with a sincere heart. Grant, I pray, that through your favour this journey of mine will be happy and successful; may I conduct my affairs to my satisfaction, and may I reach my destination and return safe in both mind and body, and give thanks to your goodness with all

* * * * *

104 Cf Ps 116 (Vulg 115):12.
105 Exod 12:5
106 Cf Rom 5:9–10; 2 Cor 5:18–19; Col 1:20.
107 Cf John 17:21.
108 Cf John 8:48.
109 Cf Gen 12:1–2.
110 Tob 5:4–12:15

who are or have been glad for my safety. I have no other prayer to make to you, preserver of the human race, who with the Father and the Holy Spirit live and reign for ever. Amen.

Prayer before Setting Sail

Lord Jesus, while you were still clothed with mortal flesh on earth you suppressed the huge raging of the winds with a single word in response to the prayers of your disciples, and in an instant turned the tumultuous waves to a great calm;[111] and you walked on the water of the waves just as if on dry land[112] – no wonder, since you are king and creator of all things whether in the heavens, on earth, or in the sea. I pray you, shine out for us instead of the heavenly twins of the pagans[113] as a true star of prosperity and safety during this voyage, so that in every element we may give thanks for your mercy: to you be honour and power for ever more. Amen.

Prayer before Battle

Almighty king of Sabaoth, that is, of armies, you determine both war and peace for the regions of the earth by means of your angels appointed for the task.[114] You gave new heart and strength to the boy David, so that although he was small, without weapons, and unskilled in war he attacked and overthrew the giant Goliath with a sling.[115] If we are fighting for a just cause, if we are forced to fight, I pray you, first, to turn the hearts of our enemies to the desire for peace, so that no Christian blood may be spilt upon the earth; or to spread the fear that men call panic;[116] or to let victory be gained with the least shedding of blood and the smallest loss by those whose cause is more pleasing to you, so that the war may be quickly concluded and we may sing songs of triumph with one accord to you, who reign in all and above all. Amen.

For the Preservation of Chastity

Spirit of God, you detest every kind of impurity, and it is your joy and delight to dwell in chaste and pure hearts:[117] I humbly pray you that through

* * * * *

111 Matt 8:23–7; Mark 4:37–41; Luke 8:23–5
112 Matt 14:25; Mark 6:48; John 6:19
113 Literally, 'the twin Castors,' ie Castor and Pollux, the constellation Gemini
114 Cf Deut 32:8, which in the Septuagint version seems to be the basis for the persuasion of some patristic and later writers that each nation or province was protected by a special angel; see DS I 484–5.
115 1 Sam 17:4, 48–50
116 The biblical paradigm for this is found at Judg 7:18–22.
117 Cf 'To the Holy Spirit' 125–6 above.

your protection I may preserve unharmed, as I owe it to your goodness to do, this precious treasure that I carry in an earthenware jar,[118] and that I may please you more and more day by day with purity of heart[119] and bodily chastity, and so attain to the life that knows no corruption, in which you live with the Father and the Son. Amen.

For a Happy Marriage

Almighty God, who alone grant success to all human actions: you have stated through the mouth of Solomon that anyone who finds a good wife has found something precious,[120] and that delight and happiness will flow to him from the Lord; and elsewhere have warned through the same authority that woman is a thing more bitter than death.[121] I pray that through your kind providence I may obtain a wife with whom I may live in harmony and cheerfulness and serve you in oneness of heart. You first gave Adam a wife for this purpose, so that joined to him as a helpmate she might dispel the monotony of solitude, and so that he might be aided in his tasks by a wife's customary obedience.[122] You fashioned her from the rib of the man in order to make agreeable to husbands and wives their essential mutual dependence and their indissoluble lifelong bond.[123] But this great boon does not come to us by chance or by our foresight, since it frequently turns out that after we have devoted all our efforts to marrying the best possible wife, we choose the worst possible; and for that reason the faithful servant of faithful Abraham, commissioned to choose a wife for his master's son Isaac, asked for a happy sign from the Lord beside the well, and obtained what he sought.[124] It is not a mark of Christian faith to demand a sign from you:[125] truly our hope is set on your goodness. This is in place of a happy augury for us, most merciful Father: you will in your kindness turn the advice of parents and friends to a successful outcome. Who live and reign. Amen.

* * * * *

118 Cf 2 Cor 4:7.
119 Cf Matt 5:8.
120 Prov 31:10
121 Eccles 7:26 (Vulg 7:27). The sayings of Qoheleth (ie 'the Preacher'), 'son of David' (Eccles 1:1), date from the third century BC, but were traditionally attributed to Solomon.
122 Gen 2:18–21; cf 1 Tim 2:11.
123 Cf Gen 2:21–4.
124 Gen 24:11–27
125 Cf Matt 12:39, 16:4; Mark 8:11-12; Luke 11:29.

Before Marriage

Most loving Father, who have created and redeemed and who continually increase the human race: at the very creation of the world you instituted the marriage of man and woman,[126] and in the same way honoured it through your only-begotten Son, born, if not from wedlock, certainly from a married woman.[127] Again you adorned it with your miraculous gift at Cana in Galilee when you turned tasteless water into wine of the best quality;[128] and you taught through your chosen vessel Paul that this union is a great mystery, applying to Christ and the church,[129] and through the same apostle you laid down the precept that the husband should love his wife as Christ loved the church.[130] I pray you in your goodness to crown with success this marriage entered into under your auspices, so that we will both be of one mind in loving and worshipping you above all things, just as you wished us to be one flesh,[131] and that when we are duly joined in marriage the love that will bind us may be chaste, mutual, and lifelong; and by your gift may we have children who will recall their father in a charming facial resemblance and bear witness to their mother's chastity,[132] and may they make a very close bond of love even closer. May we bring them up as Christians in such a way that, as they advance in age and in the possession of your graces, they may finally attain the fullness of Jesus Christ,[133] who reigns with you in the unity of the Holy Spirit for all ages. Amen.

In Time of Pestilence

It is no cause for surprise, most righteous Father, if the natural forces of this planet vent their anger upon us in various ways, sending us now earthquakes, now storms and thunderbolts, now flooding of rivers and coastal waters, now fatal conjunctions of heavenly bodies, now the noxious effect of polluted air, since we repeatedly abuse your gifts. We recognize that in this instance too the creature serves and obeys his creator, whose commandments we so often ignore; we recognize also a father's discipline, by means of which you give us a gentle reproof, recall us from our attachment to this

* * * * *

126 Cf Gen 2:18–24; Matt 19:5; Mark 10:6–7.
127 Cf Matt 1:18–25; Luke 1:26–38, 2:4–7.
128 John 2:1–10
129 Eph 5:31–2
130 Eph 5:25
131 Gen 2:24; Matt 19:5–6; Mark 10:7–8
132 Cf Catullus *Carmina* 61.214–18; Horace *Odes* 4.5.23; Martial *Epigrams* 6.27.3–4.
133 Cf Eph 4:13.

world, and draw us towards the desire of eternal life. We humbly ask you in your anger to remember your mercy:[134] you have visited these afflictions upon those who offended you; remove them now that you have been appeased. The contagion of pestilence will not cause us great harm if we remove ourselves from the contagion of sin. But in either case, Father of mercies, it is in your gift, first that we should have hearts free from the poison of malice, and also that our bodies should be safe from deadly contagious disease. Those who have fixed the anchor of their hope[135] in this life flee, when confronted by dangers of this kind, to far-fetched remedies: some to the names of certain saints, such as Roch[136] or Antony,[137] yet others to superstitious magical practices.[138] We who are convinced that no one can escape your justice consider that nothing is safer than to flee to you yourself, from the righteous judge to the fount of mercy, and to seek refuge as it were at the supreme altar of safety, since you never forsake those who place all their hope in your goodness, and under your protection those who die are also in safety.

For Spiritual Joy

Lord Jesus, redeemer and comforter of the human race: by the working of your Paraclete you have prepared, for those who through love of you reject the false pleasures of this world, far better delights of which the world knows nothing. You mitigate the troubles of this life with inner, secret consolations, and continually bestow on us as it were some new pledge of future bliss, so that we hasten towards you, refreshed and restored, with more

* * * * *

134 Cf Hab 3:2.
135 Cf Heb 6:19.
136 St Roch (c 1350–c 1380), the saint who was invoked particularly by those who suffered from bubonic plague, of which Roch himself was a victim.
137 St Antony of Egypt (251–356). He was adopted as patron by an order of hospitallers founded at La Motte in France c 1100. The hospitallers specialized in the care of those suffering from ergotism (popularly called 'St Antony's Fire'). After the advent of the Black Death in the mid-fourteenth century the order also devoted themselves to the care of victims of plague. In the Low Countries during the second half of the fifteenth century both Roch (see the previous note) and Antony were widely invoked as protectors against the plague. See Paul Trio *Volksreligie als spiegel van een stedelijke samenleving: de broederschappen te Gent in de late middeleeuwen* Symbolae Facultatis litterarum et philosophiae Lovaniensis B/11 (Leuven 1993) 278.
138 The second half of this sentence, from 'some to the names' to 'magical practices,' was condemned by the commission set up to examine Erasmus' works after the Council of Trent; see LB X 1823A.

eager spirits. I pray you that the balm of your Spirit may frequently help me to shake off the weariness I feel in the face of evil, and may gladden my heart with life-giving joy; while you lived on earth that Spirit anointed you in your human nature with the oil of gladness above your companions:[139] you who with the Father and the same Spirit live and reign for all ages. Amen.

For the Preservation of a Good Name

Heavenly Father, we have been taught by that wise prophet who had insight into your secrets that a good reputation is a treasure to be prized as highly as any other, when he stated, 'Better to possess a good name than precious ointment.'[140] But we can neither gain nor keep this distinguished boon except through your protection. The source of a good name is a blameless life: therefore this is what we seek from you above all. But since innocence is often not safe from those who harbour vipers' venom behind their lips,[141] and it is not rare to find that when we believe ourselves to be among faithful friends we are living, like Ezekiel, amid scorpions,[142] we cry out together with your holy psalmist, 'O Lord, deliver my soul from wicked lips and a treacherous tongue.'[143] But if it has pleased you in your goodness to turn the hearts of your followers towards devotion by means of this affliction as well, grant, we pray, that together with Paul, your outstandingly brave leader, we may persevere in your commandments through shame and glory, through evil and good reputation;[144] through Jesus Christ, who himself while he lived on earth heard himself spoken of as possessed,[145] Samaritan,[146] drunkard,[147] and rabble-rouser:[148] he who now reigns with you in glory together with the Holy Spirit. Amen.

For Parents

Lord God, whose will it is that after you we should hold in highest honour our parents,[149] and among the duties of an honest life, not the least is

* * * * *

139 Ps 45:7 (Vulg 44:8); Heb 1:9
140 Eccles 7:1 (Vulg 7:2)
141 Cf Ps 140:3 (Vulg 139:4); Rom 3:13.
142 Cf Ezek 2:6.
143 Ps 120 (Vulg 119):2
144 Cf 2 Cor 6:8.
145 Cf Matt 9:34, 12:24; Mark 3:22; Luke 11:15.
146 Cf John 8:48.
147 Cf Matt 11:19; Luke 7:34.
148 Cf Matt 27:63; John 7:12.
149 Exod 20:12; cf Deut 5:16; Ecclus 3:1–18; Eph 6:1–3.

to implore your goodness for our parents' protection: preserve, we pray you, my parents with all their family, first in the love of your service, then, in addition, safe from harm in mind or body; grant to me, however, that no trouble may come to them from me, and finally that as I enjoy their favour so may they enjoy yours, who are the supreme Father of us all. Amen.

PREFACE TO THE FOLLOWING PRAYERS
ADDRESSED TO DAVID PAUMGARTNER[150]

Best of young men: we have added some prayers culled from the books of
Holy Scripture, because in the very words brought forth by the Holy Spirit a
certain secret spiritual energy lies hidden. We have called them 'Ejaculations'
because they are brief; but since they are outbursts that express the feelings
of a soul set on fire, they penetrate more quickly to heaven.[151] This type of
prayer was strongly commended by St Augustine, either because the frailty
of the human heart cannot sustain its impulse for long, or because it is possible to make use of prayers of this kind anywhere, even in the midst of one's
everyday business.[152] We have simply given you these as an example and
model; the Scriptures will supply countless similar instances at every turn.

For a Reverent Fear
Grant, O Lord, that instructed by your commandments I may serve you in
fear and kiss your feet with trembling,[153] recognizing in all things your
restraining hand, lest you become angry and I perish from the righteous
path.[154] 'The fear of the Lord is the beginning of wisdom.'[155]

Against Despair
Many say of me, 'No salvation for him from his God.' But you, Lord, are a
shield around me; my glory, you hold my head high.[156]

In Mortal Danger
Most generous Saviour: give light to my eyes, or I shall fall into the sleep
of death, and my enemy will say, 'I have prevailed over him.' My foes will

* * * * *

150 Ep 2995. For David Paumgartner see n2 to the introductory note.
151 Cf the final colloquy, *Epicureus* ('The Epicurean') ASD I-3 733:489–90 / CWE 40
    1087:39–41, composed in 1533, where Erasmus says, 'Even a brief prayer gets
    through to heaven, provided it is uttered with fervent force of spirit' ('pene-
    trat autem et brevis precatio coelum, modo vehementi spiritus impetu eiac-
    uletur'). In both passages he is paraphrasing a medieval proverb, *Brevis oratio
    penetrat coelos; Proverbia sententiaeque Latinitatis Medii ac recentioris Aevi* ed P.G.
    Schmidt n s 7 (Göttingen 1982) no 35313. See further Trapman 775 n38.
152 Cf Augustine Ep 130.20 CSEL 44 62–3.
153 Cf Ps 2:11–12.
154 Cf Ps 2:12; Heb 12:5–7, 11.
155 Prov 1:7, 9:10; cf Job 28:28; Ps 111 (Vulg 110):10; Ecclus 1:14.
156 Ps 3:2–3 (Vulg 3–4)

rejoice if I stumble; but I have set my trust in your faithful love.[157] Do not enter into judgment with your servant, for no one living is righteous before you.[158] I keep the Lord always before me; because he is at my right hand I shall not be shaken. Therefore my heart is glad, and my soul rejoices; my body also rests secure.[159]

For the Same Intention
The pains of death encompassed me; the torrents of perdition assailed me. The cords of Sheol hemmed me in; the snares of death confronted me. In my distress I call upon you, O Lord; I cry to you, my God. From your holy temple hear my voice, and let my cry to you reach your ears.[160] Even though I walk in the midst of the shadow of death I fear no harm, for you are with me.[161]

For a Willing Faith
I am your servant: give me understanding, O Lord, so that I may know your decrees.[162] Your law is perfect, reviving the soul; your decrees are sure, giving wisdom to the simple. Your precepts are right, rejoicing the heart; your commandment is clear, enlightening the eyes.[163] The unfolding of your words gives light; it imparts understanding to the simple.[164] For you, Lord, grant wisdom, and from your mouth come knowledge and understanding.[165]

For the Same Intention
Make me to know your ways, O Lord, and teach me your paths. Guide me in your truth and teach me, for you are God my saviour.[166]

Seeking Pardon for Sin
I have gone astray like a lost sheep; seek out your servant, O Lord, for I have not forgotten your commandments.[167] Do not remember the sins of my youth or my transgressions, O Lord; according to your

* * * * *

157 Cf Ps 13:3–5 (Vulg 12:4–6).
158 Cf Ps 143 (Vulg 142):2.
159 Cf Ps 16 (Vulg 15):8–9.
160 Cf Ps 18:4–6 (Vulg 17:5–7); 2 Sam 22:5–7.
161 Cf Ps 23 (Vulg 22):4.
162 Cf Ps 119 (Vulg 118):125.
163 Cf Ps 19:7–8 (Vulg 18:8–9).
164 Cf Ps 119 (Vulg 118):130.
165 Cf Prov 2:6.
166 Ps 25 (Vulg 24):4–5
167 Cf Ps 119 (Vulg 118):176.

steadfast love remember me. On account of your goodness, Lord, preserve my life and rescue me; do not let me be disgraced, for I trust in you.[168] Turn my mourning into dancing; strip off my sackcloth and clothe me with joy, so that my soul may praise you in glory and not be silent.[169]

For Purity of Heart
Create in me a clean heart, O God, and renew within me a steadfast spirit.[170] Let my heart be blameless in your statutes so that I may not be put to shame.[171]

In Affliction
O Lord, grant us help against the foe, for human help is worthless. With your aid we shall triumph, and you will trample down our foes.[172] Let my soul be at rest in you alone, for my hope comes from you; you are my God and my saviour, my fortress: I shall not be shaken. In you rests my safety and glory, God of my help, and my trust is in you.[173]

After Overcoming Temptation
We have passed through fire and water, and you have led us out to a place of safety.[174] You have kept us alive and not allowed our feet to slip.[175] When cares increased within me, your comfort brought me joy.[176] I have escaped like a bird from the snare of the fowlers.[177] You have delivered my soul from death, and my feet from stumbling, so that I may walk before you, O God, in the light of the living.[178]

For the Same Intention
You have been a refuge to the poor, O Lord, a refuge to the needy in their distress, shelter from the rainstorm, shade from the heat.[179]

* * * * *

168 Cf Ps 25 (Vulg 24):7, 20.
169 Cf Ps 30:11–12 (Vulg 29:12–13).
170 Ps 51:10 (Vulg 50:12)
171 Ps 119 (Vulg 118):80
172 Cf Ps 60:11–12 (Vulg 59:13–14); Ps 108:12–13 (Vulg 107:13–14).
173 Cf Ps 62:5–7 (Vulg 61:6–8).
174 Ps 66 (Vulg 65):12
175 Cf Ps 66 (Vulg 65):9.
176 Cf Ps 94 (Vulg 93):19.
177 Cf Ps 124 (Vulg 123):7.
178 Cf Ps 56 (Vulg 55):13.
179 Cf Isa 25:4.

Against the Assaults of the Wicked

O Lord, be unto me a God, a protector, and a place of strength, to make me safe, for you are my firmament and my refuge. Deliver me, O my God, out of the hand of the sinner, and out of the hand of the transgressor of the law and of the unjust. For you are my patience, O Lord; my hope, O Lord, from my youth. By you have I been confirmed from the womb; from my mother's womb you are my protector. Of you will I sing continually.[180]

For a Blameless and Honest Life

Lead me in your way, O Lord, that I may walk in your truth, single-hearted and revering your name.[181] Let your word be a lamp to my feet, and a light to my path.[182]

In Sickness

Heal me, O Lord, and I shall be healed; save me, and I shall be saved.[183] My soul clings to the dust; revive me according to your word.[184] In your kindness give me life, and I shall keep the decrees you have spoken.[185] Sustain me, O Lord, and I shall be saved, ever to contemplate your statutes.[186] Great is your mercy, O Lord; give me life according to your justice.[187]

On Being Restored to Health

The Lord has punished me severely, but he did not give me over to death.[188] I will give thanks to you, O Lord, for though you were angry with me, your anger turned away, and you comforted me.[189]

Acknowledgment of Sin

If you, O Lord, should mark our sins, Lord, who could stand it? For with you there is merciful forgiveness, and by reason of your law I have waited for you, O Lord. My soul has relied on your word; my soul has hoped in you, O

*****

180 Cf Ps 71 (Vulg 70):3–6.
181 Ps 86 (Vulg 85):11
182 Cf Ps 119 (Vulg 118):105.
183 Jer 17:14
184 Ps 119 (Vulg 118):25
185 Ibidem verse 88
186 Cf ibidem verse 117.
187 Ibidem verse 156
188 Ps 118 (Vulg 117):18
189 Isa 12:1

Lord. Because with you there is mercy, and with you plentiful redemption. And you redeem Israel from all its iniquities.[190]

For the Same Intention, from Jeremiah

You chastised me, O Lord, and I was instructed, like a young bullock un-accustomed to the yoke. Convert me, and I will be converted, for you are the Lord my God. For after you converted me, I repented; and after you showed me, I struck my thigh: I was confounded and ashamed, because I bore the disgrace of my youth.[191]

For the Clergy

Let your priests be clothed with righteousness, and let your faithful shout for joy.[192]

For a Young Prince, from the Prayer of Solomon

O Lord my God, you have made your servant king in place of my father; but I am a mere youth, not knowing at all how to act. And here is your servant, in the midst of the people whom you have chosen, a people so vast that it cannot be numbered or counted. Give your servant therefore an understanding mind to govern your people, able to distinguish between good and evil.[193] Indeed, even one who is perfect among human beings will be regarded as nothing without the wisdom that comes from you.[194]

For the Same Intention

Send forth your wisdom from your holy heavens, and despatch her from your throne of glory, so that she may be with me and work with me, and I may learn what is pleasing to you.[195]

Against Pride and Self-Indulgence

O Lord, Father and God of my life, do not abandon me to the will of evil men.[196] Remove me from mortals who have only breath in their nostrils,

* * * * *

190 Cf Ps 130 (Vulg 129):3–5, 7–8.
191 Cf Jer 31:18–19.
192 Ps 132 (Vulg 131):9
193 1 Kings (Vulg 3 Kings) 3:7–9
194 Wisd of Sol 9:6
195 Cf Wisd of Sol 9:10.
196 Cf Ecclus 23:4.

and who seem great in their own eyes.[197] Do not let the foot of the arrogant overtake me;[198] do not give me haughty eyes, and remove all evil desire. Take gluttony away from me, do not let lust overcome me, and do not give me over to shameless passion.[199]

Against Avarice
O God, turn my heart to your decrees, and not to selfish gain.[200]

In the Morning, on Waking from Sleep[201]
I thank you, O Christ, that you have willed me to pass an untroubled night; and I pray that you will likewise bless me throughout this day to your glory and the salvation of my soul; and that you, who are the true light[202] that knows no setting, the eternal sun giving life, nourishment, and joy to all things, may in your goodness shine upon my soul, so that I may not in any way fall into sin, but by your guidance attain everlasting life. Amen.

On Going to School[203]
I pray you, Christ Jesus, who as a boy of twelve, sitting in the temple, taught the doctors themselves,[204] and to whom your Father by means of a voice from heaven gave authority to teach the human race when he said, 'This is my Son, the Beloved, with whom I am well pleased: listen to him';[205] and who are the eternal wisdom of the almighty Father: generously enlighten my mind to attain a thorough knowledge of good literature so that I may make use of it to your glory. Amen.

When These Words from Paul Are Recited:[206]
'Clear out the old yeast, so that you may become a fresh batch of dough, inas-

* * * * *

197 Cf Isa 2:22.
198 Ps 36:11 (Vulg 35:12)
199 Cf Ecclus 23:5–6.
200 Ps 119 (Vulg 118):36
201 This and the remaining *Eiaculationes* are taken over, with one exception, from Erasmus' *Colloquia*. See the discussion by Trapman 775–7. For this prayer cf the colloquy *Pietas puerilis* ASD I-3 173:1553–8 / *Confabulatio pia* ('The Whole Duty of Youth') CWE 39 92:9–14.
202 Cf John 1:9.
203 Cf *Pietas puerilis* ASD I-3 173:1578–174:1583 / *Confabulatio pia* CWE 39 92:37–93:2.
204 Cf Luke 2:42–7.
205 A conflation of Matt 3:17 and Luke 9:35; cf Mark 1:11; Luke 3:22.
206 Cf *Pietas puerilis* ASD I-3 176:1679–83 / *Confabulatio pia* CWE 39 95:23–8.

much as you are unleavened.'[207] At these words, speak inwardly to Christ in this manner: 'May I be truly unleavened, purified of all the yeast of malice! But you, Lord Jesus, who alone are purified and cleansed of every kind of malice, grant that with each day I may also more and more become purged of the old yeast and become a fresh batch, in truth and sincerity of heart.[208] Amen.'

When the Gospel of the Sower Is Read:[209]
Pray within yourself in this way: 'Happy is the one who deserves to be good soil.' I pray that since without your blessing nothing at all is good you may by your kindness turn me from barren earth into good soil, so that your word may bear fruit in me. Amen.

At the Gospel of the Wedding Feast at Cana[210]
Jesus, source of every good: at the prompting of the Virgin Mother you brought gladness to the guests by changing water into wine; grant to your servants that[211] we may be made healthfully drunk by the new wine of your Spirit.[212] Who live and reign for endless ages. Amen.

Before Receiving the Holy Eucharist[213]
I thank you, Christ Jesus, for your inexpressible love in condescending to redeem the human race by your death; and I pray that you will not allow your precious blood to have been poured out for me in vain, but will always feed my soul with your body, and enliven my spirit with your blood: so that, as I grow gradually more mature through advances in virtue, I may develop into a worthy member of your mystical body, that is, the church, and may never depart from the most sacred covenant into which you entered with

* * * * *

207 1 Cor 5:7, read as part of the Epistle on the morning of Easter Day
208 Cf 1 Cor 5:8.
209 Cf *Pietas puerilis* ASD I-3 176:1684–6 / *Confabulatio pia* CWE 39 95:28–32. The three versions of this parable are found at Matt 13:1–9; Mark 4:1–9; Luke 8:5–8. Luke's version was read as the Gospel on Sexagesima Sunday; cf *Missale Romanum*.
210 John 2:1–11. The prayer that follows is taken from the *Liturgia Virginis Matris*, where it forms the Secret (ie the 'Prayer over the Offerings'). Cf 104–5 above.
211 Here Erasmus omits the words 'eiusdem [*sc* Virginis Matris] suffragiis adiuti' from the *Liturgia*.
212 Cf Acts 2:13, 15; *Paean Virgini Matri* 31 above. See also Phillips 35, 39; and DS VII-2 2312–37 under 'Ivresse spirituelle.'
213 Cf *Pietas puerilis* ASD I-3 177:1693–1700 / *Confabulatio pia* CWE 39 95:39–96:6.

your chosen disciples at the Last Supper, when you distributed the bread and offered them the cup,[214] and through them with all who have been engrafted into your fellowship[215] through baptism. Amen.

To Christ, for True Piety[216]

I pray, Christ Jesus, that since we can do nothing of ourselves, you will in your infinite goodness never allow us to stray from the path of salvation; but that after we have cast off the shadows of Judaism[217] and the deceits of this world you will guide us through the truth of the gospel to life eternal, that is, that you will draw us to you,[218] who alone are blissful immortality. Amen.

For Unity of Doctrine[219]

O God, lover of the human race, you have generously imparted the gift of tongues, by which through your Holy Spirit you once from on high made your apostles ready to preach the gospel:[220] grant that all people everywhere may proclaim the glory of Jesus your Son in every language, so that you may confuse the tongues of the false apostles who conspire to build the wicked tower of Babel, in their attempt to dim your glory while they yearn to exalt their own;[221] seeing that all glory is owed to you alone, with your Son Jesus Christ our Lord and the Holy Spirit for endless ages. Amen.

Grace before Meals[222]

May he who with his bounty feeds the whole creation bless and sanctify whatever is served and shall be served. Amen.

* * * * *

214 Cf Matt 26:26–28; Mark 14:22–5; Luke 22:19–20; 1 Cor 11:23–5.
215 Cf Rom 11:17–24.
216 Cf the colloquy *Convivium religiosum* ('The Godly Feast') ASD I-3 234:94–7 / CWE 39 177:36–9.
217 Cf Isa 30:2–3; Heb 10:1.
218 Cf John 12:32.
219 This prayer is adapted from the colloquy *Apotheosis Capnionis*, Erasmus' tribute to the renowned scholar of Hebrew and Greek, Johann Reuchlin, printed within a few months of Reuchlin's death in 1522. See ASD I-3 273:208–15 / *De incomparabili heroe Ioanne Reuchlino in divorum numerum relato* ('The Apotheosis of that Incomparable Worthy, Johann Reuchlin') CWE 39 251:31–9.
220 Cf Acts 2:4–11, 10:46, 19:6.
221 Cf Gen 11:1–9.
222 Cf the colloquy *Convivium profanum* ('The Profane Feast') ASD I-3 198:2365–6 / CWE 39 135:20–1.

Another Grace[223]

You bring gladness to all, O Christ, and without you nothing is truly sweet. I pray that you will consent to take part in our meal, to enliven our minds with your presence, and to mingle with all our food and drink, so that nothing will lack your savour, and that you will penetrate our hearts.[224] Amen.

Act of Thanksgiving[225]

We give you thanks, heavenly Father: by your ineffable power you have created all things, by your unfathomable wisdom you control them all, by your inexhaustible goodness you nourish and give new life to them all: grant to your children that they may one day drink with you in your kingdom the nectar of immortality, which you have promised and prepared for those who truly love you,[226] through Jesus Christ. Amen.

Another, from Chrysostom[227]

May you be blessed, O God: you have fed me since my youth, you give food to everything that lives. Fill our hearts with joy and gladness, so that as we have received a sufficient measure of what is needful we may abundantly fulfil every good work, in Christ Jesus our Lord, with whom be glory, honour, and power to you, with the Holy Spirit for ever. Amen.

Another from Chrysostom's Fifty-Sixth Homily on Matthew[228]

Glory to you, O Lord, glory to you, Holy One, glory to you, O King! Since you have given us food, fill us with joy and gladness in the Holy Spirit, so that we may be found acceptable in your sight, and may not be put to shame when you repay each person according to his deeds.[229] Amen.

* * * * *

223 Cf *Convivium religiosum* ASD I-3 241:307–9, 311–2 / CWE 39 183:18–20, 23–4.
224 Cf Virgil *Aeneid* 3.89.
225 Cf *Convivium profanum* ASD I-3 214:2916–20; Erasmus also gives a Greek version of this prayer, ibidem lines 2920–6 / CWE 39 153:7–21.
226 Cf Matt 25:34, 26:29; Mark 14:25; Luke 22:15–16.
227 This prayer and the next are taken from a homily by St John Chrysostom; cf *Convivium religiosum* ASD I-3 240:291–4 / CWE 39 183:1–5; Chrysostom *In Matthaeum homilia* 56(55) 5 PG 58 545.
228 Cf *Convivium religiosum* ASD I-3 261:935–7 / CWE 39 203:1–5; Chrysostom *In Matthaeum homilia* 56(55) 5 PG 58 545.
229 Cf Rev 20:13.

A COMPARISON OF THE VIRGIN
AND THE MARTYR

Virginis et martyris comparatio

translated and annotated by
LOUIS A. PERRAUD

Helias Marcaeus (Elias Mertz), master of arts in the University of Cologne, was rector and confessor of the convent of the Maccabees,[1] a community of Benedictine nuns in Cologne who owed this name to relics in their possession of the seven Maccabee brothers and their mother, Jews whose martyrdom at the hands of the Pergamene king Antiochus Epiphanes in the 160s BC is recounted in the Old Testament apocrypha.[2] Doubtless because of his connection with the convent, Marcaeus became an enthusiastic proponent of devotion to the heroic family. By 1517 or 1518 he had become friendly enough with Erasmus to persuade him to edit and write an introduction for the fourth book of Maccabees, an extra-canonical text from the Septuagint that gives another account of the Maccabees' martyrdom.[3]

Erasmus enjoyed friendly relations with the nuns of the Maccabean convent as well as their mentor Marcaeus, and in 1523 he thanked them for a New Year's gift of sweets, with some graceful pages praising the convent for its treasured relics and the nuns for their vocation.[4] This short work, the first version of the *Virginis et martyris comparatio*, appeared in print the same year as 'filler' with a new edition of Erasmus' *Ratio verae theologiae*.[5] At Marcaeus' request, Erasmus subsequently expanded the work into a devotional treatise nearly seven times as long as the original. Froben printed this second version with Erasmus' *De immensa Dei misericordia* in September 1524.[6] The enlarged *Comparatio* was printed in the Leiden edition of Erasmus' complete works, from which it is translated here.[7]

The 1523 *Comparatio* is a tidy little piece that exhibits many of the features of panegyric oratory.[8] It begins with a classical *exordium* in which

* * * * *

1 For Marcaeus and the Cologne convent see CEBR II 381–2; cf Ep 842 introduction.
2 2 Maccabees 7:1–42
3 Ep 842 introduction
4 The introduction and conclusion of this letter are printed as Ep 1346 in Allen and CWE. (The body of the epistle, which is actually a miniature treatise rather than a letter, is omitted from Erasmus' correspondence in Allen and CWE.)
5 Cf Ep 1365 introduction and Allen Ep 1365 introduction. I cite the original *Comparatio* from Alopecius, an early printing extant in the Folger Shakespeare Library, with signature letter, leaf number, and side letter. Cf *Bibliotheca Erasmiana: répertoire des oeuvres d'Erasme* ed F. Vander Haegen 3 vols in 1 (Ghent 1893; repr Nieuwkoop 1961) 1 168.
6 See Allen Ep 1475 introduction, and Ep 1475, the prefatory letter below.
7 LB V 589–600
8 The features of panegyric are usefully summarized in John W. O'Malley *Praise and Blame* in *Renaissance Rome: Rhetoric, Doctrine, and Reform in the Sacred Orators*

Erasmus proclaims his unworthiness to deal with the high themes that the nuns have set him,[9] and ends with a fervent *peroratio* in which he summarizes his principal themes.[10] In between, Erasmus works mainly with comparisons, for example, between the contrasting excellences of martyrdom and virginity,[11] between Eve and Mary,[12] between the virgins of this world and the virgins of Christ.[13] The comparisons are enriched by a number of historical allusions: to the honours paid virgins and martyrs in the early church,[14] to the celebration of martyrdom and virginity in early Christian writers,[15] to the high example furnished by the Maccabees and their mother.[16]

In the expanded version of 1524 Erasmus draws far more widely on biblical and patristic sources,[17] and unhesitatingly incorporates non-classical techniques into the earlier piece. He deepens his interpretation of the lily and the rose, images introduced early in both versions of the *Comparatio*,[18] with an elaborate symbolic exegesis of a verse from the Song of Solomon, 'I am the flower of the fields and the lily of the valley' (2:1). From the blooms mentioned in that verse he derives the figures of Christ – archetypal rose/martyr and lily/virgin – who has human rose/martyrs and lily/virgins

* * * * *

of the Papal Court, c 1450–1521 Duke Monographs in Medieval and Renaissance Studies 3 (Durham, NC 1979) 39–42.
 9 Alopecius 05r, in the 1524 version LB V 589A–B, 159 below
10 Alopecius 08r, in the 1524 version LB V 599A–600B, 182 below
11 Alopecius 06r–07r, in the 1524 version LB V 595F–596E, 174–6 below
12 Alopecius 07r, in the 1524 version LB V 597A and 597E, 177, 178 below
13 Alopecius 07r–08r, in the 1524 version LB V 597F–599A, 179–82 below
14 Alopecius 05v, in the 1524 version LB V 594B–C, 169–70 below
15 Alopecius 05v–06r, in the 1524 version LB V 594C–E, 170–1 below
16 Alopecius 06r, in the 1524 version LB V 595B–C, E–F, 172–3 below
17 These are noted below as they occur in the text. For discussion of the biblical and patristic sources of the *Comparatio*, see William J. Hirten's introduction to Desiderius Erasmus *The Comparation of a Vyrgin and a Martyr* trans Thomas Paynell (Gainesville 1970) xxi–xxxi. H.I. Mandeville in his review of Hirten's edition, *Renaissance Quarterly* 27 (1974):57–9, suggests (59) that Erasmus chose biblical and patristic texts assigned by the breviary for singing or reading in the Common of Virgins. It should be noted, however, that Erasmus makes no attempt in the *Comparatio* systematically to cite, quote, or explain the ensemble of texts in the Common of a Virgin; that Ambrose's hymn *Iesu, corona virginum* is the only text from the Office treated at length; and that the Song of Solomon 2:1ff, the scriptural text which Erasmus treats at greatest length, does not appear in the Common of Virgins.
18 Alopecius 05v, in the 1524 version LB 590B, 160–1 below

as his beloved followers (161). These equations lend the recurring references to roses and lilies that follow a poetic resonance and a unifying power that they did not have in the version of 1523.[19] By his own admission (168) Erasmus tarries at rather uncomfortable length over St Ambrose's hymn *Iesu, corona virginum*, perhaps because the nuns to whom he was writing regularly sang it in choir as part of the Divine Office.[20] In expounding it he unhesitatingly plays the Christian *grammaticus*, or schoolmaster, furnishing a line-by-line exposition of the poem that even includes a proposed textual emendation (164).

Additions of this kind may create a work that is more diffuse and harder to classify than the original, but their scriptural and patristic riches intensify the *Comparatio*'s devotional character. Clearly, the work was most important to Erasmus himself as an incitement to holy living, for in the *Catalogus* he lists it among 'those works that train in piety.'[21] As such it seems to have found an eager audience, since it was a religious best-seller for about a century after its publication. Before 1600 the Latin text was printed no fewer than twelve times, and it was translated into German, English, and Italian.[22] Later there were translations into Dutch, French, and Flemish.[23] Thomas Paynell's English rendering (1537) is particularly notable for the melodious beauty of its prose.

Modern commentators have noticed the serene, straightforward religiosity of the *Comparatio*. Mandeville calls it 'a charmingly simple and gracious work.'[24] Hirten notes that it 'exudes peace' and 'apparently was written in a spirit free from contention and strife, either literary or theological.'[25] Yet however irenic his purpose, Erasmus was obliged by his subject to touch on controversial matters here, and it is worth reviewing his treatment of two of them, relics and virginity.

Erasmus' treatment of relics in the *Comparatio* is a good example of his desire for a popular piety that avoided 'undue trust in external forms to

* * * * *

19 See 162, 163–4, 169, 172, and 174 below. Cf Alopecius o6r.
20 The hymn *Iesu, corona virginum*, attributed to St Ambrose, archbishop of Milan (339–97), is designated by the Roman breviary for singing at Lauds and Vespers in the Common of Virgins. Erasmus' text of the hymn differs in minor points from that of the breviary, but agrees with the one printed in PL 17 1259 no 80 poem 1.
21 Allen I 40:25
22 *Bibliotheca Erasmiana* (see n5 above) 1 180–1
23 Ibidem
24 Mandeville (see n17 above) 57
25 Hirten (see n17 above) v

the detriment of inward sentiment.'[26] He sees a justification for venerating relics in the practice of early Christians, who venerated martyrs' ashes, the cells in which they were confined, the chains with which they were bound, and the swords with which they were executed (169–70). He therefore duly congratulates the nuns to whom the work is addressed on owning the precious remains of the seven Maccabees and their mother (172). He ignores, however, the relics' potential as a treasure with which to attract pilgrims or a source of miracles and treats their presence in the convent rather as a spur to virtue, exhorting the nuns in his closing peroration to imitate the Maccabees' perseverance in the face of torture and death (181).

Erasmus genuinely accepted the validity of virginity.[27] The *Comparatio*, in part a eulogy of that holy state written for nuns, quite naturally presents their calling in its most positive light, tracing virginity back to the example of Christ himself (160–1, 164) and even several times contrasting the freedom of Christ's virgins with the misfortunes of married women or the virgins of this world destined for marriage (163, 165, 166, 179–80). Yet Erasmus includes at least a hint that his position has further nuances, when he criticizes the Latin Fathers Jerome and Tertullian for exalting chastity at the expense of matrimony.[28] He lays it down as a rule that 'the excellence of virginity must not be extolled in such a way that praise of it has been joined with aspersions on chaste marriage.' The relationship between virginity and marriage suggested here will be developed more fully in the *Institutio christiani matrimonii* (216–17, 225), published two years later, in 1526. There Erasmus will present a balanced historical assessment that equally honours the two states, while perhaps according virginity less importance in the church of his own time than marriage.

LAP

* * * * *

26 The phrase is John W. O'Malley's in his introduction to the series of *spiritualia* and *pastoralia*, CWE 66 xvii–xviii.
27 See ibidem xviii–xix.
28 See 172 below, with n85.

ERASMUS OF ROTTERDAM TO THE MOST WORTHY AND LEARNED
FATHER HELIAS MARCAEUS OF THE COMMUNITY OF MACCABEANS,
WARDEN OF THEIR MOST HONOURABLE COMMUNITY[1]

I send you a book that is both short and overdue; but you would agree that it
is long and finished in good time if you knew how little leisure is left me in
which to oblige my friends in such matters by frequent periods of ill health,
by almost continuous business, especially in sending and receiving letters,
and by the toilsome research demanded by the subjects I have undertaken
to write about. If I have done what you wished, I am delighted; if not, you
must at least approve my ready desire to please, if what I hear of your good
nature is not untrue. When I have more time to spare, I will meet your pious
wishes with something more substantial. My best wishes both to yourself,
honoured sir, and to your worthy company of virgins pledged to God's
service.

    Basel, 30 July 1524

* * * * *

1 Ep 1475. This is the prefatory letter to the final and expanded version of the
  Virginis et martyris comparatio, 1524.

As Colville renders the passage describing the limitations of non-eternal beings, he does not refer to the inability of a temporal being to grasp the entire space of his life equally but rather to the impossibility of understanding the end of his life: "*nihilque est in tempore constitutum, quod ultimum uite sue spatium pariter possit amplecti*"; "And nothynge is establyshed in tyme, that may comprehend together the last space of hys lyfe" (211). Thus, instead of supporting the definition an eternity just given ("the possessyon of lyfe interminable, being hole and all together parfŷtte"), this phrasing

A COMPARISON OF THE VIRGIN
AND THE MARTYR

FROM DESIDERIUS ERASMUS OF ROTTERDAM TO THE VENERABLE
COMMUNITY OF MACCABEAN VIRGINS AT COLOGNE, GREETINGS IN
CHRIST JESUS THE SON OF A VIRGIN AND THE CROWN OF ALL
VIRGINS.[1]

Again and again,[2] best of virgins, your devotion now summons me with
certain fruits and sweets to celebrate your treasure (that you of course prize
most highly) in some literary work and to commend to you your chosen
way of life. In the first of these intentions you are led by a kind of religious
ambition, which seeks not your own glory, but that of God, who is truly
glorious in his saints. In the second, I think that you are seeking spiritual
profit, in fact are hunting after it, so as to receive presents that nourish the
soul in exchange for the ones to your guest that delight the palate. It is a
pious pursuit, it is a holy greed, it is a prudent and truly profitable exchange
and clearly worthy of wise virgins.[3] If only I were the one who could pour
out something from the perfume flasks of Holy Scripture that would refresh
your minds as much as your little gifts refresh our poor body! You do not
err in your desire, but you err in the man you select. You choose what is best,
but, indeed, you do not choose the one who can satisfy your holy wishes.

Nevertheless, lest I seem merely ungrateful, I continue to congratulate
you, virgins beloved of God, for that disposition that thirsts after nothing
but the glory of your Bridegroom. For it is also a sign of the truly chaste
bride that she consider the glory of her bridegroom to be her own. To be

* * * * *

1 This salutation opened the original 1523 version of the *Comparatio* (Ep 1346). It
was printed in the 1524 *Comparatio* despite the addition of the new prefatory
letter to Marcaeus printed above.
2 Again and again (*iam iterum atque iterum*): the opening phrase of the 1523 version (Ep 1346) was 'on more than one occasion' (*semel atque iterum*). Evidently,
the nuns sent Erasmus more candy between the two versions of the *Comparatio*.
3 Cf Matt 25:1–6.

sure, the one to whom you are particularly devoted is beautiful beyond the sons of men.[4] He is glorious in all his deeds, if someone should contemplate the admirable workmanship of this world on all sides; but he is even more glorious in the world he has redeemed than in the world he has created. By his nod he created the world and the hosts of angels, but by his precious blood he restored what he had created.

That same wisdom, which is Jesus Christ, who is also the maker of this marvellous work, in order that he might produce something yet more marvellous, by divine art constructed an eternal dwelling and a temple worthy of God. It is the church, which he, like the wealthiest king, adorned with every kind of spiritual ornament. For what is gold, silver, marble, ivory; what is the emerald, the topaz, the beryl, and the variegated splendour of gems, if it be compared to the riches of the Holy Spirit, which are prophecy, the gift of tongues, power to work miracles and cure the sick,[5] peace, purity, charity, tolerance? The whole building rises up to heaven from living stones,[6] joined to one another in admirable harmony. Christ himself is the cornerstone embracing the whole structure,[7] lest it be subject to any unsteadiness. These stones are the different orders of saints. He rejoices to be present in this temple, as he says elsewhere: 'My delights are to be with the sons of men.'[8] That great Solomon glories in these riches, nowhere more admirable, nowhere more glorious than in his saints. He has deemed them worthy of this honour, that he made them members of himself,[9] and that he made them co-heirs of the heavenly kingdom,[10] elected to the name and right of brothers.

He died for all,[11] but his special glory is in the throngs of martyrs and the choruses of virgins. These are his most precious jewels in which the church of Christ, which knows not how to glory[12] save in the gifts of her Bridegroom, accordingly takes pride and boasts. For whatever is glorious in the saints is the gift of Christ. Varied are the delights, varied are the ornaments of your Bridegroom, most excellent virgins. He makes his way adorned with the varied gems of the virtues, with innumerable varieties of

* * * * *

4 Ps 45:2 (Vulg 44:3)
5 Cf 1 Cor 12:10.
6 Cf 1 Pet 2:4.
7 Cf Eph 2:20–1.
8 Cf Prov 8:31.
9 Cf Eph 5:30; 1 Cor 12:27.
10 Cf Rom 8:17.
11 Cf 2 Cor 5:14.
12 2 Cor 10:17

flowers, but his soul takes particular delight in the roses of martyrs or the lilies of virgins. Nor is it surprising if he loves what he is himself, what he is the source of, indeed, for others. 'I am,' he says, 'the flower of the field and the lily of the valley.'[13] He is the prince of martyrs; through him the martyrs are strong. He is the leader of virgins, and through him virgins conquer the flesh with its desires.

After he came to earth, when the fire of charity had been loosed against winter and had put it to flight, these flowers appeared everywhere in our land.[14] How rare was virginity before![15] After Christ consecrated it, however, what countless thousands of young men and young women suddenly rose throughout the whole world, who freely castrated themselves for the kingdom of God![16] After he, by dying on the cross, showed that they who die in the Lord[17] are fortunate, how many swarms of men and women stood forth, who willingly and even joyfully handed their bodies over to death for the glory of Christ? Surely, this is what your Bridegroom boasts of in the Song of Songs: 'Arise, hurry, my beloved, my dove, my beautiful one, and come. For now the winter has disappeared, the rain has gone and departed, the flowers have appeared in our land.'[18] What barrenness there would be throughout our land, if that heavenly sun were not enkindling our souls with the love, if he did not nourish our minds with the dew, of his grace!

* * * * *

13 Song of Sol 2:1. For the lily of the valley in this verse as Christ, see Ambrose *De institutione virginis* 14 PL 16 327B: 'Divine prophecies testify that there is also a lily in this grain [ie the grain of life in Mary's womb] because it is written, "I am the flower of the field and the lily of the valleys, like a lily in the midst of thorns" [Song of Sol 2:1–2].' Ambrose's ensuing treatment of Christ the lily furnishes close verbal parallels to Erasmus' treatment of Christ the lily, virgin, and exemplar of virgins. (See nn20 and 26 below). St Jerome (347–419/20), priest, ascetic, and principal translator of the Latin Bible, interprets the 'flower of the field and lily of the valley' as the virginal Christ in his Ep 22 (henceforth *Ad Eustochium*) 19 PL 22 406.
14 Cf Song of Sol 2:12.
15 Cf Ambrose *De virginibus ad Marcellinam sororem* (henceforth *Ad Marcellinam*) 3 PL 16 192B: 'Indeed, after our Lord came into this mortal body and made the intimate association of divinity and humanity without any stain of admixture, then the practice of the heavenly life spread throughout the whole world and ripened in the bodies of mere men.' Ambrose goes on to argue (192C–194B) that virginity was rare or unknown among Jews and pagans before the coming of Christ.
16 Cf Matt 19:12.
17 Cf Rev 14:13.
18 Song of Sol 2:10–12

Yet what is more springlike than the spring of the gospel? What is richer? What is more lovable? The rose has its brief scarlet and the grace of lilies is brief, whence some pagan has written the phrase 'not the long-lived parsley nor the brief lily.'[19] By contrast, those special flowers in which the church is fertile never wither. For Christ is the immortal lily, and he confers immortal grace on the lilies that belong to him. He is the immortal rose whose beauty never withers, and he gives the same permanence to his own roses. He is called the flower of the field, however, because of the Jews. Fields are suitable for cultivation. Among the Jews, whom Moses and the prophets had cultivated, although they did not respond satisfactorily to those cultivators, he was bathed in his own blood.[20] He was the 'lily of the valley' amid harsh and uncultivated peoples, who were persuaded that from the virgin Mary he had been garbed in human flesh incapable of any blemish. Truly, he was the lily of the Gospel, for God the Father adorned him as Solomon was not adorned in all his glory.[21] For neither Solomon nor anyone else received as his lot flesh from a virgin, flesh unsoiled by the stain of our first parent.

Those who join themselves to this lily in faith, because they become one flesh and one spirit with him, are cleansed of stains, receive the whiteness of innocence, and themselves also become lilies. For thus in the same passage the Bridegroom, who had called himself a lily, speaks next: 'As a lily amid thorns, so is my beloved among the daughters.'[22] What is the lily amid thorns? The virgin amid wives. Matrimony is an honourable estate, but it is overgrown with thorns and briars. 'They will have,' says Paul, 'carnal tribulation of this kind.'[23] If anyone doubts whether marriage has its thorns, let him ask wives what kind of troubles a demanding husband brings, or one who is a drunkard, a gambler, an adulterer, or a spendthrift; what kind of annoyances in-laws bring, or disrespectful children; and let him deny, if he chooses, that a virgin is a lily among thorns. A virgin free from the cares of this world minds the things of

* * * * *

19 Horace *Odes* 1.36.16
20 Contrast Ambrose *De institutione virginis* 14 PL 16 327B: 'Christ was a lily in the midst of thorns when he was in the midst of Jerusalem.'
21 Cf Matt 6:29; Luke 12:27.
22 Song of Sol 2:2
23 1 Cor 7:28. For Erasmus on the difficulties of marriage, see 166, 179–80 below; cf Ambrose on the disadvantages of matrimony compared to virginity in *Ad Marcellinam* 6 PL 16 195C–197D. St Cyprian (200/10–258), bishop of Carthage martyred under the emperor Valerian, treats the superiority of the virgin's to the spouse's lot in *De habitu virginum* 22 PL 4 474A–475A.

the Lord, how she may please him.[24] A woman who has a husband is pulled hither and thither as it were, into many things, by various tormenting cares.

All those, indeed, who have put on Christ[25] are lilies, but especially virgins.[26] Among them that marvellous Bridegroom, who is not captivated by just anyone, feeds and takes delight. 'My beloved is mine and I am his. He feeds amid lilies, until the day breaks and the darkness abates.'[27] He collects such flowers in order that he may weave from them an imperishable crown[28] in heaven. In the same way, it is said elsewhere, 'My beloved comes down into his garden, to a bed of spices, that he may be fed there in the gardens and gather lilies.'[29]

To these lilies, undoubtedly, it is said in Ecclesiasticus, 'Flourish, flowers, like the lily and give off fragrance; bloom into grace and sing a song of praise together, blessing the Lord in his works.'[30] The virgin Bridegroom delights in the hymns of virgins. This is a new song,[31] unknown to the synagogue, where a barren woman was cursed because she did not give birth.[32] In the Gospel, however, innumerable persons, who have been ransomed from the earth and joined to the company of angels, sing a new song,[33] because virgins take neither husbands nor wives but follow the Lamb wherever he goes,[34] present without stain[35] before the throne of God. Many women were spotless in human eyes, but happy the ones who appear so before the throne

* * * * *

24 Cf 1 Cor 7:33–4.
25 Cf Rom 13:14; Gal 3:27.
26 Cf Ambrose *De institutione virginis* 15 PL 16 327C: 'Those who profess the passion of Christ are Christ's lilies, especially holy virgins, who possess shining, immaculate virginity.'
27 Song of Sol 2:16–17
28 1 Cor 9:25
29 Song of Sol 6:2
30 Ecclus 39:14
31 Cf Rev 5:9, 14:3.
32 Erasmus may be alluding to verses such as Isa 23:4, 26:18, and 37:3, but most probably he is simply calling to mind that barren women were often looked down upon, as was true of Sarah, Rebecca, Rachel, Hannah – and even of Elizabeth, the mother of John the Baptist. He exaggerates when he says they were 'cursed.'
33 Cf Rev 14:3.
34 Cf Rev 14:4 and Jerome *Adversus Helvidium* 21 PL 23 215B–216A: 'In this group are those who follow the Lamb, for they have not soiled their garments since they have remained virgins.'
35 Rev 14:5

of God, happy the ones who truly sing a new song to the new Bridegroom, singing psalms in their hearts[36] and calling themselves happy because they chastely sing chaste hymns to the one who is chaste.

Frequently your chorus also sings this hymn to the Bridegroom: 'Jesus, crown of virgins, whom that exalted mother conceives, the only virgin to give birth, mercifully receive these prayers.'[37] What great purity! The prince of virgins himself, both the Bridegroom and crown of virgins, is conceived in a virgin through the heavenly Spirit and is born of a virgin with the beauty of her virginity unimpaired. A husband is the glory of wives, Christ is the glory of virgins. (Further, to call attention to a point in passing, the metrical pattern requires that we read 'conceives' not 'conceived.' For 'conceives' is an alteration of tense.[38] This rhetorical device gives pleasure whenever it sets the action itself before our eyes, without distinctions of time. Otherwise, why was somebody offended by the present tense of 'conceives,' but not the present tense of 'brings forth'?)

'You who feed your flock among the lilies, surrounded by crowds of virgins, adorning the brides with glory, bestowing rewards on the bride-grooms.'[39] The shepherd, who gave his life for his sheep,[40] who even to-day has not laid aside the care of his flock, is your Bridegroom. Each day he guards it, each day he calls to it, each day he heals it, each day he feeds it. He too, however, has his own delights, which he enjoys; he has his close com-rades whom he calls bridegrooms; he has as his companions young maidens whom he calls brides. In spiritual matters there is no sex, but the designa-tions of sex or age are applied as is appropriate. There is one bride of Christ, the church.[41] She has many members,[42] each one of whom can be called a bride. He is the only Bridegroom, but he nevertheless holds certain men par-ticularly dear, and to them he entrusts his brides, so that these men also in some manner can be called bridegrooms. For if bishops are rightly called shepherds, although there is one shepherd, the Lord Jesus, what forbids these same persons' being called bridegrooms?

* * * * *

36 Cf Eph 5:19.
37 *Iesu, corona virginum* (see n20 to the introductory note) 1–4
38 Erasmus uses *hypallage temporis* or *enallage temporis* to mean a departure from the normal use of tenses, whether by error or for rhetorical effect. Cf LB VI 344E: 'The present tense adds a special grace to narrative, for we picture some past deed we are describing as being done now.' Cf also LB VI 284E, 1013E.
39 *Iesu, corona virginum* 5–8
40 Cf John 10:11.
41 For the church as the bride of Christ, see Rev 21:2, 9; 22:16–17.
42 Cf Eph 5:22–33.

Certainly the wives of this world are always puffed up with the pre-
rogatives and dignity of their husbands.[43] They flaunt and parade their own
feminine adornments. Furthermore, those who do not have a husband seem
rejected and destitute. The Bridegroom Jesus, however, decorates his brides
with spiritual gifts in place of the ornaments of this world, which they have
scorned. In exchange for the glory of the flesh, which soon vanishes, he
confers on them immortal glory. Indeed, he confers prizes on the bridegrooms as on vigorous athletes,[44] for they, in accord with the example of
the supreme Shepherd have fought even to the death for his sheep. What
prizes? Not the oak or the laurel crown, not a statue or title or other similar
reward, with which the world is accustomed to repay deeds well done, but
an imperishable crown[45] in heaven and a name written in the book of life[46]
that no future age can ever abolish.

Although he disdains no one, however humble, that delightful Bridegroom particularly rejoices in this company. For it follows: 'Wherever you
go, virgins follow, and they run after you with praises, singing, and they
make sweet hymns resound.'[47] According to the world, it is improper for a
virgin to run after the bridegroom of her own accord, but it becomes more
shameful if many maidens follow one bridegroom. In matters of the spirit
it is otherwise, for nothing is lovelier than for as many virgins as possible
to cling to the one Bridegroom Jesus. It is not surprising, however, if they
run as though maddened by the love of their Bridegroom. For he draws by
secret enticements, lovable above all human love, beautiful beyond the sons
of men, on whose lips grace has been poured,[48] whose countenance angels
consider it the highest happiness to behold. He breathes with his fragrances
on whom he wishes, and the virgins he has breathed on say, 'Draw me after
you; we will run in the fragrance of your ointments.'[49] They cannot run
unless they are drawn; they cannot love unless first they have been loved.
Those who have been drawn already wish to be drawn more fully. Those
who run desire to run nearer, that they may be joined more closely to him
whom they love. Moreover, they who say, 'Lord, where will we go? You

* * * * *

43 Cf Jerome *Ad Eustochium* 16 PL 22 403: 'Insignificant little wives are accustomed to congratulate themselves on husbands who are judges or who hold
   some special rank.'
44 Cf 1 Cor 9:25.
45 Ibidem
46 Cf Phil 4:2; Rev 13:18, 17:8, 21:27.
47 *Iesu, corona virginum* 9–12
48 Cf Ps 45:2 (Vulg 44:3).
49 Cf Song of Sol 1:2–3.

have the words of life,'[50] have felt the grace poured on his lips.[51] All who profess the name of Christ follow their shepherd Jesus, but only these inseparable companions follow wherever he goes, follow even to blows, follow even to the cross.

When the Lord Jesus was on earth, he often led behind him a huge crowd of all sorts of persons. When he went to Jerusalem to suffer death his following was smaller; but it was smaller by far when, bearing his cross, he went to Mount Calvary. Those, however, who are truly companions of the Bridegroom, who are truly virgins, are not torn away from their Bridegroom even here. When he was hanging on the cross, Peter, who is believed to have had a wife, was nowhere to be found, but virgins were clinging to the cross – Mary, the mother of Jesus, and John; the other women were standing some distance away from it, witnesses of what was being done.

Virgins follow, therefore, and, indeed, they follow eagerly and willingly. Nor do they follow mutely, but with songs and praises, and they sing sweet hymns. Women married to mortal men do not have the leisure to be present in these choruses; they do not have the leisure, and, in fact, sometimes they do not wish to sing. They must do what their husbands want; they must quarrel with maids and household servants; the children must be punished.

Our virgins, free from all the cares of this world, do nothing but sing sweet hymns to their Bridegroom in spiritual choirs. For they take no thought for themselves; they pour forth all the glory of their happiness onto him, to whom alone they owe everything. That great lover delights in songs of this kind; he wishes his gifts to be celebrated in song. He hates the songs of the Pharisees: 'I fast twice a week; I give a tenth of my goods to the poor; I am not as other men.'[52] The more chaste a virgin, the more modest she is. Hear the voice of a true virgin: 'Behold the handmaid of the Lord,'[53] and 'He has regarded the humility of his handmaid.'[54] In the Song of Songs, he calls his bride a dove, he desires to see her beauty, he hopes to hear her voice. 'Come,' he says, 'my dove in the clefts of the rock, in the hollows of the stone wall, show me your face, let your voice sound in my ears, for your voice is sweet and your face is beautiful.'[55]

* * * * *

50 John 6:68
51 Cf Ps 45:2 (Vulg 44:3).
52 Cf Luke 18:11–12.
53 Cf Luke 1:38.
54 Cf Luke 1:48.
55 Song of Sol 2:13–14

The soul too has its countenance, and it has its voice. The countenance is judged especially from the eyes. We communicate by the eyes; by the eyes we signify without speaking the intimate emotions of our souls. The eye of a virgin is simple. She does not envy, she does not intrigue, she does not suspect evil, she does not think evil thoughts.[56] A countenance of this kind delights the Bridegroom, who a little later speaks thus: 'How beautiful you are, my beloved, how beautiful. Your eyes are the eyes of doves.'[57] At this point someone may say, 'What sweetness does the querulous and moaning voice of the dove have to delight anyone? The voice of the nightingale should have been used in the comparison instead.' An exquisite and vehement love has endless complaints, but they are alluring and most pleasing to the Bridegroom. Hear the dove moaning: 'I long to be dissolved and be with Christ.'[58] And again: 'Wretched man that I am, who will deliver me from this body of death?'[59] Hear another dove: 'Woe is me, because my sojourn is prolonged.'[60] And, 'There, by the waters of Babylon we sat and wept when we remembered you, O Sion.'[61] These voices, complaining and full of sighs, are most pleasing to the ears of the Bridegroom. He delights in songs of this kind.

Because, however, the virgins had said, 'mercifully accept these prayers,'[62] it is time that they reveal what they hope for from the Bridegroom. Is it riches, is it honours, is it sensual pleasures, is it power, is it a long life? Those whom a vehement love of the Bridegroom has once seized in their very marrow are unconcerned about these things. What, therefore, is their hope? 'Yet further we pray thee, enlarge our minds, so that henceforward they may be unacquainted with all the wounds of corruption.'[63] They recognize how great a treasure is virginity, that is, an uncorrupted soul in an uncorrupted body. They recognize that everything that they possess comes from the generosity of the Bridegroom. They hope, therefore, that what he has bestowed he will increase, that he may heap kindness upon kindness. For there is no virgin so pure that she does not have some way in which she may make progress. You can scarcely find a virgin who, though her body

* * * * *

56 Cf 1 Cor 13:4–5.
57 Song of Sol 4:1
58 Cf Phil 1:23.
59 Rom 7:24
60 Ps 120 (Vulg 119):5
61 Ps 137 (Vulg 136):1
62 *Iesu, corona virginum* 4
63 *Iesu, corona virginum* 13–16

be intact, does not sometimes slip in thought.[64] Now true virginity is not found solely in the gift of chastity; every vice of the soul is a corruption of this virginity.

If someone has strayed from the straight path of Catholic faith, that person's virginity is soiled. Paul speaks of this purity, writing to the Corinthians: 'I have betrothed you to one husband, in order to present you as a chaste virgin to Christ. I fear, however, that as the serpent seduced Eve by its cleverness, so your senses are corrupted and fall short of simplicity, which is in Christ Jesus.'[65] A virgin is stained by envy, by disparagement of others, by arrogance. She is not free of the wound of corruption. Virgins pray, therefore, that the most generous Bridegroom may increase their riches and grant them to be totally unacquainted with all the wounds of corruption.[66] What does 'totally' mean? In soul and body. What does 'all' mean? Whatever human desire may suggest. This prayer could seem presumptuous were not the Bridegroom almighty and of the greatest fidelity. He does not wish his own merely to be like himself, but he wants them even to be identical with himself.

Let us grant, however, that in this life what the chorus of virgins desires happens perfectly to no one. Nevertheless, the prayer of that most pleasing choir will not be unfulfilled. What they have contemplated with the approval of their Bridegroom here on earth will fully come to pass when their Bridegroom magnifies them. The church militant has its ranks, so too has the church triumphant. (I do not know if it seems to you – I do not regret it – that I have lingered too long on the hymn written by Ambrose. For, to omit other arguments, the trisyllabic word at the end of each dimeter betrays the author.[67] In this practice, I think, that illustrious man was not so much captivated by the harmony of the metre as delighted by the symbol of the Holy Trinity.)

The church, the bride of Christ, has many hymns, but I doubt that any others are sung with greater universal rejoicing than those that celebrate

* * * * *

64 Jerome discusses the possibility of bodily purity and spiritual contamination in *Ad Eustochium* 5 PL 22 397: 'These women [ie virgins who 'have already committed adultery in their hearts,' cf Matt 5:28] are evil virgins, virgins in the flesh, not the spirit, foolish virgins shut out from the Bridegroom because they have no oil (cf Matt 25:1–13).'
65 2 Cor 11:2–3
66 Cf *Iesu, corona virginum* 15–16.
67 The lines of *Iesu, corona virginum* are in iambic dimeter, a metrical pattern which basically consists of four iambs, though certain substitutions of longs and shorts are allowed. In the hymn, each iambic dimeter ends with a three-syllable word.

the Bridegroom in the victories of martyrs or the triumphs of virgins. But that we may return to those two flowers that are by far most fragrant, the rose and the lily: as the death of Christ by its fragrance drew very many to contempt for this life, so the virginity of Christ enticed very many into the love of chastity. Those who were drawn by him, having also become flowers now themselves, have drawn others. Christ said to Peter, 'Follow me.'[68] How many have followed Peter! Who denies that a great deal is owed to the holy Doctors, who in tranquil circumstances taught the way of the Lord? How many more has the fragrance of martyrs drawn to the profession of the gospel! How many more has the example of virgins led to do the same! It is a great thing to argue convincingly and learnedly concerning the gospel, but the greatest is to die eagerly for the gospel. It is a great thing to despise the glory or riches of this world, but it is greater by far to mortify the flesh with its lusts.[69]

The church recognizes to whom she is indebted. In accord with Christ, she has honoured no one more fully than those who have willingly and gladly handed over their bodies to the cruelty of the executioner for the glory of the Bridegroom and the safety of the flock for which he himself deigned to die. The next degree of honour has been reserved for those who have voluntarily castrated themselves for the sake of God's kingdom.[70] How great was the solemn rejoicing of the whole church when a martyr had breathed forth his soul in steadfastness for Christ! What mourning, had anyone given in! How great also was the church's exultation if any virgin, who was free to marry a human bridegroom, had taken the holy veil and preferred to marry Christ! What mourning, had anyone laid aside that veil and accepted the wedding veil![71] To be sure, the loss of a treasured possession is a sad thing.

With what ardour Christians once ran to the ashes of martyrs! How holy their memory was among all the worshippers of Christ, when every day old men, young men, married women, and virgins ran to the prisons as to places consecrated by God, when kisses were pressed to the chains by which

* * * * *

68 Cf Matt 4:18–20; Mark 1:16–18.
69 Cf Gal 5:24.
70 Cf Matt 19:12.
71 Cf Cyprian *De habitu virginum* 20 PL 4 472A on corrupted virgins: 'In this way, therefore, the church often bemoans its own virgins, in this way it groans at their impurities and detestable storytelling. Thus the flower of virgins is extinguished, thus the honour of self-restraint and that of modesty are impaired, thus all their glory and dignity is debauched!'

they had been bound, when the sword by which they had been slain was preserved among the holy relics! What memory is happier or more joyful for the church than the memory of martyrs? When does the church sing more triumphantly than on their anniversaries? Nay, rather, she calls their sufferings palm branches, their torments triumphs, their deaths birthdays – and there is nothing gloomy in these celebrations, but all things are full of joy, full of thanksgiving, full of applause, full of solemn rejoicing.

Nor has the eloquence of learned men shown itself to better advantage in any other subject than in celebrating the praises of virgins and martyrs. Here Prudentius has surpassed Pindar's majestic eloquence in lyric song, has surpassed Horace's inimitable elegance.[72] Here the trumpet of Greek and Latin Christians alike has thundered out something grander and more divine than pagan epic. Here Chrysostom,[73] Cyprian,[74] Ambrose,[75] and others too numerous to mention surpass the happy abundance of Cicero.[76] What do we guess is the cause? Obviously, the greatness of the martyrs was supplying the abundance of eloquence, warmth of heart was adding power to the discourse, piety was adding enthusiasm. A rich flow of discourse is theirs on every occasion, but, whenever they have come to the martyrs and virgins,

* * * * *

72 The Latin Christian poet Prudentius (348 to after 405) praises martyrs in his collection of lyric poems, *Peristephanon liber* PL 60 275–594. In comparing Prudentius' poetry to the finest works of the ancient lyric tradition, the Greek lyrics of Pindar (518–438 BC) and the Latin lyrics of Horace (65 BC–8 BC), Erasmus boldly asserts the parity of the best Christian literature with its pagan models and rivals.

73 St John Chrysostom (c 344/54–507), patriarch of Constantinople and prolific author, composed a work entitled *De virginitate* PG 48 533–96. For three homilies entitled *In sanctos Maccabaeos* attributed to him, see PG 50 617–28.

74 On martyrs, Cyprian (see n23 above) wrote *Epistola ad Fortunatum de exhortatione martyrii* PL 4 681–702, and on virgins, *De habitu virginum* PL 451–78 (first cited n23 above).

75 Ambrose (see n20 to the introductory note) wrote several works on virginity in addition to the already mentioned *Ad Marcellinam* PL 16 187–234 (first cited n15 above) and *De institutione virginis* PL 16 305–34 (first cited n13 above). These other works include *De virginitate liber unus* PL 16 265–302 and *Exhortatio virginitatis* PL 16 335–62. *De lapsu virginis consecratae* PL 16 367–84 and *Ad virginem devotam* PL 17 579–84 are attributed to him with less certainty.

76 In *Ad Eustochium* 22 PL 22 409 Jerome recommends for reading on virginity Cyprian's 'distinguished volume' and the 'recent little works' on the subject Ambrose had written for his sister. Jerome also recommends verse and prose compositions on virginity by Pope Damasus I (reigned 366–84), as well as the lost *Ad amicum philosophicum* and other works by the African apologist Tertullian (c 160 to after 220; for Tertullian's extant works on virginity and martyrdom see n83 below).

then they sound something grander than human melody, as if by the inspiration of divine power. These things do not come about because of human exertions, but they are done by the breath of the Divine Spirit, who wishes in this way to glorify his saints, in whom he seeks to appear most glorious.

We would admit that these are human matters, save that God, who inspires the minds of the faithful, adorns the tombs of martyrs and virgins with so many miracles. Where are wicked demons put to harsher torture? Where are sicknesses that doctors cannot cure expelled more often? What emperor, what king has won such honour even in this world with any of the statues, the titles, the pyramids, the temples, the priestly colleges, the divine honours dedicated to him?

Yes, in this way God honours his martyrs, who here below seemed afflicted, humble, and dejected; in this way he honours his virgins, for, as if dead to the world, they have placed their whole hope in the Bridegroom Jesus. The glory of martyrs does not shine forth clearly except in death; virginity has its beauty even in this transitory life. Who is so barbarous as to be ill disposed to a virgin? In the midst of the tumults of war a pitiless enemy spares the virgin. If we believe legends, dumb animals and savage beasts respect virginity.[77] In how much honour vestal virgins were once held in Rome![78] Here is that innate beauty of virginity that idolaters acknowledge, that the barbarian enemy reveres, that dumb animals sense, that beasts spare. If such honour is given to the virgins of this world,[79] how much more honourable is Christ's virgin. Assume, O virgin, a holy pride, and consider whatever pleasure or honours this world boasts beneath your dignity.

* * * * *

77 The seemingly apocryphal virgin/martyr St Thecla was adored by the wild beast sent to attack her; see Ambrose *Ad Marcellinam* 3 PL 16 211C–212B. For a medieval formulation of the tradition that wild beasts spared virgins, see the anonymous *Speculum virginum* 9.710 CCCM 5 273; here the rhinoceros is apparently confused with the unicorn: 'A shapely girl, beautifully dressed, is found and placed in a spot where [the rhinoceros] frequently goes; when the indomitable beast sees her it soon runs up to her, lays aside its ferocity, grows gentle, and, kneeling, places its head in her lap. Thus, when hunters have prepared this trap, the beast is captured, but the maiden is not harmed.' I owe this reference to the courtesy of Mr Stephen Ryle of the University of Leeds.

78 The vestal virgins served Vesta, goddess of the hearth, tending the perpetual fire of her temple hearth. In historical times there were normally six priestesses who served for thirty years. They remained virgins during their term of service, but could marry afterwards.

79 In *Adversus Iovinianum* 1.41–2 PL 23 282B–286A, Jerome furnishes a long list of 'virgins of this world' (ie pagan virgins) who chose to die rather than sacrifice their virginity.

It is holy to take pride in your Bridegroom; it is pious to boast in him,[80] to whom you owe everything. It is safe, with confidence in him, to raise his crests against the world, flaunting his delights.

It is not my intention at present to rehearse completely whatever can be said in praise of martyrs or virgins. You have the books of Cyprian,[81] you have those of Ambrose,[82] you have those of Tertullian[83] and Jerome.[84] (The last two were almost excessive in their admiration of virginity. For the excellence of virginity must not be extolled in such a way that praise of it has been joined with aspersions on chaste marriage.)[85] I repeat these things, dearest virgins, that you may understand the happiness of your community, whose fortune it is to possess both things that the wealthy bride of Christ, the church, holds dear in her world.

For you safeguard those most fragrant roses that belong to the seven brothers Maccabee and their mother,[86] whose fecundity bore fruit not for her husband but for God. She filled the loss of her virginity happily indeed with the martyrdom of so many sons.[87] She did not give birth as a virgin, for that has been granted to only one among women, but she gave birth to

* * * * *

80 Cf 1 Cor 1:31; 2 Cor 10:17.
81 See n74 above.
82 See n75 above.
83 Tertullian (see n76 above) praises both virginity and martyrdom in his writings. See *Ad martyras* PL 1 691–702 and *De virginibus velandis* PL 2 935–62. He condemns worldly feminine adornments in *De cultu feminarum* PL 1 1417–48.
84 Among the works of St Jerome (see n13 above) which treat virginity are his *Ad Eustochium* PL 22 394–425 (first cited n13 above); *Adversus Iovinianum* PL 23 221–352; and *Adversus Helvidium* PL 23 193–216 (first cited n34 above).
85 For Tertullian's strictures on marriage see *Ad mulierem*, especially 1.1 PL 1 1385–9, where he exhorts his wife to remain a widow after his death. In *De monogamia* PL 2 979–1004, he violently attacks the lawfulness of second marriage; see also *De exhortatione castitatis* PL 2 963–78. Jerome argues that marriage is indeed a good, though second to virginity, for the latter belonged to man's blessed prelapsarian state whereas the former is solely a result of the fall. See *Ad Eustochium* 19–20 PL 22 405–7, and *Adversus Iovinianum* 1.3–4 PL 23 222B–225C. Erasmus criticizes Jerome's view of marriage at greater length in an addendum to Erasmus' edition of Jerome's *Ad Eustochium* CWE 61 192–3. See also his 'Life of Jerome' CWE 61 48–9.
86 These relics owned by the convent were evidently brought to Cologne from Italy in the late twelfth century. See Allen Ep 842 introduction.
87 For the martyrdom of the Maccabees in the church Fathers mentioned by Erasmus, see Cyprian *Ad Fortunatum* 11 PL 4 694A–698A; Prudentius *Peristephanon* 5.521–36, 10.751–78 PL 60 407A–409A, 502A–503A; Pseudo-Ambrose *Ad virginem devotam* 3 PL 17 584C.

virgins and martyrs. She could not furnish an example of virginity herself, but she furnished what she could with great zeal.[88] She educated her sons for virginity, she urged them to martyrdom and would also have preceded them, if she had not feared for the tender years of her sons.

The glory of virginity, therefore, did not touch a mother with sons; but in the business of martyrdom the mother's praise is so much the greater because, as a spectator of her sons' cruel torments, she suffered with each of them whatever the cruelty of the executioners could do against their bodies. (This is braver than ending your suffering once and for all with execution. Parents are tormented more savagely in their children than in themselves. Tyrants in their ingenious cruelty also know this, for they extort from parents by torturing their children in front of them what they cannot wring from their victims' own torments. So many times in this way does a wife and mother see her own entrails torn asunder!)

Where is the weakness of her sex found here? Where a parent's natural feeling (usually so strong in mothers), which sways her even less than it would a male? Obviously, duty towards God overcame her duty towards men, and the ardour of faith overcame the weakness of her sex.[89] Hail, most fortunate woman hero, who gave all males an example of courage. Hail, fairest flower-buds of the church, who anticipated the spring of the gospel like delights before their season, and who showed the power of the gospel before the gospel was proclaimed. The words of him who was born a virgin of a virgin had not yet been heard – 'Blessed are those who have castrated themselves for the sake of God's kingdom'[90] – but nevertheless you anticipate praise. The words had not yet been heard, 'He who wishes to be my disciple, let him take up his cross and follow me.'[91] You, as forerunners, foreshadow the Christ who will suffer; and indeed, your souls in heaven now follow the Lamb wherever he goes.[92] What is more, your uncorrupted bodies, which you will receive again in the fellowship of eternal happiness as you once had them as companions of your torment, could not be preserved anywhere more properly than in the holy community of virgins.

* * * * *

88 St Ambrose treats filial virginity as a compensation for marriage in his *Exhortatio virginitatis* 4 PL 16 343C. There, the interlocutor Juliana is made to say to her sons, 'You can, nevertheless, excuse your father and absolve your mother, if what is missing in them [ie virginity] is represented in you.'
89 Cf 2 Macc 7:21.
90 Cf Matt 19:12.
91 Cf Matt 16:24; Mark 8:34; Luke 9:23.
92 Cf Rev 14:4.

Now, most holy virgins, guardians of so great a treasure, my discourse will turn to you. You have in these same youths both an example of chastity, which you are to imitate, and the laurels of martyrdom, which you will proclaim, glorifying your Bridegroom, who did battle in them, who has conquered in them, who triumphs in them. You have in the same flower-basket lilies mixed with roses. Each beauty competes with the other, yet neither is obscured by the other. Each, rather, is made more brilliant by the proximity of the other, as when 'ivory is adulterated by purple' (so writes the famous author)[93] or a white gem is enclosed in tawny gold.[94]

The contest of glory between the martyr and the virgin has such doubtful results, however, that I would not dare decide which ought to be preferred to the other, should the matter be called into dispute. Each was consecrated in Christ, but nevertheless we owe more to his cross than to his virginity. He awarded the title 'blessed' to those who had castrated themselves for the kingdom of God,[95] but he required imitation of the cross.[96] However, that action seems greater which, although it is not required, nevertheless confers blessedness if someone should freely perform it; and yet, in a time of persecution, of course, a soul always prepared to endure all manner of deaths for the glory of God is what one might call a great matter. Times and circumstances, like seas, have their tranquil periods, and it is sometimes lawful to escape the hands of the executioner.

If that final contest, death, is imminent, it is both the end of bodily torment and the beginning of happiness. The virgin, however, engages in a long and uninterrupted struggle with a foe in her own household, whom it is unlawful to kill and whom you cannot escape. This, of course, is the flesh, rebellious against the spirit,[97] that we carry around with us, whether we want to or not. Let no one think that conquering it is a light task. Often we read of men overcome by the allurements of the flesh who could not be overcome by the fear of death.

Our comparison has thus far considered which of the two is braver than the other; but virginity seems to me indeed more fortunate, in so far as the flower of martyrdom, as we said before in passing, does not bloom until after death, whereas virginity even in this world has its own brightness, its own fragrance, its own grace and dignity. Virginity is a flower of

* * * * *

93 Cf Virgil *Aeneid* 12.67–8.
94 Cf Virgil *Aeneid* 10.134.
95 Cf Matt 19:12.
96 Cf Matt 16:24; Mark 8:34; Luke 9:23.
97 Cf Gal 5:17.

the soul, but through it there are also reflected in the countenance, in the eyes, and in the whole disposition of the body a kind of angelic purity and a fresh lustre untouched by age, that intends to be here on earth what all who have lived devoutly in Christ Jesus[98] expect to be after death. An unsullied and uncorrupted soul pours its vigour into the body, just as a mind infected by the vices somehow shines in, or, rather, makes horrid, the very appearance of the body. Further, lust wreaks violence against even the body that harbours it. Why will the bodies of the faithful not grow old once they have arisen? Because the soul, which is untouched by old age, will then rule them. As death comes from sin, so do sickness and old age. Destroy sin and old age will be diminished; when old age occurs, it will be healthier. A virgin, therefore, already receives in advance here and now some part of her happiness, showing forth in her mortal body some of the beauty of future immortality.

The princes of this world do not care for their soldiers with greater zeal than they do for the military training school from which they draw fresh recruits when circumstances demand; but if the school should close, from what source will you fill the army? For some centuries now, no storms have arisen under Christian princes like those at one time under Nero,[99] Domitian,[100] Julian,[101] and Maxentius.[102] Whether the circumstances of Christianity would be better under these rulers, it is not for me to decide. Certainly, through them, Christianity has been drawn into closer unity. In any case, if a storm were to befall us again that demanded martyrs, where does this band seem likely to be gathered if not from these women who have spurned all the blandishments of this world and consecrated themselves totally to Jesus the

* * * * *

98 Cf 2 Tim 3:12.
99 Nero Claudius Caesar (37–68 AD, 54–68) attempted to blame the fire which destroyed half of Rome in 64 on the Christians. He had them charged with conspiracy and arson.
100 In 95 AD, the emperor Domitian (51–96, ruled 81–96) had his cousin Flavius Clemens, his niece Domitilla (Flavius Clemens' wife), and Acilius Glabrio, consul in 91, arrested on the charge of atheism, probably for engaging in either Jewish or Christian rites. The men were executed and Domitilla exiled. During his reign pagan authorities and Jews in Asia Minor seem to have allied themselves against Christians.
101 During his brief reign (361–3 AD) Julian the Apostate (332–63) attempted to restore the old pagan religion.
102 Maxentius (died 312 AD) ruled from Rome, where he was a champion of that city's ancient status and traditional pagan faith. A rival of Constantine for supreme power in the empire, he was defeated by Constantine and killed in the Battle of Mulvian Bridge.

heavenly Spouse, who of their own accord 'have crucified their flesh with its vices and fallen inclinations'?[103] For love of the Bridegroom they have spurned that pleasure for whose sake alone most mortals would desire to live on earth forever.

A true virgin is but a step away from being a martyr. A martyr suffers his flesh to be cut by the executioner; a virgin of her own free will mortifies her flesh daily. She is, in a certain sense, her own executioner. Sometimes it is braver to subdue a captive enemy than to kill him; a martyr surrenders his body, a virgin subdues it and reduces it to slavery to the spirit. Why will Christ's virgin tremble when a man raises his hand to strike her? Will she seek the riches, delights, haughtiness, luxury, and pleasures that detain others in this life? No! She has long since renounced all of these. The woman who loves nothing in this world, who, dead to the world, lives for Christ alone, who daily utters the plaints of the dove,[104] longing to be united still more closely to her beloved Bridegroom and clasped in his embraces – will she not gladly depart from this wretched body, in which she knows that she journeys far from the Lord? What men have shown more powerful strength of soul in their torments than the virgin martyrs – Agnes,[105] Cecilia,[106] Agatha,[107] and their countless sisters? Moreover, when a virgin is handed over to the executioner, she does not begin her martyrdom but ends a martyrdom long since begun.

If these deeds seem arduous to anyone, let him also reflect that the virgin's commitment is beyond human powers; it is a dignity equal to that of the angels. Nor, indeed, are all those women virgins who are veiled in black. For, just as Paul teaches that true widows are distinguished from those who are called by the title falsely and, as far as he is concerned, one who lives

* * * * *

103 Gal 5:24
104 Cf Isa 59:11.
105 Agnes (d at Rome c 350) is portrayed in legend and cult as a girl of twelve or thirteen who refused marriage and preferred death to any violation of her virginity. For praises of Agnes, see Ambrose *Ad Marcellinam* PL 16 189C–191B, and Prudentius *Peristephanon* 14 PL 60 580–90.
106 Cecilia (third century?), according to legend, refused to break a vow of virginity by consummating her marriage with the pagan Valerian. Her own martyrdom followed that of Valerian, whom she converted, and of her brother Tibertus. She survived an attempt to suffocate her in her own bathroom, but died after three attempted beheadings.
107 Agatha (before the fourth century), virgin and martyr, died at Catania in Sicily. According to late legends, her chastity survived a brothel, and her life survived rods, rack, fire, and the removal of her breasts. She eventually died in prison as a result of her sufferings.

amid pleasures is said to be dead,[108] in precisely the same way the virgin who loves something else in this world besides her Bridegroom is no virgin. In the Gospel there are prudent virgins who had provided for themselves with many works of religion, lest the oil fail in their lamps; there were also foolish ones.[109] Jeremiah too decries impure virgins,[110] for the dignity of this title ill accords with a woman who, although she has a body untouched by a male, nevertheless through her impure thoughts holds converse in her soul with Satan her paramour. A woman who does not want to live as a celibate is already married; a woman who would be corrupted if it were permitted has already been corrupted. It is most difficult to check all the thoughts of a mind as it wanders, and yet one must fight these assailants with prayers, reading of the Scriptures, fasts, and holy deeds. To consent to them is poison.

Eve, the first virgin, spoke with the serpent and thence was the origin of all evils; she had unchaste eyes, and the enticements of the alluring fruit corrupted them. More fashionable dress, a painted face, flattering letters from young men, little gifts sent back and forth – these are the signs of a virginity about to perish.[111] To whom does a virgin pay court once she has been consecrated to Christ? Why does she seek out the company of young men, she who has taken the veil so that the world might not see what had been dedicated to the Bridegroom Christ? A married woman adorns herself for the eyes of her husband, but why should a virgin who has married Christ adorn herself for the eyes of any mortal? Hear what a famous woman says in the writings of a learned but pagan poet: 'For whom am I adorned, unhappy woman, or whom do I strive to please? He is absent, the sole cause of my adornment.'[112]

If that woman neglects her toilette because her husband is not present, with what impudence does a virgin whose Bridegroom is in heaven bedeck herself in this world? Why does she stand at the mirror once she has been

* * * * *

108 1 Tim 5:5–6
109 Cf Matt 25:1–13.
110 Lam 1:4. The Latin of the Vulgate is closer to Erasmus' meaning than the English of the RSV: 'virgines eius [sunt] squalidae' ('... her [Sion's] virgins are despoiled').
111 The patristic writers mentioned by Erasmus frequently warn of the dangers posed by cosmetics, jewellery, fine clothes, and worldly society to virgins specifically. To this question Cyprian devoted the treatise *De habitu virginum* PL 4 451–78 and Tertullian the treatise *De cultu feminarum* PL 2 1417–48. For Ambrose's views see eg *Exhortatio virginitatis* 12 PL 16 360B–361A; ibidem 355C–D.
112 Ovid *Heroides* 15.77–8. *Heroides* 15 is an imaginary letter from Sappho to the absent Phaon.

betrothed to Christ? Why not rather examine yourself in the reflecting pool of divine Scripture? Why, furthermore, does she deck herself out with these ornaments, by which he is offended? That elegance of yours is mere dirt in the eyes of the Bridegroom, that radiance is filth, those perfumes are sickening. He loves the charms of the spirit, he loves elegance of soul, he loves the colours of the mind. However many women there may be in this world who adorn themselves for worldly eyes, the virgin who belongs to Christ is more magnificently ornamented by her contempt for these things than she would be by even a profusion of them. She is adorned more becomingly by her shaved head and holy veil than any bride by silks, by gold, by jewels, and by purple. For the false glow of scarlet has always been counted a vice, even among the pagans.[113] The bride of Christ has ornaments that make her worthy in God's sight as numerous as the ornaments of this world that she has scorned for love of her Bridegroom: instead of jewels, she is adorned with virtues; instead of purple, with charity; instead of gold, with wisdom; instead of scarlet dyes, with simplicity of soul; instead of silks, with chastity and reserve; instead of jewellery, with modesty. The brightness of her soul is not obscured by the meanness of her clothes.

The special glories of virgins are clear from the writings of the ancient Fathers: to cleanse the feet of the wretched, to wash the rags of paupers, to keep company with the sick and serve them, to handle the bodies of people covered with sores for the love of Christ.[114] A virgin soiled by these things is most beautiful in the eyes of Christ. For the rest, since the situation of holy virgins is different now, let them compete among themselves in the duties of charity, let them be ready to fill the needs of the poor with their own hands. If ever a virgin should chance to talk with worldly men, let it be her care that she send them away from the conversation corrected and that she herself not leave corrupted. Let the example of the first virgin, who was corrupted by the conversation of the deceiver and hurled herself into mournful misery, make you more cautious. A youth with seductive countenance, lascivious eyes, and immodest tongue is more poisonous than any serpent. Imitate the new Virgin, the guide and ruler of your way of life. She does not speak with the serpent, but, shut away in her room, speaks with an

* * * * *

113 Cf Livy 4.44.11–12 on the vestal virgin accused of unchastity because of overdressing.
114 Cyprian exhorts virgins to care for the poor in less graphic language than Erasmus in *De habitu virginum* 11 PL 4 461B–462A: 'Let the poor realize that you are rich, let the needy know that you are wealthy. Glean interest for God with your inheritance. Feed Christ.'

angel – whence comes the beginning of all salvation.[115] A virgin who speaks with an immodest youth speaks with the serpent. A virgin who besieges God with pious prayers and who meditates on the Scriptures speaks with an angel, or, rather, with her Bridegroom. Which is safer? Which is more honourable? Which is more splendid?

If ever, therefore, a desire for what the world flaunts as sweet and beautiful excites your souls, think to yourselves – and this is the truth – that you have not renounced them, but traded with them to your great profit. Furthermore, nobody is unhappier than those who may neither enjoy the goods of this world, which they thirst after, nor, because of a soul weakened by the desires of the flesh, rejoice in their own proper delights. The virgins of this world have their companions, they have their ornaments, they have their games, they have their songs and dances; but however fine these things may be, the virgins of this world possess them only until they have sold the flower of their youth to a husband. Christ's virgins have these same things, but in their true and internal, in their enduring reality. Those other women, having soon laid aside the virgin's garland, accept the wedding veil, which is clearly a sign of subjection, as even Paul testifies.[116] The virgins dedicated to God, however, are always veiled for their Bridegroom, lest they be seen by this unchaste world. For Jesus is a jealous lover, and he does not suffer the delights that belong to him to be defiled by profane eyes.[117]

Which, indeed, is more fortunate, to be the handmaid of a husband or of Christ? 'Behold,' she says, 'the handmaid of the Lord.'[118] Whoever is truly the handmaid of the Lord is mistress of the world. Interpret your veil rightly, O virgin. It is a sign of power, not of slavery. Women who are veiled for their husbands proclaim themselves enslaved to mortals – and, O good women, the rule of husbands is not always light! Wives often chance to have as husbands difficult masters, insolent, merciless, gambling, drunken, spendthrift, in debt, rough, raging, physically abusive, not to mention for the moment any more serious crimes or illnesses. Added to these are the care of the household, the care of the children, dealing with neighbours, quarrels, the death of children, widowhood.

* * * * *

115 Cf Ambrose *Exhortatio virginitatis* 10 PL 16 357B: 'Consider how great Mary was – and yet she was never found anywhere besides her own room when someone looked for her.'
116 Cf 1 Cor 11:3–15.
117 Cf Jerome *Ad Eustochium* PL 22 411: 'Jesus is jealous; he does not want your face to be seen by others.'
118 Luke 1:38

For it is not simply affliction of the flesh that Paul points out to those who prefer marriage.[119] To list completely, in declamatory fashion, whatever inconveniences attend marriage is not part of our present purpose. It is a wretched prudence to learn them from experience. It is preferable to learn about them in the books of wise men. If, however, you mistrust even these writings, summon, O virgin, one of these women who have married happily enough. Call her to witness so that she may tell the true story of her marriage. You will hear something to make you regret your commitment less.[120] Now consider the example of virgins who have married most unhappily (and there is a great crowd of them); reflect that whatever happens to them could have happened to you.

Virgins who truly, from their hearts, espouse the immortal Bridegroom Jesus are completely removed from whatever evils and whatever calamities commonly happen to those who marry a mortal spouse. Believe me, Jesus is not a sad or unlovable spouse. He was on one occasion seen without beauty or grace,[121] but he was never more lovable than when with love of his bride he assumed that appearance. What girl would not prize her suitor more highly if he, having abandoned his father's riches, with only a rustic beech tree for shelter, should take refuge in the little cottage of a humble virgin, to obtain her hand in marriage? What, however, if he should hasten wounded to his beloved bride? Would he not seem more lovable in rags and covered with blood? Surely he would seem so to the woman who loved him. Now think whether your Bridegroom should be despised by you. For your sake he left the citadel of his Father and descended to earth and, having hidden the majesty of the divine nature, put on the form of a slave, lowering himself even to the humiliation of the cross.[122]

To the virgin who loves her Bridegroom, the convent is not a prison, as some detractors say, but a paradise. You are not permitted to roam where you please. To do so is neither safe nor virtuous for virgins, nor even to be wished for (unless, perchance, the example of Dinah pleases you).[123]

* * * * *

119 Cf 1 Cor 7:28.
120 In his *Exhortatio virginitatis* 4 PL 16 343B Ambrose puts these words into the mouth of the holy widow Juliana: 'I have known, my son, the hardships of union and the humiliations of marriage with a good husband; not even with a good spouse was I free.' Even Erasmus' suggestion that nuns turn aside from their books to talk to married women may have a literary inspiration.
121 Cf Isa 53:2.
122 Cf Phil 2:7–8.
123 See Gen 34. Dinah, the daughter of Jacob and Leah, was abducted and raped by Shechem, son of Hamor. Simon and Levi, sons of Jacob, during pretended

Virginity is not a sad or unpleasant thing. It has its pleasure gardens in the Holy Scriptures, where it can saunter with the closest intimates of the Bridegroom. Immortal God, with what wonderful intimates! With Thecla,[124] Cecilia,[125] Agatha,[126] Theodora,[127] Eustochium,[128] and countless others. Virginity has its spiritual garlands, made from the varied flowers of the virtues; it has its perfumes, so that virgins can say with Paul, 'We are a pleasing fragrance to God in every place.'[129] The Bridegroom possesses the delights of spiritual perfumes, whose fragrance surpasses all other scents. What is more lovable than the name of Jesus? His name has been poured forth as perfume.[130] What weariness can women who have been attracted by this fragrance and follow him on his way feel in this life?

The virgin also has her perfume, with which she in turn delights her Bridegroom. 'While the king was in his chamber,' she says, 'my spikenard gave out its fragrance.'[131] In the Gospel, when he is about to marry his bride, the church, he is anointed with the sinful woman's oil.[132] Virgins have their harps from David, they have their psalter, they have their songs and spiritual hymns, with which they continually sing psalms to the Lord in their hearts, giving thanks, praising and entreating him, and frequently longing

* * * * *

negotiations for the marriage of Shechem and Dinah, killed both Shechem and Hamor and destroyed their city. Jerome also uses the example of Dinah to warn virgins against going out, in *Ad Eustochium* 25 PL 22 411.

124 Thecla (supposedly first century) is a dubious saint whose cult was suppressed by the Roman Catholic church in 1969. According to legend, the apostle Paul converted her to Christianity and virginity. As a result, Thecla's parents had Paul scourged, and she herself was subjected to various attempts at martyrdom: a storm put out a fire that was to burn her; the beasts who were to kill her in the amphitheatre refused to approach her. She passed the last seventy-two years of her life in a cave in Seleucia, where the ground opened and swallowed her at her own request when some men came to attack her.

125 See n106 above.

126 See n107 above.

127 Theodora of Alexandria was a purely legendary figure said to have lived disguised as a man among monks in the Egyptian desert.

128 Eustochium (d c 419), a nobly born Roman and the daughter of St Paula, was the recipient of Jerome's *Ad Eustochium*. Both ladies followed Jerome to Bethlehem, where they directed three communities of women. Eustochium ended her life peacefully in the Holy Land.

129 Cf 2 Cor 2:14.

130 Cf Matt 26:7; Mark 14:3.

131 Song of Sol 1:12

132 Cf Matt 26:6–13 and Luke 7:36–50, which tell how a sinful woman anointed Jesus with oil.

for the presence of their Bridegroom with sweet sighs whenever he has with-drawn for a time; for sometimes he turns aside and departs, not to desert them, but to renew their love.

What do the virgins of this world have, however happy they may be, that can be compared to these consolations? A space cannot seem narrow to those for whom the immensity of heaven soon opens out; companionship cannot seem limited to those who will soon experience the company of all the saints. Why should I not say 'soon'? How paltry is the sum of this life, so paltry that old age, which touches every human being, is already at hand! Accordingly, best of virgins, recognize your good fortune and you will not envy the world its illusory pleasures; recognize your dignity and you will not seek out the world's sordid business. 'Unless you have recognized your-self,' he says, 'most beautiful among women . . .'[133] In these words, the Bride-groom threatens virgins, if they have not recognized their happiness. They do not recognize it, however, if they repent of their commitment, if they sigh for the delights of the world.

Consider what kind of Bridegroom you have espoused; cling to him with all your hearts. In him you have, once and for all, everything that is truly joyous or magnificent. Let the example of the most holy youths inspire you to perseverance. They will rejoice all the more that the relics of their bodies are preserved in your community, if they have perceived that you are imitators of their virtues, by which they pleased God. They adorn your order, and so you in turn will ornament them by the purity of your con-duct. They preferred being tortured and stripped of their flesh with many torments to eating the flesh of swine. You, in turn, consider whatever dis-pleases your Bridegroom to be the flesh of swine. If you have been imitators of their most noble struggle, you will also be sharers of their glory, with the help of your Bridegroom Jesus, who with the Father and the Holy Spirit lives and reigns for ever. Amen.

* * * * *

133 Cf Song of Sol 1:7 (Vulg 1:8). Erasmus' words are closer to the Latin version than the RSV translation suggests. Jerome wrote, 'si ignoras te o pulchra inter mulieres' ('if you do not know yourself, O beauty among the women').

ERASMI ROTEROD. EPI/
stola consolatoria in aduersis.

APVD INCLYTAM BASI/
læam AN. M. D. XXVIII.

Epistola consolatoria in adversis, title-page.
Basel: Hieronymus Froben, 1528.
Beinecke Rare Book and Manuscript Library, Yale University

LETTER OF COMFORT IN ADVERSITY

Epistola consolatoria in adversis

translated and annotated by
STEPHEN RYLE

The *Epistola consolatoria in adversis* was first published early in 1528, but the seed of this 'little flower culled from the ever-verdant garden of Isaiah' (189) had been sown some thirty years before. In 1497–8 Erasmus, living the life of an impoverished theology student, was obliged to support himself by giving tuition to young men from wealthy families. One of his pupils was an Englishman named Thomas Grey.[1] Erasmus conceived a great affection for him, and it seems to have been to Grey, under the nickname Leucophaeus, that he originally dedicated *De ratione studii*.[2] The two men had remained in touch with each other subsequently. During the autumn of 1525 Grey paid a visit to his old teacher in Basel, bringing with him his youngest son, for whom he was hoping, with Erasmus' help, to obtain a place at the Collegium Trilingue in Louvain.[3] At the same time he was also apparently thinking of other members of his family. He had at least two sisters who were members of a community of Franciscan nuns (known in pre-Reformation England as Minoresses) at Denny, about twelve kilometres north of Cambridge.[4] He would presumably have read the *Virginis et martyris comparatio* in either its original or its expanded form;[5] and it seems probable that that work, addressed to the nuns of the Benedictine monastery of the Maccabees at Cologne, suggested to him the idea on the one hand of asking Erasmus to send a letter of greeting to the Denny nuns and on the

* * * * *

1 For Thomas Grey see Allen Ep 58 introduction; CEBR II 129–30.
2 See Ep 66; ASD I-2 151 / CWE 24 662, 665. For Leucophaeus cf Ep 221:39.
3 See Epp 1624:20, 1641.
4 The abbey of Denny (variously spelt Denney or Dennye) was founded c 1159 as a daughter-house of the monastic cathedral of Ely, and its earliest occupants were Benedictine monks. About 1170 it was presented to the Knights Templars, who established a hospital there for members of their order. After the dissolution of the Templars in 1312 the property was eventually granted to Marie de St Pol, countess of Pembroke. A community of Minoresses had taken possession of Denny by 1342, and after some resistance was united with a previously existing convent from nearby Waterbeach. See further A.F.C. Bourdillon *The Order of Minoresses in England* British Society of Franciscan Studies 12 (Manchester 1926; repr 1956); *The Victoria History of the Counties of England* (London 1900–   ): *Cambridgeshire and the Isle of Ely* II 295–302; Jennifer Ward *Women of the English Nobility and Gentry, 1066–1500* Manchester Medieval Sources Series (Manchester and New York 1995) 192–4, 202–3. For a brief history and description of the surviving buildings see J.G. Coad *Denny Abbey* (London 1984; repr 1993).
5 See the introductory note to *Virginis et martyris comparatio*, 154–6 above. For the thematic links between the *Comparatio* and the *Epistola consolatoria* see CWE 66 xxxiii.

other of urging the nuns to present his former teacher with some kind of gift, such as the sweetmeats that Erasmus had received from the Cologne nuns on three (or possibly more) occasions.

The outcome has to be reconstructed from the evidence of the *Epistola consolatoria*. Erasmus duly complied with Grey's request, writing a hastily composed letter which has not survived; the nuns in their turn dispatched a gift to the great humanist at Basel. However, the gift was stolen on the way, and never reached its intended destination. Either the abbess or Grey himself must eventually have enquired whether Erasmus had received it, and the truth of the matter became clear. In order to express his appreciation of the nuns' kindness and their concern for him, Erasmus then wrote them a second letter, the *Epistola consolatoria*, on the dual themes of hope and patience.

The site of Denny Abbey would have been familiar to Erasmus, since it stands beside the Roman road running north from Cambridge to Ely. He must have passed that way on his pilgrimage to Walsingham in 1512,[6] and in the following year he apparently stayed for some time with the family of William Gonnell at Landbeach, the neighbouring parish to Denny.[7]

A further link between the Denny community and Erasmus can be documented. The abbess of Denny was Dame Elizabeth Throckmorton,[8] whose family was to figure prominently in Tudor politics. At some point between 1524 and 1528 she asked a London merchant, Humfrey Monmouth, for a copy of William Tyndale's translation of the *Enchiridion*.[9] After the dissolution of Denny in 1539 the abbess went to spend her remaining years at the home of her family, Coughton Court in Warwickshire, where she lived with two or three of the other nuns from Denny, observing as far as possible the Franciscan rule, until her death in 1547.[10]

Following its initial publication by the firm of Froben in Basel the *Epistola consolatoria* was twice reprinted during 1528, in Cracow by Hieronymus Vietor, with a preface by Anselmus Ephorinus,[11] and in Lyon by Sebastianus

* * * * *

6 See Ep 262:7–9; *Carmina* ed Harry Vredeveld 51 ASD I-7 204–5 / CWE 85 120–3, 86 520–1.
7 See Epp 274, 278, 279. For William Gonnell see CEBR II 118.
8 See CEBR III 321.
9 See *Letters and Papers, Foreign and Domestic, of the Reign of Henry VIII* ed J.S. Brewer, J. Gairdner, and R.H. Brodie 21 vols in 35 (London 1862–1920) IV-2 no 4282; Anne M. O'Donnell *Erasmus, Enchiridion militis christiani: An English Version* Early English Text Society 282 (Oxford 1981) introduction l.
10 See *Victoria History, Cambridgeshire* (n4 above) II 302.
11 See CEBR I 436–7.

Gryphius. The following year Erasmus appended it, together with several other works, to the *editio princeps* of *De pueris instituendis*, and for that edition he made a few minor changes to the text.

The Antwerp printer Simon Cock (1489–1562) issued a Flemish translation of the *Epistola consolatoria*, together with a version of *De contemptu mundi*, without indication of date. In 1713 the same two works, together with *De puritate tabernaculi* and *De puero Iesu*, were translated into French by Claude Bosc (c 1642–1715).[12] Evidence also exists to show that the *Epistola consolatoria* was read in eighteenth-century England. Samuel Knight, a graduate of Cambridge University and prebendary of Ely cathedral, printed the Latin text of the *Epistola consolatoria* as an appendix to his biography of Erasmus published in 1726. Half a century later Samuel Johnson recorded in his journal that he had read 'Erasmus to the nuns,' adding that the work was 'full of mystick notions, and allegories.'[13] Finally, the *Epistola consolatoria* was included in the collection of Erasmus' works translated into Spanish by Lorenzo Riber in 1956.[14]

For the present translation the text of LB has been collated with the Froben editions of 1528 and 1529.

SR

* * * * *

12 See J.-C. Margolin 'Erasme à l'époque des "Lumières": une traduction française inédite de *De contemptu mundi*' in *Actes du Colloque international Erasme (Tours 1986)* ed Jacques Chomarat, André Godin, and Jean-Claude Margolin, Travaux d'humanisme et Renaissance 239 (Geneva 1990) 351–86, especially 357.

13 See *The Works of Samuel Johnson* ed E.L. McAdam, Jr, with Donald and Mary Hyde (New Haven and London 1958–) I 198 (14 August 1777); Bruce Mansfield *Interpretations of Erasmus, c 1750–1920: Man on His Own* Erasmus Studies 11 (Toronto 1992) 94.

14 *Erasmo. Obras escogidas* trans Lorenzo Riber (Madrid 1956; repr 1964) 459–65

LETTER OF COMFORT IN ADVERSITY

DESIDERIUS ERASMUS OF ROTTERDAM TO THE NUNS OBSERVING
THE RULE OF ST FRANCIS, SERVING BENEATH THE BANNER OF
CHRIST NEAR CAMBRIDGE, GREETING.

The Lord gives us good advice, beloved sisters in Christ, when he urges us
to lay up for ourselves treasure in heaven, where the moth does not destroy
and the thief does not steal.[1] The gift you kindly sent me may have been
stolen, but no one, however thievish, could purloin your love or your devoted prayers, in which you so generously commend me every day to your
Bridegroom. So let us take care to enrich ourselves in the kind of wealth that
makes the one who imparts it, by sharing it with one in need, not poorer but
richer, and which cannot be stolen from the one on whom it is bestowed.
To receive little things so gratefully and eagerly means surely to long for a
greater gift.

The letter that Thomas Grey[2] insistently urged me to write – I cannot
refuse him anything – was dashed off on the spur of the moment rather than
composed; but since I understand that it gave you such pleasure, I have decided to send you together with the letter a little flower culled from the
ever-verdant garden of Isaiah, which may at the same time refresh and in-
vigorate your hearts with the fragrance of the Holy Spirit.[3] And certainly if
the scent of an earthly flower not only gives pleasure but also reinvigorates
the senses, how much more will flowers of this kind, germinated and nourished by the breath of the Holy Spirit, increase the gladness and strength of
the soul, if they are set before our minds. For there cannot be anyone who is

*****

1 Cf Matt 6:20; Luke 12:33.
2 See n1 to the introductory note.
3 Cf *Virginis et martyris comparatio* 159 above.

not occasionally[4] overcome by grief and a kind of weariness when he contemplates the evils that abound everywhere in these times, or so strong in spirit that he does not undergo some degree of mental anguish in the midst of such great disagreements over doctrine. Here then is the little flower from Isaiah for you, to give you joy instead of weariness, and to strengthen and uphold your hearts with the power of faith: 'In quietness and trust,' he says, 'shall be your strength.'[5] Who speaks these words? Not Isaiah, but the Holy One of Israel, that is, the eternal truth, which can neither deceive nor be deceived.[6]

Whenever the Lord, who chastises every child that he accepts,[7] sends us misfortunes, we should remember that he is a Father who is concerned for our salvation and is not unaware of what is good for us, so that we do not murmur against him, but patiently and in silence accept the hand of correction, painful though it may be for our natural sensitivities. This is the quietness the Lord demands through the prophet, and we should accept it not simply without murmuring but even with gladness, trusting, to be sure, that we will soon be restored to spiritual health. What afflicts us is trifling and lasts only a moment; what gives us joy is everlasting and beyond price. Love is the handmaiden of faith (as Paul says, 'faith works through love');[8] hope is the daughter of them both. Though we may grant that faith can

* * * * *

4 'Occasionally' (*interdum*) does not occur in the *editio princeps* of 1528; it was added in the edition of 1529, but omitted by LB.

5 Isa 30:15. The Hebrew term *biṭḥāh* has regularly been translated in English as 'trust,' but the Vulgate uses the Latin word *spes*, 'hope,' which Erasmus makes the principal theme of the work. See further *Theological Dictionary of the Old Testament* ed G.J. Botterweck and H. Ringgren trans John T. Willis et al revised ed (Grand Rapids 1977–   ) II 88–94; G. Kittel and G. Friedrich *Theological Dictionary of the New Testament* trans G.W. Bromiley 10 vols (Grand Rapids 1964–76) II 521–3, VI 182–92. This quotation also occurs, and is made the subject of an extended meditation, early in the second part or book of the *Speculum virginum*, a treatise of spiritual instruction for nuns written c 1140 which was widely circulated especially among Cistercian and Augustinian communities in the later Middle Ages, particularly in the northern Rhine area and the Low Countries. It is possible that Erasmus had become familiar with the *Speculum virginum* at Deventer or Steyn. See *Speculum virginum* CCCM 5 2.25–6.

6 Cf *Precationes* 130 above; Augustine *Enarratio in Psalmum 123* 10.2 CCSL 40 1826: 'veritas enim nec falli potest, nec fallere'; *Speculum virginum* CCCM 2.58–60 (see the previous note): 'sponsor fidelis et sponsio verax nec fallit facile nec fallitur, quia certe fidei veritas et consona veritati fides socia suffragatur.'

7 Heb 12:6; cf Prov 3:12; Rev 3:19.

8 Gal 5:6.

be separated from love, hope, of which we are speaking, is assuredly not born except out of faith and love. Therefore if we are children rather than slaves,[9] let us have confidence in the Father; we must love the Father, and if we believe that he has our salvation at heart, not unmindful of his boundless compassion towards all those who love him, we will derive great joy even in the midst of adversity from the expectation of divine comfort. This 'does not allow us to be tried beyond our strength, but with the testing provides a way out, so that we are able to endure it.'[10] Often it mixes sadness with joy, and always it contributes the balm of the Spirit,[11] to alleviate or bring joy even to occasions of sadness.

However, there are certain misfortunes whose end we cannot expect to see in this life, such as old age, an 'incurable disease' as the physicians say,[12] and some other kinds of sickness that baffle the skill of doctors. In these also quietness and trust are our strength. For as the poet says, 'Patience helps us to endure / The ills no human should presume to cure,'[13] and 'The sufferings of the present time are not worth comparing with the future glory which is soon to be revealed to us.'[14] And why should I not say 'soon,'[15] since the whole of this life is scarcely an instant or point of time compared with eternity? But if human hope has such power that a pagan poet has truly and justly written of it, 'Good hope gives strength, good hope confirms the heart; / One who was doomed I saw yet live by hope,'[16]

* * * * *

9 Cf Rom 8:14–17; Gal 4:6–7.
10 Cf 1 Cor 10:13.
11 Cf 1 John 2:20, 27.
12 Cf Terence *Phormio* 575; Seneca *Epistulae ad Lucilium* 108.28; *Adagia* II vi 37 *Ipsa senectus morbus est*, 'Old age is sickness of itself'; *Carmina* 2:7–9 ASD I-7 76 / CWE 85 12–13; *Epistola contra pseudevangelicos* ASD IX-1 284:22–5; Ep 1381:131–2; Allen Epp 2195:46–7, 3000:15–17.
13 Horace *Odes* 1.24.19–20, trans James Michie (London 1963)
14 Rom 8:18. In this quotation Erasmus has departed from the Vulgate, substituting 'not at all' (*nequaquam*) for 'not' (*non*) and *afflictiones* (from his own version of the New Testament) for *passiones*, and adding 'soon' (*mox*), which does not occur in either the Greek or the Vulgate text.
15 'Not' (*non*) is omitted in LB.
16 The opening four words of this elegiac couplet are based on Ovid *Heroides* 11.61, but the couplet as a whole is probably not to be dated earlier than the fifth or sixth century AD. The phrase 'one who was doomed' (*qui moriturus erat*) occupies the same position in the couplet as two very similar phrases by the fifth-century Christian elegist Orientius, *Commonitorium* 1.544, 2.392 (I owe these references to Dr Johann Ramminger of the *Thesaurus linguae Latinae* in Munich). The couplet is no 30180 in *Lateinische Sprichwörter und Sentenzen*

what will the hope that the Spirit of Christ engenders in us not achieve? Human hope is frequently deceptive, but this 'hope does not disappoint us,' as St Paul writes.[17] However, the word 'disappoint,' used by the Apostle writing in Greek, does not indicate mental turmoil, but rather shame and disgrace. For instance, if people rely on human resources and display great self-confidence, the reproach they suffer when something turns out contrary to their expectation is almost more galling than the disaster itself, and shame redoubles the misfortune. But whoever places all his trust in the Lord has a sure hope, and there is no danger that he will be deluded in his expectation and brought to shame. Although devout people seem occasionally in this life to be put to shame for a time, they are surely not put to shame for all eternity. The taunts of scorners fell upon the Lord as he hung upon the cross;[18] he heard voices more bitter than any gall:[19] 'He trusted in God; let him deliver him now if he wants him.'[20] These are the words that were heard by the head, and his members hear similar voices.[21] But just as they have an example of suffering from their head, so they have also the confidence of hope. What answer did he make to those godless taunts? None, you will find, but he placed his courage 'in quietness and trust,'[22] saying to the Father with a tranquil spirit, 'In you, O Lord, I seek refuge; let me never be put to shame.'[23]

When people see good Christians afflicted by disease, war, loss of possessions, exile, torture, and death, unbelievers say, 'Where is their God?'[24] If only this question were not also heard occasionally among Christians! But it is more serious when these sentiments resound within our hearts, sometimes even breaking out into blasphemy, when in our thoughts, overcome by sorrow and weariness, we call God cruel, unjust, lacking in concern for human affairs, and more kindly disposed towards the wicked than towards the good, since they usually enjoy greater success than those who

* * * * *

des Mittelalters (Carmina Medii Aevi Posterioris Latina ii/5) ed Hans Walther (Göttingen 1967). Erasmus certainly believed that the entire couplet was by Ovid, since he quoted it in full, introduced by the words 'notum est illud Nasonis,' in his discussion of Adagia iv iv 63: Spes servat afflictos.

17 Rom 5:5
18 Matt 27:39–44; Mark 15:29–32; Luke 23:35–7
19 Cf Matt 27:34.
20 Matt 27:43
21 Cf Eph 4:15–16; 1 Cor 12:14–27.
22 See n5 above.
23 Ps 31:1 (Vulg 30:2)
24 Ps 79 (Vulg 78):10

live devoutly. In doing so we fail to understand that our Lord passed through suffering and shame to his glory, and we forget what Paul wrote to Timothy: 'All who want to live a godly life in Christ Jesus will be persecuted in this world.'[25] If he had said nothing more we might have grown weary of unceasing affliction,[26] but now he reveals his hope that suffering will soon come to an end and be followed by bliss when he says, 'in this world.'[27]

The Hebrew sage also lays down this precept among the foundations of goodness: 'My child, if you aspire to serve the Lord, stand firm in justice and fear, and prepare yourself for an ordeal.'[28] See how the divine Scriptures agree in their opinions, though they differ in their expressions and images. Sirach[29] says the same as Peter, Paul, and Isaiah. The last speaks of 'quietness'; the first says, 'stand firm in justice and fear.' What the one calls 'trust' the other indicates by the word 'ordeal.' Anyone who stands firm is not troubled, and does not suffer distress of spirit. Anyone who stands firm in justice acknowledges his own unrighteousness, and reveres the justice of God who inflicts punishment on him. Anyone who stands firm in fear does not murmur against the one 'who can cast both body and soul into hell.'[30] Again, anyone who prepares himself is not discouraged, as for example by unexpected squalls of misfortune, but accepts with good grace whatever God pleases to send him. The apostle Peter preaches the same message in different words: 'Dearly beloved, do not be surprised at the fiery ordeal that is taking place among you to test you, as though something strange were happening to you; but rejoice in so far as you are sharing Christ's sufferings, so that you may also be glad and shout for joy when his glory is revealed.'[31] Now the person who understands that affliction is an ordeal, in other words that God is subjecting us to scrutiny, waits for perseverance, which has as its companion hope, the solace of every trouble, as the Apostle writes to the Romans: 'We also boast in our sufferings, knowing that suffering produces

* * * * *

25 2 Tim 3:12. The phrase 'in this world' (*in hoc saeculo*) does not occur at this point in the Greek or Vulgate text. Erasmus may be recalling Titus 2:12: 'sobrie et iuste et pie vivamus in hoc saeculo.'

26 'We' (*nos*) is not printed in the 1528 *editio princeps*. It was added in 1529, but omitted in LB.

27 See n25 above.

28 Ecclus 2:1. Erasmus quotes the Vulgate text; the Greek text and versions based on it omit the phrase 'stand firm in justice and fear' (*sta in justitia et timore*).

29 Ie the author of the book entitled Ecclesiasticus.

30 Cf Matt 10:28.

31 1 Pet 4:12–13

endurance, and endurance produces character, and character produces hope; and hope does not disappoint us, because God's love has been poured into our hearts through the Holy Spirit that has been given to us.'[32] It was not enough for God's goodness to make up for passing momentary sufferings with everlasting joys: even in the midst of afflictions he gives his followers the pledge of the hidden Spirit,[33] so powerful that, far from losing heart[34] in the face of evil, they boast and rejoice. And so the hope of good Christians, even if it may seem to bring them shame in the sight of others, does not in fact bring shame, as long as they sense within themselves the witness of the Spirit declaring to the human spirit that they are children of God;[35] and they rejoice that they are being tested and prepared by the hand of the most merciful Father for the heavenly life that they will inherit. This is the way the wise teacher continues: 'For gold and silver are tested in the fire, and those found acceptable in the furnace of humiliation. Trust in God, and he will uphold you; follow a straight path and hope in him.'[36] Whoever entrusts himself to God remains silent while God punishes him that he may be cured, strikes him down that he may rise again, kills him that he may have life. Allow the physician to work in his own way; only stop sinning, and God's anger will be turned into compassion. It is vain to hope for the mercy of God if you persist in the actions that arouse God's anger.

We are told in classical literature that a certain merchant, having gathered his goods together, set out for a distant country in the hope of returning home a much wealthier man. After losing everything as the result of shipwreck, he said, 'Ah then, Fortune, I realize what you want: you are summoning me to Philosophy, and I obey your summons.'[37] For him the

* * * * *

32 Rom 5:3–5
33 Cf 2 Cor 1:22, 5:5; Eph 1:14.
34 Cf 2 Cor 4:1, 16; Gal 6:9; Eph 3:13.
35 Cf Rom 8:16.
36 Ecclus 2:5–6
37 This story is told about Zeno of Citium (335–263 BC), the founder of the Stoic school of philosophy. Erasmus makes it the basis of *Adagia* II ix 78: *Nunc bene navigavi, cum naufragium feci*, 'Now that I've suffered shipwreck, my voyage has gone well.' He cites as his source 'Suidas,' the Greek lexicon of the tenth century AD properly known as 'the Suda,' N 604, ed A. Adler (Leipzig 1928–38) pars III 488, and Plutarch *Moralia* 87A ('How to Profit from One's Enemies'), one of eight Plutarchan *opuscula* which he translated and published in 1514, ASD IV-2 174:50–2. Plutarch recalls the story on two other occasions, *Moralia* 467C and 603D. See also Seneca *De tranquillitate animi* 14.3; Diogenes Laertius 7.4–5; *Stoicorum veterum fragmenta* ed H. von Arnim 4 vols in 2 (Leipzig 1903–5; repr Stuttgart 1964) I 277.

loss of his assets resulted in the maximum profit, since he changed from being an avaricious merchant and became an outstanding philosopher, richer in his contempt for wealth than in its possession. We should at least imitate his example whenever any public or private misfortune befalls us, and not give way to mental anguish or murmur against the hand of the Almighty, as the Israelites did, who perished from the bite of serpents.[38] Instead, the answer that the pagan philosopher gave to Fortune we should give to God, the sole ruler of human affairs: 'Ah then, most merciful Father, I feel your hand inviting me to repentance; I come to you, I surrender myself entirely to you; shape and reshape in accordance with your holy will this child of yours who has hitherto failed to listen to your word.'

Nowadays most people do not reflect that any adversity they suffer is sent from God. Some vent their anger on the stars, others on the human condition, others on one group of individuals or another, or on sheer mischance; and their behaviour in seeking revenge is not much more sensible than that of dogs who bite a stone thrown by a man and ignore the man himself.[39] A storm ruins the crops, merchandise is lost in shipwreck, an unhealthy climate gives rise to sickness, troops set fire to storage-barns, a malicious person takes you to court, a slanderous tongue noisily attacks you. Why do you curse sky and sea? Why do you plan revenge against an individual? That is biting a stone. Consider first that these things are sent by God, and that it does not much matter by what agency he sends them, since he makes use of the elements and of wicked people to punish us. Next, look around you: do you ever provoke God's anger by your misdeeds? And if you plead guilty – but who would plead not guilty? – first take revenge on yourself by mending your ways and turning to God, who threw the stone. But even if not, consider: 'God is testing me, to know whether I truly love him;[40] I will pray that he may increase charity in me.'

How far are most of us nowadays from such an attitude of mind! For how many years now have we been crushed by every kind of evil? The

* * * * *

38 Num 21:5–6; 1 Cor 10:9–10
39 This image is derived from the *Republic* of Plato, book 5, 469E, which Erasmus quotes in the course of his discussion of *Adagia* I x 34: *Cum adsit ursus, vestigia quaeris*, 'Confronted with the bear you go looking for his tracks'; in fact his quotation of the Greek in that passage is closer to that made by Aristotle *Rhetoric* 1406b33, where it is used as an example of the simile. Erasmus later made Plato's expression the subject of a further adage, IV ii 22: *Canis saeviens in lapidem.*
40 Cf Deut 13:4 (Vulg 13:3).

Egyptians were afflicted by ten plagues, and in response to each of them they began to come to their senses.[41] We have been worn down for so many years now by so many more evils, and we do not acknowledge the hand of the Lord. No one is in a hurry to mend his ways, but we place the blame on one another, and everyone finds excuses for himself;[42] we set vengeance in motion, as if men could do anything in the face of God's power. What variety of evil is there that does not weigh us down? What part of the world is immune from the contagion of these evils? Where on the earth is Mars not raging? And when I speak of Mars I am not speaking of any single form of evil but of an ocean of all evils.[43] Is there anywhere that is free from plague, from high prices and famine, from rapine, from pillage? In some places floods complete the picture.[44] How fierce and implacable are the quarrels of princes; what great disasters have they brought upon human affairs, and how much worse are the calamities they threaten! But these things are trivial compared with the dissensions within the church. Into how many sects are we divided, and new ones promptly sprout from them! Members of the same family, the same household, those who share the same bed, are torn apart by doctrinal disputes. In the midst of these afflictions how many people do we see contemplating the reform of their own lives or throwing themselves upon God's mercy?[45] Everyone seeks his own revenge, everyone tries to protect his own advantage, and we do nothing but redouble our evils and bring down the Lord's hand more heavily upon ourselves. We send embassies to Egypt, we load camels with treasures, we flee on swift chariots,[46] and we throw everything into confusion with senseless strife. Yet we do not hear the Holy One of Israel crying to us, 'In returning and rest you will be saved; in quietness and trust will be your strength.'[47] What does 'returning' mean? Abandoning the habits and dispositions that put us at war with God. What is 'rest'? Renouncing the desires of the flesh and submitting ourselves to God's will. Only then will that truly happy sabbath exist in our hearts, if our desires are quietened and laid to rest, and the Lord can work his will in us.

* * * * *

41 Exod 7:14–12:32
42 Cf *Liturgia Virginis Matris* 103 above.
43 Cf *Adagia* I iii 28: *Mare malorum*, 'A sea of troubles.'
44 Denny Abbey was situated in the fen country of East Anglia, which was constantly subject to flooding; and Erasmus, as a native of the Low Countries, would have been familiar with the devastation caused by floods.
45 Cf *Liturgia Virginis Matris* 103 (see n42 above).
46 Cf Isa 30:2, 6, 16.
47 Isa 30:15

What is the first concern of physicians? They empty the body of noxious humours, and the rest they leave to nature. Let us also cast out our misdeeds, and the Lord, who holds in his hand the hearts of kings,[48] will straight away turn them to the pursuit of peace and concord; he will remove from our midst the locusts[49] – the soldiers who lay everything waste – and the frogs[50] – the doctrinal quarrels; he will take away our darkness, and the truth will shine in our hearts.[51] We hear the voice of the Lord calling upon all of us to mend our ways; we should not cover our ears and harden our hearts as well, giving the same answer as the wicked in Isaiah – 'No, we will flee upon horses, and ride upon swift steeds' – in case he admonishes us again, 'Therefore you shall flee; your pursuers shall be swift!'[52] It may well be that no one now cries out against the Lord with words like these, but with our deeds almost all of us cry out.

These storms raging in the world do not disturb you so much, dear sisters. You are dead to the world[53] and already to some degree live the life of heaven on earth; hidden away with Christ your Bridegroom you take your delight, and the closer you are to him the more appropriate it is for you to commend to him the peace of the church by your devotions and sacred prayers, lifting up to the Lord not merely pure hands, with Paul,[54] but much rather pure hearts, like doves 'in the clefts of the rock and the coverts of the cliff,'[55] forever murmuring to the Bridegroom with most grateful sighs.[56] The rock is Christ,[57] and it has many clefts in which faithful souls may safely hide from the tumult of this world, and where a gentle coolness protects them from the heat of the fleshly desires that wage war against the spirit.[58]

* * * * *

48 Cf Prov 21:1. See also the colloquy *Convivium religiosum* ('The Godly Feast') ASD I-3 242:330–247:504 / CWE 39 184:4–189:4, where this text forms the basis of an extended discussion.
49 Cf Exod 10:12–19.
50 Cf Exod 8:2–14.
51 Cf 2 Cor 4:6.
52 Isa 30:16
53 This phrase, encapsulating several expressions from the Epistles of St Paul (Col 2:20, 3:3; cf Rom 6:2; Gal 6:14; Phil 1:21), is frequently used by Erasmus; see eg *Precatio ad Virginis filium Iesum* 10 above; *Enchiridion* LB V 31B / CWE 66 71; *Colloquia* ASD I-3 383:297, 688:82 / CWE 39 457:8, 40 1003:1.
54 Cf 1 Tim 2:8.
55 Song of Sol 2:14; cf Exod 33:22.
56 Cf Nah 2:7; *Virginis et martyris comparatio* 176, 181–2 above.
57 Cf 1 Cor 10:4.
58 Cf 1 Pet 2:11.

The less familiar you are with the ways of the world the more safely and happily you find shelter in these clefts, just as doves are not protected by means of their beak or claws or through strength or guile against attack by other birds, but keep safe simply through flight and concealment, and have no means of harming any of their fellow creatures. A charming simplicity shines in their eyes, for which the Bridegroom expresses love in the Canticle, and which the words of the Gospel recommend to us.[59] They do not cause a disturbance with tiresome twittering as very many other birds do, but simply console their loneliness with a delightful cooing. In accordance with this image, O most blessed sisters, you also take refuge in the coverts of Christ, placing your strength in quietness and trust.

There is a godless murmuring that is hateful to the Lord. There is also a soft and pleasant murmuring, which is made unceasingly by souls upon whom the Spirit of Christ has breathed, until imperfect things are done away with and perfection comes.[60] Such are the murmurings of doves. There is also a ruinous silence, which the ancient proverb tells us led to the destruction of Amyclae.[61] There is a sinful silence, which will not admit guilt and denies God his due glory. Without doubt this was the dumb spirit that only Jesus was able to cast out.[62] There is also a grateful and peaceful silence, and when it is joined with hope it makes the heart invincible against the attacks of every kind of evil. In this silence the desires of the flesh are stilled, but the sighs of the spirit are heard. Such were Paul's sighs when he said: 'Wretched man that I am! Who will rescue me from this body of death?'[63] Such were the sighs of David when he said: 'How lovely is your dwelling-place, O Lord of hosts! My soul longs and faints for the courts of the Lord.'[64] 'As a deer longs for flowing streams, so my soul longs for you, O God.'[65] 'Foxes have holes and the birds of the air have nests,'[66] in which they take their rest; doves know no rest except 'in the clefts of the rock and the coverts of the cliff.'[67] For this reason he was pierced with so many wounds on the

* * * * *

59 Song of Sol 1:14, 4:1; Matt 10:16. Cf the phrase 'of dovelike simplicity' (*columbinae simplicitatis*) introduced by Erasmus into his prayer to the Virgin in the 1531 edition of the *Colloquia* ASD I-3 478:312 / CWE 40 633.
60 Cf 1 Cor 13:10.
61 See *Adagia* I ix 1: *Amyclas perdidit silentium*, 'Silence destroyed Amyclae.'
62 Cf Mark 9:14–29.
63 Rom 7:24; cf *Virginis et martyris comparatio* 167 above.
64 Ps 84:1–2 (Vulg 83:2–3)
65 Ps 42:1 (Vulg 41:2)
66 Cf Matt 8:20.
67 Song of Sol 2:14; cf Exod 33:22.

cross, so that there for devout souls who have renounced all worldly aid he could be a tranquil and safe refuge. He is also called the cornerstone, binding both walls together.[68] Shelter sweetly and happily in his coverts, sisters, until you hear the voice of the Bridegroom calling you to everlasting bliss: 'Arise, make haste, my beloved, my beautiful one, and come, my dove in the clefts of the rock and the coverts of the cliff: show me your face.'[69]

Francis, the founding father of your rule of life,[70] sheltered in these coverts; in the eyes of the world he was the lowliest of creatures, but very great in the eyes of God. The most holy virgin Clare, the foundress and patron of your order,[71] sheltered in them. She relied on none of this world's safeguards, on no human resources; but strong in quietness and trust she trampled the world underfoot, overthrew Satan, and conquered the flesh, and after fleeting sorrows gained the crown of heavenly life; scorning all the pretensions and allurements of Satan she reigns with her Bridegroom, the sole object of her desire.[72] As you follow in her footsteps remain steadfast, dear sisters, and always progress towards the higher gifts,[73] so that as you now share in the struggle, so you may also share in the glory which will soon be revealed in you.[74] Do not be dismayed by tender years, the frailties of your sex, physical weakness, or the power of Satan, armed with a thousand

* * * * *

68 Ps 118 (Vulg 117):22; Isa 28:16; Matt 21:42; Mark 12:10; Luke 20:17; Acts 4:11; 1 Pet 2:6; cf *Paean Virgini Matri* 29–30 above; *Virginis et martyris comparatio* 160 above.

69 Song of Sol 2:13–14; cf *Virginis et martyris comparatio* 166 above.

70 St Francis of Assisi (1181–1226), founder of the Franciscan order, probably the best known and most widely admired saint in the calendar of the western church. Erasmus always expressed the highest regard for St Francis (see eg *Enchiridion* LB V 31D / CWE 66 71–2 and its prefatory letter, ibidem 21–2 / Ep 858:548–79; Allen Ep 1805:362–4), and even claimed late in life that the saint had appeared to him in a dream and commended his actions (Allen Ep 2700:37–41). His relations with the members of the Franciscan order in his own day, however, were often marked by mutual antagonism: they were among his fiercest critics on theological questions, and he frequently attacked them for their failure to live up to the Franciscan ideal; see eg Allen Epp 2300:117–50, 2700:20–150.

71 St Clare of Assisi (1194–1253), the first woman to embrace the Franciscan way of life, and founder of the Second Order of St Francis (the Poor Clares). See the biography by M. Bartoli, *Clare of Assisi* Eng trans (London 1993).

72 Cf *Virginis et martyris comparatio* 175–6 above.

73 Cf 1 Cor 12:31.

74 Cf Rom 8:18 and n14 above.

wiles. The rock in which you shelter is stronger than all of them; anyone who falls on it will be dashed to pieces,[75] but anyone who cleaves to it constantly will be safe.

The more a person relies on his own strength the weaker he is; but anyone who abandons all reliance on himself and looks to no other protection than Christ is capable of all things, like Paul, not in himself but in the One[76] who 'chose what is weak in the world to shame the strong, who chose what is foolish in the world to shame the wise, who chose what is base and of no account to show contempt for what seems to be of great importance.'[77] Now, even if some of you are able to boast in terms of the flesh, as Paul could,[78] we should not boast 'except in the cross of our Lord Jesus Christ':[79] since he scorned the whole glory of the world to the extent of the cross, could any who follow him not be ashamed to glory in this world? Paul, caught up into the third heaven, does not dare to boast except in his weaknesses;[80] and shall we, wretched creatures that we are, boast in our strength? He is strong in his weakness.[81] So have no fear, little flock;[82] be brave, because he who has undertaken to protect you has conquered the world.[83]

I do not think it necessary to encourage you, most devout lady, on whom the charge of the community of sisters is laid,[84] or to remind you of your duty; I would rather congratulate you, if that were not unsafe in view of human weakness, or a source of embarrassment to your singular modesty. I simply pray that you will continue your practice of remembering me in your prayers to the Lord, and that you will convey my particular greeting to the sisters of Thomas Grey.[85] May the Lord preserve you all from harm. At the same time pray in your charity for the thief, so that he may turn from a

* * * * *

75 Cf Luke 20:18; *Paean Virgini Matri* 30 above.
76 Cf Phil 4:13.
77 Cf 1 Cor 1:27–8.
78 Cf 2 Cor 11:18. Many members of the communities of Franciscan nuns in England came from families of high social status: see A.F.C. Bourdillon *The Order of Minoresses in England* British Society of Franciscan Studies 12 (Manchester 1926; repr 1956) 51–4; Jennifer C. Ward *English Noblewomen in the Later Middle Ages* (London and New York 1992) 154–6.
79 Gal 6:14
80 Cf 2 Cor 12:2, 5.
81 Cf 2 Cor 12:10.
82 Luke 12:32
83 Cf John 16:33.
84 Dame Elizabeth Throckmorton; see the introductory note, with n8.
85 See the introductory note.

kite, or rather harpy, into a dove,[86] and may at last stop playing Cretan and stealing anything,[87] in case he should provoke the hand of Christ against him, and so that his name may be changed.[88]

* * * * *

86 Cf Horace *Epode* 16.32: 'adulteretur et columba miluo.'
87 See *Adagia* I ii 29: *Cretiza cum Cretensi*, 'To play Cretan with a Cretan.' Although the proverb normally referred to the manner of dealing appropriately with liars, it could also be applied to thieves; see the closing lines of Erasmus' discussion. For other instances of Erasmus' use of this adage see Epp 119:8, 283:195–6; *De copia* ASD I–6 66:835 / CWE 24 336.
88 Erasmus is presumably expressing the hope that the thief may undergo a change for the better. He may have in mind the biblical passages Gen 41:45 and 2 Chron 36:4.

THE INSTITUTION OF CHRISTIAN MATRIMONY

Institutio christiani matrimonii

translated and annotated by
MICHAEL J. HEATH

The first edition of *Institutio christiani matrimonii*, dedicated to Catherine of Aragon, was published by Froben at Basel in August 1526. The dedicatory letter looks like a *captatio benevolentiae*: Erasmus pleads that pressure of work has delayed the appearance of a treatise promised more than two years before, and fears that haste has prevented him from portraying marriage as artistically as he might. The brief letter also includes, with unforeseeable irony, a eulogy of Catherine's own marriage and, very pertinently, a compliment on the upbringing of the ten-year-old Princess Mary: the mother's role in the education of her (female) children is an important topic of the *Institutio*. A few months later Erasmus confided to More his fear that, despite this cajolery, he had displeased the queen in discussing possible relaxation of the bonds of marriage, but both More and Mountjoy assured him that the queen had greatly approved of the book.[1]

Erasmus points out in the epistle that the style of his treatise is austere, and that its gestation was long. This is not mere bluff: the book is profoundly serious and deeply researched. It is also deliberately unconventional. The work is no routine eulogy of the married state, no pious exhortation to newly-weds; still less does it echo the traditional literary portrayal of marriage as a bleak and joyless relationship between ill-matched and restless partners, the image found in popular writing and sometimes sketched by Erasmus himself, for instance in the *Moria* and in the *Virginis et martyris comparatio*.[2] Erasmus' treatise on marriage is a detailed and painstaking examination of the institution from every conceivable angle.

Beginning with the decision to enter this honourable estate, which is also a sacrament of the church, Erasmus works his way through the successive stages of marriage. The choice of a partner raises the questions of legal consent and of the restrictions imposed by civil and ecclesiastical impediments, which Erasmus examines with a sharply critical eye. The betrothal and the wedding ceremony provoke a discussion of parental authority and of the increasing problem of clandestine marriages, to which Erasmus proposes the solution, later recommended by the Council of Trent, of more public and more formalized procedures. On the other hand, the unrestrained junketing that too often blemished the solemnity of the ceremony and of the wedding night incurs severe moral censure, and Erasmus evokes poignantly the bewilderment of the tender young couple brusquely initiated to their sexuality. Further psychological, moral, and social questions arise in his prescriptions for the early days of life together, as the wife enters upon her

* * * * *

1 See Allen Epp 1804:285–6, 1770 to More and 1816 to Mountjoy.
2 CWE 27 97–8 and 162–3 above.

domestic duties; the marital virtues of love and fidelity are completed by the embodiment of hope, in the begetting, rearing, and education of children. This last topic, the most familiar to Erasmus and to his readership, is none the less extended by an unusual discussion of obscenity. Finally Erasmus reaches the point at which a new generation, fortified by the excellence of his counsel, is ready to embark upon the dangerous seas of courtship. Thus, in the course of this circular tour, Erasmus has dealt with all the principal spiritual, theological, moral, legal, and physical aspects of this most momentous of human transactions.

Though marriage has played a vital role in almost every society, its status and function had a special importance in the early days of the Reformation. When Erasmus' treatise appeared, the 'states of life' – virginity, celibacy, matrimony, and widowhood – were the subject of intense doctrinal and theological controversy. The ex-monk Martin Luther had married his Katarina in the previous year, but this was merely the most notorious among a multitude of marriages contracted by those formerly bound by a vow of chastity. In a comment on this trend among priests and monks in Germany, Erasmus had suggested to Noël Béda in October 1525 that these religious should be allowed the 'remedy of marriage' if they could not keep their vow, in order to avoid the worse scandal of concubinage.[3] By regarding sexual activity as a natural necessity rather than a mere concession to human weakness, Erasmus was in effect recommending a breach with an ascetic tradition dating back essentially to St Paul and upheld, to cite but one interesting example, by Erasmus' close friend Colet.[4] But any contemporary discussion of matrimony necessarily invoked the issues of institutional chastity and celibacy, which St Augustine and his contemporaries had done so much to promote; what is more, monastic propaganda of the Middle Ages often took the form of declamation against marriage.[5] Here was an issue on which the divergence in the sixteenth century between Reformers and traditionalists was clearly apparent, and an entire book devoted to it in 1526 could not fail to be regarded as a contribution to the polemic.

Matrimony was traditionally considered a hybrid, being both a sacrament of the church and a civil matter, the only one of the sacraments, as

* * * * *

3 Ep 1620:60. For sarcastic comments on Luther's marriage, see eg Epp 1655 and 1697. On the whole controversy over celibacy, and Erasmus' involvement in it, see Telle 153–200 and Léon-E. Halkin 'Erasme et le célibat sacerdotal' *Revue d'histoire et de philosophie religieuses* 57 (1977) 497–511.
4 See Payne 282 n36 and, on Colet, Olsen 13–14.
5 Cf Screech 14.

Augustine and Aquinas[6] recognized, to be subject to this difficulty. For that reason doubts were frequently expressed about its status as a true sacrament, and it was not officially admitted to the list of seven sacraments until the Council of Florence in 1439. The Reformers removed it (along with four others), a move for which Erasmus has sometimes been held responsible, on the dubious grounds that he made the outpouring of grace, essential in a true sacrament, conditional upon the right intention of the participants.[7] The question is of crucial importance, since the theory of the indissolubility of the marriage bond, so resolutely defended by Erasmus' adversaries, was based essentially upon the sacramental character of the institution.

Erasmus' opinionated treatise was also bound to be viewed with grave suspicion by the orthodox because matrimony was an area over which the church had long claimed jurisdiction, especially since the great elucidation of canon law in the twelfth century.[8] Already under pressure from the less subtle attacks of Luther, the church was unlikely to welcome the critical examination to which Erasmus subjects its position with the aid of his humanist, scriptural, and patristic erudition. A survey of his principal sources will convey something of Erasmus' astonishing and often disturbing eclecticism.

His deployment of classical learning is, as usual, wide-ranging and idiosyncratic. Alongside the fundamental passages on wedlock from book 7 of Aristotle's *Politics* he places a series of *exempla* culled from his beloved Plutarch's essays on education and on marriage.[9] By favouring a moral philosopher persuaded of the value of affection and kindliness between the sexes (rather than the more austere Seneca, for instance), Erasmus signals his intention to be constructive towards womankind, but he is none the less constrained by the social prejudices of the classical heritage as well as of his own time. For example, he borrows extensively from the treatises of Xenophon and Pseudo-Aristotle on household management, both of which assume without question that a woman's place is in the home (though it should be borne in mind that the running of an extensive sixteenth-century household was no light matter). The subordinate position of women in the

* * * * *

6 Augustine *De bono coniugali* 32 PL 40 394, Aquinas *Supplementum* q 49 art 2; see also Olsen 2–6 and Payne 112–14.
7 This reading is essentially that of Telle; see nn29, 33, and 67 to the text. For objections see Olsen passim and Payne 284–5 nn46–8. Telle 291–2 further suggests that Luther and Erasmus undermined the sacrament for opposite reasons: Luther out of pessimism concerning human corruption, Erasmus out of optimism concerning human freedom.
8 See Esmein I 25–31 and 108–24, and Gaudemet 139–93.
9 *De liberis educandis* and *Coniugalia praecepta*, *Moralia* 1–14 and 138–46

ancient world is underlined by the great collections of Roman law, such as the *Digesta* and the *Codex* of Justinian, to which Erasmus also turned for enlightenment on many technical questions, though he ignored the Roman jurists' obsession with dowries. The (relatively) pure springs of Roman law, so admired by contemporary humanist exponents of the *mos Gallicus*,[10] provided examples not only of practical common sense but also of stylistic clarity; often Erasmus tacitly contrasts the elegantly expressed wisdom of the Roman emperors with the obscure wranglings of the medieval canonists. But in addition to these formal and obvious classical sources of inspiration, Erasmus as usual drew on the riches of his general reading, turning to Galen for a memorable anecdote about cosmetics, to the mimographer Publilius Syrus for a series of appropriate aphorisms, to the poets for reflections on the nature of love, both marital and profane, and, not least, to the Roman comic dramatists for a portrayal of social and family life that seemed to him universally valid. Lest such literary allusions seem frivolous or irrelevant, Erasmus often combines them with scriptural and patristic references, as he does, for example, in defending parental authority (247–8), with a breathtaking syncretic display for which he makes only the barest apology.[11]

But it is of course Erasmus' appeal to the authority of Scripture that carries the most weight. Here the position was delicate, and Erasmus' interpretations of key passages had already aroused the controversies discussed later in this introduction. The Gospels have relatively little to say on matrimonial questions (the wedding at Cana recurs as an *exemplum* with significant regularity), and some important texts, such as Matthew 19:6, where Christ severely restricts the grounds for divorce, seem potentially damaging to Erasmus' case. Similarly St Paul, so reliable a source for Erasmus on other ethical questions, appears grudging in his approval of matrimony. Erasmus often handles these texts with more ingenuity than tact, and redresses the balance where possible by amassing evidence from the Old Testament – from God's inauguration of marriage in the Garden of Eden, through the exemplary legislation of Moses, to the eulogies of good women by the patri-

* * * * *

10 Cf Lacey 102–5 and, on the general evolution of legal scholarship in the Renaissance, D.R. Kelley *Foundations of Modern Historical Scholarship* (New York 1970) especially 53–148.

11 For further discussion of Erasmus' sources, see Michael J. Heath 'Erasmus and the Laws of Marriage' in *Acta Conventus neo-Latini Hafniensis: Proceedings of the Eighth International Congress of Neo-Latin Studies, 1991* ed Rhoda Schnur (Binghamton 1994) 477–84.

archs and prophets. Similarly eclectic is his use of patristic writing, whose major function in this book is to assist Erasmus in elucidating unpromising passages of Scripture; in other respects, the well-known advocacy of virginity and celibacy by Augustine, Jerome, and Ambrose did not help his case. As Erasmus explains, abstinence and asceticism were more appropriate to their times, when unbelievers had to be won over by pious example, just as the Hebrew patriarchs, in their time allotted the duty of populating the world, were given greater licence in matters matrimonial (216).

The opinions of the Fathers were often reproduced in Erasmus' primary medieval source, the *Decretum*, the decrees collected by the ecclesiastical lawyer Gratian in the twelfth century,[12] which combined the teaching of the Scriptures with the doctrine of the early church and the more recent rulings of the papacy. Interestingly, Erasmus went out of his way to consult the legal commentaries of the medieval schoolmen who updated and embellished Gratian's basic work, though elsewhere he claimed to find their outpourings tedious and virtually unreadable. He used them for two purposes: to provide information, required, for example, to construct the remarkable account of the eighteen impediments to matrimony that occupies a central place in his discussion of the laws of marriage; and to provide opponents for his dialectic, as in his argument with Duns Scotus over the nature of vows (261). Of the commentators he names, the most authoritative are Peter Lombard (d 1160) and St Thomas Aquinas (1225–74); the former's concise *Sententiae* provided a framework for the effusions of a multitude of successors, as Erasmus wryly remarked in the *Enchiridion*.[13] Erasmus also made much use of the collected pronouncements of the popes known as the *Decretals*, which prescribed in increasing and (to Erasmus) presumptuous detail the parameters of the institution of matrimony; many of his examples of perplexing cases are based on the real-life problems presented to the medieval popes for adjudication. In his discussion of canon law, Erasmus barely disguises his habitual contempt for 'human regulations,' such as the 'papal' impediments, unknown to Roman law, of spiritual kinship and public propriety. He waxes sarcastic about rules, unauthorized by divine law, that seem designed merely to ensnare the unwary in the toils of an arbitrary ecclesiastical authority.

It is hard to know whether Erasmus was inspired by more recent treatments of the topic. Could the classical authors be bettered on ethical ques-

* * * * *

12 See n215 to the text.
13 CWE 66 9; for an account of some of the commentators, see Rummel *Annotations* 74–85.

tions? And was not his theological and legal battle essentially waged against the medieval legacy? Some of Erasmus' reflections on celibacy and divorce recall passages in More's *Utopia*,[14] but he makes no obvious allusion to this or to other recent treatises such as Luther's *Judgment on Monastic Vows* (1521) and *Sermon on the Estate of Marriage* (1522), or Vives' *Education of a Christian Woman* (1524, also dedicated to Catherine of Aragon).[15] In fact the *Institutio christiani matrimonii* itself forms part of an acrimonious debate over the nature of the institution and the implications of Erasmus' position. In particular, it is a defence of his *Encomium matrimonii*, which had been attacked as recently as May 1526 by Josse Clichtove and Noël Béda;[16] modern scholars are divided over whether the *Institutio* represents a provocative restatement and reinforcement of Erasmus' views, or simply a clarification of them.[17]

Certainly there is a change of style. The hortatory *Encomium matrimonii*, first printed in 1518 but probably written much earlier, was published separately several times, but it also reappeared, billed as a rhetorical exercise, an example of the 'letter of persuasion,' in *De conscribendis epistolis* in 1522.[18] There it was followed, perhaps as a sop to earlier critics, by a much briefer 'letter of dissuasion' in which Erasmus rehearses dutifully some of the standard misogynistic arguments.[19] The French translation of the *Encomium* pub-

* * * * *

14 Cf Olsen 14–15 and E.V. Telle 'Marriage and Divorce on the Isle of Utopia' ERSY 8 (1988) 98–117.

15 LW 44 251–400 and 45 17–49; for a survey of Luther's views, see Olsen 43–57. In 1525 (Ep 1624) Erasmus alluded to Vives' *De institutione feminae christianae* and wondered if any more need be said on the subject; in 1527 (Epp 1830 and 1847) he accused Vives of harshness towards women, a charge to which the latter pleaded justification! It is true that, by modern standards, Vives' tract takes less account than Erasmus' of female sensibilities. I can detect no allusion in Erasmus' *Institutio* to the most widely read fifteenth-century treatise, Francesco Barbaro's *De re uxoria* (1416), nor to a very recent work, Henricus Cornelius Agrippa's *Declamatio de sacramento matrimonii*, published earlier in 1526.

16 In, respectively, the *Propugnaculum ecclesiae adversus Lutheranos* and the *Annotationes Natalis Bedae*; see Rummel *Catholic Critics* II 39 and 74–8 on these attacks and Erasmus' defence of himself in later works. For earlier attacks, beginning in 1519, see Telle 315–25 (Briart, Lee, and Standish) and CWE 71 86–8.

17 See Telle 345–8 and 405–20, opposed by J.-C. Margolin in ASD I-5 367–81.

18 CWE 25 129–145; see especially 129 n1 for a succinct account of the history of the texts and of the controversies. See also the edition of the *Encomium* in ASD I-5 333–416, and CWE 71 86–95 for the brief *Apologia de laude matrimonii*, published in March 1519.

19 CWE 25 145–8; see Telle 185–7 on its alleged disingenuousness.

lished by the Chevalier de Berquin in 1525 revived the controversy with new ferocity; Berquin barely escaped with his life.[20] The *Institutio* adopts a less rhetorical and apparently more conciliatory tone: Erasmus portrays himself at one point as a delegate to a council who 'gives his considered opinion, but is prepared to yield to a better, or to be laughed out of court if he deserves it' (279). But his disclaimers are generally of a more familiar Erasmian kind: 'I have merely been giving a few reminders, and if they seem unreasonable, then consider them unsaid' (302). Understandably, his opponents refused to 'consider unsaid' a book of two hundred pages, and in modern times Emile V. Telle has echoed their impatience with what he considers Erasmus' duplicity. From the standpoint of a transcendent and immutable Theology,[21] Erasmus' barely concealed attacks upon monasticism and clerical celibacy, which he considers worthless unless they make a man free for piety,[22] are an affront to the glorious tradition of Christian asceticism; on the other hand, to credit Erasmus with the single-handed invention of divorce is to stretch hostility too far.[23]

The question of divorce (in the sense of complete dissolution of a marriage) was another on which Erasmus had recently become embroiled in controversy. In the second edition of his New Testament (1519), Erasmus had published a greatly expanded annotation on 1 Corinthians 7:39,[24] in which

* * * * *

20 See Telle's edition of L. de Berquin *Declamation des louenges de mariage* (Geneva 1976) 54–63. Berquin finally went to the stake in 1529.
21 Cf ibidem 62 n11.
22 Erasmus is less comprehensive than Luther who, in his *Judgment on Monastic Vows* (see n15 above), considers them contrary to God's word, unnecessary to salvation, a violation of the first commandment and of Christian freedom, and contrary to common sense and reason.
23 Telle's language is often intemperate: sarcasm about the 'pape de Bâle' with his blind hatred of monasticism does not make the case more plausible. A useful counterweight is the dispassionate account in Olsen, which sets Erasmus' views in the context of liberal Catholic thought (eg that of Cajetanus) as well as of the Reformers' far from unanimous views on the question. Telle returned to the attack in 'La Digamie de Thomas More, Erasme, et Catarino Politi' BHR 52 (1990) 323–32; the article includes a study of another of Erasmus' adversaries, the Dominican Lancellotto de' Politi, known as Catharinus. For replies to Telle's strictures, see J.-C. Margolin in ASD I-2 153ff and John W. O'Malley in CWE 66 xxxiii–iv.
24 LB VI 692D–703D; for summaries, see Olsen 21–7 and Payne 121–4. Erasmus added a large number of extra references to canon law in the 1522 edition; cf *Erasmus' Annotations on the New Testament: Acts, Romans, I and II Corinthians* ed A. Reeve and M.A. Screech (Leiden 1990) 467–81.

he argued on both historical and humanitarian grounds for a loosening of the church's strictures on divorce and remarriage. Once again, since his argument included criticism of the vagaries of papal decrees and further slights on monastic vows and institutional celibacy, the work attracted hostile replies; among others, Jacob van Hoogstraten and Edward Lee asserted the indissolubility of the sacrament.[25] In this annotation Erasmus cites an even larger number of Fathers and canonists than in the *Institutio*. While admitting that their evidence shows the wide and long-standing acceptance among Christians of the proposition that only death can dissolve a properly contracted marriage, he argues, in essence, that times have changed and that now Christian charity and compassion should allow 'certain marriages to be dissolved, not irresponsibly, but for serious reasons, and not by just anyone, but by the princes of the church or by lawfully appointed judges.'[26] In reply to his critics, Erasmus simply assured them that he had no wish to teach anything contrary to the beliefs of the church.

Erasmus' opinions on marriage reached a wider audience when in 1523 he published an edition of the *Colloquia* which included five new dialogues sometimes called the 'marriage colloquies.' Two of them are relatively uncontroversial, the one called simply 'Marriage' providing several precise examples of marital harmony of the kind promoted in the *Institutio*.[27] But the others, 'Courtship,' 'The Girl with No Interest in Marriage,' and 'The Repentant Girl,'[28] return without apology to the themes of virginity, vows, celibacy, monasticism, and chastity within marriage. In 1526 and 1529 Erasmus added other colloquies, more practical and less polemical, on venereal disease, breast-feeding, and extravagant clothing, which are also echoed in the *Institutio*.[29] In 1529, in *De vidua christiana*,[30] Erasmus again courted controversy by warmly recommending remarriage for younger widows at least,[31] though his eulogies of widows who have chosen to preserve their chastity does something to redress the balance. In view of his earlier praise of virginity in the *Virginis et martyris comparatio* of 1524, it seems wisest to conclude,

* * * * *

25 See Olsen 27–30; Rummel *Catholic Critics* II 25–6; and Telle 205–31.
26 LB VI 692F; see Olsen 32–3 on Erasmus' 'recantation.'
27 *Coniugium* CWE 39 306–27; cf 335–47 below. The other uncontroversial piece is *Adolescentis et scorti* ('The Young Man and the Harlot') CWE 39 381–9.
28 *Proci et puellae*, *Virgo μισόγαμος*, *Virgo poenitens* CWE 39 256–305
29 See nn370, 654, and 662 to the text.
30 CWE 66 178–257
31 Ibidem 241–4

with Erasmus himself, that each state 'has its own distinction and honour in sacred writings,'[32] and that each of us should be content with the state to which he or she has been called.

It is possible today to admire Erasmus' humane prescriptions for the preservation of marital harmony and for the upbringing of children, which are echoed in his other, more famous, pedagogical works; to admire also his uncompromising desire to raise the status of marriage in the eyes of his fellow Christians, to persuade them that the union of souls, rather than the contract, is the essence of marriage,[33] and to regularize the procedure both for entering and, where absolutely necessary, for leaving the state of matrimony. But it has to be said that his criticism of monasticism (to which he returns, like a man obsessed,[34] at the very end of the *Institutio*), his attack on the indissolubility of marriage, which was what gave matrimony its sacramental quality in the eyes of Augustine,[35] and his apparently paradoxical theory of 'matrimonial chastity'[36] were all guaranteed, and perhaps calculated, to give offence to the traditionalists, and certainly put heart into the Reformers.[37] Predictably enough, when the Council of Trent in 1564 came to revise the blanket condemnation of Erasmus' works by Pope Paul IV, the *Institutio christiani matrimonii*, along with a handful of other works, remained in its entirety a forbidden book.[38] Paradoxically the same council, though it reaffirmed the superiority of virginity and celibacy to marriage, introduced, in a bid to eliminate clandestine marriages, a set of proposals remarkably similar to those which constitute one of Erasmus' major plans for reform;[39] on this point, at least, Erasmus the would-be conciliar delegate was given a hearing.

This controversial and lengthy book was reprinted less often than

* * * * *

32 Ibidem 201; cf John W. O'Malley CWE 66 xxxiv and the *Enchiridion* CWE 66 68.
33 See Payne 118; cf Telle 356–60 on Erasmus' unusual concern for individual happiness at the expense of the ecclesiastical institution of marriage. On the less than romantic nature of marital love in the Renaissance, cf Maclean 59.
34 On the influence here of his personal experiences, see eg Ep 447, the *Compendium vitae* CWE 4 406–10, and the useful summary in James K. McConica *Erasmus* (Oxford 1991) 5–8. For full studies of Erasmus' attacks on monasticism, see Telle 15–150 and J. Chomarat 'Erasme et le monachisme' in *Acta Conventus neo-Latini Hafniensis* (see n11 above) 5–19.
35 *De bono coniugali* 6 PL 40 378
36 See 387 below. See also ASD I-5 402–4 and notes (by Margolin).
37 For Erasmus' influence on various Reformers, see Olsen 40, 76, and 113–17.
38 Cf LB X 1821A and Bruce Mansfield *The Phoenix of His Age: Interpretations of Erasmus, c 1550–1750* (Toronto 1979) 26–7.
39 See 296–7 below, and n130.

many of Erasmus' works. Froben produced two simultaneous printings (one in folio and the other in octavo) at Basel in 1526; the Latin text also appeared at Antwerp in that year, and then in two undated sixteenth-century editions, one published at Cologne and the other with no place of origin. The work takes its place in the 1540 *Opera omnia*, in the series published by J. Maire at Paris (1650), and in LB (v 613–724). Translations, some of them abridged and expurgated, exist in German (1542), Italian (1550), English (1568 and another, undated, sixteenth-century version), and French (1714).[40] The text here translated is that of the first octavo edition (Froben 1526), which has been compared with those of 1540 and LB; there are no substantial differences between them. I have corrected obvious misprints and omitted marginal headings. Translations of Scripture are my own, as in most cases no English version corresponds exactly to Erasmus' Latin. I have taken no account of the readings of the manuscript draft of the *Institutio* in Erasmus' own hand, preserved in Copenhagen,[41] as this lies beyond the remit of a translator. For their assistance in dealing with the complex issues of canon law raised in the course of this treatise, I am indebted to the valuable assistance of Msgr Alan McCormack and Dr Lynda Robitaille.

MJH

* * * * *

40 On all this, see *Bibliotheca Erasmiana: répertoire des oeuvres d'Erasme* ed F. Vander Haeghen (Ghent 1893) 110 and Telle 384 n1.
41 Cf C. Reedijk 'Three Erasmus Autographs in the Royal Library at Copenhagen' in *Studia bibliographica in honorem Herman de La Fontaine Verwey* (Amsterdam 1966) 327–49.

TO THE ILLUSTRIOUS QUEEN CATHERINE OF ENGLAND, GLORY
OF MATRONS, FROM DESIDERIUS ERASMUS OF ROTTERDAM,
GREETING.[1]

It is now more than two years, illustrious Queen, since I promised the honourable Master William Mountjoy, chamberlain of your court, that I would write something on the institution of Christian marriage. Although I never lacked the will to fulfil my promise, I was constantly interrupted and prevented from performing the task by so many other obligations, vexations, and bouts of illness that I am beginning to fear Mountjoy will think me wanting in good faith. I am now discharging my debt, late though it is, but whether I am discharging it in full, I do not know. For those who pay their debts in the correct amount but with coins that are deficient in weight and debased in alloy may be forgiven by easy-going creditors, but face serious difficulties with less flexible lenders. I might fear the same fate, except that I am dealing with the kindest and most accommodating of creditors. Moreover, if one's writing is to have life and spirit and to hold together, it is of the utmost importance to maintain, if one can, the fire and inspiration of the moment. But I have never been able to continue on my task for two days together. I shall be surprised, therefore, if you are not offended by the flat and disjointed character of the piece. But if in my picture of matrimony I have shown myself a poor artist, in the saintliness of your character one can find the perfect model of a most holy and blessed marriage. Do not suspect me here of flattery. What we admire and praise in you does not belong to you, but is a gift from God. The valiant qualities of your mother Isabella, the former queen of Spain, were celebrated throughout the world. Her spotless character was truly the sweet savour[2] of God in every place. Your qualities are known to us from closer at hand; from them we can form some idea of her virtues also, just as we recognize the skill of a painter from his picture. We expect a work no less perfect in your daughter Mary. For what should we not expect from a girl who is born of the most devout of parents and brought up under the care of such a mother? I pray the Lord may preserve this happy state to the benefit of the whole Christian world. Farewell.

Basel, 15 July 1526

* * * * *

1 The prefatory letter is Ep 1727 to Catherine of Aragon, trans Alexander Dalzell.
2 Savour: 2 Cor 2:14–15

THE INSTITUTION OF CHRISTIAN MATRIMONY BY DESIDERIUS ERASMUS OF ROTTERDAM

Although every facet of our lives requires the most meticulous attention, yet particular pains must be taken in those areas that do not merely yield immediate advantage or disadvantage, but also sow the seed of success or disaster in every other area of our moral, intellectual, and physical existence. The watchful forester knows that he cannot neglect any part of his charge, yet his primary concern is with the roots of the trees, as he knows that the trees' well-being depends entirely upon them. The officials in charge of the water supply must of course look after the pipes and the mains, but their first concern must be for the wells, since pollution of those will cause disruption to the whole community. That is why, wherever they settled in their wanderings, the venerable patriarchs, whose lives are a pattern for our own, always took pains to provide for themselves wells that gushed clean water; they fought battles over them, they dug them out if they were filled in, and their descendants respected them as a sacred trust bequeathed by their forefathers.[1]

Now I believe that the main root or principal wellspring that produces the greatest joy or unhappiness among humans is marriage; if appropriate care were taken in entering upon marriage, in cherishing it, and in seeing it through to the end, things would clearly go a lot better in human affairs than they do. And yet, quite incomprehensibly, hardly any aspect of life is treated more casually by Christians than this. The circumstances of one's birth are of great importance, and still more crucial is the manner of one's early upbringing. Matrimony, of course, involves both these wellsprings of our existence, the begetting and the rearing of children. Moreover, the prosperity of the state depends upon it, unless we happen to believe that it makes no difference what sort of family background a future statesman has, what principles he has been reared on, or what kind of example he has

* * * * *

1 Eg Abraham in Gen 21:30 and Isaac in Gen 26:18–25

been set at home; unless we think that someone whose home life is marked by habitual wickedness and sin will none the less behave in an exemplary way outside the home.

The ancient philosophers, who took nature for their guide and passed on the rules that she lays down for the good life, never wrote more respectfully or more reverently than they did of marriage. Among many others, the most eminent to have bequeathed us their thoughts on the subject are Aristotle, Xenophon, and Plutarch.[2] Again, those who have tried to promote the good of humanity by legislation have taken particular pains over marriage and made many a pronouncement about the stability and sanctity of marriage and the right way to beget and bring up children. Hence the many laws about betrothal, divorce, and adultery; about the rights of parents over their children and the duty of children towards their parents.

But for some reason that is not at all clear, Christians seem to have given far less thought to marriage than they should. I suspect that, among other things, it was because the early Christians had a certain, entirely admirable[3] enthusiasm for celibacy and lifelong purity. Many of them made a point of extolling virginity and laid down precepts to enable virgins and widows to live pious and holy lives; they did not show the same concern for married people.[4] Fortunately, however, the Lord Jesus himself went out of his way not only to show respect for the married state in a number of ways but even to lay down rules for married life.[5] Peter, the chief of the apostles, was not slow to do the same,[6] while Paul, the church's most eminent teacher,

* * * * *

2 Erasmus frequently cites below Aristotle's *Politics* 7 and the pseudo-Aristotelian *Oeconomica*, Xenophon's *Oeconomicus*, and Plutarch's *Coniugalia praecepta* (*Moralia* 138–46).

3 *Admirabilis* in Latin can also mean 'strange, astonishing'; in view of Erasmus' later attacks on monastic celibacy, one might suspect irony here. However, it is clear from Erasmus' annotation on 1 Cor 7:39 LB VI 695D, 696A, 696D, and 701D–E that, showing a sense of historical perspective akin to Augustine's (see n106 below), he considered celibacy more appropriate at certain times, such as the apostolic era, than at others, such as the present. Telle 241–2 comments on the rarity among contemporary theologians of such a historical sense, while regretting this particular application of it.

4 In similar passages in *De conscribendis epistolis* CWE 25 138 and 147, Erasmus names Jerome (eg *Adversus Iovinianum* and Epp 49 and 54) and Tertullian (eg *De exhortatione castitatis, De pudicitia*). For a much longer list, including works by Ambrose and Augustine, see CWE 66 321 n17.

5 Eg Matt 19:3–12

6 Eg 1 Pet 3:1–7

surpassed even him in his concern for it.[7] Inspired above all by their example, I too shall try my best to provide something that will inspire or assist those who are joined by the sacrament of marriage to be worthy of the most holy estate, established and sanctioned by Christ, that they have entered.

It would not be inappropriate to my subject to begin by singing the praises of marriage; the more people understand and accept the special dignity and sanctity of marriage, the more they will treat it with respect. But since it seems to me and to most people that I have written quite enough elsewhere on this topic (and far too much, according to some rather perverse critics),[8] I shall deal here only with the following subjects: how to ensure the best possible start to matrimony, how to develop and bring it to a successful conclusion, and, finally, how to bring up offspring, who are the most precious fruits of marriage.

Let us begin with the principles enshrined in nature, though of course I am not forgetting that the creator and governor of nature is God, who took particular care to ensure that everything in his creation should be provided with the means to preserve itself from harm. Nature has established no surer means of self-preservation for humanity than mutual love and good will. To this end she has joined certain people by the bonds of kinship, which no individual has the power to create or break off purely of his own volition. Close ties of kinship ensure that a sense of obligation binds parents to children, and children to parents; remarkable evidence of this can be observed in the animal kingdom, and even among savage and untamed beasts. How close are the ties of love that unite brother and sister! In fact, this natural instinct is so deeply implanted in the hearts of all peoples that the words associated with it are very widely used to convey respect, love, and concord. For example, 'father' is commonly used to describe someone who deserves our reverence and respect, 'son' someone whom

*　*　*　*　*

7 Eg 1 Cor 7 and Eph 5:22–33; all these New Testament passages play an important part in Erasmus' subsequent discussion.

8 An allusion to the controversy surrounding Erasmus' *Declamatio* or *Encomium matrimonii*, first published in 1518, though written much earlier (ASD I-5 333–416 ed J.-C. Margolin); a revised version appeared in *De conscribendis epistolis* in 1522 (CWE 25 129–45). The critics included Jan Briart of Louvain and Josse Clichtove and Noël Béda of Paris. See the introductory note 209–12 above; CWE 26 528–9 n1; CWE 66 xviii–xix and xxxiv; Telle 315–45 (and 405–20 for his controversial claim that the *Institutio* is merely more of the same); ASD I-5 367–81; and Rummel *Catholic Critics* I 59 and II 39 and 74–8. The French translation by Louis de Berquin, *Declamation des louenges de mariage* (1525), also caused a scandal; see the edition by E.V. Telle (Geneva 1976) 54–63 and ASD I-5 354–8.

we hold especially dear, and 'brother' someone whom we find particularly congenial.

Moreover, this family feeling spreads its branches and its roots far and wide in all directions. It goes back in a direct line to grandfathers, great-grandfathers, great-great-grandfathers, great-great-great-grandfathers and great-great-great-great-grandfathers; it runs forward to grandchildren, great-grandchildren, great-great-grandchildren, and great-great-great-grandchildren; to left and right it extends to brothers, sisters, cousins on both sides and beyond, to relationships with no special name. If you go back through the indirect lines, you come upon paternal and maternal uncles, paternal and maternal aunts, great-uncles, great-great-uncles, and great-great-aunts on both sides, and others for whom there is no technical name. If you go forward in the same way, you come upon a great throng of nieces and nephews by your brothers and sisters, not to mention the great- and great-great- nieces and nephews whom they provide in their turn! As you clamber about the family tree, new names are constantly added to this roll-call of family affection. Your parents are a couple: this is doubled with your grandparents, becomes eightfold with your great-grandparents, is doubled again in the next generation – and so on. Looking the other way, you encounter sons and daughters, swarms of grandchildren and great-grandchildren by them, and so on into other branches, until, after much journeying, this affection based on the ties of blood very gradually evaporates.

But then affinity, relationship by marriage, comes into play, to refresh the pool of good will, reinforcing, as it were, the bonds of natural kinship. Such relationships hover between those that nature establishes without our knowledge or consent and those that we enter into freely and deliberately. Your daughter's marriage brings you a son; your sister's betrothal brings you a brother. Even strangers, if they perform particular tasks, can be described as members of the family: the whimpering infant's wet-nurse is like a mother to him, the little child's tutor is loved like a father. Again, schoolteachers, whose sound instruction has improved their little charges, not only feel for them a kind of parental affection, but also receive in their turn the kind of respect due to a parent. Adoption, a facsimile of kinship, often establishes an even stronger bond than ties of blood. The church has also found spiritual ways to increase the reasons for mutual good will among Christians, establishing bonds of sacred kinship between those who perform the baptism, the godparents or catechists, and those who are reborn in Christ by the holy washing.

However, I think that perhaps all these relationships are surpassed by friendship, that meeting of minds which is based solely on the inclination of the will and choice. Among the ancients, as long as there remained some vestiges of honour and dignity in human behaviour, hardly any form of kinship or relationship was held in more respect than this, which extended to guests as well as to benefactors.[9] I shall not delay the reader here by recalling the laws of friendship, or by enumerating the examples of famous friendships, known to everyone from the frequent allusions to them in all the best authors. But among all relationships, natural, voluntary, or both, there is none closer or more holy than marriage, because it involves the complete and perpetual intermingling of two destinies, and connects, unites, and joins body to body, spirit to spirit in such a way that it seems to make two people one. Pythagoras described friendship as 'sharing a soul,' but marriage goes even further and also means 'sharing one body.'[10] The most important part of marriage is the union of two spirits, and so those who are joined in body but disunited in spirit are living in sin rather than in wedlock.

Technically speaking, 'marriage is a lawful and perpetual union between a man and a woman, entered into for the purpose of begetting offspring, and involving an indivisible partnership of life and property.'[11] Let this legalistic definition stand unchallenged for the moment; I have designed it specifically for the business in hand, which requires a model that includes every aspect of the question. Not only will proposing a definition of this kind help me to show that whatever makes other partnerships strong and inviolable is to be found, even stronger and more effective, in marriage, but it will also illustrate many other features of the subject. For this purpose I have painted a true and realistic portrait of marriage, to make clearer what should be the aim of anyone taking a wife or marrying a husband, for I shall not introduce into this discussion the unique and perfect marriage of the Virgin Mother, which is entirely without precedent, and shall remain so.[12] I am dealing with ordinary, everyday matrimony.

* * * * *

9 The classic discussions of friendship are Aristotle's *Nicomachean Ethics*, books 7 and 8, and Cicero's *De amicitia*. The rules of hospitality in the ancient world were elaborate and generous; cf *Institutio principis christiani* CWE 27 264 and nn5 and 6.

10 Cf *Adagia* I i 2; 'one body' is an allusion to the 'one flesh' of Gen 2:24 and Matt 19:5.

11 This definition, apparently Erasmus' own, expands the classic statements of Roman and canon law, such as *Digesta* 23.2.1 and Lombard *Sententiae* book 4 dist 27 c 2.

12 This might appear to qualify a passage in the *Encomium matrimonii* (see CWE 25 131), where Erasmus suggests that Mary's marriage may serve ordinary mortals as an example of chaste wedlock, but in fact Erasmus returns to this theme 309 below. On Erasmus' generally respectful attitude to the Virgin, see Halkin 'Mariologie.'

It may be appropriate here to borrow some terms used in scholastic dialectic.[13] The words 'lawful union' state the 'genus' of the term defined: a treaty or a contract is a 'lawful association,' although it can in no sense be called a marriage. The words 'for the purpose of begetting offspring' constitute the 'difference': they distinguish the purpose of marriage from that of every other type of lawful union. The final words, 'involving an indivisible partnership of life and property,' represent a 'characteristic property.'

The nature of a thing is also usually defined with reference to four causes. In this case, the 'material cause' consists of 'a man and a woman,' and one is thereby reminded that marriages made between those who are under age or past child-bearing cannot properly be called marriages in the exact meaning of the term, since in the one case they are not yet man and woman, and in the other they have ceased to be so. As for the efficient cause, that is 'lawful union.'[14] The law is the immediate source of true matrimony, but of course God is the source of the law: he first joined male and female and soon after ordained the laws of marriage, declaring, 'And the two shall be one flesh.' And, 'For this reason shall a man leave his father and mother and cleave to his wife.' And again, 'Increase and multiply and replenish the earth.'[15] Thus marriages that are not made lawfully (that is, under the authority and auspices of God) cannot truly be called marriages, although the church in its indulgence has allowed certain kinds of union, by no means 'lawful,'[16] to be loosely called marriages.

The formal cause is represented by 'union and partnership of life': there can be no marriage unless there is agreement between the partners as

*　*　*　*　*

13 Erasmus subjects his definition of marriage to formal analysis in the style of Aquinas (on marriage, *Supplementum* q 49); Erasmus exploits the terminology of scholastic logic to demonstrate the superiority of marriage to other contracts. He was usually more scathing about the 'quibbling' of the medieval schoolmen; see the memorable passage in the *Moria* CWE 27 126–30.

14 According to Isidore of Seville, quoted in Gratian's *Decretum* pars 2 c 27 q 2 c 1, the 'efficient cause' of marriage is consent: Aquinas agrees, *Supplementum* q 45 art 1. Erasmus thus emphasizes the scriptural rather than the legal foundation of marriage. But all agree that the 'final cause' is the begetting of offspring (ibidem q 54 art 3). The 'four causes' mentioned here are Aristotelian in origin (*Analytica priora*).

15 The quotations are, respectively, two sentences from Matt 19:5 (= Mark 10:7–8) and Gen 9:1.

16 Γνήσια in the text, a term used by Xenophon *Cyropaedia* 4.3.1 to distinguish 'wedded wives' from mere concubines. Erasmus may be alluding to marriages arranged, for financial or political reasons, between couples below or beyond child-bearing age.

to the purpose of marriage. Thus liaisons for mere fornication and forced marriages are ruled out by my definition. The final cause of marriage is the 'begetting of offspring,' which means that no true marriage can be made between those too old for child-bearing, or those who are irremediably sterile – according to the strict definition of marriage I have proposed, although the church does not rule out certain types of marriage, of the second and third kind, which I shall touch on later, should an appropriate opportunity arise. For the moment I am simply attempting to make it clear that the different things that give strength to various other kinds of partnership are all to be found, united, in matrimony alone.

There are three things, above all, that bind and consolidate human society: nature, law, and religion. Nature includes not only the ties between parents and children, between siblings, between those related by blood or marriage, but also any true relationship that our innate reason commands us to respect, warning that it would be wickedly sinful to violate it. No legal penalty is prescribed for a faithless or ungrateful friend, but do we not all condemn the betrayal of friendship and ingratitude towards benefactors? Civil law did not penalize such misdeeds for the simple reason that it was unable to devise a punishment to fit the crime and considered that universal condemnation was easily punishment enough. It is worse to break a friendship than a legal agreement because it is entered into on trust alone, without documents, witnesses, or sureties, and arises from disinterested good will towards another. No legal instrument could be more binding than a bond established by some unsolicited act of kindness, especially if the donor has acted so spontaneously that he leaves himself no right to ask for recompense or to reproach the other, because of course he assumes the recipient's good will towards him, and does not harbour any suspicion of ingratitude in his heart.

But where is there a closer union of hearts, where is there greater trust than in matrimony, where both partners willingly place themselves in each other's power and even to an extent surrender their bodies to each other? And so little do they consider the possibility of divorce that it is considered the worst of omens even to mention the word at the wedding! The laws of the Jews and the pagans apparently granted husbands the power to repudiate their wives,[17] but by common consent divorce has always been

* * * * *

17 See especially Deut 24:1, modified by Christ in Matt 5:31–2. Divorce and remarriage were relatively easy under imperial Roman law; see *Codex* 5.17.1–10 and *Digesta* 24.2.1–11; in the later *Novellae* 117.8–15 the Christian emperors sought to restrict the possibilities of dissolution by reducing allowable

reckoned among the most sinister of deeds, the equivalent of ingratitude and the betrayal of a friend.

Another reason why the bond of marriage surpasses any friendship, however close, is that there is nothing to prevent one person from having many friends; and of course affection cannot have the same strength when it is spread among a number rather than concentrated on a single person, as it is in marriage. The Scythians considered it unseemly for one person to be a friend to many (the Greeks call this *polyphilia*);[18] Hesiod is not keen on *polyxenia*, any more than on *axenia*.[19] Although we read that *polygynaecia* was allowed to certain patriarchs and kings,[20] it is certainly not permitted nowadays. Nature effectively cements these bonds in another way, through the natural inclination felt by each sex towards the other; the deeply implanted desire to beget children complements the union of hearts. So much for nature's contribution.

Now, how has the law tried to prevent the breaking of partnership agreements? It has introduced contracts, witnesses, documents, guarantors, securities, penalties. Which of these does not apply far more strictly in marriage, the true, properly conducted marriage with which we are concerned? The authorization of the families is required, legal documents and witnesses play their part in betrothal, and a prescribed form of words is used to make the contract between bride and groom. Under Roman law a

* * * * *

causes. By the twelfth century, although annulment was permitted on various grounds (see n148 below), total divorce in the modern sense had been virtually replaced by the limited *divortium quoad torum*, separation from the marriage-bed (Esmein II 85–98; Telle 353–4). The etymological meaning of *divortium* is 'separation,' and Erasmus later exploits the flexibility of the term in a way impossible in English (cf Telle 350–1). His subsequent plea for a more humane approach to the indissolubility of marriage was of course echoed by the Reformers, who widened the causes beyond adultery alone; see Olsen passim and Gaudemet 284–5 (also 70–88 for the Fathers' strictures on divorce and remarriage). For later claims that Erasmus directly inspired the Reformers' actions, see Bruce Mansfield *The Phoenix of His Age: Interpretations of Erasmus, c 1550-1750* (Toronto 1979) 41, 151 n4, and 204.

18 An opinion cited in Lucian *Toxaris* 37; cf *Adagia* III vi 37: *Neque nullis sis amicus neque multis*, 'Be a friend neither to none nor to many'; and Plutarch's essay *De amicorum multitudine* ('On Having Many Friends'), *Moralia* 93–7.

19 Hesiod *Works and Days* 715; the words mean 'hospitality to many' and 'lack of hospitality.'

20 The Old Testament contains many examples of polygamists, eg the patriarchs Abraham (Gen 16) and Jacob (Gen 30), and the kings David (1 Sam 25:43) and Solomon (1 Kings 11:3: seven hundred wives!).

solemn oath was sworn, in a prescribed form, before the censor. Remember Aulus Gellius' story of a man who got himself fined by the censor: he was asked, in the customary way, 'On your conscience, are you satisfied that you have a wife?'; to which he replied, with rather inappropriate humour, 'Yes, I have a wife, but by heaven I'm not exactly satisfied!'[21] Nowadays marriages are contracted in public before a priest or in private before witnesses. The forthcoming ceremony is announced to the people, in case somebody knows of some factor that may subsequently render the union invalid; everyone sees the bride taken in solemn procession to the church and back again, helping to ensure that no pretext will be found to undermine the union once it is effected. Again, what pledge could make a contract more binding than having children together (which is why Latin calls children 'pledges')?[22]

Another point: there are three kinds of penalty for violating the laws of matrimony. The first, which I consider the least serious, is execution: by stoning under Jewish law, and by the sword under Roman law.[23] The second is ostracism.[24] The third is divine vengeance, which no guilty creature can escape. But there will be a better opportunity to discuss these later; for now, let me finish what I was saying.

For the most secure guarantees of their contracts, people look to religion, which indeed used to consist very largely of such things as oaths, vows, obtestations, sacrifices, and other rituals. Even among the pagans, those scrupulous worshippers of demons, weddings were performed with much religious ceremony.[25] They had Jupiter Gamelius,[26] who was supposed to watch over marriage alliances and to punish those who desecrated them.

* * * * *

21 Aulus Gellius *Noctes Atticae* 4.20.2, also found in Cicero *De oratore* 2.64.260 and Quintilian *Institutiones oratoriae* 8.5.1. A variant reading in Gellius and in Erasmus' text, which would translate '*You* are not exactly satisfied!' seems to weaken the joke.

22 *Pignora*, a common metaphor used also of other close relatives; cf Quintilian *Institutiones oratoriae* 6.1.33 and Pliny *Epistles* 1.12.3.

23 Deut 22:24 and *Institutiones* 4.18.4; see also n248 below and a passage in the *Institutio principis christiani* CWE 27 269 and n31.

24 Used among the Greeks: Aristotle *Politics* 7.16.18 (1336a1) and Plato *Laws* 6.784E. See also n250 below. Paul prescribes this penalty for incest in 1 Cor 5:13.

25 Cf the laudatory account of ancient marriage ceremonies in *De conscribendis epistolis* CWE 25 135; but here Erasmus goes further in establishing syncretic parallels with Christianity.

26 A Greek epithet meaning 'pertaining to weddings,' applied to this aspect of Zeus or Jupiter

Then there was Juno Pronuba,[27] under whose auspices marriages would prosper, and also Venus, who was supposed to have in her gift procreation, which is of course the fulfilment of matrimony. Marriages were made under their auspices and, as it were, in their presence. A sacrifice was made to Juno, Venus, and the Graces,[28] to reinforce all the other elements: the contract of betrothal, the solemn oath, which was held most sacred among the ancients (to the great shame of modern Christians); the curse pronounced against potential desecrators; the joining of right hands, the symbol of trust, and the exchange of kisses, the sign of mutual love; the written contract and the dowry. Juno was believed to encourage fidelity and Venus fertility, and the Graces to ensure continuing affection between the couple. Those people and their unholy symbols could give us some lessons in holiness. Let us give thanks to God that our impiety is different in kind from theirs, and that his mercy has freed us, through his Son, from the heathenish worship of demons.

None the less, we ought to be ashamed to call ourselves Christians if we neglect something that the pagans thought deserved such careful attention and if our true beliefs do not inspire us to treat marriage with reverence, since their vain superstition induced them to do so. Instead of Jupiter Gamelius, we have God the Father, who instituted marriage in the Garden of Eden; he it is who rewards those who observe the laws of marriage he made and punishes those who infringe them. Instead of Juno, we have the Son of God, who hallowed a marriage by his presence and by the very first of his miracles.[29] Instead of the Graces, we have the Holy Spirit, who breathes into those who take this sacrament as they should a secret breath of mutual love; thus they are joined by more than the human affection engendered by the body's desires and, inspired by the gift of heavenly love, are more closely united by their devotion to God than by their physical union with

* * * * *

27 The queen of heaven as the patroness of marriage, the divine counterpart of the Roman matron (*pronuba*) who attended the bride throughout the wedding ceremonies
28 As Erasmus points out, Venus was traditionally associated with fertility; the three Graces, daughters of Jupiter and the sea-nymph Eurynome, usually represented harmony and reconciliation.
29 The wedding at Cana (John 2:1–11), an incident often evoked in the wedding liturgy: see Stevenson 10 and 65–6. In the *Encomium matrimonii* CWE 25 131, Erasmus uses this example to bolster his argument that marriage is the greatest of the sacraments; his tone here is deliberately more restrained. Telle 373–5 argues, however, that in the next sentence ('as they should') and elsewhere Erasmus denies the automatic outpouring of grace (*ex opere operato*) during the ceremony, an essential component of a true sacrament.

one another. In place of Venus, we have Holy Church, whose authority sanctions and embellishes all lawfully contracted marriages. Finally, this holy act (as it undoubtedly is) is performed in a holy place, a duly appointed minister of the sacraments officiates, auspicious prayers are offered, the Gospel is at hand, and the sacrifice made is not of cattle but of the spotless Lamb,[30] who bequeathed to us this most sacred token of a covenant that must never be broken.

Thus the consecration of a marriage is attended by much religious devotion – and yet are there still among us Christians unafraid to desecrate it as though it were merely a secular institution? In order that marriage might be the more sacred to us and that, as Paul's teaching has it, 'wedlock might be honourable to all, and the marriage-bed undefiled,'[31] to some extent God held matrimony in greater honour than virginity,[32] although the latter has its particular glories, by which it rises to the heights of the angels. For what does the church hold more dear or more sacred after God than the seven mysteries, which Christ the Bridegroom left for his bride, as guarantees of his return and as most precious reminders of himself during his absence (in the corporeal sense, at least)? He chose to include marriage among these precious pledges, these priceless jewels, these holy memorials to himself – and virginity cannot lay claim to the same degree of honour.

To comprehend more clearly the true majesty of that word 'sacrament' ('mystery' in Greek),[33] you should know that in lawful marriage, as in almost all the other sacraments, there are three things to look for: a symbol, a pledge, and an example. By a symbol, I mean an outward sign, a likeness which evokes an archetype; the 'pledge' is the gift of spiritual grace that is poured out as if guaranteed through the administration of the sacrament; the 'example' is the element in the ceremony that we are encouraged to emulate. The more exalted the person a statue represents – a prince, a saint, or the supreme godhead – the more respect it will receive; similarly the sacraments command respect and honour by virtue of the hidden meaning they convey.

* * * * *

30 A reference to the nuptial mass
31 Heb 13:4
32 On the controversy aroused by this view, see the introductory note 205 above.
33 τὸ μυστήριον: cf n66 below. Marriage was the last of the seven sacraments to be acknowledged officially, at the Council of Florence in 1439 (*Decretum pro Armenis*, Denzinger 1327). For conflicting views on Erasmus' treatment of its sacramental character, see Payne passim, especially 104–25; and Telle 257–71 and 367–82.

What then is the meaning to us of this visible union of a man and a woman? First, it represents that supreme mystery, which the very angels worship,[34] whereby the divine nature joined itself to human nature by an ineffable bond; in one and the same hypostasis[35] were joined the Son of God, a human soul, and a human body, and an indissoluble link was forged between the heavenly and the terrestrial, the eternal and the mortal, the visible and the invisible, the infinite and the finite, the created and the un-created, the highest and the lowest. What could be more divine than this alliance? Such diverse natures come together in a single being, though their essences remain distinct; but such is the harmony of this hypostatic union that one and the same being may truly be called God and man, the Son of God, God from God, an immortal from the Immortal, born outside time yet in time born as a man of mankind; at the same time creator of all things and creature, dead yet giving life to all that lives, reviver of the dead yet him-self consigned to death. In both cases we observe perfect unity: in the one a single hypostasis from God and man, in the other the image of this unity: 'And the two shall be one flesh.'[36] In the one, two natures are joined but not mixed together, in the other the two sexes are linked but not merged.

In that divine union, where two natures are joined but not mixed, their respective positions are maintained and the mightier enfolds the weaker, that is, the divine nature embraces the human. In a contract of marriage, the husband retains his authority, by which, none the less, he so cherishes and enfolds the weaker sex that their life together is based on partnership, not tyranny. The man represents the principles of form and action, the woman, of matter desiring form.[37] See how duality is by some inexpressible means reduced to unity[38] in God and man, in husband and wife; God is the first

* * * * *

34 Cf Heb 1:6.
35 The union in one person of the divine and human natures; this mystery of faith concerning Christ, who is both perfect God and perfect man, was fully established (against various heresies) by the Council of Chalcedon in 451 (Den-zinger 300).
36 Gen 2:24. For a detailed commentary on this passage and its 'extravagant' blending of different 'mysteries,' see Telle 369–71.
37 A reference to Aristotelian-Thomistic physics, in which matter and form are the primary essential principles of changeable being; cf the colloquy *Puerpera* ('The New Mother') CWE 39 601–2. In *De generatione animalium* 1.1.2 (716a5), Aristotle states that, in the begetting of children, the father provides form and the mother the material; Aquinas quotes this in *Supplementum* q 52 art 4.2. See also Maclean 8–10 and 40–1.
38 Erasmus uses the grecisms *henas* (unity) and *dyas* (duality), recalling Plato's discussions of the special kind of unity that defies mathematical analysis (eg *Philebus* 15A; see also *Parmenides* 149C and *Phaedo* 101C).

cause of both unions, with love as intermediary. The Son took on human nature, but the operation was performed by the godhead as a whole. What are we told concerning matrimony? 'Whom God has joined, let no man put asunder.'[39] If God can be separated from man in the person of Christ, a husband can be separated from his wife in marriage. When divorce occurs, it appears that it was never a true marriage. If the man who said, 'Friendship that could end was never true friendship,'[40] was right, it would be even more true to say, A marriage that could be dissolved was never a true marriage. And let people say what they like, I call a true marriage not one that is approved by the law but one that is cemented between equals in virtue by true affection; a union founded on moral qualities will very rarely fall apart.

I have thus established one parallel to show how closely a human institution can reflect the divine reality. You see how two disparate parts become one in an indissoluble union, how both have the same cause, and how love is the intermediary in both cases. What else but his ineffable love persuaded the Son of Man to share our nature? Similarly, a marriage that is not based on mutual affection does not deserve the name. But what of the fruit of this union? After taking our form the heavenly Bridegroom, clothed in human shape, stepped out from his chamber. His first task was to expel his rival and then to claim his bride, the church, whom he set free by his death, whom he washed and purified with his blood, whom he endowed with the mystic gifts of his spirit. How numerous and how blessed are the offspring that Christ fathered (and continues to father) by his bride! She is impregnated with the heavenly seed of God's word, as the apostle James writes: 'Of his free will he begot us by the word of truth, that we should be, as it were, the beginning of his creation.'[41] Paul is no doubt justified in saying, 'For I have given you birth in Christ Jesus through the gospel,' and again, 'You are my children, to whom I give second birth as Christ is formed within you.'[42] But how much more just it is to acknowledge Christ as the creator and leader of this new generation of children, 'who were born, not of blood, nor of the human will, nor of the desires of the flesh, but of God.'[43]

The church is of course that abundantly fruitful bride of Christ whom David was inspired by the Spirit to foretell: 'Your wife shall be like a fruitful vine growing all round your house.' The church is like a single house

* * * * *

39 Matt 19:6. On the increasing liturgical importance of this text at the time of the Reformation, see Stevenson 76 and index under 'Matthew 19.'
40 Aristotle *Eudemian Ethics* 7.5.3, cited in Erasmus' *Adagia* II i 72
41 James 1:18
42 1 Cor 4:15; Gal 4:19
43 John 1:13

for all her children, and they are the delightful throng of offspring hymned by David in the same verse: 'Your children shall be like olive-shoots surrounding your table.'[44] The old olive trees have been rooted out, and now new olive plants are growing in their place, tender in their innocence but heavy with the sweet fruit of faith and love. They stand round the Lord's table, whence they are refreshed with heavenly food and drink, the body and blood of their redeemer.

That nameless Hebrew sage was contemplating this wonderful progeny with his mind's eye when he exclaimed, 'O how fair is that chaste generation, and how bright!'[45] No wonder they appear fair and chaste, since the Bridegroom has washed away their sin and adorned them with so many heavenly treasures! No wonder they seem bright, since the true Sun of the world, 'who enlightens everyone that comes into this world,'[46] has shone upon them! The church is the new bride who seemed barren to the synagogue, since the Jews thought they had destroyed the Bridegroom, though in truth he had ascended to heaven. For a while he did indeed withdraw his physical presence, but he left the powerful seed of God's word in her; he continued to meet her and, through the hidden ways of the spirit, to steal into the bosom of his bride and thus beget every day a numerous progeny from every nation under heaven. Even she is astonished by this bountiful supply of children, and says, in Isaiah: 'How did I come by all these children? I was sterile and barren, an exile and a captive: who reared them? I was deserted and alone: where were they all?'[47]

Why has the synagogue so few offspring? Because it has killed its husband, and instead of the Bridegroom it embraces Moses, who is long past the age of fatherhood. But the new bride, just when she was most harassed by the Jews and the gentiles, by exile, torture, and death, none the less gave the Bridegroom a multitude of legitimate sons and daughters. Of course, she claims no credit for her fertility, but gives thanks to the Bridegroom, saying, 'Here am I and my children, whom the Lord gave me.'[48] Thus the first and greatest of all the mysteries is that the Son of God joined himself to human nature as to a bride, making a single hypostasis from the two. In the same way, man and woman are made one flesh in matrimony.

* * * * *

44 Ps 127 (Vulg 128):3
45 Wisd of Sol 4:1 in Jerome's version of the Septuagint PL 29 430C; the reading has been rejected since Erasmus' time and does not appear in English versions.
46 John 1:9
47 Isa 49:21
48 Isa 8:18

The second mystery is that the one of whom John the Baptist says, 'It is the bridegroom who possesses the bride,'[49] has joined the church to himself by an unbreakable bond, exactly as the rest of the body is linked to the head. Body and head sound like two separate things, but they become one and the same by this communion. Hear how the Bridegroom prays in the Gospel for his bride, from whom he will not be separated: 'I ask it not only for them, but for all those who shall believe in me through their word; may they all be one, as you, Father, are in me and I am in you; may they all be one in us. Holy Father, in your name protect those whom you have given me, that they may be one as we are one.' A little later he says, 'I in them and you in me, may they be perfectly one.'[50] And to show us that in this mystical marriage good and evil alike are shared, he says, in the Gospel, 'Whatever you do, even to the least of my followers, you do it to me.'[51] In the Acts of the Apostles he cries out, as Saul attacks the Bridegroom's children, 'Saul, Saul, why are you persecuting me?'[52] Obviously he would have said, 'Why are you persecuting my followers?' were it not that the bride and groom are one.

Such a union knows no divorce: 'I give them eternal life,' he says, 'and they shall never perish; no one shall pluck them from my hands.'[53] The devil gets his name from the Greek word for slander;[54] he is watchful and cunning, ever ready to foment discord between brothers and quarrels between the bride and her groom. He is furious that his handmaiden has been taken from him and raised to such an honourable estate, and he tries every means to engineer a divorce between those who are happily united. But he must fail: the church's Bridegroom is all-virtuous, and will not reject his beloved; he is all-powerful, and cannot be ousted by force; he is all-knowing, and cannot be deceived by Satan's wiles. That old fox procures abortions and sterility by witchcraft, but the Bridegroom turns all this sorcery to his bride's advantage. Thus in the simile of marriage you can also find an image of the lawful union of the bride and groom, of the indissoluble bond in which everything is shared, and of the fruit of their union, heavenly offspring or, as Paul puts it, 'a new creature.'[55]

* * * * *

49 John 3:29. On the infrequent use of this image in the wedding liturgy before the Reformation, see Stevenson 9–12, 43, and 125.
50 John 17:20–1, 23
51 Matt 25:40
52 Acts 9:4
53 John 10:28
54 διάβολος
55 2 Cor 5:17

In this respect the sacrament of marriage reminds us of baptism. Through marriage we are born into this world, through baptism we are reborn in Christ. This rebirth is of course more momentous than birth, but were we not first born through marriage none of us could then be reborn in Christ through baptism! The fact that, as Paul says, marriage also produces 'the children of wrath'[56] is not the fault of matrimony itself but of the devil, the cause of that first unhappy divorce when nature, created good, was corrupted by sin. Marriage existed before sin, and, but for its intervention, matrimony would have produced nothing but joyful and utterly beloved[57] offspring. Some scholars – Jean Gerson[58] is one – believe we cannot altogether discount the view, if we base our hope on God's boundless mercy, that should a child born to devout parents happen to die without receiving, through nobody's fault, the gift of baptism, it will not necessarily be condemned to eternal torment. But whatever the church's judgment on this (for I am not seeking to impose my own opinion here), it is clear that, even if nowadays every Christian marriage produces 'the children of wrath,' they are born with hope of receiving grace. For baptism is denied to none and, in an emergency, may be administered by anyone.

It may not be inappropriate here to consider another mystery symbolized by marriage: the heavenly Father begot a Son equal to himself before time existed, and then, having created the world through his Son, the Father begot him again, in a certain sense, in the race of mortals; then God fathered his Son once more, though more materially, through the Virgin Mary. I feel that it would not be irreverent to picture God the Father as the bridegroom, the holy Virgin as the bride, the angel as the intermediary,[59] the Holy Ghost as the agent of conception; the newborn child as both God and man, the offspring of God and man, a creature of mixed race, as it were, which in Latin

* * * * *

56 Eph 2:3
57 Erasmus uses the rare grecism *erasmius* in what is perhaps a rather bitter allusion to his own family circumstances.
58 Jean Gerson (1363–1428) *Sermo in festo nativitatis beatae Mariae virginis* in *Oeuvres complètes* ed P. Glorieux 10 vols (Tournai 1960–75) v 349–50, discussing the implications of Christ's sanctification in the Virgin's womb. The Sorbonne theologian Noël Béda had been urging Erasmus to read Gerson's work for some time; Erasmus replied in March 1526 (Allen Ep 1679:84) that he had just obtained a copy and begun to read it. Although welcoming Gerson's humane view here, Erasmus formed no great opinion of him, to judge by remarks in the *Ecclesiastes* LB V 857D and in the Annotations on Luke LB VI 228E, and he rarely cites him subsequently. On the fate of unbaptized infants, see NCE II 63–4 and 69–71, and VIII 762–5 (under 'Limbo').
59 *Paranymphus*, meaning an advocate or spokesman in general, but in particular a friend of the bridegroom acting rather like the best man or groomsman today

is called a hybrid – not, of course, a word to be used casually in speaking of the divine, but one that I have used here to clarify the illustration. After all, the holy Fathers are not afraid to write of the Virgin Mother as the bride of God,[60] and the church does not hesitate to apply to her Solomon's words about the church and Christ in the Song of Songs.[61]

So many of the details remind us of marriage. Gabriel,[62] the messenger, receives the Virgin's consent, and the power of the Most High overshadows her (as he embraces her, no doubt). The Holy Spirit, the agent of that inexpressible conception, comes to her, the Virgin's womb swells, and she gives birth to that miraculous Geryon,[63] a giant formed of three substances; his first journey was from the heights of heaven to the Virgin's womb, then from the cross to the underworld, thence to the throne of divine majesty, where he now sits, victorious, at his Father's right hand. The apostles denied the Lord; only the Virgin, according to pious belief, remained faithful to their union[64] – an example of that stable kind of marriage which knows nothing of divorce.

Perhaps we might examine here a fourth symbolic aspect of matrimony: just as the whole church, which includes every true believer from the beginning of the world to its end, may be considered the one bride of Christ, the one spotless dove, so, according to the moral sense,[65] each individual soul

* * * * *

60 Erasmus himself calls Mary the 'bride' of God in his *Precationes: ad Virginem Matrem* ('To the Virgin Mother') 126 above, and his early *Paean Virgini Matri* (20–38 above) is permeated by the imagery of Old Testament wisdom literature; see Halkin 'Mariologie' 36.

61 Song of Sol 4:7: 'Thou art all fair, my love; there is no spot in thee'; cf *Apologia adversus monachos* LB IX 1036C; see also Halkin 'Mariologie' 42.

62 This account is based on Luke 1:34–5.

63 A triple-headed or triple-bodied giant, shepherd of Gades, killed by Hercules in his tenth labour. The comparison is unexpected: elsewhere Erasmus mentions Geryon in a satirical context, in *De conscribendis epistolis* CWE 25 45, and in Ep 541:142 as a compliment to Wolfgang Capito, who was armed with the 'three languages,' Latin, Greek and Hebrew. For another giant as a type of Christ, see *In psalmum quartum concio* CWE 63 230. See also *Paean Virgini Matri* 21 n11 above; *Liturgia Virginis Matris* 101 n96 above.

64 See Matt 26:56–75 on the disciples' desertion, and John 19:25 on Mary's presence (with John) at the crucifixion. Erasmus may have in mind the *Stabat mater*, the celebrated thirteenth-century liturgical sequence that describes the scene at the crucifixion. For Erasmus' views on such 'pious beliefs,' see Halkin 'Mariologie' 51 and Halkin's edition of the *Liturgia Virginis Matris* ASD V-1 104–5.

65 One of the four senses of Scripture (cf *Moria* CWE 27 134), the 'tropological sense,' in which Scripture is applied to the individual believer; Erasmus' exposition of the First Psalm, for example, is conducted 'principally on the tropological level' (CWE 63 8).

chosen to share eternal bliss is also a bride of Christ; for all eternity it cannot be separated from its husband, to whom it has borne many children in the form of the virtues with which it was endowed and the people whom it brought to the love of Christ by wholesome teaching and a holy way of life. Thus there are so many symbolic representations of the divine mysteries in lawful matrimony that Paul was right to say, 'I tell you that this is a mighty sacrament, in Christ and in the church.'[66] I think I have now said enough for our purposes about marriage as a symbol.

On the question of the gift of grace the Doctors' opinions are divided.[67] The older theologians seem to have associated matrimony with the word sacrament in so far as they recognized in it an outward symbol of the most sacred things; I have already discussed this. But since they denied that a special sacramental grace is poured out during the ceremony, they excluded matrimony from the formal list of the sacraments, in which, as all the Doctors of the church agree, there must be an efficacious sign, a sign guaranteed to be efficacious by the divine goodness itself. However, later theologians have won acceptance for their less rigorous view that in matrimony, properly undertaken, as in the other sacraments, a special gift of the Spirit is poured out, by which the participants are granted greater stamina to live in perpetual harmony, greater strength to face together the perils of this life, and greater wisdom to bring up their children in the ways of piety. But just as in other sacraments, so it is in matrimony: unless they are received aright, grace will be replaced by wrath.

You married people must not be made downhearted by the lustre attaching to the professions of nun or priest; your calling has its own glories.

* * * * *

66 Eph 5:32; in his own *Novum Testamentum* LB VI 856A Erasmus uses *mysterium*, echoing Paul's μυστήριον; but in order to advance his argument in this text (as in the *Encomium matrimonii* CWE 25 131), he reverts here to the Vulgate translation *sacramentum*. See Olsen 6–10; Telle 367–82; Payne 112–15; and Rummel *Catholic Critics* I 158–60 on the controversies over this translation. On the history of the question, see Lacey 33–51.

67 Cf n101 below, on Augustine. Erasmus discusses this question fully, though from a different perspective, in his annotation on 1 Cor 7:39 LB VI 699D–700A, citing Augustine and Jerome among others; there he is denying that marriage is indissoluble simply because it is now a sacrament. It was not formally listed among the sacraments until 1439 (see n33 above), but Aquinas, eg, describes it as such, with certain reservations based on its other, natural functions, in the *Supplementum* q 42 art 1–4 and q 50 art 1.1. Telle 373–4 views this passage as an insincere capitulation by Erasmus to the attacks of Zúñiga, Lee, and Béda – insincere in particular because he places restrictions on the outpouring of grace, dependent according to him on the intentions of the human participants ('properly undertaken' below).

There is much in it to boast of, 'but if you must boast, then boast in the Lord.'[68] You will be 'boasting in the Lord' if, when you extol the glories of marriage, you ensure that the glory of its symbolism and the magnitude of the gift are matched by the reverence of your conduct. Otherwise, so far from raising you up, the glory of this calling will condemn your irreverence all the more severely. You know the principles: 'marriage is honourable before all, the marriage-bed undefiled,'[69] a union witnessed and favoured by God, to which divorce is unknown and dissension a stranger, free from all immorality, rich in works of holiness that multiply and improve as each day goes by. Again, we should not ignore the theologians' assertion that there is in matrimony a sacrament, that is, a sacred sign indicating two or three kinds of reality. For the outward ceremony of union, which involves the contract, the dowry, the joining of hands, the kisses given and received, and other solemn rituals, symbolizes the mutual affection of the couple, but also the mysterious and inexpressible joining of divine and human nature, of Christ the Bridegroom and the church his bride, which I have already described. Finally there is the sacramental gift that is poured invisibly, according to God's covenant, on those who enter upon matrimony in the proper manner.

What I have called a symbol, they call a sacrament or sign; the meaning of the symbol they call a reality. But nothing prevents the same thing from being both a reality and a sacrament, if we look at it from different angles. The sign has two functions, the demonstrative and the efficacious. Similarly the reality has two aspects: the one we live and the one we take as our model. The union of male and female does not actually effect the mystical unions in Christ that I have described, but it represents, by means of a symbol, their archetype, as it were, showing what must be imitated; from this the theologians conclude that the union of man and God in the hypostasis[70] of Christ is a reality only and not also a sign. They say that the mutual love between spouses is also a reality and not merely a sign, but that this case differs from the previous one because nuptial union, performed by visible rites, is to some extent the cause of the reality that it symbolizes, that is, of love and marital harmony, but much less obviously is it the cause of the outpouring of sacramental grace. It is not that the minister of the sacrament or the signs themselves confer grace, but that through them God covenants, as it were, to bestow this special gift whenever the sacramental ceremony is performed as it should be.

* * * * *

68 1 Cor 1:31; 2 Cor 10:17
69 Heb 13:4
70 Cf n35 above; for a commentary on the theology here, see P.L. Hanley 'Sacramental Character' in NCE XII 786–8, and Payne 119–30.

And though some may disagree with this view, still the sacrament draws our attention to love and harmony, and thereby urges us, as it were, to practise them. Moreover, as it says in the comedy, 'Giving advice is very like giving assistance.'[71] Now the indivisible union of hearts is not perceptible to the physical senses, and thus cannot perhaps be described as an outward sign, though it may properly be called a symbol or likeness. When anything is conceived according to some model, it acquires the likeness of the thing it imitates. But why should it not also be a sign? After all, a statue, representing a man or a god, is called a sign [*signum*] in Latin, even when it does not seem to be one.

The sacrament therefore first of all signifies something for you both to revere and to imitate, revealing the source of all spiritual gifts and the archetype of all Christian harmony; it also demonstrates the duties which, in imitation of the archetype, must be performed on each side, and it adds the heavenly gift with whose aid you can perform what is expected of you. The gift is ready and waiting, if you will make room for it in your heart. However, all this can be discussed more fully at another time, if the occasion arises, as I am sure it will.

Now, I tried earlier to show that of all human agreements, partnerships, treaties, none is more stable or more sacred than marriage. No contract between human beings is so binding that it cannot be abrogated, under human law, as a result of changing circumstances; uniquely, death alone unties the knot of matrimony, and in a sense not even death does so. True love, situated as it is in the soul, is not ended by the death of the body, and, as I have said, the most important element in marriage is spiritual union. A widow who loved her husband with all her heart will not consider her marriage ended by his death. She takes pleasure in her memories of him and looks forward to making the same journey in a little while and to being reunited with the one man she chose from all others. She will think it a kind of adultery to take a new bridegroom into her husband's bedchamber, reciting to herself these words of Virgil inspired by true conjugal love: 'He who first was joined to me took all my love; / Let him possess and guard it in his grave.'[72] As a concession to human frailty, to our bodily weakness, second marriage is permitted, but monogamy wins praise whereas digamy is merely tolerated.[73] Though it may sometimes happen that a woman whose husband

* * * * *

71 Plautus *Curculio* 460
72 Virgil *Aeneid* 4.28–9
73 See eg 1 Cor 7:8–9 and Gratian *Decretum* pars 2 c 31 q 1 cc 9–13, quoting Chrysostom's disapproval of remarriage, followed by its grudging acceptance

has died is obliged to remarry, none the less monogamy was in her thoughts and prayers when first she wed; she chose to spend her life with one man, if it were possible. It is even a kind of virginity to be known by only one man.

Some women do not approach matrimony in this frame of mind, that is, they refuse to accept that marriage should, if possible, be permanent on both sides, and, though marrying one man, can envisage a second marriage. While such women may be considered wives on earth, in God's eyes they are more like concubines than wives. The law punishes those who break up their marriage by desertion and by adultery committed through physical union, but God's judgments are still more rigorous: for him, a woman who merely has eyes for another man is already an adulteress; one who has longed for her husband's death is a murderess; if she has even thought of leaving him, she has as good as ended the marriage. Indeed, if she does not get on with her husband, even though they share a home, a room, a bed, yet the best part of the marriage is destroyed because they do not share a union of hearts.

The very words generally used by the different nations for these things proclaim an indivisible union and partnership in everything. It is well known that *coniunx*, a spouse, and *coniugium*, marriage, are derived from *commune iugum*,[74] the common yoke, a metaphor relating to oxen, who find the yoke attached to them easier to bear as they grow used to it and start to work in harmony. But if they are yoked to strange or ill-matched beasts, they will resist and try to shake off the yoke. Exactly the same image is used in the Greek σύζυγος. St Paul uses the word in Philippians 4[:3], 'yoke-fellow.' Some believe that this refers to the Apostle's wife, whom he had turned into a sister for the sake of God's gospel.[75]

* * * * *

by Jerome and Augustine; the latter's *De incompetentibus nuptiis* eg 1.10–11, 2.2–4 PL 40 457–8 and 471–3 allows remarriage only after the death of the spouse; Augustine's adversary Pollentius argued that an adulterer might be considered 'dead.' On the similar controversy over Erasmus' apparent view, see Telle 349–65 and Rummel *Catholic Critics* II 25–6. In the different context of *De vidua christiana* Erasmus does not rule out remarriage, but praises widows like Anna (Luke 2:36–8) who devote themselves to God rather than take another husband (CWE 66 200ff).

74 Cf Isidore of Seville *Etymologiae* 9.7.9 PL 82 365 and Gaudemet 164.

75 An early witness to this supposition is Clement of Alexandria, quoted in Eusebius *Historia ecclesiastica* 3.30; Erasmus mentions this debate in his annotations on Phil 4:3 LB VI 875–6 and 1 Cor 7:8 LB VI 687E–88C, but reaches no conclusion himself. See also his annotation on another piece of 'evidence,' 1 Cor 9:5 LB VI 706C.

A yoke is not always a symbol of enslavement, but sometimes of good will. Remember Horace's lines: 'When the casks are drained to the lees, / Friends abandon us, / Too sly to bear the yoke with us.' And, again: 'She [Venus] brings them together beneath a yoke of bronze.'[76] The ancients defined friendship as ἰσότης, equality. A yoke establishes equality, but it is not perfect equality unless both creatures are already tame and in harmony with one another. The Lord too has a gentle yoke[77] that he uses to repress the wildness of our flesh. Those who together accustom themselves to the yoke will find matrimony easy to bear; those who struggle against it will merely bring twice the trouble upon themselves. They were free not to accept the yoke, but once accepted it is not to be shaken off. For similar reasons, some think that γάμος, marriage, is a corruption of δυάμος, because it joins 'two' (δυάς) together; others prefer γεννάω, I beget, as the source; but the closest to the idea of con-iugium is the view that γάμος is connected with δαμάζω, I tame, since the yoke tames and domesticates the untamed. Homer, for example, calls a girl who has not yet put on the yoke of marriage παρθένος ἀδμής, an untamed girl.[78]

Another point: the verb nubere, to marry, which in Latin is now used only of women, who are thus called nuptae, brides, was once used of both men and women. But the ancients used obnubere to mean 'to cover' or 'to enwrap' because at that time the bride's head was covered by a veil either, as the apostle Paul believes, to remind her that she was placing herself in her husband's power,[79] or for modesty's sake, as St Ambrose says, writing on the marriage of Abraham (book 1), 'For when Rebecca was told that her future husband Isaac was there, she got down from her camel and began to cover her head with a cloak.'[80] In Rome the bride's head was already covered by a veil when she stepped out of her father's house; she was turned round in a circle and then taken to the bridegroom's house to prevent her, supposedly, from finding her way back to her parents' home.[81]

* * * * *

76 Horace Odes 1.35.26–8 and 3.9.18; on friendship as equality, cf Adagia i i 2.
77 Cf Matt 11:30.
78 Homer Odyssey 6.109. The etymology of γάμος is uncertain; none of the suggestions here is considered likely by modern philologists.
79 1 Cor 11:1–12; cf Isidore of Seville Etymologiae 9.7.10 PL 82 365.
80 Ambrose De Abraham 1.9.93 PL 14 477A, quoting Gen 24:64–5
81 On the red bridal veil (flammeum) cf Pliny Naturalis historia 21.8.46, and on its Christianization see Stevenson 31. The ceremonial procession to the bridegroom's house, in domum deductio, was apparently an essential part of the Roman marriage rite (Digesta 23.2.5).

Although this symbolic covering of the head is in fact practised only by the female sex, the thing it symbolizes is applicable to both: a girl who is now promised to one man is veiled, lest she draw the eyes of many others; but the bridegroom too is veiled, that is, he is satisfied with the girl promised to him. Why should a girl want to attract the eyes of other suitors, when she has already obtained everything she could hope to gain by her appearance (if, indeed, mere external appearance should be used to attract a husband)? For whom does a young man dress up, when he is promised to another? To seek to please more than one is immoral and a kind of adultery.[82]

The Latin and Greek words for husband, *maritus*[83] and ἀνήρ, are synonymous with masculinity, telling us that marriage was principally established so that from the partnership of man and woman should be born children. Just as the Latin *vir*, a man, is connected with *vigor*, so the Greek ἀνήρ comes from ἀνύω, I achieve or perfect, as though it were ἀνυήρ. For power rests with the man, as does the primary responsibility for the act of procreation. He is also called πόσις, which sounds very like the word for a drink;[84] just as rain makes the land it falls on fertile, so the wife is barren unless impregnated by her husband.

It is thought that *uxor*, wife, comes from *ungere*, to anoint, as if the word were *unxor*, anointer.[85] It is derived from an ancient custom, described by Pliny,[86] in which the new bride, before entering her husband's house, anointed the doorpost with wolf's grease to prevent harmful drugs crossing the threshold. *Axungia*, made of pig's grease and so called because it is used to grease axles, holds pride of place among medicines as a powerful treatment for many different ills. It is in general fast-acting and easily available, but it has a particular application in marriage: the unsalted ointment, when used as a pessary, nourishes foetuses that are in danger of miscarrying. Also, when taken from a sow that has not yet farrowed, it helps to soften women's skin.

I imagine that the ancient custom was supposed to signify, first, that doctors would not be welcome in the house. If anything went wrong, it

* * * * *

82 An echo of Augustine's *De sancta virginitate* 11 PL 40 401. On the ceremonial use of veils in both western and eastern rites, see Stevenson 27–37 and 98.
83 Derived from *mas*, 'male,' according to Isidore of Seville *Etymologiae* 9.7.2 PL 82 363
84 ὁ πόσις, husband; ἡ πόσις, drink
85 Cf Isidore of Seville *Etymologiae* 9.7.12 PL 82 365, with reference to the custom described below.
86 Pliny *Naturalis historia* 28.37.143; the next example is from the same work, 28.37.139.

could quickly and easily be put right by the mother herself, using baths and ointments. Indeed, ill health in the family could be avoided altogether by a frugal diet and a healthy way of life, and to that end medicine was smeared on the doorpost to ward off evil. Second, this symbol was like a prayer for successful childbirth and against miscarriage. Finally, if I am not mistaken, it advised the bride to give up painting her face since she had now found a man whom she could impress by her obedience and her upright conduct rather than by her cosmetics. *Axungia* is particularly useful for healing limbs that are 'ruptured, torn, strained, and dislocated';[87] thus the grease smeared on the doorpost can be seen as a way of excluding from the house all tumult and discord. Add to all this that marriage is rather like a chariot resting on two axles: if they are oiled by courtesy and integrity, the horrible grinding sound of arguments will not be heard in the family, and, as they work together in harmony, everything they undertake will turn out all the more successfully. Maybe the wolf's grease has another meaning: as Xenophon remarked, it is characteristic of a virtuous and prudent matriarch to extract some advantage for her household even from its enemies.[88] This possibility, and the various ways of achieving the desired result, have been discussed by those most reliable authorities, Xenophon and Plutarch.

If anyone finds this kind of allegorizing ridiculous, let him remember St Ambrose, who could extract a moral lesson from anything in nature; for example, how many different ways did he find to make the mating of the snakes and the eels demonstrate the duty of a spouse towards his or her partner?[89] In fact, we ought to find the examples of the pagans even more striking than our own. It would be quite shameful for Christians to disobey the teaching of heaven when those idolaters, whose only guide was nature, were so careful of their marital obligations. The Greek words for husband, ἀκοίτης or παρακοίτης, and wife, ἄκοιτις, all mean 'bedfellow,' thus commending fellowship and discouraging separation. Similarly in Greek a spouse is called συνοικῶν, sharer of the home, and a wife is called σύνοικος.

* * * * *

87 A quotation from Pliny ibidem 28.37.140; however, the interpretation of these customs appears to be Erasmus' own.
88 Xenophon *Oeconomicus* 1.6; cf Plutarch *Moralia* 86B–92F, 'How to Profit by One's Enemies,' a work translated by Erasmus (LB IV 23–30).
89 Ambrose *Hexaemeron* 5.7.18 PL 14 227–8; Ambrose draws the lesson of marital fidelity, however poisonous the spouse, from the fabled mating of the *echidna* (viper) with the *murena*; the latter is supposed in this context to be the harmless Moray eel or lamprey, but references in Greek drama (Aeschylus *Choephoroi* 994 and Aristophanes *Frogs* 473–5) suggest that it was a sea-snake, associated (as a term of abuse) with the *echidna*.

There is one more rather thorny problem concerning the vocabulary of marriage, which is why 'matrimony,' rather than 'patrimony,' is used (for the woman who becomes a mother, *mater*, naturally makes her husband a father, *pater*).[90] In the first place, the term immediately serves as a reproach to anyone who enters upon matrimony out of lust or a desire for status or wealth. Only the hope of progeny must summon people to chaste wedlock. But since the business of the home is to give birth, nourish, bring up, and educate young children, and this is the special domain of the matriarch within the walls of her home, the ancients preferred 'matrimony' to 'patrimony.' The husband goes out into the world, to the market-place, into government, to the provinces, to the counting-house, in order to increase their patrimony. The wife protects and manages their property, staying at home to take care of her youngsters and her household. Husband and wife govern the same little province, but each has a different role. If each performs it in perfect harmony with the other, they will lead a life of extraordinary bliss; if not, no kind of life is more dreadful than marriage. However, I shall say more about this in the appropriate place, when discussing the best way to govern a household.

A most important factor in marriage is the choice of a partner. This requires the greatest caution and deliberation because, as the proverb says about war, your first mistake is also your last.[91] You can always send a friend packing, and yet Pythagoras warns against casually offering your hand to just anyone.[92] Those we care for must be chosen with care.[93] We will usually love for ever what at the outset we chose with care to love. Although the law prescribes no punishment for breaking off a friendship, no wise and honest person will befriend someone unless he is prepared to love him for ever. Even if, as so often happens in this world, something occurs to prove his choice wrong, or if his friend changes beyond hope of amendment, none the less, out of respect for the principle of friendship, the relationship is allowed to fall apart gradually and is not sundered at a stroke.

Thus, if Christian law permitted divorce, as the laws of the pagans and of Moses did, greater care would still have to be exercised here even than in choosing a friend. If a friend has deserted you, he is but one of a number; only a wife is a companion for life, a partner in everything, and no

* * * * *

90 This problem is discussed at length by Aquinas *Supplementum* q 44 art 2.
91 *Adagia* III i 31; in his commentary on the adage, Erasmus also cites marriage – and entering orders.
92 See *Adagia* I i 2.
93 Erasmus puns here on *deligere*, 'to choose,' and *diligere*, 'to love.'

man can dismiss her completely. He has always taken something from her, especially if he repudiates a woman whom he married as a virgin. He may dismiss her, but he has already robbed her of her most precious treasure, her foremost claim to an honourable place in society.

If you have had children too, how will you dismiss her? Will you send her away with the children? You are renouncing your own children, not repudiating your wife. Will you dismiss the mother without the children? You are keeping what is not yours; you have no more than half a right to your children. If a friend is rejected, he may perhaps blurt out secrets entrusted to him in friendship; but who knows a man's every secret better than a wife – even if he never confided in her? Moreover, the sex is naturally talkative and vengeful (I am speaking of the ordinary run of women, of course). Finally, if someone causes offence by ending a friendship, he offends only one person. But if a man repudiates his wife, having signed registers and contracts and exchanged gifts, he is faced with the relatives, who must be appeased, and indeed he is faced with the general public, who will always embellish a broken marriage with spicy tales.

All these many factors should persuade us not to rush into matrimony. Nowadays, when Christian law leaves no lingering hope of putting asunder what has once been joined in matrimony, you must make haste very slowly towards it.[94] You will get no chance to reconsider. In other areas it is shaming to have to say, 'I wasn't thinking,'[95] but in this matter it is not only shaming, but too late! In the past,[96] we read, a man would quite often refuse to take up office or would resign because he was dissatisfied with his colleague. If such caution is to be applauded in respect of a post lasting a year at most, how much more should it be applied to the choice of a 'colleague' in the domestic sphere, where you will have to collaborate to the end of your days with someone who cannot by law be changed once she is chosen? The home is a smaller domain than the state, but it contains your most precious charge. You are responsible for a smaller number, but they must take precedence over everything else.

* * * * *

94 Cf *Adagia* II i 1, the celebrated *Festina lente*.
95 This echoes a famous remark by Scipio Africanus about ill-prepared generals (Plutarch *Moralia* 187A; Seneca *De ira* 2.31.4; and Cicero *De officiis* 1.23.81), applied to princes by Erasmus in the *Institutio principis christiani* CWE 27 218.
96 Reading *aliquando* rather than *aliqua* (LB); the original editions abbreviate the word. The reference is to the Roman magistrates appointed in pairs, such as the consuls and censors.

Similarly, who does not wish to have children who are physically healthy and morally sound? A wife must be chosen with this in mind, if nothing else, unless perhaps we think it unimportant what sort of family people come from, how they have been brought up, or what principles and examples have been instilled in them, forming and educating them from their earliest years. When invited to a feast, we make our excuses if there is going to be a guest of whom we disapprove; we refuse to share a carriage or a boat with just anybody; and yet in taking a wife no one troubles to choose with anything like the same care. Marriages are often arranged secretly, furtively even, between virtual children who may be quite drunk, by panders and bawds – and this among Christians, when even pagan laws refused to recognize such marriages. This is of course the reason for so many unhappy and precarious marriages among us, when each partner holds the wolf by the ears, as the saying goes, and cannot hold it or drop it.[97] It is the reason for all these wretched divorces, and husbands who marry ten wives in a row. The bawds who arrange these marriages know our lawyers' maxim, 'Words in the present tense make a marriage valid.' And indeed words in the future tense, once physical union has taken place, are changed to the present tense, and the marriage is not only valid, but consummated.[98]

That is why the bawds ensure that intercourse takes place practically as soon as the words have been spoken; modesty and reason are overcome by a flowing bumper of wine, off come their clothes, and they are left alone. What unchristian marriages! Is there much difference between a drunken adolescent and a lunatic? What sense can a girl have left, when the alliance of Venus and Bacchus has doubled her madness, and the voices of panders and bawds cast a spell of insanity upon her? And this is called lawful consent! It is all part of a plot, a trap, as it were, laid for weak-minded youth, without the knowledge of parents and guardians who, if they knew, would forbid

* * * * *

97 *Adagia* I iv 25
98 The point at issue is the form of words exchanged by the couple: the difference, eg, between 'I take you for my wife' and 'I shall take you for my wife.' The rules were elaborated by twelfth-century French theologians to clarify ambiguities concerning betrothal (eg in Gratian *Decretum* pars 2 C 27 q 1); the formulas *verba de praesenti* and *verba de futuro* seem to have been coined by Peter Lombard *Sententiae* book 4 dist 27 c 3 (cf Esmein I 124–67 and Gaudemet 165–7). Aquinas in particular (*Supplementum* q 45 art 5) allows unions made by *verba de praesenti*, if no impediment supervenes; on *verba de futuro*, 'words in the future tense' followed by consummation, cf ibidem q 45 art 3 and q 46 art 2, and the *Decretales Gregorii* IX 4.1.2 and 5 CIC 2 661–2.

it. Yet among Christians, who number matrimony among the sacraments of
the church, this is called a marriage, and there is no question of waiting
for puberty or coming-of-age. If they are bad enough, they are old enough,
they say, and this maxim[99] gives those who are far too young the freedom
to contract marriage. Moreover, free men, they say, have a natural right to
control their own bodily activities, including the propagation of the species,
and so indeed have slaves; parents cannot take it from their children, nor
masters from their slaves.

I am not describing here some aberrant practice passed down to us by
our forebears. It is now that human wickedness patches together troubled
and unhappy marriages by exploiting regulations that were quite appropriate to their own times. How I wish that our leading churchmen could
or would lend their authority to some programme of reform! For I do not
think it right or conducive to the repose of the state to allow personal whim
to play a greater role than official institutions in rescinding our predecessors' decrees. Both imperial law and the decrees of the Roman people are at
pains to ensure that no litigation can possibly arise from civil contracts. Yet
such is human perversity that no kind of contract causes more trouble than
matrimony. This arises partly from the nature of the institution itself and
partly from a conflict between the two kinds of law. The secular laws of the
pagans laid down very careful rules about betrothal, and about contracting
and dissolving marriages. The statutes of the Christian emperors generally
followed them.[100]

However, papal law then seized the main responsibility for this matter, changing so many things in the princes' laws that the whole business
scarcely seemed to make sense any more. The theologians' pronouncements
continue the same process. For since matrimony is numbered among the
sacraments of the church, and since the Gospels and Paul's writings make
a great many rulings on it, the popes thought it appropriate to claim the

* * * * *

99 *Malitia supplet aetatem* (literally, 'malice compensates for youth'), a legal maxim
cited for instance in *Decretales Gregorii* IX 4.2.14 CIC 2 678; cf Gaudemet 197.
100 The principle of continuity is stated in the first preface to Justinian's *Digesta*
of 530 AD, *De conceptione Digestorum*, reproduced in the *Codex* 1.17.1. The connections between Roman law and canon law, and the superiority of the latter, are demonstrated eg by Gratian *Decretum* pars 1 D 10 cc 1–13 (cf Esmein I
25–31). Examples of the restrictions imposed by canon law, discussed later in
this work, are the widening of impediments such as consanguinity and affinity, the imposition of new ones such as spiritual kinship and public propriety,
vows of celibacy, and strictures on divorce.

power to deal with the subject in their own right. Nowhere did imperial law yield more fully and more respectfully to papal decree than on the question of matrimony.

Now, although there has never been a time in the church's history when it has not given a measure of respect to marriage, yet in the days when the church was just beginning to expand marriage was treated with less respect than it had been, or than it is now. It is possible to deduce from the writings of the early Fathers that it was not yet placed among the sacraments of the new law, according to the strict definition of the term.[101] Those who married wives received the rather limited commendation that they were not sinning, whereas those who 'made themselves eunuchs for the kingdom of God'[102] were rewarded with praise and blessing. Paul said: 'If a virgin weds, she does not sin. A man who cannot contain himself does not sin if he takes a wife; for it is better to marry than to burn.'[103] And the Lord called blessed those not born eunuchs or made eunuchs by men, but who castrated themselves out of zeal for piety and the gospel.

The church used to hold virgins vowed to God in such honour that their exaltation almost completely overshadowed the glory of marriage. The Holy Spirit infused into human minds such a love of chastity that not only did young men and girls willingly abstain from marriage, but even those who, before they professed the gospel, had married wives, 'had them as though they had them not.'[104] Some turned their wives into sisters, others abstained from the marriage-bed by dint of constant prayer – so much so that Paul was compelled to make some new rules to temper what one might almost call this immodest enthusiasm for purity. He ordained that they should sleep apart only if both consented, and should return soon to the duties of wedlock; that a wife who had left home should be reconciled with her husband; that she should not part even from an unbeliever, so long as he permitted her to practise her own religion. He even urged

* * * * *

101 See Payne 113–15 and, on the general question, Olsen 2–6. In *De bono coniugali* PL 40 373–96, which seems to lie behind Erasmus' discussion here, Augustine describes marriage as 'a kind of sacrament' ('cuiusdam sacramenti res,' 378) in view of its indissolubility and its symbolism of the union of Christ and the church, but is silent on the question of grace; cf 232 above. See also n33 above and the introductory note 205–6.
102 Matt 19:12
103 Erasmus conflates 1 Cor 7:8–9 and 28. He then repeats the allusion to Matt 19:12.
104 1 Cor 7:29

younger widows to remarry, since both their vulnerable age and their previous experience of pleasure suggested little hope of firm and permanent continence.[105] Some would have tried to dissuade all Christians from marriage, had not Paul spoken out loud and clear in its favour. But although he wishes widows to marry, at that time second marriage was held in very low esteem.

God, the ruler of all ages, instilled at once into human minds (especially those of women) at the creation, when the human race needed to be propagated by marriage, a rare appetite for procreation. Similarly, soon after the redemption of mankind, when a new generation needed to be propagated by the gospel message, he inspired people's minds with a similar desire for chastity – an appropriate emotion for that period, no doubt. The harvest was great.[106] The whole world lay before them, and therefore that tiny band had no time to make children for the world while working to beget heirs to heaven. They were pleased to call their children all the souls they won for Christ. They did so well that within a few years the church could glory in her numberless progeny throughout the earth.

However, when the seeds of Christianity had been planted in every nation on earth, there was less reason why they should abstain from marriage. Virgins were still held in high esteem, but respect for marriage began gradually to increase. For a long time traces of the old predilection lingered among the bishops, especially the bishops of Rome. In the time of St Gregory,[107] for example, the custom of the Roman church laid down that anyone who had slept with his wife should refrain for a short period from entering a church and still more from partaking of the Lord's body, and was not to enter unless he had washed. St Gregory also agreed with St Augustine that intercourse between husband and wife could not be performed with-

* * * * *

105 The successive allusions are to 1 Cor 7:5, 11, and 13; and 1 Tim 5:11–14.
106 Cf Matt 9:37. See n3 above on the 'difference of times,' which explains the apparent promiscuity of the patriarchs and is a central theme of Augustine's *De bono coniugali* (9 and 15–19 PL 40 380 and 383–7). See also Gratian *Decretum* pars 2 C 32 q 4 cc 1–7, a lengthy discussion of the same question based on Ambrose, Jerome, and Augustine; also Lombard *Sententiae* book 4 dist 33.
107 Gregory I (the Great) was pope from 590 to 604; the two passages in question occur in a reply to enquiries from St Augustine, the first archbishop of Canterbury: *Epistolae* 11.64.8 PL 77 1196B and 1197B. Cf Lombard *Sententiae* book 4 dist 32 c 4 on Jerome's similar view. The preceding reference to 'the bishops of Rome' hints at the more liberal attitude to marriage in the Greek church; cf n181 below.

out sin if they had exercised their marital rights out of lust rather than to beget children. Moreover, the early Fathers forbade the exercise of marital rights on certain days of the year.[108]

These rules were not imposed on people against their will, but the Fathers' regulations gave the seal of their approval to something that human piety often accomplished of its own accord. It seems very likely that in many other areas custom gave rise to the law, rather than the opposite, as in the case of the Lenten fast and of the prohibitions on the consumption at certain times of meat and dairy produce.[109] Thus the devoted shepherds of the church, as if congratulating their flock on this spontaneous display of piety, drew in the boundaries of marriage to encourage a wider spread of fellowship among Christians for other reasons; at the same time they provided more opportunities for chastity to be preserved.

They narrowed the boundaries here by reducing the degrees of blood kinship and by adding the impediments of spiritual kinship and spiritual affinity, but they give a plausible enough reason for doing so. However, it is not so easy to explain why in a different area they relaxed the procedure for contracting marriage. The papal statutes assert that a valid marriage can be made by a simple declaration of consent, using words in the present tense,[110] and the theologians underwrite this decree with great unanimity. However, Emperor Justinian does not permit sons to take wives without the consent of their parents, who have legal authority over them. He thinks that here natural law and legal practice come together, since nature has given parents authority over their children and Roman law reinforces this until the

* * * * *

108 See eg Ambrose, who recommended abstinence on feast days and processional days in his commentary on 1 Cor 7:5 PL 17 229A, and Pseudo-Augustine *Quaestiones veteris et novi testamenti* 127 PL 35 2385. See also n150 below, and 391 and n587.

109 As Erasmus points out in his critical discussion of fasting, *De esu carnium* LB IX 1197C–8A / ASD IX-1 19–20, in the early church the paschal fast was spontaneous rather than compulsory; unregulated and relatively short, it perhaps corresponded to the time supposedly spent by Christ in the tomb (Eusebius *Historia ecclesiastica* 5.24 PG 20 503). The Council of Nicaea (325) first prescribed a forty-day fast. In the colloquy Ἰχθυοφαγία ('A Fish Diet') CWE 40 682–6, the characters agree that fasting originated in voluntary abstinence for dietary or humanitarian reasons. Erasmus' constitution made him particularly vulnerable to the rigours of statutory fasting, from which he obtained dispensations (see Epp 1353 and 1542). On the controversies surrounding his views, see Rummel *Catholic Critics* I 181–4 and *Annotations* 146–52.

110 Cf n98 above.

ceremony of emancipation has been performed.[111] I believe that he came to the same conclusion in the case of wards and minors placed under the legal tutelage of guardians.[112] If it had been legal to contract marriage without the parents' knowledge, there would have been no point in putting the question, 'Can the son or daughter of a madman contract a marriage without the consent of the father?' Justinian permitted it, but only on practical grounds.[113]

Similarly, in Holy Writ those seeking a bride ask their parents for one, and there is no proviso concerning the inclination of the children themselves, though in any case it is likely enough that at that time the children wished only to do what was pleasing to their parents. Thus Abraham obtained Rebecca for his son Isaac, and she was married according to her father's wishes.[114] At his father's command Jacob sought out his uncle Laban and, under their agreement, accepted the two sisters; the one who was pushed into his tent as he slept did not complain, nor did the other who was overlooked, even though she expected to be wed after her week of days. The whole business was conducted according to the father-in-law's wishes.[115] Similarly, in Deuteronomy 22[:28–9] the ravisher of a virgin not yet betrothed pays her father the fifty shekels, and marries her if her father is willing; there is no mention of the girl giving consent. The son of Tobias accepted Sarah from the hands of her parents.[116] Exodus 22[:16–17] says the same: 'If a man shall seduce a virgin not yet betrothed and sleep with her, he shall give her a dowry and marry her; if her father refuses to give her, he shall pay a sum equivalent to the usual dowry of virgins.' Here too, you see, the decision over marriage lies with the father. In the same book, chapter 34[:12–16]: 'Take heed, and never make a covenant with the inhabitants ... etc, nor take a wife for your sons from among their daughters ... etc.' It is not the sons who are instructed not to marry, but the father, told not to take a daughter-in-law from an outcast tribe. Again, in Genesis 21 the exiled Hagar, having no husband to give permission, herself accepts a wife for her son. There are many similar examples in the Old Testament to show that the

* * * * *

111 *Institutiones* 1.9–10; the first of these chapters deals with *patria potestas*, paternal authority, which was remarkably extensive in Roman law. The ceremony of emancipation at majority was akin to the freeing of a slave; see *Institutiones* 1.12.6.
112 Cf *Institutiones* 1.21.
113 Ibidem 1.10 preamble
114 Gen 24
115 Gen 28–9
116 Tob 7:10–13. Cf 308 n311 below.

right to contract marriage lay with the mother and father rather than with the children.

The same thing is made clear in the first letter to the Corinthians, chapter 7[:36–8]: 'But if a man feels that he is behaving unjustly towards his unmarried daughter because she is now ripe for marriage, and that something must be done, let him do as he wishes; he does no sin if he gives her in marriage. But if a man is steadfast in his heart, being under no compulsion and in control of his will, and has decided in his heart to preserve her chastity, he will do well. Thus he who marries his daughter does well, but he who does not marry her does better.' This passage obviously hands complete control over marriage to the father. Theophylact reads it in the same way, and so does Ambrose, though he rules out the use of compulsion or force on a girl who has no inclination at all to marry.[117] The first of all marriages was made in the same way. God created Adam and gave him a wife. It was not that Adam cried, 'I need a wife,' but that his creator's providence decreed, 'It is not right that Adam should be alone; let us make him a helpmeet like himself.'[118]

To sum up: I know of no example in Holy Writ of a marriage contracted without the knowledge and consent of the parents. Even the common expressions in Latin 'to give in marriage' and 'to settle one's daughter'[119] are evidence that parents had the right to choose a husband for their daughter. It may perhaps seem inappropriate to cite here the evidence of tragedies and comedies, but in fact they reflect the life of the ancients as in a mirror. For example, when Tyndareus realized the risk he would run in choosing a husband for Helen, he relinquished to her the right to choose. But before she made her choice, he had all the suitors swear an oath that if anyone should try to take her by force from her chosen husband, all the rest would band together to punish the seducer.[120] Again, Danaus and Belus arranged the

* * * * *

117 Cf Erasmus' annotation on this text of Corinthians LB VI 691F–692C. Some commentators take it to refer to a partner in celibacy rather than an unmarried daughter, an opinion that Erasmus rejects, following Augustine and Theophylact, the eleventh-century 'archbishop of the Bulgars' (PG 124 654–5; on Erasmus' increasing confidence in his scriptural scholarship, see Rummel *Annotations* 67–8). Ambrose gives his view in *Commentarius in epistolam ad Corinthios primam* 7.37 PL 17 237B.
118 Gen 2:18
119 *Dare nuptum* and *elocare filiam*; the latter means, literally, 'to hire out a daughter'!
120 Tyndareus was king of Sparta and husband of Helen's mother Leda. He feared to displease the other suitors by choosing one of them; the expedient described

marriages between their sons and daughters.[121] In comedies, too, marriages depend on the permission of the parents. For example, Pamphilus is told, 'You are marrying a wife today; it is my wish.' He also hears that 'no one will give his daughter to a husband like that.'[122] There are many similar examples.

Moreover, if an agreement to marry had been made without the parents' knowledge, they would tear it up if they disapproved of the match; if they approved, they would give their consent. Thus, in the *Andria* Pamphilus is sent away from his mistress Glycerium, and in the *Phormio* Antipho is sent away from his bride, though in both cases an unexpected misunderstanding finally comes to the rescue. Again, in Catullus' *Epithalamium* the bridegroom speaks these words to his bride:

> Do not resist this husband, girl.
> It is not right to fight the man your father gave you,
> Your father and your mother, whom you must obey.
> Your maidenhead is not your own, in part it is your parents',
> A third part for your mother, a third part for your father.
> A third alone is yours; do not resist the other two
> Who, with the dowry, grant their rights to him.[123]

Simo is prepared to disinherit his son and renounce the name of father because Pamphilus has taken a wife in secret and had a child by her. The old man says: 'What! Do you call me father? As if you needed a father, when you have taken on a house, a wife, and children against your father's will.' A speech threatening disinheritance – and what does the young man reply? 'I put myself in your hands, father. Command me, give me any task; do you want me to marry this girl? Do you want me to break with her? I shall bear it as best I can.'[124]

* * * * *

here was suggested to him by Ulysses. The story is told by Apollodorus *Bibliotheca* 3.10.

121 According to Apollodorus *Bibliotheca* 2.12–20, Danaus, after leaving his native Egypt and becoming king of Argos, engaged his fifty daughters to the fifty sons of his brother Aegyptus (their father was called Belus in this account). The precedent is not a happy one, since, to circumvent an oracle, all but one of Danaus' daughters murdered their husbands on the wedding night!

122 Terence *Andria* 388 and 395–6. The next two examples summarize the plots of the plays in question. In all these examples the authority of the father is supposedly absolute.

123 Catullus *Carmina* 62.59–65

124 Terence *Andria* 890–1 and 897–8

But it seemed inhumane that parents could force children into unwanted matches, which might indeed be almost harsher than selling them into slavery; the slave is at least consoled to some extent by the hope of freedom, whereas the chains of matrimony can be broken only by death. Therefore both imperial and canon law[125] decreed that a marriage would not be valid without the consent of the children. They also decreed that wicked parents should not, for financial or any other reasons, force their children to remain unmarried or thrust upon them spouses they did not want. It was to help children that this purely human regulation declared that a marriage was valid, even without the knowledge or consent of the parents, when contracted between adults using words in the present tense. But the same thing often happens to a legislator as happened, we are told, to Hercules: as he cut off a horn from the river Achelous, the waters rose up and threatened him from a different direction, or – an even better example – whenever he cut off one of the Hydra's heads, several more grew.[126] It is true not only that, as the saying goes, good laws come from bad behaviour,[127] but also that, thanks to the perversity of humankind, from the best of laws comes the worst of behaviour.

I believe that the decree stating that 'marriage is made by consent alone'[128] is a purely human one, so that the person who made the law to meet particular circumstances can abrogate or alter it when circumstances change. And yet now, as a result of this law, how many well-born youths, how many girls even of the highest rank have we seen and do we see embroiled in unfortunate and chaotic marriages, bringing immense grief to their parents and kinsmen and sometimes indeed great peril to the state? I shall refrain, as a matter of prudence, from giving examples.[129]

* * * * *

125 *Digesta* 23.1.11–13; Gratian *Decretum* pars 2 c 27 q 2 c 1 and c 31 q 2 c 1
126 The first story is told in Ovid's *Metamorphoses* 9.1–97; the river god Achelous fought Hercules for the hand of Dejanira and in the course of the combat changed himself into a serpent and an ox; the severed horn became the cornucopia (see *Adagia* i vi 2). Hercules' battle with the many-headed Hydra of Lerna had become proverbial; see *Adagia* i x 9.
127 *Adagia* i x 61
128 Gratian *Decretum* pars 2 c 27 q 2 c 1; a celebrated maxim of Ulpian (*Digesta* 23.1.4) made the same provision in Roman law.
129 Erasmus had also remained prudently silent on the opposite topic of arranged marriages in his chapter on the marriage alliances of princes in *Institutio principis christiani* CWE 27 277–9; the earlier work was dedicated to the Habsburg prince Charles, whose family was notorious for its exploitation of dynastic marriage. It is less clear whom Erasmus does not wish to offend here.

This window, which was already open wide enough to admit human wickedness (the true cause of clandestine marriages),[130] is opened another crack by the following provision: words in the future tense will have the force of the present tense if sexual intercourse subsequently takes place.[131] This holds true even if the words are spoken during intercourse, when their minds are elsewhere, or even if the girl trapped the young man into doing it by some cunning device and there is clear and plentiful evidence that he did not speak from the heart. He spoke, he entered her, he must have her to wife. I am not saying this to condemn the decree, but to alert young men and women to the dangers of contracting marriage. It is not my place to challenge laws accepted by the church, but it is the task of the legislator to change the law to meet present circumstances.

There are a number of other cracks in the law through which one may crawl into matrimony. To the question, Can a marriage be contracted with a nod of the head alone? the answer is yes. To the question, Can a marriage be made by correspondence? the answer is yes. To the question, What about the use of a token, such as giving half a broken coin to the girl? the answer is that the match is made. To the question, Can a marriage be made by proxy between people who are absent? the answer is yes, if the proxy has received authorization from one of the parties concerned to contract a marriage with the other. To the question, Can an action make a marriage valid, for example if the young man were to say, 'If you take me for your husband, give me a kiss'? the answer is yes. To the question, Can a marriage be made by silence? If, for example, the girl's father says to the young man's, 'I give my daughter as wife to your son,' and the suitor's father replies, 'And I give my son as husband to your daughter,' what if the young man and the girl do not

* * * * *

130 On the background to the contemporary scandal of clandestine marriages see CWE 39 271 n48; Telle 389–90; and Screech 44–54. However, Gratian, whose decree is under attack by Erasmus here, himself condemns clandestine marriages in another chapter (*Decretum* pars 2 c 30 q 5 c 1); but later canon law certainly implies that they must be tolerated unless some diriment impediment be involved: *Decretales Gregorii* IX 4.3 CIC 2 679–80. By the decree *Tametsi* of 1563, the Council of Trent attempted to remedy the situation, largely in the way proposed by Erasmus, by imposing more precise and public forms for the ceremony: with parental consent, the banns were to be read three times and the marriage solemnized before a pastor and two witnesses, and the details entered in an ecclesiastical register (Esmein II 151–239; Denzinger 1813–16).

131 Cf n98 above. Gratian *Decretum* pars 2 c 27 q 2 c 37 quotes Augustine *Confessions* 18.3, Jerome, and Ambrose in support of this proposition; the conversion to 'words in the present tense' is clarified by decrees of Alexander III and Innocent III quoted in *Decretales Gregorii* IX 4.1.15 and 22 CIC 2 666–7 and 669.

refuse, but merely keep silent? the answer is that the marriage will be valid. Finally, if the man can, in any way whatsoever, give the woman a sign that he consents to the union, the marriage is valid.[132]

All this would be well enough, were not human beings so prone to fickleness and deceit. First of all, none but God alone can truly judge whether consent is wholeheartedly given. But since the church can judge only about outward signs, there often arise cases of matrimony where the ruling is confused: couples who were joined in true matrimony are separated, and others who are united rather by fornication or adultery are put beneath the yoke. Suppose that someone has contracted a marriage, saying the words in the present tense but lying in his heart, and that he then binds himself wholeheartedly to another; even if they have sworn an oath and followed it with intercourse and offspring, none the less he is compelled to return to the first woman.[133] If he abides by the church's decision, he will provoke God's anger; if he does not, he will be anathematized. What should he do? Let him choose the lesser of two evils, and resign himself to accepting man's thunderbolt,[134] lest God's thunderbolt condemn him to eternal perdition. He cannot blame the bishop, who has simply done his job. As Plato says, you have only yourself to blame if a false promise, on an apparently trivial matter, exposes you to severe punishment.[135] And yet the other woman, who has done no wrong, cannot now marry with a clear conscience; she has a husband whom she can neither claim nor reject.

From the same source arises another problem, that of the form of words used: which are present tense, which future? To God it does not matter which words you use to signify your readiness to marry; I am dealing here with human judgment. The words 'I take you for a wife' and 'I take you for a husband' are a contract of marriage. Perhaps it would be safer to add the possessive 'my' in each case, since the father too accepts 'a wife' for his son. But there would be more to worry about if the man said, 'I take you for mine,' and she replied, 'And I take you for mine.' In this case mere friendship might be understood. Verbs in the infinitive cause a good deal of

* * * * *

132 Signs were valid forms of consent in the case of the deaf and dumb; cf *Decretales Gregorii* IX 4.1.23 and 25 CIC 2 670. On proxies and letters, relatively common means of betrothal, cf *Digesta* 23.2.5; on more bizarre signs of consent, see Gaudemet 169.
133 This case is based on Aquinas *Supplementum* q 45 art 4 resp 3.
134 That is, the punishment of the church; it was commonplace to describe excommunication, in particular, as the pope's thunderbolt; see eg *Julius exclusus* CWE 27 170 and *Ciceronianus* CWE 28 384.
135 Plato *Laws* 4.717D, quoted in *Adagia* III i 18

confusion: if they both say, 'I wish to enter into matrimony with you,' the words are apparently in the future, and there is no contract of marriage unless physical union follows. But if they say, 'I wish to have you for a wife, and I you for a husband,' the marriage is made. But there is much disagreement among the lawyers here, some saying one thing, others the opposite, and others calling for further discussion.[136]

On the one hand, if the man says, 'I shall provide for you as a wife,' the marriage is valid, provided that she also says something similar. Again, if he replies, 'I am willing,' to the question 'Are you willing to take this woman as your wife?' and the woman makes the same reply, the marriage is legitimate; in fact, I am surprised that this should be called into question, since there can scarcely be a surer method of contracting a marriage than with this formula. On the other hand, if the man says, 'I shall not leave you, for better or for worse,' some believe that the marriage is valid, but others are not so sure. Finally, if the man says, 'I promise you that I shall have you for my lawful wife,' and the woman replies in kind, they think that with these words, though they are in the future tense, the marriage is contracted in the present. It would be different if he said, 'I promise that I shall marry you.' The reason is that in the words 'I promise you that I shall have you,' the words 'from this time forth' are understood. Of course, something else might be understood, such as 'some day' or 'soon,' but the lawyers say that the words to be understood must be those most favourable to the contract of marriage.

Hundreds of similar examples can crop up, but there is even more confusion over nods of the head and other signs.[137] Gestures do not mean the same thing in every country, and some head movements are so ambiguous that they often mislead the person at whom they are directed. For example, we use the same head movement to threaten and to yield, and nod in the same way to give a boy permission to play and to refuse a coin to a beggar. The Italians shrug their shoulders to show that they do not know the answer, but the gesture is fairly meaningless to a Sicambrian![138] Practically the same

* * * * *

136 See eg the *Decretales Gregorii* IX 4.1.7 and 4.1.26 CIC 2 663 and 670–1 on obscure and misleading formulas, and Aquinas *Supplementum* q 43 art 1 on valid and invalid formulas. A particularly detailed list of acceptable formulas is given in the thirteenth-century *Speculum* of Guillaume Durand, bishop of Mende (4.4.2– 4, ed of Basel 1563, pp 413–14). The form of words varied considerably from one diocese to another; cf J.-B. Molin and P. Mutembe *Le Rituel du mariage en France du XIIe au XVIe siècle* (Paris 1974) 102–22 and Stevenson chapter 2.

137 See n132 above.

138 The Sicambri were an ancient tribe of western Germany; here the name presumably stands for a northern European, such as Erasmus himself. Gestures

applies to messages from the eyes. Very often your expression will tell one story while your words tell another, to the extent that an action for slander could be brought against you for calling someone a good chap while pulling a horrible face! It is safer to refrain from playing these games. Some people will interpret nods, gestures, and other signs only in the light of the words that have gone before. If the words were jocular, the signs will be considered a joke; if the words were in the future tense, the nods and signs will relate to the future, but if in the present, the marriage will be in effect now.

When a marriage is contracted in the absence of the couple by letter or by proxy, if before the ceremony the sender changes his mind about his agreement with the girl or about the reply in her letter, the marriage will be invalid. There is a similar uncertainty over whether the man is bound by a contract when he says, 'I want you for a wife; do you want me for a husband?' and the girl replies only after a long interval. He could have changed his mind in the meantime. On such cases opinions differ; the lawyers think it advisable that the woman should reply immediately or, if there is some delay, that the form of words used to make the marriage should be repeated. Another problem arises here: when young children are betrothed at their parents' behest and reach adulthood without actually rejecting what was done at that time, does this make a valid marriage? The answer is no, unless the couple give some sign of wishing to reaffirm their consent. Yet among the Benedictines, I am told, if a boy reaches adulthood without saying anything, his silence is construed as a desire to make his profession.[139] Again, there is a great debate over what signs are sufficient to confirm it.

Still more uncertainties arise over oaths and conditions. If a man simply says, 'I accept you as my wife,' and later says the same words to another woman but also swears an oath, then even if this is followed by sexual intercourse, he will be held to the first contract and the second will be invalid. In fact, as the decretals show, the opinions of the Roman pontiffs on this subject have been divided.[140] For example, if a man contracted marriage with

* * * * *

still have regional idiosyncrasies; see the tables in D. Morris et al *Gestures* (London 1981) 272–3.

139 On this not uncommon form of 'tacit profession,' and its acceptability in canon law, see J. Hourlier *Histoire du droit et des institutions de l'église en Occident* vol 10 *L'Age classique, 1140–1378: les religieux* (Paris 1974) 188–9; cf Aquinas *Summa theologiae* II–II q 189 art 5. The position on betrothal here reflects Gratian *Decretum* pars 2 c 30 q 3 and, more closely, the *Decretales Gregorii* IX 4.2.8 CIC 675–6. Once more Erasmus cannot resist the polemical contrast between marital and monastic practice, to the detriment of the latter.

140 Erasmus discusses these disagreements in greater detail in his annotation on 1 Cor 7:39 LB VI 696E–697C. For pronouncements by various popes cf n131 above

a girl using the future tense, followed by an oath, and then contracted with another using the present tense but without an oath, the second woman is his wife. An oath does not have the same power as physical union.

No contract, least of all marriage, is valid if it includes dishonourable conditions. It will be valid if it includes an honourable condition which is fulfilled. 'I take you as a wife, if you are a virgin': this condition may be thought dishonourable, and yet the marriage is valid, since the law of Moses punished with death a woman who claimed to be a virgin but was found by her husband to be defiled.[141] In this case certainly the clemency of Christian law is to be admired. It is extraordinary that they should think that a marriage can be made if impossible conditions are attached, such as 'I take you, if you can touch the sky with your finger'![142] Anyone who makes conditions impossible to fulfil is clearly indicating that he does not consent, so what becomes of the famous maxim, 'Without consent a marriage cannot be contracted'?[143]

Similarly, another host of problems arises over the purpose of consent. If someone takes a bride but intends to abandon her soon afterwards, some think that this does not make a marriage. Again, if someone knowingly marries a sterile woman and would not marry her if he thought she could give birth, some believe that the contract stands, others the opposite. A worse case: if someone takes an old woman not to live with her but to steal her dowry, some think that it is a marriage, while others do not. Those who have weighed this question most carefully conclude that general consent to the union is sufficient to contract a marriage, even if the man has decided not to live with her, share their property, raise children, or keep faith with his wife – even if, in fact, he marries a woman in order to sell her or put her on the streets. Others are not sure whether a man who takes a wife for her dowry or her body, and has no other motive for marrying her, can contract a true marriage. This involves making very fine distinctions, and cutting through the knotty questions[144] of primary and secondary intentions.

* * * * *

and *Decretales Gregorii* IX 4.1.30–1 and 4.4.1 CIC 2 672 and 680. The question is discussed at length by Lombard *Sententiae* book 4 dist 28 cc 1–2.
141 Deut 22:13–21
142 This is given as an example of an impossible condition in *Institutiones* 3.19.11.
143 Cf n128 above.
144 Cf *Adagia* I i 6: *Nodum solvere* on Alexander and the Gordian knot. 'Distinctions' and 'primary and secondary intentions' were much discussed by the scholastic philosophers, many of whom were also commentators on canon law; Erasmus obviously wishes the reader to associate these legal quibbles with this despised and outmoded tradition.

In addition, the statement that sexual intercourse changes a promise for the future into present reality cannot be accepted without qualification. The man has made a promise, quite sincerely, but he has lain with her not in the true spirit of wedlock, as a husband should with his wife, but rather as he might with any girl. Therefore if he has later contracted marriage with another, using words in the present tense but without intercourse, the first contract is invalid before God, though not in the eyes of a human judge.

It quite often happens these days that one of a couple who have given verbal consent and been united physically will deny that either has taken place. What is to be done, if both are prepared to swear an oath? Some think that the oath should be administered to the man if the woman was not a virgin before their consummation, but the opposite if by their intercourse he has made a virgin into a woman. Another question: should a woman continue to bestow her favours on a man who, after enjoying her body for some time, admits that for him their contract of marriage was a sham? She must not believe him, they say. But what if he convinces her, and she cannot persuade him to make a proper contract? The woman is left in a wretched state.

I shall deliberately pass over countless other perplexing and labyrinthine problems in order to spare the reader, whom I must also ask to bear with me for a while longer on this subject, until I reach the final point I wish to make. I have good reasons for lingering over these matters, however obscure and unpleasant they may be. I have shown how many problems are caused by the ease with which marriage may be contracted. It might seem more acceptable if there were an equally simple way of ending the contract, which would provide a remedy for mistakes or hastiness. Nowadays it is extremely easy to enter the net, but there is no way out. Even the right to repudiate an adulteress, which the Gospel appeared to grant, has been interpreted very narrowly by the Fathers to mean separation from the marriage-bed rather than the freedom to marry again.[145] The licence granted by Moses' law to repudiate a wife on almost any ground[146] was rightly curtailed by the Lord. But now we have more or less closed even the one loophole which,

* * * * *

145 See Matt 19:9, restricted in particular by Augustine in his severe *De incompetentibus nuptiis* (*Ad Pollentium*) 1.1–11 PL 40 451–8. Erasmus cites this in his annotation on 1 Cor 7:39 LB VI 694A, but points out that most other patristic writers, including Tertullian and Ambrose, accept Christ's words at their face value. On 'separation from the marriage-bed,' see n17 above. Erasmus uses the image of marriage as a net again in the Paraphrase on 1 Cor 7 LB VII 878D; it is a favourite image of the sardonic fifteenth-century French tales *Les Quinze Joyes de mariage*.

146 See Deut 24:1–3.

it seemed to some, he left open. It is not much comfort to have sent an adulteress packing if the innocent party is condemned to miserable solitude for as long as his repudiated wife lives. However, the argument over divorce is so complicated that it clearly requires a Delian swimmer,[147] as they say. The greatest minds of ancient and modern times have laboured long and hard over it.

To these complications, difficult enough in themselves, are added eighteen impediments to marriage.[148] Some are of the kind that do not dissolve a contract but prevent one from being made in the first place; if you fall foul of these you are liable to criminal charges, but not to the loss of your wife. Some suspend the contract temporarily, while others both prevent it being legally made and destroy it if it has been. Some of them dissolve a legally valid marriage that has not been consummated. A few will dissolve any contract so thoroughly that not even the Roman pontiff can mitigate the rigour of the law, whereas in a few other cases he can if he wishes ratify a contract improperly made. Again, some break up the home and the marriage-bed, while others restore the male and female to their former condition. There are some that do not break the lifelong bond or the sharing of the marriage-bed, but merely remove the right to demand one's conjugal rights, usually from one partner but sometimes from both. And around every one of these impediments swarms a host of questions and countless disputes among the human commentators.

The first impediment is interdiction by the church, which can be either general, as in the prohibition on clandestine marriages, or particular.[149] If the interdiction is a permanent one, the dissolution of the contract will also be permanent.

* * * * *

147 *Adagia* I vi 29; a very skilful swimmer
148 Impediments to marriage were of two kinds, prohibitive (or impedient), which rendered a marriage illicit but not invalid, and the more severe diriment, which rendered a marriage invalid; cf Lacey 69–76. Most canonists from the twelfth century onwards provide a list of the impediments (cf Esmein I 205–20 and Lacey 131–41), though the precise number varies. The clearest and most comprehensive list is perhaps Aquinas' (*Supplementum* qq 50–62), but the basis for most of the increasingly voluminous scholastic commentaries is the list in book 4 of Peter Lombard's *Sententiae*, dist 26–42. The closest to Erasmus' list that I have seen is in Angelus de Clavasio *Summa angelica* (Lyon 1523) fols 225–35. See Telle 391–404 for a commentary on Erasmus' list. The Reformers, led by Luther, reduced the list considerably; see Olsen 45–7.
149 See n130 above. A 'particular' case of interdiction by the church might merely involve delay while the circumstances were investigated by the competent authorities (Gaudemet 218–19).

The second impediment is similar: 'Marriages must not be made at unlawful times of the year;[150] if they are, they will have to be dissolved.' However, lawyers think that this forbids the ceremony and consummation, but not the actual making of a contract. There is some doubt as to whether the husband commits a fresh offence each time he lies with his wife.

The third impediment is the making of conditions, of four kinds: honourable, dishonourable, indifferent, and impossible; these engender a thousand different interpretations and mighty differences of opinion that it would take far too long to enumerate.[151]

The fourth impediment is error, which can be of two kinds: mistaken identity and misrepresentation of status or fortune. Suppose that the error occurs in some basic element of the marriage, affecting its very substance, as it were – mistaken identity, for example, when Barbara is substituted for Margaret, or misrepresentation, when a girl is given to a slave alleged to be a free man[152] – then the marriage cannot stand. In the first case, consent was not given by both the persons specified, while in the second the man is not free to fulfil his marital duties. Another case would be the marriage of a eunuch, incapable of intercourse, masquerading as a whole man. This impediment also gives rise to innumerable distinctions, hypotheses, and arguments.

Now, I am not questioning the commitment and diligence of the commentators, I am only surprised that ignorance of your partner's true circumstances cannot stand in the way of legal matrimony. There are worse things to be than a poor slave: who would not prefer to live with a slave than with a leper or a syphilitic? For such a marriage is valid if the woman agrees to join her husband in his master's service. And there are defects of character much uglier than epilepsy or leprosy. A girl cannot truly give consent if she marries a man, supposedly honest and in good health, whom she would

* * * * *

150 Particularly during Advent, Lent, and Rogation Week: see Gratian *Decretum* pars 2 C 33 q 4 cc 8–11 and *Decretales Gregorii* IX 2.9.4 CIC 2 272. Cf the passage 391 below on sexual abstinence at certain times.
151 This impediment is discussed in detail in *Decretales Gregorii* IX 4.5 CIC 2 682–4.
152 On this case see Gaudemet 215–18. Such cases are discussed by Gratian *Decretum* pars 2 C 29 and in the *Decretales Gregorii* IX 4.9 CIC 2 691–3. Aquinas explains (*Supplementum* q 51 art 2.3 and q 52 art 2) that in the latter case a slave cannot (theoretically) give his body without his master's consent. In his annotation on 1 Cor 7:39 LB VI 694C, Erasmus cites Ambrose's example of a woman marrying a pagan whom she believed to be a Christian; he returns to the general theme in the colloquy Ἄγαμος γάμος, *sive Coniugium impar* ('A Marriage in Name Only, *or* The Unequal Match') of 1529 (CWE 40 851).

never have married had she known the truth about him, especially if she has been the victim of some shameless deception. If a condition had been made, such as, 'I accept you if you are free from such diseases,' I believe that the marriage would not be valid if it were then discovered that he was not free from those ills.

In fifth place they list the vow of chastity. This can take two forms: one is the solemn vow made with due ceremony in church, the other is the simple vow made without ceremony of any kind. Scotus adds the further categories of the public and the private vow.[153] Human laws[154] make the following distinction between them: a simple vow prevents you from lawfully making a contract of marriage, but if you make one, the marriage is not rendered invalid by the vow; a solemn vow of chastity, on the other hand, not only prevents you from making a contract, but also renders null any contract you have made, even if you swear that the contract has been consummated by intercourse. The solemn vow is held in such esteem that a person who is betrothed, or properly wedded but not yet bedded, is permitted to make a solemn vow without the partner's consent and, once the profession has been made, a bridegroom cannot demand his rights from his wife, and a bride is free to marry another.[155]

But here again various questions arise. For example, if the bridegroom forces his bride to lie with him, does the girl lose the right to make a solemn vow? Those who favour the religious orders say that she does not; others claim that the husband has done no wrong in exercising his marital rights and that the girl has done wrong in denying him something she is not permitted to deny. In fact different rules apply to the priesthood and to the monastic profession.[156] Someone who is legally married and is later ordained to

* * * * *

153 In his commentary on Peter Lombard's *Sententiae* book 4 dist 38 c 1: *In primum [– quartum] sententiarum quaestiones subtilissimae* 4.38.1 scholium 1 (eg ed of Antwerp 1620, II 403). On Erasmus' generally hostile view of the scholastic theologian John Duns Scotus (1266–1308) and his colleagues, see Rummel *Annotations* 80–4 and 142–6. The question of vows and marriage is discussed at length by Gratian *Decretum* pars 2 c 27 q 1 cc 1–43 and c 33 q 5 cc 1–11, by Lombard *Sententiae* book 4 dist 38 and Aquinas *Supplementum* qq 53 and 61, and in the *Decretales Gregorii* IX 3.32–4 and 4.6 CIC 2 579–96 and 684–7; see also Telle 398-420.

154 *Decretales Gregorii* IX 4.6.3 CIC 2 685, a decree of Alexander III (c 1160)

155 Cf *Decretales Gregorii* IX 3.32.2 CIC 2 579 and especially Aquinas *Supplementum* q 61, expanding Lombard *Sententiae* book 4 dist 27 c 7.

156 On a priest's duty to his wife, see Gratian *Decretum* pars 1 D 28 c 14 and D 31 cc 11–13; see ibidem pars 2 c 17 q 2 c 2 for the case of a married man being

the priesthood becomes a priest but does not cease to be a husband, even though he cannot insist on his marital rights and cannot refuse them to his wife if she demands them. Another difficult question is whether a girl should be compelled to remain unmarried until her fiancé makes his vows, which usually takes a year or more. The prevailing opinion – from among a great many – is that the woman must postpone any new marriage until the time of his solemn profession (out of respect for his vows, I suppose). But what if her fiancé is less than serious and wanders from one monastery to the next, turning one year's novitiate into several? A conundrum indeed!

A different problem[157] arises with the simple vow: does someone who makes a simple vow of chastity and then gets married commit a mortal sin every time he lies with his wife, or only once, the first time? Opinions are divided, but almost all agree that under these conditions he has no right to demand his marital rights, though he can and must allow them to his wife if she so wishes. A second point: if such a husband's wife dies, is he free to contract another marriage? Some say yes, others no. The more humane think that the entire force of the vow is destroyed by the first act of intercourse. If a marriage is made between a couple both of whom are bound by a simple vow of chastity, the marriage is valid, but neither has the power to insist on his or her marital rights, though neither does wrong if he or she gratifies the other's needs.

Other problems that are far from simple arise here. First, why should a vow invalidate a legally contracted marriage, but not if it has been consummated? In both cases the marriage is legally complete, and although greater harm has been done to a girl who has been deflowered than to one who has not, yet any girl who has been married suffers no mean hurt to her reputation: there are lingering suspicions that she is not really a virgin, and even if intercourse has not taken place, many other things may have happened that no man could accept with equanimity in his bride. Then again, many will suspect that she was discarded because of some concealed physical or moral imperfection.

* * * * *

dissuaded by Augustine from taking monastic vows; in Augustine's view (*De bono coniugali* 15 PL 40 383), he cannot live in chastity without his wife's consent. The case that follows is based on *Decretales Gregorii* IX 3.32.11 CIC 2 582 or Lombard *Sententiae* book 4 dist 27 c 8.

157 This is raised by Lombard *Sententiae* book 4 dist 32 c 2 and by Aquinas *Supplementum* q 53 art 1.3; the solution had been suggested by Augustine *De bono coniugali* 15 PL 40 383–4.

Someone might also ask why, if the Lord clearly refused to allow married couples to be parted except for adultery,[158] a solemn vow should have the power to make a married couple single again, apparently against the Gospel's teaching (I am merely thinking aloud, not passing judgment). If it is always true that the greater good must prevail over the lesser, the priestly calling seems preferable to marriage, especially since a profession of chastity is tied, so they say, to priesthood. Indeed, someone might with some show of reason ponder whether the priest's profession is not of higher religious status than the monk's (I refer to monks who have not taken holy orders). A priest swears obedience to his bishop; in some countries he even makes an explicit vow of chastity[159] (usually in places where it is least likely to be observed). Thus the monk is superior only in virtue of the vow of poverty, but against this may be weighed the dignity and duty of the sacrament conferred on the priest; monks do not gain access to some new sacrament, unless I am mistaken.[160] But let that go. One may perhaps doubt whether monastic vows should be allowed to take precedence over the duties of marriage.[161] The monk's profession is in every respect an invention of mankind, whereas the dissolution of a marriage violates the very basis of a sacrament, since the Lord said, quite explicitly, 'What God has joined, let no man put asunder.'[162]

The papal ruling on vows is clear enough, but the most distinguished theologians have put considerable effort into explaining the reasons behind it.[163] Some contend that a solemn vow is given precedence over marriage to avoid scandal, whereas a simple vow does not constitute a stumbling-block to faith. This neat explanation can be rejected on two counts. First, a simple vow can sometimes cause no less scandal than a solemn one, and may be just as widely known. Second, since the Holy Scriptures declare that marriage cannot be dissolved, they deny that any possible scandal can outweigh and undermine the authority of the gospel teaching. In fact, the

* * * * *

158 Matt 19:9
159 Cf Lombard *Sententiae* book 4 dist 37 c 1 and Aquinas *Supplementum* q 53 art 2.3.
160 On the controversy over Erasmus' attacks on monasticism, see the introductory note 212 above. The different functions and capacities of priests and monks are outlined by Gratian *Decretum* pars 2 c 16 q 1 cc 1–40. A man could, of course, be a monk without being a priest and vice versa.
161 This position is implied by a decree of Innocent III reproduced in the *Decretales Gregorii* IX 3.32.14 CIC 2 583–4.
162 Matt 19:6
163 Eg Lombard *Sententiae* book 4 dist 38 c 2 and Aquinas *Supplementum* q 53 art 2. The sentence following echoes Rom 14:13.

taking of vows in such circumstances ought to offend true believers more than the breaking of them. One may also dispose of the argument that the greater good must not be impeded by the lesser. According to this theory, even a consummated marriage would be nullified by a solemn vow because the monastic life would be considered better than any marriage, even one that had been consummated. However, the act of consummation does not make a marriage more of a marriage, only stronger. Again, as I said earlier, the priestly state is better than the married state, and thus a husband can dissolve his marriage to take holy orders.

Some commentators cite civil law:[164] before intercourse the bridegroom has not taken full possession of the gift of his wife's body, whereas in taking monastic vows he at once gives himself, body and soul, to God. This stronger and fuller commitment must supersede one that is weak and incomplete. This argument has been refuted as follows: if 'possession is nine points of the law,'[165] it would follow that if a man had made a verbal contract of marriage with, let us say, Catherine, and then contracted a marriage with another woman, followed by physical union with her, the first contract would be invalid – which is the opposite of the church's position.[166] It should follow, then, that such a man's profession would be unlawful, though valid once the vows had been taken, just as it is a sin to get married after making a simple vow of chastity. Some argue that there is solid evidence when a solemn vow has been taken, as is not the case with a simple vow. Scotus rejected this, on the ground that sometimes a simple vow becomes public knowledge but can still be nullified by marriage.[167] He distinguishes four

* * * * *

164 Although Ulpian's famous maxim (see n128 above) gave consent priority over consummation, the *Codex* 5.17.10 suggested the contrary. See also 250 above on the effect of consummation after *verba de futuro*, words in the future tense. The argument here is presented by Aquinas *Supplementum* q 43 art 3.6.

165 *Potior est conditio possidentis*, a maxim found for example in the *regula iuris* of Boniface VIII (*Liber sextus decretalium* 5.12.65 CIC 2 1124) and quoted in this context by Aquinas *Supplementum* q 53 art 1 resp 1

166 See 251 above; this assumes that the contract with 'Catherine' was made using the present tense. Erasmus' argument here had been used by the canonist Guillaume Durand de St Pourçain (1270-1334) in his *Resolutiones et decisiones*, a commentary on the *Sententiae* of Peter Lombard, 4.27.2 (6) (ed of Paris: J. Petit, 1508, fol 418v). The same work (4.38.1, fols 434v–435r) may have provided most of Erasmus' material on simple and solemn vows. Erasmus cites Durand by name below (see n172); in the *Enchiridion* CWE 66 10 and in Ep 396:101 he figures in lists of mediocre theologians.

167 In the passage identified n153 above. The 'more plausible explanation' cited next is also used by Scotus there.

kinds of vow: public, private, simple, and solemn; but simple and public can be one and the same.

Some advance a more plausible explanation. When a monk makes his profession, he yields his body to the power of the man to whom he makes his promise, that is, the abbot, to dispose of according to the terms of the vow; therefore he cannot allow his spouse to use his body for some other purpose. But even this is unconvincing: a man yields his body to God when he makes a simple vow of chastity, and yet he yields his body to his wife for the opposite purpose. The argument used by some that God refuses to allow anyone to yield his or her body to him except through a human agency is nugatory and is as easy to refute as to advance, since in such matters the will of God cannot be determined. Another hypothesis to be rejected is that the simple vow merely embodies a promise, whereas the solemn vow actually gives possession to the one to whom the vow is made. But an agreement freely and willingly made between God and man has just as much force in a simple vow as in a solemn vow.

The lawyers say that no better reason can be given than that the church has so decided. But the theologians[168] will not accept even this, and say, 'If the rulings of mere human beings have such power, then they can also decide the opposite, namely, that marriage is not nullified by the taking of solemn vows.' If we could accept this, the controversy would be at an end, but we are afraid to say it now, because it might appear that mere humans have the power to dissolve a marriage that God has made. They allow the pope the right to declare certain people incapable of contracting a marriage, or to decide that a marriage was not entered into lawfully, but they will in no circumstances grant him the power to dissolve a marriage that has been properly contracted.

We must therefore seek a sheet-anchor[169] on which we may rely when tossed by these conflicting views, although not everyone agrees even on this. Passing over many others, here is Aquinas' argument: 'By its very nature (and not by the decision of the pope) a solemn vow not only prohibits a marriage being contracted, but also dissolves it if it has been made, since by his vow a man loses control over his body.'[170] But this again begs the

* * * * *

168 Including Erasmus himself, who argues strongly, if somewhat speciously, that there is nothing to prevent the popes reversing their predecessors' rulings on the indissolubility of marriage, in, eg, the lengthy annotation on 1 Cor 7:39 LB VI 696A and 697C–D

169 *Adagia* I i 24; in Latin the sheet-anchor was called the 'sacred anchor.'

170 Aquinas *Supplementum* q 53 art 2.3

question of the simple vow, and Thomas makes his point so feebly that he appears dissatisfied with it himself. This is what he says next: 'And because a marriage that follows such a vow is null and void, so such a vow is said to dissolve a marriage that has been contracted.' He dared not say 'dissolves' but merely 'is said to dissolve.' This looks like resolving one controversy with another, or at least answering one doubt with another; the precise question he is discussing is why a solemn vow dissolves a properly contracted marriage, despite Paul's contention that only by death may either partner be released.[171]

I am not sure whether Durand's argument[172] is convincing or merely ingenious. In marriage, he says, there are two kinds of union: a spiritual union through consent and a physical union through intercourse. Similarly, death takes two forms: physical death, when the soul is separated from the body, and spiritual death, when someone becomes dead to the world. Therefore, just as physical death dissolves a consummated marriage, so spiritual death dissolves a valid marriage that is unconsummated. If this were so, the property of those entering religious orders would go to their relatives, as it does when somebody dies, and in fact, as Jerome writes, such a law was made by the Christian emperors to check the avarice of the clerics and monks.[173] Nowadays, since this symbolic death has no such effect on property, it seems it should have still less effect on marriage, which the Lord allows to be dissolved for one reason only. An exile is dead to the state, and yet that symbolic death does not preclude the exile from inheriting or possessing property.

Thus people who enter a notoriously disreputable monastery, where chastity is ignored and private possessions are allowed, should not be freed from a binding marriage contract.[174] The same applies to anyone who becomes a monk just so he can automatically be made an abbot. It is obvious that such people are by no means dead to the world. Finally, if that sort of death had enough power to free people from marriage, it would have more than enough to release them from their debts, and it would be useless to ask

* * * * *

171 Cf 1 Cor 7:10–11.
172 In the work cited n166 above, 4.27.2 (9) fol 418v
173 Jerome Ep 52 [2].6 (*Ad Nepotianum*) PL 22 532; Migne's note alludes to a constitution of Valentinian to Pope Damasus, c 370. There are several rulings on the obligation of monks to leave their property to relatives in the *Novellae* (5.5.76 and especially 122.38).
174 A case of this kind is considered by the thirteenth-century canonist Hostiensis *Summa aurea* 3 de voto 17 (ed of Lyon 1548, fol 179r).

those about to make their vows whether they owed anything to anyone, or whether they had promised anything to a girl. In fact, true spiritual death occurs in baptism, as the apostle Paul plainly taught us,[175] and yet the acceptance of baptism does not free a man from a bond of service or from a bond of matrimony according to Paul's teaching,[176] so it is still less likely that the pseudo-death (not mentioned in Holy Writ) of taking one's vows could have those effects.

The distinction that some make between priest and monk – that the latter is dead, the former merely maimed[177] – does not seem very satisfactory. In fact the priest, if bound by a vow of continence, is equally dead as far as the principle of marriage is concerned. To be different from the others, Scotus alleged that the church made anyone who swore a solemn vow incapable of marriage or, to use his expression, 'illegitimated' them for marriage, but the same was not true of a private vow.[178] In this way he avoids opposing the Lord's decree and undermining the strict rules of matrimony; the status of matrimony is preserved, but the stuff of which the marriage was made is rendered unsuitable. You may ask why the same power does not make the person bound by a simple vow incapable of matrimony, especially since he is committing a deadly sin by contracting a marriage with the intention of lying with his wife. The answer is that he has placed himself in God's hands in a different way from the other, who has placed himself in the church's hands, as far as the act of matrimony is concerned, and thus the church can free from the bonds of matrimony someone who has bound himself to the church's judgment. But the other one, who has pledged himself to God without the church's intervention, is left by the church to answer to his own conscience. Someone may ask why the pope does not, in the case of the simple vow, take away the right to contract a marriage, as he does with the solemn vow; or else absolve him from sin, as he does with the solemn vow, where dissolving the bonds of marriage even receives praise as a work of piety. Here Scotus replies with a perhaps: 'Perhaps,' he says, 'a greater evil will follow.' I imagine that the reader will see easily enough, without my telling him, how many different ways there are to pull

* * * * *

175 Rom 6:1–11; Col 2:12–13
176 See 1 Cor 7:12–14, 20–4.
177 Probably a commonplace of the canonists, mentioned by Guillaume Durand, in a passage adjoining those cited by Erasmus above (see nn166 and 172), 4.27.2 (10); Durand is himself quoting his predecessor Hostiensis (see n174 above).
178 Scotus *Quaestiones subtilissimae* (see n153 above) 4.38.1 scholium 2 (II 404). Erasmus mocks his unclassical style here.

up this sheet anchor![179] I merely wished to illustrate the difficulty of the question.

The sixth impediment to marriage is holy orders.[180] The Roman or western church first removed priests from their priesthood [if they married], then deacons too, and finally subdeacons. There is some hesitation over the lesser orders, hence the compromise that if clerics in the western church have wives, they may keep them, but they will be disqualified from performing their functions and deprived of their benefices, if any. The Greek church today maintains its own rules,[181] I am told.

The seventh impediment is consanguinity, which is defined in terms of degrees and lines.[182] The direct line goes back to great-great-great-grand-fathers, their fathers and grandfathers, and so on; the rest of these relationships have no special name in Latin, and the general term for them is ancestors or progenitors. The direct line goes forward through sons, grandsons, and others to great-great-great-grandsons, their sons and grandsons,

* * * * *

179 Cf n169 above.
180 On Erasmus' views on priestly celibacy, see in particular Léon-E. Halkin 'Erasme et le célibat sacerdotal' *Revue d'histoire et de philosophie religieuses* 57 (1977) 497–511. In Ep 1539 and in the *Encomium matrimonii* CWE 25 137 Erasmus openly advocates marriage for priests (and monks) as a corrective to current immorality, pointing out that some of the apostles were married, despite the greater need for single-minded evangelists in their time. In his annotation on 1 Cor 7:39 LB VI 697A, Erasmus cites with distaste, via the *Decretum* of Gratian (pars 1 D 31 c 1), the rulings of the sixth-century popes Pelagius II and Gregory I which resulted in the imposition of celibacy on subdeacons. The successive decrees prescribing celibacy for all orders from subdeacon upwards are collected in Gratian *Decretum* pars 1 DD 27–34, the decrees concerning minor orders in *Decretales Gregorii* IX 2.3.1–9 CIC 2 457–9. For contemporary opinion in favour of marriage for priests, see Telle 189–91 n1; for the history of the question, see A. Stickler *The Case for Clerical Celibacy* (Fort Collins 1995).
181 That is, it permitted men already married to become priests, as it still does; cf Lacey 103–11. The difference seems to have been tacitly accepted by the Roman church in the eleventh century; cf Gratian *Decretum* pars 1 D 31 c 14. Aquinas discusses it in the present context in *Supplementum* q 53 art 3.2.
182 The ancient incest taboos codified by Moses (eg Lev 18) were developed into a complex system of prohibitions both in Roman law (eg *Institutiones* 1.10.1–7) and in canon law (Gratian *Decretum* pars 2 c 35, source of much of the material here). Joannes Andreae, the fourteenth-century canonist frequently quoted by Erasmus in his annotation on 1 Cor 7:39 LB VI 694D ff, produced very detailed diagrammatic 'trees' of consanguinity and of affinity (see 270 below), which went into dozens of editions in the early sixteenth century. They were based on earlier versions such as those of Isidore of Seville *Etymologiae* 9.6 PL 82 359–63 and Durand de Saint-Pourçain (see n166 above) fols 439–40.

and others; the general term for these is descendants or posterity. Some believe that marriage is always prohibited in this line, adding jokingly that if Adam were still alive he would have to remain single. Others consider that the right to marry is restored from the fifth degree onwards. On this subject imperial law concurs with the decrees of the church, both in the numbering of the degrees and in the prohibitions on marriage. Both count as many degrees as there are persons, minus one.

In the indirect line, called the collateral branches, the right to contract marriage is restored after the fourth degree (so long as the degree of kinship is calculated according to canon law rather than to civil law). If the male and the female belong to different generations and are thus related in different degrees to the stock[183] (for example, one of them might be three degrees from him, the other five or seven), some think that they can get married, others do not. On this point divine law, civil law, and canon law disagree. Divine law removes the right to contract marriage only from a few of the closest degrees of kinship.[184] In the beginning of the world it was essential that brother should have children by his sister, and on this pretext some even condone Lot's daughters' incest with their father.[185] When the human race increased, the right to marry was restricted, but only in respect of a few degrees, notably the first and second, as Leviticus 18 tells us. There you are forbidden to marry your mother, your sister (even if one parent is different), your grandchild by a son or daughter, and your maternal or paternal aunt (your mother's or father's sister). The same rules apply to the female sex. It was therefore permitted to marry the offspring of one's brother or sister, as Abraham married his niece Sarah, his brother's child (Genesis 20), and as Caleb's brother married his daughter (Joshua 15).

It is in the calculation of degrees of consanguinity in the collateral lines that disagreement first occurs between the civil laws and the papal statutes.

* * * * *

183 Degrees of kinship being calculated in canon law according to the distance of each party from the common ancestor (the stock), it was perfectly possible for the number of degrees to be different. The different methods of computation are set out in Gratian *Decretum* pars 2 c 35 q 5 c 2, quoting Alexander II's lengthy comparison (made in 1065) of the church's prescriptions with those of Justinian (*Institutiones* 3.5 and 3.6). I am grateful to Ladislas Orsy for checking the translation on this impediment.
184 Cf n182 above; the need to people the earth is pointed out by Gratian *Decretum* pars 2 c 35 q 1, following Augustine *De civitate Dei* 15.16, and by Erasmus in the *Ratio verae theologiae* LB V 87–8, a broad picture of historical evolution and of the church's changing needs; cf n3 above.
185 Gen 19:30–8; cf for example Lombard *Sententiae* book 4 dist 33 c 1.

The latter lay down the following rule: people are related to one another in the same degree as they are related to the stock, their common ancestor, whereas the former lay down that, when they belong to the same generation, the number of degrees from the stock must be doubled to establish their degree of kinship. Again, when they belong to different generations, the church's rule is that the degree of kinship is simply that by which the further distant of them is related to the stock, whereas civil law says that it is the total number between both of them and the stock, not counting the stock himself. Thus Caius[186] is forbidden to marry his sister, his sister's daughter, granddaughter, and great-granddaughter, that is, any woman descended from his sister's son or daughter, or her grandson or granddaughter, who is Caius' great-great-niece, and is distant from Caius in the fourth degree, according to the calculations of canon law. He is also forbidden to marry his paternal or maternal aunt, and indeed his paternal or maternal great-aunt (his grandfather's or grandmother's sister), because they are considered more or less as his own ancestors, nor yet their daughters, granddaughters, or great-granddaughters. It is also unlawful for him to marry his maternal or paternal great-great-aunt (the sister of his great-grandmother or great-grandfather), or their daughters, granddaughters, and great-granddaughters.

The same principles apply to the female sex. Tulliola, Caius' sister, cannot marry her brother, her paternal or maternal uncle, her paternal or maternal great-uncle or her paternal or maternal great-great-uncle. She is also not permitted to marry her brother or his grandsons and great-grandsons. At one time papal law used to prohibit marriage up to the seventh degree in the indirect line, so that any contract of marriage within it would have no effect. This prohibition has been mitigated by later rulings so that it does not extend beyond the fourth degree.[187]

Further, according to civil law there are three classes of indirect relationships, the first being ascending relationships, the second descending ones, and the third the strictly collateral ones.[188] In the first two classes the

* * * * *

186 Caius was the conventional name used in Roman law, the equivalent of 'John Doe.' The feminine Caia was also used (cf 369 below), rather than Tulliola (the pet name of Cicero's daughter), which Erasmus seems to use for 'Jane Doe' below.

187 Successive reductions in the prohibited degrees are demonstrated by Gratian *Decretum* pars 2 c 35 qq 2–3. The Fourth Lateran Council of 1215 (see n199 below) reduced the number to four.

188 *Digesta* 38.10.1. This paragraph also draws on Gratian *Decretum* pars 2 c 35 q 5 c 2; in canon law the calculation was based on the contention that brother and sister are 'one flesh.'

rules are the same in imperial and papal law, and in fact marriages in the fourth degree of the collateral line are valid in both. As I said earlier, the calculation of the degrees in the direct line is the same in both systems of law. In the indirect line brother and sister are in the second degree according to imperial law, but in the first degree according to papal rulings (the reason for this difference is irrelevant to our discussion here). The reckoning of imperial law still applies in questions of inheritance and guardianship, but the papal law applies to matrimony. It makes no difference whether consanguinity was established within or outside wedlock.

The eighth impediment arises from adoption. This falls into two categories. One goes under the general name of adoption, the other is called adrogation; dependent children are adopted, but independent persons are adrogated.[189] Adrogation has a special feature: the person adrogated comes under the legal power of the adrogator, but so also does his family; his children, if any, acquire the legal status of grandchildren just as he takes on that of a son. Adoptive relationships fall into three categories. The first is between different generations, for example between an adoptive father and his adopted son or daughter, or equally between an adoptive grandfather and his adopted grandson or granddaughter; it is possible to be adopted not only as a son, but also as a grandson or great-grandson. Within this first category marriage is prohibited entirely, as if it were in the direct line of consanguinity, so that even if the adoption comes to an end, the prohibition remains. The second category involves a kind of collateral relationship between the natural son and daughter of an adoptive father and his adopted son or daughter; for as long as the adoption lasts, they may not marry; when the adoption is ended by coming-of-age or some other means, they may contract marriage. The third category is the relationship between an adoptive father and the wife of his adopted son, or between an adopted son and the wife of his adoptive father; marriage between them is entirely prohibited, so that even if an adopted son achieves his independence, he cannot marry the woman who was the wife of his adoptive father, because she is regarded as his stepmother. And conversely, an adoptive father cannot marry his adopted son's wife, since she is regarded as his daughter-in-law.

* * * * *

189 The distinction between adoption and adrogation was enshrined in Roman law; see Gaius *Institutes* 1.97–107 and in particular the *Digesta* 1.7.1.1, probably Erasmus' source. Adoption applies to *filiifamilias*, children still under *patria potestas* (cf n111 above), whereas adrogation applies to a free individual (*sui iuris*) and requires his or her consent, and sometimes that 'of the people.' On this impediment canon law, as expounded for example by Aquinas *Supplementum* q 57, was heavily influenced by Roman law.

The ninth impediment is unknown to the laws of the gentiles, to imperial law, to Moses' law, and also to the Gospel's law; it was introduced through the piety and extreme generosity[190] of the early popes. It is called spiritual kinship, and it results from the administration of the sacraments – not all of them, but two only: baptism (which also involves catechizing and the appointment of godparents) and confirmation. Here again a host of tricky problems arises: for example, is there any difference between baptizer, godparent, and catechizer? How far does this kinship extend in invalidating marriages? In which cases does it not dissolve contracts, although it prohibits the making of them? I shall try to convey the gist of the matter briefly: spiritual kinship does not have established degrees of its own, but is divided into three categories. The first they call 'paternity,' with its attendant term 'filiation' (new words are needed for new institutions), and it exists between those who baptize, confirm, or stand as godparents and those who are baptized, confirmed, or sponsored by them. The second is called 'compaternity,' and exists between those who baptize, confirm, or stand as godparents and the natural parents of those who have received the sacraments. The third is 'symbolic brotherhood' between those who are baptized, confirmed, or made godchildren and the natural offspring of those who perform these duties.

In all three categories it is generally true that the spiritual relationships contracted by the husband apply also to a wife with whom he has lain, but not to a virgin bride, since it is only after physical consummation that what applies to one of the partners is understood to apply to the other as well. Thus if someone has been betrothed to a woman and stands godfather to your son before lying with the woman as a husband, you may lawfully wed her. Similarly, if someone is godfather at the baptism of my wife's son by another man, he does not enter into 'compaternity' with me through her. These rules apply even if a layman has to perform baptism in an emergency.

* * * * *

190 The expression Erasmus uses, *ex abundantia*, was often used ironically, eg by Quintilian *Institutiones oratoriae* 4.5.15 and in the *Digesta* 33.7.12.46; Erasmus clearly implies that to him *cognatio spiritualis* is a superfluous further obstacle to matrimony. According to Gratian *Decretum* pars 2 c 30 q 1 c 1, it was first introduced in the fourth century by Pope Julius I and confirmed by Innocent I and Celestine I in the fifth; see also *Codex* 5.4.26. Subsequent developments, through to the case of emergency baptism, are collected in Gratian *Decretum* pars 2 c 30 qq 1 and 3–4, in the *Decretales Gregorii* IX 4.11 CIC 2 693–6, and especially by Aquinas *Supplementum* q 56, who argues that the spiritual bond is holier than the physical (q 56 art 1.4) and discusses most of the problems mentioned by Erasmus.

Thus there are twenty cases in all in which spiritual kinship prohibits marriage: ten arise from baptism, and the same number from confirmation.[191] The first is between the baptizer and the baptized, the second between the wife of the baptizer (if he has previously lain with her) and the baptized, the third between the baptized and the children of the baptizer, the fourth between the baptizer and the parents of the baptized, and the fifth between the wife of the baptizer and the parents of the baptized. Five more cases, but involving godparents and godchildren, follow the same pattern. Ten similar cases apply to confirmation, five concerning the confirmant and the confirmed, and as many concerning the sponsor and the confirmed. In these twenty cases spiritual kinship prevents a marriage being contracted, and dissolves any such contract.

Following upon these is the tenth impediment, which arises from affinity.[192] According to civil law affinity arises only from marriage, but according to ecclesiastical law, from any sexual intercourse, though there is some doubt about incomplete or unnatural sexual acts. There is no small difficulty over such questions as whether the relationship was established before or after the event, how far it extends, and the nature of its effect: does it both prohibit and dissolve contracts, and can it be relaxed? But this impediment is no fabrication.[193] It is derived both from Roman law and from Leviticus 18,[194] where you are prohibited from marrying your stepmother or your stepmother's daughter, your daughter-in-law (that is, your son's wife, though I am not sure if it applies to a wife repudiated by your son while he is still alive), and your brother's wife – perhaps only during his lifetime, since, if he dies without issue, his surviving brother is ordered to provide

* * * * *

191 This is probably a standard list; the same twenty cases are enumerated, though in a different order, by Joannes Andreae (see n182 above) *Tractatus de sponsalibus et matrimoniis* (ed of Paris: G. Philippes, 1509, fols 62v–63r).

192 Existing relationship by marriage or, according to canon law, through any previous carnal relations. In Mosaic law it had been restricted to cases of wedlock, but from the eighth century canonists interpreted Gen 2:24 ('They shall be one flesh') as applicable to all carnal relations (cf Bede *Ecclesiastical History* 1.27.5 PL 95 60). This impediment, and its extension to the seventh degree of kinship, is expounded by Gratian *Decretum* pars 2 c 35 q 2,3 c 16 and q 5 c 3; in the *Decretales Gregorii* IX 4.13–14 CIC 2 696–704; and most comprehensively by Aquinas *Supplementum* q 55; see also n182 above. For its limitation to marriage alone in Roman law, see *Digesta* 38.10.4.3.

193 Another indication (cf n190 above) that Erasmus considered the impediment of spiritual kinship spurious and unnecessary.

194 Lev 18:8–16, modified by the injunction to Onan in Gen 38:8 to raise up seed to his dead brother, which is echoed in Matt 22:24, Mark 12:9, and Luke 20:28

offspring for his dead brother. Herod was rebuked by John because he had married his brother's wife during his lifetime.[195] Again, you are prohibited from marrying your wife's daughter by another man, or the daughter of your wife's son or daughter, or from taking your wife's sister as your concubine, even though Jacob joined two sisters to himself in matrimony.[196] Here secular laws are in almost complete agreement with the decrees of the church except that, as I have said, according to papal theories affinity can arise from any sexual intercourse, lawful or unlawful.

The technical terms[197] for these relationships are father-in-law, mother-in-law, son-in-law, daughter-in-law, stepfather, stepmother, stepson, and stepdaughter. Thus a bridegroom would say: 'My father-in-law is my wife's father, and I am his son-in-law; my grandfather-in-law [*socer magnus*] is my wife's grandfather, and I am his grandson-in-law [*progener*]. Conversely, my father is my wife's father-in-law, and she is his daughter-in-law; my grandfather is my wife's grandfather-in-law [*socer magnus, prosocer*], and she is his granddaughter-in-law [*pronurus*]. My wife's grandmother is my grandmother-in-law [*prosocrus*], and I am her grandson-in-law [*progener*]; my mother is my wife's mother-in-law, and she is her daughter-in-law, and my grandmother is her grandmother-in-law [*socrus magna*], and my wife is her granddaughter-in-law [*pronurus*]. My stepson is my wife's son by another man, and I am his stepfather, while my wife is called the stepmother of my children by other women, and they are her stepchildren. My brother is my wife's brother-in-law [*levir*], and my sister her sister-in-law [*glos*].' In Greek the wives of two brothers are εἰνάτερες, sisters-in-law. There is no technical term in Latin for my sister's husband, nor for my wife's brother.[198]

It is unlawful for any of these to be joined in matrimony on the ground that affinity makes them like parents and children to one another. Whenever this relationship is established by sexual intercourse between a man and a woman already related by blood, affinity is established (in the same degree as the existing consanguinity) between the woman's blood relatives and the man, and the man's blood relatives and the woman. However, there

* * * * *

195 Matt 14:3–4; Luke 3:19
196 Gen 29
197 It will be seen that Latin is far richer than English in such terms. Lists of them appear in anthologies of both Roman and canon law, eg *Institutiones* 3.6 and *Digesta* 38.10.15–18; Isidore of Seville *Etymologiae* 9.5–6 (in a form similar to that here); PL 82 353–64; and Gratian *Decretum* pars 2 c 35 q 5 c 6, though Gratian finally runs out of names!
198 This curious fact is pointed out by Lombard *Sententiae* book 4 dist 41 c 4.

is no prohibition when there is not, and has not been, a relationship by blood in the fourth degree or closer between one of the persons concerned and the spouse of the other. Thus, any woman who is a blood relative of my wife, up to the fourth degree, is my relative by marriage in the same degree, and vice versa. Therefore I cannot marry my wife's mother, sister, grandmother, great-grandmother, great-great-grandmother, great-great-great-grandmother, maternal aunt, great-aunt, and great-great-aunt, nor paternal aunt, great-aunt, and great-great-aunt. Nor can I marry my wife's daughters, nephews, and nieces down to the fourth degree, nor any of those I have listed under affinity above.

At one time the decrees of the popes identified three types of affinity;[199] when one person was joined to another by sexual intercourse, it changed the type of relationship but did not change the degree. But of the three the second and third have been abolished, and thus I am not prohibited from marrying my brother-in-law's wife, whom he married after my sister's death; this had not been allowed formerly, because a marriage had taken place establishing affinity of the first type, in the second degree. Affinity of the first type, like blood relationship in the fourth degree or closer, prevents marriage being contracted or dissolves any contract that is made.

The eleventh impediment is called public propriety,[200] which was introduced by the popes primarily as a counterpart to affinity in much the same way that spiritual kinship corresponds to consanguinity; thus it dissolves marriages up to the fourth degree, as affinity does. So much weight

* * * * *

199 The first type arose from sexual relations of any kind (cf n192 above); the second prohibited marriage between a man and the *affines* of the woman by the first type, and vice versa; the third, between a man and the *affines* related to the woman by the second type, and vice versa. In other words, one could not marry one's in-laws' in-laws' in-laws. The second and third types were abolished by canon 50 of the Lateran Council of 1215 (*Decretales Gregorii* IX 4.14.8 CIC 2 703).

200 Cf Gratian *Decretum* pars 2 c 27 q 2 cc 14–15 and especially *Decretales Gregorii* IX 4.1.3–4 and 8 CIC 2 661–3). This impediment prohibited marriage between a widow and her deceased husband's kinsmen, or else identified propinquity or quasi-affinity arising from simple betrothal, or from an unconsummated marriage (an argument used in Henry VIII's divorce); such imperfect unions created an impediment to marriage with the blood relatives of the other party. Erasmus' example of the monk suggests that the impediment arose even from a manifestly illicit contract or union. The impediment was unknown to Roman law, being quite different from the concept of *honestas*, which applied to socially undesirable matches, eg with actresses or courtesans; cf *Digesta* 23.2.41–50.

is given to this impediment that even a monk is considered to be able to consent to a contract from which public propriety arises, dissolving an established marriage, according to some. It arises in fact when a betrothal has been properly and formally arranged, by words either in the present or in the future, but the marriage is not yet consummated; from the moment of betrothal the impediment exists between the fiancé and his fiancée's blood relatives, and between the fiancée and her fiancé's blood relatives. However, there has been some relaxation in the definition of public propriety as it affects second marriages. Caius' widow has married another man and had children by him: once, these children could not contract marriage with any blood relation of Caius, but now they can. Moreover, this 'propriety' dissolves only later betrothals and marriages, not preceding ones. Betrothals between those who are less than seven years old do not give rise to the impediment of public propriety.[201]

The twelfth impediment is custom or regulation.[202]

The thirteenth impediment is criminal guilt, and there is much debate about this.[203]

The fourteenth is a disparity of cult, meaning difference of religion; for example, marriage between a Christian and a pagan or a Jew. In fact, Paul does not want a wife to leave her pagan husband, unless he refuses to live with her, but he does not allow a free woman who is already a professed Christian to marry 'except in the Lord,' that is, unless her husband is of the same religion.[204] I am therefore surprised that some modern writers assert

* * * * *

201 Infant betrothals were prohibited under Roman law (*Digesta* 23.1.14) and under canon law (Gratian *Decretum* pars 2 c 30 q 2), but the decree cited by Gratian does not disqualify the participants from marrying in later years, provided that both consent to the match. The specific link with 'public propriety' is made in the *Decretales Gregorii* IX 4.2.4 CIC 2 673.

202 Erasmus is unspecific here because customary law varied throughout Christendom; 'regulation' probably means an external decision, such as a papal decree, for which the Latin used here, *constitutio*, is quite usual.

203 Some specific cases are discussed in the *Decretales Gregorii* IX 4.19.1–2 CIC 2 720; see also 289–90 below. Aquinas (*Supplementum* q 60) identifies the most common case by his heading 'De uxoricidio.' One recent contributor to the 'debate' had been Luther, who pointed out, in *De captivitate Babylonica ecclesiae*, 1520, that David's removal of Uriah (2 Sam 11) did not prevent him from marrying Uriah's widow Bathsheba; see Telle 393 n24.

204 1 Cor 7:13, 39. In the *Ratio verae theologiae* LB V 87F, Erasmus attributes the movement away from Paul's teaching to the influence of Augustine and Ambrose, although marriage between Jews and Christians was formally outlawed by Constantius in 339 (*Codex Theodosianus* 16.8.6). Heretics and pagans were

that it is lawful to marry a Jew or a pagan. If it is enough merely to be male and female, why then a brother and sister are male and female.[205] If a prohibition based on God's law has any power to move us, Paul forbade such a marriage.

The fifteenth obstacle to marriage is fear.[206] If consent is not freely given, it is not consent, and is made no more convincing by the swearing of an oath.

The sixteenth is a previous commitment. Formal betrothal is considered to have no legal force if one of the parties has already contracted marriage with another using an operative form of words. The same rule applies if consent using the future tense was given before, even if an oath has been sworn since. The question arises here as to whether, since a husband's death frees his wife, she is also set free if her husband is absent for a very long time, with no apparent prospect of his return but no certain news of his death.[207]

The seventeenth impediment is physical inability to fulfil one's marital duties[208] (not applicable if the problem arises after consummation). If it is a matter of a chronic physical condition or of the size of the genitals, the marriage is dissolved; something can be done about temporary disabilities, since doctors can remedy some physical defects, and the passage of time increases the size of the body.

Finally there is deprivation, when someone lacks certain senses and cannot understand what marriage is, or signify consent; for example, someone who is blind, deaf, and dumb.[209]

* * * * *

added at the Council of Chalcedon in 451, and the prohibition had obtained universal acceptance and effect by the twelfth century (Gratian *Decretum* pars 2 c 28 q 1).

205 Probably aimed at the schoolmen, who used such arguments as part of their dialectic; see eg Durand de Saint-Pourçain (see n166 above) 4.39.1, fol 437 and Aquinas *Supplementum* q 59 art 1, who would in fact allow marriage with a baptized heretic.

206 Cf *Decretales Gregorii* IX 1.40.1 and 4.1.13–14 CIC 2 218 and 665–6.

207 The question is discussed in *Codex* 5.17.2; Gratian *Decretum* pars 2 c 34; and the *Decretales Gregorii* IX 4.1.19 CIC 2 668.

208 Discussed in Gratian *Decretum* pars 2 c 27 q 2 c 29, c 32 q 7 c 25, and c 33 q 1 cc 1–3, and in some detail in *Decretales Gregorii* IX 4.15 CIC 2 704–8 and by Aquinas *Supplementum* q 58 art 1. It is noticeable that Erasmus does not couple this question with that of witchcraft, as most canonists do.

209 'Deprivation' (*privatio*) is thus the eighteenth impediment. However, it was possible for someone suffering only two of these disabilities to give consent; cf n132 above.

I have listed all these impediments to make it plain how many difficulties and dangers there are to contracting a valid marriage, though, once the contract has been made in one way or another, it cannot be broken, according to the firm principle of the Gospel.[210] By its very nature marriage is a difficult subject, and the Gospel's ruling, which takes from married couples the Jewish right to divorce, has added to the problems; but by far the greatest difficulty arises out of papal rulings and, not least, from differences of opinion among men over particular cases – not to mention the human wickedness that turns good laws to evil purposes. In other contracts, where the worst that can happen is that someone will lose money, people take great pains to avoid being cheated. Yet in making this contract, much the most difficult of all, on which depends lifelong happiness and to a large extent the salvation of our souls, they take no precautions at all, and many plunge into it as into a pit from which there is no escape. This explains, of course, the universal cries of complaint from the unhappily married, but it is here, as nowhere else, that the proverbs 'Make haste slowly' and 'Feet on the ground' must be applied.[211] We observe that someone using a ladder to descend into the deepest well will emerge without a scratch, whereas anyone falling into a shallower well will be seriously injured, breaking his limbs if not his neck. A surgeon can mend a broken or dislocated limb; no doctor can be found for someone unhappily chained in the fetters of matrimony. I even think that death may be a lighter affliction than an unhappy marriage, where the living suffer the torments of hell[212] and utter the wails of the damned on earth. When buying a horse, you look carefully for faults, and stipulate that your money shall be returned if any latent defects show up; you investigate the local customs and law applicable to the transaction, and, unwilling to trust your own eyes, you bring along someone more expert than you are; and yet three words and an embrace will make a marriage between a mere boy and a frail girl. When buying a house or a farm, you explore and investigate every angle: Is the vendor's title sound? Are there easements involved? Is there some charge upon it? The records are produced, witnesses are summoned, and an agreement drawn up; why, then, so much haste and carelessness in contracting marriages?

For example, how many people – and I am thinking not just of these boys and girls, but of adults too – how many know that the words in the future are changed to the present if intercourse follows? How many know

* * * * *

210 Matt 19:6
211 *Adagia* ii i 1 and ii i 2, here quoted in Greek
212 *Suos patiuntur manes*, an allusion to Virgil *Aeneid* 6.743

that digamy arises if a man discovers later that the girl he married, believing her to be a virgin, is not? How many know how to calculate their kinship, in every branch, to the fourth degree? Indeed, how many people know who all their relatives are? Even fewer give any thought to spiritual kinship, and, similarly, the rules of affinity are generally little known. Yet all this ought to be learned before you enter upon matrimony. Otherwise, it will cost you very dear to learn of one small regulation, if you have learned of it only to your detriment. After the marriage is contracted, there is a great rush to the lawyers, and the theologians are bombarded with queries; would it not be greatly preferable to do all that before making the contract? 'Now – too late, alas – the Trojans are made wise.'[213] The lion, caught in the hunter's net, always says, 'If only I had known before . . .' Not only is it no use to say, 'I wasn't thinking . . .';[214] it may be disastrous, and no allowance is made for inexperience.

Some people try to undermine the authority of canon law in order to excuse their own foolhardiness. However, it is not merely seditious but even impious to allow individual irresponsibility to override something duly established by public authority; so much so that even if one bishop or another has made an ill-considered decision, either because he took too little care over it, or because he was badly advised, or because he was led astray by some private interest, Christian restraint (which, as far as possible, seeks to be fair to all) demands that we put up with it and remain silent, unless such forbearance involves impiety as well. How much less right, therefore, have we to reject the decrees of properly convened universal synods, especially if they meet with general approval among Christians? Thus, although decrees are amended by decretals[215] and decretals sometimes conflict with one

* * * * *

213 *Adagia* I i 28
214 Cf n95 above.
215 The twelfth-century *Decretum* of Gratian included early conciliar decrees and enjoyed general favour among Renaissance humanists; the later *Decretals* included many papal pronouncements on clerical privilege and secular subjects, and were thus more controversial; cf Gaudemet 278. Erasmus makes little distinction between them in the *Antibarbari* CWE 23 86–90, but his later scepticism about the *Decretals* is barely disguised, both here and in his annotation on 1 Cor 7:39 LB VI 695–7, a series of conflicting papal rulings. Rabelais satirically attributes all the world's miseries to the suffix, in the episode of the Papimanes:

> Depuys que *Decretz* eurent *ales*,
> Et gens d'armes porterent males,
> Moines allerent à cheval,
> En ce monde abonda tout mal. (*Quart Livre* chapter 52)

another (they are usually papal rescripts),[216] yet the worldwide acceptance of their practical effectiveness greatly enhances their authority. Whenever there is a difference of opinion among men, it is best to adhere to whatever seems least risky. The true Christian who desires a totally tranquil marriage will take pains to fulfil all the requirements of justice, first of all satisfying God's demands, then complying with men's, as far as he may. Those who go too fast at the beginning nearly always arrive too late at the end; in this matter, those who are unnecessarily hasty in their plans never achieve their aims. The decision to marry should imply a desire to enjoy a pious, tranquil, and honourable existence with another person; but passion and impatience stand things on their heads, and with their alluring promises of ephemeral pleasure they drag humanity down into endless and inescapable anguish. Whereas the application of a little reason will ensure that the best course, not the softest, is chosen, and in time it will also become the most pleasant. Since the source of true joy and tranquillity is a clear conscience, what true pleasure can there be in it when the source is polluted?

In certain cases even the pope's authority[217] may not be able to offer a remedy, and such relaxations of the rules as he offers can themselves often bring problems: some detail may be left out, or expressed wrongly; you may get what you did not ask for. Thus it is safer, as the comic poet said, not to catch the disease than to try to cure it.[218] Moreover, although the Roman pontiff may quiet your conscience, he cannot still the tongues of men. Thus, in their wisdom, the ancients[219] tried to reduce the possibility of deception by allowing to proceed towards marriage any betrothal between minors that had been agreed by the parents, so long as the children were not younger than seven, at which age, although the judgment is not yet formed, they have some knowledge of the world but are still entirely willing to accept what they are told. But the marriage was not finalized before the young man's fourteenth year, and the girl's twelfth, the ages at which puberty generally occurs. In fact, in some countries puberty occurs later, and it does not happen to everyone at the same age, even in the same region; the reasons are the different rates of physical development and the sound or pernicious influence of the upbringing. But by this means the prince also wished to

* * * * *

216 A rescript was a written reply on a point of law. Erasmus points out that the *Decretals* contain both decrees and rescripts.
217 A marginal note in the original editions refers specifically to dispensation.
218 Probably a reference to Persius' famous admonition (*Satires* 3.64) 'venienti occurrite morbo' ('Meet the disease on its way').
219 Cf *Digesta* 23.1.14 and 17. The 'prince' mentioned later is Justinian.

serve the interests of decency and of respect for the children's age and sex, since previously puberty was usually determined by a physical examination of the couple.

Thus, in those days, a considerable time elapsed between betrothal and marriage, so that the partners were no strangers to each other; if the youngsters had remained agreeable to each other for so many years, their parents could entertain hopes of a stable and well-favoured marriage. At present Christian law does not prescribe a long engagement,[220] and enjoins us to consider valid a marriage contracted between adults by words in the present tense, or even in writing or by nods of the head, indicating the same thing as the spoken words; none the less it does commend the diligence of parents who do not rush their children straight to the altar, but use betrothal to eliminate deceit, so that the actions of older relatives or guardians will be invalid unless they have the consent of their offspring or wards.

Thus if one looks back to the situation at the time when so many Christians were filled with enthusiasm for chastity and, since charity had not grown cold, wickedness was not yet flourishing among them, one would say that the papal decrees on marriage were right and godly. But if one looks at social life today, if one considers the many thousands throughout Christendom who are enmeshed in the toils of marriage, then charity, which desires the good of all, may perhaps lead us to wish that an indulgent Mother Church, always attentive to the edification and not the destruction of her children, will allow some relaxation, will arrange things a little differently, exactly as a learned and trusty physician will vary his prescription to suit the climate and the age and condition of his patient. Remedies for the body are found in drugs, and doctors are the disciples of Hippocrates;[221] in society, papal rulings are the drugs, and the popes, the successors of Christ, are the doctors. If the decretals amend certain earlier decrees, if one decretal amends another, if the Roman pontiff (different individuals, of course) relaxes the rigour of his rulings and, in their interpretation of those rulings, one theologian differs from another, one lawyer from another, and theologians from lawyers generally, then I believe that the church could, for the

* * * * *

220 Cf Gratian *Decretum* pars 2 c 30 q 2 and *Decretales Gregorii* IX 4.2.8–12 CIC 2 675–7; on the forms of consent, see nn132 and 136 above.
221 Hippocrates was regarded as the divinely inspired founder of medicine, though his authority was being challenged at this period by more empirical systems; see Margolin 481–2. The simile of the doctor is a favourite with Erasmus, as it was with the ancient writers.

benefit of its flock, alter the laws it has made and give a clear lead on the matters in dispute; I shall offer a few suggestions.

But since these are turbulent times, when one group rejects entirely the authority of papal and episcopal rulings[222] while their opponents consider them equal, or even superior, to the Gospel, I must say first that my discussion is not intended as a defence of the mockers or as a set of orders for the princes of the church. My only aim is to find some way of soothing the consciences of the unfortunate, and doing so by the authority of those leaders to whose vigilance the Lord's flock is entrusted. Thus I wish everything I am about to say to be treated as if it were a speech made by one individual from among all those gathered at a council to discuss these matters; he gives his considered opinion, but is prepared to yield to a better, or to be laughed out of court if he deserves it.

In the first place, it seems to me that matrimony would be a much less complicated business if the rulings on spiritual kinship were to have the status of exhortations rather than the force of law. These exhortations would extol the piety of those who showed such respect for persons with whom they had established a spiritual relationship; but this purely theoretical kinship would not prevent the sort of marriage that God established and Christ commended. The reasons for these rules put forward by lawyers or theologians may be pious enough, but they do not have the weight to enforce the dissolution of a properly contracted marriage; if they had, surely these rulings would have been promulgated already in the days of the apostles, in whom zeal for chastity burned so brightly.

Let us now look at additions made by the moderns. Argument by analogy with greater, lesser, or even equal things does not always carry conviction. Physical kinship dissolves a marriage, spiritual kinship even more so, they say. But it does not follow that, because physical kinship involves inheritance, therefore spiritual kinship does so even more. Again, the pope cannot allow anyone to marry his sister, they say, and therefore he cannot allow anyone to marry a girl whom his father or mother held over the baptismal font. Again, physical kinship extending in every direction, to the fifth degree, prevents marriage, and therefore, they say, spiritual kinship does the same (which is not in fact the case). Again, since at birth no one has more than two parents, a male and a female, therefore, they say, at one's spiritual

* * * * *

222 Presumably Luther's followers. In his annotation on 1 Cor 7:39 LB VI 696A–7D, Erasmus had given numerous precise examples of popes reversing or modifying the rulings of their predecessors on marriage law.

rebirth no more than two should be present; nowadays, in fact, one may have as many as desired – but all are bound by this theoretical kinship.

Second, if we are to give so much importance to this symbolic kinship, it would be more appropriate to apply it to a teacher of the gospel rather than to a person performing baptism. Rebirth is really brought about less by baptism than by teaching, for this is what Paul writes to those whom he had not baptized, but to whom he had preached the gospel: 'My little children, to whom I give second birth until Christ is formed in you.'[223] And, elsewhere: 'For in Christ Jesus I have begotten you through the gospel.' He calls Onesimus his son, whom he had 'begotten in his bonds,' obviously by means of his teaching. In those days the apostles' assistants generally performed baptisms. The word of God is the seed by which humanity is reborn, and thus spiritual kinship is established between all who listen to the same evangelist – between pupil and teacher, between a husband and the wife he has converted. In my opinion, those who are called catechists have more right to be called fathers than the godparents, provided that they live up to their name. Yet it was more or less legal for catechists to marry their pupils, had not Boniface VIII interpreted something that was 'hardly' true as, none the less, true without qualification.[224] This, despite the fact that saying, 'I can hardly believe it,' really means that you do not believe it, and therefore that something that is 'hardly' an impediment could be interpreted, in favour of matrimony, to mean that catechizing is not a sufficient impediment to matrimony.

But anyway, where are the catechists nowadays when infants receive baptism? The sponsors, called godparents, seem now to have taken over the role of sureties, or to have taken over both parts, replying on behalf of the infant, 'I believe . . .' St Dionysius makes it clear that this is the correct procedure, in his *Ecclesiastical Hierarchy*.[225] However, what role do godparents now play at baptism beyond a pale imitation of the ancient custom? They make solemn promises for the future, but what need is there for godparents

* * * * *

223 Gal 4:9, followed by 1 Cor 4:15 and a reference to Philem 10
224 *Liber sextus decretalium* 4.3.2 CIC 2 1068; Boniface VIII (pope 1294–1303) makes this impediment to marriage prohibitive but not diriment.
225 Pseudo-Dionysius *De ecclesiastica hierarchia* 2.2.1–7 PG 3 393–5. St Augustine echoes this view in a sermon quoted by Gratian *Decretum, De cons* D 4 c 105. The sense is that the godparents now play the role of the catechist in standing surety for the beliefs of the candidate for baptism. In the early church formal catechesis, primarily the responsibility of the bishops, was directed mainly to pre-baptismal adults. The instruction of children was left to Christian parents. See NCE III 225–6 and 234.

when parents and priests are bound to do this by virtue of their position? Since, therefore, modern practice is no more than a relic of an ancient custom, I do not see any serious reason why the consciences of partners in marriage should be troubled by these extra worries. Anything that can dissolve a marriage lawfully contracted between lawful partners should of necessity be serious indeed, especially since the Lord says, 'Those whom God has joined, let no man put asunder.'[226]

I hear you object that the pope can make certain persons ineligible, and that God has not truly joined those who have contracted marriage in defiance of the church's rulings; moreover, that it is useful to establish different ways of spreading fellowship among Christians. Of course I do not reject these arguments, but I am afraid that they will undermine God's law if they should fall in with ungodly shepherds of the church. But for the moment I am content to say that any rule established by human authority can by the same means be changed for the benefit of the Christian community.

Finally, if spiritual kinship is more important than physical kinship, in which the pope will not relax the rules governing degrees of consanguinity, he should not have done so in the former. If it is less important, this weakens the arguments that are so often rehearsed for us, and not only on this matter. For example, there would seem still less reason to establish kinship through the anointing of the forehead in confirmation. In baptism we are reborn, but at confirmation it is as though we are receiving a donative before we take up arms against the enemy,[227] and in this there is no symbolic birth. I do not intend to undermine the decrees by this discussion, but rather to determine whether the experts' arguments have enough weight to invalidate so important an institution. In fact they do proffer explanations as to why spiritual kinship does not arise from the other sacraments, of which one may say that they are plausible but far from conclusive.

I feel the same about 'public propriety,' which arises from a symbolic version of affinity. For since marriage was established by divine law, I do not see why it should be prohibited because of scandal arising from this artificial type of affinity. My reasoning is similar concerning interdict and unlawful days:[228] since these arise from human decisions, they can be changed by human decision, if it is conducive to the common good. The case of interdict

* * * * *

226 Matt 19:6
227 The donative was a gift distributed on special occasions to Roman soldiers by the emperor; Erasmus echoes the terminology of his *Enchiridion*.
228 That is, occasions on which marriage could not be performed; papal interdicts usually contained this prohibition. On unlawful days, see n150 above.

does not arise so frequently, but these days a valid marriage contract can be made on an unlawful day, and only the ceremony is prohibited.

In adoption there is a symbolic representation of both consanguinity and affinity, as between the adopted child and the adoptive mother. Similarly, there is symbolic consanguinity between the adopted child and his new father's natural son, and between the adoptive father and his adopted son's wife, and vice versa. Imperial law attributes such importance to this that in the first and last case, even when the adoption has been ended, the prohibition against marriage remains; the reason given is the special deference that adoption creates.[229] However, in the case of fictive kinship in the indirect line, the ending of the adoption restores the right to marry.

Here again are a number of rules that could be relaxed by papal indulgence without any threat to true religion. For if marriage is a sacrament of the church and is made by a declaration using words in the present tense, it has to be considered whether a human ruler has the right to nullify this contract on the ground of symbolic consanguinity or affinity, or of a hypothetical respect for decency. Whom should we respect more than our teachers? And yet respect for them does not prevent marriage. Youth must respect age, by divine command, according to Leviticus 19[:32]: 'Stand up in the presence of grey hairs, honour the persons of the aged, and fear the Lord your God.' The relationship between young and old is, in theory, like that between children and parents, and yet the church accepts marriages between septuagenarians and girls scarcely in their teens, despite the offensive spectacle of a grandfather apparently wedding his own granddaughter, or a girl her aged father. There would be far fewer problems with contracts of marriage if the limits of prohibition were within those prescribed by the Lord in Leviticus 18, whether between relatives by blood or by marriage.

Someone may say that these restrictions are a legal matter, and have effect only because the church sanctions them. They seem to me, however, to arise largely from moral considerations. A natural instinct impels us to respect those persons whom we are for that very reason forbidden to marry. However, there is a view that the pope can pronounce certain people ineligible to marry (a power denied him in respect of the other sacraments) because marriage is a contract, and contracts are subject to human law. I agree that marriage is a contract, but it is a sacramental one; if it is correctly performed according to the prescriptions of divine law, what possible cause can there be to nullify it? I am not saying that the church had no power to restrict the

* * * * *

229 *Digesta* 23.2.14 and 55

right to marry or that those restrictions were wrong. I am suggesting, rather, that we need to consider whether it would be useful, in our own times, to ease troubled consciences by showing the sort of understanding that, in the past, led the church to impose restrictions, and thereby encouraged and fostered the people's spontaneous and urgent desire to practise chastity and charity.

The question of matrimony is made more complicated by the ruling that affinity, like consanguinity, can arise from any sexual liaison, since many such relationships, the result of furtive couplings, will remain concealed. The civil law takes the simpler line of recognizing no affinity unless established by lawful wedlock.[230] The dissolution of any union established according to God's decree is hateful. Moreover, if it is desired to extend respect for consanguinity or affinity beyond the bounds established by God's law, let this be considered an admirable end in itself, without undermining God's decree. If we remain within his law, there will be no need to invoke interdict or regulation or local custom to dissolve a marriage.

Many of the pitfalls surrounding matrimony would be avoided by abolishing the category of things 'that prevent a contract being made but do not dissolve an established contract.'[231] If a contract cannot be dissolved, how can we forbid its being made? Or, if an impediment is so powerful that it can make people ineligible to marry, it should also nullify a contract between them. At the moment, taking holy orders, even as a subdeacon, invalidates any subsequent contract of marriage. If orders are taken afterwards, the marriage is neither dissolved nor maintained but remains a half-marriage: the man has no wife, but the woman is neither spinster nor wife and, through no fault of her own, is trapped within an ignominious and unblessed marriage. If celibacy is a natural appurtenance of priesthood and the other orders, it would be easy either to dissolve the contract of marriage and give the woman her freedom, or to remove the man from holy orders. In the past priests could be turned back into laymen, and it still happens, I hear, among the Greeks if a priest is convicted of a crime.[232] If the Roman

* * * * *

230 Cf 270 above, and n192.
231 Those few impediments, such as simple vows, that are considered prohibitive but not diriment. The subsequent example is based on Aquinas *Supplementum* q 53 art 4.
232 The custom in the eastern church dated back to the sixth-century *Novellae* of Justinian, 113.20–1. In the western church, a decree of Alexander III (*Decretales Gregorii* IX 1.11.4 CIC 2 118; c 1160) ordered the degradation of criminal priests only if their crime were public; otherwise, they were to undergo condign penance and be denied further preferment.

pontiff can, for the reasons already stated, make people ineligible to consent to matrimony, he can also make them ineligible to receive the imprint of holy orders; as this cannot be undone once it has been done, it should at least be possible to prevent it being done in the first place. Again, just as a second marriage is considered invalid on the ground that making one contract removes one's freedom to consent to another, so a man who has been married has lost the right to make a second contract and thus, it seems, cannot consent to ordination. I am putting forward these ideas only for the sake of argument.

Why, nowadays, are only priests and monks (from whom the right to marry is withdrawn) allowed a form of consent which, though it is of no use to anyone, is held to have an effect on other people's marriages on the ground of public propriety? The rigour of the civil laws could be used like the hatchet of Tenes[233] to cut out most of the problems by removing from our midst someone who makes mock both of matrimony and of the church by entering the priesthood after marrying a wife. He wrongs the poor woman and behaves insultingly and impiously towards the church when by a sacrilegious trick he steals the sacrament of orders. Simple theft is punished by death, but this crime is worse than any theft. In all this the good reputation of holy orders is given as justification, but nothing is said of the damage done to matrimony: what kind of reputation will holy orders acquire, if room is left to slither into them by evil tricks?

There is another distinction whose removal would greatly simplify the problems of matrimony. The taking of monastic vows dissolves a ratified marriage, but not if it has been consummated.[234] The church could decide, in accordance with the gospel decree, that nothing may dissolve a marriage, ratified or consummated, except death or adultery. If marriage was established by divine law and can be sealed by a form of consent in the present tense, how can it be dissolved by mere mortals making a verbal distinction between 'ratified' and 'consummated,' or between a simple vow and a solemn vow? If the popes can make people within certain degrees of

* * * * *

233 *Adagia* I ix 29, a proverbially effective instrument for settling intractable disputes, and appropriate here since its owner, King Tenes, sometimes used it to execute adulterers. Erasmus is here attacking those who enter orders to escape from marriage; as we have seen (n180 above), he had no objection to married priests.

234 Cf Aquinas *Supplementum* qq 61–2. A 'ratified marriage' (*matrimonium ratum*) is made when two baptized persons exchange consent in a valid marriage ceremony; the unconsummated union is approved by the church as a valid sacramental covenant.

kinship ineligible to marry, they can also make those who marry ineligible to make a vow without the consent of their spouse. Furthermore, that consent would have to be approved by their bishop, and only reluctantly accepted, in these particularly uncertain times, because experience may show that such divorces will rarely turn out well.

The excuse for this regulation is that it gives support to the religious orders, which the church rightly supported in days gone by when in their way of life the nobility and the people were beginning to slip back into paganism, and it seemed that only among monks and nuns was the gospel maintained in full vigour. How I wish that we could make the same boast today! But even at that time, when the piety of the monks was most deserving of support, there is no record of a concession which allowed just anyone to desert his hapless wife and plunge into the monastic fraternity.[235] Care is taken to ensure that the taking of monastic vows does not harm the novice's creditors, though the debt owed to a spouse is more sacred than any other contract. If the monk is returned to his wife, there is no harm done; if he stays, the girl will suffer, for the reasons cited earlier. I shall go no further into this business, to avoid delaying the reader unnecessarily. I am merely showing what the church might do and what the present circumstances demand. For the rest, I defer to the judgment of those who stand at the helm of the church.

Since many very complex problems are caused by vows, it would be a service to all Christians to advise them to abstain from all unnecessary and indeed useless vows. If you are keen to visit Jerusalem or Compostella,[236] you may gratify your whim, but there is no need to include a vow in your plans. If something prevents you, remember that something that is far from essential must always give way to what is more vital to your salvation and closer to Christ's teaching. If you have doubts about this, you are free to consult your bishop, your parish priest, or some other grave and learned man. If you have no doubts, follow your own judgment, so long as your conscience is clear. A Christian vow must be quite different from those pagan vows whereby people promised a tenth of their goods to Hercules if he

* * * * *

235 Erasmus uses the term *contubernium*, literally, 'tent-companionship.' It was used in Roman law (*Digesta* 40.4.59) of 'marriage' between slaves, and ironically (eg Petronius 92.4) to mean 'concubinage.' Doubtless Erasmus was aware of this range of meaning!
236 With Rome itself, the most important centres of pilgrimage, mentioned in Erasmus' satires on the topic *De votis temere susceptis* ('Rash Vows') CWE 39 37–9 and *Peregrinatio religionis ergo* ('A Pilgrimage for Religion's Sake') CWE 40 619–74.

would boost the family fortunes, or pimps made some vow to Venus if she would increase their takings, and so on and so forth. Jephthah's vow should not be taken as an example either.[237] Other Jewish vows either related to their phantom Law, or were easy to perform, or could be revoked.

What is more, any vow must be freely made and carefully considered. What kind of vows, then, are those that are wrung out of us, during illness, at sea, or in battle, by the fear of death or some other mental affliction verging on insanity? In these circumstances a true Christian's vow should have nothing in view but eternal salvation. If it is clear that a vow will lead less surely towards that goal than something else, then the less certain path to salvation must surely be abandoned for the better one. I am talking about common vows, which, in my opinion, it is safest not to make at all or, if they are made in a rash moment, to consider null and void. No one should think that I would cling to this view unless it should gain the full backing of the church, which has the power to do what I have proposed – if it wishes.

The case of the vow of continence is far from simple.[238] Some deny that a monk breaks his vow if he fornicates (unless he has got married!), because a vow is a renunciation of something previously permitted to you, and it cannot really be called a vow if someone promises never to be a whoremonger. However, leaving aside these somewhat irrelevant thoughts: the cause of matrimony would be greatly advanced if the church were to decree that a vow of chastity should be invalid unless ratified by a bishop, who must be very exacting on this score. Also there need not be so sharp a distinction between a simple vow and a solemn vow. If a simple vow has been taken first, the marriage is halved, whereas if a solemn vow is taken, even afterwards, it dissolves a legally valid marriage. The same penalty should be inflicted, in either case, on someone who wrongs his wife by taking orders or professing monastic vows, and it should be considered more of a scandal if a husband becomes a priest or a monk than if he returns to his wife, to whom he owes a lifetime of companionship, unless the lady gives her consent freely and after due consideration. Paul had 'begotten Onesimus

* * * * *

237 Judg 11:30–40; his imprudent vow compelled him to sacrifice his daughter.
238 For Erasmus' strictures on such vows and the controversy over them, see Rummel *Catholic Critics* I 182 and II 74–8, and Telle 88–94. The personal tenor of much of this discussion is suggested by its resemblance to passages in the autobiographical Ep 447, eg lines 610–21 and 709–45. On the contemporary background and the Pauline foundation of Erasmus' views, see Screech 69–71.

in his bonds,'[239] and no vow could be more sacred than that. He served the apostle Paul when he was enchained for the gospel's sake, and no service could be more holy. None the less, Paul sent him back to his master Philemon. And yet it is supposed to be impious if a wife is sent back to her husband? For it is harder if a wife makes a vow against her husband's will than vice versa, since authority remains with the husband. It all seems even worse if one considers present conditions in most of our monasteries and nunneries, and how few of the inmates live the true monastic life! People were always permitted to come together and profess the gospel against the will of parents and husbands; even slaves were allowed to do so. However, the Apostle did not allow a Christian slave to leave his pagan master or a Christian wife to desert an idolatrous husband.[240] And yet, apparently, we deem it ungodly to compel a monk or a priest to return to his Christian wife.

Now I can almost hear someone say, 'Parents and spouses can have no sway over someone who has been inspired by the Holy Spirit to dedicate himself entirely to God.' So what happens at baptism? Is half the child dedicated to God and the other half to the devil? How I wish that all who take monastic vows were inspired by the Holy Spirit! No one would have the right to stand in their way, even if they were throwing themselves into the river! But it is well known that many are inspired by a spirit of folly, irresponsibility, madness, ambition, avarice, idleness, lust, and self-indulgence. Certainly those who in secret or against the will of their parents (whom God's law commands us to obey)[241] devote themselves to a way of life from which they cannot subsequently extricate themselves, seem more likely to be inspired by an evil spirit, which drives them into the arms of the monks despite the protests of their doubtless devout and honourable parents. Papal decrees give parents the right to withdraw their son from a monastery if he is under twelve.[242] That was a good rule in its time, but

* * * * *

239 Philem 10
240 See Paul's letter to Philemon and 1 Cor 7:13 respectively.
241 Eph 6:1; cf Exod 20:12 etc.
242 Gratian *Decretum* pars 2 c 20 qq 1–2, quoting councils of the seventh and ninth centuries. These decisions are endorsed by the *Decretales Gregorii* IX 3.31.1 and the age raised to eighteen in certain cases (3.31.6), but another conciliar ruling (3.31.2 CIC 2 569) allowed parents only one year in which to extract their children, even those under age. In Epp 447:712 and 858:523–5 Erasmus suggests that thirty would be a suitable age for the decision. Luther thought that seventy or eighty might be about right (*De votis monasticis*, Telle 143).

now I think it would be better to extend this parental right to the age of twenty-five. There might be fewer monks, perhaps, but they would be better monks.

In days gone by, a son who was still legally subject to his father[243] was not free to be baptized secretly, if his parents were available to give their consent, and baptism did not free him from his duty to obey his father, unless he were asked to commit some act of obvious impiety. For example, the son was obliged, if asked, to bring his father the incense to offer to Jupiter, although he was also obliged, if asked, not to perform the sacrifice himself. But God desired that the bonds of matrimony should be closer than those between father and son: 'For this reason a man shall leave his father and mother and cleave to his wife.'[244] Therefore I do not think it would be an affront to true religion if the church were to decree that a solemn vow should not deprive a husband of his bride. The husband will still have someone to obey, someone to whom he owes obedience; he will achieve poverty, if he gives his possessions to the poor and believes that his property belongs to the community, not to himself. I admit that chastity is only partly under his control, but this little drawback should be weighed against the many other good works he can perform: visiting the sick, aiding the poor, distributing alms, attending sermons, educating his children, governing his household, preparing with his own hands what he will give to the needy.[245] Nowadays such duties are almost never performed by monks and nuns, who are most appreciated for their show of holiness – although in the beginning Jerome, Ambrose, and Cyprian prescribed such duties for the virgins dedicated to

* * * * *

243 On the power of *patria potestas* under Roman law, cf n111 above. It was weakened under the Christian emperors; eg, Justinian (*Novellae* 81) frees officeholders and bishops from *patria potestas*. On such cases, cf Augustine (Ep 75 [250]) to Auxilius, quoted by Gratian pars 2 c 24 q 3 c 1.
244 Gen 2:24; Matt 19:5
245 Erasmus suggests that the monastic vows of obedience, poverty, and chastity can be fulfilled more satisfactorily within marriage than in a monastery, though he is less outspoken on chastity here than in the *Encomium matrimonii* CWE 25 137. See also Ep 858, a preface to the *Enchiridion* (CWE 66 18), in which Erasmus dismisses those who call his advocacy of near-celibacy within marriage 'Marcionite' (referring to a heretical ascetic sect). St Jerome's tract *Adversus Iovinianum* set out to refute the idea that the married state was equal to that of virginity; he was supported by Augustine in *De bono coniugali* and *De sancta virginitate*. See also Telle passim for a hostile analysis of Erasmus' views; he suggests (43–8) that the model for this 'marital celibacy' might be Thomas More.

God.[246] I am not attempting to equate monks with married people in every respect, but I wanted to point out, without detriment to the religious life, some things that are more appropriate to marriage, which is our subject here.

Next, there is the question of criminality, of various types, and once again a host of problems arises. Things might be easier if we were told to tolerate certain less serious crimes, such as a man fornicating with his future wife before the marriage. However, if the crime were very serious, either the civil law would free one partner by executing the other, or the innocent party would be released completely from the marriage by having the partner (who has deserved death) considered dead – unless the innocent partner actually objected to being separated from the guilty. It is reasonable not to separate those who are partners in crime, as in adultery, which nowadays we treat as a joke, although in the ancient world no crime attracted a harsher penalty. A thief who came by night and broke into another's house was not to be killed, unless caught in possession of a weapon.[247] In short, the law allowed a private individual to use the sword only in two circumstances – when violence had to be countered, or when a husband caught an adulterer in the act, though not with impunity unless he killed both of them; having done the deed, he risked conviction for murder, unless he could prove to the court, with witnesses and evidence, that he had killed both of them after catching them in the very act. Allowance was made for a husband's outrage, but not indiscriminately.[248]

* * * * *

246 Cf the *Vita Hieronymi* CWE 61 29, where Erasmus contrasts in detail monastic life in the fifth century (as he imagines it to have been) with its degenerate modern descendant; see also the preface to the *Enchiridion* (Ep 858) CWE 66 21–2, and Telle 71–8 and 123. For examples of the Fathers' prescriptions, see Jerome Ep 108 (*Ad Eustochium*) PL 22 896–8; Cyprian *De habitu virginum*; and Ambrose *De virginibus ad Marcellinam sororem*.

247 Gaius *Institutes* 3.189, relaxed by *Institutiones* 4.1.5. However, a canon of the *Decretales Gregorii* IX 5.12.3 CIC 2 794, based on St Augustine, lifted the charge of murder from the killer of a nocturnal thief, on the authority of Exod 22:3 and of the ancient Roman law (by night it was considered impossible to distinguish between a mere thief and a potential assassin).

248 Erasmus also contrasts the Roman penalties for theft and adultery, and deplores modern laxity towards the latter, in the *Encomium matrimonii* CWE 25 133–4 and in the *Institutio principis christiani* CWE 27 269. On the severe *lex Iulia de adulteriis coercendis* passed by Augustus, see Tacitus *Annals* 3.24; *Institutiones* 4.18.4; and especially *Digesta* 48.5.1–45. The relatively mild medieval sanctions against adulterers are tabulated in the *Decretales Gregorii* IX 5.16 CIC 805–7.

The law of Moses lays down that a woman taken in adultery is to be stoned by the people;[249] adultery was also a capital offence for the Greeks[250] and Romans. Of course, I do not disapprove of the church's clemency in preferring repentance to death for the malefactor. However, it seems a perverse kind of clemency when the civil laws will nail to the cross an ordinary thief, even a first offender,[251] but consider undeserving of punishment someone who is tainted by a score of adulteries. Once, it is true, the shepherds of the church used to prescribe penalties for malefactors, and for the church's sake the princes often connived at certain excesses, but the church's justice, however severe, never wielded the sword for the civil power. The church heals the soul; the bodies of criminals are the law's concern, and if it spares the adulterer but the wife cannot bring herself to live with him, it seems not unreasonable that he should be considered dead to her (since he deserves death) and that the innocent party should be set free. However, I realize that our predecessors produced some very weighty arguments in drawing up the rulings on matrimony that apply at present. Thus I have made these points only for the sake of argument.

As for conditions:[252] I have already said that no one could seriously argue that a contract containing an impossible condition will make a valid marriage, for example, 'If you are a virgin I take you as my wife,' when you know that she has been seduced and has had a child. Similarly, I do not see why a condition like the following should be thought dishonourable: 'I take you in matrimony, if I find that you are a virgin'; if the girl has a guilty conscience, she must not deceive a man whose concern is honourable. In Deuteronomy 22[:13–21], for example, severe punishment is prescribed for a man who has married a girl as a virgin and then pretends to find out that she is not. If guilty, he is beaten as well as being fined. But the punishment is much harsher for a bride who has not kept herself for her husband: she is taken outside the city walls and stoned by the people.

These days, however, there is a more serious reason why a bridegroom might make a fuss about the girl's virginity, because if, even unwittingly,

* * * * *

249 Deut 22:24
250 As Erasmus mentioned earlier (see 223, and n24), Plato and Aristotle prescribed for adulterers *atimia*, public disgrace and the loss of civil rights, but according to Plutarch *Solon* 23.90F, at one time an adulterer caught in the act could be killed out of hand.
251 Erasmus uses ironically a Greek adjective applied to a bride by Theopompus *Comicus* 94.
252 The general question is expounded in the *Decretales Gregorii* IX 4.5 CIC 2 682–4; a particular case similar to those here is described ibidem 2.24.25 CIC 2 368–9.

he has married a woman who is not a virgin, he will be barred from the priesthood as a digamist. If every contract stipulated virginity, there would probably be husbands demanding their money back every day, since it is no less difficult to prove than to preserve, but it is the law's permissiveness that has opened the way to such corruption. Thus, if it is desirable to avoid such obnoxious inquiries, it should at least be no obstacle to the priesthood that a man has unknowingly married an unchaste woman. In this case Paul's authority[253] is not conclusive for us, even if a man has knowingly married an unchaste woman, or if he has remarried after his first wife's death, for the simple reason that in the same statement the Apostle includes many other things that do not nowadays remove a man from the priesthood.

Certainly natural reason does not reject the idea that a contract of marriage can be dissolved if one of the partners accepts a condition so vital that, had he or she not concealed a breach of that condition, the marriage would in all likelihood not have taken place; for example, if a beggar pretended to be a millionaire's son, if the child of an incestuous union pretended to be a scion of some noble house, or if a victim of leprosy, epilepsy, or the so-called Neapolitan pox[254] pretended to be in perfect health. The partner who imposed the condition before giving consent should be released from the contract, and the other, who has tainted the sacrament with deceit, should be punished. A heavier penalty is required for those who pervert the sacred, such as those who use sacramental confession for pimping, or sorcerers who pervert the Eucharist. When deception is combined with impiety, it not only harms individuals but brings the church of God into disrepute. In fact, even if the condition were not made explicit, none the less one of the parties to the match would still be considered to have been deceived in his or her expectation. It would seem only just to destroy a contract entered into under false pretences if the injured party will not overlook the deception, and especially if it is clear that the other party engineered the whole thing. Examples abound in popular tales, and they are not all fictitious. If consent depends on a condition that is not fulfilled, there can be no consent.

* * * * *

253 See 1 Tim 3:1–13. Erasmus returns 298 below to this passage on the qualities required in a bishop.
254 Syphilis, called 'le mal de Naples' by the French and the 'French pox' by most other nations, was supposedly introduced to Europe by Columbus' returning sailors and spread by the French army returning from its invasion of Naples in 1494–5. For a full discussion and bibliography, see Margolin 501–2 n185. Cf n370 below.

It is truly said by the lawyers that nothing is less compatible with consent than error; where there is error there is no consent. But although a case of mistaken identity releases the person who has been deceived, errors over quality or fortune do not.[255] But what if such an error causes greater problems than a case of mistaken identity? It might be less distressing to marry John, who you thought was Peter, than to marry a lunatic, a leper, or an epileptic whom you believed to be healthy. People planning to get married will of course take every precaution against deception. But in matters of such moment, and where every trick cannot be foreseen, the pope's authority could give some help to the party who has been deceived by pronouncing such marriages invalid, and so could the civil laws by ensuring, rigorously, that no one should go unpunished for trifling with matrimony. Marriage was not instituted to permit innocence to be ensnared in deceit but to join one partner to another for their mutual benefit. It is not marriage but capture when one partner lays hands on the prey he was hunting, while the other, ensnared, can only weep; or would you prefer to call this a kind of rape? Yet today quite a few are considered clever and resourceful for the very fact that they constantly move around, marrying first one, then another, up to a dozen maybe, and make their living from it. These godless impostors and plagues of mankind should be hoisted on crosses.

Now, I think that marriage would be less open to manipulation if marital crime were to be punished in another way. At the moment, if the bridegroom has seduced the bride's sister, the marriage is simply dissolved (this seems to be, in fact, a case of affinity).[256] There should be another way to prevent him enjoying the fruits of his wickedness while allowing a marriage contracted by free and lawful consent to stand. It would be easy to put a stop to such dissolutions if both parties were to be freed, as in a crime punished by execution the civil law frees the other partner. In this and many other cases the authority of the popes could pronounce people capable or incapable of marriage: thus either the contract would be null and void, or its terms would be accepted in their entirety, and both partners equally bound by them or released from them.

* * * * *

255 Cf Gratian *Decretum* pars 2 c 29 q 1 cc 2–4; Lombard *Sententiae* book 4 dist 30 c 1; and *Decretales Gregorii* IX 4.1.26 CIC 670–1. In the last case some doubt is expressed over the possibility of annulling a consummated 'marriage' with someone masquerading as 'John.'
256 Cf Gratian *Decretum* pars 2 c 32 q 7 cc 21 and 23, and particularly Aquinas *Supplementum* q 58 art 4.

Quite rightly, the laws of the church condemn clandestine marriages,[257] but I wish that it would condemn them these days so clearly that any marriage contract made in secret should be considered no contract, unless confirmed by the families and by a solemn undertaking on both sides, such as used to be made before the censors in Roman times, accompanied by the swearing of an oath, as I outlined earlier.[258] I do not think that there are any examples in Holy Writ of dependent children or wards contracting secret marriages which remained valid against the wishes of those in authority over them.[259] At one time parents had the power of life and death over their children, and although it is unfair that parents should force their children into celibacy after puberty, some holy Doctors, including Ambrose,[260] think it fair that parents should have the right to choose from among a number of suitors. If parents are so inhuman as to treat their children like slaves or cattle, and either refuse to give any thought to their marriage or, for their own reasons, impose on them husbands or wives who are plainly unsuitable, then certain people could be nominated to help the children. Uncles, grandparents, state officials, bishops, for example, could be entrusted with this duty.

Seeing that imperial law protected slaves who were too harshly treated by their masters or subjected to insult and abuse,[261] is it not much more necessary to protect children and minors from the wickedness of parents, tutors, and guardians? Anyone who seeks to gain advantage at his children's expense is no longer a parent but a tyrant. Is it really any wonder that Christian morality has sunk so low, when you may come across people today who, horrible to relate, prostitute their own children for sordid gain? Guardians and trustees are even less reliable. In Britain the sons of noblemen whose fathers have died are put in the charge of guardians. This right is bought or obtained from the king. Whenever this power falls into the hands of a different family, the property of the ward is often managed in such a way that, unless he marries the wife chosen for him by his guardian, he will get precious little return from his acres; the period of tutelage lasts until the twenty-second year. But these are considered proper marriages, although the civil law does insist that tutors or guardians cannot marry the wards

* * * * *

257 See n130 above.
258 The censors were Roman magistrates concerned mainly with social affairs; see 223 above.
259 Cf the examples 246 above.
260 *De Abraham* 1.9.91 PL 14 476B
261 Eg Gaius *Institutes* 1.53; *Institutiones* 1.8.2

entrusted to their care, and neither can their children (though canon law does not forbid this).[262]

Thus neither guardians nor parents should have the authority to impose a spouse on unwilling children or wards; none the less, the reins should not be so far relaxed, at this somewhat reckless age, that they should be allowed to contract marriages – that is, take a sacrament of the church – in secret, or rashly, under the influence of drink or sorcery, by saying the right three words while in the act of coupling. How I wish that the old sense of mutual obligation between parents and children were still alive, when parents looked after their children's interests as if they were their own, and children never mistrusted their parents' intentions. When Paul writes of the virgin, he gives all power to the father. Of the widow, he says, 'Let her marry whom she wishes, but in the Lord.' He does not say that a virgin may marry whom she wishes, but 'If a virgin marries, she has done no wrong.'[263] It is as though he were allowing virgins to marry even against their parents' wishes, but not allowing them the choice of a husband.

However, it seems most equitable that such an important step should not be taken without the consent of those whom it exposes to most risk. That is why forced marriages are to be condemned. If young men or young women object violently to the partners whom their parents wish to thrust upon them, they must not be forced to comply with their parents' wishes immediately, but must be given time to consider, to see whether this youthful rebelliousness can be overcome, and matters be settled in a rational way. But if they persist, and their inclinations are not entirely unreasonable, then affectionate parents may be persuaded to yield a little of their authority, as in the comedy, when Clitipho rejects the girls his mother has found for him, and his father lets him marry the girl of his choice.[264] There must be a middle way whereby parental authority is not completely undermined, nor a child's freedom of action completely given up. The consent of the contracting parties must prevail and triumph – but that consent must be genuine, free, and lawful, especially in a matter that not only is the most complex of all, but also is irremediable if anything goes wrong.

Can consent be freely given where fear plays a role, especially when it affects a youth of tender years or a girl handicapped by both her youth and her sex? Withdrawal of the family's support will be a powerful weapon

* * * * *

262 For the Roman law, see Gaius *Institutes* 1.115.
263 See 1 Cor 7:36–8 (on paternal authority); the quotations are from 1 Cor 7:39 and 28 respectively.
264 The comedy is Terence's *Heautontimorumenos*.

against them; some are more afraid for their reputation than for their virtue. Parents may use force, a thrashing even, to repress youthful wantonness, but when it comes to marriage, compulsion must always yield to persuasion. Similarly if, under the influence of a bawd, of wine (the father of madness), of lustful caresses, of the night (the enemy of honour), of magic incantations,[265] the three words are exchanged between virtual children, can there be any true consent, since their every sense is reeling and their minds are gripped by the threefold madness of drink, lust, and sorcery? A valid contract cannot be made with someone who is insane, or has not yet reached puberty or the legal age. Yet a treaty of marriage, the most important of all, is legally valid even if it is made at an age when otherwise the law intervenes, even in minor contracts, because of the child's inexperience and lack of judgment. When drunkenness rules, it is worse than a mere fit of madness, in that sometimes constant drunkenness leads to permanent insanity. Anger is called a brief madness;[266] a long sleep may barely clear a drinker's head.

In days gone by, the judge used to ask, 'On your conscience, are you satisfied that you have a wife?'[267] Can there be any question of conscience, when your mind is bewitched in more ways than one? To argue with a drunkard is, as the proverbs put it, like talking to yourself,[268] and although a lad who makes a drunken marriage with a drunken girl may in fact be talking to someone else, if you were to wake him up and ask him what he had said or done he would remember very little. Words have no weight if they are spoken by someone of unsound mind, unless it is obviously during a few moments of lucidity. Words forced out by fear are considered invalid because the mind is neither free nor in control; why then should they be valid if spoken in a bout of madness coupled with violence? For to use these arts to take over the minds of girls and young men is not merely to trick them, but to do them violence. I have read of people whom torture could not subdue being conquered in the end by sensual pleasures. Some girls are taught these tricks to help them find a rich husband, and young men use them to hunt down large dowries. Should these devices fail, magic incantations and sorcery are brought to bear.

How many young men of breeding and wealth have I seen trapped by girls whose reputations were as low as their income! Imagine their parents'

* * * * *

265 Erasmus uses the grecism *epagoge*, meaning in Greek an invocation drawing down a god but in Latin merely a rhetorical device.
266 Cf Horace *Epistles* 1.2.62.
267 Cf 223 above.
268 Cf Publilius Syrus *Sententiae* 12.

grief, their family's sorrow! They would try separating them, with the groom banished to France, the bride to Holland. The female might be pushed into a convent, with poison at hand if she refused. The man, to keep the rich pickings from the church he used to enjoy, would wait for news of his new bride's death, but she might escape and pursue him; his parents would disinherit him. In short, everything would be tried – in vain. The marriage was indissoluble. Are the Lord's words appropriate to a marriage like this: 'What God has joined, let no man put asunder'?[269] Would it not be better to say, What the devil, through his servants, has joined, let God, through his servants, put asunder? The Roman pontiff cannot invalidate a statement of consent between two individuals legally entitled to make one. Very well, but he can, unless I am mistaken, declare that such consent is not lawful, nor indeed the individuals legally entitled to give it, if they are not in their right mind. If the Roman pontiff can make people joined by spiritual kinship ineligible to marry, I should be surprised if he could not make these deluded people ineligible to make contracts. Not only should the marriage be considered invalid, but punishment should be inflicted on those who use these black arts to cement such marriages.

If you were to say, Let them learn from their misfortune to be more careful, I would agree – if people were permitted to exchange or sell back their wives. But once this die has come up with the wrong number, no trick can change it. The civil laws are not slow to give assistance to wards and minors, restoring the status quo if a contract is injurious to the ward, or letting it stand if it is to his advantage.[270] They make allowance for youth, too easy to trick, and punish those who set traps for the innocence they should protect. Should not the church's laws be yet more compassionate than the civil laws?

All these controversies – over the form of words in the present and future tense, over valid and consummated marriages, over signs, nods, and letters – could in large measure be resolved if the church's leaders could bring themselves to decree that no marriage would be legally valid unless it were made before specially appointed magistrates and in the presence of witnesses. Each party, sober and free from constraint, would agree to the marriage using an unambiguous form of words that would be written down and preserved. As for dealings in secret: if intercourse were involved, it would be considered fornication, and if consent had been given using no recognized form of words, it would be considered mere words. There

* * * * *

269 Matt 19:6. It is not known whether Erasmus had some specific case in mind here.
270 Eg *Institutiones* 3.14.1 and 4.7. For the image of the die, cf *Adagia* I iv 32.

would be no marriage until consent to matrimony had been given, using an approved form of words, before judges and witnesses, by two sober and independent people. The same conditions should apply, I think, to those who cannot speak but can signify their wishes by signs or nods.

In other contracts precautions are taken against fraud, enabling the agreement to be rescinded, but in this most lofty and sacred matter it helps to be a trickster, and innocence lies exposed to deceit. The crook profits from his villainy, and innocent youth is saddled with the loss. I have no doubt that the princes of the church would find more and better remedies than those I have suggested, if God filled their hearts with concern for a problem which is not, in my opinion, an unimportant one. I must repeat once more that it is not my intention to undermine in any way the rulings and customs established for the public benefit, but to use the wisdom of our predecessors to try to ensure stability and happiness in every marriage.

In pursuit of this goal, it would be particularly useful if the impediments, which are like traps, could be removed as far as is possible without harming true religion, and if we could adhere as closely as possible to the decrees of Holy Writ; if anything has to be added to the Holy Scriptures, it should aim above all to ensure that the contract of marriage is entirely clear and unambiguous. These days, as I said earlier, it has been made a great deal easier in some respects to make a contract of marriage, on grounds derived more from the lawyers' opinions than from Holy Writ; in other areas, where the rules might have been relaxed on the basis of Holy Writ, they have been tightened. For example, a man who has married a girl in good faith, thinking her a virgin, and who then discovers that she has been seduced in some furtive fornication, is considered a digamist. He is barred from priesthood, however keen his vocation, by this hypothetical digamy or, to put it rather better, by a quite blameless ignorance of things that a husband could neither foresee nor prevent. If it had happened before baptism, I suppose that he would also have to be ejected from the priesthood as a digamist, just as a first wife is laid to a man's charge, even if the marriage and her death occurred before his baptism, when he marries another after his baptism – a rule against which Jerome protested in vain.[271]

I admit that St Paul wishes a bishop to be 'a man of only one wife,'[272] because at that time he was obliged to earn the respect not only of Christians,

* * * * *

271 Jerome Ep 69 [83] (*Ad Oceanum*) PL 22 653–64, cited by Gratian in his discussion of this question, *Decretum* pars 1 D 26 cc 1–5. Gratian quotes Augustine and Ambrose in opposition to Jerome's more liberal view based on ethical and rational arguments similar to those of Erasmus.

272 1 Tim 3:2

but also of the pagans and Jews whom he was seeking to win to the gospel. At that time bishop, priest, and elder were the same thing;[273] thus, Paul's remarks on the bishop of those days have been extended to apply to all priests. For the safety of the gospel, they had to be irreproachable in every way, being exposed to the gaze of unbelievers as well as believers. What was a tiny band nine hundred years ago has grown so large, however, with teeming swarms of priests throughout the world, that there is now no danger that someone will find the gospel repugnant simply because a man is taken into holy orders who has knowingly been a widow's husband before – so long as everything else about him upholds the dignity of his orders.

These days, if you look at the majority of bishops, you will find that something more serious than a wife who was not a virgin could act as a stumbling-block to the people, if they were to judge the gospel's teaching by the bishops' example.[274] This is not to mention the effect on heretics, schismatics, Jews, and others who are strangers to Christ's name. Therefore, since the times have changed, the reason why Paul does not want the bishop to be twice married – that taking another wife is evidence of incontinence – has ceased to apply. Yet we still harp on just a few of Paul's words, 'a man of only one wife,' as if this were the only rule the Apostle laid down for the choice of a bishop. In fact, he goes on to demand that he should be 'irreproachable, sober, courteous, prudent, chaste, hospitable, a good teacher, not given to drinking or to brawling; forbearing, not litigious; no lover of money.' A little later: 'He must not be a neophyte, lest the sin of pride bring upon him the devil's judgment.' Paul demands much the same of bishops in his letter to Titus: 'For a bishop, as God's steward, must be free of all guilt, and be neither proud, irascible, bibulous, violent, nor a lover of money; he must be hospitable, kind, sober, just, holy, chaste, clinging to the true doctrine he has been taught, that he may be equipped to preach sound doctrine even to those who seek to contradict him.'[275]

Why, from the many 'headings' in the Apostle's 'ruling,'[276] is the little wife alone considered reprehensible, while the horde of harlots and

* * * * *

273 An argument derived from Jerome's letter (see n271 above) PL 22 656
274 Erasmus frequently deplores the worldliness of contemporary bishops; see eg passages in the *Moria*, *Julius exclusus*, and *Institutio principis christiani* CWE 27 137–40, 177, and 280.
275 1 Tim 3:2, 3, and 6, and Titus 1:7–9 respectively
276 Erasmus parodies the language of the papal decree. In fact Gratian, after dealing with the question of episcopal celibacy, does go on to illustrate, with reference to papal pronouncements, the necessity of the other qualities enumerated

congregations of concubines are not laid to his charge? If the only people admitted to the office of bishop or priest were those who had preserved their chastity intact, it would seem highly appropriate to combine the dignity of the priesthood with the honour of virginity in order to increase respect for the bishop in the community. Nowadays, however, chastity is not a prerequisite, but a second wife, or one who was not a virgin, is laid to their charge, and so rigorously that no allowance is made even for unavoidable ignorance. The digamist is not barred from the duties of priesthood for committing a crime; he has done no wrong in marrying a wife lawfully, and even deserves praise for respecting chaste and holy matrimony and bringing up children in a Christian way. So why is he barred? Presumably because among the people, who are always inclined towards slander, and even more among the enemies of the Christian name, anyone who marries again lays himself open to suspicions of incontinence. The bishop must guard not only against evil but against even the appearance of evil-doing, lest this teacher of the gospel philosophy, this steward of God's mysteries, this light placed on the candlestick to shine through the house,[277] should by some mischance become a stumbling-block for unbelievers or the weak in faith.

Now, this reasoning was acceptable in the days when absolute purity was required in a bishop. Nowadays only this least important element is a requirement, and many other things that would better befit a bishop are ignored. 'Anyone who lies with a harlot,' says the Apostle, 'is made one body with her.'[278] Someone who has unwisely married a woman who is not a virgin is now said to have shared his body with her, whereas someone who has slept with a host of harlots has not shared his body and, as if he were pure and wholesome ($\tau\acute{\epsilon}\lambda\epsilon\iota\sigma\varsigma$, the Greeks say), is appointed to four or, if he prefers, five bishoprics.[279]

If a man who has married a second wife is barred not for a crime but because of a trifling suspicion, or rather fear, among the people that he is incontinent (which also gave digamy a bad name among the pagans), what

* * * * *

in 1 Tim 3:23 (*Decretum* pars 1 DD 35–49). However, Erasmus has in mind here the precedents cited in the *Decretales Gregorii* IX 1.21 (*De bigamis non ordinandis*) CIC 2 146–8, especially chapter 6, which deals with the question of 'several concubines in succession.'

277 Cf Matt 5:15.

278 1 Cor 6:16

279 The Greek word means both 'unblemished, immaculate' and 'perfect, complete.' For another attack on episcopal pluralism see *Julius exclusus* CWE 27 183.

is it that disqualifies the man who married a widow? Should the prohibition in Moses' law of a priest marrying a widow or a woman not a virgin[280] be applied to someone who was not at the time contemplating the priesthood? Having two concubines did not stand in Augustine's way,[281] yet nowadays a wife who was once enjoyed by another, in secret and unbeknown to her future husband, can be laid to his charge. If we accept the Apostle's rigorous decree that bearing the yoke twice bars a man from a bishopric, how can we accept someone whose whole life has been defiled by all manner of vice? If Paul considers suitable for the priest's task someone who 'governs his household well, and has obedient and carefully educated children,'[282] why should someone who fulfils these conditions be considered unworthy of the very name of priest simply because he was mistaken when he chose his partner? The Roman pontiff will not temper the severity of the Apostle's ruling, even for those who seek to enter the priesthood for the holiest of reasons, unless they become monks; in that case they are considered dead to the world and, with a quick change of name, digamous Laurence is reborn as monogamous Thomas.[283]

If we really wanted to get it right, how could we ignore the first 'heading' of this law: 'The bishop must be irreproachable'?[284] Paul did not say, 'not convicted and condemned for a crime,' but ἀνέγκλητος, which means of such blameless character that no plausible suspicion of any misdeed could attach to him. If people say that digamy is visible to all and that a life of vice is not so obvious, what shall we say of the neophyte? A man can be elected a bishop even before being baptized, as happened to St Ambrose.[285] In fact, St Jerome tells us that in his day people apparently thought that being a neophyte was the holiest of all states.[286] The purity of Ambrose's life

* * * * *

280 Lev 21:7, 13–14
281 Augustine was faithful to his first mistress but, at his mother's insistence, put her away in order to be married; his bride being under age, however, he took another mistress in the meantime. The story is told in his *Confessions* 6.15.25. Cf *Enchiridion* CWE 66 103.
282 1 Tim 3:4
283 Cf Erasmus' satirical remarks on this subject in the colloquy *Virgo* μισόγαμος ('The Girl with No Interest in Marriage') CWE 39 291.
284 1 Tim 3:2
285 Ambrose, the provincial governor, was elected bishop of Milan by the warring Catholics and Arians while still a catechumen; he was baptized and ordained within a few days, and consecrated bishop on 7 December 374. Gratian *Decretum* pars 1 D 61 cc 8–11 discusses the precedent set by his elevation.
286 See Ep 69 [83] (*Ad Oceanum*) PL 22 663, where Jerome points out ironically that there is nothing easier than for a neophyte to enter holy orders: 'Yesterday

before his baptism recommended him and removed any fear that this neophyte would be 'swollen with pride and fall into the snares of the devil.'[287] In this case the Apostle's decree was relaxed; only in the case of the wife is it not relaxed.

What are we to make of the manifest crimes committed by some priests and bishops? A man who has led his troops into battle many a time or who has openly and publicly admitted to murder is awarded a whole series of livings, and a man who ought to have been convicted and punished by the civil laws is welcomed to the office of bishop. If Paul's rule still applies and the mere suspicion of incontinence attaching to second marriage disqualifies a man from the priesthood, then surely appalling self-indulgence will disqualify him all the more. Similarly, if someone is prevented from becoming a bishop on the ground that he may possibly be guilty of an offence, notorious guilt should all the more certainly ensure a man's removal from office. Thus it is not really the Apostle's strict decree that removes the digamist from the priesthood, but (as not even the theologians deny) a human regulation. One might wish that Paul's rules be rigorously observed in every particular, but nowadays, although the reason for Paul's concern has disappeared, digamy remains as an impediment, applying even to a first marriage to a widow, or to a woman who is not a virgin, and even when the husband suspected nothing; whereas so many other rules are either ignored completely or relaxed, without difficulty, by the Roman pontiff's indulgence.

If human authority has enough power to dissolve a contract of marriage, I wish that the self-same authority would take the trouble to rescind marriages cobbled together between virtual children by means of furtive copulation and the black arts, or else to order that the contracts be considered null. I wish, moreover, that it would lay down clear rules governing the establishment of valid and lawful marriage contracts. This would be the way to help many thousands now struggling in the toils of disastrous marriages. Further, we know that certain rulings discussed earlier, for example on extra degrees of consanguinity and on spiritual kinship, were established as a result of the great enthusiasm for chastity among the Christians of an earlier period; these could now be changed, in the light of present circumstances.

* * * * *

a catechumen, today a pope, yesterday in the amphitheatre, today in the church ...' Paul's prohibition on neophytes was confirmed by the Council of Nicaea in 325, and the *Novellae* 6.1.2 debars uneducated or lay persons from the episcopate.

287 1 Tim 3:6

Human laws, like doctors' prescriptions, can be modified according to the needs of the patient.

But this will of course be the prerogative of the church's leaders, once the spirit of Christ has inspired them with the will to act. I have merely been giving a few reminders, and if they seem unreasonable, then consider them unsaid. I cannot, of course, give orders to those whom the Lord has chosen to lead his flock, and I do not hold the church's rulings in contempt. If anything that I, in my simplicity, have said about them finds favour, I shall be delighted to have given some help in unravelling some of these questions of conscience. If none of it finds favour, my avowed commitment to charity and my concern for piety will obtain for me, if not praise, then at least pardon. At the very least my lengthy discussion of these matters will have made people aware of the problems surrounding marriage and make them more careful in embarking upon it. The precautions I have suggested so far not only can but must be taken, as far as is possible.

None the less, finding a wife who is suitable – compliant, teachable, and eager to apply what she has learned – is not really in the suitor's power. We must beg God, the author and benefactor of every marriage, to bestow good fortune and success on our enterprise. This is obviously Solomon's advice: 'A home and riches are passed on by your family, but a prudent wife is a special gift of God.'[288] Ambrose points out the particular slant given to this in the Greek version, which translates the idea in this way: 'Parents pass on a house and resources to their children, but a wife is fitted to her husband by the Lord.'[289] A marriage cannot be successful unless harmony reigns in it, and harmony comes from similarity of temperament and character and from mutual good will. These are the main things that engender and foster concord.

Paul used the same Greek verb, ἁρμόζω, in Corinthians: 'I have "fitted" you to one wife.'[290] Discord and misunderstanding make for a miserable yoke, not a marriage; a song without harmony sounds dreadful. Solomon once more: 'A man who finds a good woman finds a good thing, and will enjoy favour from the Lord.'[291] Here again, where our Latin version has *bonum*, a good thing, the Greek reads χάριτες, meaning 'favours.' The sense is much the same: the Latin implies by 'good thing' something outstandingly good, a

* * * * *

288 Prov 19:14
289 Ambrose *Expositio in Lucam* 8.9 PL 15 1858B; Erasmus quotes both the Greek and the Latin texts.
290 2 Cor 11:2
291 Prov 18:22

world of good things, as it were, while the Greek uses the plural to indicate the magnitude of your good fortune. If your own carelessness has saddled you with an unhappy marriage, admit your responsibility and try to bear with patience a misfortune that you have brought upon your own head. If it was not your fault, you must still accept it, since it was God's will for reasons hidden from us. He knows better than you what is necessary for your salvation. If, however, you find peace and prosperity, do not ascribe it to your own foresight, but acknowledge that, as the wise Solomon tells us, this joy comes from the Lord; give him thanks as the true patron of the feast.[292]

Sirach confirms Solomon's words: 'A good wife is the best gift; those who fear the Lord will be given this best of gifts for their good deeds.'[293] Every good thing, as James testifies, flows from God;[294] he distributes his gifts among us according to his inscrutable will. Ordinary people imagine that those who are born handsome, rich, or noble owe most to God; but what does Ecclesiasticus tell us? That the man who has been allotted a good wife has received the best of gifts. This gift is not casually bestowed on just anyone, but on those who fear God and have pleased him by their good deeds. Solomon also includes this among his proverbs: 'The wise woman builds her house, the foolish woman pulls it down with her own hands.'[295] Moreover Ecclesiastes, having reviewed everything under heaven, finds at the last 'the woman who is more bitter than death.'[296] If a bad wife is so bitter a thing, think how great a gift of God is a good wife.

What about those[297] who consult the stars to discover the luckiest day to marry or use magic to enrapture a young man or woman? If their marriage turns out badly, as it nearly always will, they will be unable to blame God. They will have to sue the stars for false pretences, and accuse the demons of misrepresentation – or rather themselves, since they chose to trust ungodly spirits instead of our most bountiful God, who enriches all who call

* * * * *

292 Erasmus uses *auspex*, literally, a 'diviner,' but also a protector and, more technically, a witness to the marriage contract in ancient Rome, who might also be appointed to ensure that the ceremonies were properly performed; cf Cicero *De divinatione* 1.16.28.

293 Ecclus 26:3

294 Cf James 1:17.

295 Prov 14:1

296 Eccles 7:26

297 In Latin *ubi sunt?*, 'where are they?', an echo of one of the most famous topoi (denoting ephemerality) of both classical and scriptural writing; cf E. Gilson 'De la Bible à François Villon' in *Les Idées et les lettres* (2nd ed Paris 1955) 9–38; see CWE 66 145 n101 for further references and parallels.

on him. The ancients, though ignorant of true religion, had enough religious scruples to take the auspices on serious matters only by invoking some high deity in a religious ceremony: before going to war they would sacrifice to Mars, before sailing, to Neptune, before trading, to Mercury, and before marrying, to Juno and Venus.[298] Yet we Christians embark on matrimony as though it were a trifle, to be shrugged aside whenever the fancy takes us, although in fact lifelong happiness – or misery – depends on it. Shall we vow some gift to St Nicholas as we set off with our merchandise,[299] and yet implore no heavenly aid as we embark on matrimony? Who better to grant us a successful marriage than the one who established marriage and made it holy? Shall we try to ward off ill health by prayer, but not a bad wife, more dreadful than death? Shall we pray to God for a good harvest but not for a happy marriage?

Only Christians possess the sacraments of the church, outside which there is no true religion. The gentiles' religion was split into a thousand different sects, and there were some races so barbarous that they barely knew any sort of deity at all; yet there was none so uncivilized and wild that it did not treat marriage with a certain religious awe. Aristotle, Xenophon, and Plutarch knew nothing of Christ, yet they wrote with more reverence and awe of marriage than of any other subject. The Peripatetic philosopher, though generally unmindful of God, speaks thus of marriage: 'A well-intentioned wife must realize that her husband's authority will determine the rules by which she must live, rules imposed on her by God through union in matrimony and partnership.' Who taught this unbeliever that marriages are made by God? A little later, he says again: 'Therefore anyone who makes light of marriage appears to make light of the gods too. Thus, for the gods, before whom he sacrificed and married his wife . . .' etc.[300] The man who denies that the world was created by God[301] none the less admits that a marriage cannot be made without God.

* * * * *

298 These are the appropriate deities, since Mars was the god of war, Neptune that of the sea, and Mercury that of merchants (among many other attributes). On Juno and Venus, see 224 above.

299 Best known as the prototype of Santa Claus, the fourth-century St Nicholas of Myra was, among other things, the patron saint of merchants.

300 Pseudo-Aristotle *Oeconomica* 3.1 and 3.2. The third book of this supposititious text survives only in a medieval Latin version and is of uncertain date; it may well have been influenced by Christian views on marriage. Erasmus casts doubt on its authenticity in Ep 2434.

301 A reference to Aristotle's discussion of 'becoming' (eg *De generatione* 317), which Aquinas for one took to be a denial of a divine act of creation (*Summa*

What about Xenophon? When he has Socrates ask Ischomachus whether he had himself taught his wife how to run a successful household, the latter replied, 'No, but I sacrificed to the gods, to all the gods, but especially to Zeus, praying they would permit me to teach her what things are best, and permit her to learn them.' He concludes that his wife's prayers had been similar, on the ground that 'she has shown herself docile and obedient to her husband's advice.'[302] Plutarch, too, describes the sacrifice that was customarily made to Juno as patroness of marriage.[303] Again, Juvenal reveals that the marriage-bed itself was sacred to a guardian spirit, as he inveighs against adulterers:

> It is an old and well-established custom, Posthumus,
> To rattle on another's bed,
> And mock the genius of the sacred couch.[304]

To all these, ignorant of true religion, marriage was a sacred thing; to us, adherents of the true religion, it is profane and trivial.

If we find pagan examples unconvincing, we must surely consider the example of the patriarchs, set before us in the Holy Scriptures. How was Isaac joined to Rebecca?[305] By secret couplings? By sorcery or magic? No; he allowed his father to choose him a wife. Abraham assigned the mission, as the most important of all, to a servant of proved loyalty, and first bound him by a most sacred oath, so that in essence he was entrusting the matter to eternal God. These are his words: 'The Lord of heaven and earth, who took me from my father's house and from the land of my birth, who spoke to me and swore to me, said, "I shall give this land to your seed." He shall send his angel before you, and you shall take a wife for my son from there.' Again, when the servant arrived at his destination, he prayed beside the well and begged the merciful God to bless the marriage. Then, when all his prayers had been answered, he fell down and worshipped God, thanking him for the favours that had brought about the desired result. Moreover, the girl

* * * * *

theologiae 1 q 44 art 1–2). Cf Erasmus' *In psalmum quartum concio* CWE 63 196 and the discussion of Aristotle in the colloquy *Puerpera* ('The New Mother') CWE 39 601–3.
302 Xenophon *Oeconomicus* 7.7
303 Plutarch *Moralia* 141E–F (*Coniugalia praecepta*)
304 Juvenal *Satires* 6:21–2; the Roman marriage-bed was sometimes ornamented with the figure of the genius or tutelar deity of marriage in bronze.
305 The story is told in Gen 24; the quotations below are verses 7 and 50.

was not taken without her family's consent; they gave their daughter, full of hope for the future, and said, 'The word has come from the Lord; we can say nothing to you except by his decree.'

This is the way, believe me, that happy marriages must begin. The son, unquestioning in his obedience, loves none but the bride given to him by God through his father; the faithful and devoted servant carries out his mission scrupulously, ever mindful of religion and duty, and reflecting the order of the entire household. The story does not say that Abraham consulted his son over the choice of his wife, nor was Rebecca asked whether she wanted this husband. Neither had seen the other, and yet there was between them a strong and enduring love which made Isaac forget the grief his mother's death had caused him. No doubt, had it been necessary, he would have been ready to leave his mother and cling to his wife; now his mother's memory gave way, in some sense, to his love for his wife. There was no mention, on either side, of age, or beauty, or income; it was enough for his father- and mother-in-law that it was God's will.

I have not told this story to suggest that I approve of forced marriages. I simply wanted a vivid example to demonstrate how far from the true form of Christian marriage are these immoral weddings arranged in secret, without the knowledge or consent of the families, under the auspices of lust and drink or by means of the black arts. Far too many Christian marriages come closer to the example of Shechem the Hivite, who, after abducting and defiling Jacob's daughter Dinah, asked for her hand in marriage through his father Hamor and offered them anything they wanted. What was the outcome of this violent and unnatural marriage? After three days every male in the city was slaughtered and all their property seized as booty.[306] The girl and the young man were in agreement, but their families were not. I once knew a young man of noble birth who landed from a ship by night and slipped into a certain castle; he then abducted a girl, along with her aged father, and carried her off to his lair – and all the courtiers thought this a very neat trick. That was how this drunkard, spendthrift, robber, and madman acquired a well-dowered wife of excellent character from an illustrious family, while she acquired perpetual torment and endless trial of her piety.

Another example: did not the blessed Isaac pass on to his son Jacob the procedure for matchmaking he had learned from his own father? He specifies the family from which the bride is to be chosen; Jacob raises no objection and undertakes a long and dangerous pilgrimage. He never considers

* * * * *

306 See Gen 34.

violence, he never sets a trap for the girl, but, after his vision of angels, he worships the Lord and sets up the stone on which he lays his head to sleep – incidentally, what a commentary on the softness of our modern suitors, whose heads can scarce endure a pillow stuffed with goose feathers – and makes a vow to God. Thus fortified, he meets the girl, but does not speak to her of marriage in secret. He agrees with her father Laban to serve him seven years before marrying Rachel, and in the meantime he does not touch the girl he loves, though living in the same house and working in the same pastures. Finally, when Leah is fraudulently thrust upon him, he does not ask for a divorce, but, such is his love, he renews his agreement and fulfils Leah's week; once more he shows such restraint that over all these years no opportunity to lie with her tempts him to enjoy his wife in some furtive coupling before the agreed date.[307]

These days, very few Christians seem to celebrate their weddings without reversing the proper procedure and lying with their wives before the wedding and indeed, more often than not, before the betrothal. Some suitors are so overcome by lust that they will violently assault the poor girl, not merely taking her virginity but putting her very life in the utmost danger. Why are we Christians so surprised when such unions, undertaken without a thought for God, turn out so badly?

Let me tell you the outcome of this marriage begun in holiness. Jacob had twelve sons, the chieftains of the tribes of Israel; he blessed them, gave them his commands, and then drew his feet up on to the bed and was gathered to his people.[308] Esau, however, refused the wife his father chose and, greedy for wealth and beauty, married three wives from the people of Canaan.[309] The sons they bore him were the founders of the impious and accursed tribes that made constant war on Israel. Hence God's contrasting pronouncements on these contrasting brothers: 'Jacob have I loved, but Esau have I hated.'[310] A marriage entered into under God's protection will mean not merely that you will live a pleasant life beside your wife, but that your children will be dutiful and pleasing to God. That is why the Lord constantly forbade the Israelites to make mixed marriages with godless and profane tribes.

* * * * *

307 See Gen 28–9. 'Leah's week' refers to the seven-day wedding feast (cf Judg 14:12) that had to be completed before the marriage was considered valid.
308 Cf Gen 49:33.
309 Gen 36
310 Rom 9:13, based on Mal 1:2–3

Another example: Tobias' son,[311] led by an angel and guided by God, found a wife and married her with God as his sponsor and Raphael as his messenger. Her father gave the young man his daughter together with all his property, and said, 'The God of Abraham and the God of Isaac and the God of Jacob be with you, and unite you, and pour his blessings upon you.' To guarantee the validity of the marriage, he sent for some paper and wrote out the contract; then the bride and bridegroom spent three days and nights in the same chamber, engaged in pious prayer and chaste conversation with God. Finally, on the fourth night they lay together, but with restraint and, as Raphael had taught them, in fear of the Lord, intending to satisfy their desire for children rather than their lust, so that a blessing might fall on their offspring. This is what the book says. Marriages with a happy future are those that God favours; their prospects are determined not by astrologers or silly prognostications, but by pious prayer. Let me tell you how well this marriage turned out: two grief-stricken families were filled with joy, the evil spirit was driven out and the bride freed from the curse; Tobias the father's eyes were opened and fervent thanksgiving filled the air.

Was ever a marriage more blessed than that of the holy Virgin and Joseph? And did that depend on clandestine couplings? Of course not. Matthew tells us that she was betrothed, and, as Luke puts it, 'The angel was sent to a virgin betrothed to a man whose name was Joseph, of the house of David.'[312] By whom was she betrothed? By her parents, naturally, who had chosen for their young daughter a husband from the appropriate tribe, as the Law prescribed; the will of God was at work in her holy parents. The betrothed couple lived together beneath the same roof, perhaps even in the same bedchamber, and yet Mary's honour was entirely safe. The marriage-bed was devoted not to intercourse but to pious prayers. The bedchamber became a temple where they made sacrifice to God, with a daily outpouring of reverent prayer; they were awaiting a message from on high and did not consider it proper to enter upon marital relations beforehand. The duty they owed to their parents brought them together, but their duty to God kept them from intercourse.

* * * * *

311 Erasmus resumes the apocryphal book of Tobit, a favourite source for Evangelical commentators on marriage; see Screech 46–7. The quotation that follows is not found exactly in English versions, but is Tob 7:15 in the Vulgate; this blessing appears very frequently in wedding liturgy (Stevenson 6–7 and index under '"Raguel" prayer'). In the Vulgate both father and son are called Tobias; hence Erasmus' circumlocutions here.
312 Luke 1:26–7, preceded by an allusion to Matt 1:18

Nowadays, I see a great many worshippers of the Blessed Virgin, who sing her praises, deck her statues with votive offerings, and light candles to her; but where are those eager to follow her example (a form of worship much more acceptable to her)?[313] Why do people seek a happy marriage in the stars or in fortune-telling? It should be sought in examples like these. The Virgin's example was provided not for us to imitate in every detail but to follow as far as we are able. The story tells of a girl betrothed by her parents, and thus you should not expect your marriage to be happy if you come together, against your parents' wishes or without their knowledge, in a furtive union consisting of words in the future tense and copulation in the present. If your parents are unable or unwilling to do their duty, there are always other relatives, there are men of experience, there are magistrates and bishops whose advice can help you make a successful match.

The story tells of a couple living together but without physical contact. This is not expected of you, but this shining example should at least persuade you that you marry a wife to beget children, not to slake your lust, and that marital relations should be infrequent and restrained. It was granted only to the Virgin to bear a child such as hers in that special way, but if you make every effort to follow this example of a marriage lawfully contracted and chastely conducted, you may hope for children who will be devoted to her son. She bore the Son of God without knowing a man; if you inculcate true religion in your legitimate offspring, you too will have children of God, the joint heirs of Christ;[314] this will bring you joy in abundance.

But we observe so many miserable marriages among Christians because we fail to follow not only the saintly examples commended to us in the Scriptures but even those provided by the pagans, who disallowed certain kinds of marriage which we permit. Children should be given the right not to be forced into marriage against their will; parents should be given the power to prevent their children marrying without their consent. If the parents lack judgment or probity, in the present degenerate moral climate, let a judge be appointed to give impartial advice to the children. We have magistrates to approve or rescind ordinary contracts and even officials who check the accuracy of wine-measures, but this vital contract is made by

* * * * *

313 Cf Erasmus' *Liturgia Virginis Matris* 92–9 above, where he deplores superstitious practices and recommends instead imitation of Mary's piety. The canonists had already pointed out that the non-consummation of the Virgin's marriage gave it a unique quality; eg Lombard *Sententiae* book 4 dist 26 c 7, dist 28 c 3, and dist 30 cc 2–3.
314 Cf Rom 8:16–17.

and between the most frivolous people and in the absence of any reputable witnesses.

Since much depends on the judgment of both sides, parents and children, it will be useful to examine the factors that may impair or improve our judgment. For we must not cease to exert ourselves simply because we must trust only to God for a successful outcome to all our striving. He has decreed that in all our acts two things should be combined: complete confidence in him, and a readiness to act, on our part, as far as lies within our power, or rather as far as lies within the measure of the gifts he has given us.[315] He wishes us to depend on him not as an infant depends on its mother but as a general depends on his king. Our tasks must be performed actively and energetically, but within the limits he lays down; we must trust to him for the outcome, since everything remains beneath his almighty dominion.

Thus the first thing to do, as I have said, is to pray to God for correct and wise judgment. Next you must decide upon your aims, and this above all will determine whether your judgment will be sound or faulty. If in choosing a son- or daughter-in-law the principal consideration is beauty, youth, wealth, nobility, or political influence, you will usually end by arranging an unfortunate match, not a happy one, since the chief source of happiness lies in an appropriate choice of partners, whose virtue and compatibility will ensure lasting harmony.

The Lord will provide the rest, and he will ensure that what is best for you will also prove most successful. Nothing done with God's approval can be called unsuccessful, whatever the outcome. All too often what the world calls the height of success is in fact utter disaster. I can understand why Pittacus' dictum 'Marry an equal'[316] is so well known among scholars, since, as the proverb says, like attracts like, and they stick together.[317] Equality is to be measured in terms not simply of wealth but of every kind of attribute. The proper order must not be reversed, as it usually is by ordinary people: 'Money first, morals last!'[318] In a proper account, the first entry in the ledger should be the good things of the mind, then those of the body, and finally

* * * * *

315 A statement of the anti-Pelagian or synergistic theology espoused by contemporary Evangelicals, derived from such texts as 1 Cor 3:9 and 2 Tim 2:20–1 and illustrated for example in the colloquy *Naufragium* ('The Shipwreck') CWE 39 356–9; see M.A. Screech *Rabelais* (London 1979) 182–7 and 345–50.
316 Quoted in Diogenes Laertius 1.80 and expounded at length in *Adagia* I viii 1
317 *Adagia* I ii 20
318 Juvenal *Satires* 3.140

those called external.[319] Moreover, there is a hierarchy among the attributes of the mind; some do not infallibly make their owners virtuous. Willingness to learn, for example, or a good memory, scholarship, eloquence, ingenuity, promptness can all be perverted to immoral ends. But chastity, sobriety, self-restraint, moderation, truthfulness, prudence, reticence, honesty, and vigilance make their owners virtuous whenever they are present. If your partner seems inclined towards these qualities, it is a very hopeful sign that she can be moulded to your character, and an even more hopeful one if a naturally virtuous disposition is reinforced by a sound upbringing. You should use a similar process to judge of her faults.

Now there are some moral attributes that are, as they say, written on the forehead,[320] such as modesty, chastity, kindness, and self-restraint, but speech still gives the most reliable indication of character. 'Speak, young man,' said Socrates, 'that I may see you.'[321] The philosopher's eyes are in his ears, not in his face. Many people think it enough to have seen the girl whose hand they seek, but if they really want to see her, they should talk to her. To avoid disappointment, careful enquiries must be made as to how and by whom she was brought up. It is important, of course, to be well born, but much more important to be properly brought up.[322] It is not at all uncommon to see young men and women of excellent family, endowed with remarkable natural abilities, deteriorate, if their upbringing is neglected, until they seem worse than by-blows and foundlings. By contrast, some bastards, given a liberal upbringing by virtuous tutors, surpass legitimate children in the probity of their character.

Here again, it is important to look not only for natural abilities, but also for a temperament that will make for a harmonious union; too close a resemblance is not always a good thing. If the young man is rather lethargic by nature, he will need a bride with a more active disposition; if the husband is inclined to extravagance, he will need a thrifty wife who is better at looking after the pennies. If he is a hot-tempered young man, he will be best suited by a more restrained wife, who will know the time to give in and obey. Since such temperamental differences are to be found even in the best

* * * * *

319 Cf Aristotle *Nicomachean Ethics* 1.8 (1098b13ff) and *Politics* 7.1.3 (1323a25), and Plato *Laws* 5.743E.
320 Cf *Adagia* I ix 88.
321 The aphorism is expanded in Erasmus' *Apophthegmata* 3.70 LB IV 162D.
322 The vital role of nurture in complementing and improving upon nature is a constant theme of Erasmus' educational writings; see eg *De pueris instituendis* CWE 26 311–17.

natures, a marriage may be none too happy unless appropriate provision is made for them.

However, the most important of all the moral qualities to be observed in a partner are the amount of their respect for their parents and the extent of their devotion to God. If they have learned this respect and devotion, they can acquire all the other virtues. But you must take care not to marry someone who is superstitious rather than pious; if true piety implies an agreeable flexibility, superstition means a harsh inflexibility, and it tends to infect women more often than men. Of course, there are some trifling superstitions that a husband may as well tolerate until his wife knows better. Paul allows a Christian wife to remain with a husband who has not yet chosen to confess Christ, so long as he does not object violently to a partner of a different religion; but he does not allow a woman to marry unless the man is a Christian.[323] Tertullian says that Christians took little notice of this,[324] and these days it seems advisable that a husband should bear with his wife, or a wife with her husband, since perhaps the one can correct the other should they disagree somewhat on those doctrinal questions which are today a subject of controversy throughout the world. This does not apply if impiety has driven one of them so mad as to deny Christ entirely, along with the Holy Scriptures and the Apostles' Creed, which is manifest apostasy. It would be imprudent to make a match if one of the partners were a zealous adherent of some reprobate sect. The Apostle teaches that mixed marriages must be upheld if they were contracted through no fault of our own, but that they must not be contracted in other circumstances.

It is up to the individual to decide whether it is more advisable to marry an untutored virgin or a widow with experience. I know that some people concur with what appears to be the opinion of Xenophon's Ischomachus[325] that it is better to marry an inexperienced girl who brings the bridegroom nothing from her parents' home except chastity, modesty, and a willingness to be guided in all things. Differences of temperament mean that there can be no single educational method and that the same education will not suit everyone; it is not uncommon to see two entirely virtuous individuals who would be completely unsuited to lifelong companionship. Thus a man who chooses a well-favoured but untutored bride will try, if he is a good crafts-man, to fashion himself a wife to suit his own temper, and will succeed, with God's aid, so long as his own character reflects the moral code. Con-

*****

323 1 Cor 7:13; 2 Cor 6:14
324 Tertullian *Ad uxorem* 2.2 PL 1 1403–5
325 Xenophon *Oeconomicus* 7.5–6

versely, a man who wants to escape the drudgery of educating her, which
is a long and not always successful job, may prefer a widow who is already
broken in and formed. It is not a bad idea, so long as he takes into account
her behaviour towards her previous husband and what means and methods
he used to instruct her. You may be fairly sure that she will be compliant
and docile towards you if she showed herself obedient to her dead husband.

The point here is less that your wife should be your equal than that she
should suit you. Pittacus' dictum[326] includes both: τὴν κατὰ σαυτόν, meaning
'fitting for you.' Sometimes things fit together which are not alike or even
similar. However, it would be the height of folly if, in order to demonstrate
your forbearance, you deliberately took a shrewish wife into your home, as
we read that Socrates did. His friends were astounded that he put up with
his two peevish and unmanageable wives, but he replied, in his ironical way,
that he was learning tolerance at home so that he could use it abroad.[327] That
may not have been the real reason, yet it is extraordinary that a philosopher
did not either choose more docile wives or else instruct them as he ought.
Maybe he took more thought for the state than for his domestic affairs.

Now I will admit that sometimes the state's business should take priority over domestic matters, but none the less a wife, children, and a household
do demand special attention from any good husband. In fact, if everyone
were to neglect his family, the state, whose stability depends on families,
could not survive. A good husband or a virtuous wife will have enough
to do in coming to terms with things in his or her partner which cannot
be changed or improved; it would be madness to go looking for trouble.
Even if we have taken every precaution, the vicissitudes of human existence, always tending towards the worst, bring us troubles enough; there is
no need whatever to go running after them.

Just as only a craftsman can properly judge his craft, so only a virtuous man – and a man of experience too – can properly judge questions
of virtue. Anyone who wants to choose himself a virtuous wife must first
make himself virtuous. On this point the advice of older relatives and of
parents will be more than valuable, not only because young men and women
are usually led astray by love, which is, as they say, a blind judge,[328] but

* * * * *

326 See 310, and n316 above.
327 Aulus Gellius *Noctes Atticae* 1.17.1–4; cf CWE 25 136 and Diogenes Laertius 2.37
     and, on Socrates' two wives, ibidem 2.26 and Erasmus' *Apophthegmata* LB IV
     161D.
328 Cf *Moria* CWE 27 97; Cupid is, of course, traditionally portrayed wearing a
     blindfold.

also because people of more mature years, with all their experience, weigh things up more carefully than young people, who are guided more by desire than by reason. Their inexperience, as a laudable ancient maxim[329] has it, makes them over-confident – and scorn for danger will bring the danger closer.

Love often mistakes the worst things for the best, as Theocritus wrote;[330] it deceives itself and will see a suitor's violence and arrogance as strength, his extravagance as generosity, and use a euphemism, such as *gynaecophilia*,[331] to describe his unbridled lust. Similarly, love will call a girl's loose chatter polite conversation and will claim that the lewdness of her looks, walk, and gestures merely shows that she is friendly. Some people think that good behaviour is merely a matter of making the right gestures. If a girl has learned, let us say, to be forever curtseying, joining her hands, and pursing her lips in a prim smile, if she will touch as little food and drink as possible at a party (having stuffed herself in private beforehand), not stick out her left hand when it should be the right, touch food only with her fingertips, not show her teeth when laughing; if she has mastered such trifles as these they think she has learned enough to earn a husband. But on the contrary virtue should have been so deeply inculcated in her that it shines out candidly from her brow, her eyes, her face and in her every movement, in the same way that physical fitness is revealed unconsciously in the healthy glow and alertness of someone's body.

In reaching the right decision, a not unimportant role will be played by the girl's reputation. Of course, hearsay is often wrong, 'as often the bearer of lies and slander as the herald of truth.'[332] But Hesiod was not unjustified in saying, 'What popular report noises abroad / Is not always without foundation.'[333] A bad reputation, however undeserved, can bar a man from the priesthood, and similarly anyone wishing his marriage to be successful in every respect must take care to choose a partner about whom even rumour fears to lie. Gaius Caesar repudiated his wife on suspicion of adultery, even though, when called as a witness, he said that he did not

* * * * *

329 *Adagia* IV v 54
330 Theocritus 6.18–19
331 Literally, 'love of women'; Theocritus 8.60 applies the derived adjective to Zeus in a derogatory sense. The normal adjective, without pejorative overtones, is *philogynes*.
332 Virgil *Aeneid* 4.188
333 Hesiod *Works and Days* 763, quoted in *Adagia* I vi 25

think her guilty; but Caesar's wife must be not only innocent of any crime but also above any suspicion of crime.[334]

If he was right, how much more justifiably will a young man refrain from marrying a girl who, though innocent, is the subject of widespread rumours. If a husband repudiates his wife, he stains her reputation for ever; if a suitor withdraws from his engagement, it appears merely that he has not gone through with it, and the girl retains the right to marry another. Olympias was right to criticize a young man who had married a girl of great beauty but unsavoury reputation: 'This idiot,' she said, 'has married with his eyes but not his ears.'[335] So long as you marry with your ears and eyes open, there will be no danger, if your ears and eyes are like the philosophers' – ears in the eyes and eyes in the ears. The eye that sees only physical beauty and charms that are skin deep is no philosopher's eye. The philosopher's eye sees through the flesh the beauties of the soul and prefers to bestow its love on them. A blushing cheek, a shy glance, an expression, an attitude – all speak volumes to the wise man. She may keep silence but her voice will be heard by any observer who has ears in his eyes, though in fact eyes in the ears are a surer judge than ears in the eyes.

Another point to be considered in choosing a husband or wife is whether they have learned or practised some skill. If their means are slender, knowing a craft is essential; even if they are comfortably off, possessing a skill will have two advantages. First, should some mischance suddenly deprive them of their substance (and such possessions are particularly vulnerable to fortune's whims), they will have some means of escaping poverty without resorting to crime. Not only will skill fill your hand, in any land, as the proverb says,[336] but it will fill any position in life; or, put a better way, skill will support any position in life. Second, it will leave less room for idleness, so often the ruin of morality. Solon is said to have made a law providing that a son whose parents had taught him no skill was not obliged to support them when they were stricken with age or reduced to poverty;[337] and yet the oldest of laws, written in the hearts of every people, is that if children are reluctant to repay their parents at least to the extent

* * * * *

334 The source of this famous dictum of (Gaius) Julius Caesar is probably Plutarch *Caesar* 10.6 (712C); see also Suetonius *Julius* 6 and 74.
335 Olympias was the mother of Alexander the Great; the anecdote appears in Plutarch *Moralia* 141C and in Erasmus' *Apophthegmata* LB IV 320F.
336 *Adagia* I vii 33
337 Plutarch *Solon* 22 (90D)

that the stork's chicks do,[338] they should be treated like faithless traitors and put into irons. Yet Solon judged parents unworthy of this aid if they had neglected to provide their children with the means to support themselves. It does seem rather shameless to demand that others do their duty when you have failed in your duty to them, and it seems unjust to want to reap where you did not sow at the proper time.[339] If children who were neglected when young by their parents managed later to make themselves rich by their own efforts, the legislator did not prohibit them from showing compassion, but he did free them from any obligation to help. His aim was to encourage parents to teach youngsters a useful skill, which would also help them to avoid temptation at an age when inexperience makes them prone to idleness and lust and, as the poet said, like wax in the hands of evil.[340]

There are of course differences between the arts; the main division is into liberal and mechanical arts.[341] The liberal arts, which include rhetoric, arithmetic, geography, and the study of law, require intellectual discernment above all. The mechanical arts, such as architecture, involve practical skills. Some, such as sculpture, painting, and medicine, lie between the two, although practical skill is only a small part of these, and the intellectual side is the more important. The most reliable protection against poverty is the art of medicine (the opposite of the science of 'mendicity'!).[342] Next best is jurisprudence, cousin to politics. Grammar feeds quite a few, but does no more than feed them; it includes poetry and, as things are at present, rhetoric. Married men are banned from the temples of theology, the result less of papal proscription than of a theologians' conspiracy.

Among the political arts the more reputable, or at any rate the less violent, are those practised in peacetime, such as oratory and jurisprudence, rather than those used in war. Not that military skill, the ability to protect the lives and property of your countrymen against enemy attack, is not admirable, but nowadays an ancient custom has taken root, so that most wars are waged by cruel and barbaric soldiers who fight for

* * * * *

338 The family affection of storks was proverbial: the young were supposed to feed their aged parents. For references, cf *Querela pacis* CWE 27 294 and n7.
339 Cf Matt 25:24–6.
340 Horace *Ars poetica* 163
341 On this long-standing division, see eg Cicero *De oratore* 3.32.127 and *De officiis* 1.42.150; and Quintilian *Institutiones oratoriae* 1.4 and 2.17–18.
342 Erasmus puns on *medicandi* (doctoring) and *mendicandi* (begging). Doctors, like the lawyers who follow them here, were proverbial for their greed; cf *Moria* CWE 27 107.

money, like the Carians.[343] In fact, so perverse is the human mind that many girls think they have made a splendid match if they marry one of these Carian mercenaries whose only motive is profit, a butcher for hire who will abandon his wife and children at the first sniff of a war. Yet women think it heroic to be united to a man who is defiled by sacrilege, pillage, carnage, rape, and other wickedness; they even expect a reward from heaven for putting up with such husbands, if they cannot change their ways. If I had my way, no girl would ever marry such a man if anyone else, however humble, were available, so long as he knew some harmless trade.

As for the arts that are both healthy and profitable, the ancients all agreed in awarding the prize to agriculture; in days gone by it was an honourable calling even for mighty kings and aristocratic senators, but now it is turned over to the lowest members of society, who do all the work while their idle masters reap all the rewards. We have sunk so low that nowadays a girl married to a farmer is considered beneath contempt. But if physical fitness, which must surely be considered one of our greatest assets in life, is our aim, there is no healthier life than this; if it is thrift, no one lives more economically; if it is profit, there is no more harmless way to earn money; if – and this is the most important consideration – our aim is to live an upright life, nowhere is there less temptation.

However, I am not here to sing the praises of the country life! It has already been done very gracefully by many eloquent writers, especially by Xenophon in Greek and Virgil in Latin.[344] But wise men should not succumb to popular error and rate something that is intrinsically superior lower than things that are inferior to it; they should instead take it up and restore it to a place of honour by their laudable example. Even those whose civic duties prevent them from living in the country permanently could none the less become amphibians, as it were, and divide their time between the two. For example, they can make for the country whenever they have time to spare from their urban occupations, and the more often they do so, the better

* * * * *

343 Cf *Adagia* I vi 14. The Carians, a people of Asia Minor, were fierce warriors proverbial for treachery and for being prepared to fight as mercenaries, an unusual profession in the ancient world. On Erasmus' long-standing horror of mercenary soldiers, cf *Institutio principis christiani* CWE 27 282–3 and n5, and *Querela pacis* ibidem 309.

344 A reference to Xenophon's *Oeconomicus* (see especially 5.1–17) and to Virgil's *Eclogues* and *Georgics*. There are also echoes here of Juvenal's fourteenth satire, and of the pseudo-Aristotelian *Oeconomica*, eg 1.1.2–3; on this text, see n300 above.

the yield from their farms. Moreover, they themselves will return fitter and keener to their civic duties and, by alternating between them, will never grow tired of either country or town. Meanwhile their wives can stay at home to store and distribute what their husbands have had brought in from the fields.

This way of life is so much happier and healthier – and safer – than the commercial business in which so many are engaged these days, which takes a man far from his family for much of the year, compelling him to flit over mountains and seas and roads infested with brigands, in danger of losing his life as well as all his goods. These men's wives are little more than widows; their minds are never free from anxiety and fear for their husbands or their goods, and usually for both! All may be well in fact, but they are terrorized by the slightest rumour and often by nightmares. It is safer – and also harmless to others – to 'do business' with your trusty farm, which returns with interest whatever it receives. This is a respectable kind of usury, and the greater the effort you put in, the larger the return; should one harvest disappoint your hopes, the next will make good the loss. Not only does the land take the farmer and return him safe, but if he arrives a little under the weather,[345] it sends him back fighting fit.

This business knows nothing of deceit, whereas normal commerce can barely survive without trickery; only the slippery and the sly find easy pickings there. For a Christian dishonest profit is no profit but a loss; no Christian can be happy with something that gnaws away at his conscience. As Solomon teaches, 'Better a dry crust and joy than a house full of feasting and strife.'[346] With a guilty conscience, you will always be at odds with yourself; you cannot escape, wherever you turn. Solomon again: 'Better a pittance honestly earned than great gains ill gotten.'[347] The psalmist agrees: 'Better the little the righteous has than the riches of the wicked.'[348] However small your substance, with God you possess a great treasure; without God, a guilty conscience will make everything seem tawdry and shallow. 'The possessor must be healthy in body and mind,' says the poet,[349] but for the wicked that part of them is sick which, when it is well, can turn misfortune into joy.

* * * * *

345 In Latin *sublanguidus*, literally, 'somewhat languishing,' and apparently an adjective coined by Erasmus
346 Prov 17:1
347 Prov 16:8
348 Ps 36 (Vulg 37):16
349 Horace *Epistles* 1.2.49

What is more, ill-gotten gains usually disappear the same way; as the character in Plautus said, 'Evil come, evil go!'[350] How often do we see great riches, painstakingly acquired by usury, monopoly, and other dirty tricks, destroyed in a moment by fire or storm, or confiscated by princes, who cunningly sell a monopoly, let the buyer soak up cash like a sponge, and then, at the right moment, squeeze him dry. I need hardly mention charlatans and hucksters, like those who make their money from paste jewellery or pinchbeck gold, or trick the gullible with alchemy or bogus magic, or those who cater for our lower appetites, such as confectioners, pastrycooks, and pimps, or flute-players and rope-dancers. What about card-sharps and gamblers? Some people make their living that way. Any girl who knowingly marries one of these deserves to suffer, as an accessory to evil. If she says, 'I cannot be a spinster all my life, and no one else was available,' I can promise her more happiness if she marries the meanest cobbler than one of these fine 'craftsmen.'

But enough of these male professions! A girl whose parents have taught her to manage a household has acquired a skill that is by no means to be disdained. She will never find any shortage of jobs to do in the home, and will get enough exercise to keep her healthy if she visits the various parts of the house regularly – the kitchen, the men's and women's quarters, the bedroom, the attics – and either does the housework herself or tells others what needs to be done. Spindle and distaff are indeed the ideal female instruments for discouraging idleness, which is bad for anyone but particularly harmful to young people and women. Some men deal with important business by mental activity alone; unless a girl is given something to occupy her mind, her thoughts turn inevitably towards evil.

Families who will not let their daughters learn a trade because of their status and position in society or because they are already well off are none the less quite right to instruct them in tapestry-work, silk-weaving, or playing an instrument, to enable them to cheat boredom; they would do even better to have them instructed in the humanities. Weaving, for example, is an occupation that leaves the mind free to listen to young men's chatter and to reply to their banter, but a girl intent on her books has no thought for anything else. What is more, once she begins to enjoy study, it will sharpen and stimulate her mind more than any other occupation; others may discourage idleness, but study has the advantage that the more you do the greater the pleasure you obtain, and it will keep you occupied even into old age.

* * * * *

350 Plautus *Poenulus* 4.2.22

Finally, reading good books not only forestalls idleness but also fills girls' minds with the best of principles and inculcates virtue.

Telemachus sends Penelope back to her spindle and distaff for a while, and we learn that she was also skilled in tapestry-weaving;[351] in fact the poets make nearly all their heroines adept in this sort of work. So where does that leave parents who believe that their children are letting them down if they learn any skill but dancing, feasting, and swapping silly stories? Cyrus, the mighty king of the Persians, boasted to Lysander that with his own hands he had planted rows of trees in oblique lines so that the regularity of the angles and the placing of the promenades between them made every prospect a delight to the eye.[352] At Rome the ruling classes thought so highly of agriculture that distinguished figures such as Cato and Varro were by no means averse to publishing detailed instructional books on the subject.[353] Nowadays, however, even the common people, if they have just enough money to get by without engaging in manual labour, will not allow their children to learn this harmless trade, but bring them up to enjoy idleness and sensual pleasures, thinking it better to be known as a skilled gambler than a skilled farmer.

To sum up: in judging your bride's moral qualities, the first thing is that you should know what you are talking about. Generally speaking, someone who is himself virtuous will recognize and appreciate virtue. In this area, as I have said, the assessment of parents or elders will be more reliable than the children's; it is better to trust them, since they have learned from their own and others' misfortunes what to look for and what to avoid, rather than to give youthful inexperience the chance to learn wisdom from its own mistakes. Second, reasoned advice must prevail over mere whim; here again, it is preferable that children should defer to their parents' judgment, as the latter are beyond the reach of Cupid's darts, which all too often afflict the young. Third, moral qualities themselves must be sifted: some are better than others, but the greatest of all is piety. There are some that do

* * * * *

351 See Homer *Odyssey* 1.356–9; Ulysses' son Telemachus excluded his mother from a discussion with the suitors because she had wept at a minstrel's song about the Trojan war. Penelope's skill in weaving was proverbial (*Adagia* I iv 42) because she used it as a device to postpone choosing a new husband.

352 Xenophon *Oeconomicus* 4.20–4. The technical term for the arrangement is *quincunx*, the shape of the five spots on a die.

353 Cato the Censor (d c 150 BC) rose to all the honours of the state, but also left a treatise on agriculture, *De re rustica*; Varro, who died in 28 BC, was a lieutenant of Pompey and reputedly the author of five hundred treatises, of which only two, including the *Res rustica*, survive.

not immediately make their possessor virtuous: a good weaver is not necessarily a good woman, and a good lawyer can be a bad man. Fourth, you should look not just for attractive qualities, but for appropriate ones. Although to a Christian nothing will appear suitable unless it is also good, yet even some attractive quality will not always suit everyone. Compatibility is so important that sometimes people who are dissimilar, but right for one another, will live in greater harmony than those who are more alike, despite the very proper saying that similarity breeds good will;[354] not everyone, after all, likes the same things, and in fact the variety of people's tastes is astonishing. Fifth, in examining her moral qualities, you must rely less on your eyes than your ears and, in order to appraise the girl's character and temperament, use every scrap of information: about her family, since normally virtue breeds virtue; about her upbringing, even more important than her family; about her earlier life and her reputation, which her family should guard as jealously as her virginity, since their main concern must be to hand her unsullied to her husband; even if her body is untouched, she will not be unsullied if her reputation is besmirched. Such considerations will enable you to see your future much more clearly than any flight of birds or sacred chickens gobbling corn;[355] clear thinking is the best prophet.

Now although I would want you to investigate all this very thoroughly, I would expect you still to show consideration for other people's honour and reputation, especially those of young girls. For some suitors, seeing that someone else is preferred to them, invent and spread damaging rumours about the girl; they cannot have her, so they would rather appear contemptuous of her than rejected by her. Would it not be more in keeping with Christian charity to dissemble, and conceal anything untoward that you might find out about the way of life or character of a marriageable girl? It is no disgrace for a young man to go looking for a partner, but a girl cannot, and it does no great harm to his reputation if he fails, since she cannot marry more than one suitor.

For this reason, whenever a girl has several suitors it would be better to leave the choice to her parents and thus reduce the chances of ill feeling against her. If, on closer acquaintance, the girl fails to please the suitor, it will

* * * * *

354 Cf *Adagia* i ii 20–1, two proverbs meaning 'like attracts like.'
355 Erasmus uses two technical expressions, *praepetes aves*, birds whose species, number, and path of flight were regarded as prophetic, and *tripudium solistimum*, the most favourable omen given by the sacred chickens, devouring their feed so greedily that it dropped from their beaks; cf Cicero *De divinatione* 1.15.28 and 2.34.72.

not be hard to invent some reason why he should not go through with the wedding. A customer who disparages the jewels for sale in front of everyone else is considered most uncouth: if the price is right, why disparage them? If not, it costs nothing to keep silent. But it is much more churlish to invent slurs upon the reputation of a girl you cannot have, simply to prevent her marrying another. A good way to avoid this would be for the parents to exclude other people from these negotiations and conduct them in private; if something goes wrong, there will be less scope for backbiting and ill will, and the quest will be more likely to succeed than if the news gets out and produces a crowd of rivals.

Now someone will ask, 'Since there is always a great shortage of good people, what is to become of all the bad ones, if the good are allowed to marry only one another?' Why, let the punishment fit the crime,[356] and those who sinned outside marriage repent within it. Surely those who have wickedly enticed innocent girls to fornicate with them should be urged by all honest citizens to marry those they have defiled, or at the very least be compelled by law to find them a husband and provide a dowry. Why are Christian laws so reluctant to do this? Because fornication is a daily sport among the great men whose opinions make and unmake our laws. But divine law will continue to press for it, and that should carry more weight, with Christians at least, than human laws.

I feel that I have said enough about choosing a wife according to her moral qualities; now I must deal briefly with physical qualities, though I shall not enter a debate with the Stoics and Peripatetics over whether they should be called 'good' or merely 'useful.'[357] On this subject, ordinary people's judgment is nearly always topsy-turvy; they prize youth and beauty above all else, but where these alone are the motives for love there can be no lasting affection. The flower of youth is fleeting and beauty fades, not only with the passing of the years but from many another cause; affection also must perish if its source dries up. Thus if we wish friendship to last it must be based on things that are not exposed to the buffets of fortune or withered by age. Listen, Christian suitor, to a wise man's counsel: 'Charm is a delusion and beauty vain,' he says. 'It is a God-fearing woman who is

*****

356 A free translation of the proverb *similes labra lactucae*, 'like lips, like lettuce' (*Adagia* I x 71)
357 Aristotle (eg in *Politics* 7.1) numbered physical qualities among the 'good things' (*bona*), but the Stoics, with their characteristic contempt for the body, considered physical attributes mere *commoda*, 'useful or serviceable things'; see eg Seneca *Epistulae morales* 74.17 and 87.29 and 36.

honoured.'[358] The flower of youth enraptures you; you cherish a rose that is soon to fade; beware! 'Charm is a delusion.' You marvel at her looks, but hear this: 'Beauty is vain.' Why vain? because it shines but for a moment. Why vain? because too often it misleads: it is deceit, not beauty, that conceals an ugly soul beneath a beauteous skin. Why then do your eyes dwell on her outward form? View her with philosophers' eyes and see the beauties of her soul. These alone will suffice to engender constant affection, but if her body too is fair, like a jewel set in gold, then 'the gifts of the gods are not to be rejected,' as Homer puts it,[359] so long as your priorities are right.

Turn your eyes, therefore, upon those beauties compared to which the others are but pretence and lies. Where are they to be found? Look, the wise man points them out in the verse I have just quoted: 'It is a God-fearing woman who is honoured.' Here is the flower of the soul, the everlasting human beauties truly to be prized: piety and respect for God. A soul that fears God will not transgress against his decree and thus will have neither wrinkle nor stain.[360] What use is an unblemished skin if your soul is stained and spotted all over with sin? Isaiah cries, 'All flesh is grass and all mankind's glory is like the flower of the field; the grass withers and the flower falls, but the word of the Lord endures for ever.'[361] The prophet is told to shout these words, not speak them, presumably because people turn deaf ears to them. If all material things are like the flowers and the grass, how much more is it true of youth and beauty? But here is a different kind of beauty, which remains springlike even into ripe old age: 'The word of the Lord endures for ever.' Where the word of the Lord flourishes, the unfailing beauty of honour will start a friendship that will never die.

However, since matrimony is a union of body and soul, some thought must be given even to physical suitability, to ensure that here too some equality or similarity exists. A philosophical nature will ignore completely outward appearance, however unfortunate, provided that intellectual and moral gifts compensate for these shortcomings. We see deep marital affection continuing to flourish between decrepit old folk, though not a trace remains of their former good looks. Should not reason produce the same effect in a wise man that habit has produced in these others? Someone who marries only to beget children or curb his lust will find his wife quite

* * * * *

358 Prov 31:30
359 Homer *Iliad* 3.64–5
360 Cf Eph 5:27.
361 Isa 40:6–8

acceptable simply because she is a woman; someone who is not philosopher enough to be content with moral qualities should choose a girl of only moderate looks, such as might be called regular or wifely, neither so loathsome as to put him off nor yet so charming as to attract adulterers or ugly gossip. But if he should happen to find a girl of outstanding beauty, ideal character, perfect thriftiness, and simple demeanour, he can easily avoid or reduce these dangers: the jewel of beauty is nowhere safer than at home, and no place is more appropriate for a virtuous wife to live. Sarah was in danger, but only on the journey; Dinah was defiled, but only among strangers.[362] God preserved Sarah's chastity because she accompanied her husband on a pilgrimage ordained by God; Dinah was raped because, against her father's orders, she wandered through a foreign city, to see and to be seen.

It is not at all easy to lay down precise rules about the age of your chosen bride. If you are looking for an untutored girl whom you can bend to your own ways, a girl of tender years is best, when she is at her most adaptable. If you prefer a woman whose character is already formed, you will choose a woman of more mature years, into her thirties perhaps, not yet showing her age and still quite capable of bearing children. Aristotle suggests, in the *Politics*, that the bride should be eighteen and the groom thirty-seven.[363] If people get married younger, he says, their children may lack respect for them because of the closeness of their ages; if they are older, the parents may die too soon to make the most of their children. He recommends the ages I have quoted for three reasons: first, because there is a reasonable age difference between parents and children; second, because both male and female are physically mature at that age; third, because partners of this age would cease to be fertile at roughly the same time, the woman at around fifty, the man at around seventy. Generally speaking this is true, although many people produce children later, just as quite a few stop doing so earlier; in this respect it is not so much years that count as the state of the body. There are some temperaments (the doctors' word is *crases*)[364] so unfortunate that they grow old before reaching the prime of life, let alone

* * * * *

362 See Gen 20 and 34.

363 Aristotle *Politics* 7.16.3–10 (1334b39–1335a35). He acknowledged, however (*Historia animalium* 4.6 and 5.14), that boys of fourteen and girls of twelve were biologically capable of reproduction. These were the minimum ages allowed for marriage by both civil and canon law (*Codex* 5.4.24 and Aquinas *Supplementum* q 43 art 2).

364 A technical term for bodily temperature, which was supposed to have a determining effect on both physical and mental processes

old age. However, it must be the parents' concern to ensure that no couple is married unless their bodies are fully grown and they have both reached puberty; this will prevent not only premature intercourse, which may injure or even destroy a body that is still delicate, but also the possible birth of weak and unhealthy children, caused by semen that is still too watery and less mature than is necessary.

None the less, there are a number of reasons for not waiting as long as the doctors and the philosophers may rule. Paul did not presume to specify any particular age: 'If he cannot contain,' he says, 'let him marry whom he wishes.'[365] However, to prevent precocious young people giving way to their lust, much importance must be attached to careful upbringing, parental discipline, a healthy diet, constant occupation of their time, virtuous company, and instruction in the gospel teaching. If children are brought up by over-indulgent or, rather, neglectful parents in idleness and luxury, frolicking with other youngsters or servants who are dissipated, idle, and wanton, playing stupid games and telling filthy stories, it cannot be surprising or unexpected if they are overwhelmed by lust long before they reach adulthood. If warnings and other curbs on immorality are no use, it is safer to allow them to marry, lest worse befall. Jerome recounts with amazement that Solomon had a son while still a boy, and that a nurse was made pregnant by a mere boy with whom she was sleeping.[366] These days it is not a rare occurrence, especially in France, for a girl barely ten years old to be a wife and to become a mother in her eleventh year. However, such monstrous precedents should not be called into play; instead, every possible practical remedy should be tried to restrain the wantonness of youth, an age that is more concerned with pleasure than with health; but they must be persuaded rather than bullied into exercising self-control.

Something else that seems monstrous, but none the less sometimes occurs, especially in Britain and Italy, is that a very young girl is married to a septuagenarian. If such a marriage turns out well, the spouses must have made a great sacrifice to Venus,[367] as they say. Still more absurd – but I have seen it happen – is a woman of sixty-six marrying a youth of barely twenty summers. However old he is, a man can make a young woman pregnant, but an old woman cannot be made a mother by a young man. There is an

* * * * *

365 1 Cor 7:9
366 Jerome Ep 72 [132] (*Ad Vitalem*).1–2 PL 22 673–4. The computation was based on 1 Kings 14:21: Solomon having reigned forty years, since the age of twelve, his son Rehoboam succeeded him at the age of forty-one. Jerome suggests alternatively some form of overlapping joint rule between father and son.
367 *Adagia* III i 30

ugly side to both cases: the aged husband appears to be sleeping with his daughter, not his wife, and the aged bride appears to have married her son, not a husband. If the love of money inspires such marriages, it is disgusting; if it is lust – even more disgusting! Yet the church's laws do not dissolve such marriages, though they are the butt of jokes and witticisms among the people.

None the less, some people oppose marriages between two people in the flower of their years, claiming that the heat of sexual ardour will be cooled if a young girl is joined to an older husband: it seems unnatural for the bride to be older than her husband, for if a man marries an older woman he will have to live like a bachelor for much of the marriage. But even this kind of marriage can be defended with reference either to incontinence (intemperance is so unseemly in an old person) or to the fact that they will be able to do things for one another (harmony is valuable at any age).

Ancient wisdom gives pride of place among physical qualities to good health,[368] and the second place to beauty. Thus the most discerning judges will observe first of all how healthy, active, and temperate their partner's body is, whatever their age. A woman married to an invalid has taken on an old man; a man married to a sickly wife has taken on an old woman. Some illnesses, such as fevers and colds, do not last long, and sometimes even leave the body stronger afterwards; others, such as gout, dropsy, epilepsy, apoplexy, or paralysis, never leave their victims entirely. Some conditions are more distressing than any ordinary illness, such as leprosy or what is commonly called the Neapolitan pox,[369] probably worse than any leprosy. There are also diseases of the mind, frenzy, derangement, lethargy. Other things cannot be called diseases, but debilities or handicaps, such as blindness, lameness, mutilated or missing limbs (a squint is more damaging to the appearance than to the health). There are also minor defects that are none the less annoying in a partner, such as foul breath, a bad stammer, or partial deafness, but none of these is so terrible as to be intolerable in marriage, and if they appear after the wedding, both partners must accept them as their destiny, since no mortal can know what the future will bring. It is only right that a husband should tolerate in his wife something that, had the powers above so willed it, she might have had to tolerate in him.

However, I am still staggered by the folly of some parents, who will hand over a pure and healthy virgin to a husband riddled with the new

* * * * *

368 Cf Aristotle *Rhetoric* 1.5.10 (1361b3).
369 See n254 above.

leprosy.[370] This pox differs from leprosy only in that it causes worse pain and greater danger to life, and is easier to catch. Shall an innocent virgin be joined to a walking corpse? If the girl had killed her father, I ask you, could anyone have devised a worse punishment? Does health not enter into the equation, when her age is reckoned, her looks inspected, her dowry counted? Has anyone ever deliberately married a daughter to a leper? What matter that the disease is not called leprosy, when it is more horrible than leprosy? What affection can a wife feel for a husband who hangs such a garland round her neck at the very start of their marriage? What respect will children feel for parents who have given them a life more loathsome than death? Again, since princes and their officials are supposed to take thought for everything that affects our health and well-being, I am truly astonished that they have ignored this plague for years and allowed it to spread far and wide, especially since in Holy Writ we are commanded to banish lepers and shown how to do it.[371]

Perhaps this disease is being treated lightly because it is thought to have originated with the aristocracy, like elephantiasis, of which Pliny writes, 'This disease is native to Egypt and, although kings were attacked by it, it was fatal to the people.'[372] Ringworm, a foul and disgusting disease if you like, spared women and the lowest orders.[373] But the pox spares no one, of whatever race, sex, age, or condition, and affects even unborn children. The slightest suspicion of leprosy will get you expelled from our cities, but these pox-carriers are allowed to drink, sleep, eat, talk, kiss, and even marry among us, and spread the disease throughout the world, apparently just to please the aristocracy.

One peculiarity of this disease is that those who have it take delight in passing it on to others; this is no doubt the work of some devilish spite. Someone who has come to grief through his own fault is intent upon forcing as many others as possible to share his plight. How such people should be handled by those whose job it is to safeguard public

* * * * *

370 Syphilis: Erasmus returned to this theme, with much vehemence, in the 1529 colloquy Ἄγαμος γάμος, sive Coniugium impar ('A Marriage in Name Only, or The Unequal Match') CWE 40 842–59.
371 Lev 13:42–6; cf Matt 8:4; Luke 5:14.
372 Pliny Naturalis historia 26.5.7; Erasmus fails to explain that it was 'fatal to the people' because the treatment administered to the kings required baths prepared with warm human blood!
373 Ibidem 26.3.3; the term used by Pliny and Erasmus, lichen, is used of a number of skin diseases, even of leprosy, but modern scholars conclude that ringworm is meant in this passage of Pliny.

health is another matter, but it is certainly the business of parents, who worry about so many minor details when they choose their children's partners, not to ignore this awful disease, which promises certain death not only to their daughter but to her offspring. Let them answer me this: if by some mischance their daughter had been seduced by a leper, would they not have the seducer burned, if they could? So are they not mad to deliver their innocent daughter, knowingly and willingly, into the arms of a leper? Similarly, if a girl of marriageable age should inexplicably contract leprosy, would not her whole family, all her relatives, be consumed with heart-rending grief, and even strangers cry out for pity? But now, when a daughter, with all her children, grandchildren, and future descendants, is exposed to leprosy, everyone dances and sings at the wedding as if it were a triumph!

Who in his right mind would not rather be stripped of all he possessed at a stroke than buy a vast increase in his wealth at the price of leprosy? You will make a better match for your daughter if you give her to a humble potter or a healthy gardener instead of a leprous lord. It is difficult to know which is the more guilty – parents who expose their children to die, or who choose them partners like this; at least the former, if the worst happens, will make a quick end, whereas the latter will die a lingering death. Then again, we know that for quite a few exposure ended happily,[374] but what consolation can the others find, unless we count it a blessing that sometimes, in our distraction, we find pleasure in our woes because we do not recognize them as such?

Why should a marriage made with a man incapable of sexual intercourse be rescinded, and yet a contract be valid with a man who produces pus instead of semen and begets pox instead of children? What are we to make of this, when a mind affected by bodily illness cannot be sound either, and yet parents who consider themselves sane thrust their sons and daughters upon such monsters and take less trouble over choosing a son-in-law than they would over choosing a horse? With the latter, they flush out hidden defects and look carefully for things that the seller does not have to disclose; but in contracting a marriage, in our wisdom, we ignore the obvious.

* * * * *

374 The obvious example being that of Romulus and Remus, the founders of Rome, who were rescued and brought up by a she-wolf (Livy 1.4.5; Cicero *De republica* 2.2.4). Exposure was practised in the pagan world (cf Aristotle *Politics* 7.16.15 [1335b19–22]), but was strictly prohibited by later Roman law: *Codex* 8.52.2 and *Novellae* 153. In Erasmus' time babies were frequently abandoned in churches; see Margolin 502–3 nn188–9 and 194.

Thus, after weighing up his character, our next concern must be his health. Some physical infirmities are not contagious, such as lameness, blindness, missing or mutilated limbs, or other unnatural deformities; in fact, if both have some defect it may add to the harmony of their marriage. I knew a priest in Britain, a tall, healthy, upright man, who told me that he had eleven brothers, all with an equally fine physique; but their father had withered legs and had to be carried everywhere in a chair. He was also rather poor, so he married a blind woman and gave the following explanation: 'We shall be better friends because of it; we shall bear with one another, being united in misfortune, and neither of us will be able to find fault with the other.' And the man's judgment was perfect: every word they exchanged was friendly and fond. God rewarded their devotion with a happy issue; their life together was tranquil and blameless and their children numerous and well-favoured.

It remains to discuss external qualities,[375] which are to some extent beyond our control (for example, being born of a distinguished or wealthy family) but can to some extent be obtained and improved by our own efforts. In this area the first place goes to family distinction, especially when it has been won by true virtue. All too often, 'nobility' is no more than inherited wealth, and it is not uncommon for wealth to be the proceeds of crime. By contrast, the true aristocrat, if he values more than a mere reputation for virtue, will have an example of the right way to live close at hand, from his ancestors, and if they have failed to provide one, his family tree will serve no purpose other than to make their immorality all the more notorious.

In some countries nowadays a mere title of nobility can confer immunity on a criminal.[376] If a commoner commits piracy or highway robbery, he is broken on the wheel; if he is a knight, or a claimant to some minor title, or the owner of some ruined castle (more like a den of thieves),[377] then it is called war, which can apparently be declared by somebody without a foot of land to stand on.[378] What gives such people the right to declare war?

* * * * *

375 The third of the Aristotelian categories of 'good things,' after those of the mind and those of the body; cf n319 above.
376 Cf the colloquy Ἱππεὺς ἄνιππος, sive Ementita nobilitas ('The Knight without a Horse, or Faked Nobility') CWE 40 884–8, on knights doing as they please, their insolence passing for wisdom, and Adagia I ix 44 (CWE 32 204–5), on the excesses of the German Junkers.
377 Cf Luke 19:46.
378 Adagia I v 7

What gives them the right, under the pretext of some trumped-up 'war,' to rob anyone they please on the public highway or on other people's land? Whenever they run out of money for their gambling, whoring, and drinking, they rush to so-called war – making sure that their chosen enemy has something worth plundering. The princes, and the emperor in particular, would do humanity a great service if they would get rid of such monsters, with their horses and castles; when they are caught red-handed, let their titles give them just the one privilege – of being hanged higher, as their exalted status demands!

Parents must be mad if they imagine it to be in their daughter's best interests to marry her to one of these knights rather than an honest farmer or a skilled artisan. Bewitched by an empty parade of nobility, they prefer a son-in-law who will waste good money on bad living to one who will preserve and increase his portion by his own efforts. The girls themselves may be forgiven this mistake; their age and sex make them too eager for glory, unable to judge rationally or to look beyond the excitement of the moment. But no such allowance can be made for their parents, who to their shame bewail – afterwards – a calamity that they could have prevented. Given all the previous examples of such marriages, they should have learned from others' misfortunes.

Away then with these empty pretensions to nobility, acquired by crime, stained with sin, faked,[379] or assumed! Only impostors will pass themselves off as noblemen, but some do so in order to commit their crimes with more safety and impunity; only fools who glory in shadows will buy nobility. The wise man will scorn even true nobility. There is some merit in being descended from distinguished and honourable forebears, but much more in being brought up and educated in a manner befitting your lineage. Thus, if the family tree does enter the equation, so must the young man's disposition, character, and upbringing, to avoid tears later, because, as the Greek proverb puts it, the children of heroes are a bane.[380] Take account of the virtues, not the nobility, of his family. You must not be impressed by aristocrats whose only nobility lies in the portraits in the hall; a man of outstanding virtue is noble enough, and anyone born of a lawful union cannot be considered ignoble.

* * * * *

379 *Ementita*; cf the title of the 1529 colloquy cited n376 above, which develops fully the themes sketched here (CWE 40 880–90).
380 *Adagia* I vi 32; the rest of this paragraph is based on the commentary on this adage. The remarks on the virtues of the illegitimate obviously have personal overtones for Erasmus.

Indeed, although people always suspect the worst of bastards and by-blows, they are very often wrong, since the evidence shows that the worst of children can be born to the best of parents, while we sometimes see an irregular union produce the most distinguished of men. Jephthah the bastard is enrolled among the Hebrews most distinguished for their virtue, and the name of bastard cannot tarnish the glory of Themistocles. By contrast, Socrates left children whose very names are unknown, and apparently Cicero's son was a drunken sot quite unlike his father. That most reviled of Roman emperors, Commodus, was the son of Antoninus, the most admired of them.[381] I think that this must be laid to the charge of the wives, who bear the children and see to their early upbringing. Socrates' wives were dreadful women, Cicero's Terentia deserved to be repudiated, and the emperor Antoninus' wife was notorious for more than one adulterous affair.[382] Thus it is useful to consider the character, as well as the lineage, of both parents.

If there is nothing else to choose between a bastard and a legitimate child, an aristocrat and a commoner, then you should opt for legitimacy and nobility. But if the commoner outshines him in true virtue, then a mere title should not persuade you to make your daughter live with a man who is distinguished only by others' achievements, rather than with a man capable of ennobling even the humblest stock by his own good qualities. I admit that a row of family portraits seems a plausible guarantee of a man's honour, but since the customary pursuits of most noblemen today are dicing, playing cards, drinking, dancing, acting the fool, and whoring, anyone who wishes to provide his daughter with a good Christian marriage must weigh up the suitor's upbringing and character, the things, in other words, that belong to him rather than to someone else. Here, I would give some weight to public opinion concerning the suitors' families, so long as the difference between the young men in terms of virtue is slight. The principal objectives of Christian matrimony must always be

* * * * *

381 On Jephthah, see Judg 11–12. According to Plutarch's *Lives*, the Athenian general and statesman Themistocles was the son of an obscure Athenian and an alien mother whose very name and country are in doubt, while Cicero's son Marcus, despite rising to the consulate, was best known for his boasts of heavy drinking. The saintly and philosophical Marcus Aurelius Antoninus (emperor 161–80 AD and author of the *Meditations*) was succeeded by his worthless son Commodus (d 192 AD).

382 On Socrates' two wives, see n327 above. After divorcing Terentia for adultery, Cicero married again, but he also repudiated his second wife. Marcus Aurelius' wife Faustina was suspected of infidelity and of instigating plots against her husband.

that the marriage should be first of all lawful, then holy, and finally harmonious and tranquil; if these three conditions are met, it cannot be thought unsuccessful.

Ancient fables tell of the demigods supposed to be born of unions between gods and nymphs or mortals; Aeneas was supposedly born of Venus and Anchises, Bacchus of Semele and Jupiter, Hercules of Jupiter and Alcmena.[383] Some people imagine foolishly that this is like intermarriage between patrician and plebeian. But this idea, mocked even in pagan times by the philosophers, must be entirely banished from the thoughts of Christians. Through baptism we are all reborn as the legitimate children of God, and the same inheritance awaits us all. The nobleman here is he who best represents the image of his creator, the common Father of all who live devoutly, and he who comes closest to the example set by God's only-begotten Son, who honours us all with the name of brother.[384] If nobility is important to you, then here is true nobility. Paul says that a pagan husband can be made holy by a Christian wife, and vice versa;[385] how much more should an illegitimate or plebeian wife be ennobled by a patrician husband, and vice versa?

Now slavery is an odious thing, which Paul tells us to escape if we have the chance;[386] it should have been abolished among Christians long ago. Nothing could be more unseemly than that among Christians, whom Christ redeemed equally by his precious blood, one man should consider another not as his brother and joint heir to the heavenly kingdom, but as hardly human, buying him for cash like a packhorse and selling him again at a whim – owning him and treating him like a brute beast, and in fact sometimes using his Christian brother more harshly than his horse. A man who knew nothing of Christ exhorts us to remember that slaves are human beings.[387] The apostle Paul wants a baptized slave to be given the name of brother; he commends Onesimus to the master from whom he had escaped: 'Receive him, therefore, as a part of myself.' A little earlier he had called him 'my beloved son, whom I bore in my chains.' A little later, he says: 'Receive him now, not as a slave, but as more than a slave, as a beloved brother. If you count me a partner, receive him as you would

* * * * *

383 Stories of heroes begotten out of wedlock are commonplace in classical mythology; Erasmus names three of the most celebrated.
384 Cf Matt 12:50, 25:40; Mark 3:35.
385 See 1 Cor 7:14.
386 See 1 Cor 7:21.
387 Cato *Disticha* 4.44

me.'[388] Such was the power of the baptism they shared that a former slave, a runaway slave, became a 'beloved son' to Paul and a 'beloved brother' to his master.

The Apostle does not want a slave to leave his master unless he has been freed, as this might impede the progress of the gospel; for the same reason he does not want a Christian wife to turn from a pagan husband. If human laws insist on the right of property, then at least the slave's attitude can be changed, if not his status. Slaves should not perform their duties out of fear, serving, as Paul said, only as far as the eye can see, but do everything willingly, 'fearing the Lord in the simplicity of their hearts,'[389] knowing that if the men they serve are impious or inhuman, yet they shall receive from Christ, for whose love masters become slaves, the ample reward of their eternal inheritance. In return, masters must show humanity and give them what is fair and just, as brothers, as fellow slaves, and as fellow heirs. As brothers, because they have been reborn to the same Father through baptism; as fellow slaves, because a human slave is no less valued than his master by the Lord that both serve; as fellow heirs because, in the distribution of rewards that the Gospel promised to believers, masters have no advantage over slaves: status will help no one, but piety will decide all. But perhaps all this is better discussed elsewhere. I merely wished to point out here the need for caution, lest you unknowingly marry a servant thinking her a free woman. In fact, human laws will also disallow such a marriage, but it is better to walk round a trap than to extricate yourself after falling into it. Servants and maidservants who use some knavery to put themselves forward as free-born should be appropriately punished by the law.

Now, money should be the least important question, especially if both partners have enough income to live on decently, or a trade instead of an estate. In comedies,[390] as it happens, marriages are called into question when an impoverished bride marries a rich husband, on the ground that she is entering into slavery rather than matrimony. However, among Christians, whom Christ has made equal in so many ways, the size of the dowry should not be so important; in fact, as I have said, things usually turn out better if a rich husband takes a bride without a dowry, rather than the reverse. It is entirely laudable that a rich man should take in marriage a girl of slender means but of good character; the greater the disparity in their fortune, the

* * * * *

388 The quotations are from Philem 10–17.
389 Allusions to Col 3:22; Eph 6:5–6
390 Eg in the *Aulularia* and *Mercator* of Plautus

more his generosity will be admired. However, financial equality may play a far from negligible part in establishing harmony between those of lesser means, if at the same time it is balanced against the other advantages and disadvantages, and if the order of priorities I have established is preserved.

If all marriages were made in this way, that is, with the support of the parents (or after due consultation with the older generation), by choosing with care and sound judgment, and above all by placing our hopes in God, then the world would not see so many unhappy and burdensome marriages, nor so many separations. It is God alone who joins human hearts in endless love and brings us success by his favour. We cannot do better by him than to live according to his decrees, placing all our expectations of success in him, since he alone knows what is good for us. All that he sends us is truly blessed and auspicious, even if it sometimes appears calamitous to the superficial mind. Therefore, if you find a wife who fulfils your heart's desire, you must give thanks to God; if not, you must believe that, just as he draws some people to him and purifies them through illness or the loss of their worldly goods, so you have been given a shrewish wife to test your virtue, as happened to those holy men Job and Tobias.[391] If such a one has fallen to your lot, submit to the will of God and, if you cannot mend the faults in your wife, embrace the God-given opportunity to display your patience, saying, like Paul, 'Virtue is made perfect by weakness.'[392] He will put an end to your troubles; like the wise doctor he knows the right time to act, and the precise moment that is best. You must know that there can be no unhappiness wherever there is purity of intent and will.

Finally, besides all that has been said, there is always that inexplicable element of liking – or dislike – between two people. Thus it happens that, for no apparent reason, a man is well disposed towards one person rather than another, that he likes the first more than the second; similarly, he may recoil from someone but be quite unable to explain why he dislikes him. The ancient sophists' theory was that people's presiding geniuses[393] were either compatible or incompatible. Whatever we may think of this clever explanation, we do detect this unexplained affinity or disharmony between people's natures, as in the oft-repeated epigram

* * * * *

391 See eg Job 2:9–10; Tob 2:13–14, 3:1–6.
392 2 Cor 12:9
393 The widespread classical notion of the tutelary deity, the *genius* or *daemon*, aroused much interest among Erasmus' contemporaries. According to some, each person had both a good and an evil genius; Erasmus depicted the evil genius of the pope in *Julius exclusus* (see CWE 27 168 and n1).

I do not love thee, Doctor Fell;
The reason why I cannot tell;
But this alone I know full well,
I do not love thee, Doctor Fell.[394]

This instinct should not be entirely trusted, especially in women, because it is often thoughtless and merely temporary. But if it persists, if it is constant and unshakeable, then it is no use 'fighting the gods,'[395] in my view; we must give in to this inexplicable natural inclination, which is also observable in animals, plants, and trees.[396]

Thus, once a lawful marriage has been made with all due care and consideration, the next thing will be to ensure that harmony and good will are established and encouraged between the partners.[397] For in some cases friendship disintegrates at the very beginning, before it has been cemented, before they have the chance to know and grow accustomed to each other. The parents and older members of the family have a primary responsibility here. They must warn the bride and groom beforehand that they will have to lay aside that aggressiveness which is so characteristic of inexperienced young women and hot-blooded adolescents and that each will have to take up the common yoke with docility and make allowances for the other, until growing familiarity and intimacy enable each to understand the disposition and character of the other. If this is done, it will be none too difficult for them to avoid upsets by considerate behaviour and to lay the foundations of a lasting affection that, once established, will not easily be destroyed. You could compare them to little pots stuck together with glue.[398] If you knock them while the glue is still wet, they will break at a touch, but if you wait until the glue has hardened and they are firmly stuck, they will be very

* * * * *

394 Martial *Epigrams* 1.32; the nursery-rhyme translation is by Thomas Brown.
395 Erasmus uses the Greek expression found in *Adagia* II v 44 and III ix 22.
396 A gloss on this remark is provided by *De pueris instituendis* CWE 26 312: in the animal and plant kingdoms, says Erasmus, it is natural to 'avoid anything that would cause harm and suffering.' He goes on to give a precise example concerning trees.
397 Many parallels exist between the following passage on the ideal domestic way of life and the 1523 colloquy *Coniugium* ('Marriage') CWE 39 306–27. In both texts, as Craig Thompson (ibidem 306) notes, Erasmus solves all problems 'with the invincible assurance of a confirmed bachelor'; in the colloquy, however, Erasmus provides four detailed examples of wedded bliss from his own observations.
398 The simile is borrowed from Plutarch's treatise on marriage, *Moralia* 138E.

difficult to break, even with fire or a sword. Even things joined by nature are more easily broken than those that are glued together in this way.

Thus the girl needs to be told by her parents to be obliging and compliant towards her husband and, if he should upset her, to give him the benefit of the doubt, or at least put up with it. She must not rush headlong into recrimination and arguments, nor flounce out of the house; in time, when life together has bred intimacy between them, it will ensure that things that upset her at first will now amuse her, and that what once seemed intolerable will prove very easy to bear. However, it is best to try to avoid such problems altogether since, as Homer's epic tells us, 'Discord is swift, reconciliation is slow.'[399] It will not be difficult for one of them to make amends for some trifling offence, if it is done at once, but if they both retaliate the quarrel is likely to grow and become so deep-rooted that it will be very difficult to eradicate without leaving some traces of bitterness behind. It will be like a broken limb or a deep wound, which is rarely so completely healed by medical science that an occasional twinge of pain does not remind us of the accident, or an ugly scar allow us to forget the old wound. A mere bruise or a graze is easily healed and eventually quite forgotten.

Just as no one is blessed with a personality completely free from flaws, so almost no one can have a character so hopeless that there is not some admirable, or at least tolerable, trait among all the defects. Epictetus is worth listening to here: he says that we must always grab the handle that we can see, not look for another one that isn't there![400] There is a type of person who is disenchanted with every aspect of human existence, and no wonder, since they refuse to consider anything but the evils that beset our mortal condition. Take, for example, Heraclitus and Democritus:[401] whenever they went out into the world, the former would weep and the latter laugh; I don't know which of them was the madder. Somebody said, 'It would be best either not to be born, or to be snuffed out as soon as possible.'[402] On the other hand, Metrodorus, who managed to discern inherent advantages in everything, had nothing but praise for every aspect of life.[403] But the

* * * * *

399 Homer *Iliad* 9.502, where discord and reconciliation are personified as Ate and Litae; cf *Adagia* I vii 13.
400 Epictetus *Enchiridion* 43; cf *Adagia* I iv 4.
401 Pre-Socratic Greek philosophers proverbial for their contrasting reactions to the spectacle of humanity
402 A venerable utterance reported in this form by Pliny *Naturalis historia* 7.1.4; cf *Adagia* II iii 49.
403 Cf Plutarch *Moralia* 142A. Metrodorus, a physician, was a disciple of the laughing philosopher Democritus.

wise man will always weigh advantages against disadvantages, if he has the liberty to be dispassionate. If he is not free to change his way of life, he must turn his eyes from the disadvantages to the advantages, to help him bear what cannot be changed. You will find this easier to do if you will admit that other people may perhaps have to put up with a good deal from you. God, in whom there is no evil for others to put up with, none the less puts up with our errors and sins, with immense forbearance; so how can you, a prey to so many vices, refuse to put up with some fault in your lifetime partner, whom you must tolerate even if you find her intolerable?

If husband and wife are as bad as each other, then mutual forgiveness is more like appeasement than tolerance, more like a settling of scores than an act of generosity. The jurists define four types of contract: I give that you may give; I give that you may do; I do that you may do; I do that you may give.[404] What merit is there in someone offering forgiveness simply in order to be forgiven when he does something wrong? If yours are the worse misdeeds, it is merely cynical for you to shudder at the wart on your partner's face while expecting your own great tumours to be overlooked! If you surpass your partner in virtue and generosity, that is all the more reason, as Paul taught, to look after the weaker part.[405] Remember that your strength is a gift bestowed by God to enable you to help those weaker than yourself, and especially your partner. 'No man hates his own flesh' or shrinks from it, however corrupt, 'but instead cherishes and sustains it.'[406]

Now in some circumstances a husband should give in to his wife now and then, even though she is the 'weaker vessel';[407] but the wife must defer much more to the authority of the head, 'for the husband is the head of the wife,' as Paul said.[408] The husband is to the wife what the spirit is to the body.[409] The spirit is the greater of the two, but it is for the body's benefit; the spirit does not dominate and overwhelm it, but makes concessions to assist it. The affection the husband feels for his bride will enable him to recognize the right time either to tolerate or to correct the girl's inclinations. Similarly, if the girl gives her husband a wife's love together with

* * * * *

404 On the basic forms of contract see eg *Digesta* 45.1.75 and *Institutiones* 3.15.1.
405 This conveys Paul's meaning in such chapters as 1 Cor 7 and Eph 5, but is closest textually to 1 Pet 3:7, cited a few lines later.
406 Eph 5:29
407 1 Pet 3:7
408 Eph 5:23, a principle enshrined in canon law with the approval of Augustine and Jerome; cf Gratian *Decretum* pars 2 c 33 q 5 cc 13–20.
409 A comparison found in Plutarch's treatise on marriage, *Moralia* 142E

appropriate respect for him, which nature's laws seem to require in view of his sex and position, she will not be tempted to argue with her husband but will win his affection by obedience and compromise.

At the outset, even the sweetest things may have their unpleasant side, a sort of bitter taste which, with the passage of time, turns to sweetness. What is more pleasant than wine? And yet it comes from grapes, which are bitter at first. Thus any man who recoils instinctively from his virgin bride, finding her unbearably sour and immature, is acting as irrationally as someone who tastes an unripe grape and, disgusted by the acid taste, rejects it and leaves the sweet taste of the ripened grape to others.[410] You are prepared to wait until new wine has lost its sharpness; you must also wait a little until your new bride has matured. Put the unripe apples to one side until in time they become more appetizing. Such rawness is often evidence of a natural vigour and firmness. People who mature too soon often have less strength and grow old before their time. As the proverb says, neither honey nor bee.[411] If you require sweetness, you must accept that it may have its unpleasant side. Nature so frames human life that nothing is so sweet as to be free from all bitterness. Young men, too, not yet forearmed with any great experience of the world, can be somewhat rough and arrogant until the passage of a few years calms them down. Thus girls who recoil from their husbands and immediately begin to feud with them are acting as rashly as someone who is stung by a bee and therefore leaves the honey to others. The most beautiful rose grows among thorns. You do not dig up your rose garden as soon as a thorn pricks you; you accept the pain for love of the flowers.

They say there was a custom among the Boeotians[412] that a bride on her way to her husband was veiled – and crowned with a garland made of asparagus. This seems so absurd that of course it invites the observer to seek a hidden meaning. No doubt the ancients intended it to signify that in the union of an inexperienced young man and an untutored and spirited virgin there was bound to be some friction and difficulty at first, but that, if

* * * * *

410 Another comparison borrowed from Plutarch, *Moralia* 138E
411 *Adagia* I vi 62
412 This example and the preceding one of the rose are found in Plutarch *Moralia* 138D–E. The Boeotians were proverbial for their stupidity, but Plutarch and Erasmus do their best to rehabilitate them here. Judging by the subsequent description of the plant, there may be some confusion with the *aspalathus*, a prickly shrub that yielded a fragrant oil; see Pliny *Naturalis historia* 12.24.110.

they persevered, their difficulties would give way to a most agreeable way of life, just as asparagus is a prickly plant – all prickle, in fact, as it has no leaves – which none the less produces a fruit that is both delicious to eat and most useful in medicine. However, asparagus is always just asparagus, and does not bear fruit in every season, whereas the young couple's prickliness will change into endless sweetness and produce everlasting fruit, if only they will work together towards mutual harmony.

Even with the virtuous and the well-born, there are certain quirks of character, if not actual faults, that can be annoying unless you are used to them. It is the same with certain wines, which you cannot justly call sour or bitter but which have their own peculiar taste, commonly called the tang of the soil,[413] which may be somewhat unpalatable to anyone unused to it; but on a few days' acquaintance the distaste may be overcome. Would you begrudge doing for your wife what you do for your wine?

Again, there are minor blemishes, like moles on the skin, that it is best to ignore. That carping attitude which the Greeks call μικρολογία [pettiness] can cast a blight over all life's pleasures; it is like quarrelling over goat's wool, as the saying goes.[414] One thing that will contribute much to preserving affection between you is an unfailing courtesy, striking a balance between indulgence and austerity so that it does not lose you respect, but equally does not mar the pleasures of family life. It should ensure that any necessary rebuke will not give offence, if it is timely, delivered in a pleasant manner, and tempered with praise and a little flattery.

Thus it will be essential, to avoid problems and to encourage total harmony between you, that each should study and be familiar with the character and disposition of the other; here again the parents could help by giving advice to the bride and groom. As Virgil put it, 'You know the tactful and the timely way to approach a husband.'[415] The slave in the comedy says something similar: 'I understand his disposition very well.'[416] As the proverb has it, you should understand a friend's character, not hate it.[417] All this will be even more necessary in marriage. Everyone has different tastes and a different temperament; people are attracted or repelled by different things.

* * * * *

413 *Sapor soli*; cf French 'vin du terroir.'
414 *Adagia* I iii 53; goat's wool – if it may be called that – is of course more or less worthless.
415 Virgil *Aeneid* 4.423; Dido is addressing her sister Anna.
416 Terence *Adelphi* 533
417 *Adagia* II v 96

In this case, there is nothing wrong with 'friendship won by submissiveness.'[418] A modest silence or a pleasant, soothing reply will often defuse a serious quarrel. Why should you refuse such things, which you would often enough grant a servant or an employee, to your spouse, with whom, willy-nilly, you are to spend the rest of your life?

However, although there must be mutual respect, both nature and scriptural authority lay down that the wife should obey her husband rather than the opposite. Paul recommends love and gentleness to husbands: 'You men,' he says, 'love your wives, and do not be harsh with them.' But what does he prescribe for the women? Obedience and submissiveness: 'You women,' he says, 'be subject to your husbands as to the Lord.'[419] For this very reason nature has endowed the male sex with a certain ruthlessness and fierceness, but the female with softness and gentleness. You may find the following comparison far-fetched, but it is apt enough to illustrate my point. The first thing that trainers of animals, wild beasts, or unbroken horses try to find out is what things will annoy or calm them. Lions are annoyed when they are looked at sideways; bulls are enraged by the colour red; lynxes are so maddened by the sound of drums that they will claw themselves to pieces; elephants are frightened by the squealing of a pig, and think it shameful to be caught in the act of coition.[420] A plunging horse can be calmed by stroking and by clicking the tongue. There are countless other examples; animal trainers always know the best ways to avoid upsetting their charges, and use them to calm unsettled beasts. They are thus able to handle safely animals that are by nature dangerous and fierce.

If a married couple will do the same, they will soon begin to enjoy a life of tranquillity, and if some disagreement should arise, it will not be hard to resolve it peacefully. Some otherwise virtuous people are by nature quick to anger, but it soon evaporates if they are not opposed. What could be easier than to remain demurely silent in such cases, or to soothe them with appropriately amiable words? Some people cannot stand being answered back when they are upset, and even refuse words of comfort as long as the hurt is fresh in their minds. An easy and economical solution here is to postpone one's reply until such time as the wound is less sensitive. Some husbands

* * * * *

418 *Adagia* II ix 53
419 The quotations are Col 3:19 and Eph 5:22.
420 Most of these examples had already appeared in the colloquy *Coniugium* ('Marriage') CWE 39 312. The original sources are book 8 of Pliny's *Naturalis historia* (lions 19.52; elephants 9.27 and 5.13) and Plutarch's *Moralia* 144D–E for the bulls and lynxes (tigers in Plutarch).

enjoy boisterous parties; in this case a more serious-minded wife should not raise an eyebrow, but make some allowance for her husband, provided that her matronly modesty and the respect she should feel for her husband are not affected. Some people cannot bear to be told a lie, even in jest, some detest make-up, others like or dislike particular foods or particular colours and styles of clothing. Even in such trivial cases, a measure of complaisance will avoid upsets and encourage affection. Certain kinds of story appeal to some tastes but not to others; an offensive tale can often be interrupted and toned down by a timely interjection. I knew a man, rather irascible by nature but easily placated, who never got so annoyed with his wife that he would not, if called on for a song or one of his poems, at once begin to recite or sing, apparently forgetting all that had gone before.

It is not too surprising that some wives do not get on with their husbands, when they take every opportunity to be contrary. If their husband is sad, their faces beam with joy; if he is happy, they look downcast; if he is laughing and joking, they will talk about something serious and sad; if the husband is feeling amorous, they suddenly become ostentatiously chaste and forbidding. No doubt this illustrates that witty saying, 'With a husband, life isn't very lively.'[421] But living together means sharing pleasures and cares, fun and seriousness, joys and sorrows. It is not enough for a wife to be honest and chaste unless she is also sympathetic to her husband's moods. No one would think much of a mirror,[422] however crusted with gold and jewels, if it did not give a faithful reflection; similarly, a rich, noble, and beautiful wife is no use if she does not fit in with her husband. If a mirror showed a laughing face weeping or a happy face as sad, would it not be considered unreliable and useless? But a wife who is happy when her husband is sad or sad when he is happy appears not only unsuitable but even hostile. Again, there are some women to whom nothing is so delightful as their husband's absence, while his presence makes them restless and foul-tempered; you could compare them to the moon,[423] which is dull and dark when close to the sun, but ever brighter as it moves away. A good wife should do the opposite: when her husband is by her, she must share his joy; when he is away, she must stay indoors and behave as if she were a widow.

Similarly, some husbands make the bad mistake of being morose and stern at home and merry and gregarious everywhere else; by denying their wives a share in their pleasures at home, they are encouraging them to

* * * * *

421 Cf *Adagia* iii ix 80: *Conviva non conviva*.
422 The image is developed from Plutarch *Moralia* 139F.
423 Another image developed from Plutarch's treatise on marriage, *Moralia* 139C

seek amusement and laughter elsewhere. However, a good wife will not revenge herself by imitating her husband's faults; instead, she will encourage him to appreciate home life by her pleasant and accommodating manner. When grafting new shoots onto a plant, gardeners always take great care to meld the parts together, smearing them with a mixture of clay and oakum, and as Virgil elegantly put it, 'They teach the shoot to grow in the moist bark.'[424] This prevents even slight damage to the new graft; when in time a scar has covered the wound, they pull off the poultice and need give the graft no further special care. Similarly, there is a greater danger of discord in the very first stages of a marriage, when the union is still fresh and fragile, but each day's acquaintance makes it stronger. We may observe how animals of the same species, such as horses, do not necessarily get on until they have grown used to one another, but that we may see peaceful relations even between a dog and a cat, or a wolf and a lamb,[425] once acquaintance has been established. We must surely expect even better of human beings, creatures born to social life, and still more of a man and a woman, whom nature has so fashioned that they cannot live without each other – unless a power greater than nature has breathed upon them.[426]

Thus it is excellent advice that the first lovemaking between husband and wife should be made as easy as possible. This is believed to be the reason for the ancient marriage ritual in which the bride was taken into the husband's bedchamber in the dark. This custom was obviously exploited to deceive the patriarch Jacob, when Leah was substituted for her sister Rachel.[427] Commentators suggest two reasons for the custom: to protect the girl's modesty, and to prevent anything in this first sexual act, which is often the most difficult, from offending the husband's eye.

Solon apparently made provision not only for fastidious eyes, but also for the most delicate nose.[428] He decreed that, before the bride was brought into the bedchamber for the intimate meeting with her groom, she should nibble a quince apple to purify her breath. Such attention to

* * * * *

424 Virgil *Georgics* 2.77
425 A most unlikely occurrence according to *Adagia* iv vii 91: *Ut lupus ovem amat*, 'As a wolf loves a sheep'
426 A reference to the divine gift of chastity; cf Matt 19:10–12 and 1 Cor 7:7.
427 Gen 29:23–5; the custom is also mentioned by Plutarch *Moralia* 280A (*Quaestiones Romanae* 65).
428 Solon, the celebrated Athenian lawgiver, as quoted in Plutarch *Moralia* 138D and 280A. The subsequent comparison with the training of children recalls Erasmus' *De civilitate* 5 CWE 25 286–8.

detail might seem unworthy of a legislator, were it not that the merest trifles all too often destroy human relationships. However, I am quite ready
to accept the view that that wise man aimed to conceal a deeper meaning in his statute, namely, that it is vital that a new bride should not, in
their first conversation, let slip from her mouth anything that might offend the young man's ears or mind. Speech issues from the lips but is
the most reliable image and witness of the soul; from her words he will
see more clearly what she is like than by examining her whole body under a spotlight. When we send our children with a message to some worthy citizen, we teach them the correct form of address and the right answer to each question, so that nothing offends the company. How much
more should parents ensure that the couple's first conversations be harmless, infused with modesty and politeness? They must learn that, whereas
among close friends even insults can be laughed off, in a first conversation
between strangers the most harmless observation may give offence. But no
quince apple, no brand of perfume or unguent smells as sweet to a wise
young man as modest, sober, prudent, and respectful words dropping from
the lips of his new bride and bringing with them the reflection of a lovely
nature.

Furthermore, there is nothing better than conversation to establish,
confirm, and maintain friendship. It was conversation that drew human beings, who used to roam the earth like wild animals, together in cities; it also
joined city to city, people to people, kingdom to kingdom. It distinguishes
the king from the tyrant, since the tyrant compels but the king persuades.
Now marriage is rather like a kingdom, but must be far from any semblance
of tyranny. Nothing is accomplished there by force; all is done by persuasion and good will. Plato will not let a law prescribe anything unless it can
be defended on moral as well as practical grounds, and I do not see why
Seneca attacks his view.[429] The husband is indeed the director and head of
the woman and rules her: not, however, as the farmer drives his cattle, but
as the spirit rules the body.[430] His character provides unwritten laws for his
wife's behaviour, as Aristotle rightly said;[431] but they are Platonic laws, persuading not compelling her, guiding her willingly, not dragging her along
by force.

* * * * *

429 Plato *Laws* 4.722–3; Seneca *Epistulae morales* 94.38. In fact Seneca is merely quoting Posidonius, and himself agrees with Plato; cf *Institutio principis christiani*
CWE 27 265.
430 Cf n409 above.
431 Pseudo-Aristotle *Oeconomica* 3.1; on this work, see n300 above.

According to Greek writers, the ancients used to associate Mercury with Venus.[432] You may well wonder what Venus has to do with Mercury. The ancient sages explain that good relations between a couple are established not so much by a sharing of physical pleasures as by a meeting of minds; the cement between them is courteous and friendly speech. On her own Venus is both intemperate and violent and, as the poet says, 'forces many beneath her brazen yoke.'[433] But speech, which in antiquity was the province of Mercury,[434] can establish lasting friendship on sound and honourable terms. 'Do not be,' says the psalmist, 'like the horse and the mule, in which there is no understanding.'[435] The Lord makes a similar complaint in Jeremiah: 'They have become like lustful and roving stallions, each one neighing after his neighbour's wife.'[436] Similar were the husbands, followers of Venus and not Mercury, whom the demon Asmodeus slaughtered one after the other.[437]

I wish that, among Christians too, the lustful husband were not praised to the skies. Does it augur well for his marriage if he makes love to his wife for the first time as if he were raping a prisoner? He rips off her underwear, tears her clothes and anything else that impedes his stallion's lust. You would say that the groom behaves more like a madman than a lover, and that nothing could be less like a sacramental union. There is more dignity in the mating of most dumb animals. And it is not finished yet: the details of that first night are recounted and spread abroad ... How unchristian a marriage is this marriage between Christians! A wife must obey her husband, of course, but Mercury must also be there, to join their hearts before their bodies, to urge but not to force them to physical intimacy. While on the subject, we must remind the bride not to instigate their lovemaking herself, as this may diminish his affection for her;[438] on the other hand, she must not show herself too unwilling or forbidding when he suggests it. The first attitude, for some reason, makes a woman cheap and less attractive to a man,

* * * * *

432 Plutarch *Moralia* 138c
433 Horace *Odes* 3.9.18
434 Best known as the messenger of the gods, Mercury was also, among other things, the patron of orators. Cf *Adagia* II x 10: *Mercurius infans*, where he is described as the father of eloquence and of the arts.
435 Ps 31 (Vulg 32):9
436 Jer 5:8 in the Vulgate; English versions are rather different.
437 See Tob 3:8 and 6:13–17 on the demon who killed Sarah's seven husbands on their wedding night, finally thwarted by Tobias, who, as Erasmus approvingly relates 346 below, talked and prayed with his bride on their wedding night.
438 Similar advice is given by Plutarch *Moralia* 140c.

the second changes love into hatred. A respectable married woman will not be provocative, a chaste woman will know how to refuse gently, but only a false wife will persist in her protests.

Again, I am rather afraid that someone will say, 'Why are you stuffing your Venus and your Mercury into Christian ears?' Come now, the gods' names may be changed, but the argument is the same. We have a Mercury of our own, the Word of God the Father, who reconciles all things both in heaven and on earth.[439] Let us make him the witness and sponsor of Christian marriage, so that no impurity may soil relations with a spouse; let the husband persuade his wife, through God's decrees and laws, to do willingly and joyfully what she has learned is pleasing to the Lord. Let both partners first pray to him in unison to bestow his favour on their marriage; after prayer, let them engage in pious conversation. Finally, let their lovemaking be modest and virtuous, the opposite of fornication and rape.

I know that there will be some – fine, witty fellows in their own estimation – who will find all this ridiculous, but let these fine unchristian fellows go hang; I am writing this treatise for good Christians. However, let those who think Christ's teaching worthless at least hearken to the old man in the pagan comedy, who said to his son, 'Go home, and pray to the gods that your bride may be brought to you.'[440] That pagan will not have the bride brought from her home, nor does he expect the marriage to be blessed by heaven, unless the bridegroom prays to the gods. But you consider it unfashionable, before you lay hands on your wife, to pray together to the one who first joined wife to husband, and to ask him to make your marriage stable, chaste, and blessed. If you are not ashamed to be called a Christian, do not be ashamed to do what most befits a Christian.

Perhaps you need a form of prayer? I shall be pleased to provide one. It will be appropriate to pray along these lines: 'O creator, redeemer, and propagator of the human race, God, who first in paradise consecrated the marriage-alliance between the founders of our race; whose only-begotten Son commended this sacrament to us in many ways, first when in an inexpressible way he joined our nature to himself, as if in marriage; then again when he chose the congregation of all the saints as his bride, being born for this purpose within wedlock but without need for a human father; then when he honoured a wedding with the first of his miracles, turning water into the best wine; and finally, when he decreed that this holy union, to reflect its mystic origins, should be indissoluble, saying, "What God has

* * * * *

439 Cf Col 1:20.
440 Terence *Adelphi* 699

joined, let no man put asunder":[441] we pray that, since we have joined lawfully in this holy union, according to your decrees, you will deign to prosper with your perpetual favour what is yours, that we may obey your will with equal humility and equal zeal. May all uncleanness and all discord be banished from our home; give us that true peace the world cannot give;[442] give us enough to satisfy our needs; give us offspring to bring up in your name, so that, continuing together under your commandments here below, we may deserve to come together into the inheritance of heavenly life.' If you can think of some better form of words, use that.

You can find a model for your conversation in the book of Tobit: 'We are the children of holy men,' he says, 'and we cannot be united in the manner of the pagans who know not God.'[443] You could also borrow a form of prayer from the same book, if you do not like mine. But the following exchange seems appropriate to Christian spouses; the husband begins as follows: 'My dearest one, my sister in religion, my partner in marriage: God has seen fit to join us together in the holy bond of matrimony, and I have gained something I must prefer even to my parents, whom, after God, I hold dearer than anything else; you too have been given something that you are told to hold dearer than your progenitors. We are closely joined to our parents by the ties of blood, but as the scriptural prophecy says, in matrimony we two have in a certain way been made one flesh, that is, a single person. We have accepted a yoke that cannot be lifted from us as long as we live; we must not even think of separation, but rather direct our energies towards establishing a tranquil and blessed partnership. If there is harmony between us, we shall live pleasantly and happily, however slender our means; on the other hand, if – God forbid – our bodies are united at bed and board but our hearts disunited by discord, then, however abundant our wealth, we shall spend our lives in vexation and misery. Thus let there be between us that special love that unites the body and the soul, Christ and his church. If our friendship is based only on youth, or beauty, or physical attraction, or wealth, there will be no genuine or lasting harmony between us. But if our hearts are united by equal devotion to God and similar reverence for religion, then no earthly misfortune – not poverty, nor illness, nor age – can impair our joyous partnership through life. I shall

* * * * *

441 Matt 19:6; the preceding allusion is to the wedding at Cana (John 2:1–11). On the mystical significance of marriage, see 225 above.
442 Cf John 14:27.
443 Tob 8:5 in the Vulgate; English versions are rather different. The prayers of Tobias and Sarah follow in verses 7–10 (5–8 in English versions).

try my hardest to be a husband you will not regret; I am sure that you on your side will strive to match or surpass my efforts. I have married you to beget children, not out of lust; if, as Paul admonishes, we wish our marriage to be honourable and our bed undefiled,[444] let our life together be pure and gentle, let our lovemaking be modest and infrequent; let us devote ourselves to bringing our children and the rest of the household to holiness, but in such a way that our greatest confidence and principal trust lies in help from God, who favours even the least favoured of his servants. The union of our hearts and the purity of our consciences will provide us with all the pleasure we need. We shall divide the management of the household into two parts: you shall have particular charge of matters pertaining to the home, and I to those outside, but in such a way that neither shall exclude the other. Since it is impossible that we mortals should always be wise, I hope you will believe that, if ever I admonish you, I shall be looking to your interests rather than my own, and if you should see me doing something wrong, I shall not resent admonition from her who shares all that is mine. But the authority nature has given to the husband, and which the apostles confirmed and sanctioned, will not harm you; our mutual affection will smooth every path. Let us therefore enter upon this holy enterprise, inspired by God, united in heart, and equal in resolve. Thus may we live a tranquil and innocent life, like a pair of doves: you shall guard the nest and I shall fly out to seek and bring home the necessities of life. We shall be one and, as it is written, "God shall have mercy on the two who are as one." '[445]

What shall the Christian bride reply to all this? Perhaps she might begin as follows: 'Best of husbands, whom I must not only love but honour, I count myself especially fortunate to have been given a husband who, beyond his other gifts, shows himself both wise and devout. I bring to you from my parents' house a body that is chaste and undefiled; I promise you a heart obedient to your wishes, to all your commands, concerning not only household tasks but also religion and worship. You must decide how to form and instruct me. I have the highest hopes that God will prosper all that we undertake in love.' Christian matrimony should always begin with such preliminaries, with such exchanges; today, instead, we see many marriages that are no more honourable than concubinage, and not much less repulsive: as their beginnings are marked by impiety, so their course is full of troubles and their ending is despair.

* * * * *

444 Cf Heb 13:4.
445 Tob 8:19 in the Vulgate

The course of our discussion now almost compels me to deal with the separate duties of husband and wife. I shall indeed embark on that once I have given a few words of advice on the wedding ceremony, the prelude to marriage, in which ordinary Christians usually make worse mistakes than any pagans do, or ever did. There is more than one reason for these mistakes: people are led astray by ambition, extravagance, intemperance, and licentiousness. First of all, it is unacceptable to subject a bride and groom, who are about to embark on so important and so serious an undertaking, to so many ridiculous little rituals, devised in another time and place to cater for mere human caprice, as if it were a trivial and a frivolous matter for a young man to be united with a pure and chaste virgin. This sacrament need involve no more than the bride's journey to the church, the performance of the ceremony itself, and her return home. What then can justify the general rowdiness and merrymaking, the wanton frolics that go on from breakfast to suppertime, to which the blushing bride must admit all comers – open house for the whole town! The poor girl is obliged to shake hands with drunkards, syphilitics, sometimes with criminals, who have come with an eye more to larceny than dancing; in Britain, she even has to kiss them![446] After a riotous supper, more dancing, another bout of drinking; the exhausted couple are not allowed to retire before midnight. Only a few hours later a mad din and tumult break out again outside their bedroom, everyone charges in to make obscene remarks, and the madness starts up all over again. In some countries this Corybantic frenzy[447] goes on for three days. What could be more inhuman, more uncivilized than to weary with such nonsense these anxious hearts, and these bodies about to take up new burdens? How much more pleasant it would be to hold the nuptial feast quietly and soberly with just the parents and a few close relatives.

But here, as everywhere else, ambition, with extravagance in train, encourages a host of evils. The wedding will be considered beggarly unless a horde of aristocrats, *grandes dames*, plutocrats, and other notables is invited to the feast. A so-called respectable wedding is one where vast sums of money are squandered on frippery, where as many guests as possible throw up or take a fever from intemperance and exhaustion, and where licence is freely granted to filthy language and silly pranks. What a splendid start to the life of chastity, self-denial, and sobriety on which the groom has

* * * * *

446 Erasmus had offered a less morose view of such English customs in a jocular letter of 1499 (Ep 103).

447 Cf *Adagia* III vii 39; the Corybantes were priests of Cybele proverbial for the abandon of their rituals.

embarked, tossing aside the follies of his earlier life! What an atmosphere in which to take a wife and teach her chastity and self-denial! Whose doctrine is it that the holy state of matrimony should begin with the Bacchanalia?[448] Is this the way to take a sacrament? Shall a girl on the threshold of matrimony be initiated into extravagance, wantonness, ambition, and the rest, all so incompatible with true marriage? Christians, it is like celebrating the festival of Flora in the temple of Vesta![449] Are these happy omens for a marriage? It used to be unlawful to speak words of ill omen at a wedding; what worse omens than filthy language, obscene behaviour, and lewd stories?

In ancient times the bride was brought to the groom with her face veiled; why show her to everyone now that she had found a husband? Only one man need set eyes on her, since she is allowed to please only one. In Italy they go to great lengths to keep unmarried girls at home. In Venice, they never go out without a chaperone and a veil down to their shoulders; you would think they were nuns. In fact it would be more acceptable for a girl who has not yet found a husband to be unveiled and paraded in public; but why on earth should a girl to whom it is now forbidden to seek to please other men be paraded bareheaded through the streets? For whose benefit is she unveiled now? For whom is she painted and prinked?

No less absurd is the custom of distinguishing a virgin from a woman of experience by letting her wear her hair loose.[450] Is it not enough that her husband is satisfied as to her virginity, without the public being called to witness? What does such nonsense achieve, except to make impertinent tongues wag about a maiden who is, more often than not, quite irreproachable? The public is eager for scandal, and the envy provoked by this pointless display is a deadly sin. What awful things are sometimes shouted at young girls as they process back and forth in full view of everyone, with the cantor in the lead more or less inviting the public to see the show? What is the point of exposing the glory of virginity to the evil tongues and taunts of men? That treasure is safer if it is hidden. And again, what is the point of reproaching women about to remarry with their previous marriages? Granted, before

* * * * *

448 The Bacchanalia were riotous festivals in honour of the wine-god Bacchus.
449 The Floralia were an extremely licentious Roman celebration of the goddess of spring, supposed originally to have been a courtesan; Vesta was the goddess of fire and the hearth, and patroness of the celebrated vestal virgins, whose shrine no male might enter. These references to pagan festivals have an obvious satirical edge.
450 Cf De vidua christiana CWE 61:230–1, where Erasmus muses cynically on the chastity of brides wearing their hair loose.

marriage there is a distinction between married and unmarried, widow and virgin, but now that a marriage has been arranged, what use is this distinction? Those married once and those married twice will both be honoured before God. But it is humiliating, not honourable, for a blushing young virgin, her hair unbound, her head bare, painted and apparelled like a harlot, to be exposed to the lustful eyes of the young men and the slanderous tongues of the people. Is it an honour for a virgin, whose dowry is, above all, her chastity, to be attended by the sighs and catcalls of young men? It is no honour, but a kind of prostitution.

The Gospel declares that anyone who has looked on a woman with lust has committed adultery,[451] and not the least part of virginity is an unsullied reputation. Thus a virgin has lost something of her chastity if she has delighted so many eyes, has awoken desire, has been pursued by lustful cries and perhaps appeared by night in someone's dreams and suffered defilement, so to speak, as the plaything of a phantom. Indeed, in the ancient myth Juno was offended merely because Jupiter subjected a cloud to Ixion in her place;[452] it was not enough that the adulterer had not touched her, but she judged it a kind of adultery to have been defiled even through an image and an illusion. Virginity is a fragile thing, like a milk-white rose that loses its fresh bloom in the gentlest breath of wind. Therefore, you parents, allow the bride to bring her virginity unsullied to her husband's chamber; she will be all the dearer to her husband, and her reputation will be all the safer.

Marriage is a holy and a chaste institution, and the ceremony should be equally pure and holy, to convince the bride and groom from the outset how sober, modest, and gentle are the ways that become marriage. Do you believe that marriage is a sacrament of the church? You so believe. Do you believe that it was established by God in person? Of course, you so believe. Do you believe that the gift of the Spirit is poured out on those who perform this sacrament aright? You so believe. Why then is something so solemn and so holy accompanied by such unholy rites?

Come, tell me: when a virgin takes the veil of St Francis or St Dominic, who would allow the occasion to be celebrated with silly games, laughter, lutes, pipes, foolery, and dancing? On the contrary, the novice is purified by confession, prays, puts off the garments of worldly pride, prostrates herself,

* * * * *

451 Matt 5:28
452 Ixion, king of Thessaly, was transported to heaven by Jupiter; attempting to seduce Juno, he was beguiled by a cloud made in her image, from which the Centaurs were born. Ixion was hurled into Tartarus.

is veiled and given the host, and with all that listens to a holy exhortation. Nothing indecent or foolish about these rites, although a girl entering this marriage is taking no new sacraments.[453] And yet you approach the great sacrament of marriage, which God chose to establish and which the Lord so often commended to us both directly and through his apostles, with stupid nonsense and extravagant and immoral customs, as though it were a secular ceremony. If you receive a sacrament unworthily, your reward will be not grace, but God's wrath. Even in the church itself the nonsense continues: at the entrance the young men exchange blows with the bridegroom,[454] and during the service silly gestures and nods are exchanged and rude remarks are passed. Who would believe that a solemn act was being performed? Is it not a disgrace that the pagans who worshipped idols had holier marriage customs than Christians? Everyone seeks a bride who is thrifty, chaste, and unassuming – and at the very outset we show her extravagance, immodesty, and arrogance. When a deacon is ordained, he cleanses his conscience, he readies himself for worship that he may receive the holy mystery in a holy frame of mind. How much more appropriate would such holiness be at weddings, instead of the goings-on we see now?

There is intense competition to see who can produce the finest clothes, the most sumptuous banquet, the best presents. It appears kind to give the newly-weds something for the house, but how has it become the custom that the bridegroom has to impoverish himself making gifts that none the less bring him more odium than thanks? Some think that these are presents not given but returned, while others think of them as the repayment of a debt. Many, seeing others get more expensive presents, angrily consider themselves slighted, and jealousy increases among the recipients; as a result the bridegroom loses popularity and antagonizes – at his own expense – the very people he has been trying to please. And thus Christians judge the quality of a wedding by the amount of money thrown away on presents! Not to mention the crazy cost of the bride's dress, and I mean crazy: I have seen people borrow so much money to deck the bride in her finery that

* * * * *

453 Erasmus does not neglect the opportunity to contrast the non-sacramental character of monasticism with the sacrament of marriage: cf 260 above, and n160.
454 A widespread custom attested as early as the fourteenth century and as far afield as Scandinavia; the blows were presumably intended to impress on the young men that the bride was now beyond their reach. Rabelais exploits the custom's comic potential in the episode of the *noces de Basché* (*Quart Livre* chapters 12–15); see R. Marichal 'René Dupuy, seigneur de Basché, et les Chicanous' BHR 11 (1949) 132–4.

within a couple of months they have been compelled to sell off their clothes and their crockery for a good deal less than they paid for them.

What is the point of all this costly display? Are you afraid that your bride will neglect her toilet or her appearance? Are you afraid to appear more intelligent than the last fellow to bankrupt himself by such extravagance? Are you really keen to make your less wealthy neighbours all too conscious of their poverty? Is not poverty enough of a burden in itself? You may think you risk humiliation if you lose this dire competition, but you cannot win; even if you surpass all your predecessors, the next man will cap even your insanity! Does not your affluence already expose you to envy, without your boasting and flaunting it before everyone? Even so, nothing is so thoroughly wasted as money laid out on food and drink: nobody really thanks you for laying on a public feast, and some even curse the host for giving them a fever and indigestion. None the less, people splash out three years' income on such nonsense; do Christians have no sumptuary laws or censors[455] to restrain such behaviour? Marriages are arranged so that even people who are not very rich may, following Paul's advice, supply their family's needs by the work of their hands, and bestow something too upon those who are dogged by poverty.[456] And yet, outrageously, well-off Christians pour their money away on the doorstep of matrimony and leave nothing to pass on to the needy or to spend on their family.

Now the fact that girls from poor backgrounds also celebrate their nuptials with great pomp, though it is either hired or borrowed, will be recognized by the more clear-sighted as a kind of momentary respite from their poverty, which these days is not just a burden but also a humiliation. But why do rich girls ostentatiously display their good fortune, which they refuse, of course, to share with lesser mortals? They enjoy tormenting the needy instead of helping them. The rich should be content with their good fortune without reminding others of their poverty and increasing the burden they have to bear.

Indeed, the richer and more powerful you are, the more you should set an example of economy to others, which would have the dual effect of making the rich less envied for their luck and the poor less burdened by their poverty. What is so wonderful about some egregious prima donna strutting down the street exhibiting her expensive jewellery, gold, purple, and furs? She can play with them at home whenever she likes. In fact, she would be

* * * * *

455 The Romans in particular imposed severe legal restrictions on consumption; see *Institutio principis christiani* CWE 28 527 n28. On the censors, cf n258 above.
456 Cf Eph 4:28.

truly admirable and truly dazzling if she wore a simple, unadorned outfit and thus rebuked the ambition of the lesser mortals who use such things to advertise themselves beyond the domestic sphere. Which is the greater compliment: to hear foolish or vulgar women, gaping at your dazzling gold and jewels, say, 'How much of her money has she got on her back? The cheapest thing she's wearing is the gold!' but nothing about your figure or your mind? Or to hear wiser spirits saying, 'What honesty and modesty in a wealthy woman! How little are her ways affected by her fortune!'? This homespun simplicity does her more credit than all the sumptuous display of others. Will not ordinary people, who have barely enough to live on, be ashamed in the future recklessly to throw around money that exists more in their minds than in their wallets?

Such examples of sobriety and economy will be all the more striking if they are set by you, princes and noble ladies, rather than by anyone else. Your inferiors readily copy whatever example you set them, and thus the less well off will be shamed into restraint, as it were, from shameful indulgence in luxury, when they see that you disapprove strongly of flaunting one's wealth. They will realize that it is done on purpose, since otherwise the size of your fortune and the independence of your life would make extravagance quite justifiable in the people's eyes – but you have decided against it. Christians must always be mindful of thrift and moderation. So far from wasting money on riotous living, they should rather spend even less on essentials and set aside a portion to relieve the needs of their neighbours.

Even if there appears to be some excuse for pomp, extravagance, and wantonness in other areas, surely they must be entirely excluded from a wedding, which sets the pattern for married life. But these days the poison has crept even into this holy remedy – for what else is the profession of matrimony but the abjuration of a young man's dissipation, debauchery, gluttony, prodigality, and gambling and (if applicable) a young woman's haughtiness, excessive pride in her appearance, or wantonness? And yet in our society marriage is an initiation into these evils!

What is baptism but an abjuration of Satan? But nowadays, even there, pride makes people competitive. The godparents are chosen either because of their social standing or because they may bring expensive presents. But Paul taught that anyone under instruction in the faith should give a share of all his worldly goods to his teacher;[457] these days, perversely, those who

* * * * *

457 Gal 6:6

play the catechist's part[458] make the gifts, though more out of habit than out of conviction. If you wanted to show kindness to the poor, it could be done in secret, or under another pretext; why tarnish a sacrament with self-advertisement? At the very least, death, which levels rich and poor, high and low, should teach us moderation and thrift. But what could be more ostentatious and less frugal than our funerals?

But enough of this lengthy criticism of ordinary people's behaviour; if only I could improve it and turn my reproaches into praise! My discussion will now return to the subject I interrupted earlier. I have set out the rules for embarking upon matrimony clearly enough, I think, and shown that the final result nearly always corresponds to the beginning. As I said earlier, people who throw themselves into wells, or fall in by accident, will get badly hurt, but those who climb down step by step, even into the deepest well, will emerge unscathed. Similarly, men who marry in haste, without thinking, usually end up complaining – far too late – about their unhappy marriage, but you will find very few people disappointed in marriage who, with the advice of their elders, have made a careful and deliberate choice and taken a wife whom they can love for ever more. Anything that is the result of a whim will not last; any decision based on reason and judgment will be stable and lasting.

Now, to prevent the discussion wandering off too aimlessly, I shall confine the rest of this discourse to just three subjects, but in such a way that I shall not diverge from the plan I established at the beginning. Paul considers three things supremely valuable: faith, hope, and charity,[459] and these three words also seem to contain the secret of any successful marriage. And the greatest of these is charity; if it is present, all the rest is easy and straightforward. Closely allied to it is faith, without which mutual good will cannot subsist between the partners. Finally there is hope – the hope of a happy issue. The reward of a truly Christian marriage is children who are obedient and virtuous.

First of all let us continue our discussion of charity, or love. It must first be born, then nourished and strengthened, and finally healed and restored if it should happen to break down. It is born, nourished, and maintained mostly by the following: natural disposition, similarity of character, equality, mutual deference and service, worthy advice and exhortation, and children; it is destroyed by their opposites. Love that changes to hatred for some

* * * * *

458 That is, the godparents; cf 280 above.
459 See 1 Cor 13:13.

trivial reason was not true love. Just as a blazing fire made with hares' fur[460] or dry straw will quickly go out unless there is more solid material underneath to keep the flames going, so love that is based on physical attraction or some other trivial cause, though it may seem overwhelming for a while, cannot last, any more than the things on which it was based. Denser material, such as iron, is slower to ignite, but once alight it retains heat for a long time. Again, some materials make a fire smoky or crackly, and others produce an unpleasant smell; such is the 'love' established between immoral people for shameful reasons – soured by quarrels and brawls, life together is impossible, and then it is time for infamy's trumpet to sound. We can observe this sort of noise and smoke in certain ill-fated marriages which reach the point where the husband is driven from the house, and sometimes the wife too; both become the subject of general mockery. A clean fire is made with woods called for this reason *acapnos*, smokeless. A sweet-smelling fire is made with cedar wood. You will get a quiet, bright flame from pure wax smeared on clean linen, or from asbestos cloth (called 'quick flax' because it is not consumed by fire)[461] dipped in oil that has been thoroughly aged to remove any watery residue. This is not the kind of love that is bred in sinful and foolish hearts by sensuality, ambition, the thirst for riches, or a shared predilection for evil, but the kind that virtue cements between those who are devout and temperate. Nothing is more truly lovely or more lovable than this, and if it were visible to our physical sight it would inspire many more to love it than any physical beauty or adornment. Again, certain materials are quicker to put out fires than to kindle from them. Some people have personalities like that, being so rebarbative that they cannot even love themselves, let alone maintain a friendship with someone else.

It is no wonder that relationships are brief and unhappy if they are bred by Cupid, since he is both blind and winged. I am speaking of the earthly Cupid, son of the terrestrial Venus,[462] who impudently inspires shameless and immoral love in first one and then another. He is depicted as blind, because such feelings are the product not of reasoned judgment but of heedless

* * * * *

460 The image is borrowed from Plutarch *Moralia* 138F.
461 Asbestos cloth (*linum vivum*) is described by Pliny *Naturalis historia* 19.1.19. *Acapnos* is a grecism used by Martial *Epigrams* 13.15.
462 Erasmus distinguishes between the popular association of Cupid and his mother with sensuality and their spiritualization by philosophers, particularly Platonists, drawing on Plato's *Symposium* 180–1; cf *Enchiridion* CWE 66 116. A roll-call of the various deities called Cupid and Venus is given by Cicero *De natura deorum* 3.59–60.

physical passion; he is winged because this tainted love changes rapidly to hatred. By turns it brings war, peace, a truce, war again, but nothing constant, nothing peaceful and enduring. For this reason the poets call the violent passions of lovers 'frenzy' rather than love.[463] And rightly so, for when reason is dead and buried, what is left but madness?

However, the philosopher says that there is another Cupid, the child of the heavenly Venus, and that none is more clear-sighted than he.[464] He does not blind those whom he strikes with his darts, but instead cures their blindness and gives them sight. He shows them the beauties of the spirit, which reflect the Supreme Beauty. Once it is glimpsed, the lover is transported by love for it; it creates and fosters those faultless relationships that grow ever deeper and better. There can be no doubt that the source of all true beauty is God himself; everything in him is unalloyed goodness, absolute purity, complete wisdom. He does not begrudge his beauty to others, but shares it generously, as James the apostle teaches: 'Every good gift and every perfect gift comes not from the earth but from on high, from the Father of light.'[465] For he showers sparks of his light upon the hearts of his chosen ones, and from them is kindled among the virtuous a kind of loving and chaste fire of mutual affection, reflecting its source. For just as God's light knows no clouds, nor the play of passing shadows, so the love it inspires is always cloudless and serene, and knows nothing of transient quarrels and jealousies. There is no need for contracts, witnesses, and documents between those whom this bond has united; true virtue can never perish.

Thus it is inward beauty, inward riches, inward nobility that must inspire Christian marriages, and if affection should arise from some other cause, it must none the less be transferred from there to ensure that it survives. The order of nature decrees that we move on from things that are accessible to our physical senses towards those that can be perceived only through the workings of the mind. Christian piety must not reject entirely this order of things; it gradually pulls feeble humankind away from these physical preliminaries and leads it by the hand towards the things of the mind. Thus someone enraptured by some example of physical beauty is

* * * * *

463 Eg Horace *Satires* 2.3.325; Propertius 1.13.20; and Virgil *Aeneid* 4.101. In Plato's *Phaedrus* 244–5, on the other hand, the frenzy of love is one of the four divinely inspired madnesses that raise humans above their mortal condition. For a commentary on the Platonic themes here, see M.A. Screech *Ecstasy and the Praise of Folly* (London 1980) 140–52.
464 Plato *Symposium* 180D
465 James 1:17

being made aware, as if in a dream, of that other, truly supreme beauty of which Plato thinks some memory is awakened in us,[466] since humans seem to have an innate inclination towards good that apparently does not exist in animals. When the dream has been shattered, the lover will turn his mind's eyes towards the hidden beauties of the soul, and the phantom of insubstantial beauty will yield to the truly beautiful.

The newborn child is nourished by its mother's milk, and adults too thrive best on such basic food; similarly, true love is nourished by much the same things as gave it birth. Love that is inspired by sensuality or wealth is no more true love than those are truly desirable things. A man who takes a wife with a large dowry but would never have married her without this inducement, is in love with money, not his wife. A man who marries a beauty out of lust is motivated by love of himself, not of his wife. Nobody calls it friendship when people cultivate childless old folk in the hope of an inheritance. It is no more justified to call a young man a lover if he ensnares a girl in order to rob her of her dearest possessions – her chastity and her good name. Tell me, could an enemy do more? Do enemy soldiers subject the girls they capture to worse outrage? Love must be born of honour and nourished by honourable conduct.

The girl whom virtue makes lovable possesses the most effective of love potions. If you would be loved, be sure you are lovable – and nothing is truly lovable but virtue. This makes those women seem all the more insane who try to inveigle men into loving them by using cosmetics or spells and sorcery. In Xenophon, Ischomachus cleverly used cross-examination to reprove his wife's vice.[467] He had noted that she was using white lead, antimony, rouge, and other cosmetic colours to prettify herself, and also built-up shoes, like those worn by goddesses and heroines in tragedy, to make herself taller. 'Tell me, wife,' he said, 'was not one of the conditions of our marriage that we should share all our possessions?' She nodded. 'Well, would you have been pleased if, after you had made your contribution as agreed, I had given you paste instead of jewels, pinchbeck instead of real gold, gold-plated glass instead of gold bracelets, and, instead of genuine necklaces, wooden beads covered with gold, silver, and jewelled coatings? Would you reckon such trumpery gifts more precious than the possessions – all I own

* * * * *

466 An allusion to Plato's theory of reminiscence, expounded in the *Meno* 80–6 and the *Phaedo* 72–7
467 Xenophon *Oeconomicus* 10.1–9. 'Cross-examination' translates *isagoge*, literally, 'bringing a case to court.' White lead (*cerussa*) was used to whiten the face and antimony (*stibium*) was the equivalent of mascara.

– that I have in fact put into our pool?' When his wife replied that she could not possibly love a husband who would use her so deceitfully, he continued, 'But of course the major point of our agreement was that we should surrender our bodies to one another; true?' The wife nodded once more. 'Am I more agreeable to you,' he asked, 'will I be dearer to you, if I give you my body as it is, untouched by artifice, or if I offer you lips and eyes bespattered with red dye?' She declared that her husband's eyes could not be any dearer to her painted with red than in their natural state, and he concluded, 'Believe me, I feel the same, and take more pleasure in your natural complexion than I do in that unnatural face you put on with white lead and antimony.' Accepting this timely advice, the woman threw out all her warpaint and other supposed aids to beauty.

A made-up face is not a face but a mask, and no husband, however complaisant, will allow his wife to wear a mask. Moreover, when a woman knows what her husband likes but paints her face and does her hair in some other way, she is admitting a desire to please other men – not the action of a virtuous woman, whose greatest achievement is to satisfy just the one man to whom she was betrothed and given in marriage, for whom she put on her veil. For a marriageable girl to have her face painted is a sort of confidence trick; for a married woman to be made up is a kind of adultery. What husband is so foolish as to be taken in by his wife's cosmetics, if he knows she is wearing them? And is any husband so unobservant as to miss the fact, either in the morning, when she is at her toilet, or when she takes a bath, or sweats, or on some other occasion when the make-up comes off, as in Galen's story?[468] A game of 'follow my leader' was being played at a party, he tells us; each guest had a turn at being the leader. A little harlot called Phryne, seeing that many of the women present were wearing layers of nail varnish and rouge, ordered that everyone should put both hands in a basin of water she had brought in and should at once rub them over the face, then wipe off the water with a towel. When it was done, the women's make-up was ruined and their faces looked hideous; the make-up had peeled off in some places, but patches of it remained in others, and it was smeared and blotchy. Only Phryne looked clean, and seemed even prettier than before, because she was wearing no make-up.

* * * * *

468 The story is told in Galen's *Exhortatio ad artium liberalium studia*, translated and published by Erasmus in April 1526 (LB I 1054E–F); it is used again in Ep 2431. The cosmetics mentioned here are *purpurissa* (rouge) and *anchusa* (oxtongue), another red dye obtained from the plant of the same name and used for painting both the nails and the face.

This was probably sufficient punishment for the whores who were, I imagine, the guests at that party; but a Christian wife who tries to deceive her husband with cosmetic tricks deserves something more severe. Either she is extremely foolish, or she takes her husband for a complete fool, if she expects to hoodwink him, and she shows scant respect for her husband's tastes if she believes that this phoney complexion will give him any pleasure. What would a man say if he asked his wife for a kiss and she offered him a cheek smeared with tar? You might as well look at your husband through a glass screen as through a film of antimony. Even if she has managed to find a husband so stupid that he enjoys being taken in by all these cosmetic lies, it is indecent for a Christian bride (who has chosen to be a wife, not a mistress) to pander to the desires of such a husband. She must give her husband modest physical satisfaction, not the exotic services of the harlot.

Thus marriage should have no truck with love potions, drugs, pills, and paint; unadorned beauty and a wholesome appearance are all that is needed. Love based on deception or constraint is not love. If the husband is easy to please, her sex alone will be sufficient recommendation; if he is more fussy, pleasant manners and cheerful conversation will be the most effective spell or induction.[469] At the court of Olympias, mother of Alexander the Great, a certain woman, with whom Philip was desperately in love, was accused of using magic potions to enrapture the king. The queen ordered her to appear, but when she came and proved to be handsome, self-assured, and well-spoken, Olympias said, 'We can forget the charges of witchcraft; the only potion you need is yourself.'[470] How much more easily can a wife, who lives constantly at her husband's side, arouse his love. Circe, after all, is supposed to have been a skilled enchantress; she used to turn the men she attracted into various kinds of beast.[471] But in so doing she could not accomplish her desires, nor would they love the woman who had wronged them, should they return to their senses. Ulysses' companions, whom she turned into pigs, did not make very agreeable company – unless perhaps she was a devotee of grunting! She truly loved Ulysses alone (whom she failed to bewitch), struck by his character and his words rather than his appearance; but he could never love

* * * * *

469 Erasmus uses the rhetorical term *epagoge*, an opening statement or preamble presenting the facts of the case.
470 The story is told in Plutarch *Moralia* 141B–C, and quoted again in Erasmus' *Apophthegmata* 7 LB IV 320F.
471 Circe is the enchantress in Homer's *Odyssey* 10.

Circe or Calypso[472] for long, since both used magic on him. He was steadfast in his love for Penelope, who, instead of make-up and magic, used modesty.

Christians should not waste much time on their physical appearance; our self-restraint should be apparent not only in the naturalness of our appearance and the sobriety of our meals, but also in our dress. The body is a kind of clothing for the soul, and dress is a covering for the body; just as the body projects a certain image of the mind, through gesture and expression, the brow and the eyes, so dress can be a sure sign of physical chastity and modesty. What an outcry there would be if the dress of a man entering Benedict's or Francis' order did not correspond to his profession! It would be no less shocking if someone who has in baptism renounced the world and all of Satan's trappings should in his attire parade the world and the trappings of Satan! If a woman were married to a man who had not yet confessed Christ, perhaps Paul would forgive her for dressing a little too ostentatiously in deference to her husband's ways.[473] She could echo Esther: 'Lord, you know the compulsion I am under, and that I hate the symbol of pride and glory that I wear on my head when I must appear in public.'[474] But when a Christian woman has married a Christian, she must reckon that nothing pleases her husband more than to see her dress as a professed Christian should; and if the husband happens to forget Christian principles himself, she must adjure him to remember them. If she cannot persuade him to change at once, she must acquiesce, but within certain limits, helping him gradually to see the truth; if he cannot be won over by shock tactics, he may be swayed by constant reminders. Virtue is a powerful weapon if you persevere with it. If a monk puts on a soldier's tunic instead of his Franciscan habit, he is called an apostate.[475] If instead of everyday clothes a Christian wears all-silk garments, which even the Roman emperors found distasteful,[476] or, worse, cloth of gold studded with jewels, then he has thrown off the dress of *his* order and is thereafter in some sense an apostate, unless his soul protests that he is under duress.

* * * * *

472 Calypso is the nymph who detains Ulysses for seven years on her island in *Odyssey* 5.
473 Cf 1 Cor 7:13–14.
474 Esther 14:16
475 Erasmus had himself incurred the charge of apostasy by abandoning his Augustinian habit; see Epp 446–7 and 517–18.
476 Cf *Codex Theodosianus* 15.9.1.

There is a good way for a wife to soothe a husband who is annoyed by the modesty of her attire; she could reproach him – tacitly[477] – in the following words: 'My dearest husband, did we not agree that we would both practise, with equal zeal, the religion in which we were baptized?' 'Yes.' 'Now, where can we find better religious principles than in Holy Scripture?' 'Nowhere better.' 'And you will not insist that I obey you, if you tell me to do something that is plainly contrary to its teaching?' 'I'm not so wicked as to ask you to do anything of the kind.' 'That's exactly what I thought ... and yet St Paul, writing to Timothy, clearly laid down rules about the appearance expected of respectable women: "Similarly," he says, "women must dress in an appropriate manner, modestly and soberly, without elaborate hairstyles, gold, pearls, or costly clothes, but as befits women professing godliness through good works." '[478] Paul here requires a wife to conceal her body, not parade half naked through the streets, and to conceal it beneath a dress befitting a woman who professes godliness. Decorous appearance does not consist in carefully styled or dyed hair, in necklaces of gold or jewels, or in costly purple and fine linen, but in the true adornments of the heart – your virtues.

Peter makes the same point still more clearly: 'Similarly, women are to be subject to their husbands, so that even if the latter do not believe, they may be won over without a word being said, by their daily contact with their wives, as they observe with respect your holy way of life. Your beauty should reside not in your hairstyle, your gold bracelets, or your fashionable clothes, but be hidden in your hearts, in a spirit that is imperturbably calm and modest, a most precious ornament in the eyes of God. Thus too in days gone by the best of women placed their hopes in God and adorned themselves with obedience to their husbands.'[479] If the prince of the apostles counselled simplicity in their attire even to women who had married unbelievers, to help in their conversion, how much more unseemly it is for a Christian husband to demand of his Christian wife an appearance that is neither suitable for a respectable woman nor effective in safeguarding her modesty. Would it not be infinitely preferable that the money squandered on adorning her body be spent in relieving the poor?

* * * * *

477 Erasmus plays on the double meaning of *compellare*, both 'to reproach' and, simply, 'to address.'
478 1 Tim 2:9–10; on this topic, see Maclean 15–16.
479 1 Pet 3:1–5

The ancients were quite right to say that similarity, especially of character and temperament, was the father of love.[480] But the precise nature of this similarity is very important. It is no good if people are brought together because they have the same faults. There will be little stability in a union based on things that are subject to the whims of fortune, to mishap, or to the passing of time, such as physical attraction, youth, beauty, a dowry, health, or strength. Only a set of shared virtues will tie the 'Herculean knot' used, we are told, in ancient wedding ceremonies.[481] The Greek proverb, too, is not far wide of the mark: 'People are brought together less by misdeeds than by misfortune.'[482] For example, a bastard will get on well with another, or an exile with an exile, a maid with a serving-man, a lame woman with a cripple, a monster with a monster.

By similarity, we really mean equality. Of course, there can be similarities between those who are not equals, and equality between those who are not alike. When a pauper marries a millionaire, there is neither similarity nor equality between them, and we may rightly consider her sold into slavery, not given in marriage.[483] Again, when a woman of noble birth marries a commoner, the match is unbalanced and exposed to scandal. When people are matched in wealth, age, family, and appearance, then both similarity and equality are present. But when the daughter of a noble but impoverished house marries a plutocratic plebeian, there is no similarity but a certain equality between them. Again, when an eminent scholar marries a noblewoman, or a distinguished doctor weds a wealthy woman, there is a certain equality between these dissimilar people, so long as they put their different qualities to equally profitable use.

But in any case Christians should not bother with these niggling calculations, since the Lord Jesus, who presides at weddings, made us equal in so many ways.[484] He redeemed us by the same death, he washed us in the same blood, he justified us with the same faith, he refreshes us with the same Spirit, he strengthens us with the same sacraments, he honours us with the same name, calling us his brothers and the children of God, and he has summoned us all to share the same inheritance of heavenly life. Why, then,

* * * * *

480 Cf *Adagia* I ii 21.
481 *Adagia* I ix 48; the bride's girdle was knotted at the ceremony, and untied only by the bridegroom in the nuptial chamber. This was apparently a fertility ritual, since Hercules had seventy children.
482 *Adagia* II i 71
483 Cf 333 above, and n390.
484 Cf 332 above on the guarantees of human dignity provided by Christ.

are you calculating her income? Why are you consulting the annals about her family tree? Forget about your birth, and hers; what about your rebirth? Can you consider her beneath you, when God accepts her as a daughter, and Christ as a sister? How can she be poor, when she shares Christ's inheritance? An honest Christian will appreciate his wife by scrupulously weighing her good points. If she happens to be less than beautiful, observe the beauty of her soul; she is pretty enough if she is chaste, restrained, and modest. She may be penniless, but hard-working and thrifty, quick to acquire property and careful to look after it; her dowry will be large enough if she is endowed with these qualities.

Here, of course, you must view her with the honest, dovelike eyes of the gospel, not with the squinting, devious gaze of the Pharisee.[485] There are certain optical instruments that enlarge objects, and others that make them seem smaller; some make things lighter, others darker, and still others make it easier to see things in the distance though they make closer things indistinct. But the eye of the Pharisee is inconsistent and looks askance, since even the smallest faults in other people appear very large to him, while his own faults, however great, appear very small when he turns his gaze on them. Indeed, either he fails to see them at all, like a blind man, or else he hallucinates or, to use a more expressive Greek word, παραβλέπει, he sees things wrong, judging a vice to be a virtue and condemning others' virtues as vices. He is perspicacious, even lynx-eyed,[486] about things that are at a distance but purblind to those closer to him; he reminds us of those vampires[487] who were said to blunder into things at home, whereas outside nothing could be concealed from their eyes. Very different are the kind and dovelike eyes I mentioned, which will wink at many of their neighbour's faults, either by giving him the benefit of the doubt or by making light of them; but they are harsher judges of their own faults. If you have eyes of this kind, then inequality will not trouble you too much.

However, experience suggests that inequality will matter less if it is the husband who outshines his wife; he is more powerfully swayed by reason,

* * * * *

485 Cf *Epistola consolatoria* 198 above, where Erasmus derives the expression 'dovelike eyes' from the Song of Songs (1:14 and 4:1) and 'the Gospels' (presumably Matt 10:16). For Erasmus the Pharisees of the Gospels frequently represent bigotry, legalism, and lack of charity.

486 Cf *Adagia* II i 54; the classical expression refers not to the lynx but to Lynceus, the sharp-sighted Argonaut.

487 *Lamiae*: cf *Adagia* I vi 85, based on Plutarch *Moralia* 515F. In some versions of the legend, the monsters actually removed their eyes when at home.

whereas feelings have a stronger hold on her. Given the slightest excuse, a woman's feelings will rapidly bring her to despise her husband. But a truly charitable Christian will treat his wife with even greater consideration if she happens to be much poorer than he in the things ordinary people prize than if they were on an equal footing. The less well off are always apt to be touchy, so that often they take an unguarded remark or a joke as an insult. If you playfully call a pretty girl an old hag, she will not mind; but it might offend an older or less pretty woman. Paul taught us that those parts of the body considered less honourable must be treated with greater respect;[488] to do so is to increase our respect for ourselves. By analogy, is not a husband who disparages his wife also demeaning himself? Each partner must always show respect for the other, but especially in the presence of other people or when the partner is absent. No one will look down on a wife, however lowly her origins, if it is clear to all that she is precious to her husband, that she is dear to him above all else. You must not say to yourself, 'She is of low birth; she brought me almost nothing.' Say instead, 'She is my wife.' Still less should a wife be thinking, 'This man does not deserve my loyalty and obedience.' She should instead be saying, 'He is my husband; the allegiance I give him, I give to the Lord.'[489]

Again, a husband may defer to his wife in the sense that he will sometimes swallow his pride, but he will never surrender his authority; he will be consistently friendly and obliging, but he will never grovel. Nature has ordained this, the Scriptures teach it, and indeed it works to the advantage of women themselves. Even among the Persons of the Trinity there is a hierarchy, though it demeans none of them. Where there is no order, there is no respect. If the plough drives the ox[490] – if, that is, the established order is overturned – the result will be disaster.

It is possible to err in two different ways here. Some husbands are so inept in handling their rich and well-born wives that they try to repress them and bring them down until they are sufficiently humiliated to be dominated without difficulty. This strikes me as altogether inadvisable: you might as well teach a large and spirited horse to bend its knees to let you mount because you are too short, weak, or clumsy with horses to get on by yourself.[491] You can also find friends and rulers of this kind. People belittle and

* * * * *

488 Cf 1 Cor 12:33.
489 Cf Eph 5:22; Col 3:18.
490 *Adagia* I vii 28; one of the examples of incongruity given in the commentary is that of a wife giving orders to her husband.
491 The simile is borrowed from Plutarch *Moralia* 139B.

humiliate their friends to make them more deferential, and certain princes enhance their own power by attacking and enfeebling their subjects and their neighbours. Anyone treating friends that way quickly changes from a friend to a master, and ends up with slaves and flatterers instead of friends. Similarly, any prince who manages to enhance his power only at the expense of his subjects and neighbours has clearly sunk from king to tyrant; citizens and allies have now become bondsmen and covert enemies. If the nation he is called on to govern[492] is insignificant, a skilful prince will work to raise its prestige; if it is already rich and renowned, he will accept the challenge to match or even outshine the glories of his new realm by the noble virtue and diligence with which he rules it. These principles are still more vital in friendship; without some measure of equality the very notion of friendship cannot survive. Thus, if your wife possesses outstanding qualities, do not try to bring her down, like a muleteer trying to flatten a pack-saddle by putting rocks in the part that sticks up; instead, you should yourself strive for moral improvement and rise to your wife's level. In any case, no one will begrudge a wife her glory if he bears in mind that, legally, in marriage all property belongs to the husband rather than the wife!

These insecure husbands show a similar attitude towards their household, envying it as they would an individual; they cannot bear independent spirits and will put up only with the most abject toadies: to these alone will they give houseroom. I can well believe that they would like to turn their servants into asses; it would make them that much easier to enslave. The famous playwright is relevant here: 'Misgovernment will bring down the best government.'[493] It is no great feat to govern asses, or people who are little different from asses, but it is a noble achievement to govern properly a community of independent, free, and lofty spirits. In this sphere the wife yields to her husband, but takes a share in the government and protects his flank.[494] Thus husbands are quite wrong to try to turn their wives into mere maidservants.

No less misguided are spineless husbands who allow their wives to become their rulers, as Epictetus, rather crudely but none the less truthfully, warns us.[495] Physical passion prompts them to indulge their wives' every whim while they are young and beautiful. They court them with gifts, which

* * * * *

492 An echo of *Adagia* II v 1: *Spartam nactus es, hanc orna*, a famous essay whose theme is briefly resumed here
493 Publilius Syrus *Sententiae* 380
494 See Juvenal *Satires* 3.131.
495 Epictetus *Enchiridion* 40; for 'crudely' (*crassa Minerva*), see *Adagia* I i 37.

was forbidden, not without reason, even by the laws of the pagans.[496] They allow them to do as they please – wear whatever clothes and make-up they like, eat what they like, go where they please. They flatter and grovel, calling them 'mistress,' and themselves 'willing slaves.' By the time their wives' youthful beauty has withered, they have in fact become mistresses, and tyrannical ones at that, but the husbands cannot really complain, since they were responsible. It smacks of tyranny to undermine your wife's self-esteem so you can order her about like a maid, but to surrender to a wife's rule is the height of foolishness. A spirited horse will repeatedly throw a rider who cannot rein him in, but a skilful horseman will be safe on his back.[497]

Thus many husbands err in one of these two ways, and it is the same story with the women. Some of them are discontented, envious, it may be, of their husband's distinction, and keep complaining that they have been sold into slavery, not given in marriage; they could avoid this if they would only buck up and remember that a husband's good fortune is shared by his wife. Whom do you envy, woman, if you envy your husband? Why, no one but yourself! Most people will confess their hates, but no one will admit to jealousy, because to be envious is to admit your inferiority. If it is so shaming to envy someone else, is it not much worse to envy yourself?

By contrast, some women aim to bend their husbands to their will, and to lead them by the nose like oxen. They unhinge them with drugs, called *philtres* in Greek, which they think will force the man, however unwilling, to love them. But what in the end do they gain by these black arts? They spend their lives like Circe with her pigs and asses; how else to describe men bewitched by drugs and magic incantations?[498] What sort of mentality have such women, who prefer to rule over senseless, dumb madmen than to obey wise and sensible husbands? On a journey, any rational person will prefer to follow someone who can see and who knows the way, rather than to lead a blind man.[499] If lethargy, mental derangement, or some accident has impaired a husband's faculties, will not his wife complain that she is the most wretched of women, condemned to spend her life with a lunatic? And yet these women think themselves lucky if they can make a sane man lose his mind!

* * * * *

496 See eg *Digesta* 24.1.1–67; but Erasmus is probably following Plutarch *Moralia* 143A and 265E.
497 Cf Xenophon *Oeconomicus* 1.8.
498 This passage on drugs is inspired by Plutarch *Moralia* 139A. On Circe, see n471 above.
499 Cf Xenophon *Memorabilia* 1.3.4.

I said a few words earlier about flexibility. There is no personality so completely rounded that one could not wish it changed in some way or other. Nor will you easily find a pair of human beings so completely reconciled to life together that a certain weariness with each other's company will not arise – unless each in turn gives way to the other when appropriate. As the father in the comedy says, 'It is not essential that a husband should have things all his own way.'[500] Still less is this true of a wife. A little rain often stills a mighty wind,[501] and similarly a quarrel, which may get out of hand if both parties stand their ground, may be patched up and settled by a soft and conciliatory answer, sometimes even by a timely witticism. A soft answer turns away wrath,[502] and silence sometimes does the same. Some people are easily moved to anger, but their anger subsides as quickly as it arose, unless they are provoked further. With them the simplest way to avoid the worst trouble is to keep quiet for a while, until they return to their normal selves. As a result, friendly relations are not only preserved intact but actually improved; the man, regaining his senses, realizes that he has been upset for no good reason, and is annoyed with himself; he is thus even better disposed towards a wife whose gentle nature compensates for his pointless tantrums. Therefore, if something crops up that requires a warning to her husband, a wife will find him much more willing to listen at an opportune moment. Also, she will be ill advised to recall any particularly unpleasant thing he may have said while angry, especially as he may not remember saying it! Instead, she should tell herself, 'That was anger speaking, not my husband.'

In such situations keeping silence, always an ornament in a virtuous wife, will also provide a ready cure. Not the kind of silence where her tongue is still but her face speaks volumes, betraying her obstinacy and her disregard for her husband; such eloquent silence is worse than any words. No, her face should be respectful and grave, reflecting the feelings in her heart, but without a trace of resentment or scorn. However, although some people do not like to be answered back, others find silence more than a little offensive. In this case, as the Greek proverb says, the best doctor for a hurt mind is gentle but salutary advice,[503] a few well-chosen words, halfway between silence and a full riposte. You could say, for example, that things are

* * * * *

500 Terence *Adelphi* 51–2
501 Pliny *Naturalis historia* 2.47.129, a proverb not found in the *Adagia*. The French version is exploited scatologically by Rabelais in the *Quart Livre* chapter 44.
502 Cf Prov 15:1.
503 *Adagia* III i 100

better than they seem, or that it will be easy to put things right, or that what is done cannot be undone by shouting. But if there is a danger that your words, however soothing, will upset him, the safest course is to keep silent.

In any case, even when your husband is entirely calm, you must never give him the rough edge of your tongue. A wife who makes war on her husband is making war on God, who said, 'You shall be in your husband's power, and he shall be lord over you.'[504] Charity softens this rule, but it does not remove the husband's power; thus Paul commands women to be silent in church, 'because they have a sign of authority on their heads.' He also calls the man the head of the woman.[505] Thus religious obligation makes the woman subject to the man. But even if this had not been laid down in Holy Writ, reason alone would convince us that soft words or silence will be more effective than rage. An intelligent wife will naturally want her husband to grant her wish; if a gentle and modest request will achieve this more surely than a harsh and haughty demand, why start a quarrel, which will usually do no more than turn his anger into fury? Not to mention that sometimes hard words are answered by hard blows. Boreas is the fiercest of the winds: he drives the clouds, calls up thunder, shatters the oaks, and heaves up earthquakes.[506] By contrast, Zephyr is the gentlest of the winds: his breath coaxes the flowers from the earth. Yet when Boreas tries to snatch a traveller's cloak, what happens? The traveller pulls it tighter or puts on a thicker coat. But when the gentle breeze Favonius[507] begins to blow, he will take off both cloak and jacket of his own accord. A wife should learn from this example how much better it is to deal gently with her husband than to quarrel and brawl. 'Do not strike fire with a sword,' said Pythagoras,[508] and the noble playwright was right when he said, 'A good woman rules her husband by obeying him.'[509]

The most honourable victory is that won by patience, and for a woman the best way to rule is through obedience. If the wife is upset by that streak of cruelty that nature instilled in the male sex, she should remind herself

* * * * *

504 Gen 3:16
505 See 1 Cor 14:34, 11:10 (the quotation), and 11:3.
506 Boreas is the north wind. In his essay on marriage (*Moralia* 139), Plutarch describes a similar contest (itself based on a fable of Aesop) between the north wind and the sun; Erasmus substitutes Zephyr, the west wind, a favourite Renaissance symbol of gentleness, warmth, and fertility.
507 An alternative name for Zephyr
508 Cf *Adagia* I i 2.
509 Publilius Syrus *Sententiae* 108

that this harshness, however unpleasant at times, could be the salvation of the household. It is a kind of seed-bed of the courage a husband needs when he must risk his life for his wife and children. Would a wife want her husband to be lacking in manly spirit then? When his wife's honour is at stake, what will a husband not dare? Therefore you women must put up with your husbands' innate roughness in everyday life; you may find that it will save your lives if the need arises for a man of courage. When you and your children, your lives and your possessions, must be saved from an enemy's assault, would you rather have a monkey or a lion for a husband? A lion, of course. Give your lion the respect he deserves, careful not to stir him to justified anger against you. More people will treat you, the lion's wife, with respect if you always show respect for your lion. It is better to be a lioness, the obedient mate of a friendly lion, than to be the playmate of an ape. In ancient times, it was customary for the bride, when first brought into the bridegroom's house, to say, 'Wherever you are, Caius, there shall I, Caia, be.'[510] Similarly, you must say to yourself, 'Wherever you are, my lion, there shall be your lioness; where you are the master, I shall be the mistress; where you are the lord, I shall be the lady; where you are ruler of the house, I shall rule by your side.' But if you try to be Caius and not Caia, there will soon be no house and no household.

None the less, there are some areas in which the husband should yield to his wife now and then, either because they are unimportant, or because they fall within the province of womankind, or because they are specifically domestic matters. An example of the first kind would be if the wife preferred some particular form of dress (so long as there was nothing indecorous about it), or if she had her own special fasts or prayers. A husband might well wink at these for a while, although it is generally safer to get the wife accustomed to fall in with her husband's wishes in small matters as well as in great. Thus it will be more a matter of winking at them than of yielding to her explicitly. But in matters that are the province of women, such as cooking, shopping, looking after the small children, and supervising the maids, the husband will not be too quick to intervene, unless he sees something that really needs to be rectified, and he will not mind giving way if he sees that his wife knows better than he does.

* * * * *

510 See *Adagia* I ii 62, based on Plutarch *Moralia* 271F (*Quaestiones Romanae* 30). On Caius as the customary name in Roman law, see n186 above. On Renaissance views of the physiological and psychological difference between the sexes, see Maclean 41–6.

In more important areas, too, the female sex can sometimes give advice worthy of a man, for example in urging him to abandon some feud of his. The philosophers grant that women are often ready with the sort of impromptu advice they would not manage after long deliberation, as a man might; in fact, a man's judgment is often impaired if he yields to a sudden impulse. In such a case, a man should not be ashamed to listen to good advice from his wife. Abraham deferred to his wife Sarah and allowed her opinion to prevail when they disagreed: he sent away the maidservant and her son.[511] At first he found it hard to accept: 'Send away your son and his mother.' But the Lord told him, 'Do not think it hard on your son and your maidservant; listen to Sarah and all that she has told you.' You husbands must accept that the Lord says the same to you, whenever your wife's advice affects your reputation or your welfare; you must believe that God dictates whatever reason tells you to do. Many have found it profitable to follow their servants' advice, and so you should be all the more eager to accept your wife's. Of course, some people are so contrary that if something seems right to their partner, they will oppose it for the very reason that the other supports it; there is no matter so trivial that the one will deign to give way to the other. No wonder that 'charity grows cold'[512] between such people.

Now, there is embedded in human nature a certain ἀψίκορον, a sort of fastidious impatience with things as they are, which means that nothing pleases them for very long, and that they quickly get tired even of the most agreeable things. There are two remedies for this affliction: intermission[513] and service.[514] To break off marital relations for a while may serve to renew the pleasures of friendship, while performing little services for each other may rekindle your mutual affection, like blowing gently on a fire.

Intermission is a useful way to improve a relationship that is becoming tedious. However, total separation of husband and wife is not the aim; for many, such as businessmen and courtiers, it comes with the job, and in their case wedded bliss is imperilled more by these lengthy absences than by constant companionship. Paul laid down precise rules about sleeping apart;[515]

* * * * *

511 See Gen 21:10–12.
512 Matt 24:12
513 *Intermissio*, interruption, used here in the restricted sense of breaking off marital relations temporarily
514 Here, *officium* might equally be translated 'favours' or 'courtesy,' but Erasmus later introduces the notion of obligation, which is the most common meaning of the term in Latin.
515 See 1 Cor 7:5.

if it is done tactfully and by mutual consent, it may contribute much to preserving the freshness of the couple's affection for one another.

Giving small presents is a crude way of gaining affection. Love cannot be bought, unless perhaps the gifts commend themselves not so much by their cost as by their symbolism or the evidence that some thought has gone into them, or if they make a tasteful joke: things like letters, poems, antique medallions, original drawings. However, it is rather risky to introduce such ideas into a discussion of matrimony, as I may open a window on things prohibited by the law.[516] The very word 'service' includes all the things that a husband must do for a wife, and a wife for a husband. Such obligations also exist between parents and children, masters and servants, and this will be touched on later; without them, harmony cannot reign in the household. At the moment I am thinking of less weighty kinds of service, but ones that will increase and preserve mutual affection and help to soothe potential hostility. For example: send your husband off on a journey with a kiss and good wishes, and greet his return with a smiling and eager face; when he is off to business or the court, accompany him to the door, and welcome him joyfully when he returns; include words of love and respect in any complaint you have to make. A wife should not say too much about her absent husband, not even in praise of him; if she must, she should make it brief and respectful, either concealing or making light of any fault in him. Again, if she knows that something is precious to him, a little bird, a dog, or anything else, she must take special care of it. These are small things, but of no small importance in maintaining affection between husband and wife. The husband will compete with his wife in performing these little services. If something goes wrong, these services will make things better; if nothing is wrong, their affection will be aroused and renewed by them.

Again, any children married couples have together, bind chains of adamant around their married love. Of course, anyone can perform little services for another, but not everyone can have children. We have a natural instinct to show love and devotion to them. Moreover, the more they love their children, the less a husband and wife will find to quarrel about. Those nations who lived with nature as their sole guide called children 'pledges.'[517] Now a pledge is normally something given to guarantee a contract, in the same way that hostages are exchanged; indeed, princes attempting to make a lasting treaty will give and receive as hostages those who are dearest to them, and sometimes it is the worse for them if one of the parties goes back

* * * * *

516 Cf 365–6 above, and n496.
517 Cf n22 above.

on his word. But how much more sacred is the pledge devised by nature! When a wife has a child by her husband, each gives the other a hostage in which both of them live and breathe, like two beings made one; the child will be dearer to each than they are to themselves. Artful nature ensures that the husband gives a hostage to the wife, and the wife to the husband. Thus they refuse to be parted, from innate love of their children, and they cannot be parted, since the possession of children is indivisible. When people go different ways, they can usually say, 'Take what belongs to you.' But when it comes to children, who shall say to whom, 'Take what belongs to you'? In this case neither of you can take what belongs to you without taking what belongs equally to both of you.

Here we may contemplate nature's marvellous attention to detail: both partners are delineated in the same face, both are represented in the same little body. The husband sees a portrait of his wife there, the wife sees an image of her husband. Often some feature of a grandparent's face will reappear in the child, or it may be the image of its great-uncle or great-aunt: all the more reasons for feeling affection and obligation towards your children. Anyone who turns a deaf ear to nature's message here has not merely ceased to be a Christian but has ceased to be human; he has fallen to a level below the beasts, become fiercer and wilder than a lion or tiger.

I believe that this is why there is no special injunction to parents to love their children, in the same way that no one is ordered to love himself. Solon was asked why he had decreed no punishment for parricide, although he had prescribed punishments for much less serious crimes. He replied that he never thought so heinous a crime would be committed in his city.[518] Nature has so engraved this law in the innermost hearts of all that a man-made law seems quite superfluous. It is indeed wonderful that nowhere are more examples of devotion to duty to be found than in areas where there is no law to prescribe one's duties. The historians recount such things of friends, though not so many; human history overflows with examples of fathers who did not hesitate to lay down their own lives to save their children. We read of Aeneas that 'all the loving father's thoughts were for Ascanius.'[519] The Lord cries out in Isaiah, 'Can a woman forget her infant, and not take pity on the child of her womb?'[520] But alas, for human

* * * * *

518 Cf Diogenes Laertius 1.59 or (closer to the version here) Cicero *Pro Roscio Amerino* 25.70. Erasmus cites the example again in his *Apophthegmata* LB IV 324A and in the *Hyperaspites* of 1526 (LB IX 1351C).
519 Virgil *Aeneid* 1.646
520 Isa 49:15

wickedness! There are women in Christendom who will murder newborn babes, who will procure abortion and kill the unborn child.[521] But let us dismiss from this discussion what are more like rare and terrible freaks than true examples. Thus, if you have children, you have hostages for your love for one another; but even if you have not, where there is love there is no barrenness. Remember how Elkanah consoled his wife: 'Why is your heart full of grief? Am I not more to you than ten sons?'[522]

Now, not only is the wife's education[523] of great importance in sealing the love between them, but it is also largely the husband's responsibility. What the comic poet said of children is no less applicable to a wife: 'What any man wants her to be, that is what she is.'[524] Just as a husband must choose to marry a girl who shows that she is willing and able to learn, so once they are married the husband's first and most important concern must be to imbue his wife with the precepts of Christian philosophy, gradually instilling in her a love of study and of true virtue. If their circumstances allow her the time, it will be most valuable for the girl to be instructed in Greek and Latin. If slender resources mean that she must work with her hands, still she must be instructed to the extent that she can read the vernacular language fluently; no little wisdom can be imbibed from translations. To prevent her thoughts drifting off, as women's do, into idle dreams, her husband must prepare her for reading by expounding certain basic principles himself, and must supervise her reading until she is used to swimming without a lifebelt.[525]

I am not suggesting that all this will permit the wife to miss sermons in church.[526] On the contrary, she will get more out of them in this way: she must listen to them carefully and often, but she will bring home from them more sound instruction if she has gone to church prepared by her reading.

* * * * *

521 Cf the impassioned diatribe against abortionists in *De conscribendis epistolis* CWE 25 138–9.

522 1 Sam 1:8

523 Erasmus had dramatized many of the themes here in the 1524 colloquy *Abbatis et eruditae* ('The Abbot and the Learned Lady') CWE 39 501–5, which also includes a satirical contrast with monkish ignorance. On the general question, see R. Kelso *Doctrine for the Lady of the Renaissance* (Illinois 1956), and J.K. Sowards 'Erasmus and the Education of Women' *The Sixteenth Century Journal* 13 (1982) 77–89.

524 Terence *Adelphi* 399 (adapted)

525 *Adagia* I viii 42

526 Cf the role played by sermons in the education of More's daughters, Ep 1233:142–9.

If there is to be no reading, then her husband, her tutor, will take the place of books, and he must train her not only to understand what she hears but also to remember it. So many things escape an untrained mind that it might as well not have listened; such people think that the human mind cannot possibly remember a long speech, whereas to the trained mind nothing is simpler. It will therefore assist her understanding and her memory if, before going to a sermon, the wife has studied a digest of the subject on which the preacher is to speak. The husband will at the same time ensure that she gets used to listening only to the best preachers; chosen at first because they are the best, in time they will also come to be the most enjoyable. After the couple have been to hear a sermon together, the husband will choose a time and place to ask his wife what she has heard; these first examinations must not be too rigorous, but softened with praise and flattery, until her untutored mind has developed. At the same time the husband will carefully explain how the preacher began, what themes he dealt with, how he moved from one subject to the next, what memorable things he said about each, whether he made use of any digressions,[527] and whether he added anything new in his conclusion. All this will improve the woman's judgment and her memory. It will not be inappropriate to point out some correct or incorrect methods of argument, and the use of similes and examples; the latter, being drawn from life, are accessible to everyone and can be expounded even to the thickest, as it were, of Minerva's followers.[528]

When this has gone on for a month or two and the wife's judgment and memory have become more dependable, it will be a good idea for each of them to attend a different sermon, on the understanding that the wife will tell her husband what she has heard, and vice versa. In this way the intellectual benefits will double, and the two will also find a certain pious pleasure in their discussions. Gradually the husband will remove all commonplace and muddled notions from his wife's mind, and replace them by true, philosophical ones. A woman cannot give birth to a proper child unless her husband has impregnated her with fertile seed; anything else she may bear will be without form and composed merely of corrupt humours, what doctors call a 'mole.'[529] Still more corrupt will be the offspring of the

* * * * *

527 Erasmus uses the rare technical term *parergum* (parergon); as in the *Ecclesiastes* LB V 862, Erasmus expects a sermon to be rhetorically effective as well as spiritually edifying.

528 *Crassior Minerva*: cf *Adagia* I i 37; one might translate Erasmus' comparative here 'the more artless.'

529 The 'mole,' *molas*, is described by Pliny *Naturalis historia* 7.15.63. But the source of these remarks is probably Plutarch *Moralia* 145D–E, who describes them as

female mind, unless a man has instilled in it healthy ideas, like fertile seeds, from which there will quickly grow a crop of the finest virtues – piety, sobriety, chastity, and self-restraint. When the woman realizes how much her husband's instruction has changed her, and compares herself with what she was before, she will begin to congratulate herself: 'Oh, how lucky I was to find such a husband! What a mindless creature I would have been without such a teacher!' She will now begin not only to love him as a husband but to admire him as a teacher and respect him like a father; or, to put it in a more Christian fashion, to venerate God in her husband. Now trivial infatuation will yield to this new Cupid, and she will no longer believe that her happiness depends solely on her husband making her a mother. She will admit that he has sown in her a much superior seed, whose offspring will never grow weak and old, but will wax stronger with the passing of the years.

Hecuba is numbered among fortunate women: she was queen of Ilium, and her children were both numerous and highly gifted. All this she owed to her husband Priam. But what of it? When her fortunes changed for the worse, the violence of her grief transformed her, it is said, into a she-dog.[530] If she had learned from her husband not to be downcast by misfortune or complacent about good fortune, or that it is only in the mind that good or evil makes us happy or unhappy, she would have owed him more than if he had made her queen of all Asia. In Homer, Andromache says to Hector, 'You are at once a father, a revered mother, and a brother to me.'[531] Are these mere names – father, mother, brother, husband – so very important? More fortunate by far is the woman who can say: 'Under your tutelage I have changed from an animal to a human, from a weak creature to a strong and resolute woman, from a Pharisee to a true Christian. I laugh at witchcraft; I no longer swoon at eclipses, thunder, or earthquakes, having learned that all have natural causes. I give thanks to God for both good and ill fortune, knowing that whatever happens is sent by him, and that whatever he sends is for our good. I try my best to do good to everyone, and do not allow God's grace to remain idle in me.[532] None the less, I place my hopes of salvation not in my deeds or my merits, but in the boundless compassion of the Lord

* * * * *

'fleshlike uterine growths originating in some infection.' Such products of phantom pregnancies are sometimes called 'mooncalves.'
530 According to a post-Homeric legend recounted by Ovid *Metamorphoses* 13.536–75, this transformation occurred after Hecuba attacked Polymnestor, murderer of one of her many sons, Polydorus.
531 Homer *Iliad* 6.429–30, quoted in a similar context by Plutarch *Moralia* 145C
532 Cf 1 Cor 15:10. The following reference to 'boundless compassion' recalls the theme of Erasmus' *De immensa Dei misericordia* (1524) CWE 70 77–139.

Jesus, who will not desert those who trust in him with all their heart. Thus I am not weary of life, yet I look forward cheerfully to my last hour. Must I not conclude that the man who taught me all this was performing God's task?'

A husband may think he has done his duty if he buys his wife a dazzling dress or an expensive ring, but in reality he has done her wrong. A husband has done his duty if he has persuaded his wife to despise fine clothes, gold, and jewels, and to blush to wear such trappings; to realize that chastity, self-restraint, sobriety, and generosity to the poor are much more precious adornments; to agree that it is pleasanter to read a book in a quiet corner than to go to dances and wild, noisy parties, or to dash off and join the circles of gossiping women from which no married woman, however virtuous, returns home unscathed.

These are just some of the services that will naturally produce a constant and lasting affection between husband and wife. Of course, to produce such attitudes in your wife, it is essential that you should first adopt them yourself; she will accept that you sincerely believe what you are teaching her only if she sees the principles you have taught her shining through every action of your life. The most effective kind of teaching is to practise what you preach, and for that very reason there is nothing to prevent a wife teaching her husband a thing or two. Although it may not be very ostentatious, a life of probity can be a powerful spur to emulation.

This is probably the appropriate place to discuss briefly the principles of household management. The ancients dealt with this in some detail,[533] but it will not be inapposite for a Christian to pass on some ideas to his fellow Christians. First of all both partners must firmly believe that they have been joined in matrimony by God's will, and that their marriage cannot be unhappy if they persevere in the paths laid down by God and place all their expectations of bliss in his goodness. This then must be like a solid wall around them, the first and most important point of agreement between the partners. The two of them, male and female, are not united simply in order to pay that debt to nature that a man without a woman or a woman without a man cannot pay, but for another and higher purpose; even the beasts of the field mate, give birth, and cherish their offspring. A Christian woman is joined to a Christian man in order to protect her modesty; to make swifter

* * * * *

533 The treatises exploited most fully by Erasmus are Xenophon's *Oeconomicus* and Plutarch's *Coniugalia praecepta* ('Advice to the Bride and Groom') *Moralia* 138A–146A. On Renaissance acceptance of the wife's domestic role, see Maclean 55–60.

progress, by their combined efforts, towards virtue; to produce offspring, not just for nature's sake but for God; and finally to win another household for Christ.[534] It is no small task to achieve all this; it is an achievement to enhance the Sparta[535] that God has entrusted to you.

However, we do not lavish praise on someone who has succeeded in building and developing a city but is incapable of governing it; similarly, it is no great feat to expand your family with children, servants, and property unless you can look after your new possessions properly. Just as a kingdom is made of many cities and a city of many houses,[536] so a house is a kind of city, and indeed a kingdom. By kingdom I mean a place that is governed with no hint of tyranny, but whose ultimate destiny rests upon one man: in this case, the head of the household.[537] However, no kingdom or city can hold together without harmony among its members, and similarly the family will disintegrate if there is discord, especially between its leading citizens, the husband and the wife. There can be no enduring harmony where injustice rules, but, equally, there is bound to be rebellion unless some kind of order is imposed. Rules must therefore be made to guard against both possibilities. The husband will have the right to frame these, but in such a way that no member of the household observes them more scrupulously than he. The worst injustices occur when one spouse takes advantage of the other; the most deadly rebellion occurs when children plot against their parents, or a wife against her husband. A family must therefore be governed by rules and a recognized hierarchy.

A household can be divided basically into people and property. Hesiod's precept describes the bare essentials of a household: 'First get a house, a wife, and an ox to pull the plough.'[538] The wife is essential, to provide children, and the ox, to provide food and a tangible asset. Male and female servants[539] are needed to help with the work; they were once part of the property and could be inherited, like land and cattle, and their master had the right to sell them. These days nearly all servants are hired. Thus a complete household consists of the following parts: husband and wife, who are

* * * * *

534 The last phrase has a Pauline ring; see eg 1 Cor 9.
535 See *Adagia* II v 1; the sense of this famous adage is 'Do well what you have been given to do.'
536 Cf Xenophon *Memorabilia* 3.6.14.
537 *Paterfamilias*, a legal term denoting both ownership and responsibility, as defined in *Digesta* 50.16.195
538 Hesiod *Works and Days* 405, quoted in Greek and translated
539 *Famuli* and *famulae*, meaning domestic attendants; under Roman law they were indeed the property of the *paterfamilias*.

the senate, as it were; children, who are like the equestrian order; servants, who represent the common people; and property.[540]

To establish a household you must exercise judgment, and to manage it you must use reason. The choice of a wife has already been dealt with, and the best way to ensure that children are honest and upright from the start will be discussed in the appropriate place. But servants must be employed who are not only good at the household tasks they are required to perform, but also of impeccable character, or at least capable of being trained to be honest. However, just as no more furniture than necessary should be bought, so the establishment must not be burdened with a great rabble of idle servants. Some people today like to show off by keeping a horde of useless and worthless retainers, showing as little intelligence as those who beggar themselves raising horses and birds for their entertainment. When so many members of Christ are dying of hunger, how unchristian it is either to store up your treasure for the moth and the thief[541] or to squander it on worthless pleasure, when it could be used to rescue your brothers from poverty.

As for property: what is the best investment? It is generally supposed to be land, and the next best is bricks and mortar. Certainly farming is the most admirable of occupations.[542] It is all a matter of judgment. But whatever your chosen profession, be sure that you do your work honestly; always remember that ill-gotten gains are not profit but loss. 'A righteous man's pittance is better than all the riches of the wicked.'[543] You may count as your possessions only those you have obtained without harming anyone else. Many people boast of their wealth, but if you subtract what they owe to others, they are more or less penniless. But the crime is compounded when ill-gotten gains are even worse spent. It is a sin for Christians, who like to talk about their compassion, to waste money on cosmetics, extravagant clothes, luxuries, and gambling. You commit sacrilege, you windbag, when you fritter away what belongs to the poor, or rather what belongs to Christ, who through his members begs for refreshment.[544] Thus your establishment

* * * * *

540 Erasmus represents the household in terms of the Roman republic; the 'equestrian order,' the knights, ranked between the ruling senators and the plebeians. The image may be traced to Plato *Republic* 8.590–1, like the similar depiction of man in the *Enchiridion* CWE 66 42.
541 Cf Matt 6:19–20; Luke 12:33.
542 Cf 317 above.
543 Ps 36 (Vulg 37):16
544 Cf Matt 25:35–40.

must be neat but economical – neither mean nor anything like luxurious. If your income dries up, thrift is a great source of revenue.[545] If some accident should reduce you to poverty, misfortune will be easier to bear if you are used to living modestly.

It is most important to ensure that everything we own should serve a useful purpose. One reason for raising children is that, eventually, they in turn will look after their aged parents. Xenophon even counts friends among our possessions (in fact, he puts them before oxen!) because they can be so useful to us.[546] Now, one should not try to make enemies, of course, but it is equally true that one should not be on intimate terms with everyone. Anyone with just a few real friends has enough. Hesiod also mentions neighbours; bad neighbours are a trial, but good ones can be a great boon.[547] However, if we want good neighbours we must be good neighbours; all too often we make very bad neighbours ourselves.

Xenophon even counts enemies among our possessions.[548] Anything that we find useful apparently belongs among our possessions, and if we know what we are doing, enemies can be very useful to us, just as friends can often be extremely dangerous if we do not use them as we should. A full account of how to make the best use of enemies is given in an excellent essay by Plutarch.[549] For the purposes of our discussion, there are two ways in which enemies can be useful: first, by their example, and second, by their eagerness to do harm. You observe, for instance, that your enemy is shunned by all the best people because of his unguarded tongue, and you say to yourself, 'The same thing must not happen to me.' You observe how petty-mindedness leads him to envy others their prosperity, and you say, 'I must not allow his disease to infect me.' On the second point, the more alert he is for the chance to harm you or your reputation, the more alert you will be to avoid conduct unbecoming a man of honour. If he makes some reproach to you, be sure to give him no ground for a second complaint. If he has made some unwarranted accusation, look about to see whether you have unintentionally given him some ground for it. If the accusation is true, you should be glad of the warning; you would thank a friend for doing you this service, though of course you owe no gratitude to an enemy. If it is false,

* * * * *

545 A maxim quoted in Cicero *Paradoxa Stoicorum* 6.3.49 and in *Institutio principis christiani* CWE 27 262
546 Xenophon *Oeconomicus* 1.14
547 Hesiod *Works and Days* 346
548 Xenophon *Oeconomicus* 1.6
549 *Moralia* 86B–92F; cf n88 above.

rejoice in your innocence, spurning the chance of revenge and thus adding to your virtue. If ever you are seized by a wicked impulse to play some dirty trick, remember your enemy first; imagine how he will be filled with glee, how cleverly he will distort what you are doing, what he will say and do against you. Such thoughts will do much to cool your enthusiasm.

Similarly, if as a wife you are thinking of leaving your husband after a quarrel, of making your private drama public knowledge, you should call to mind any particularly malevolent or jealous women you know. 'Won't so and so be pleased, when they hear what I have done?' Or: 'Won't the men be delighted to see me living alone, without my husband? Imagine how they will all embellish the story! Is it not much better to make it up quietly with my husband than to provide my enemies with so much entertainment at my expense?'[550] Since the female sex is said to be vindictive, you could have no finer revenge than to behave better with every day that passes – the ideal way to burn and torture those who wish us ill! Such thoughts will increase your determination to bring up your children and run your household properly, so that spiteful tongues will find nothing credible to say. Thus, just as human ingenuity has found ways to make dangerous beasts serve humanity – we wear their skins, we use snakes' flesh in medicine[551] – so you may profit more than somewhat from your enemies, if you know how to go about it.

It remains true then that in a well-run household everything must have a specific purpose, and this will be easier to achieve if all the members are given the jobs for which they seem most suitable. One may broadly divide the tasks into two groups, the domestic and the external. The outside jobs are the husband's affair; inside the house is the woman's domain,[552] especially the provision and cooking of food, as well as allotting their daily tasks to the servants and checking their work. The children's upbringing is also the wife's province while they are still young, but when they have reached the age at which they must be trained for a future career, the husband will take over. Similarly, both will be involved in finding husbands for their daughters, but the husband has the final say.

However, the husband will not lightly intervene in what are his wife's responsibilities, unless he observes something too important to be ignored. The wife may also intervene, but much more rarely, in her husband's affairs. When the situation compels her to do so, she must seek a suitable time

* * * * *

550 This example is inspired by Plutarch *Moralia* 86D.
551 Examples culled from Plutarch *Moralia* 86D
552 Cf Xenophon *Oeconomicus* 7.22; Pseudo-Aristotle *Oeconomica* 3.1.

and place, and tone down the harshness of her criticism by broaching the subject with due deference and using all her charm. In the partnership of marriage the same law equally binds the husband to the wife and the wife to the husband, but, as the Apostle decreed, the wife has no power over her husband: 'I do not permit a woman to be a teacher or to domineer over a man; she must be silent.'[553] He does not permit her to speak in church at all, though she is allowed to discuss things at home in order to learn; but nowhere is she given authority over her husband. Now of course the wife must show much respect for her husband, but the husband too must show some respect for his wife, just as parents who want their children to respect them must first show respect for the children, and not do and say whatever they please in front of them. Thus there is the same rule for husband and wife, but it applies in different proportions.

Similarly, although husband and wife share all their possessions, the husband has the right to apportion them, and everything is reckoned as his property. If you dilute wine with water, it is still called wine – even if there is more water in it than wine.[554] In the same way, even if the wife has brought more to the marriage than the husband, all their possessions must be considered the husband's. It would be absurd to call some things the husband's and others the wife's, but even more absurd to call them all the wife's.

For the rest of the household, the primary authority after the husband's must rest with the wife, especially when he is absent. The servants also can be divided between them. Some are particularly involved with the husband's business affairs; the wife should not order them about, though they must show all the more respect for their mistress and not provide an example of insolence for the others. Servants must work, and in return they will receive food and clothing – nothing extravagant, but adequate for their needs. Lazy ones must be prodded into action; quick and industrious ones should be praised and, if they keep it up, be given some reward to encourage the others to work harder. The wife will greatly advance the servants' work if, without doing the work herself, she makes the sluggish ones buckle to their task, reminds them of their duty, demands that they do it, shows them how things should be done, approves some good piece of work, or points out what is wrong. If giving advice has no effect, she must reprimand them, but only with the necessary degree of unpleasantness, like a doctor's medicine; excessive scolding will not spur the servants on but

* * * * *

553 1 Tim 2:12, followed by an allusion to 1 Cor 14:35
554 The example is taken from Plutarch *Moralia* 140F.

make them disaffected. Once servants used to be punished with the lash, but nowadays when they are all hired it would be better to refrain from striking them, unless they are too young to be reasoned with. But an adult who cannot be shamed into doing better, who does not respond to gentle advice or stern reprimands, will not be improved by a beating either. He cannot be reformed, but he can be changed – for another. The instruction of children will be discussed in the appropriate place.

Thus if the lady of the house keeps a watchful eye on everything that happens there, observing what needs to be done in the bedrooms, in the living rooms, in the nursery, in the servants' quarters, in the yard, and in the garden, her contribution will be great, even if she performs no specific task herself. The famous sculptor Phidias made for the people of Elis a statue of Venus standing on a tortoise.[555] At first sight it seemed ridiculous to have that slender and delicate goddess stand on a creature generally agreed to be fearsomely ugly, instead of placing her on dainty sandals amid rose petals. This apparent incongruity provoked everyone to ask what the artist was getting at. That wise man was indicating that a housewife wins esteem for two things in particular: silence, and attention to her domestic duties. The tortoise, you see, has no voice, and never crawls out of its house (the Greeks call it φερέοικος[556] for this reason); if it is frightened, it withdraws completely into its shell. Similarly, a wife should move slowly through the house, carrying the house with her, as it were. If she looks out, it should be no farther than the yard, the playground, or the garden next to the house; these are the boundaries of the housewife's realm. If ever she is afraid, she knows that nowhere will she be safer than at home.

So far this interpretation seems quite apt, but what about representing a woman as silent (a tortoise has no more voice than a snail)? It is not that the wife is deprived of speech, but she must cut out idle noise and chatter. If there is something important to be said, it is best for the wife to say it as if on her husband's behalf; this will enable her to speak with greater authority, like someone who uses a herald to give his words more weight. She does not have to shout: 'I want this! I command that!'; it will be more effective to say things like: 'It is the master's wish . . . I would not want my husband to

* * * * *

555 Phidias lived in the fifth century BC, retiring to Elis in the Peloponnese after being banished from Athens. The statue is described by Pausanias *Description of Greece* 6.25.1, and the interpretation here is given by Plutarch *Moralia* 142D and 381E.
556 Literally, 'carrying its home'

find out . . . You know what the master told you to do . . . Have you forgotten what your father said?' In this way any dispute arising among the servants or the children, or between the servants and the wife, will be easily and quickly resolved with a little artfulness on both sides. But if you do nothing to eliminate such quarrels, they may grow and put down roots: 'The quicker the cure the better it is.'[557]

If some quarrel arises between husband and wife, it will be much less desirable to gloss over it. As the man in the play said, 'It is like living a lie.'[558] The son, in despair, had run off to join the army, and the old man, missing his son, was cruelly tormenting himself; and all because neither would open his heart to the other. There must therefore be a quick but amicable confrontation, followed by a full and friendly reconciliation. Any dispute arising within those four walls must be settled within them, to prevent any breath of animosity reaching the servants or the neighbours. A wife must first take up her complaint with her husband; if it is too serious to be settled without some outside intervention, she should take it to her husband's relatives rather than her own. It must not look as though she is seeking an end to the marriage.

Xenophon thought it necessary to insist at great length that every item of household equipment should have a particular place assigned to it.[559] Thus it would always be to hand when needed, and it would be easier to see if something was missing or in the wrong place; if you do not know where something is, you might as well not have it. This can often cause pointless quarrels, when something is thought to have been thrown away but in fact is lying unnoticed somewhere. Thus the first task will be to obtain whatever equipment the household seems to need, and then to look after it and keep it ready for use. This may seem a rather humdrum piece of advice, but it will contribute a great deal to the smooth running of the household.

Plutarch records an old-established custom in the Libyan city of Leptis, whereby a woman, the day after moving into her husband's house, would

* * * * *

557 In Greek in the text, the equivalent of the Latin saying quoted n218 above and found in the *Proverbs* of Apostolius 3.90 *Corpus paroemiographorum Graecorum* ed E.L. a Leutsch 2 vols (Hildesheim 1965) II 308. I am indebted to Dr Roland Mayer for this reference.
558 Terence *Heautontimorumenos* 154, followed by a summary of the play's plot
559 Xenophon *Oeconomicus* 8.10; he compares the orderly household to a well-run ship.

send a message to her mother-in-law asking to borrow a jar. According to custom, the mother-in-law would refuse, saying that she had none.[560] They say that this custom meant that the girl, having had a quick taste of her mother-in-law's ways, was all the more appreciative of her husband's generosity to her, and was also reminded of her own mother's past kindnesses to her. What is more, if in the future her mother-in-law treated her or spoke to her rather harshly, she would be less upset; for it is a characteristic of all mothers-in-law to be ill disposed towards their sons' wives.[561] But I think that it also means that the good housewife will make sure that she has everything she needs in her own home, remembering that rather wise saying, 'I would rather buy than beg.'[562] It is more blessed to give than to receive. 'Let your well overflow into the road,' says the book, 'and share your water with the street; drink water from your own cistern and running water from your own spring.'[563] It is better to have a surplus at home that you can share with a needy neighbour than to have to borrow what you need.

I want the house to be decorated in such a way that its appearance reflects the lifestyle of the people who live there: a pleasing simplicity everywhere, with no hint of luxury. There should be no gilded ceilings, no pricey tapestries, no paintings that cost as much as several farms, no silk curtains – nothing looks neater than linen. If you have money to spare, do not waste it on empty display but bestow it on the poor. Just as dirty talk has no place in the family circle, neither have licentious pictures. A silent painting can be very eloquent and work its way stealthily into people's consciousness. It seems that there is no limit to the filth that modern painters and sculptors will depict, and yet some people decorate their living-rooms with this charming stuff, as if young people were not already exposed to enough evil influences. If modesty requires that we conceal our own bodies, why are they stripped bare in pictures? If there are actual sights that you think will endanger the morals of your sons and daughters, why allow them constantly to be placed before their eyes? There is a well-known story of a young man who left the marks of his lust on a statue of Venus.[564]

* * * * *

560 Plutarch *Moralia* 143A
561 For another disobliging account of mothers-in-law, see the *De vidua christiana* CWE 66 224.
562 *Adagia* I iii 20
563 Prov 5:15–16, preceded by a reference to Acts 20:35
564 The statue of Venus Euploea was at Cnidos in Caria, and was regarded as the masterpiece of the great sculptor Praxiteles; the young man's story is told by Pliny *Naturalis historia* 36.4.21.

Some artists introduce their own evil thoughts into even the most uplifting subjects. When depicting an episode from the Gospels, they will include some stupid and impious detail; for example, in painting the Lord's visit to Mary and Martha,[565] they will show the Lord talking to Mary, but at the same time young John will be in a corner whispering into Martha's ear, while Peter drains a tankard. Or again, Martha will be standing behind John at the table, resting one hand on his shoulder while with the other she seems to be mocking Christ, who is oblivious to all this; or else Peter will be bringing a ladle dripping with red wine to his lips. And although these images are blasphemous and impious, some people seem to find them witty. Pictures on sacred subjects should show the same reverence as a discourse on them. If you wish to hang an instructive picture, what could be more suitable in a Christian house than the life of Christ or the deeds of the saints? If you want something more light-hearted as well, you could have depictions of moral fables or of the countless different trees, plants, flowers, and animals.

There must thus be nothing in the house that will either corrupt the inmates or give visitors a bad impression of life in the household. When a guest sees that everything is in its place, that there is nothing superfluous, that all are intent upon their tasks, that nothing is overlooked, that everything is neat but not showy, and that there is no impropriety in gestures, speech, dress, or pictures, he will take away an excellent impression of the family and, if he is a wise man, will imitate their example in his own house. A wife schooled in this way of doing things will realize what joy is to be found in good judgment, what peace in a clear conscience, and what comfort in a properly run household; and also what a good name, even here on earth, all these things will win her. Will she not then love more than ever the husband who showed her this way of life? Especially if she reflects on the disasters and the ill repute that have befallen many other families for the lack of such a guide. Moreover, the husband who enjoys all this at his wife's side will surely hold her especially dear since he has found her in all things so dutiful and helpful.

*****

565 On the popularity of this subject, see Louis Réau *Iconographie de l'art chrétien* 3 vols (Paris 1955–9) II-2 328–9; a famous example of a less than reverent treatment is Giovanni da Milano's fresco in Santa Croce, Florence. The story of Christ's visit to Mary and Martha is told in Luke 10:38–42; Erasmus was fond of using it to illustrate the virtues of the contemplative life – cf M.A. Screech *Ecstasy and the Praise of Folly* (London 1980) 180–2 – which may explain his indignation here.

I cannot conclude this section on love without a few words on faith, as I promised, since love depends on faith.[566] I shall therefore return to love after tidying up the question of faith, or fidelity. The wife owes many things to her husband and the husband to the wife; I have already discussed this. But fidelity is mutual and equal between husband and wife, as Paul says in 1 Corinthians 7[:3–5]: 'The husband must give the wife what is due to her, and the wife similarly to the husband. The wife's body is not her own, but her husband's; similarly, the husband's body is not his, but the wife's. Do not deny yourselves to one another, unless perhaps you agree to abstain for a while to devote yourselves to prayer.' The text would be quite acceptable if it merely said, 'The wife's body is not her own, but her husband's.' In some countries husbands used to have the power of life and death over their wives,[567] and Paul too asserted that the husband was the head of the wife, which makes another of his statements rather hard to swallow: 'The husband's body is not his, but the wife's.'[568] It will be easier to accept if properly interpreted. It does not mean that the wife has complete power over the husband's body, and vice versa, but only as far as sexual intercourse is concerned. The principal object of marital union is to beget children, and a secondary purpose is as a remedy against incontinence. In these matters, their rights are equal: the husband cannot beget children without the wife any more than she can without him, and in the second case, the female sex is no less weak and imperilled than the male, and thus the husband must be as ready to do his duty as the wife.

A husband has different powers over a wife and a maidservant. A maid can be offered for sale, a wife cannot. He cannot demand certain kinds of work from his wife if there are servants who can do it. And yet in certain circumstances the wife will not hesitate to do things that a maidservant would consider beneath her. Again, he cannot demand that a maidservant submit to him physically, as a remedy for incontinence, but he has the right to ask it of his wife; similarly the wife cannot ask it of a manservant. Under the old Law the wife does not seem to have had the same rights over the husband as the husband over the wife; otherwise Rachel could not have bought from her sister a night with her husband, in exchange for the mandrakes,

*****

566 Cf 1 Cor 13:13.
567 Presumably a reference to the laws of the Hebrews and of the ancients concerning adultery; cf nn248–50 above. Gratian *Decretum* pars 2 c 33 q 2 c 5 interprets an apparently similar regulation of Pope Nicholas i as referring only to the spiritual sword.
568 1 Cor 11:13; Eph 5:23

if she had had the right to demand it.[569] But the Apostle's decision is very clear, and natural reason supports his ruling.

Now certain questions arise here concerning physical relations, their timing and frequency, of which some can scarcely be discussed in decent language. Therefore, to save time and blushes, the most important thing for Christians is to remember the Apostle's dictum: 'Let your life together be honourable in every respect, and your marriage-bed undefiled.'[570] Thus the husband has no right to ask his wife to perform any kind of perverted act, and she is not bound by the rule of obedience here. Indeed, even the sort of physical contact that is unavoidable should be as chaste as possible. In the begetting of children, infrequent rather than regular intercourse is more successful, and the remedy is intended for our inescapable natural weakness, not for perverted lust. Compare this with the fact that servants are entitled to their food, but that it need not be as plentiful and tasty as some of them, whose greed is boundless, would like; let it be merely of a quality and quantity to satisfy their physical needs. Nature's requirements are confined within certain boundaries; intemperance and lust know no limits.

Therefore, just as good Christians will discipline their bodies not to demand choice food or to yearn for more than is necessary to allay their hunger and thirst, so they must become accustomed in their physical relations to have a marriage that is restrained, modest and chaste, and, as far as is possible, like the state of virginity. But a household that resounds with the noise of frequent rowdy parties, lewd stories, singing, dancing, and silly games is unlikely to be restrained in all the rest. Lust is the companion of idleness and extravagance, while chastity is the companion of hard work and thrift. These days many husbands teach their wives intemperance, while the wives in their turn provoke their husbands' lust; their physical relations take such a form that one might speak of fornication and adultery within marriage. Their talk, their little games, their gestures, their wantonness are such that she seems more like a mistress than a wife, and he more like a lover than a husband; it is shocking to describe how they vie with one another in depravity.

Even pagan literature teaches us that the pleasures shared between husband and wife must be enjoyed in secret, away from prying eyes. Titus Flaminius was expelled from the senate by Cato the Censor because,

* * * * *

569 Cf Gen 30:14–16. But Erasmus has reversed the roles of the sisters: it was Leah, spurned by Jacob, who bought the night in which she conceived Issachar.
570 Heb 13:4. On this topic, see Alan W. Reese 'Learning Virginity: Erasmus' Ideal of Christian Marriage' BHR 57 (1995) 551–67.

during a thunderstorm, he tried to calm his wife by embracing her – in his daughter's presence.[571] There was no lust involved; it was to ease a weak woman's fears. So what crime had he committed, grave enough to have a man of senatorial rank removed ignominiously from his position? He had not shown respect for a virgin's modesty. This misdeed seemed to Cato, who knew nothing of Christ, to warrant so heavy a penalty. But these days is there anything that cannot be said and done in front of children? What secrets of the bridal chamber could survive our drunken parties? But the bridal chamber alone should witness these joys of married life. Even the animals can give us lessons in modesty. Elephants know nothing of adultery; they will mate only in secret, and then on no more than five days in a year; after mating, they will not rejoin the herd without washing thoroughly in a river.[572] Such is the innate sense of decency of these beasts; how, then, should a Christian behave?

'Where is this leading?' someone will ask. 'Surely anything is allowed in the bridal chamber? With lights out and clothes off, should not modesty be laid aside as well?' Not at all; it was a very foolish poet who wrote of his wife, 'Let her Lucrece all day be, / Thaïs in the night to me.'[573] Herodotus wrote that when a woman takes off her clothes she also takes off her modesty,[574] and a certain woman, being dragged off by King Philip, cried: 'Let me go! In the dark, all women are alike.' Perhaps both these remarks are true of the ordinary run of women, but for a properly educated married woman the opposite is true; it is particularly when she takes off her clothes that she puts on wifely modesty, and she treats her husband more respectfully than ever when the lights are out, on the ground that she is then most completely in his power. A husband must not think, either, that the marriage-bed is a

* * * * *

571 The story is told by Plutarch *Cato* 17.7 and *Moralia* 139E. Erasmus is quoting from memory: Plutarch calls the offender Manilius, but Erasmus confuses him with another of Cato's victims, Lucius Flaminius, expelled from the senate for executing a prisoner of war. Lucius' brother Titus, a celebrated general, quarrelled with Cato over this.

572 This information is transcribed from Pliny *Naturalis historia* 8.5.13.

573 Martial *Epigrams* 11.104.21–2, translated by Robert Herrick ('What Kind of Mistress He Would Have'). Lucretia, the archetype of chastity, was raped by Tarquin and would not live with the shame; Thaïs was the most notorious of Greek courtesans, mistress of Alexander and Ptolemy. A seventeenth-century emendation of Martial transforms her into Laïs, but the effect is the same, since the latter was a famous Corinthian courtesan.

574 Herodotus 1.8, quoted with disapproval by Plutarch *Moralia* 37D and 139C; Plutarch is also the source of the next example, *Moralia* 144F.

place dedicated to debauchery, but rather a temple of restraint and modesty. A bed that witnesses the joint prayers of husband and wife in the evening as they go to bed, and again when they rise in the morning, will also witness pleasures that are chaste and permissible.

Let that be enough for the moment on this type of obedience and physical self-restraint. However, it would be worthwhile to discuss Paul's rules about sleeping apart, that is, about suspending the exercise of marital rights: 'Do not deny yourselves to one another, unless perhaps you agree to abstain for a while to devote yourselves to prayer; afterwards return to one another, in case Satan should tempt you through your incontinence.'[575] The verb used here, *fraudare* [deny], implies a mutual obligation; in its usual sense, *fraudare* means to refuse to pay a debt, or to disappoint someone's expectations. Thus, although continence is an excellent thing, neither partner is free to practise it without the other's agreement.[576] A sacrifice involving harm to another is unacceptable to God, and in marriage nothing good can be achieved without harmony. If the wife favours continence, let her indeed give up her right to lie with her husband; but if he demands his rights, she must comply. The Apostle permits couples to sleep apart, but only by mutual agreement, for a limited time, and to allow them to pray. How cautious Paul is in permitting the suspension of conjugal rights! He does not accept just any reason for sleeping apart, but only the need to pray. And, in case 'for a while' seems unemphatic, he repeats and underlines the idea: 'afterwards return to one another.' Why such attention to detail? 'In case Satan should tempt you through your incontinence.' The Apostle knows what a skilful craftsman Satan is; he frequently deceives people by a semblance of piety and knows the weaknesses of the flesh; nor is he ignorant of the many temptations and attractions of lust, once its fires have been lit. Thus Paul wants the period of separation to be brief because danger lurks everywhere.

It may be that this passage was particularly relevant to the Corinthians, to whom the letter was addressed; the Greeks seem to have been more promiscuous than other races, and Corinth more corrupt, depraved, and debauched than anywhere. Paul rebukes them for their excesses: 'One of you is hungry, another is drunk.'[577] But although I am sure that there are races less depraved than the Greeks, yet wherever there is the slightest danger, Paul's advice must be heeded. Nor should a vow of perpetual chastity be

* * * * *

575 1 Cor 7:5
576 Cf Gratian *Decretum* pars 2 c 33 q 5, citing 'many authorities' on this point; the most eminent is Augustine *De bono coniugali* 6 and 15 PL 40 377 and 383.
577 1 Cor 11:21

taken lightly, even if there is mutual agreement. 'The spirit is indeed will-ing, but the flesh is weak,'[578] and Satan never sleeps. It is safer to turn the Lord's gifts to account without taking a vow. Bishops must not be too ready to turn a husband and wife into a monk and a nun, unless their advancing years make permanent chastity more likely; but even old age may not be entirely safe.

There is about physical contact something coarse that conflicts with the life of the spirit. That is why, under the law of Moses, priests did not so much as enter the houses where their wives were for as long as they were responsible for the services, but remained in the temple.[579] David and his companions were not allowed to eat the holy bread until they had under-gone several days of purification.[580] While the Law itself was being given to the people, they were commanded to keep from their wives.[581] But every Christian is to some extent a priest,[582] and his sacrifice is prayer, the incense and perfumed smoke most pleasing to God. Thus when a married couple perform this priestly function and turn their thoughts to the deeds of holi-ness, they give up their marital relations to make their sacrifice more accept-able to God. Someone may ask whether, since Paul told us to pray without ceasing,[583] we shall not have to keep from our wives for ever. It was indeed Paul's wish that everyone could be like him,[584] but he dared not turn his wishes into commands, for fear of exposing the weak-willed to still greater danger. Thus daily prayer need not preclude a moderate exercise of marital rights.

St Ambrose thinks that Paul is talking here about receiving the Eu-charist, which is when one's prayers must be at their most pure, and accom-panied by fasting.[585] I am not sure whether he is right or not, for in Paul's

* * * * *

578 Matt 26:41
579 Cf Lev 21:12–13 and the commentary in Gratian *Decretum* pars 1 D 31 c 4.
580 1 Sam 21:4–6, used as an example by Christ in Matt 12:4
581 Exod 19:15
582 Cf 1 Pet 2:5. The idea was thus grounded in the New Testament, but it was becoming increasingly controversial because of Luther's championing of the 'priesthood of all believers.' On the 'incense of prayer,' cf Ps 140 (Vulg 141):2.
583 1 Thess 5:17
584 Cf 1 Cor 7:7–9.
585 Probably a reference to the *Sermo de esu agni* attributed to Jerome, where 1 Cor 7:5 is interpreted in this way, and linked with the prohibition on eating the shewbread in 1 Sam 21:4 (cf n580 above); Ambrose's less specific reading of 1 Cor 7 is quoted alongside Jerome's view in Gratian *Decretum* pars 2 C 33 q 4 cc 1 and 4; cf Aquinas *Supplementum* q 64 art 1.1.

time most people received the body and blood of Christ every day, but in Ambrose's time it was usually only on Sundays. These days love has grown so cold[586] that people hardly receive them once a year, and even then reluctantly and grudgingly. The more reasonable conclusion therefore is that whenever the occasion or your state of mind encourages you to pray more intensely than usual, for that period you should agree to abstain from marital relations; for example, on those days on which the church has forbidden the celebration of marriages,[587] such as from Advent Sunday until the octave of Epiphany, from Septuagesima until the octave of Easter, from the first day of Rogations until the octave of Pentecost, and on any other feast days that encourage continence in the same way. However, Paul does not seem to insist even on this, but to permit it to those who want it. The rights of marriage are eternal; this relaxation of them is permitted, but not obligatory. Moreover, those who are weak must implore the aid of God, who alone bestows continence, that they may make good use of his gift. Those who receive this gift from God in such measure that they engage in physical relations only for the procreation of children will have far more time to devote to prayer, to visiting the sick, reading holy books, hearing sermons, and giving alms.

When the wife is pregnant, she will rest from intercourse, as she will for a period of recovery after the birth; already, when she has her monthly flux, necessity not religion obliges her to abstain from intercourse. God forbade it in Leviticus 20[:18]: 'If a man has lain with a woman during her monthly flux and uncovered her shame, and she has laid bare the source of her blood, they shall both be cut off from among their people.' Of course, this severe sanction has been lifted today, yet this natural reason, supported by the Law, must carry enough weight with Christians to prevent husbands from pestering their wives at that time, and give wives good ground for refusing if their husbands seek what they should not.

When a marriage is founded on fidelity, it will be safe from adultery and jealousy. It is clear enough from the penalty imposed by Moses on adulterers that theirs is a most serious crime. These are his words in Leviticus

* * * * *

586 Cf Matt 24:12.
587 Cf n150 above. Erasmus goes on to suggest sexual abstinence for several weeks around the great festivals of Christmas, Easter, and Pentecost; an octave is the day week following a festival. Septuagesima falls nine weeks before Easter, and Rogations start three days before Ascension Day and thus fourteen days before Pentecost. There is a comparable set of suggestions, based on Augustine, Jerome, and others, in Gratian Decretum pars 2 c 33 q 4.

20[:10]: 'If a man commits adultery with another man's wife, if he commits adultery with his neighbour's wife, both the adulterer and the adulteress shall surely be put to death.' But among Christians, since matrimony is a sacrament, any who commit adultery, besides the unbearable wrong and betrayal they perpetrate, also defile themselves with sacrilege; even the pagans imposed the capital sentence for adultery.[588]

How then has it come about that, for Christians, adultery is a game and a joke? A man convicted of a single theft dares not show his face, but another, renowned for a thousand adulteries, is considered one of the best. Papal laws[589] allow an adulteress to be thrown out of the house, and a wife has the same right in theory, except that in this area the male sex has arrogated all power to itself. An adulterous husband does not have the right to put away his adulterous wife, since he has taught her the ways of wickedness. Christian compassion should prompt forgiveness even here, especially if it is a mere lapse and not calculated wickedness, and if there is hope of amendment. But if, after discovering your wife's adultery, you make love to her, you lose any right to repudiate her. This is what human regulations decree.

However, I do not see why anyone should lose his rights as a result of showing mercy. If a husband forgives his wife time and again when she confesses and promises improvement; if he restores her to favour and does not abstain from her bed, hoping to give her less cause to fall again, why should he be deprived of his right to put her away if he sees she is incorrigible? It is as though he were encouraging another's wickedness. But, you will say, that is the meaning of the law. But I say that charity sees everything in the most favourable light. Let Christian moderation therefore be content with the penalty of separation, the kind in which he will live henceforward as a celibate, since he will not be free of the marriage bond while his wife is living. However, if he can bear to live with an unfaithful wife, begging her all the while to change her ways, first, he will receive from God a reward for his forbearance, and second, he will not lack a remedy for his own incontinence. For the right to kill both the persons taken in adultery, which the ancient laws allowed to outraged husbands,[590] must be completely eradicated

* * * * *

588 See nn248 and 250 above.
589 Cf Gratian *Decretum* pars 2 c 32 q 6; the *Decretales Gregorii* ix 5.16 CIC 2 805–7; Lombard *Sententiae* book 4 dist 35; and especially Aquinas *Supplementum* q 62 on the questions raised subsequently. There is a similar passage in Erasmus' annotations on 1 Cor 7:39 LB VI 697E; in Ep 1211:227–40 Erasmus describes a particularly involved and painful case of this kind.
590 See nn248 and 250 above.

from Christian practice, especially since, although the law of Moses allows a husband to accuse his wife of adultery, it does not permit him to have her killed for his personal satisfaction.[591]

Now jealousy is the usual companion of extramarital affairs, but of course this disease will rarely arise among those who are joined by Christian love. Those who love one another with all their hearts will take every precaution against any suspicion that might cloud their relationship, as it were. Thus it is very wrong of people to tell wives untrue stories about their absent husbands, to stir up suspicion in those female minds; but it is still worse for husbands deliberately to arouse their wives' suspicions. Such jesting should have no place in a marriage; instead, everything should be directed towards fostering and increasing their love for one another, as Paul taught:[592] 'Whatever is true, whatever is pure, whatever is right, whatever is holy, whatever is lovable, whatever is of good repute, all that is virtuous and praiseworthy: think on these things, and do them.' What will be your reward? 'And the God of peace,' he says, 'will be with you.' And 'the peace of God, that passes all understanding, will watch over your hearts and your thoughts, in Christ Jesus.'

Thus we must refrain not only from evil, but even from things that have an appearance of evil, as the Apostle teaches in his letter to the Thessalonians.[593] Certain actions, springing from naïvety and innocent enough, none the less arouse suspicion. Coquettish nods, suggestive laughter, a saucy reply, unexpected animation, flirtatious notes, little gifts, secretive whispering – all these things may be accidental or quite innocent, but as they have an appearance of evil, they must be scrupulously avoided. Doctors reckon that a fever that creeps up on its victim, and whose cause is trivial or obscure, is more to be feared than one whose cause is obvious and serious. Similarly, suspicions based on such flimsy grounds are often less easy to allay, and may grow very rapidly.[594] Frequent and enthusiastic attendance at dances and parties, or lengthy trips without your husband, are not ideal ways of disarming jealousy, especially if your youth and beauty make you vulnerable and a perfect target for wagging tongues. A married woman is

* * * * *

591 Probably an allusion to the 'trial of jealousy' described in Num 5:12–31. A jealous husband might charge his wife with adultery, without evidence; she was made to drink contaminated water by the priest, and the result testified to her innocence or guilt.
592 The quotations following are a rearrangement of Phil 4:7–9.
593 1 Thess 5:22
594 This simile is borrowed from Plutarch *Moralia* 141B.

nowhere safer or more respected than at home or by her husband's side, and that is where she should be most glad to be; she was taken from his side and she should not leave his side.[595]

It is commonly said that a household cannot run on smiles, and it is true. Sometimes a friendly warning is required, sometimes a complaint, and from time to time a reprimand; but such things should be done without rancour or unpleasantness. It is a good idea to temper the severity of a necessary reprimand with soothing or appreciative words, such as the following: 'I have always admired the way you restrain your tongue, so I was surprised by that remark you made at dinner today.' Or: 'Is such behaviour worthy of you? I would not like to see such a blemish on your record of good deeds.' 'If you could see in a mirror how much modesty suits you, you would never take it off.' 'You know how this virtue shone forth in that excellent woman your mother; I would not like to think you could not live up to her standards.' Warnings like these are more effective than shrill reprimands. In ancient times, the priests sacrificing to Juno Pronuba cut out the victim's gall-bladder and threw it behind the altar before slaughtering the animal.[596] The purpose of this law was to advise the bridal couple that in their life together they must put aside all bitterness, which does nothing to right wrongs, but merely stirs up hatred. The good Samaritan poured wine and oil into the traveller's wounds:[597] wine has a mild acidity that clears up pus and infected blood, but this is made less painful by the addition of the soothing oil. That is the kind of rebuke to use if you want to cure the disease without harming the patient.

I have now fulfilled my promise to deal with faith, I think; let us return to charity or love, which must be the most important thing shared by a husband and wife. Yet the Apostle specifies that the man must feel love, the woman respect; since authority and power rest with the husband, he may become a tyrant if his powers are not tempered by a great deal of love. Because the woman has a lower status and belongs to the weaker sex, she is told to respect her husband, and this will fence her off, as it were, from selfish passions. Paul has much to say on this in his letter to the Ephesians: 'Husbands,' he says, 'love your wives, as Christ loved the church and gave himself for it, that he might sanctify and cleanse it with the washing of the water in the word, that he might present the church to himself all glorious,

* * * * *

595 A punning allusion to the birth of Eve (Gen 2:21–2)
596 This example is borrowed from Plutarch *Moralia* 141E–F; Pronuba is the surname of Juno as patron goddess of marriage.
597 Luke 10:34

having no stain or wrinkle or any such thing, that it should be holy and without blemish. In the same way men must love their wives; in loving his wife a man is loving himself. No one hates his own body, but nourishes and cares for it, as Christ does the church; for we are limbs of his body, his flesh and his bones. For this reason a man will leave his father and his mother and cling to his wife, and the two shall be one flesh. This is a great mystery, and I refer it to Christ and the church, but each one of you must love his wife like himself, and the wife must respect her husband.'[598]

St Paul says more than once that the man is the head and the glory of the woman and excels her for many reasons: because he was created first, because the woman was made from the man, not the opposite, or because the woman was led astray and took the lead in prevaricating before God.[599] Therefore he requires the woman to be subject to her husband, as he says again in the passage I have just quoted. Someone will think that, if all power rests with the husband, who is also the more aggressive and stronger of the two, the wife is nothing but a servant consigned to slavery. That is why the Apostle immediately says that love must be added to the husband's authority; where there is love, there is no room for tyranny. The word 'husbands' is redolent of authority, but the words 'you must love' exclude the possibility of enslavement. The authority of a loving husband is designed to advance the interests of the woman entrusted to his power. In the same way, the spirit rules the body, not to crush it but to protect it. And in case we think that the love required in marriage is something mundane, he cites an example. Which one? Not Penelope, or Alcestis, or Portia,[600] or any of the other women famous for their outstanding love for their spouses, but, he says, 'as Christ loved the church.' He could not give a more perfect example: Christ is the bridegroom of the church, the church is the bride of Christ. All of you who are in the church and part of Christ must strive to follow the pattern of the bride and bridegroom laid down by Paul, strive to follow it with all your might, even if you may not entirely succeed.

How did Christ love his bride? 'He gave himself up for her.' He gave himself up to all the ills of our earthly condition, to insult, scourging, and

* * * * *

598 Eph 5:25–33
599 The allusions are to 1 Cor 11:3; Eph 5:23; and Gen 2–3.
600 Penelope was the faithful wife of Ulysses (see also n351 above), Alcestis volunteered to die in place of her husband Admetus, and Portia took her own life at the news of her husband Brutus' death. Erasmus gives longer lists of virtuous wives in the *Encomium matrimonii* CWE 25 141 and *De vidua christiana* CWE 66 201.

finally the cross. You see the depth of his love. You owe the same love to your wife; you must be prepared to risk your own life to protect the life, chastity, or reputation of your wife. Is it enough to defend your wife from physical attack? Not at all. If you truly love your wife, you will protect her from all kinds of danger. A wife is very far from safe if she has a dead soul in a living body, and it will be dead if she loves the things of this world. Paul continues, 'that he might sanctify and cleanse it with the washing of the water in the word.' He loved it when it was unclean, he washed it with his blood to make it clean and undefiled, for the power of the blood he shed derives essentially from its accompaniment by the word that brings life, the word of faith. If you have a pagan or a Jewish wife, do not cast her out but do your best to ensure that an unbeliever may be sanctified by a believer. If you have a wife who is baptized but is so caught up with this world that she never thinks of Christ, you must take every opportunity to chip away at her bad points and replace them with good ones, until she becomes a wife after your own heart, 'all glorious' before God, with an unsullied reputation among men, 'without stain or wrinkle, or any such thing, that she may be holy and without blemish.'

Christ's church has not yet reached that state on earth, but each day he washes and purifies it so that some day it shall be free from all blemish, and there will remain in it no more propensity to sin, no error, no fall from grace. Christ bears with his bride while she is still beset by the weakness of the flesh; you too must bear with your wife, as indeed you share her weakness. Your wife may grow in physical beauty and health, but you will find it more gratifying if her character is free from wrinkles and stains. You cannot give your wife such gifts, but the Lord will bestow them through you, since he often chooses to bestow his gifts on one person by means of another, so that the one has the pleasure of helping, while the other is enriched by receiving the gift. Remember that your wife was joined to you so that you might care for and protect her. Do not make excuses, saying that it is too much like hard work or that your wife is unteachable; the Apostle's words urge you to persevere. Why tell yourself that there are two people involved, one giving and the other receiving? Husband and wife are one; to help your wife is to help yourself, and to neglect your wife is to neglect yourself.

Christ is the head of his church,[601] the church is the body; from him all grace flows into the church. But are not the head and the body the same

* * * * *

601 Cf Eph 5:23.

thing? Christ cries, 'Saul, why are you persecuting me?'[602] And in the Gospel
he says that whatever is done for the least of his members will be considered to be done for him.[603] Similarly, the husband is the head of the wife,
and she is the body; but who ever hated his own flesh? On the contrary, we
feed it when it is hungry and care for it when it is sick. These words epit-
omize gentleness and compassion; and he adds, 'as Christ does his church.'
Consider how gently God deals with the weakness of his members; sometimes he sends misfortune to chide them, sometimes good fortune to encourage them, and he finds many other ways to draw them to him. You will
not resent having to bear your wife's infirmities, until she improves, if you
remind yourself that whatever you do for her you are also doing for yourself. When God presented Eve to Adam, the man recognized their oneness:
'"This is bone of my bones, flesh of my flesh." For this reason shall a man
leave his father and mother and cling to his wife, and they shall be one
flesh.'[604] After God, no one deserves your devotion more than your father
and mother, and yet marital love surpasses the closest ties of filial affection.
Christ avows his body, and you husbands must avow your flesh. In a sense
Christ left his Father, when he came to earth, and later left his mother, the
synagogue; he clings indivisibly to his bride, nourishing and caring for her
with the utmost gentleness and compassion, treating her not as a stranger
but as his own body.

It is easy enough to understand how husband and wife are joined as
one by the union of their bodies and their spirits. But much obscurity sur-
rounds the manner in which Christ joined the mystical body of the Church
to himself through faith, so that he too became one with his members; Paul
calls it 'a great mystery'[605] because it remains unexplained for the present,
but he uses it as an example to show couples the importance of perfect harmony. It is as if he were saying, 'I cannot at present expound the mystery
that is hidden here; it is enough to have demonstrated that a husband and
wife are one, as Christ and his bride the church are one, to show the importance of perfect love between man and wife, and that every man should
love his wife as he loves himself.' Similarly, to show wives the importance
of obedience, it is enough to say that the church is subject to her bridegroom,
Christ, whom she loves and worships, to whom she bends the knee every
day, to whom she gives credit for all that she has. The well-being of the

* * * * *

602 Acts 9:4
603 Cf Matt 25:40.
604 Gen 2:23–4
605 Eph 5:32; cf 225–6 above.

church depends on her submission to the bridegroom, for those who are not subject to Christ cannot be members of him. In the same way the wife must submit to her husband as her head; if she withdraws from their partnership she exposes herself to much misfortune and to dishonour.

Again, in his letter to the Colossians, Paul asks that the husband's rule be tempered with love; if not, authority may become harshness. 'Husbands,' he says, 'love your wives and do not be harsh with them.'[606] Love is the great equalizer, the smoother of paths; it is able to make the master play the part, often enough, of the servant. Who could be more exalted than Christ? Yet he came to earth to serve, not to be served.[607] Love can make pleasant even things that are intrinsically disagreeable. Husbands therefore are given the right to rule, reprove, and punish, but they are also bound by the rule of love – and 'love is kind, it is not puffed up, it does no wrong.'[608]

Now let us hear what Paul has to say to wives: 'You women,' he says, 'be subject to your husbands as to the Lord, since the man is the head of the woman, just as Christ also is the head of the church; Christ is the saviour of the body, but just as the church is subject to Christ, so must women be to their husbands in everything.'[609] This was God's first law after the fall: 'You shall bear your children in pain; you shall be under your husband's power and he shall be your master.'[610] Since the wife first led her husband into evil paths, guiding and tempting him towards death, she is commanded to follow his lead towards redemption. This law, which God laid down for all wives, must be borne with patience. Now Paul did not merely say, 'be subject,' but added, 'as to the Lord.' Some, including St Jerome,[611] interpret this to mean that a wife is subject to her husband as a maidservant is subject to her master. But if the Apostle had meant this, he would have written, 'are subject to their husbands as their lords,' whereas he actually wrote, 'as to the Lord.' Therefore I think it more likely that 'as to the Lord' refers to the Lord Jesus, because a wife who obeys her husband is not so much submitting to a man as to the Lord, who is represented by the husband, and to whom the Lord wishes the wife to be subject. The preceding verse reads, 'Be subject to one another in fear of Christ.' A little later

* * * * *

606 Col 3:19
607 Cf Mark 10:45.
608 1 Cor 13:4
609 Eph 5:22–4
610 Gen 3:16
611 In his commentary on Eph 5:22, Jerome makes a comparison with Sarah's obedience to Abraham, whom she called *dominus*, 'lord' or 'master,' in Gen 18:12 (PL 26 564B).

he writes, 'Servants, obey your earthly masters with fear and trembling, single-mindedly, as serving Christ.' A few lines later: 'Serving the Lord and not men.'[612]

It may be that the husband to whom the wife must submit is unworthy, but the Lord is not unworthy, and it was he who ruled that she should be subject to him simply because he is her husband. It may be that the husband is unpleasant, but she will receive a reward for her obedience from the one for whose love she has served an unworthy husband. The man is the head of the woman, because she was created from the man, just as Christ too is the head of the church. For the church had its beginnings in Christ, and from him flow all the gifts of grace that the church receives. But in his role as head of his wife, the husband must take as his model Christ as head of his bride. In the human body, the head holds sway over all our limbs, since it is placed at the top and contains all our senses and intellectual faculties, but it uses its power for the good of the body; the head does not hear, see, smell, taste, think, and remember for itself alone, but for the whole body. That is why Paul added, 'Christ is the saviour of the body.' We cannot resent a regime that ensures our salvation, and similarly a wife should be pleased to obey her husband for her own good.

You may say that the church's subjection to Christ is quite fitting but that some husbands' behaviour would be barely tolerable to the maidservants. The husband has of course an example to follow in Christ, but if he deviates from this he does not lose his authority, since that would upset the proper order of things; remember that Paul tells us to obey those in authority over us, not only the good and the easy-going, but also the bad and the troublesome.[613] If what your husband tells you to do is merely unpleasant, you must obey, thinking not of his faults but of the Lord's command. If he tells you to do something that is contrary to religion or morality, you must gently refuse and, if he insists, remember that 'God must be obeyed before man.'[614] If you obey an order that is unholy, you are not obeying God through your husband, but Satan through one of his members. And yet the Apostle prescribes submission in all things. The authority of husbands is very great, although you must exclude wrongdoing from its scope. 'I please all men in all things,' said Paul,[615] and yet he always refused to compromise over some common practices, such as sacrificing to idols and eating the food consecrated to them.

* * * * *

612 The quotations are Eph 5:21, 6:5, and 6:7.
613 Cf Heb 13:17.
614 Acts 5:29
615 1 Cor 10:33, followed by allusions to 1 Cor 8–10

It would be worth looking at the terms used by Peter, the first of the apostles, in his advice to both husbands and wives; he was not unversed in the ways of marriage. Like Paul, he foresees a proselytizing role for the woman: 'Similarly,' he says, 'you women must be subject to your husbands; if any of them are unbelievers, they may be won over without a word by their wives' behaviour, observing the reverence and piety of your behaviour.'[616] Paul gives the same advice, that a woman converted to Christ should not leave her husband if he is prepared to accept a wife of a different faith: 'For how do you know, woman, that you will not win your husband for Christ?'[617] It is certainly a good sign that the husband does not shrink from sharing his bed with a woman who frequently crosses herself, who bends the knee at the name of Jesus, who adores the holy bread. And when the husband sees that his wife is changed for the better, that she is more than ever chaste, sober, patient, obedient, respectful, it will be no surprise if his wife's way of life leads him to think well of Christ. A husband will not tolerate a preaching wife; this sort of practical message will be more effective. 'Observing,' says Peter, 'the reverence and virtuousness of your behaviour.'[618] The gospel's righteousness is not condescending; a good wife will respect a godless husband more than a bad wife will revere a godly husband. Peter calls this respect 'fear'[619] because it is careful to give no offence, even inadvertently. What a wife will do for a pagan husband must also be done for those who have no more Christianity than the fact of baptism. I personally know some men who admit that they owe their souls' salvation to their wives, and I know others whom their wives could not recall from a life of sin by any means, be it obedience, patience, or tears.

Peter now paints us a picture of the good Christian wife: 'Her beauty will reside not in her elaborate hairstyle, her gold jewellery, or the pretty dresses she puts on, but in the inmost centre of her being, with that imperishable ornament, a gentle, quiet spirit, which is most precious in the sight of God.'[620] The female sex is particularly prone to two faults: women try to impress by their appearance, a failing that arises from their thirst for vain glory, and, second, they cannot suffer insults and are always eager for revenge.

* * * * *

616 1 Pet 3:1–2
617 1 Cor 7:13 and 16 (the quotation)
618 1 Pet 3:2, with slightly different wording from the previous quotation (cf n616); the question is discussed in Erasmus' annotation on the text (LB VI 1048E).
619 The Vulgate reads *in timore*, literally, 'in fear,' but in this context the sense is obviously closer to the subsidiary meaning 'with respect.'
620 1 Pet 3:3–4

This imperfection is caused by the weakness of their reason and their ignorance of true superiority; the truly superior mind ignores any hurt that it suffers. To be upset and to rush to vengeance is the sign of a mean spirit.

Thus a woman is governed by her feelings and judges success in life by externals, in which she cannot bear to be outdone. Some foolish women are upset if they see their neighbour better turned out or more richly dressed than they are. Not content with their natural appearance, they paint themselves with cosmetics, tint their hair with special dyes, curl it and crimp it. They wear jewelled earrings, gold necklaces, and clothes of fine linen and silk, not to mention the furs whose price has been pushed through the roof by competition. All this is mere external embellishment, and the more splendid it seems, the more it sullies the inner being, which neglects outward appearance in proportion to its inward beauty. When therefore a husband sees his wife's personality change so that, in spite of her sex, she rejects the outward show and the accoutrements of pride, and instead willingly gives whatever she can to the poor, content with the ornaments of the soul that are most precious to God, whom alone she strives to please; or when, after provoking her by some insult, he sees that there is no decrease in her love or in her willingness to obey him, but that she carries on in the same conscientious way, bearing everything with a gentle and calm spirit, then he will realize that the gospel is no empty name, but a power that changes character. Then at last he will be stung into emulating her, fearing humiliation if his wife can achieve what he cannot. Thus, without a word, the husband is won for God by living in the company of a godly wife.

One may perhaps come across women who manage to scorn outward appearances, but the woman who, harming none and helping all, can preserve her calm and restraint in the face of insults and reproaches is truly inspired by the spirit of Christ. And such women quite often find themselves married, by God's will, to husbands who are drunkards, spendthrifts, plunderers of the poor, adulterers, gamblers, so that they may win their husbands for God.

Thus it is all the more necessary for wives to be entirely obedient to good and reasonable husbands. To encourage them, Peter cites the example of the most renowned of women: 'Thus it was long ago, when pious women fixed their hopes on God and adorned themselves with obedience to their husbands, as Sarah obeyed Abraham and called him her lord. You are now her daughters, if you do good and do not fear any perturbation.'[621] At the

* * * * *

621 1 Pet 3:5–6

time when God instructed Abraham about circumcision and promised him Isaac, his name was lengthened from Abram to Abraham, but his wife's name was shortened from Sarai to Sarah.[622] The more reason commands us, the less power our passions have; if evil desires are cut off, the flesh and the spirit will be at ease together. But the flesh should follow the lead given by the spirit, and not the opposite. Moreover, we read that Sarah called her husband 'lord' in Genesis 18[:12]: 'Now that I am aged,' she said, 'and my lord has grown old, shall I care about pleasure?' If she had called him 'lord' out loud, you might think it just a sop to her husband's vanity, but in fact she said it to herself, thinking that no one could hear; that makes it plain that she meant what she said.

If anyone requires a precise example of Sarah's obedience to her husband, we could look at chapters 12 and 20 of Genesis. As they approached Egypt, Abraham was afraid for his life because of his wife's great beauty; he implored her to pretend to be his sister and disguise the fact that she was his wife. Whereupon that virtuous woman did not protest or say, 'My chastity is no less precious to me than your life is to you; find some other way of protecting yourself and do not expose me to seduction by these unbelievers!' No, she obeyed her husband, preferring to endanger her chastity rather than her husband's safety. Then Abraham undertook a journey at the Lord's behest, and Sarah did not hesitate to go with him. The husband obeyed God, as God is the head of the husband; the wife obeyed her husband, as the husband is the head of the wife. It is always safe to follow when your leader is himself guided by the spirit of God. And so, following the instructions of the godhead, Abraham was given a kind enough reception, and Sarah's chastity remained intact.

Abraham cannot be blamed for taking a beautiful wife through a succession of barbarian tribes.[623] He obeyed God over his wife, as he did over his son; in both cases the patriarch's faith shone out and his fears for the two of them were not realized. His wife kept her chastity, his son kept his life. But what excuse can there be for husbands who parade their wives, extravagantly and eye-catchingly arrayed, at rowdy parties, in the marketplace, or at the public baths? Some even allow them to set out for Jerusalem

* * * * *

622 *Sara* in Latin; the change of name from 'Mockery' to 'Princess' (Gen 17:15) is a greater transformation than Abraham's (from 'High Father' to 'Father of a Great Multitude'; Gen 17:5), but Erasmus' point is that, phonetically at least, the wife's name became less ostentatious.
623 By pretending that Sarah was unmarried, Abraham exposed her to seduction – but only at God's behest.

or Compostella! There's many a slip 'twixt cup and lip, but even more slips 'twixt Holland and Jerusalem.[624]

Sarah obeyed Abraham on this occasion, and there can be no doubt that she did so, with all due respect, on every other occasion. The Jews boasted that they were the children of Abraham, but the Lord punctured their pride, asking how they could be Abraham's children when their lives were so unlike his.[625] For Abraham's family spread wider, to include all those who could emulate his faith. Similarly Peter wants all women to be called the daughters of Sarah if their good deeds recall those of their mother Sarah. Abraham is called the father of many nations; in the same way, Sarah is the mother of all good wives, 'whose daughters you are,' he says, 'if you do good.'[626] In spiritual matters, kinship is thus not a matter of blood relationship but of similarities in character. Why does St Peter add the words 'and do not fear any perturbation'? It is a woman's nature to be afraid. Yet any woman who has submitted wholeheartedly to God's will may depend on God's aid and have no fear, just as Sarah stout-heartedly followed her husband on his journey among the fierce and cruel tribes. Anyone who does good has nothing to fear from evil; she has God's protection, and against him no power of men or demons can prevail.

Having dealt with the wives, Peter now turns his thoughts to the husbands. 'You men,' he says, 'must live with your wives in a similar way; use your understanding and honour them as the weaker vessels, since they share the inheritance of living grace; in this way your prayers will not be hindered.'[627] What does 'live in a similar way' mean? With honesty, with contempt for self-indulgence and ambition, concerned only to adorn your inner nature, with the kindness and moderation of a spirit at peace, with love and respect; ruling your wives with understanding, not blinded by power or lust; requiring of them only what is useful and permitting them nothing that might be harmful or corrupting to their virtue. For anyone who has the power to give orders must also have an understanding of what is desirable and what is not. The tyrant demands whatever he wants and seeks his own

* * * * *

624 The proverb is *Adagia* i v 1; as the *Moria* and the colloquies *De votis temere susceptis* ('Rash Vows') and *Peregrinatio religionis ergo* ('A Pilgrimage for Religion's Sake') remind us, pilgrimages to Jerusalem and to St James of Compostella were among the longest, costliest, and most dangerous; they were also the most prized (CWE 27 122, CWE 39 37–8, and CWE 40 623).
625 Cf John 8:39.
626 1 Pet 3:6
627 1 Pet 3:7

advantage; the husband considers also what is best for the person receiving the orders.

He should not look down on his wife because she plays a lesser role in the partnership of marriage, being weaker in body and mind. On the contrary, he should honour her the more, and make a husband's love compensate for nature's deficiencies. Husband and wife are one body but, as Paul teaches, we must give greater honour to the weaker members;[628] whatever honour you do your wife, you also do yourself. In this case 'honour' is not so much a matter of how you address her, or of her position at table; it applies rather to the conduct of every aspect of your married lives. If God held women in such esteem that he made them equal to men in offering the inheritance of heavenly life to those who believe, how then can a human husband disdain them? If God implanted in women the same spirit as in men, why should a husband be reluctant to provide the necessities of life for his wife, as though they did not share all their earthly possessions? There is a grace that deludes and a beauty that is vain,[629] but there is also a grace giving life, that is, the loving favour of God, through his Son Jesus, which offers eternal life to all who place their trust in him. How can you shun your wife's company, when you are joint heirs to such a treasure?

Peter adds, 'in this way your prayers will not be interrupted.' The apostle insists that your prayers be assiduous, and he brooks no interruption. Arguments, for example, interrupt prayer. The Christian's offering is prayer, but God may not accept it if the wife has some justifiable complaint against her husband, or vice versa; even if the wife has forgotten the wrong, the husband must repair the damage before offering up his gift of prayer. The prayers most acceptable to God are those poured out in unison by a husband and wife whose hearts are united.

Since Peter alludes to women's dress and to prayers, it is worth recalling Paul's teaching on the same points in his first letter to Timothy: 'I want men to pray in every place, lifting up hands that are clean, free from all anger and resentment. Similarly, women must dress in a modest and becoming manner, adorning themselves not with gold, pearls, costly clothes, and elaborate hairstyles, but, as befits women professing godliness, with good works.'[630] Both apostles recommend constant prayer: Paul prayed on his knees by the seashore, and at Philippi he even prayed in prison.[631] Any

* * * * *

628 1 Cor 12:23
629 Prov 31:30
630 1 Tim 2:8–10
631 Acts 21:5 and 16:25

place is holy to one who prays in the spirit. The Samaritans used to worship on the mountain,[632] the Jews at Jerusalem; the Christian, knowing that God is present everywhere, will pray anywhere. It is not the place but the heart that makes a prayer pure or impure, which is why Paul speaks of 'lifting up hands that are clean.' Those who are sullied by wicked deeds do not have clean hands; remember what was said to the Jews in Isaiah: 'Your hands are full of blood.'[633] Those who live by theft, who cheat the poor of their wages, who plunder their subjects, or who slander the innocent have unclean hands, and even if they were to pray in the little room where the Lord was born, their sacrifice would be unacceptable to God. Lift up your hands, so long as they are clean, but it is better still to lift up a pure heart. If you hurt another, your hands are not clean; if you are yourself hurt and angry, your heart is not yet ready to pray. Forgive your neighbour's offence from your heart, and your heart will be pure.

'Free from all anger and resentment,' says Paul. Anger breeds revenge, but resentment is less serious; you wonder whether to forgive someone, saying to yourself, 'I have done him so many favours, and this is how he repays my kindness; if I let him get away with this misdeed, he will soon do it again.' Do not measure the gravity of his offence or whether he is worthy of forgiveness; consider only that he is your neighbour and that the Lord commanded us to forgive unreservedly our erring neighbour.[634] I think that this illustrates Peter's words 'Do not allow your prayers to be interrupted.' A prayer is no use if it is disrupted by such thoughts. There is a covenant between us and God: 'Forgive, and you shall be forgiven.'[635] It is therefore most impertinent to ignore the covenant and demand God's forgiveness while harbouring a grudge against your neighbour.

Similarly, Paul wants women also to pray, but he does not add, 'in any place.' A woman's modesty may not be preserved in just any place. In their dress women must adorn themselves 'in a modest and becoming manner.' It is characteristic of the sex that they enjoy dressing up to go out; is Paul perhaps worried that wives may come to church unsuitably dressed? Yes, but he also prescribes another kind of ornament: 'adorning themselves,' he says, 'in a modest and becoming manner.' Their appearance will reflect and proclaim their virtues.

* * * * *

632 The chief shrine of the Samaritans was the temple on Mount Gerizim built by the renegade Manasses as a rival to Jerusalem's temple.
633 Isa 1:15
634 Cf eg Matt 6:12; 18:35.
635 Luke 6:37

Writing to the Corinthians, Paul decrees that women shall cover their heads in church, and keep silent.[636] How little the Apostle's rule can mean to a woman who appears in church looking like nothing so much as an actress playing a tragic heroine! So far from being decently covered, her hair shines glossily through a net and her bodice is open practically to the waist. In other ways, too, she looks as if she has just stepped off the stage: her face is painted with white lead and rouge and her eyes are daubed with mascara. Her looks are mirrored in her slinky walk, and, as the prophet says, in the dancing of her feet[637] and her bold stare as she swivels her gaze from side to side. She is going to a play, not to pray. Woman, how little such airs and graces befit your profession! You may ask, 'What profession? I am not a Benedictine or a Franciscan.' No, but you have professed true religion, and that costume of yours is for women who profess irreligion. Why do you, having renounced all the pomp of the world and Satan, flaunt them everywhere, even in church? How can you take pleasure in an outfit so alien to your religion? You were born to serve Christ, not Venus. How can you take pleasure in an outfit belonging to so alien a cult? You seem to outdo even the pagans in the extravagance of your dress. You may claim to be pious, but you must show your piety by good deeds. It must shine out from your face, your movements, your eyes, from every lineament of your body. I hear Christian words but I see pagan deeds. Modesty and chastity are the true ornaments of a married woman, and such adornments are devalued by artful curls, by gold, pearls, fine linen, and silken cloth. Sell all these stains on your modesty to help the poor, and your good works, which are the most apt of adornments for a wife confessing Christ, will add immeasurably to your true beauty.

Let the wife therefore demonstrate her chastity and modesty in this kind of appearance; the very fact that she is unadorned will make her seem most richly attired. If to this she adds silence, she will lack none of the adornments of a wife. 'Let the wife,' says Paul, 'learn in silence with all obedience.' He made this clearer in his letter to the Corinthians: 'If they wish to understand something they must ask their husbands at home.'[638] If in an assembly women are not allowed to speak, not even to seek instruction, what are we to make of those who now chatter endless nonsense in church? He adds, 'with all obedience.' Just as a wife is adorned by contempt for ornament, so when she submits in all things she is exalted, whereas if she gets above herself she becomes truly abject and ignoble.

* * * * *

636 1 Cor 11:5, 13; 14:34
637 Cf Prov 7:10–13.
638 1 Tim 2:11; 1 Cor 14:35

Now for the final part of this work, on the rearing of children. The subject is in fact raised in the same chapter of Paul, where he concludes as follows, 'Yet she will be saved through motherhood, if only women persist in faith, love, and holiness, with a sober mind.'[639] To bring up children properly is an onerous task, but there is a great reward: 'She will be saved,' he says. As she looks to her children's salvation, she obtains salvation for herself. You surely did not think, wife, that you had discharged your obligations when you had 'borne a few children in pain'?[640] Salvation is promised only to those who have persisted in faith, love, and holiness, with a sober mind. You will not be a true mother unless you have bestowed all these on your children. You may say: 'But it is beyond my power to make my children handsome or ugly, and it is just as far beyond me to ensure that they do not abandon faith, love, holiness, and sobriety. Why should I be punished for others' misdeeds?' The Apostle did not mean to say that a mother will be punished if her children are impious, provided that she has done her duty; but he did demand that mothers take the greatest pains to rear their children properly. He considered their influence so vital that children carefully brought up in this way would hardly ever fall by the wayside. Children rarely turn to impiety unless their parents are at fault.

Many parents have wrong ideas about three particular subjects: conception, pregnancy, and child-rearing. First of all, it is a very common notion that good people produce good children,[641] and bad people bad, just as, often, good-looking people have good-looking offspring, and ugly people have ugly children. But the fact that we rarely come across bastards who are virtuous has more than one explanation, it seems to me. First, they are born to unchaste women, and almost always bear some temperamental resemblance to their mother, even if their father is a man of upright character. Certainly both of them were uneasy in conscience as they lay together, and in that secret workshop of nature state of mind as well as of body is of the utmost importance. Second, they are brought up more casually than legitimate children. Third, the defect of their birth excludes them from the more noble aspirations in life, and they nearly always resort to the tricks and subterfuges of the servant class. Thus Euripides very wisely wrote, 'A man

* * * * *

639 1 Tim 2:15
640 Cf Gen 3:16.
641 See *Adagia* I vi 32–3 for contrasting proverbs on the question of hereditary virtue. Erasmus' own defective birth gives the following passage on bastards a particular interest, implying that he at least had risen above his natural handicap.

becomes a slave, however brave his heart, / When he learns his father's and his mother's sin.'[642] By contrast, to be the offspring of virtuous parents confers on a child the precious gift of freedom.

Thus men who go round casually getting women pregnant are not worthy of their children's love, since they have done them a great wrong even before they see the light of day. The children are unable to inherit, they are debarred from civic honours, from the priesthood, and from public office. They are insulted, called 'spurious,'[643] told to find out who their father was, and are barely thought of as anyone's children. In short, they are hardly given a chance to struggle towards virtue. These are the penalties inflicted on these innocents for their parents' incontinence. The Greeks name Themistocles and the Hebrews Jephthah as the only distinguished men to have been illegitimate.[644]

Thus your first duty towards your children is to have them by your lawful wife; I have already discussed the proper way to choose a wife.[645] The next condition is that husband and wife, whenever they set out to have a child, should not be out of sorts because of anger, hatred, or an excess of food and drink. Their bodies must be healthily sober and their minds tranquil, for in some mysterious way the mind's infirmities can infect the body, and vice versa. For example, illness or old age often produces peevishness, and it is well known that love can make the body waste away, just as spite and anger can produce heat, and fear produce coldness and trembling. If we can observe such effects in healthy adult bodies, what effect do we imagine they will have on those formless fluids from which human beings are fashioned? When Diogenes chanced to see a young man much the

* * * * *

642 Euripides *Hippolytus* 424–5, quoted in the same context by Plutarch *Moralia* 1C
643 *Spurii*, a legal term applied to the offspring of an adulterous liaison; according to canon law (*Decretales Gregorii* IX 4.17.6 CIC 2 712), such children could not be legitimized, whereas the natural children of unmarried parents could be legitimized by the subsequent marriage of the couple. The term would also apply to Erasmus if his father was in major orders (cf CWE 4 189) when he was born. That it was derogatory is suggested by its supposed derivation: Gaius *Institutes* 1.64 connects it with *spernere*, 'to scorn,' and with the Greek σποράδην 'casually, indiscriminately'; see also Plutarch *Moralia* 288E. Isidore of Seville *Etymologiae* 9.5.23 PL 82 356 applies *spurius* to the child of a noble mother and servile father, and *nothus* (used by Erasmus in the previous paragraph) to the child of a noble father and servile mother.
644 Themistocles was an Athenian general of the fifth century BC; according to Plutarch's *Life* 1, he was the son of an Athenian nobody and a nameless foreign woman. Jephthah was the son of Gilead and a prostitute; see Judg 11:1–2.
645 302–35 above

worse for drink, he did not blame him, but his father: 'Young man,' he said, 'your father was drunk when he made you.'[646]

The doctors say, not unreasonably, that young parents will produce weaker offspring than older ones, because their seed is more fluid and less mature.[647] It seems logical also that temporary physical incapacity will produce the same result. Although Christian philosophy teaches that all souls are equal, the physical envelope in which they are placed must make a difference. We can see that some people are naturally prone to anger, vindictiveness, or envy, and it is generally agreed that this is connected with their physical constitution.

If we are to believe students of natural science, sometimes parents are to blame not merely for offspring who are blind, lame, maimed, or in some other way damaged or misshapen, but also for those who are dull, stupid, and prone to conspicuous misbehaviour.[648] Drunkards produce madmen, violent parents produce ill-tempered children; the children of debauchees are prone to epilepsy, and those of silly buffoons turn out light-headed and worthless. Like father, like son.[649] Therefore, you Christian couples about to start a family, be sure that your physical and mental condition is such that you may both wish and hope that your children will be like you. I will not go into all the wearisome details of Aristotle's argument that people should not start a family until they are mature and fairly advanced in years.[650] But our physical vigour lasts for about five times seven years, that is, until our thirty-sixth year approximately, and our intellectual vigour for seven times seven years, that is, until our fiftieth year, roughly. From that age he thinks that men should refrain from begetting children, as he believes that the children will be born both physically and mentally weaker. Second, he considers that winter is a better season for procreation than summer, and judges that among the winds the north is the most advantageous and the south wind the least. It is certainly true that it is the wrong time to make children when the stomach is stuffed full; it is better to wait until digestion is complete.

* * * * *

646 Diogenes the Cynic, quoted in Plutarch *Moralia* 1D–2A, and again in Erasmus' *De pueris instituendis* of 1529 (CWE 26 315), a work that 'recycles' much of the material in this section of the *Institutio*, itself heavily dependent on Plutarch's *De liberis educandis* ('On the Education of Children') *Moralia* 1–14. On Erasmus and childhood in general, see R.L. DeMolen *The Spirituality of Erasmus* (Nieuwkoop 1987) 143–64.
647 Cf Aristotle *Politics* 7.16.6 (1335a15) and the passage cited in the next note.
648 Cf Aristotle *Historia animalium* 7.6 (585a–b).
649 Cf n641 above.
650 Aristotle *Politics* 7.16.1–11 and 16–17 (1334b29–1335b38)

Anyone who finds all this laughably trivial obviously does not care whether his children are healthy or sickly, intelligent or stupid. Husband and wife share the responsibility here, but the next stage is the special concern of the pregnant woman. As the foetus is being fashioned in nature's workshop, growing and taking shape, it is constantly influenced by its mother's physical and mental condition, which is, as it were, the wet soil in which it grows; a seedling assimilates the characteristics of the soil in which it is planted.[651] Thus the expectant mother's first care must be to have a clear and untroubled conscience, as this is the source of true psychological satisfaction. She must then avoid anger, hatred, envy, and all the other passions, which begin as diseases of the mind but then infect the body. She must eschew over-indulgence, intoxication, immoderate laughter, dancing, and anything else that will disturb her physical equilibrium.

Pregnant women are not expected to fast, but they have every reason to observe moderation at all times, for this is also part of rearing a child. It is not yet born, but already, in the recesses of its mother's body, it is learning something of the right way to live. Too much abstinence from food will harm it, as will an excessive intake of food and drink. The type of food may also be wrong: anything excessively hot or cold will be harmful, or anything causing a sudden reaction in the body. Above all you must avoid rare and spicy foods, which contract the womb or cause a discharge of urine (the medical term is diuretic) and often cause miscarriage. You must also avoid excessive or unusual physical exertion. No woman will hesitate to observe these precautions scrupulously if she remembers that two lives are at risk within a single body. You revile women who will procure a miscarriage with drugs, or murder their newborn babies, and you are right to do so; but you must also consider that anyone who brings on a miscarriage through drunkenness, dancing, or some other kind of intemperance is not so far from committing the same crime.

Immediately after the birth she has the task of breast-feeding. Here every gun must be brought to bear against the perverse but extraordinarily widespread practice of mothers handing their infants over to hired wet-nurses. However, I will not detain the reader over this; it is fully discussed by Phavorinus in Aulus Gellius,[652] Plutarch did not omit it from his writings on the rearing of children,[653] and I myself have said a good deal on the subject, particularly in the colloquy entitled 'The New

* * * * *

651 The comparison is from Aristotle *Politics* 7.16.14 (1335b19).
652 Aulus Gellius *Noctes Atticae* 12.1
653 Plutarch *Moralia* 3C–D

Mother';[654] you can look at these if you wish. I will simply repeat that nothing is more unnatural than that a mother should refuse to feed her offspring. To banish a newborn babe to the arms of some woman who will feed it for money is like exposing it to the elements, and mothers who allow this to happen are barely worthy the name. What is more, hardly anything is so conducive to the physical and moral health of a child, and to mutual affection between parent and child, as to have a baby suckle at its mother's breast. If illness or some other problem prevents this, at least the greatest care must be taken to ensure that the infant is entrusted to a nurse who is physically healthy and sober and upright in character; if not, the helpless child may imbibe with its milk both physical weakness and moral corruption.

Those who have learned to train mules or horses make much of their skills, but no skill is more difficult to learn than how to fashion a human being, and it is a skill that all parents ought to have. If they did, there might not be such a shortage of virtue in the world. It is something to be well born, but upbringing is still more important. You could say the same about it as Demosthenes said of the orator's delivery: asked what was the first requirement in rhetoric, he replied, 'Delivery.' The second? 'Delivery.' The third? 'Delivery.'[655] In other words, he made delivery the supreme requirement in all public speaking. The same idea would apply even better to upbringing, which can overthrow Nature, however powerful she may otherwise be; and although a child's nature is not hard to change, habits acquired during its upbringing cannot be changed.

In every sphere of learning three things are necessary above all to enable you to succeed: nature, training, and practice or experience.[656] By nature, I mean a certain aptitude for learning what you are taught; training

* * * * *

654 *Puerpera* ('The New Mother'), published in February 1526; see CWE 39 590–618, especially 595–6, where Erasmus discusses the medical and psychological benefits of breast-feeding. In the *Ecclesiastes* LB V 875F–876E, to illustrate the art of subdividing a topic, Erasmus gives thirteen reasons why 'a woman should not allow her child to be nursed by another woman.'

655 The celebrated orator Demosthenes is quoted in Quintilian *Institutiones oratoriae* 11.3.6.

656 Repeated in *De pueris instituendis* CWE 26 311 and inspired by Plutarch *Moralia* 2A, including the agricultural simile that follows. Cf also Quintilian *Institutiones oratoriae* 2.19.2; and Aristotle *Politics* 7.13.11 and *Nicomachean Ethics* 10.10. The latter identifies the same three stages but places 'practice' second, on the ground that an infant is conditioned by experience before it is capable of reasoning. As Margolin 64–6 and 513 n280 suggests, Erasmus' second term, *ratio* (literally, 'reason'), has in this context overtones of 'method' and 'learning,' as in his title *De ratione studii*.

provides rules by which you may judge what to avoid and what to pursue; practice turns rules into habits. Let me try to make my meaning clearer by a simile. Imagine that the child is an uncultivated field, that the moral code is the seed, and that practising what has been taught is like cultivating the field. From conception until the seventh year, the fallow ground is simply prepared for the sowing; but we can either help and improve on nature, or worsen it by our mistakes. During this period the farmer's tasks are not negligible: he must drain marshy places and water dry ones; he must open up shady spots and level uneven ground; he must prune fruit trees, grub up roots, spread fertilizer, and break up the soil. The mother has similar tasks to perform for her nursling, protecting him from anything that may harm him physically or morally. The farmer's next job is to sow the finest possible seed in his field. This is also the mother's task from the seventh year, though the father has a role too. But the labour of both will be in vain unless the growing child is given the chance to practise virtue, so that it quickly and easily becomes second nature to him. If he can see the practical advantages of good behaviour, as well as its theoretical excellence, he will willingly pursue the course that he has learned is the best. What a splendid harvest will be reaped from their children by parents when they have reached this point; it will bear out the truth of Solomon's maxim 'A wise son brings joy to his father; a foolish son is his mother's sorrow.'[657] And even if they reap no reward from their children, perhaps because they die before reaching maturity, yet they reap God's reward of eternal life.

Let us therefore return to the nurture of the infant. The principal elements in this are food and drink, sleep, exercise, clothing, the child's surroundings, and the company it keeps. Some children are given both the wrong sort and the wrong amount of food: some parents think it amusing to give small children wine, or highly spiced or salty food, whereas it can do serious harm. Others are afraid that their children will be too thin, and stuff them with food even when they have had enough, like capons being fattened up for market. The first of these will predispose their children to alcoholism, gourmandise, and 'Attic desserts';[658] the others, if we are to believe Aristotle, will make their children lazy, lumpish, and dull[659] – as will too much sleep.

Infants must therefore be weaned on milk products and other appropriate foods, and in moderate quantity, so that their minds are not dulled

* * * * *

657 Prov 10:1
658 Attic desserts were reputed to be particularly toothsome; see *Adagia* II iii 100.
659 Aristotle *Historia animalium* 7.12 (587–8)

by excess or their bodies weakened and impaired by hunger. However, just as too much sleep enfeebles the body and the mind, so the child should not take too much exercise, especially as it gets bigger; nature gives younger children a certain vital energy, whose heat gradually increases the size of their bones, and exercise helps to strengthen them.

As for clothing, there are again two common mistakes. Some parents push their young children out of the house, half naked in the depths of winter, intending the north wind and the frost to toughen them up. They are not much more civilized than those German tribes who, history tells us,[660] made every father place his newborn child on his shield and dip it into the Rhine. If it took to the freezing water and seemed to be trying to swim, it was acknowledged as legitimate; if not, it was rejected as a bastard. However, Aristotle thinks that a little exposure to the cold will help make children healthy.[661]

I suspect that many modern parents are even more misguided when they encumber their children's little bodies with the same kind of showy clothes that vanity makes adults wear.[662] On a skull that is still soft they place a double cap with broad fringes, a great heavy thing such as not even an old man would have worn ninety years ago. Then there is a thick vest with stockings attached to it, above which is worn a shirt, and over all that a topcoat, weighing down youthful shoulders and loins with its thick padding; boys are supposed to enjoy wearing such finery. Girls are treated still more cruelly. Their heads are burdened with ribbons and head-dresses, sometimes even with men's caps. They wear a shift, and above their linen undergarment a gown of the most ornate kind. The bodice of the gown, far too heavy to be practical, flows from the shoulders to the ground in such wide billows that this one part is enough of a burden for an entire outfit; but then there is a ruffled skirt falling from the waist, weighing down the hips with its many pleats, and, as if that were not enough, a huge train is attached to the back, unfolding from the waist and inflicting yet another burden on this slender body. The stockings and the shoes with their heavy soles and

* * * * *

660 Less a historical allusion than a rhetorical commonplace, often coupled with the legend that the eagle exposes its unfledged young to the sun; see eg a letter attributed to Julian the Apostate (*Epistulae* 383D; variously numbered 16, 59, or 191) and a poem by St Gregory of Nazianzen (PG 37 1516:143–4).
661 Aristotle *Politics* 7.17.2 (1336a12–15)
662 On extravagance in dress, cf the colloquy *Senatulus, sive* Γυναικοσυνέδριον ('The Council of Women') CWE 40 909–10, and *De civilitate* CWE 25 278–9; on the incongruity of outdated fashions, as described here, see Ep 1479 and *Ciceronianus* CWE 28 381.

double straps on each side look tough enough for a football match. What is the effect of all this? Tender young bodies are injured by the weight, and moreover the limbs are confined and not free to develop properly. Money is tossed away on such nonsense, and, what is more, young people gradually acquire a foolish vanity about their clothes that will be very difficult to unlearn when they grow up. If parents are really besotted by such trifles, they would do better to practise their foolishness on dolls or monkeys, and not on their children.

The environment in which infants are weaned is not unimportant, either. Damp surroundings bring on ill health, and so does excessive heat, although most German children are brought up in steaming heat, like fire-worms;[663] you would sometimes think they were being roasted alive. A place exposed to draughts, or else to loud noise and disturbance, is no good; these may damage the child's brain. Baths and ointments are good for children if properly administered.

My next point may seem irrelevant to some, but I think it of primary importance that, as far as possible, infants should be brought up in the company of children of equable temperament and good character, since any physical or moral defect in a playmate seems, in some mysterious way, to be contagious. If doctors are right to advise even adults to consort with those who are physically fit and of a calm and sunny disposition, since one's natural condition may be improved or worsened by contact with others, how much more likely is this to be the case with children, who are physically unformed and pliable, and thus capable of taking any direction? However, it is nature's rule that bad things, such as eye trouble or stammering, spread more rapidly than good things. It is said that Aristotle had something of a stammer and that Plato had round shoulders – and that their pupils came to resemble them in these respects.[664] It is generally recognized that some diseases are highly contagious. But not everyone realizes how beneficial or harmful can be the temperament of the person with whom you spend your time, because the benefits, and the harm, creep in gradually and in small amounts. You do not notice the mischief as it creeps in, but after a time you realize that it has. Some children, even at that age, are lachrymose, grumpy, irritable, and somehow malicious; if at all possible, keep your child well away from them! Someone may say that it is unchristian to make such a

* * * * *

663 Cf *Adagia* I ix 51 on this favourite image of a winged insect reputed to live in fire. On the German predilection for heat, cf the colloquy *Diversoria* ('Inns') CWE 39 371 and 376 n9.
664 Cf Plutarch *Moralia* 26B and 53D.

fuss about physical health. I am not advocating a lot of fuss, but I do see the need for care, for the simple reason that a properly developed body will help make the mind more receptive to education.

The ancients often argued about the age at which schooling should begin. Many felt that a child should not be troubled with the burdens of book-learning until its seventh year,[665] but Aristotle thinks that formal education should begin from the fifth year.[666] Others believe that a child is teachable as early as its third year. My view is that they are all right! Some things may be inculcated very early into a tender and unformed young mind, but gently, and only the sort of thing to which that age is highly responsive; in this way the child of tender years will not be distressed but the teaching will not be wasted. Children can learn, in play, to recognize Latin and Greek letters, draw their shapes, and imitate their sounds, whereas an adult learning to read can take a long time over this. There are certain preliminaries to formal learning that make it easier for us to learn later. This is true not only of school subjects, but of moral and spiritual education too: for example, to bend the knee at the name of Jesus,[667] or when meeting some distinguished person; in church, to clasp the hands together and venerate the Eucharist, to kiss a crucifix, to stand quietly by when the blessing is asked for the meal or thanks are given – these are some of the beginnings of piety.[668]

In these years all harshness must be avoided, although the child must be taught respect. The child must sometimes be tricked into learning when it thinks it is playing, and encouraged to learn by kind words, praise, promises, and little gifts, rather than coerced by threats, curses, and blows. Some wrong-headed teachers, by their grim and cruel methods, teach their pupils nothing – except to hate learning.

I have known some mothers who fancied themselves great experts on the rearing of children, and who succeeded in ruining a naturally virtuous character by their cruelty.[669] A boy, barely eight, lost his wits. A girl, barely able to talk, was carefully trained in the manners of the court. The most important of these was that she must punctuate each sentence, when talking

* * * * *

665 In *De pueris instituendis* CWE 26 319, Erasmus attributes this opinion to Hesiod, probably by way of Quintilian *Institutiones oratoriae* 1.1.16.
666 Aristotle *Politics* 7.17.14 (1336b35–7)
667 Cf Phil 2:10.
668 On the usefulness, at least at this early stage, of outward tokens of piety, cf passages in *De civilitate* and *De pueris instituendis* CWE 25–6 279–80 and 318.
669 For more precise (and horrifying) examples of the results of maltreating children, see *De pueris instituendis* CWE 26 326–30.

to her mother, with the phrase 'Madame ma mere'; if she had to say no, instead of 'Nany' she must say, 'Salve vostre grace, Madame.'[670] To help her learn, the child, still in her fifth year, was beaten until she fainted. As this happened more and more frequently, she learned one further lesson: that when she was beaten she must not let slip any tears, sobs, or wails, but bottle them up; if not, she would be packed off to the torturer's.[671] And this was a girl of faultless character in every respect. I saw her practically choke to death as, threatened by her mother, she was forced to swallow her sobs and stop her tears.

The ancients actually had laws to prevent this kind of thing, though Aristotle disagrees with the legislation and thinks that such suppression and inhibition of the spirits helps to strengthen the infant's frame.[672] This might be true if it were a matter of modest self-restraint; but this violence done to nature was already reflected in the girl's eyes, brimming with suppressed tears; she had a glazed look in them, like someone scared witless by a ghost. The mother was herself no more than twenty-six, but a widow so confident of her own skills that she refused to heed the warnings of her brothers and relations; in fact she did not beat her daughter unless she was thoroughly angry. But I concluded that the mother deserved a beating much more than the daughter. She was not merely misguided: even if she had had something serious and important to teach her daughter, she should have refrained from cruelty and violence, in view of the girl's age; but in fact she was torturing the child over the trivialities of court life. Other parents similarly vent their fury on children for using their left hand instead of their right,[673] but overlook far more important things. Even when there is some valid reason for taking the cane to a child, it should be done without rancour, and once the punishment is over, the child should always be comforted in some way.

Nature already gives some indication of a child's character before its seventh year; children will appear relatively bad-tempered or mild-mannered, humourless or affable, obstinate, artless, or devious and cunning. At this stage great care must be taken to encourage any virtues and discourage any vices that appear. You have in your hands a slender and

* * * * *

670 'No [= Nenny] ... Begging your pardon, madam'
671 *Ad carnificinam*, literally, to the hangman's or to the rack, but in Erasmian terms, to a school; he frequently alludes to schools and schoolmasters in these terms in *De pueris instituendis* eg LB I 505A and 506–7 / CWE 26 326 and 329–31.
672 Aristotle *Politics* 7.17.6 (1336a34–9), a comment on Plato *Laws* 7.792B
673 Cf Plutarch *Moralia* 5A.

infinitely flexible twig, a piece of the most malleable wax, of damp clay;[674] you must play the skilful craftsman.

So much for 'preparing the fallow field,' the first stage of education, which we have decided to call 'nature'; now we turn to the sowing of seed, which I have called 'training.' Exactly what you plant in a child's mind is of the utmost importance, since nothing sticks in the mind for longer than what is absorbed in these early years. Everyone parrots Horace's dictum, but few take heed of it: 'A new jar will retain the smell / Of the first thing ever poured into it.'[675] Our earliest habits often still seem the best. In his *Politics* Aristotle tells of one Theodore, an actor, who would never let anyone else go on stage before him because he thought that the spectators always applauded the first performer more loudly than the rest.[676]

There are two sides to education, the one concerned with scholarship itself, the other with piety and morality. There is nothing to prevent the two being pursued side by side, but piety must always have priority. I have said a few words about book-learning already here, and a good deal on the subject in other works, particularly the one *On Education for Children*, and in my *Education of a Christian Prince* and *Colloquies*.[677] Anyone wanting more information should consult Plato's *Republic* and *Laws*, and Aristotle's *Republic*, especially books 7 and 8. They prefer public schooling to private education; these days public education is in the hands of the elementary schoolmasters, who ought to be selected with the greatest of care, but in fact it is usually sordid and worthless men, some of them barely sane, who are appointed. They are given sordid premises and a pitiful salary, and you would think they were raising pigs, not educating the free-born sons of the citizenry.[678] The very future of the state is endangered in such places. But it goes still worse with those children who receive an illiberal education[679]

* * * * *

674 Cf *Adagia* III ii 33.

675 Horace *Epistles* 1.2.69–70, a favourite image of Erasmus. See *Adagia* II iv 20; *Puerpera* ('The New Mother') CWE 39 596; *De pueris instituendis* CWE 26 306.

676 Aristotle *Politics* 7.17.13 (1336b27–31)

677 *De pueris instituendis*, though not published until 1529, was composed c 1509 (see CWE 26 292); the *Institutio principis christiani* CWE 27 203–88 was first published in 1516, and the *Colloquia* from 1519 onwards.

678 Schoolmasters are a frequent target for Erasmus, eg in the *Moria* CWE 27 122–3; *De pronuntiatione* CWE 26 382–4; and especially *De pueris instituendis* ibidem 324–5.

679 Cf the full title of *De pueris statim ac liberaliter instituendis* ('Early Liberal Education for Children'), where Erasmus rails against the 'houses of the Brethren' in which an illiberal education was sometimes provided for cash, though they

in the caves of certain creatures of darkness, since this trade is practised in some monasteries by a kind of men halfway between monks and laymen – so many evil things have crawled into the world under the cover of religion!

But let us pass quickly over all that and concentrate on ways of inculcating piety into children. The first seeds of religion are to know that God must be feared and loved above all else: God who created, restored, and governs the universe, who is all-pervading, all-knowing, all-seeing, and who has offered eternal life to all those who keep his commandments[680] and trust in him through his Son Jesus, who with the Father lives in the hearts of the faithful through the Holy Spirit. But they must also know that just as God rewards all goodness, so he punishes all wickedness. Thus no one is denied the reward for his good deeds, even if mere mortals return evil for good, and likewise no one, however secret his sins, can escape God's vengeance, unless the sinner repents and is reconciled with God.

The name of Jesus must be brought to children's attention in such a way that they take him to their hearts and love him above all else. Then they must be told that children are always accompanied by angels who watch and note all their deeds, their thoughts even, and that they delight in chastity, modesty, sobriety, love, and friendship and deplore their opposites; when the angels observe these virtues in their charges, they shower them with gifts from God to make them better still.

The next task is to ensure that the child holds the Holy Scriptures in the greatest reverence, for in them, as from an oracle, God speaks eternally to humankind. The child will conceive this esteem for them more readily if he sees that the sacred books are always treated with respect, if he learns to kiss the gospel text, if no one invokes Holy Writ in jest or in anger, but soberly and respectfully. Let him also learn to contemplate the beauty of the skies, the rich bounty of the earth, the bubbling of the springs, the winding of the rivers, the vastness of the oceans, the boundless variety of the earth's creatures, and remember that all this was created to serve humanity's needs, so long as humanity serves its creator, God. Let the child learn of those gifts that God has especially bestowed upon his chosen flock through his only Son, and that are poured out daily through the Holy Spirit, and, finally, of the rewards awaiting the righteous

* * * * *

were hostels rather than schools (CWE 26 325 and n97 and Margolin 548 n546). For Erasmus' own bitter experiences at the hands of such teachers, see *De pronuntiatione* CWE 26 385–6; Ep 447:109–14 and n108; and R.J. Schoeck *Erasmus Grandescens* (Nieuwkoop 1988) 36–8.

680 Cf Matt 19:17.

and the punishments awaiting the unrighteous. Let the child be told of the obligation he accepted at baptism to remain true to his commander, Jesus, in whose service he has enrolled; let him keep spotless the white tunic he has put on. Let the child also be told of the close ties of kinship that exist between all Christians, who are like the members of a single body. This will accustom him to treat fellow Christians with brotherly affection for the simple reason that they are Christians; let him understand that Christ is both wounded and healed in his members. Let the child learn that no one who dwells in Christ is unhappy, or could ever be unhappy, whatever befalls, be it good times or bad, be it life or death. In adversity we must give thanks to God, who scourges us for our salvation's sake; nor must we take prosperity for granted, but worship God for his kindness.

The child must be taught how to conduct himself towards his parents, his elders, his equals, and his inferiors; he will learn not to scorn the poor, and to be friendly to his equals, respectful to his elders, and devoted to his parents. He should know that, in performing a service for any of these, he will be earning God's approval, since in so doing he obeys God's commandments. Let him be given examples of virtue, drawn above all from the life of Christ, and then of others, especially those whose holiness is attested by the Holy Scriptures. Let him be told how ugly it is to fall prey to envy or anger or hatred, and how becoming it is to speak with restraint, modesty, and circumspection; he must hold his tongue, except when it is essential to speak, and not betray his ignorance. Finally, let him learn that there is nothing worse than lying, or slandering someone, especially in the person's absence. If these and similar principles are instilled in a child's tender mind, they will eventually blossom into a life of outstanding virtue.

You should be aware that when children reach their fourteenth year their potential is at its highest, and they are most receptive to everything that is worth knowing; if this opportunity is missed, it will not recur. At this stage, therefore, you must concentrate single-mindedly upon the best ways of consolidating the child's moral development and completing his academic education. It will greatly advance our hope that the children will turn out as we wish if we have first set ourselves before them as a pattern. Children have a particular gift for imitation; if they see that their parents' lives are filled with piety, chastity, sobriety, and moderation, they will copy the things they see every day, out of habit, as it were, just as living with a stammerer will make you begin to stammer. Mere words of advice will have little effect if the child sees that his parents' lives are quite different from their words, and it will be hard to convince him that their advice was serious when they take no heed of it themselves.

Another important matter will be the choice of tutor or teacher.[681] Parents are in fact extraordinarily negligent over this. They pick very carefully the man who will look after their horses, but they will entrust their children to almost anyone. Some mothers treat their lap-dogs[682] better than their children, and a stable boy or a falconer is paid more than the children's tutor. Even princes are, generally speaking, less fortunate here than elsewhere: few are handed over early in life to god-fearing and honourable tutors.

What should be looked for in a tutor is not so much erudition as moral integrity. You must make an unbiased and considered choice; do not take on anyone who pushes himself forward, who campaigns for the post by flattering you, or who is thrust on you by your friends. When you are ill, or your ship is foundering, do you listen to your friends? 'Send for this particular doctor, for my sake; he's a relative, a friend of mine.' 'Give the wheel to this chap; he's very keen to have it!' You will of course reply, 'I may pander to your whims some other time, but now I am in danger, and the best doctor for me will be the one most likely to cure me; the skipper I want is the one who knows best how to handle a ship.' You should do the same in choosing the person to whom you intend to entrust your child's formative years. But if you find a suitable candidate, do not put the whole burden on him and abdicate your own responsibility; you must act like an overseer,[683] and look in from time to time to see how your child is getting on.

Your tenant farmer may be an honest man, but you still pay frequent visits to the farm and, if you find something wrong, demand that he take action; if he has failed to perform some essential task, you want to know the reason why. And if the farmer clearly fails to live up to your expectations, you get rid of the slacker and put in someone better. If you will do all that for a parcel of land, will you not do as much for the intended heir to your entire estate? Is a child worth less than a field? You do all you can to leave your child well-off, but make no attempt to teach him what to do with his inheritance.[684] That is no less absurd than buying him the finest of lutes but forgetting to arrange any music lessons for him.

* * * * *

681 This section, largely inspired by Plutarch *Moralia* 4A–E, is echoed vigorously in *De pueris instituendis* CWE 26 313–14; cf Margolin 477 n42.
682 Literally, 'Maltese puppies'; cf *Adagia* III iii 71.
683 Erasmus uses *episcopus*, 'bishop,' but originally meaning 'overseer' in Greek; perhaps a comment on the true role of the bishop; see n274 above.
684 Erasmus is echoing the rhetorical question posed by the philosopher Crates, quoted in full (via Plutarch *Moralia* 4E) in *De pueris instituendis* CWE 26 304.

Teaching the very young is no mean skill, and educating adolescents requires outstanding talent. Our lives on this earth are influenced most powerfully by three groups: by teachers, who form the young; by preachers, who instruct the people; and by princes. When Diogenes was being sold at auction, the auctioneer asked him how he would like to be described, and he replied, 'Say that I am a man who can handle children.' A rich man who had young children at home heard the announcement, bought Diogenes, and made him tutor to his children.[685] But a single drachma would be too much to pay for a bad man, or a bad teacher. For in fact not every good and learned man is necessarily suited to teaching the young; many lack gentleness, others lack patience. But anyone who is a specialist in this field cannot be paid too much; a good tutor is worth whatever you think your child's well-being is worth. Aristippus, probably the most quick-witted of all philosophers, was asked by a very rich man what salary he would want to take on the man's son; he demanded a thousand drachmas. The rich man, scandalized by his effrontery, exclaimed: 'What! I could buy a slave for that much!' 'Yes,' replied Aristippus, 'but if you pay me you will be getting two slaves: your son, and the man you've hired for your son.'[686] I do not disapprove of people who employ a tutor at home while the children are still small; the young children are even better cared for, and the parents can look more closely at the character of their instructor.

People often ask whether it is more advantageous for children to be educated at home by a tutor or to have lessons with a crowd of other children[687] in what the ancients termed a *paedagogium*,[688] nowadays called a college, or in some places a *bursa*.[689] There is also, as I mentioned

* * * * *

685 The story, found in Diogenes Laertius 6.74, is told at greater length in *De pueris instituendis* CWE 26 326.

686 The story is told in Diogenes Laertius 6.86 and Plutarch *Moralia* 4F–5A.

687 The question is discussed most thoroughly by Quintilian *Institutiones oratoriae* 1.2.1–29, who opts for a medium-sized school. Erasmus is most concerned that schools should be under public and preferably secular control; see Margolin 85–6 and 549 n550.

688 The word *paedagogium* may have pejorative overtones, being originally a school for slaves and metaphorically a school for vice; cf Pliny *Naturalis historia* 33.12.152.

689 *Bursa* is a puzzling term, more likely to be applied to a student's financing (cf French *bourse*, 'grant') than to his place of study. C. DuCange *Glossarium ad scriptores mediae et infimae Latinitatis* 6 vols (Niort 1883) 1 790, having recognized the association with *bursarii* (students subsidized from the public purse), defines *bursa* further as a meeting place, or an illicit meeting, also a secondary meaning of *collegium*, which Erasmus has just used; we may suspect further irony on Erasmus' part.

earlier,[690] a kind of men, halfway between monks and laymen, who will take charge of anything up to a couple of hundred youngsters in a single building. It cannot be denied that isolation is unprofitable to children, and that there are many advantages in mixing socially. None the less, it must be admitted that in a large group there are always some bad characters, who will infect many of the others, and that individuals cannot receive the same attention when it has to be divided among so many. Moreover, you cannot choose the teachers there, as they are appointed and removed at the behest of others. There is one particular disadvantage with colleges, which is that they do not teach grammar with sufficient intensity.[691] It should be the most carefully taught subject of all. There are two reasons: first, students are too quickly whisked away to those subjects that lead to the degrees of Bachelor and Master; the young people are dazzled by the prestige and informality of the subjects, and the masters make more profit out of them. Teachers of grammar are so little esteemed that they will appoint a mere boy to teach the other boys, even if he is barely sixteen and got his qualifications only the day before yesterday. Yet no one can teach grammar properly unless he has studied all kinds of writing on all sorts of topics and is a practised writer himself.

For these reasons many people prefer a middle course and have five or six children taught by a single tutor. This solution provides the comradeship that lively youngsters require, though the tutor can still give his attention to individuals, and it easily avoids the corruption that flourishes in larger groups. The next best course is to give each of the pupils who live or learn in a college a personal tutor who will give him some private lessons. Someone will object, 'This is good advice for the rich, but what about the poor?' I wish that I could give useful advice to everyone! But at least the rich can be reminded that if they spot any naturally talented children from poor backgrounds, they could pay for their education, or let them join their own children and be taught with the same care and attention by their teacher. There are many kinds of alms-giving, by which the rich try to buy into the kingdom of God, but they should know that this kind of alms-giving is particularly pleasing to God.

Whatever the system of training adopted, it is essential that all children be taught first to speak clearly and accurately; then they must learn to read

* * * * *

690 Cf n679 above.
691 A criticism made with greater vehemence in *De pronuntiatione* CWE 26 380; much of this discussion of schools is echoed in that dialogue, published in 1528.

and write fluently. Books are a major source not only of instruction but of recreation, but no one can take much pleasure in reading if he cannot read quickly. Those who can afford it should also study one of the nobler mechanical arts, such as painting, sculpture, clay modelling, or architecture. I know that the ancient philosophers had no time for such arts,[692] but we cannot despise them since we worship Christ the carpenter, known as the carpenter's son.[693] Such studies will keep them from idleness, and if they fall on hard times, they will have something to keep them going, if we believe the popular saying that having a skill never hurt anyone.[694]

Some people consider that a girl's education is complete if she has been shut away until her marriage and has never set eyes on a man or been seen by one; in the meantime she lives among foolish and inconsequential women, from whom she may imbibe more corruption than if she were living among men. I admit that it is a great achievement to have preserved a daughter's virginity, but the truly chaste woman is the one who knows herself what chastity means, and how it can best be preserved. A girl's mind must be filled with the religious arguments that will enable her to do so rationally and wholeheartedly. People in general consider it a waste of time to give girls a literary education, but wiser heads know that there is no better way to improve their minds and safeguard their virtue. In this area, however, people must make their own decision, according to their circumstances and means. It is certainly true that a growing girl will need more careful protection than a boy. Both are on a very slippery path, but more pitfalls await a girl, and she is less strong-minded; once she has fallen, rumour's trumpet will sound more harshly for her. The merest touch, or a breath of wind, and your milk-white rose will lose her bloom.

To sum up: that most precious treasure, virginity, is irrecoverable, and so, as I have said, your first concern will be to fill the girl's mind with holy thoughts and teach her to know what is right and then to love it. Your next task will be to protect her from any taint of immorality; for as long as possible, she must know nothing of sin, and she must never find it attractive. Third, she must be kept busy, as idleness is the bane of good character. Immoral company plays a big part in corrupting innocent minds; I would expect a father and mother, above all, to say and do nothing immoral in front of their daughter, however young she may be. I do not know why, but we are all very precocious when it comes to learning to do wrong; even if she

* * * * *

692 Cf Xenophon *Oeconomicus* 4.2–3.
693 Cf Matt 13:55; Mark 6:3.
694 Cf *Adagia* I vii 33.

cannot understand what she sees or hears, it will remain in her mind like a corrupt seed that will one day grow into a poisonous plant. 'A boy must be treated with great consideration,'[695] but a little girl even more so; if you parents are thinking of doing something immoral, do not imagine that your little daughter is too young to understand. Where can children go to avoid bad company if even their parents school them in wickedness?

This is how girls are brought up at court in certain countries: in the morning, they get busy with the curlers and the make-up, then off to mass to see and be seen; breakfast, followed by some gossip, followed by the midday meal. After that, take your places for some mindless chatter! The girls sink down here and there, and the men rush to put their heads in their laps. The girl who never refuses one is highly praised for her manners. Then it is time for some silly games, most of them rather coarse as well; so the afternoon is whiled away until it is time for supper. After supper, more of the same amusements as after the previous meal.

It is in such an atmosphere that the sons and little daughters of princes are brought up. But they are not much better brought up in the country. The sons and daughters of the gentry spend their days in the company of greasy, idle servants, who are often slovenly and immoral into the bargain. How else are they to pass the time? Well, they could pass the time a lot more profitably weaving tapestries. Aristotle wants high-born children kept away from the slaves because of their low character and lowbrow humour.[696] The ancients had special rooms in which the men could meet, other rooms set aside for the women, and the parthenons, or maidens' chambers, where the girls could spend their time.

To learn how carefully a girl's chastity must be safeguarded, listen to that wise man Sirach: 'You have sons: train them and bend them to your will from their earliest years. You have daughters: protect their bodies and do not let them see you smile.'[697] What kind of advice is this? How can a father not love his daughters, especially if they are dutiful and god-fearing; and if he loves them, how can he look upon them with an unsmiling face? But in fact, if you truly love your daughters, that is why you will hide your smiles when you see them. Where is the danger? It is important that girls of that age should always be constrained by feelings of respect, and too much cheerfulness in their father's face will detract from this not a little. If his daughters do something unbecoming, they are rebuked by a stern glance

* * * * *

695 Juvenal *Satires* 14.47
696 Aristotle *Politics* 7.17.7 (1336a39–b3)
697 Ecclus 7:23–4

from their father; if they have done nothing wrong, their father's expression still must be serious (but not harsh) to remind them not to err.

What would Sirach say if he could see some of these modern fathers who, in the presence of their growing – and even fully-grown – daughters, boast in their cups of their own youthful indiscretions, spotlighting the temptations of adolescence? Even worse, they blurt out the secrets of the marriage-bed. And yet, if their sons go astray, these fathers will disinherit them; and if anything happens to their daughters, they will confound heaven and earth.[698] Why rage at your children, you faithless father? It is yourself you should punish, since you put them up to it; can you be surprised if the young people do things of which they have heard you boast so often? 'What words will you find to upbraid your son?' as the woman in the play said.[699] It is worse to boast of your misdeeds than to commit them, but it is worst of all to do it in front of your children. Are you surprised that your offspring do not respect you, since you have no respect for them? What chance of your children having decent moral standards, when they are undermined by you, who should be their most scrupulous guardian?

Some people use obscenities so often that they sometimes slip out unexpectedly. I witnessed a remarkable example of this in Brussels, at the church of St Gudula.[700] The church was crowded with people when a certain married lady, of impeccable reputation and excellent family, came in. The floor was slippery with snow from people's shoes, and suddenly she slipped and fell; in her surprise, she uttered a loud cry, naming, as many women do out of habit, the male member. Everyone roared with laughter, and she blushed with shame. It just slipped out, but why do people get into such bad habits? Could they not learn, just as easily, to name Jesus or Mary when something unexpected happens to frighten them? Some people have a similar habit of cursing when something goes wrong, or of swearing when they tell a story; but when they say, 'A hundred devils!' might they not just as well say, 'God be good to me'? Some people can scarcely utter four words without swearing; children take in such things from an early age.

* * * * *

698 *Adagia* I iii 81
699 Terence *Phormio* 1042
700 St Gudula's is the cathedral church of Brussels. This anecdote was added to Erasmus' manuscript draft on a separate slip of paper; see C. Reedijk 'Three Erasmus Autographs in the Royal Library at Copenhagen' in *Studia bibliographica in honorem Herman de La Fontaine Verwey* (Amsterdam 1966) 346.

Love stories, which are so influential with the young, very easily take hold of immature minds, and a good many of them contain an element of coarseness. Storytellers who corrupt innocent minds with their far from innocent tales must be kept away from young girls, for it is poison that they drip into those tender ears.

In some countries these days, as a sort of annual ritual, new songs are published for the girls to learn. They all have similar themes – a husband deceived by his wife, a girl escaping her parents' vigilance, a secret tryst arranged with a lover; these tricks are recounted with approval, and successful debauchery is applauded. The style in which these poisonous tales are told is so foul, so full of innuendo and suggestiveness, that pure filth could not be filthier. A lot of people, especially in Flanders,[701] earn a living from such stuff; if the law were more vigilant, the authors of these lullabies would be flogged by the hangman, and made to sing dirges, not dirty ditties. And yet these brazen corrupters of youth make a living from their crimes, and there are even parents who think that learning such songs will count as a social grace in their daughter.

The ancients considered that music belonged to the liberal arts; but since those rhythmic sounds have such power to affect the human spirit, some concluded that the soul itself was music, or at least contained musical harmony, since like attracts like. Thus they carefully distinguished between the different modes, among which the Dorian took the palm, and considered music so important that they thought it necessary to make laws prohibiting the import into the state of any music that might corrupt the citizens.[702] And is not our music, leaving aside the foul language and disgusting themes, full of frivolousness, not to say madness? There used to be a kind of performance in which, without using words, the actors could represent whatever they wished by no more than the movements of their

* * * * *

701 See J.-C. Margolin *Erasme et la musique* (Paris 1965) 16–23 for a discussion of the contemporary vogue for the erotic *chanson* in France and Flanders, promoted by composers who were also ecclesiastics, such as Jannequin and Passereau. In 1525 the Parisian engraver Pierre Haultin devised movable characters which permitted staff and notes to be printed simultaneously, and this led to a huge expansion in the printing of such texts. The remainder of Margolin's monograph provides a useful commentary on Erasmus' decided views on music here.

702 See Aristotle *Politics* 8.3.2–10 and 8.7.12 (on the superiority of the Dorian mode); Plato *Republic* 3.398–401, *Laws* 7.800–3, and *Timaeus* 47D. Much of this echoes a passage in Ep 1304:381–430. Patriotic Greeks considered the Dorian the only authentic national mode, and disparaged the 'barbarian and Asiatic' Lydian and Phrygian, and their derivatives.

bodies.[703] It is similar with these songs: even without words, you can guess the obscenity of the subject from the style of the music, not to mention the frantic shrilling of the pipes[704] and the thumping rhythm of the drums, all adding to the frenzy – and we let girls dance to this music, get a taste for it, and think it can do them no harm.

In fact we have even brought this kind of music out of the dance-halls and taverns and into the churches; still more ridiculous, we pay people huge salaries to wreck the dignity of the services with their absurd warbling. I would not ban music from services, but I would insist on settings that are worthy of them. Nowadays the sacred texts are accompanied by the most unholy sounds; you might as well dress Cato in Thaïs' clothes.[705] These licentious singers even include obscene words. If the law will not take action, priests and bishops should be on the watch for this.

As Aristotle said, 'A foul mouth will not shrink from foul deeds.'[706] The question is, what is obscene? Some deeds, such as theft and murder, are foul, but the words describing them are not considered obscene. Similarly, some things are not offensive in themselves, but if you describe them in unvarnished language they become obscene – for example, to have one's wife, to discharge one's belly, to pass water. No part of the body is shameful, since God created all parts good and beautiful; yet in some cases decency demands that they be concealed, and even that they should not be named directly, but indicated by some modest circumlocution. Vulva is a blameless word, and so is womb, and yet the ignorant consider them disgusting. You may say 'a woman's nature' without giving offence, when you mean her pudenda; there are similar euphemisms for the male pudenda. A similar reticence must be observed in describing the actions of these organs that I discussed earlier. Thus the first definition of obscenity is to name directly things that, for decency's sake, should be described more guardedly.

The second definition is to describe indecent acts, though not in crude language, in such a way as to make indecency seem acceptable and laudable.

* * * * *

703 A reference to the art of *pantomimus*, a sophisticated form of what is now called mime, very popular in imperial Rome. *Mimus*, on the other hand, was more akin to modern farce.

704 *Corybanticae tibiae*, an allusion to the frenzied priests of Cybele, renowned for their wild dancing; cf *Adagia* III vii 39.

705 Cato the Censor, the epitome of moral rigour (or his equally strict great-grandson Cato of Utica); on the courtesan Thaïs, see n573 above. On Erasmus' distaste for the 'absurd warbling' in church, and particularly for polyphonic settings of the liturgy, see his paraphrase on 1 Cor 14 LB V 731C–F.

706 Aristotle *Politics* 7.17.8 (1336b5–6)

For example, it is not obscene to use the word adultery, but if someone describes in lurid detail the methods used by the wife to deceive her husband and receive her lover, that is obscene. If it is essential to describe indecent acts, it must be done with loathing, just as good deeds must be described with every sign of approval. However, other people's misdeeds should never be recounted unless some useful purpose is served by it. It is also obscene to put a vicious interpretation on some perfectly innocent act, but worse than obscene to adapt some blameless piece of writing to a filthy theme, as did Ausonius in his *Cento nuptialis*, a work utterly unworthy of a Christian.[707] Again, although it is not obscene to speak of theft or murder, there are none the less certain monstrous crimes, most of them the products of lust, that boys and girls ought not to hear mentioned unless it is absolutely necessary, and even then with great circumspection and detestation. Paul speaks of this in Ephesians 5[:12]: 'The things they do in secret it would be shameful even to mention.'

Sometimes changing usage creates obscenity, although neither the word nor the deed is intrinsically obscene: the same word seems quite proper in one time or place, but not in others. For example, *bini* [a couple] is a perfectly proper word in Latin, but not in Greek,[708] and *patrare* [to perform or father] used to be improper, but has no obscene overtones now. But in modern times the verb *amare* [to love], which used to be an acceptable euphemism for sexual intercourse, is now so discredited that you cannot decently use it even in an entirely innocent context; it is considered offensive and obscene even to say that you 'love' your mother.

I have run through all these different kinds of filthy language to help you avoid any hint of obscenity. I said something earlier about obscene pictures: Aristotle believes that lewd pictures and sculptures are so detrimental to morality that the state should impose laws prohibiting the possession of any image containing a hint of lasciviousness.[709] The tongue speaks to the ears, a picture speaks[710] to the eyes, but a picture is more graphic by far than words and generally makes a deeper impression on the mind. Aristotle also prescribed a severe penalty even for an indecent utterance. What

* * * * *

707 Ausonius' *Cento nuptialis* is a compilation or patchwork of Virgil's lines, written at the request of the emperor Valentinian c 368, and includes an epic and graphic description of the wedding night!

708 βινέω describes illicit intercourse, as opposed to ὀπυίω, which is used both of marrying and of intercourse.

709 Aristotle *Politics* 7.17.9–10 (1336b8–16); for the earlier passage, see 384–5. The punishment Aristotle prescribes relates to the communal meals that were an important part of Greek civic life.

710 Cf *Adagia* III i 48.

was it? If the offender were free-born but not yet old enough to join the men at table, he would be refused that honour; if he were older, he would be scourged, the treatment reserved for slaves, since he had committed a slave's offence.

An undisciplined tongue is indeed the kind of servile fault that should be unthinkable in any noble spirit, but even more in those whom Christ's blood released from enslavement to sin into the freedom of the children of God.[711] You have heard the pagan philosopher's view; should not Christians be all the more ashamed to lionize, as witty and jolly fellows, the most foul-mouthed reprobates? Not to mention the licentiousness of our signs and paintings, which depict and set before our eyes things normally too disgusting even to name. These subjects are on public display in the taverns and market-squares and meet our eyes whether we like it or not, images 'that would inflame even the desires, long extinguished by age, of a Priam or a Nestor.'[712] Alas, the indifference of our law and its officers!

The philosopher hammers away at all obscene images, except those of certain gods whom the laws associate with licentiousness.[713] I imagine that he is referring to images of the naked Venus and Cupid, of the keeper of the gardens, of satyrs, and of the phalluses of Bacchus; in their festivals certain ritual indecencies were performed.[714] What a strange religion the philosopher proclaims! He permits such indecency to be associated with the gods, who above all should hold aloof from such things. Gods should be worshipped in purity by the pure and in chastity by the chaste. Similarly, Seneca attributes to long-established laws the fact that the people indulge in foolish rituals to worship the gods, doing what the laws command rather than what is holy.[715] But even Aristotle requires that young people be excluded from such ceremonies.[716]

* * * * *

711 Cf Rom 8:21.
712 Juvenal *Satires* 6.325–6. The wise king of Pylos, Nestor was proverbially associated with old age; see *Adagia* I vi 66, and, for Nestor with the venerable Trojan king Priam alongside, *De contemptu mundi* CWE 66 152 and the colloquy νηφάλιον συμπόσιον ('The Sober Feast') CWE 40 925.
713 Aristotle *Politics* 7.17.10 (1336b16–19)
714 The 'keeper of the gardens' was Priapus, son of Venus and Bacchus, and a god of fertility, both human and agricultural. The satyrs, part human and part goat, were renowned for their lechery. Giant phalluses were carried in procession during the festival of Bacchus, the Bacchanalia (cf n448 above).
715 See eg Seneca's *Epistulae morales* 95.47–50. But this is possibly a reference to Seneca's lost work on superstition described and quoted by St Augustine *De civitate Dei* 6.10, and mentioned by Erasmus in the *Ratio verae theologiae* LB V 80C.
716 Aristotle *Politics* 7.17.10 (1336b17–18)

Thanks be to God that our worship contains nothing that is unchaste and impure! But this makes it all the more sinful when people introduce indecency into subjects that are by nature innocent. First, why is it necessary to have certain stories depicted in church at all? Why a youth and a girl lying in the same bed? Why David watching Bathsheba from his window and summoning her to be defiled, or embracing the Shunammite who was sent to him? Why the dance of Herodias' daughter?[717] The subjects are indeed taken from the holy books, but why has so much artistic licence been used to depict the women? There are things surrounding the altars where the Eucharist is performed that would not be allowed into any decent home.

Thus you must keep out of your house all loose-living, idle, and pampered young people, together with drunken servants, gossiping women, dancing-girls, mountebanks,[718] actors, actresses, and indecent pictures – in short, anyone or anything that could poison the minds of the young through their eyes or ears, or in any other way. So far from such people and influences being brought into your home from outside, should you find that any of them have crept unnoticed into your household, they must be ignominiously expelled at once.

I feel compelled to ask why Christian law is so forbearing. Some people make a living from this trade: they obtain a good-looking girl from somewhere and teach her, young as she is, to perform erotic dances and mimes; they worm their way into the banquets of the nobility and even of bishops. As soon as she is old enough, she is made a whore, and one poor ruined girl earns enough to keep three strapping youths and a woman who claims to be her mother; these libertines get a gold piece or two from every satisfied client. If magistrates ever took any thought for morality, it would be here: they would ask the vagabonds where they found the girl (and perhaps discover that she had been spirited away from a respectable home) and why, despite being perfectly fit, they had chosen to lead this idle and

* * * * *

717 The stories of David, Bathsheba, and Abishag the Shunammite are told in 2 Sam 11 and 1 Kings 1; an example is Hans Memling's *Bathsheba at Her Toilet* (c 1485, now in the Staatsgalerie, Stuttgart); see M. Brion *The Bible in Art* (London 1956) plate 175. The story of Salome, Herodias' daughter, is told in Matt 14:1–12 and Mark 6:14–29; an example might be Benozzo Gozzoli's *Dance of Salome and Beheading of St John the Baptist* (c 1490, now in the National Gallery of Art, Washington); see G. Ferguson *Signs and Symbols in Christian Art* (New York 1961) plate VII. On licentious depictions of religious subjects in general, cf 384–5 above.

718 *Atellanarum histriones*, 'actors in Atellan plays,' which were popular farces in ancient Rome, described by Livy 7.2.12

vicious existence. To help them make a full confession, they would deserve at the very least the honour of a public thrashing and banishment from the city. This topic would provide abundant material for a tirade,[719] but I must set a limit to my complaints and complete my task.

Idleness is in fact a danger to anyone, but it is most dangerous by far to impressionable youth. Children must therefore always be given something to keep them occupied, even a game, if you wish, so long as it is worthwhile. Idleness is still more dangerous if accompanied by wealth and isolation. The celebrated playwright's dictum is not far from the truth: 'The thoughts of a woman alone always turn to evil.'[720] There are few women who have achieved that masculine strength of mind that enables them to debate important matters with themselves, and never to be less alone than when they are alone.[721] It is certainly true that solitude is unprofitable to boys and girls. The philosopher feared for the youth whom he saw standing alone, lost in thought, and asked him what he was doing. 'I am talking to myself,' he said. 'Are you sure that you are not talking to a rogue?' replied the philosopher.[722] But if a girl is intent on her prayers or on her book, she is neither idle nor alone; in prayer, she is talking to God, and in reading the sacred books she is listening to God's word.

But there is no end to the advice I could give, much of it passed on by the ancients, and as much by modern writers. The subject would require much briefer treatment if parents knew what to advise, and if children obeyed their parents. For at this early age it is not yet possible to put children in the best category, of those who are both wise in themselves and ready to accept good advice. There is of course the opposite category, those totally feckless people who have no wisdom in themselves but will not be guided by the counsel of others. It is enough if children fall into the middle category, of those who cannot yet see for themselves what it is best to do but who willingly accept good advice. That is why the apostle Paul required only one thing of children: obedience. 'Children,' he says, 'obey your parents in all things, for this is God's will.'[723] When he says, 'in all things,' he does not include unchristian demands; he is using hyperbole to underline the importance of obedience. Of course some parents are too strict, laying down arbitrary rules and punishing where there is no crime. Children will

* * * * *

719 Like that in the *Institutio principis christiani* CWE 27 267–8
720 Publilius Syrus *Sententiae* 376
721 An echo of a dictum of Scipio quoted in Plutarch *Moralia* 196B
722 An anecdote told of Crates by Seneca *Epistulae morales* 1.10.1
723 Col 3:20

obey in all things, until it is a question of going against their religion; the duty we owe to our parents must yield to the greater duty we owe to God. To those who rebel and claim that their parents are wicked, the Apostle has a concise reply: 'For this is God's will.' Let this be enough to quell all rebellion: 'This is God's will.' The rule of obedience is the same for slaves and free children.[724]

It will be best if each side performs its function aright; unless the man in authority is lapsing into tyranny, it is best that subordinates should obey their masters. Nothing is more ruinous than rebellion. It may be that a drunken and witless father does not deserve his son's obedience, but 'that is God's will.' Offer that much obedience to the Lord, and he will grant you the reward of obedience. Paul commands, in his letter to the Ephesians: 'Children, obey your parents in the Lord, for it is right that you should. Honour your father and your mother, which is the first commandment with a promise attached: "That it may be well with you, and that you may live long on the earth." '[725]

Why did he add 'in the Lord' to his rule of obedience? 'In the Lord' means both 'for love of the Lord,' who will reward you for it, and also 'in things that are not against the piety the Lord taught us.' The first tablet of the commandments contains those that pertain to God, and the second those that pertain to man.[726] But since, after God, we must first honour our parents, from whom we received life itself, Paul is right to call this the first commandment, because it precedes the others in its own category. He also added, 'with a promise attached.' It is indeed true that to this one commandment is attached a reward, albeit a temporal one, to make the children more eager to obey, given that young people are not as much moved by spiritual rewards. These are the words in Exodus 20[:12]: 'That you may live long on the earth which the Lord your God gave you.' Those who have been obedient to their parents do not always live long on the earth, and of course in some respects the quicker you leave this earth the better; certainly we are not being guaranteed immortality in the land of the living, since anything that will end so soon cannot be called long.

* * * * *

724 Erasmus puns on *liberi*, which means both 'children' and 'free people' – which in this case they are not. There is probably an echo here of Paul's similar advice to children and slaves, eg in Eph 6:1–8.

725 Eph 6:1–3, quoting Exod 20:12

726 Tradition has it that, of the two tablets given to Moses on Mount Sinai (Exod 32:15–16; Deut 4:13), the first contained the first three commandments and the second the remaining seven; cf NCE IV 6–7.

Some may prefer Ambrose's theory that the promise 'that it may be well with you, and that you may live long on the earth' applies not to the children, but to the parents. He writes as follows: 'This promise appears in Exodus, that parents should be honoured, and it will be well with them, and they will live to a great age.'[727] But I think that the text means, 'As you treat your parents, so will your children treat you.' There are children whose behaviour causes much anguish to their parents; in some cases they are even brought to an early grave, which is undoubtedly a kind of parricide. By contrast, obedient children ensure a healthy and long old age for their parents. There is nothing more agreeable and reassuring to parents as they grow old than to see their children turn out well. As the blessed elder, father to so many, put it, 'I have no more abundant joy than to see my children walk in the paths of truth.'[728] Thus you can expect from your children the kind of treatment you gave your own parents.

The Apostle awards the highest authority to parents, but he tempers this by advising that it should be exercised without harshness: 'And you fathers,' he says, 'do not provoke your children to anger, but bring them up in the teaching and the discipline of the Lord.'[729] Some people take their children to task as though they were aiming not to improve them, but to terrify them and make them worse than they are. But paternal discipline should be applied in the same way that a doctor gives medicine to a patient; he gives him a bitter-tasting draught but at the same time comforts him with the hope of a cure.

The Latin *educate* [bring up] translates Paul's ἐκτρέφετε.[730] Some fathers make no allowances for youth (they expect their children to be born old!), but an infant must be cherished and allowed to mature gradually. This is the sense of ἐκτρέφετε. 'In the teaching,' *in disciplina*, ἐν παιδείᾳ, is connected etymologically with the education of children, since παιδεύειν [to rear or educate] comes from the Greek word for a child παῖς; that is the period of life most suited to learning. Thus the ignorant are called ἀπαίδευτοι because, having usually frittered away their childhood in idleness and play, they can never acquire true learning. παιδεύειν means to teach under strict discipline[731] (not simply to teach, which in Greek is διδάσκειν), to prevent

* * * * *

727 Ambrose *Commentarius in epistolam ad Ephesios* 6.3 PL 17 422A
728 3 John 4
729 Eph 6:4
730 This linguistic discussion echoes Erasmus' annotation on the passage (LB VI 856F).
731 A secondary meaning of the Greek verb is 'to punish.'

the child's becoming intellectually developed but morally lax. Paul adds νουθεσία, 'in the discipline (or admonition) of the Lord,' and you may want to know what, exactly, 'the Lord's discipline' means. Paul's letter to the Hebrews makes it clear: 'The Lord disciplines those whom he loves, and scourges every child whom he acknowledges.'[732] This is the model for paternal discipline, which must be tempered by love, and indeed born of love.

It appears that Paul is speaking here of older children. How can we surmise this? First, because here he bestows all authority upon the father, not even mentioning the mother, and second, because he limits parental discipline here to verbal chastisement and does not mention beating, although Solomon says, 'A father who spares the rod hates his child, but one who loves him keeps him in order.'[733] Thus there is an age at which beating is useful and another at which verbal chastisement is enough. A Trojan, says the proverb, can be cured only by a flogging.[734] But a self-willed child who is not moved by fear of God, respect for its parents, shame, or conscience will not be improved by a thrashing either.[735] Another point: fathers must not hand out a thrashing or a reprimand while they are in a rage, but a woman, less able to give physical vent to her emotion, will refrain from beating, especially from beating boys; she will delegate this task to her husband.

In his letter to the Colossians, the Apostle again tries to temper paternal authority: 'Fathers, do not provoke your children to wrath, for fear they become disheartened.'[736] The Latin clause 'for fear they become disheartened' is more forceful in Paul's Greek: μὴ ἀθυμῶσι, 'for fear they become depressed, or despairing.' Some fathers are so excessively violent in their reproaches and rattle on so interminably that finally the browbeaten youth will take himself quietly off, either to the army, or to a monastery, or to some other perilous place; he takes out his father's rage upon himself.

A father must temper his authority with reason. Young people frequently go wrong through ignorance or thoughtlessness. Ignorance can be cured by παιδεία, instruction with discipline, and thoughtlessness by νουθεσία, admonition, which is a remedy for ἀθυμία, faint-heartedness. Training by means of reasoning and example will show what is to be sought and

* * * * *

732 Heb 12:6
733 Prov 13:24
734 *Adagia* I viii 36
735 Cf Quintilian *Institutiones oratoriae* 1.13.13–14; for strong protests against corporal punishment, and against cruelty to children in general, see *De pueris instituendis* CWE 26 326–34.
736 Col 3:21

what is to be avoided, and will explain to the pupil why these things are to his advantage. Νουθεσία [putting in mind] is so called because it recalls to the pupil's mind what thoughtlessness has allowed to escape, and restores his faltering judgment.

It was a waste of breath for Demea to yell: 'O heaven! O earth! O Neptune's oceans!'[737] Far more subtle was that mild father who shamed the young man into tears of remorse, and then delivered a fatherly rebuke: 'What country do you think this is? You have wronged a girl whom you had no right to touch. I hope that you will not be so stupid again.' His mildness persuaded the young man to obey him in everything. However, gentleness can sometimes be the wrong answer, and complaisance misguided. For example, Eli the priest was a holy man, but his sons were distinctly unholy, and the old man's exhortations had no effect on them 'because the Lord meant that they should die.'[738] When people stray from the path, allowance must always be made for human frailty, but when their wrongdoing has reached the point that they do not hesitate to wrong either gods or men, then the sinner who cannot be reformed must be removed from our midst to prevent further damage. Most people are awed by Brutus, who had his own sons beheaded for trying to reintroduce Tarquin's tyranny, but few applaud him.[739]

There are several reasons why young children are quicker and easier to teach.[740] First, their minds are empty, like a blank tablet on which you may write whatever you wish. Second, everything impresses them, and they firmly retain these impressions. Finally, even small children have a talent for imitation, the first sign of understanding. Thus the early years must be fully occupied, before love affairs and other infatuations bring their distractions, and the special gifts that God has bestowed upon children must be exploited to guide them into the paths of virtue. Since they will always remember the first things they learned, only the best must be instilled in them. You must therefore inculcate the principal virtues with a small but carefully chosen selection of maxims; it would be best to take them from the sacred

* * * * *

737 Terence *Adelphi* 790, followed by lines 685–6 and 695. The contrasting attitudes of the fathers, Demea and Micio, in this play were a favourite illustration for Erasmus; see cwe 26 500 n32.

738 1 Sam 2:25

739 Lucius Junius Brutus, the great hero of early republican Rome (sixth century BC), whose story is told in Livy 2.5.5–9; cf a famous passage on him in Virgil *Aeneid* 6.817–23. Tarquin was the last king of Rome.

740 Cf the similar development in *De vidua christiana* cwe 66 228 and in the first chapter of the *Institutio principis christiani* cwe 27 209ff.

books, although there are many in the pagan texts that are not unworthy of a Christian. Similarly, since they readily copy anything they see done, make sure they see nothing that it would be wrong to copy.

When finally they reach the parting of the ways (not Pythagoras' fork,[741] since they must choose the path of virtue from their earliest infancy) and must decide what career to choose, parents should be wary of forcing their sons and daughters to follow some way of life for which they are unsuited, especially if it is one of those from which there is no return, like entering holy orders or a monastery.[742] Parents have different reasons for their mistakes here. Some, burdened with large families, destine a number of their children for the priesthood or the monastic profession and, to guarantee that they cannot escape, ensure that they have taken some orders, or been spirited away to a monastery, before they reach puberty. A subdeacon cannot return to the world; he has been put in bonds, and yet all too often the victim does not realize that he is bound. If the parents fear that, when his judgment matures, he will overturn their decision, they obtain a bull from the pope enabling him to be initiated into the priesthood earlier than is permitted. The parents' reasoning is, 'If our property is divided among so many, our family will lose its standing; as it is, our son may well become a prior or an abbot, we can go and sup with him, and he will be no burden to us.' Others, less pragmatic, are concerned for the child's safety: considering the frantic lifestyle of the adolescent, they are afraid that he will meet some ignominious death, or fall foul of the law. Their fears are allayed by the tonsure and the cowl! Others make religion their excuse: 'I want,' they say, 'some of my children to be dedicated to God, so there is someone to pray for me after my death.' I see; so the rest are dedicated to the devil, are they? Or is it that only priests and monks can pray? All this would be more acceptable if they tried persuasion on their children; as it is, they simply force them into

* * * * *

741 Cf *Adagia* I i 2; Pythagoras used the letter gamma to illustrate how at some point we must all choose to follow either the path of virtue or that of vice. Erasmus considers that a true Christian has no choice to make.

742 Erasmus returns for a last thrust at a primary target of this work (see 258–65 above), which of course reflects his own experience; cf Epp 296 and 447 on his unsuitability for the monastic life. These problems are dramatized in the colloquies *Virgo* μισόγαμος ('The Girl with No Interest in Marriage') and *Virgo poenitens* ('The Repentant Girl') CWE 39 279–305, which date from 1523. For the debate over the validity of a monastic profession enforced by the parents, see Gratian *Decretum* pars 2 C 20 q 1 cc 1–8, where most of the precedents cited uphold its validity.

it, and say that they will not die in peace unless their wishes have been carried out.

An even better solution would be for parents who observe that their children incline towards such a career not to approve their choice immediately, but to investigate their children's vocation, and see whether it comes from within, or from some outside prompting.[743] If they discover that the Pharisees are involved, hunting proselytes for their own purposes,[744] the parents must tell them to keep away from other people's children. If the vocation comes from within, let them first consider whether the rest of their children's lives correspond to it; if they find that they are steeped in lust and corruption, they will know that their vocation is not prompted by God. In fact some parents even connive at their children's wickedness, saying, 'Let them have their fling, and afterwards they will hate vice all the more.' What a foolish idea, to make someone worse to make them all at once better! If, however, their lives correspond to their intention, the parents must still not agree on the spot; just as young people, rushing with youthful enthusiasm to enter an Olympic contest, must be shown how much pain and effort go to make a champion, so the parents must warn them of the difficulties and troubles of that way of life, and paint them a picture of a true monk or priest. Then they must assess their physical and mental aptitude for the life they propose to lead. If the child has replied quietly and sensibly to every question and has persisted in his desire for some time, there is every chance that a good spirit is guiding him, and the parents must not prolong their opposition excessively; they may well be resisting God's will.

There must be many men and women today who have learned, as they grow older, that their parents used trickery and force to push them into a way of life for which they were unsuited by nature; far from praying for their parents, they will curse them and vow them to hell.[745] Children must be brought up in such a way that, whether they incline towards holy orders or towards the married state, it is a case of 'the pure approaching the pure.'[746] If a young man rejects marriage not for love of religion, but to

* * * * *

743 Erasmus expresses similar doubts about monastic vocations in the final chapter of *De contemptu mundi* CWE 66 172–5 and in *De vidua christiana* ibidem 223.

744 Cf Matt 23:15. Erasmus often equates Pharisaism with the rigid insistence on ritual regulation characteristic of certain monastic orders; see eg Epp 164:29–31 and 447:626–729.

745 Literally, 'to the Furies,' *Diris*, the daughters of Hell and Night, who, in classical mythology, persecuted the shades of the guilty

746 Cf Titus 1:15.

facilitate his debauches, he must be induced to see reason for the good of his soul; but if he rejects it instinctively, or on rational grounds, he must not be discouraged. The same principle may be applied to the choice of studies and to all the rest of our innumerable undertakings; people almost always do better if they have a natural aptitude for something.

I see that this debate has come full circle: we began with the age at which marriage is appropriate and desirable, and now the course of our discussion has brought us back to that point – a suitable moment at which to close this work.

WORKS FREQUENTLY CITED

SHORT-TITLE FORMS FOR ERASMUS' WORKS

INDEX

WORKS FREQUENTLY CITED

This list provides bibliographical information for publications referred to in short-title form in introductions and notes. Erasmus' letters are cited by number and line in the CWE translation unless Allen or another edition is indicated. For Erasmus' other writings see the short-title list following.

Acta Torontonensis	*Acta Conventus neo-Latini Torontonensis* ed A. Dalzell, C. Fantazzi, and R.J. Schoeck, Medieval & Renaissance Texts & Studies 86 (Binghamton 1991)
Allen	*Opus epistolarum Des. Erasmi Roterodami* ed P.S. Allen, H.M. Allen, and H.W. Garrod (Oxford 1906–58) 11 vols, plus index
Alopecius	*Ratio seu methodus compendio perveniendi ad veram theologiam, per Erasmum Roterodamum* ... (Cologne: Alopecius, 1523)
Aquinas *Supplementum*	Thomas Aquinas *Supplementum tertiae partis summae theologiae* PL series 2 vol 4 917–1444
ASD	*Opera omnia Desiderii Erasmi Roterodami* (Amsterdam 1969–)
BHR	*Bibliothèque d'humanisme et Renaissance*
CCCM	*Corpus christianorum, continuatio medievalis* (Turnhout 1971–)
CCSL	*Corpus christianorum, series Latina* (Turnhout 1954–)
CEBR	*Contemporaries of Erasmus: A Biographical Register of the Renaissance and Reformation* ed Peter G. Bietenholz and Thomas B. Deutscher (Toronto 1985–7) 3 vols
CIC 2	*Corpus iuris canonici* ed A.L. Richter and A. Friedberg vol 2 *Decretalium collectiones* (Leipzig 1881)
Codex	*Codex Iustinianus* ed P. Krueger, *Corpus iuris civilis* vol 2 (Berlin 1906)
CSEL	*Corpus scriptorum ecclesiasticorum Latinorum* (Vienna and Leipzig 1866–)
CWE	*Collected Works of Erasmus* (Toronto 1974–)
Denzinger	H. Denzinger and A. Schönmetzer *Enchiridion symbolorum definitionum et declarationum de rebus fidei et morum* 35th ed (Barcelona 1973)

Digesta	*Iustiniani Digesta* ed T. Mommsen and P. Krueger in *Corpus iuris civilis* vol 1 (Berlin 1928) 57–994
DS	*Dictionnaire de spiritualité ascétique et mystique: doctrine et histoire* ed M. Viller et al (Paris 1932–95) 17 vols in 19
DTC	*Dictionnaire de théologie catholique* ed A. Vacant, E. Mangenot, and E. Amman (Paris 1899–1950) 15 vols
ERSY	Erasmus of Rotterdam Society Yearbook
Esmein	A. Esmein *Le Mariage en droit canonique* (Paris 1891) 2 vols
Gaudemet	J. Gaudemet *Le Mariage en Occident: les moeurs et le droit* (Paris 1987)
Gratian *Decretum*	*Decretum Gratiani* PL 187
Halkin 'Mariologie'	Léon-E. Halkin 'La Mariologie d'Erasme' *Archiv für Reformationsgeschichte* 68 (1977) 32–54
Institutiones	*Iustiniani Institutiones* ed T. Mommsen and P. Krueger in *Corpus iuris civilis* vol 1 (Berlin 1928) 1–56
Lacey	T.A. Lacey *Marriage in Church and State* 2nd ed (London 1947)
LB	*Desiderii Erasmi Roterodami opera omnia* ed J. Leclerc (Leiden 1703–6; repr 1961–2) 10 vols
Lombard *Sententiae*	Petrus Lombardus *Libri sententiarum quatuor* PL series 2 vol 1
LW	Martin Luther *Works* ed Jaroslav Pelikan and Helmut T. Lehmann (St Louis 1955–86) 55 vols
Maclean	I. Maclean *The Renaissance Notion of Woman* 2nd ed (Cambridge 1983)
Margolin	J.-C. Margolin *Erasme: Declamatio de pueris statim et liberaliter instituendis (étude critique, traduction, et commentaire)* (Geneva 1966)
Marienlexikon	*Marienlexikon* ed Remigius Bäumer and Leo Scheffczyk (St Ottilien 1988–94) 6 vols
NCE	*New Catholic Encyclopedia* prepared by an editorial staff at the Catholic University of America (New York 1967–79) 17 vols

Novellae	*Iustiniani Novellae* ed R. Schoell and G. Kroll, *Corpus iuris civilis* vol 3 (Berlin 1928)
O'Donnell 'Women Saints'	Anne M. O'Donnell 'Mary and Other Women Saints in the Letters of Erasmus' ERSY 11 (1991) 105–21
Olsen	V. Norskov Olsen *The New Testament Logia on Divorce: A Study of Their Interpretation from Erasmus to Milton* (Tübingen 1971)
Otto	August Otto *Die Sprichwörter und sprichwörtlichen Redensarten der Römer* (Leipzig 1890; repr Hildesheim 1971), cited by proverb number
Pabel *Conversing*	Hilmar M. Pabel *Conversing with God: Prayer in Erasmus' Pastoral Writings* (Toronto 1997)
Pabel *Erasmus' Vision*	*Erasmus' Vision of the Church* ed Hilmar M. Pabel, Sixteenth Century Essays and Studies 33 (Kirksville 1995)
Payne	John B. Payne *Erasmus: His Theology of the Sacraments* (Richmond 1970)
PG	*Patrologiae cursus completus ... series Graeca* ed J.P. Migne (Paris 1857–1912) 162 vols
Phillips	Jane E. Phillips 'Food and Drink in Erasmus' Gospel Paraphrases' ERSY 14 (1994) 24–45
PL	*Patrologiae cursus completus ... series Latina* ed J.P. Migne (Paris 1844–1902) 221 vols
PL series 2	*Patrologiae cursus completus ... series secunda* ed J.P. Migne (Paris 1846–53) 4 vols
Raby	*The Oxford Book of Medieval Latin Verse* ed F.J.E. Raby (Oxford 1959)
Rummel *Annotations*	Erika Rummel *Erasmus' Annotations on the New Testament* (Toronto 1986)
Rummel *Catholic Critics*	Erika Rummel *Erasmus and His Catholic Critics* (Nieuwkoop 1989) 2 vols
Salzer	Anselm Salzer *Die Sinnbilder und Beiworte Mariens in der deutschen Literatur und lateinischen Hymnenpoesie des Mittelalters* (Seitenstetten 1886–94; repr Darmstadt 1967)
Screech	M.A. Screech *The Rabelaisian Marriage* (London 1958)

Stevenson

Kenneth Stevenson *Nuptial Blessing: A Study of Christian Marriage Rites* (New York 1983)

Telle

Emile V. Telle *Erasme de Rotterdam et le septième sacrement* (Geneva 1954)

Tracy *Erasmus*

James D. Tracy *Erasmus of the Low Countries* (Berkeley and Los Angeles 1996)

Trapman

J. Trapman 'Erasmus's *Precationes*' in *Acta Torontonensis* 769–79

Warner

Marina Warner *Alone of All Her Sex: The Myth and Cult of the Virgin Mary* (London 1976)

SHORT-TITLE FORMS FOR ERASMUS' WORKS

Titles following colons are longer versions of the same, or are alternative titles. Items entirely enclosed in square brackets are of doubtful authorship. For abbreviations, see Works Frequently Cited.

Acta: Acta Academiae Lovaniensis contra Lutherum *Opuscula* / CWE 71

Adagia: Adagiorum chiliades 1508, etc (Adagiorum collectanea for the primitive form, when required) LB II / ASD II-1, 4, 5, 6 / CWE 30–6

Admonitio adversus mendacium: Admonitio adversus mendacium et obtrectationem LB X

Annotationes in Novum Testamentum LB VI / CWE 51–60

Antibarbari LB X / ASD I-1 / CWE 23

Apologia ad Caranzam: Apologia ad Sanctium Caranzam, or Apologia de tribus locis, or Responsio ad annotationem Stunicae . . . a Sanctio Caranza defensam LB IX

Apologia ad Fabrum: Apologia ad Iacobum Fabrum Stapulensem LB IX / ASD IX-3 / CWE 83

Apologia adversus monachos: Apologia adversus monachos quosdam Hispanos LB IX

Apologia adversus Petrum Sutorem: Apologia adversus debacchationes Petri Sutoris LB IX

Apologia adversus rhapsodias Alberti Pii: Apologia ad viginti et quattuor libros A. Pii LB IX

Apologia contra Latomi dialogum: Apologia contra Iacobi Latomi dialogum de tribus linguis LB IX / CWE 71

Apologia de 'In principio erat sermo' LB IX

Apologia de laude matrimonii: Apologia pro declamatione de laude matrimonii LB IX / CWE 71

Apologia de loco 'Omnes quidem': Apologia de loco 'Omnes quidem resurgemus' LB IX

Apologiae contra Stunicam: Apologiae contra Lopidem Stunicam LB IX / ASD IX-2

Apologia qua respondet invectivis Lei: Apologia qua respondet duabus invectivis Eduardi Lei *Opuscula*

Apophthegmata LB IV

Appendix de scriptis Clithovei LB IX / CWE 83

Appendix respondens ad Sutorem LB IX

Argumenta: Argumenta in omnes epistolas apostolicas nova (with Paraphrases)

Axiomata pro causa Lutheri: Axiomata pro causa Martini Lutheri *Opuscula* / CWE 71

Carmina LB I, IV, V, VIII / ASD I-7 / CWE 85–6

Catalogus lucubrationum LB I

Ciceronianus: Dialogus Ciceronianus LB I / ASD I-2 / CWE 28

Colloquia LB I / ASD I-3 / CWE 39–40

Compendium vitae Allen I / CWE 4

Concionalis interpretatio (in Psalmi)

Conflictus: Conflictus Thaliae et Barbariei LB I

[Consilium: Consilium cuiusdam ex animo cupientis esse consultum] *Opuscula* / CWE 71

De bello Turcico: Consultatio de bello Turcico (in Psalmi)

De civilitate: De civilitate morum puerilium LB I / CWE 25

Declamatio de morte LB IV

Declamatiuncula LB IV

Declarationes ad censuras Lutetiae vulgatas: Declarationes ad censuras Lutetiae vulgatas sub nomine facultatis theologiae Parisiensis LB IX

De concordia: De sarcienda ecclesiae concordia, or De amabili ecclesiae concordia (in Psalmi)

De conscribendis epistolis LB I / ASD I-2 / CWE 25

De constructione: De constructione octo partium orationis, or Syntaxis LB I / ASD I-4

De contemptu mundi: Epistola de contemptu mundi LB V / ASD V-1 / CWE 66

De copia: De duplici copia verborum ac rerum LB I / ASD I-6 / CWE 24

De esu carnium: Epistola apologetica ad Christophorum episcopum Basiliensem de interdicto esu carnium LB IX / ASD IX-1

De immensa Dei misericordia: Concio de immensa Dei misericordia LB V / CWE 70

De libero arbitrio: De libero arbitrio diatribe LB IX / CWE 76

De praeparatione: De praeparatione ad mortem LB V / ASD V-1 / CWE 70

De pueris instituendis: De pueris statim ac liberaliter instituendis LB I / ASD I-2 / CWE 26

De puero Iesu: Concio de puero Iesu LB V / CWE 29

De puritate tabernaculi: De puritate tabernaculi sive ecclesiae christianae (in Psalmi)

De ratione studii LB I / ASD I-2 / CWE 24

De recta pronuntiatione: De recta latini graecique sermonis pronuntiatione LB I / ASD I-4 / CWE 26

De taedio Iesu: Disputatiuncula de taedio, pavore, tristicia Iesu LB V / CWE 70

Detectio praestigiarum: Detectio praestigiarum cuiusdam libelli germanice scripti LB X / ASD IX-1

De vidua christiana LB V / CWE 66

De virtute amplectenda: Oratio de virtute amplectenda LB V / CWE 29

[Dialogus bilinguium ac trilinguium: Chonradi Nastadiensis dialogus bilinguium ac trilinguium] Opuscula / CWE 7

Dilutio: Dilutio eorum quae Iodocus Clithoveus scripsit adversus declamationem suasoriam matrimonii CWE 83

Divinationes ad notata Bedae LB IX

Ecclesiastes: Ecclesiastes sive de ratione concionandi LB V / ASD V-4, 5

Elenchus in N. Bedae censuras LB IX

Enchiridion: Enchiridion militis christiani LB V / CWE 66

Encomium matrimonii (in De conscribendis epistolis)

Encomium medicinae: Declamatio in laudem artis medicae LB I / ASD I-4 / CWE 29

Epistola ad Dorpium LB IX / CWE 3 / CWE 71

Epistola ad fratres Inferioris Germaniae: Responsio ad fratres Germaniae Inferioris ad epistolam apologeticam incerto autore proditam LB X / ASD IX-1

Epistola ad graculos: Epistola ad quosdam imprudentissimos graculos LB X

Epistola apologetica de Termino LB X

Epistola consolatoria: Epistola consolatoria virginibus sacris, or Epistola consolatoria in adversis LB V / CWE 69

Epistola contra pseudevangelicos: Epistola contra quosdam qui se falso iactant evangelicos LB X / ASD IX-1
Euripidis Hecuba LB I / ASD I-1
Euripidis Iphigenia in Aulide LB I / ASD I-1
Exomologesis: Exomologesis sive modus confitendi LB V
Explanatio symboli: Explanatio symboli apostolorum sive catechismus LB V / ASD V-1 / CWE 70
Ex Plutarcho versa LB IV / ASD IV-2

Formula: Conficiendarum epistolarum formula (see De conscribendis epistolis)

Hyperaspistes LB X / CWE 76–7

In Nucem Ovidii commentarius LB I / ASD I-1 / CWE 29
In Prudentium: Commentarius in duos hymnos Prudentii LB V / CWE 29
Institutio christiani matrimonii LB V / CWE 69
Institutio principis christiani LB IV / ASD IV-1 / CWE 27

[Julius exclusus: Dialogus Julius exclusus e coelis] *Opuscula* / CWE 27

Lingua LB IV / ASD IV-1A / CWE 29
Liturgia Virginis Matris: Virginis Matris apud Lauretum cultae liturgia LB V / ASD V-1 / CWE 69
Luciani dialogi LB I / ASD I-1

Manifesta mendacia CWE 71
Methodus (see Ratio)
Modus orandi Deum LB V / ASD V-1 / CWE 70
Moria: Moriae encomium LB IV / ASD IV-3 / CWE 27

Novum Testamentum: Novum Testamentum 1519 and later (Novum instrumentum for the first edition, 1516, when required) LB VI

Obsecratio ad Virginem Mariam: Obsecratio sive oratio ad Virginem Mariam in rebus adversis, or Obsecratio ad Virginem Matrem Mariam in rebus adversis LB V / CWE 69
Oratio de pace: Oratio de pace et discordia LB VIII
Oratio funebris: Oratio funebris in funere Bertae de Heyen LB VIII / CWE 29

Paean Virgini Matri: Paean Virgini Matri dicendus LB V / CWE 69
Panegyricus: Panegyricus ad Philippum Austriae ducem LB IV / ASD IV-1 / CWE 27
Parabolae: Parabolae sive similia LB I / ASD I-5 / CWE 23
Paraclesis LB V, VI
Paraphrasis in Elegantias Vallae: Paraphrasis in Elegantias Laurentii Vallae LB I / ASD I-4
Paraphrasis in Matthaeum, etc (in Paraphrasis in Novum Testamentum)
Paraphrasis in Novum Testamentum LB VII / CWE 42–50
Peregrinatio apostolorum: Peregrinatio apostolorum Petri et Pauli LB VI, VII

Precatio ad Virginis filium Iesum LB V / CWE 69
Precatio dominica LB V / CWE 69
Precationes: Precationes aliquot novae LB V / CWE 69
Precatio pro pace ecclesiae: Precatio ad Dominum Iesum pro pace ecclesiae LB IV,
  V / CWE 69
Psalmi: Psalmi, or Enarrationes sive commentarii in psalmos LB V / ASD V-2, 3 /
  CWE 63–5
Purgatio adversus epistolam Lutheri: Purgatio adversus epistolam non sobriam
  Lutheri LB X / ASD IX-1

Querela pacis LB IV / ASD IV-2 / CWE 27

Ratio: Ratio seu Methodus compendio perveniendi ad veram theologiam (Methodus
  for the shorter version originally published in the Novum instrumentum of
  1516) LB V, VI
Responsio ad annotationes Lei: Liber quo respondet annotationibus Lei LB IX
Responsio ad collationes: Responsio ad collationes cuiusdam iuvenis gerontodidas-
  cali LB IX
Responsio ad disputationem de divortio: Responsio ad disputationem cuiusdam
  Phimostomi de divortio LB IX / CWE 83
Responsio ad epistolam Pii: Responsio ad epistolam paraeneticam Alberti Pii, or
  Responsio ad exhortationem Pii LB IX
Responsio ad notulas Bedaicas LB X
Responsio ad Petri Cursii defensionem: Epistola de apologia Cursii LB X / Allen
  Ep 3032
Responsio adversus febricitantis libellum: Apologia monasticae religionis LB X

Spongia: Spongia adversus aspergines Hutteni LB X / ASD IX-1
Supputatio: Supputatio calumniarum Natalis Bedae LB IX

Tyrannicida: Tyrannicida, declamatio Lucianicae respondens LB I / ASD I-1 / CWE 29

Virginis et martyris comparatio LB V / CWE 69
Vita Hieronymi: Vita divi Hieronymi Stridonensis *Opuscula* / CWE 61

Index

This book

was designed by

VAL COOKE

based on the series design by

ALLAN FLEMING

and was printed by

University

of Toronto

Press